Portuguese Jews and New Christians in Colonial Brazil, 1500–1822

Portuguese Jews *and* New Christians *in* Colonial Brazil, 1500–1822

A New Geography of the Atlantic World

ALAN P. MARCUS

UNIVERSITY OF NEW MEXICO PRESS | ALBUQUERQUE

© 2024 by the University of New Mexico Press
All rights reserved. Published 2024
Printed in the United States of America

ISBN 978-0-8263-6716-7 (cloth)
ISBN 978-0-8263-6717-4 (paper)
ISBN 978-0-8263-6718-1 (ePub)
ISBN 978-0-8263-6719-8 (pdf)

Library of Congress Control Number: 2024947870

Founded in 1889, the University of New Mexico sits on the traditional homelands of the Pueblo of Sandia. The original peoples of New Mexico—Pueblo, Navajo, and Apache—since time immemorial have deep connections to the land and have made significant contributions to the broader community statewide. We honor the land itself and those who remain stewards of this land throughout the generations and also acknowledge our committed relationship to Indigenous peoples. We gratefully recognize our history.

Cover illustration: Map of Brazil by Samuel Augustus Mitchell, 1874
Designed by Felicia Cedillos
Composed in Adobe Caslon Pro

Contents

List of Illustrations   vii

List of Tables   ix

Preface   xi

Acknowledgments   xvii

Introduction   1

Chapter One. The Portuguese New Christian "Uniqueness" in the New World   39

Chapter Two. The Portuguese Inquisition and the Impact on Portuguese Jews and New Christians   75

Chapter Three. The Portuguese World and Portuguese-Jewish Diasporas   103

Chapter Four. Sugar and the First New Christians in Colonial Brazil   135

Chapter Five. The First Jewish Settlement in the Americas   169

Chapter Six. Results from the Examination of the Portuguese Inquisition Dossiers in Brazil   205

Conclusion   233

Afterword   239

Appendix   245

Glossary   261

Notes   263

References   335

Index   363

Illustrations

Figures

Figure 5.1. Map of Olinda   186

Figure 5.2. Maurício de Nassau   186

Figure 5.3. Map of Recife, known as Mauritsstadt   187

Figure 5.4. Portrait of the first rabbi in the Americas: Isaac Aboab da Fonseca (1605–1693)   187

Figure 5.5. Map of Friburgum Palace, Recife, Brazil, 1656   188

Figure 6.1. Occupations for those arrested for Judaism   217

Figure 6.2. Breakdown of social status for arrests for all heresies in Brazil   218

Figure 6.3. Totals for all arrests in Brazil by century   226

Figure 6.4. Total arrests only for the crime of Judaism by century   226

Maps

Map 1. Brazil and Latin American neighbors today   70

Map 2. Age of Exploration: Portuguese and Spanish territories in the late fifteenth and sixteenth centuries   70

Map 3. Inquisition tribunals in Portugal   77

Map 4. Portuguese diasporas and exploration   132

Map 5. *Capitanias* (Brazilian captaincies)   133

Map 6. Northeast sub-regions   138

Map 7. Map of Sertão, Pernambuco   147

Map 8. Map of Bahia (Recôncavo Baiano) 147

Map 9. Dutch Brazil 173

Map 10. Synagogue in Recife 183

Map 11. Breakdown of results: arrests of Judaism by century and state in Brazil 223

Tables

Table 6.1. Immigrants from Portugal Arrested for Judaism in Brazil: Place of Origin   210

Table 6.2. The Youngest Individuals Imprisoned by the Portuguese Inquisition in Lisbon   211

Table 6.3. Members of the Paredes Family Arrested in Rio de Janeiro   214

Table 6.4. Breakdown for Social Status in Arrests for All Heresies in Brazil   218

Table 6.5. Location of Arrests for All Heresies in Colonial Brazil   224

Preface

This book is about the experience, presence, and importance of Portuguese Jews and New Christians and their descendants in colonial Brazil and beyond. They were deeply involved in the colonial enterprise in Brazil from the time the Portuguese first arrived there in 1500, and comprised among the New World's first sugarcane industry experts, skilled laborers, merchants, rabbis, calligraphists, playwrights, poets, writers, pharmacists, medical doctors, real estate brokers, and geographers—facts that remain largely unknown in most public and academic spheres. Their presence and prominence in colonial Brazil merit recognition and acknowledgment in the biography of Brazil, and more broadly, Latin American geography. Moreover, the importance of migration and mobility to, within, and beyond Brazil and throughout the Americas, become salient themes, explored here through multi- and interdisciplinary approaches.

When most people think of Brazil today, they probably first imagine the Amazon rainforest, soccer, tropical beaches, Carnaval, samba, and a country well known for its harmonious joie de vivre and the exuberance of its people, or for the iconic "Christ the Redeemer" statue overlooking Guanabara Bay. Yet the importance of a Jewish legacy and the impact of the Portuguese Inquisition activities in colonial Brazil will likely be absent from this universal imagination. As Thomas Skidmore points out, "Brazil has created, beneath a façade of harmony, a contradictory society."[1]

That is, beneath these popular imaginations, there lies a sinister side in Brazil's DNA. Brazil's colonial biography developed under unprecedented historical, social, and geographical circumstances through the interaction of the Portuguese and three disenfranchised populations: Indigenous, African, and Portuguese of Jewish origin. Altogether they participated in the making of an incipient nation as they merged into an unfamiliar context of New World encounters. These new conditions in Brazil were shaped by the contingencies of Catholic orthodoxy, colonialism, cultural genocide, persecution, and the institution of slavery. These populations lived among each other, often intermarried, and produced offspring that evinced the unique mark of Brazilian hybridity (*mestiçagem*), so characteristically "Brazilian," yet at the same time, one that emerged from the encumbrance of new circumstances.

Here I explore the story of one of Brazil's first immigrants: Portuguese Jews and New Christians (i.e., Jews who had been converted to Christianity mostly by force, and their descendants) who migrated or were sent as penal exiles to Brazil. Their story is inherently tied to the geography of colonial Brazil. As a geographer, I have framed this narrative specifically within the context of spatial relationships and migration processes, since this is a story steeped in geography.[2]

The more I researched this topic, the more I realized the extent of its significance and importance. However, I noticed the conspicuous lacuna in the annals of geography (despite a mountain of scholarship written by historians in the past fifty years, mostly published by Brazilian scholars in Portuguese). I wanted to fill that gap.

What factors cause people to leave their place of origin and drive ("push") them to migrate to another place? Perhaps war, jobs, socioeconomics, drought, famine, poverty, unhappiness, or religious persecution and discrimination? What factors attract ("pull") them to that place of destination? Perhaps religious freedom, socioeconomic mobility, and opportunity, or curiosity, adventure, and the geographical imagination? Yet penal exiles or slaves, for example, do not have a choice and are forced to move from one place to another. Population movements, then, include not only voluntary migrants, but also involuntary, coerced, reluctant, or clandestine migrants, and a nuanced historical insight of multifaceted and interrelated variables are needed to understand the full scope of such processes. That is, the wide range of dimensions involved in studying migration processes then are evidently not as neat or linear as a mathematical formula. Furthermore, what happens in those places of destination after migrants arrive? Do they continue to migrate to other places Basic questions like these intrigued me and had first prompted me to think and write about these themes almost two decades ago.[3]

These complex intersections warrant careful navigation. I noticed that many scholars tend to habitually conflate Spanish with Portuguese Jews whenever they discuss Iberian Jews or Sephardic Jews, and most focus on Spain, and on Spanish Jews and New Christians (I noticed this in popular spheres as well).[4] Moreover, due to the large migrational influx of Ashkenazi Jews to Brazil during the twentieth century, most people associate the word "Jew" exclusively with "Ashkenazi Jew," with little or no knowledge about the significance of Portuguese Jews and their role in colonial Brazil (commonly known under the ambiguous umbrella term, "Sephardic Jews" or "Sephardim").[5]

Several people with whom I spoke had never heard about this migration enterprise to Brazil, or that Portuguese Jews had established the first Crypto-Jewish communities in the Americas in Brazil and had founded the first synagogue in the Western Hemisphere. Nor had they heard about a former Jew, a New Christian known as Mestre João ("Master John"), who first determined the location of the constellation of the Southern Cross when the Portuguese arrived in Brazil in 1500. The same Southern Cross, *O Cruzeiro do Sul*, that today emboldens Brazil's national flag, has become a Brazilian symbol of nationhood. During the mid-seventeenth century, Portuguese Jews played an important role not only in establishing the first official Jewish congregations and synagogues in Brazil, Suriname, and throughout the Caribbean islands, but also in founding the first Jewish communities in North America (i.e., today Newport, Rhode Island, and New York City). The establishment of these first Jewish communities in the Americas was specifically tied to the exodus of Portuguese Jews from Recife, Pernambuco.

So how, and why did the processes by which Portugal and its institutional powers in Brazil make this Jewish and New Christian legacy and memory "submerged?" To answer this question, I introduce an interrelated sevenfold approach in the next chapter. These seven intersectional possibilities help to answer this fundamental question throughout this narrative. As Toby Lester states in his study on the early cartography of the Americas, the roles of New Christians in the New World "is an aspect of the early colonization of the Americas that deserves more attention."[6] Thus, I felt compelled to examine further this important facet of Brazil's colonial geography.

As I continued to research this topic, I also learned more about the activities of the Portuguese Inquisition in Brazil and the persecution of those

New Christians and their descendants. Even though they were nominally Catholic in public, they could be accused of practising Judaism in secret; a heretical crime listed in the Inquisition dossiers as *crime de judaismo*, "crime of Judaism" (hence, they were "Judaizers," *judaizantes*). I decided to research the impact of the Portuguese Inquisition's activities in Brazil and examined 19,775 digitized dossiers available online at the National Archives in Portugal (Arquivo Nacional, Torre do Tombo). From those dossiers, I found that a total of 1,033 individuals had been arrested in Brazil; a little over two-fifths were arrested for Judaism (449 individuals). The Inquisition dossiers became an important repository of information and new data patterns and insights emerged.

My intention here however, is not to callously glorify the Portuguese world or trumpet the achievements of New Christians and Jews and their arrival in Brazil at the expense of overlooking, or remaining indifferent to the contingencies of imperialism, colonialism, genocide, and slavery (contingencies that I also address).[7] Prior to the arrival of the Portuguese in 1500, Indigenous populations, the original inhabitants of Brazil (i.e., Tupiniquim, Tupinambá, and Janduís, among millions more at that time) were already part of a complex and interconnected South American network of trails and paths, with several tribal, trade, regional, and cultural linkages with an ancient and sophisticated sociocultural heritage. They left indelible cultural imprints and had already modified Brazil's landscapes (as well as in the rest of the Americas), yet were eventually decimated by genocide, wars, and diseases, and reduced to less than 1 percent of Brazil's total population today.[8] Instead, I highlight the importance of a much-needed inclusion of the presence of Portuguese Jews and New Christians within the biography of colonial Brazil, between 1500 and 1822.

A few clarifications are in order. The terms "Jew," "New Christian," and "Judaizer" ("Crypto-Jew") are not interchangeable, bound, or static. New Christians straddled a unique condition living as nominal Catholics and at the same time, as descendants of Jews who were not fully Jewish nor fully Christian, living betwixt and between religious and sociopolitical categories.

The terms "anti-Semitism" and "anti-Jewishness" connote different things at different times in the literature. For example, the term "anti-Semitism" does not appear until the nineteenth century and its semantics in modern vernacular carry specific biological and racial connotations. Therefore, I have made a concerted effort to make that distinction whenever possible and use the terms "anti-Semitism" and "anti-Jewishness" within their appropriate and respective historical contexts.

I am also cautious to avoid falling into the theoretical pitfall and approach known today as "groupism." As explained by sociologist Rogers Brubaker, this approach perpetuates stereotypes of individuals in a group as unchanging and absolute, instead of being fluid and subject to changes and contexts of time and place. In the milieu of this narrative, this becomes an important consideration given the spectrum of ambivalence, nuances, and malleability of Portuguese New Christians and Jews in colonial Brazil.[9]

By "Luso-Brazil," I mean Portuguese-speaking and Portuguese-influenced Brazil, where "Lusophone" is a Portuguese speaker, from the term "Lusitanian": the aboriginal population that lived in the region prior to the Roman conquest of Iberia and that became known as "Lusitania," which is today the modern country of Portugal. Today, Lusophone countries include the countries of Portugal, Brazil, Cape Verde, Guinea-Bissau, Equatorial Guinea, São Tomé and Príncipe, Angola, Mozambique, Macau, and East Timor. Also, Brazil never received the official nomenclature of "colony" by Portugal; that is, it was either referred to as simply *"Brasil"* or *"Estado do Brasil."* However, for simplicity I use the term "colony" loosely to refer to the historical period from 1500 to 1822 (a period known as *Brasil colonial*, "colonial Brazil").

This emphasis on the Portuguese world, Luso-Brazil, the Portuguese diaspora, and Portuguese Jews and New Christians stems from the need to counterview the narrative of New World encounters that has been projected all too often in anglophone academic and popular spheres as an exclusive "Spanish story."

Acknowledgments

The research work conducted here was partially funded by grants awarded by the Department of Geography and Environmental Planning, and by the College of Liberal Arts Faculty Research Grant at Towson University, Maryland. Several people have helped me throughout the writing process, and without them the completion of this book would not have been possible.

I want to begin by thanking Paporn Thebpanya for her work producing all the maps used here, and for helping me sort them out; Derrick Marcus, David Marcus, Kent Barnes, David McCreery Jr., and Wim Klooster, who read early rough drafts, and for their helpful and insightful notes and suggestions. Anne Lapedus Brest who kindly shared the work of her uncle, Irish historian Bernard Shillman, with me. Historian Rita-Costa Gomes, who shared important materials with me and made many insightful observations and suggestions. I am also grateful to Rita for inviting me to participate at the PIMA meeting (Pre-Modernists Iberianists of the Middle Atlantic) at Towson University, March 11, 2022, to discuss one of my chapter manuscripts in this book.

I am indebted to historian Laura Jarnagin Pang for her continuing suggestions and thoughtful comments, and who kindly took the time to meticulously read my manuscript drafts. I am thankful for her generosity and ongoing encouragement.

I also want to thank the Department of Geography and Environmental Planning and the College of Liberal Arts at Towson University, and especially my Department Chair, Charles Schmitz, for his ongoing encouragement and support. I am thankful to geographer Andrew Slyuter for his comments and suggestions, Patricia Kot, the copyeditor, for her meticulous work and attention to detail, the anonymous reviewers, and to Michael Millman, senior acquisitions editor at the Univerisy of New Mexico Press, for enthusiastically taking on my project and seeing it through from the early stages to its final publication.

Last but not least, I want to thank my wife, Debbie Marcus, who read several drafts and made helpful suggestions, and who always encourages me and makes me smile. I am thankful for her patience and support, without which I could never have finished this project. Although I received help and assistance in the writing process, any missteps, and errors here are entirely mine.

Introduction

HOW DID PORTUGUESE NEW Christians and Jews become one of the first immigrants to settle in Brazil? To ask this question presumes that their presence in Brazil might seem like an oddity, given that Brazil was among the world's largest and staunchest Catholic nations.[1] However, their presence should not appear to be all that surprising considering the anti-Jewish sentiments spurred for almost three centuries by the Portuguese Inquisition, the Crown, and the Catholic Church. Thus, escaping persecution and migrating to the New World would seem like a logical undertaking. However, by offering multidimensional insights into migration, mobility, colonial Brazil, and more broadly, the Atlantic world, this narrative shows how these migrants were more than a mere "exotic oddity" in the tropics.

The migrations of New Christians to Brazil were not restricted to the northeast region of Brazil (e.g., Pernambuco and Bahia).[2] Brazilian historian José Gonçalves Salvador, for instance, described how their presence throughout colonial Brazil had been well documented, from Amazonia and the northern region to Rio de Janeiro, Minas Gerais, and the Rio da Prata ("River Plate") in the southernmost regions. By 1632, a Portuguese priest wrote a letter back to the inquisitors in Lisbon relaying that the majority of European inhabitants in Brazil at that time were (former) "Jews."[3] Historiographers of Brazil nonetheless perpetuated a narrative wherein fundamental historical figures tied to Brazil's colonial biography hailed exclusively from Portuguese nobility and Old Christian families, yet as José Gonçalves Salvador points out, many of them were, in fact, New Christians (e.g., José de Anchieta, Martim Afonso de Sousa, and Salvador Correia de Sá e Benevides, among many others).[4] According to another historian, Angelo Adriano Faria de Assis, the significance of their presence in Brazil offered an "escape valve" for New Christians—the possibility to project their new livelihoods far away from the economic stifling, discrimination, and persecution in the Old World.[5]

My goal in this book is to offer a broad synthesis of the movement, presence, and prominence of Portuguese Jews and New Christians and their descendants in colonial Brazil, and I highlight their migrations, mobility, contributions, and importance.[6] I have focused on the period between 1500, when the Portuguese first arrived in Brazil, and 1821, the year the Inquisition ended, and a year before Brazil's independence from Portugal in 1822. Given the vast temporal, thematic, and spatial scopes of this topic, this study has its inherent limitations.[7]

This book does not comprise a comprehensive analysis of *all* Luso-Brazilian Jewry or *all* New Christians, nor is it about Judaism or the Portuguese Inquisition. I have not conducted a specific regional or temporal study, or a biographical case study either. Instead, this book offers a holistic overview using multi- and interdisciplinary approaches, with important deliberations on migration, place, and spatial interrelationships that are vital to the biography of colonial Brazil. Altogether, these considerations help us understand the role of Portuguese Jews and New Christians in the development of complex demographic processes and environmental contingencies in colonial Brazil.

In most popular and academic spheres, perhaps more is known about other religions and cultural legacies in colonial Brazil than about the migration and legacy of Portuguese Jews and New Christians.[8] As Stuart B. Schwartz comments, "the early infamy of Brazil as a colony settled by New Christians . . . began to fade somewhat as the colony became profitable and the origins of the first settlers were forgotten."[9] Brazilian collective memory, in light of this "infamous" presence, should be interpreted through a careful framework and a nuanced understanding. To carry the social marker "New Christian" meant that a person was a carrier of "tainted blood": a descendant of former Jews. To this day, to be *judeu* (a "Jew") still carries a strong and widespread negative social stigma in modern Brazil (as I discuss in the Afterword).

The diaspora of the Portuguese Jews and New Christians is often considered one of the largest European diasporas of the early modern period.[10]

Moreover, Portuguese Jews not only played an imperative role in the founding of the first Jewish congregations and synagogues in Recife and Olinda, Brazil, Suriname, and throughout the Caribbean, but they also played an important role in establishing the first Jewish communities in North America (today New York City and Newport, Rhode Island).[11] They were active participants throughout the Americas, beginning in the sixteenth century. More importantly here, they were important participants in the "making" of colonial Brazil—a fact that remains unacknowledged within most popular and academic spheres, especially within Latin American geography.

Geographers have contributed to the general topic areas explored here, of colonialism, landscape, sense of place, free and forced migration, and, of course, Brazil. This book would therefore join that growing literature with an innovative contribution.[12] At the same time, there is growing interest among historians in the roles of Jews in the region, as I outline ahead; a topic to which geographers have not contributed much at all—until now.

However, this book is about much more than just Brazil because it explicates networks of mobility throughout the Atlantic world, from Brazil to Africa, Europe, the Caribbean, and North America. It therefore has relevance for students not only of Brazil but of the more extensive networks of the Atlantic. It will be of interest to geographers, historians, Brazilianists, Latin Americanists, and scholars in Jewish studies, the Humanities, and the social sciences (e.g., Brazilian studies, Portuguese studies, Luso-Brazilian studies, Latin American studies, and migration studies), as well as to non-academic readers.

Toward a New Geography of Colonial Brazil

So, what is new here? Some readers may be disappointed after reading this book, since there is nothing "revolutionarily new," and historians have been writing about this topic for quite some time now (*Nihil sub sole novum*). However, what *is* new is a narrative in the English language written as a broad synopsis that is not restricted to a particular historical period or geographical region. Some of the topics that I discuss here may be familiar to a Brazilian audience, but not to an anglophone one, while other points may be unfamiliar to both. This synthesis in the English language is new (especially since most of the literature on this topic is published in Portuguese) and yields insights that are not available in the scholarship that has focused only on regional and temporal approaches.

I have conducted a new study consisting of an analysis of 19,775 *processos* (archival dossiers) available online at the National Archives, Portugal (Arquivo Nacional, Torre do Tombo).[13] From these digitized archival dossiers, I found that 1,033 individuals had been imprisoned in Brazil for all heresies.[14] Only New Christians accused of the heretical "crime of Judaism" in Brazil were burned at the stake (i.e., New Christians accused of practicing Judaism in secret: judaizantes).[15] The "crime of Judaism" is a literal translation from the Portuguese, "crime de judaismo," as listed in the Inquisition dossiers. I show that the Inquisition specifically targeted New Christians and their descendants, who represented 70 percent of all individuals arrested in Brazil for all heresies (and not just for Judaism)—and who comprised the single largest cohort of all arrests in Brazil. A little over two-fifths of all individuals in Brazil were arrested for the "crime of Judaism" (449 individuals, accounting for 43 percent of all arrests).

The first person arrested for the crime of Judaism in Brazil was Salvador da Maia in 1591; aged 40, born in Lisbon, living in Ilhéus, Bahia, and listed as a merchant (processo 2320). The last individual arrested for Judaism in Brazil was José Ricardo de Morais in 1778, in Vila Boa de Goiás, Goiás; originally from Meia Ponte, Rio de Janeiro, and listed as a farmer (processo 16953).[16] Other varied heretical crimes (a total of 584) accounted for 57 percent of all arrests. After Judaism, bigamy accounted for the second largest single cohort of arrests, followed by: heretical propositions, sodomy, blasphemy, witchcraft, sorcery, and superstitions, respectively, and a wide range of other heresies (See Chapter 6 and the Appendix for a full list of heresies).[17]

I found thirteen inviduals from Brazil who were burned at the stake, and three burned in effigy (post-mortem)—all of them for the "crime of Judaism." I found individuals who were as young as 10 and as old as 100 years old. For example, Helena da Cruz from Rio de Janeiro arrested in 1718, aged 12, was among the youngest arrested for the crime of Judaism in Brazil (processo 8200). Among the oldest individuals arrested for Judaism in Brazil were Ines Aires, who was arrested in Rio de Janeiro in 1713, aged 80, and widow of André de Barros, a local merchant (processo 13099), and Ana Rodrigues, aged 80 (wife of Heitor Antunes), a New Christian arrested in 1593 in Bahia (processo 11680)—discussed in Chapter 4.

Brazilian historian Anita W. Novinsky conducted a study from the Inquisition dossiers over twenty years ago in 2002 which yielded slightly different results than mine; for example, they showed a higher number of arrests in Brazil, with a total of 1,076.[18] Some of the differences between my results and hers, of course, stem from the fact that the dossiers that I examined were from the digitized online material available (with the downside that several were incomplete or missing dossiers), while the study she conducted was in situ from dossiers stored at the National Archives at Torre do Tombo ("hard copies"). Novinsky found the names of 29 individuals who were burned at the stake, and seven in effigy. However, she included Brazilians who were living in Portugal at the time of their arrest (which I did not do since I only included those who were arrested *in* Brazil), and which may account for this difference in totals. She also found slightly fewer arrests for Judaism: 322, which accounted for 41 percent of total arrests in her sample (conversely, I found 449 people, which accounted for 43 percent in my sample). Novinsky found different totals for the arrests in Bahia (345 arrests), Rio de Janeiro (249), Pernambuco (135), and Minas Gerais (60). Conversely, in my sample the top four places for most arrests found were in Rio de Janeiro, Pernambuco, Bahia, and Minas Gerais, respectively.[19] However, it is not clear how Novinsky considered exactly under which jurisdiction those arrests were made at different times, and its equivalent modern state name (as I explain ahead here). In my examination, for example, I discuss the location in the equivalent modern states today, no matter under which jurisdiction it fell at different periods (i.e., Pernambuco comprised different territory boundaries over different historical periods). Moreover, I point out that arrests in respective regions varied significantly depending on the century. For example, during the sixteenth-century arrests for Judaism were virtually exclusive to Pernambuco and Bahia, while during the early eighteenth century, arrests for Judaism occurred mostly in Rio de Janeiro. My results, nonetheless, broadly overlap and corroborate Novinsky's results, despite a few contingencies and differences.

This book marks a new contribution to anglophone scholarship, especially in geography. The only full book publications available today that have discussed Jews and New Christians *throughout* colonial Brazil (i.e., from 1500 to 1822), are either published in Portuguese by Brazilian historians and have not been translated into English, or are outdated.[20] For example, the only book in the English language available on the topic, *Jews in Colonial Brazil*, a well-known synopsis written by historian Arnold Wiznitzer, was published in 1960, well over half a century ago. Nonetheless, I have relied on these important publications that provide a contextual and scholarly backdrop for this book.

One of the problems that I found in other recent historical studies is that they tend to focus either on one geographical region or place alone (e.g., Northeast Brazil; or Minas Gerais, Bahia, Rio de Janeiro, or Pernambuco, etc.), or a specific historical period. I wanted to fill this gap.

The dossiers from the Portuguese Inquisition examined here represent a mere glimpse into the magnitude of the presence of Jews and New Christians in Brazil, since there are no data on the exact numbers of how many went to Brazil. Therefore, I have not attempted to offer a comprehensive study to quantify this migration, and instead I provide a broad, educated impression of this phenomenon.[21] I have expanded and built upon previous studies and pieced together snippets of scholarship to offer a new synthesis and analysis that now receives a new veneer, painted with broad strokes.

I discuss two additional components in this book: (1) I underline the importance of the Convivência period, which would later influence Portuguese colonial encounters in the New World. These connections to Portugal's past then dovetail with the first Portuguese arrivals in Brazil and the transference of the Portuguese world to Brazil. Known as *gente da nação* ("people of the nation"), Portuguese New Christians and Jews established commercial networks and communities throughout major global ports and entrepôts, for instance from Sofala, Porto d'Ale, Joal, Petite Côte, Luanda, and Goa, to Rouen, Bordeaux, Amsterdam, Antwerp, Hamburg, and London, and throughout Latin America and the Caribbean (e.g., Suriname, Brazil, Curaçao, Jamaica, Barbados, Mexico, Peru, and Bolivia). I include discussions here that show the unambiguous connection between Portuguese Jews and New Christians with the broader Atlantic world and its global commercial enterprises and kinship networks. (2) I include discussions that specifically distinguish Portugal and Spain's colonial approaches and encounters in the New World and expand on explaining the differences between Portuguese New Christians and their Spanish *converso* brethren.

This is a story about Portuguese Jews and New Christians (they were not Spanish), and in this regard, I highlight the Portuguese participation in New World encounters. These discussions underline the predicaments often found in anglophone scholarship and popular spheres that has traditionally lumped Spanish and Portuguese Jews and New Christians together in studies about Latin America, and that perpetuate an imaginary geography of a Latin America that is more "Spanish" than "Portuguese."

Geography Matters and Beyond

Until now this topic has not received the attention of anglophone geographers, as it has been studied almost exclusively by historians (especially Brazilian historians). Yet why should this matter? First, because this is indeed a quintessential "geographical" narrative that involves cardinal elements and themes of geography that engage with spatial and migration processes, place, environment, region, and movement (i.e., the "stuff" of geography). That is, the framework of this narrative underlines the inherent involvement of Portuguese Jews and New Christians in various sociocultural and ecological interactions in Brazil since 1500 (i.e., human-environment interactions). These interactions, therefore, are inherently tied to the biography of colonial Brazil and to the geography of Brazil: for instance, from the first interactions with Indigenous populations and the first "western" scientific and geographical location of Brazil, an observation based on the constellation of the Southern Cross made by a New Christian, Mestre João, on board Pedro Álvares Cabral's fleet when he first landed in Brazil (as I discuss later); to the introduction of the sugarcane cultivation and industry in the rich, dark fertile *massapê* soils of the Brazilian northeast by New Christians in Pernambuco and Bahia; and to the exploration of gold and diamonds in the Brazilian center-west region (*centro-oeste*: discussed in Chapter 4).[22]

Brazil's first colonial economic boom, for example, began with the exploitation of *pau brasil*, "brazilwood" (*Ibirapitanga* in the Tupi language), and was an enterprise that had been assigned by the Crown to be undertaken specifically by New Christians. The subsequent economic boom was sugar, which was also introduced in Brazil by New Christians since they were known for their expertise in the sugarcane industry. The next boom was gold, precious stones, and diamonds—all of which also involved commercial and kinship global networks of the "people of the nation." Hence, as active participants throughout the Americas, their presence and prominence merit attention within the annals of Latin American geography.

Second, the various spaces, sites, and scales of surveillance and of denouncements to the Portuguese inquisitors include spatial themes and topics that are also conceptually rooted in geography. Thus, multifaceted spatial interrelationships emerge through these interactions that illustrate the role of their presence and prominence in colonial Brazil. Third, although this following adage has been repeated many times, it is still worthwhile reiterating: there is no history without geography, and no geography without history; they are interrelated disciplines, albeit each with its own respective approaches and theoretical foci. At a larger geographical scale, as Irene Silverblatt argues, "'The heretical' was much more than a dimension of religious doctrine: it played a critical role in the making of the modern world."[23]

Fourth, the central themes of migration, mobility, and spatial processes emerge as important ones; for example, the conditions that were right ("site"), and the significant connections between places ("situation"). Portuguese New Christians were constantly moving from one place to another—they were extremely mobile. To most people of the sixteenth and seventeenth centuries, being "Portuguese" equaled "New Christian," which equaled "mobility." They self-identified as *gente da nação Portuguêsa* ("people of the Portuguese nation") or simply, "gente da nação." This group came to represent and project their capacity to move around the world with access to various global networks available to them, moving commodities, ideas, and people at a much larger scale than before. As Daviken Studnicki-Gizbert explains, the "people of the nation" were inherently involved in a "circulatory movement of migration, maritime labor and trade."[24] In this case, migration was not a static or unilateral endeavor. As we shall see ahead, many of them did not simply migrate to one place and stay there; several went back and forth between places, and they were notably decentralized and autonomous.[25] For example, "people of the nation" moved from Brazil to Peru and Mexico and back to Brazil, or to Barbados, Jamaica, Curaçao, and other Caribbean islands, for instance; and to Suriname, Amsterdam, Antwerp, Hamburg, or the British Isles, and some even returned to Portugal. In today's vernacular gente da nação projected the definition of "transnationalism" par excellence, and as Francesca Trivellato aptly puts it, "Nação thus stood for the translocal identity (at the same time real and imagined)."[26]

These discussions then include examples of "push-pull factors" that precipitated migration movements which did not occur in a sociocultural and political vacuum. Hence, a main thread that is weaved throughout this book underscores the movement of "people of the nation" within a complex web of nuanced political, religious, and socioeconomic forces, and at the same time, within discrimination policies, along with the sites, spaces, and methods of surveillance imposed upon them for almost 300 years. Subsequently, they were inherently involved in the geographical transformations of physical, demographic, and cultural landscapes in colonial Brazil. As Brazilian scholar Nachman Falbel aptly claims that New Christians, Judaizers or not, were a fundamentally important component of early colonial Brazil.[27]

Toward an Approach of Using Historical Geography to Understand the "Biography of Place"

To highlight a geographical premise here, the following theoretical component will further illuminate my point. Geographer Kempton E. Webb outlined the concept of the landscape evolution in the tradition of historical geography. He asserted:

> The cultural and physical processes that shape any landscape interact continuously, in varying degrees of intensity with each other *and also* with the earth's surface; this surface becomes altered, thereby presenting a continuously changing base upon which subsequent interactions occur.[28]

That is, Webb embraces a concept that is both comprehensive and at the same time, one that offers dynamic views. While Webb's ideas were developed almost half a century ago, they are still effective and especially fitting here in this examination. Moreover, he conceived this idea while he was conducting research about the northeastern region of Brazil in situ—which becomes an even more suitable idea to reiterate here.[29] Webb asks, "What does the biography of this landscape reveal of the causes and processes that have produced the present situation?"[30] Thus, by using this question as a theoretical launching pad, we can then incorporate its premise as an effective strategy to uncover and reveal submerged cultural and physical landscapes in Brazil's colonial heritage and memory—albeit, contested and dynamic. This approach can then also be used as an investigative tool for a perspective on "biography of place."[31] That is, the causes and processes in the geography of Brazil then emerge and can offer important insights into the gradual changes in environmental and sociocultural contingencies occurring over time throughout that nation. Webb claimed, "if there were ever an area of Brazil where traditions have persisted, it is Northeast Brazil, so it is toward the early Portuguese experience there that we must look for enlightenment."[32] A starting point associated with Webb's claim then is to first look at the place of origin of Brazil's first immigrants: the Portuguese.

It is important to point out that Portugal's population was already historically heterogenous even before the Portuguese first migrated and settled in Brazil. Consider that Portugal's amalgamated culture stemmed from centuries-old migrations and influences that ranged from the Phoenicians, Romans, and French and English knights, to Moors (Muslims), Gypsies/Roma, Jews, Dutch, and north and sub-Saharan Africans (e.g., black Africans were once estimated to comprise about 10 percent of the total population of Lisbon, Évora, and Algarve).[33] For example, it is estimated that urban African slaves in Lisbon in the 1630s numbered about 15,000 out of a population of 100,000.[34] In addition, the Gypsies/Roma in Portugal, for example, were forbidden to speak *Giringonça* (Romany), and they were expelled from the nation in 1573, and many migrated to Brazil. However, many still stayed in Portugal, and by 1718, all Gypsies in that nation were rounded up and sent to Portuguese overseas colonies (including Brazil)—this policy of "removal" continued as late as 1745.[35] Other studies point to the complexity of the Portuguese people, and show that even Japanese, Chinese, and (East) Indian ancestries are found among the Portuguese population due to the extensive Portuguese overseas global explorations over the centuries.[36]

Therefore, whenever we hear the modern ascription "Portuguese," discussed as a national monolithic group (i.e., "European") or as a category coded in contemporary racial overtones (i.e., "white"), we will also likely find, at the same time, a contested categorization that has been deeply marked over the centuries by a diverse population with an ambiguous ancestry. Moreover, this ancestral ambiguity of the Portuguese people was only magnified when they settled in Brazil, where widespread mestiçagem ("miscegenation") took place over centuries through the intermingling of Indigenous, African, New Christian, and Old Christian populations, resulting in a complex and hybrid Luso-Brazilian human geography.[37]

Considering Layers of Cultural Landscapes and Palimpsest

Geographers have referred to syncretic and amalgamated sociocultural phenomena as "palimpsest"—a term taken from the medieval parchment that was scraped away to be reused, yet left residual writing on it. In this case, the metaphor of palimpsest used in geography refers to the "layers" of cultural landscapes that have been built on top of other layers over time, be it architecture, urban layout, housing, or names of streets, for example (e.g., a synagogue was built where a mosque used to be, which eventually became a Catholic church). Therefore, over time, cultural mosaics with syncretic elements become apparent as "cultural layers." Malyn Newitt offers a vivid example during the 1520s:

> A taste was acquired for Flemish art which came to adorn not only merchants' houses in Portugal but churches and residences in Madeira and the Azores. Meanwhile ceramics imported from the Netherlands cross-pollinated with the Moorish tradition to produce the *azulejos* ["tiles"] that became the art-form most characteristic of Portugal.[38]

That is, the spatial processes within migration movements and the idea of "place" consist of the human cultural imprints on Earth that have developed over time—the very substance of place-making—as in Carl O. Sauer's well-known conceptualization of cultural landscapes.[39] However, over time, new places "cover up" cultural landscapes of the past. As Alan Marvel and David Simms explain, "a landscape often shows traces of older forms and symbols, not just recent features. Therefore, what exists in any given place are layers of meaning that are waiting to be revealed, interpreted, and understood by those who encounter them."[40] Furthermore, they clarify, "these layers of meaning help to establish a sense of place and can include attributes such as geography, history, culture, socioeconomics, arts, architecture and language."[41]

Therefore, "place" as a complex concept, effectively combines both material and mental representations.[42] Tim Cresswell offers an example: "a church, for instance, is a place. It is neither just a particular material artifact, nor just a set of religious ideas; it is always both."[43] In this case, places often carry a double meaning or even multiple meanings over time, which brings us back to how places over time become submerged, covered under intersectional sociocultural layers of memory. Experiencing "place" is inherently imbued with human attachment, symbolism, meaning, contexts, and tensions.[44] Places evoke powerful emotional responses and attachments in people, as they hold strong personal ties to them, and often they become the focal point in territorial conflicts or wars, for example.[45] We see this, for instance, in the city of Jerusalem and its evocative emotional attachments, particularly for those of the Abrahamic faiths—where Jerusalem is more than just a city or just a capital—it is a powerful "idea." However, at the same time, ironically a "sense of placelessness" pervades in the deeply imbedded spirit of Jews in their global diaspora—as one scholar explains, "Diaspora is part of the condition of Jewishness."[46]

The examination of the central theme here of migration processes then helps us understand important clues to these nuanced cultural layers of place that have been built upon each other over time, especially as migrating populations leave cultural traces in each respective place-biography, sometimes obscuring and hiding sociocultural layers.[47] Keeping the concept of palimpsest in mind then, an important backdrop for this theme of a submerged legacy and memory in colonial Brazil emerges.

The idea of "sense of place" becomes even more complex when we consider that many Portuguese New Christians (former Jews and their descendants) in fact returned to Portugal after having fled, despite the ongoing persecution and discrimination. David L. Graizbord, for example, provides a sophisticated and nuanced discussion about such returnees, and how

Portuguese New Christians who returned were emotionally connected to place (e.g., sense of place), as they "felt a deep emotional and intellectual attachment to their countries of origin," which had "shaped their collective heritage and personal histories."[48]

It is also vital then to consider the importance of the "culture of times," to borrow Stephen J. Gould's term.[49] That is, since places are by nature contested, and the symbolisms they are imbued with are based on arbitrary sociopolitical and cultural constructions, they convey powerful symbolic meanings and experiences to different people at different times—place-making is indeed an arbitrary and contested process.[50] Moreover, the "culture of times" is contingent on the culture at any given historical period, and is inherently tied to the interpretation of these complex constructs of place. That is, the "culture" of a particular period plays an important role in the decision-making in migration processes and upon migrants who then act as agents of change, via diffusion processes, and take that "culture" to places of destination.

Central Themes of Migration and Mobility

Richard Morrill situated the importance of migration studies within geography, stating, "Migration is indeed a quintessentially spatial social process, in which the environmental, place, and space components of geography are essential to a full understanding."[51] Giving continuity to this framework, I discuss the theme of migration and explore the complexities of spatial processes and migrant interrelationships with places of origin and places of destination.[52]

Therefore, the study of place, and of spatial and migration processes, are quintessential geographical themes, and we can use geographical concepts here to understand the complex "push-pull factors" involved in the movement of Portuguese Jews and New Christians to and within Brazil. Whether these migrations were coerced, forced (e.g., "penal exiles," *degredados*), voluntary, or reluctant (e.g., having to flee because of persecution, without wanting to leave), their movement to Brazil increased in size and scale after their systematic persecution and repression in Portugal, and over time, amplified kinship ties were made available to them. The networks generated from migrations to and from Portugal's forts and trading outposts (*feitorias*) and territories around the world, and were forged into a wide range of trade, commercial, and familial contacts, which further facilitated increased migration influxes to those places of destination (i.e., "chain migration," where one family member moves to a place of destination and is subsequently joined by other family members and loved ones).[53]

During a period of two hundred years (1500–1700), it is estimated that about 700,000 individuals left Portugal mostly for Portuguese territories, of which at least 100,000 went to Brazil (most of whom were men, which contributed to the chronic sex ratio imbalance in that nation for almost two centuries after the first Portuguese arrivals).[54] On a larger scale, overall between 1500 and 1800, over 1.5 million people left Portugal, and after the late sixteenth century most of them migrated to Brazil, with a steady movement to that nation that continued throughout the seventeenth and eighteenth centuries.[55] While we have several accounts of their presence, and evidence from the existing Inquisition dossiers, it is unknown how many of these migrants were New Christians. However, recent genetic studies suggest that they comprised a significant proportion of migrants to Brazil. For example, one study suggests that about 30 percent of Brazilians today can trace their heritage to those Portuguese Jews who fled the Portuguese Inquisition.[56] That would be equivalent to about half a million Brazilians today.[57]

The total population in Brazil increased from over 100,000 by 1590 (i.e., 30,000 Portuguese, 28,000 Indians, and 42,000 Africans) to an estimated 390,000 in 1760 (when Europeans and their descendants comprised less than 30 percent of the total population). The population density in Brazil was concentrated in Bahia and Pernambuco during the sixteenth and most of the seventeenth centuries because of sugar cultivation and the concentration of Africans and Indians used as slave labor. However, after the mid-seventeenth century, with the discovery of gold and diamonds, that population density shifted to the southeast region—mainly Rio de Janeiro and Minas Gerais—and eventually in the late nineteenth century to São Paulo (today the city of São Paulo is the most populated city in South America).[58]

It is important to also point out that Portuguese Jews and New Christians had also migrated to Amsterdam, Antwerp, and Hamburg, for example, in the late sixteenth and early seventeenth centuries, establishing important

Portuguese-Jewish communities there.[59] Many of the members from the main community in Amsterdam would eventually migrate to the New World—mostly to Brazil, as well as to Suriname and the Caribbean islands, such as Barbados, Jamaica, and Curaçao, and eventually to New Amsterdam (today New York City). The traditional push-pull factors in migration processes, then, play an intrinsic part in how scholars view circumstances that prompt people to leave their place of origin ("push factors") and those that attract people to move to a place of destination ("pull factors").[60]

Another basic strategy is to examine the transformations in various sites, spaces, and situations precipitated by Portuguese immigrants, for example, by asking questions such as: In what region did they first settle in Brazil, and in what historical period? What can we learn about their encounters with Indigenous and African populations? How were Brazilian landscapes and economies transformed, for instance, with the extraction of brazilwood, pau brasil, and the implementation of sugarcane mills, and to what extent were New Christians involved in these economic activities? How did New Christians, who were also Crypto-Jews, integrate into colonial Brazilian society? These questions facilitate the understanding of the broader geography of colonial Brazil that are addressed in subsequent chapters.

Push-pull factors signal the behavior of migrants who ostensibly make rational and economic choices in their selection to maximize and optimize their benefits by migrating to a place of destination. However, migrants may also make decisions based on non-rational or non-economic reasons (e.g., escape, curiosity, adventure, or the "geographical imagination").[61] The major push factors for (former) Jews to migrate out of Portugal, for example, may have been economic and sociopolitical stifling, discrimination, persecution, and fear of the Inquisition. The pull factors include: the idea of settling for a livelihood without discrimination or fear in Brazil: opportunity; the pursuit of curiosity and adventure; the idea that socioeconomic upward mobility could be achieved without surveillance or persecution; and a search for the "promised land."[62]

The decision-making process of migrants has often rested on migrants' perception of how the benefits of moving might outweigh the risk of staying. In this case, Marcos Chor Maio and Carlos Eduardo Calaça propose that these migrations of New Christians to Brazil involved a two-fold strategy:

(1) New Christians in Brazil were searching for upward mobility, especially as sugarcane planters and sugarcane industry experts were thus able to enter the "Portuguese aristocratic structure" (i.e., living as "local noblemen"), where they were free from business restrictions imposed on them in Portugal. (2) They could distance themselves geographically from the tentacles of the Inquisition in a new place that was more difficult for this institution to police.[63] While the statutes of "blood purity" (*pureza de sangue*) were still applied throughout Brazil, compared to Portugal they were enforced with relatively less rigor.[64]

Throughout this book, I have highlighted the continuous migration of Portuguese Jews and New Christians to, within, and out of colonial Brazil. Migration, as an important theme, then, also emerges along with a vital component in "race matters": from the first encounters with Indigenous populations and intermarriages, and mameluco offspring, to the advent of the transatlantic slave trade from Africa, and the subsequent intermingling of Indigenous, Portuguese (Old and New Christians), and African populations, miscegenation became even more accentuated in Brazil.

On "Race Matters"

Why discuss "race" and Brazilian social scientist, Gilberto Freyre, here? The constructs of "race" in Brazil require careful historical navigation (although it is not the focus of my book). However, this section is necessary since this component helps explain an important facet of Brazilian human geography, and it is especially pertinent later, when I examine the results of my study of the Inquisition dossiers in Chapter 6.

It is worthwhile to reiterate that "race" connoted different things to different people in different places at different times. Our "modern" interpretation of "race" merits attention as I examine the experience of Portuguese Jews and New Christians and their encounters overseas (especially in Brazil). For instance, Peter Mark and José da Silva Horta explain the case in West Africa (i.e., Joal and Porto d'Ale), and within the context of Portuguese Jews and New Christians, where the idea of "race" "had different connotations in the sixteenth century and was not ineluctably linked to skin color, even in the early 1600s."[65] They explain, "skin color was not a deterrent to the selection of a mate and . . . did not preclude the subsequent incorporation of any offspring into the Jewish social and religious community."[66] In the case of Senegal, for example, Portuguese "Jewish men followed the widespread practice of Portuguese in Africa of establishing relationships with local women."[67] As I discuss ahead, there are many parallels to be made between this particular case in West Africa and Luso-Brazil.

Research by Peter Mark and José da Silva Horta also shows that in both Suriname and Senegal, the "Eurafrican" Jewish population "could claim Jewish identity through the paternal line (contrary to traditional Jewish law, where Jewish identity is passed on through the maternal side). In Senegal, "white" or "Portuguese" identity depended upon several factors, including language and profession; having European ancestry could be a parameter, but it was not essential."[68] Again, the case of Brazil shares commonalities with Luso-African society in seventeenth-century Suriname as well as West Africa, albeit with some major differences—as I point out later. I found that Indigenous, African, and "mixed-race" populations (i.e., mulato, mameluco, pardo, etc.) appear prominently in the Inquisition dossiers among those arrests for the crime of Judaism in Brazil. However, constructs of "race" were fluid, and not static. That is, the meaning and significance of these constructs depended on the historical period, and on the sociocultural and geographical context. Therefore, it is necessary to provide a brief backdrop on the influence of Gilberto Freyre within Brazil's national imagery and Brazil's emblematic schema of "race."

Today Brazil's traditional conceptualization of its national hybrid cultural and racial formation stems from an imaginary triad consisting of three major ("racial") groups based on Indigenous, African, and Portuguese ancestral elements. These three main groups comprised the basis for Brazil's colonial demography, and over time produced a hybrid population make-up, as outlined by Gilberto Freyre.[69] While Freyre is today virtually demonized in current scholarship, and his musings are also mired with a set of contemporary theoretical and historiographical problems, it is worthwhile to briefly discuss a few key points that he made in the context of "race," and of Portuguese New Christians and Jews—albeit almost a century ago—which yet received international and national attention. That is, Freyre's perspective highlights the syncretic importance of the Old and New Christian

Portuguese populations, as well as that of Indigenous and African sociocultural elements in Brazilian colonial society.[70]

A native of Recife, Pernambuco and the grandson of a *senhor de engenho* ("sugarcane plantation owner"), Freyre claimed that the critical elements that helped to form and unite the Portuguese nation stemmed from "individuals of Semitic origin or stock [Jewish], individuals endowed with a mobility, a plasticity, and adaptability social as well as physical that are easily to be made out in the Portuguese navigator and cosmopolitan of the fifteenth century."[71] Freyre was referring to the widespread trade and commercial networks engendered by the flourishing transatlantic mercantile world of Portuguese-Jewish and New Christian enterprises, a topic that I explore in Chapter 3. Freyre also discussed their presence and importance in Brazil (particularly in Minas Gerais, in his second book, *Sobrados e Mocambos*, published in 1936).[72] Consequently, Freyre observed, "it was the Semitic element, mobile and adaptable as no other, that was to confer upon the Portuguese colonizer of Brazil some of the chief physical and psychic conditions for success and for resistance."[73] He concluded that Portuguese imperialist expansion had been based upon Jewish prosperity, and that Portuguese Jews were specifically known for their worldwide influence "through commerce, mercantilism . . . and scientific culture."[74] More important, he stated, "the history of patriarchal society in Brazil is inseparable from the history of the Jew in America."[75] As Ella Shohat and Robert Stam point out, "Freyre . . . sees Sephardi/Semitic [Portuguese-Jewish] 'blood' as an integral part of the [Brazilian] national mix."[76]

In his 1933 milestone publication, *Casa Grande e Senzala* (translated later into English as The Masters and the Slaves), Freyre famously claimed that Brazil's hybrid population and its approach to race were more "advanced" in comparison to the cultural perspectives on race in the United States.[77] While a student at Columbia University, under the tutelage of anthropologist Franz Boas, Freyre had published his doctoral dissertation that famously celebrated rather than eschewed Brazilian miscegenation and hybridity. Freyre claimed that Brazil's hybrid population was based on a nation built on "racial tolerance," something that stood out at the time, particularly since his book was published in 1933, the same year that Adolf Hitler became chancellor of Germany, and at a time when Jim Crow profoundly affected blacks in the southern United States through discrimination and official segregation. Freyre stated that contrary to Germanic and British societies, Brazilian society was not governed by "race" and uniformity alone, but rather it was inspired by a diversely hybrid society and its Portuguese-style colonial legacy.

"Racial democracy" and mestiçagem remained embedded within Brazilian national collective thinking.[78] However, they mean two different things, as Marshall C. Eakin aptly points out.[79] That is, mestiçagem becomes convenient to explain Brazil's idea of collective nationhood, as long as "whiteness" eventually eclipses "blackness." Although Freyre did not use the term "racial democracy" until later in the 1960s, it is often associated with him (yet it was Artur Ramos who originally coined the term in the 1940s). Scholars have castigated Freyre's romantic vision of mestiçagem and Luso-tropical civilization that annihilates "African identity" in Brazil.[80] Moreover, critics accuse Freyre of silencing Brazil's history of rape, sexual violence, and slavery. For example, in *Slavery Unseen*, Lamonte Aidoo discusses how the Inquisition dossiers from Brazil reveal several cases of sexual violence inflicted upon slaves by their masters, including male slave rape, "cloaked beneath the language that denies the real nature of these events."[81]

Hence, Freyre's critics have also disparaged the lack of statistical evidence and the shortcomings of his historical method, and of overly romanticizing Luso-Brazil, as well as for being unrealistic, shortsighted, and Eurocentric.[82] That is, scholars have countered the widespread world perception that Brazil was/is a "racial paradise." Abdias do Nascimento, for example, long argued that Brazil's diverse populations developed through rape and violence, and not through consensual sex and a benign miscegenation, as Freyre would have it when he said: "the milieu in which Brazilian life began was one of sexual intoxication."[83] Over the past sixty years, as Thomas Skidmore pointed out, Brazilian censuses have illustrated that "race" was a critical independent variable affecting key life chances, such as education, mobility, and income.[84] Therefore, given the statistics available today, Freyre's overly romantic perception that the hallmarks of Brazil's biography stemmed from "racial tolerance" are problematic and do not hold true for Brazilian blacks or Indians, past and present.[85] In addition, some scholars have also criticized Freyre's allegedly anti-Semitic sentiments in his work.[86] Other scholars have pointed out yet another angle: that Freyre inserted a positive notion of the integration of Jews and New Christians into Brazilian society as an example of the unique plurality of Luso-Brazilian identity.[87]

Despite Freyre's polemic racial narrative and sociocultural shortcomings, the importance of his early musings on Brazil's hybridity underlines how a myopic US-based binary "racial" worldview ("white/black") obfuscates Brazil's diverse and complex human geography. As one scholar asks, "How is it that the same person can be considered black in the United States . . . and white in Brazil?"[88] To answer such a question it is necessary, then, to contextualize these complex geographies—something that Freyre began to illuminate almost a century ago. This means we need to clarify the processes in which the historical geography of early Brazil unfolded, as it directly affects our reading of the Inquisition arrests and the plight of New Christians and Jews in colonial Brazil.

During most of the sixteenth century, due to a chronic shortage of European women in Brazil, Portuguese men (Old Christians and New Christians alike) were encouraged to have sexual intercourse and intermarry with local Indigenous women, which, in turn, produced a new hybrid "Brazilian" population. As Alida Metcalf explains, miscegenation "was very much a part of the biological story of Brazil . . . Mixed-race and bicultural children became an integral part of the Portuguese settlements."[89]

However, the contexts of language and cultural translations by anglophone scholars present a few problems. For example, the contemporary clearcut US-based interpretation of "race" (i.e., the rigid binary black/white optic) is not useful or appropriate here, in the case of Portuguese Jews and New Christians in Brazil, and cannot be applied effectively to understand Brazilian populations, past or present.[90] Stanley E. Blake is more emphatic and states, "the use of Portuguese racial terms is . . . problematic. Historians need to avoid injecting modern and foreign racial terminology into their analyses."[91]

One big difference between the modern interpretation of "race" in the United States and Brazil, for example, is that today's Brazilian census surveys use the term *côr* (color) instead of *raça* ("race").[92] It is well known that anthropologists have found in their studies hundreds of "colors" that Brazilians use to self-identify in contemporary surveys. For instance, the term "pardo" may have derived from the word *pardal* ("sparrow"), known for its dark feathers, while *moreno* is tied to the term "Mouro" (in Portuguese), stemming from the term "Moor," connoting light dark skin—somewhere between pardo and white.[93] The term "moreno," derived from "Moor" (also meaning "Muslim"), stems from the Latin *maurus*, meaning "a native of Mauritania" in North Africa (*moro* in Spanish; *mouro* in Portuguese; and *maure* in French).[94] However, "moreno" is not used in official Brazilian census surveys, despite its widespread popular usage. The term "mulato" ("half black, half white") was recognized in early Brazilian censuses but not anymore, and "indicates that mixed-race people had a social and political status in Portuguese America."[95] This discussion is important since I examine the arrests for Judaism in Brazil where a variety of ascribed ambiguous and nuanced "colors" appear under the category of "social status."

Moreover, the varieties of Brazilian and physical appearances that may perplex the foreign researcher—that is, phenotypes, as well as regional quasi-ethnic groups that are not included in the Brazilian census (e.g., *caboclo*, mameluco, *cafuzo*, mulato, *ribeirinho*, etc.)—make it difficult, if not impossible to discern who is "black" and who is "white" through the current US-based binary racial optic ("black/white"). In short, Freyre viewed the conceptualization of "color" in Brazil differently from US perceptions of "race."[96]

Furthermore, in Chapter 6, I discuss several cases of New Christians accused of Judaism in Brazil who were of Indigenous and/or African parentage, or were born in Africa, or were Indigenous, resulting in a wide gamut of "colors" and ancestries. The fact that the Inquisition was far more concerned with targeting New Christians and the "imagined Jew" instead of discriminating and persecuting individuals specifically based on their biology (i.e., "race") and skin color alone, is telling. The Inquisition did not follow or care about the Judaic tradition of matrilineal descent (i.e., where a person is considered Jewish through their mother's genealogical side), and was more concerned about whether an individual was a "Judaizer." This fact also underlines how the focus of the Inquisition's activities in Brazil was placed upon the "Jewish problem," and that lingered for almost three centuries, impacting the lives of New Christians and their descendants with plural and hybrid ancestries.

It is important to point out that the myths of "racial democracy" and of the "cordial Brazilian" are social constructions used to sustain the narrative of an imagined Brazil, and often obfuscate and deny "African-ness," Indigeneity, and "Jewish-ness." However, from the time the Portuguese first arrived in Brazil, violence, a strict Catholic hierarchy, and a patriarchal economic system based on slavery dominated the colonial period that would serve to benefit the social elite, the Crown, and the Church.

Race and racism (as we know it today), however, have traditionally—until relatively recently—been rendered "private" concepts and sentiments among Brazilians, despite Brazil being the last country in the Western Hemisphere to abolish the institution of slavery. Ironically, racism in Brazil was never institutionalized as it was in the United States by law and formal segregation—it was silenced and "denied." However, today, racist sentiments in Brazil have been politically enabled by a more explicit and public form of hatred.[97] That is, myths of "racial democracy" and of a "cordial Brazil" are being reintroduced to legitimize the façade and to rewrite the historical narrative of social and racial harmony in Brazil. Under this perceived harmony and using these myths, it then becomes much easier to deny Brazil's past of slavery, misogyny, and anti-Semitism. Yet it is beneath these same Brazilian social and cultural myths that we find the inherent intolerance and violence that realistically forged the nation of Brazil, and which were deeply embedded in its past.

On New Christians

Could New Christians be Judaizers? Yes, but not all of them. In fact, over time most New Christians had become devoutly Catholic. Yet many New Christians in sixteenth-century Brazil adhered to old Judaic practices in secret; for example, the well-known cases of Branca Dias in Camaragibe, Pernambuco, and Heitor Antunes and Ana Rodrigues in Matoim, Bahia, discussed in detail in Chapter 4. Some New Christians returned to openly profess the Jewish religion in northeast Brazil during Dutch rule (the only period when Judaism was allowed in Brazil: between 1630 and 1654).

Would New Christians still have been considered "Jews?" In the eyes of the Inquisition, New Christians were considered "potential Jews" since they carried *sangue infecto* (the "taint of Jewish blood"), even if most New

Christians over time had, in fact, become devout Christians and were not Judaizers. That is, if they carried sangue infecto, and could not claim pureza de sangue ("blood purity"); then *fama pública* ("public rumors") could circulate about their genealogy or religious practices. A mere hint of Jewish descent could have raised suspicions and presumption of Crypto-Judaism, and which, as David L. Graizbord explains, "included mechanisms deeply rooted in Judeophobia."[98] Although New Christians were nominally Catholic, at the same time, they were not considered fully Christian or fully Jewish either (at least according to Judaic laws). David L. Graizbord aptly claims that they lived in a "cultural liminality," and "inhabited a cultural threshold . . . neither fully insiders nor fully outsiders of either world but were simultaneously part of both."[99] Therefore, the terms "Jew," "New Christian," and "Crypto-Jew" are not interchangeable, static, or bound categories.

Some New Christians were aware of their Jewish ancestry but were extremely fearful of revealing it in public, while at the same time, other New Christians who claimed to be devoutly Catholic secretly practiced Judaism— they were judaizantes ("Judaizers"). Some scholars, in fact, assert that many New Christians still clung to Judaic practices generations after the conversions occurred, as Yosef Kaplan explains:

> A systematic study of the large amount of evidence preserved in the files of the Inquisition . . . of many hundreds of Conversos . . . in the 16th and 17th centuries and their return to Judaism leave no doubt as to the tremendous number of Conversos who secretly maintained their contact with Judaism, despite the serious dangers that threatened them.[100]

Antônio José Saraiva explains that the term "Marrano" referred to New Christians who were Judaizers, and was used as a "taunt of scorn and opprobrium" (i.e., from Arabic, *muharram*, meaning "anathema" and also meaning "pig/swine" in Castilian, a derogatory term and a pernicious reference to pork avoidance in Jewish law).[101] Notably, the term "Marrano" is never found in Portuguese-Brazilian official documents; therefore I have not used it here.[102] The term *cristão-novo*, "New Christian," appears in the Portuguese Inquisition dossiers that I examined—not converso (as it was used in Spanish cases)—and therefore I use the term "New Christian" here.

The most important task for the Inquisition was not to punish Jews proper, but to discover, suppress, and punish those individuals who were Catholics on the surface, yet who were Judaizers or Crypto-Jews in secret. In the eyes of the Inquisition (and the Crown and Church), once an individual was labelled "New Christian," it did not matter if the forced conversion of an individual's ancestor from Judaism to Catholicism had occurred one generation or several generations ago or, for example, if they were de facto nuns, priests, friars, or devout Catholics.[103]

If someone studied their genealogy and found out that they had any hint of Jewish ancestry, they became suspects as potential Judaizers. More important was the concept of fama pública. That is, if others believed through gossip or "public opinion" that someone was a Judaizer, for whatever reason, then that person invariably embodied that perception. James E. Wadsworth clarifies, "even when records existed, real weight rested on public opinion or fama pública."[104] The Inquisition would verify whether rumors were accepted as "true" using records or local memories—as Wadsworth explains, none of which were infallible.[105]

A Backdrop of the Portuguese Inquisition Dossiers

The documentation that survives today in the 19,775 online processos from the Portuguese Inquisition dossiers, includes extensive genealogical and personal information. However, another estimated 24,000 additional processos are physically available ("hard copies") at the National Archives of Portugal at Torre do Tombo (Arquivo Nacional, Torre do Tombo), but were not examined here. According to Francisco Bethencourt, the total number of dossiers available at the Torre do Tombo is estimated at 44,817, of which 9,726 were under the jurisdiction of the Inquisition tribunal of Lisbon, with the remaining dossiers under the tribunals of Évora, Coimbra, and Goa.[106] However, exactly how many dossiers existed in the past is unknown, since it is estimated that hundreds of them were destroyed in the big Lisbon earthquake of November 1, 1775, which was followed by the most destructive tsunami ever to strike Europe, and hundreds more dossiers were also lost or damaged in the transferal to their new archival home at the current location in Torre do Tombo.[107]

In my examination, after the online dossier numbered 16,000, the subsequent numbering available was not sequential, and several dossiers thereafter were either repeats or were missing in full, and dozens of dossiers were not processos proper; instead, they were correspondences, denouncements, or testimonies. Each dossier describes a repressive act and classified the "reality" of how the inquisitor would subsequently act with a specific religious intent, that is, to get the accused to conform to Catholic orthodoxy.

The entries for occupations of those arrested varied widely, ranging from nuns, priests, friars, and professors (*mestre*), to slaves, peasants, merchants, lawyers, doctors, sailors, fishermen (*homem do mar*), bankers, soldiers, agricultural workers, farmers (*lavrador*)—of manioc, corn, or tobacco—hairdressers, chocolatiers, cobblers, painters, shoemakers, bakers, construction workers (*pedreiro*), and tailors, for instance.

I plotted all the locations/places in Brazil where those individuals were living during the time of their arrest. My specific interest here was to focus on the presence of those accused of Judaism in Brazil. In the Inquisition dossiers the category of "social status" (*estatuto social*) indicated whether the accused showed if one of their ancestors was Jewish at one time (e.g., ranging from New Christian, half New Christian, one-quarter New Christian, three-quarters New Christian, or part New Christian). The Inquisition maintained meticulous genealogical records, even if an ancestor had converted generations ago; in the eyes of the Inquisition those descendants remained "New Christian"—that is, they were "tainted" with a marked social status that was not recognized as being fully Christian or Jewish—and they were treated as "potential Jews" ("Judaizers" or "Crypto-Jews").

I examined every entry in the 19,775 processos in the digitized catalogue made available online at the National Archives at Torre do Tombo (Arquivo Nacional, Torre do Tombo). The online entries were not organized according to any systematic format, alphabetical or chronological, so I needed to enter each entry individually and organize and categorize each one myself. Whenever I found an individual who was living in Brazil, I copied that registration onto a spreadsheet. I also focused on the category of "residency" (*morada*) in Brazil; that is, the place where the accused was residing at the time they were taken to trial. Notably, hundreds of Brazilian-born families were also residing in Lisbon at the time when the Inquisition imprisoned them. However, since they were living in Lisbon and not in Brazil, I did not examine those cases.[108]

I wanted to learn where they were living in Brazil, their age, the accusation/crime, where they were originally from, their marital status, their social status, and the sentence and punishment they received. After the late sixteenth century, Portuguese Inquisition activities could be found throughout Brazil in all five Brazilian regions (i.e., north, south, southeast, center-west and northeast) and 70 percent of all arrests for any heresy in Brazil—not just Judaism—comprised New Christians and their descendants, whereas Old Christians comprised just 15 percent.

Scholarship Available

I relied on primary sources and the examination of the Portuguese Inquisition online dossiers made available at the National Archives, Portugal (Arquivo Nacional, Torre do Tombo, Portugal).[109] I also consulted original reports and documents recently translated into English by Clive Willis and Stuart B. Schwartz in *Early Brazil: A Documentary Collection to 1700* (some translated into English for the first time); the official online Brazilian Census Office, *Instituto Brasileiro de Geografia e Estatística/IBGE* (the Brazilian Institute of Geography and Statistics); and the online Archive of Amsterdam (Archief Amsterdam) of the Portuguese-Hebrew Congregation Register of Regulations and Decisions (5409–5414), 1648–1654 (Recife, Pernambuco), Inventaris van het Archief van de Portugees-Israëlietische Gemeente—this was the register of the first synagogue in the Americas in Recife, Pernambuco.[110] In addition, I found a wealth of information of original seventeenth- and eighteenth-century documents and publications of Portuguese Jews, which have been digitized and made available online at the Archival Collection at the Ets Haim Library in Amsterdam (Ets Haim Bibliotheek Livraria Montezinos), the world's oldest functioning Jewish library, founded in 1616 and today under the UNESCO Memory of the World Register (with a 30,000-volume collection). The library used to be a part of the Ets Haim Seminary, which was Amsterdam's first Portuguese-Jewish seminary.[111] I consulted materials made available online through the Portuguese-Israelite Congregation of Amsterdam (Portugees-Israëlietische Gemeente te

Amsterdam)—today, the oldest continuous Jewish congregation in the Netherlands.[112] I also used complementary non-scholarly sources (e.g., dictionaries, encyclopedias, textbooks, readers, surveys, and newspapers) to provide a contemporary context, and to include broader perspectives from public and popular spheres. Thus, I have pieced together a broad narrative here using multi- and-interdisciplinary approaches.

Most bibliographic guides to articles and books on the Portuguese Empire are more extensive in their coverage in Portuguese-language publications; however, as Timothy J. Coates points out, they are "weak in their coverage in English-language publications."[113] In this case, beginning in the 1840s, the earliest studies about the Portuguese Inquisition were pioneered by Lusophone historians Alexandre Herculano and António Joaquim Moreira.[114] Until then, this topic rarely received any mention.

Notably, in his colossal three-volume *History of Brazil*, English historian (and also eminent poet) Robert Southey made several references to New Christians in Brazil, albeit now outdated and written two hundred years ago; nevertheless he offered important insights and described the impact of fear of the Inquisition in Brazil (the first part was published in 1810 and then the subsequent three volumes in 1822).[115] Southey also highlighted the importance of the first Jewish settlement in the Americas, in Recife, Pernambuco, during Dutch rule (1630–1654), an episode which at that time was rarely discussed in anglophone historiography.[116] It is important to also mention that Cecil Roth and Samuel Oppenheim were among the first anglophone historians to study the phenomenon of New Christians and the diaspora of Portuguese Jews.[117]

Since the Portuguese Inquisition archival dossiers were kept secret and only made available to the public and studied after the late 1960s, according to Fernanda Olival, "the subject seemed to be lying dormant, appearing only irregularly and almost completely disappearing from historiographical analyses."[118] That is, the historiography of the activities of the Inquisition in Brazil received little more than scant scholarly attention until then, with some exceptions.[119]

Later, scholarship on the Portuguese Inquisition and Jews in Brazil increased throughout the 1960s, after the files of the Inquisition were made available to the public.[120] For over half a century, the late Brazilian historian Anita Waingort Novinsky, at the University of São Paulo (USP), pioneered studies of Jews and New Christians in Brazil. She stated in 1973, "Practically nothing is yet known about the role of this large group of Jewish people, during centuries, in the creation and the development of Brazil."[121] Almost thirty years later, in 2000, Novinsky would continue to comment that studies on the Jewish diaspora to the Americas were left with an "enormous lacuna: Portuguese America. No serious author has yet considered the importance of the settlement of Sephardic [Portuguese] Jews in Brazil."[122] She concludes, "It was Brazil that received the greatest number of immigrant descendants of the *Anussim* ["coerced ones" in Hebrew]. Demographic studies on the Marranos in Brazil are still in their initial phase."[123] Novinsky has since founded the *Laboratório de Estudos sobre a Intolerância/Museu da Tolerância*, or Laboratory for the Studies of Intolerance/Museum of Tolerance, in São Paulo. Her doctoral dissertation in 1972 was published in the well-known book, *Cristãos-novos na Bahia*.

However, research studies on this topic have flourished in the past thirty years and today they are extensive and are almost exclusively written by historians.[124] The more recent scholarship on Jews and New Christians, and on the Inquisition during colonial rule in Brazil, has continued to produce new and important insights.[125] As Ana Isabel López-Salazar points out, over the last few years, an abundant historiography with new PhD theses and scholarship has been produced, largely through new research funded by public institutions, both in Portugal (e.g., FCT—*Fundação para a Ciência e a Tecnologia*, or Foundation for Science and Technology) and in Brazil (e.g., CNPq—*Conselho Nacional de Desenvolvimento Científico e Tecnológico*, or National Council of Scientific and Technological Development).[126] Most scholarship on the impact of the Portuguese Inquisition in Brazil has been produced by a new generation of Brazilian researchers at the Universidade de São Paulo (USP) in São Paulo and the Universidade Federal Fluminense (UFF) in Rio de Janeiro.[127] The breadth of this available scholarly corpus has provided an important backdrop to this narrative here.[128]

Omissions in the Scholarship

While Brazilian historians have produced a mountain of scholarship on this topic, I found a conspicuous absence of the topic in anglophone literature in geography as well as anglophone Latin American studies.[129] There is nothing written about the presence of Portuguese Jews or New Christians in colonial Brazil (or in the rest of Latin America for that matter), and Portuguese Jews and New Christians are completely absent in the anglophone pedagogy of the Americas.[130] Yet this important geographical narrative within New World encounters merits attention and requires a much-needed insertion within the biography of colonial Brazil (and especially within the pedagogy of Latin American geography, which includes the Caribbean). I have also noticed that conspicuous omissions of this topic abound within the broader anglophone social sciences.[131]

Notably, Carl O. Sauer, the eminent geographer who for decades headed the famed Department of Geography at the University of California, Berkeley, over a century ago, influenced generations of US geographers and the subfield of Latin American geography in the United States, and published on the historical geography of the Americas, did not write a word about the presence of Portuguese Jews and New Christians in the New World.[132]

Take this statement for example: "Brazil's first Jewish settlement was in Belém, at the mouth of the Amazon River, dating from the 1830s."[133] This is a reference to the estimated 1,000 Mashriq Jews who migrated to Brazil much later, to the Amazonian town of Belém, Pará.[134] However, the first official Jewish settlements in Brazil existed in Recife and Olinda, two hundred years beforehand. This reference to Jews in Belém refers to another migration influx from the Ottoman Empire—that is, Mashriq Jews coming from the Levant (i.e., the Ottoman Empire), and Maghrib Jews coming from French- and Spanish-speaking North Africa—who began to make Brazil a center of the Mahjar ("countries of emigration" or "Arab diaspora") much later in the nineteenth and twentieth centuries.[135] Perhaps that author was referring to Belém as the oldest "continuous" Jewish settlement in Brazil, but it was not the first.

With few exceptions, most of the recent academic corpus in anglophone social sciences today has ostensibly produced a framework for understanding modern Latin American Sephardic Jewry within a specific context of Spanish Jewry, focusing exclusively on Spanish-speaking America and the Spanish Inquisition. Despite a few marginal references, virtually nothing has been written about the Portuguese Inquisition, Portuguese Jews and New

Christians in Brazil (or in Portugal), or the first Jewish settlements in the Americas in Brazil.[136]

Why a "Submerged" Legacy and Memory?

So why, and how, is this topic largely omitted and "submerged" in the historiography of colonial Brazil, and broadly the Atlantic world? To answer this important question, I propose seven possibilities below which I reiterate throughout this book. The following proposed reasons are interrelated, are not mutually exclusive, and, when combined they offer strategies to illustrate how and why this memory and legacy became submerged over time.

First, an overall combination of language and academic/disciplinary barriers has contributed to the scholarly obfuscation of this topic.[137] Consider, for example, the glaring disproportionate Spanish-speaking research emphasis and the language barrier of Portuguese-speaking research within US academia.[138] According to a report by the Brazilian Studies Association, for example, Portuguese has been on the US Department of Education's list of Less Commonly Taught Languages (LCTL) for over fifty years, even though Portuguese is the seventh most widely spoken language in the world, with approximately 237 million speakers worldwide, and roughly one out of every three South Americans speaks Portuguese.[139] There are thousands of undergraduate programs in Spanish, compared to fewer than one hundred in Portuguese, and for several decades, US university enrollments in Portuguese language classes have lingered around 7,000 students, compared with more than 650,000 in Spanish language classes.[140] Therefore, there has been a tradition and an academic Anglo-American preference to examine the Spanish-speaking New World which has led to an overall ignorance of the Portuguese world, and subsequently of Brazil.[141] In addition, a traditional tendency in anglophone academia has often ignored the scholarship produced in the global South, particularly by Brazilian scholars writing in the Portuguese language.[142] As Archie Davies explains, " . . . the Anglophone world is exceptional in being largely monolingual. Academics and practitioners from other language traditions can overwhelmingly also speak and read English (and very often third and fourth languages) and have access to a wider and more eclectic range of theorizing."[143]

Despite a few exceptions in the English language, most of the primary research remains in the Portuguese language and therefore is not accessible to an English-speaking audience.

Second, most scholarship in the social sciences use the framework of the "Hispanic world," or discussions framed around "Hispanic/Latinos" or "Hispanic Jews," often lumping Latin America into an oversimplified, monolithic Spanish-speaking landmass. This type of framework obfuscates the important differences between Spain and Portugal's colonies in the New World, and as a result they neglect Luso-Brazil. Within the anglophone literature in the social sciences, Latin America then has become virtually synonymous with the Spanish Empire, and Portugal has all but disappeared from these narratives of New World encounters. Furthermore, when discussed at all, anglophone scholarship frequently disregards the distinctions between Portuguese Jews and New Christians, and Spanish conversos (as in "Iberian Jews" or "Sephardim") and ignores the distinction and salience of Portuguese Jews and New Christians in Brazil. Consequently, Portugal and Portuguese Jews therefore ironically become a virtual footnote, an inconsequential afterthought. I will return to this discussion in detail in the next chapter.

Third, there was the perpetuation of an internal secrecy. Many New Christians in Brazil wished to keep their ancestry a secret for fear of constant surveillance and the threat of social, economic, and political retribution, and lived in a "culture of secrecy." They feared ongoing surveillance at various sites and spaces, and being accused of something that an individual knew nothing about, or questioned about an unknown Jewish ancestor, for example. They feared being ostracized (e.g., denied entry into prestigious orders such as the Order of Christ, and denied ecclesiastical and political positions). They feared social banishment—the imminent danger of being denounced through fama pública ("public rumor")—and then to be arrested by the Inquisition and risk financial ruin and confiscation of all assets or sentenced to be burned at the stake. Altogether, these were policies conducive to families maintaining their Jewish ancestry a secret. New Christian families often tried to "fudge" or hide their family's Jewish genealogical ancestry tree, or made a concerted effort to marry off their children into Old Christian families, or bought fake titles or "blood purity" certificates from corrupt officials.[144] Many families who achieved a new socioeconomic status in Brazil managed to manipulate their family genealogies to avoid persecution.[145] Evidence shows that some New Christians in Pernambuco's original sugar aristocracy had tried to disguise this ancestry and would quickly have their offspring marry into Old Christian families.[146] As Ernst Pijning points out, there were three steps New Christians had to do to avoid Inquisition persecution: "acquisition of social status, accommodation to local society, and denial of Jewish ancestry."[147] Arguably, this "denial of Jewish ancestry" lingers to this day in modern Brazil. That is, to be known as judeu, "Jew" still carries a deeply ingrained negative social stigma in public spheres.

Fourth, the Portuguese Inquisition dossiers were kept a secret, even long after this institution ended in 1821, and the documentation of thousands of detailed dossiers on Brazil (estimated at over 40,000 today) were not open to the public and studied in detail until the 1960s. Consequently, this fact led to a lag in studies about the Portuguese Inquisition activities; moreover, it also resulted in the significant delay in the broader scholarship produced on its activities in Brazil (however, as discussed above, today it is extensive).

Fifth, the emergence of the powerful joint venture between the Catholic Church, the Portuguese Inquisition, and the Crown, and their vehement abhorrence of Crypto-Jewry, had attempted to conspicuously wipe out any trace of New Christian Judaizers in Portuguese territories, and thus to wipe out the "infamous" idea that Brazil had been dominated and colonized by New Christians with sangue infecto (i.e., individuals with Jewish ancestry). Consider, for instance, that New Christians were restricted by *limpeza de sangue* ("blood purity laws") and were under the threat of denunciations and fama pública, which lingered throughout colonial Brazil. In this light, Alberto Dines asserts that the Portuguese Inquisition had attempted to eradicate the New Christian and Jewish presence and contributions in Brazil from Brazilian historiography, and points out its zeal to exterminate these communities.[148] Ironically at the same time, the Inquisition left behind thousands of dossiers, which in fact provide ample documentation of the New Christian and Jewish presence in Brazil.[149] The legacy of Old World anti-Jewish sentiments transferred to the New World, and eventually the modern anti-Semitic political and academic environment in Brazil, have together produced a rhetoric and a political climate that would prefer to keep this historiography and legacy submerged. This political climate of anti-Semitism, for instance, was exacerbated after the 1930s, during the Brazilian military dictatorship (1964–1985), and continues today, with the recent spike in neo-Nazi groups and the rise of attacks on Jews in Brazil, along with recent overtly right-wing, pro-Brazilian military dictatorship sentiments espoused by many Brazilian politicians (I discuss modern anti-Semitism in Brazil in the Afterword).

Sixth, while the historiography has cited rough estimates for the number of New Christians living in Brazil at different times, there are no concrete figures to rely on; therefore, the discussion of their presence in Brazil is also submerged. The number of arrests of New Christians by the Inquisition in Brazil, of course, represent only a tiny fraction of what the realistic figures may have been.

Last, we must consider that the presence of New Christians and Jews in Brazil is viewed in many public and academic spheres as an "infamous" presence. That is, consider the profound universal dislike or hatred of Jews and Jewry, in other words, blatant modern anti-Semitism.

Thus, I have integrated these seven interrelated reasons for the theme of a "submerged memory" throughout this book, and altogether they shape the basic framework for my discussions articulated ahead.

Periodization

As the focus of this book concerns Jews and New Christians living in Brazil only during the colonial period (1500–1822), a periodization of their presence is useful here. The following schema was first proposed by Salamão Sarenbrenick in 1962, and since then has only been reiterated in 2008 in *Judeus no Brasil* by Nachman Falbel, who also critiqued it, pointing out some of its conceptual problems.[150] However, it serves the purpose here of providing a basic framework for a chronology of events since 1500. I have expanded and modified it slightly, adding a few components to Sarenbrenick's original periodization:[151]

> 1500–1570: Increasing immigration from Portugal and Portuguese Atlantic islands to Brazil and integration of Portuguese New Christians in Brazil's economy under three subperiods:

a) First explorations (1501–1515). Arrival of first Portuguese New Christian degredados ("penal exiles").

b) First colonization (1515–1530). Exploration and exploitation of pau brasil (brazilwood) for its red dye.

c) Systematic colonization (1530–1570). Occurred mostly in few coastal northeast and southeast regions. Hereditary captaincies were established in 1534 (*capitanias hereditárias*). In 1532, the captaincy of São Vicente was established by Martim Afonso de Souza, and another in 1534 by Duarte Coelho in Pernambuco, which introduced the first sugarcane plantations (*engenhos*) in Brazil and welcomed the arrivals of the first Portuguese New Christians (former Jews) from the mainland and Portuguese Atlantic islands, known as specialists in the sugarcane industry. In 1549, the first capital of Brazil was established in Salvador, Bahia, under Tomé de Sousa, Brazil's first governor-general.

1570–1630: A tumultuous phase, characterized by anti-Jewish discrimination and the arrival of the first Inquisition visitations to Brazil. The Iberian Union (1580–1640) of Spain and Portugal was established. Beginning in 1580, bandeirantes from São Vicente and São Paulo (many of whom were believed to be New Christian Crypto-Jews) started their expeditions into the Sertões ("hinterlands"), reaching across into Spanish domains and Jesuit settlements in Paraguay. Jesuits knew them as "Jewish banditti."

1630–1654: Development characterized by the apex of the Jewish collective presence and Dutch rule in Recife and Olinda in Pernambuco, and the establishment of the first Jewish community in the New World (the first synagogue, cemetery, and arrival of the first Rabbis in the Americas).

1654–1700: Critical phase in the livelihoods of Jews in Brazil, and migrations to the Caribbean (Suriname, Barbados, Jamaica), Europe (Amsterdam), and North America (New Amsterdam, today, New York City), and the disintegration of official Jewish communities in Recife and Olinda. Gold and diamonds were discovered in the hinterlands of Minas Gerais and Goiás starting in the 1690s, driving migration of New Christians to that region.

1700–1770: The Age of Gold (i.e., ciclo do ouro). A period of heightened persecutions of New Christians by the Portuguese Inquisition, particularly in Rio de Janeiro and Minas Gerais. Most of these New Christians were involved in the gold and diamond trade or were medical doctors and merchants. The 1750s saw the decline of the ciclo do ouro, coinciding with fewer arrests for Judaism in Brazil.

1770–1824: A period of progressive liberalization, assimilation of Jews into Catholicism, and the end of the Portuguese Inquisition. The end of the status of "New Christian" with the Pombaline Reforms.

I consider two parallel and inherent problems in the analysis for this study: one is conceptual, and the other is geographical. First, Crypto-Jews did not always comprise all New Christians in Brazil; that is, not all New Christians were secretly practicing Judaism—in fact, most were not, especially by the eighteenth century (albeit they were still stigmatized by their Jewish ancestry, sangue infecto). Yet many communities in Brazil made up of New Christians still held on to old Judaic practices. Moreover, as Stuart B. Schwartz warns about the trials of the Inquisition and its documentation, "confessions were not necessarily expressions of true belief, nor were charges and accusations free of other motivations."[152] Therefore, it is difficult to confirm that all accusations or confessions of Judaism (or other heresies for that matter) were in fact "true." However, it is possible to piece together fragments from the documentation of their place of birth, residence, origin, social status, occupation, and genealogical information provided by the Inquisition to obtain a better idea about any given individual's social and cultural backdrop—and then triangulate pieces of information from various secondary sources. Hence, not all accusations or confessions of Judaism were monolithic or static, and we need to interpret them cautiously.

Second, the other problem is a geographical one. That is, the location entries in the Inquisition dossiers where New Christians were arrested in Brazil can raise problems, especially if we consider that those places at one point in time or another were under a different captaincy, bispado (or "bishopric," "diocese") or province for example, depending on the historical period.[153] That is, since 1500, those respective jurisdictions, borders, and boundaries changed, over time. A given territory or captaincy listed as a hamlet or town in say, Pernambuco, Rio de Janeiro, or Bahia, for instance, may be equivalent to a completely different modern-day state today. For example, the captaincy of Pernambuco lasted from 1613 to 1821, and its subordinate captaincies were Ceará (1654–1799), Rio Grande do Norte (1701–1790), Paraíba (1755–1799), Alagoas (1654–1817), and Itamaracá, which was only incorporated into Pernambuco in the mid-1700s.[154] Until 1676, Pernambuco was subordinate to the bishopric of Bahia, and after 1676, the captaincy-general of Pernambuco included lands as far as Minas Gerais, and so on.[155] These geopolitical changes create confusions for a clear analysis, especially as they relate to their equivalent modern-day state names. In 1822, Brazil gained its independence from Portugal and became an empire led by D. Pedro I, and then by his son, the monarch D. Pedro II. It was not until 1889, the end of the Brazilian monarchy, when Brazil became a federal republic—that is, Brazilian provinces then became states. In this case, I have located the name of the geographical jurisdiction at the time with the equivalent modern-day geographical location name.

Outline of This Book

The discussions in each chapter here are ordered thematically; however, I have kept each of those discussions in each chapter in chronological order. In the footsteps of geographer Kempton Webb and anthropologist Charles Wagley, who formed a successful and strong interdisciplinary program focused on Brazil at Columbia University in the 1960s, I believe that inter- and multidisciplinary approaches and collaborations are imperative enterprises that result in, and foster, an increased interest in Brazil and Brazilian studies. Therefore, I use and follow an inter- and multidisciplinary approach in this book, in the hopes of drawing more attention to Brazil within Latin American studies and Latin American geography.

In Chapter 1, I discuss the contributions of major figures in Brazil's biography and insights about their connections to their Jewish ancestry, and the omissions in the literature about the differences between the Spanish and Portuguese colonies in New World encounters and within the conception of Latin America today. Furthermore, I discuss why those differences deserve serious consideration, and highlight the importance of being Portuguese and "people of the nation."

In Chapter 2, I offer an overview of the Portuguese Inquisition, its methods of denunciation and punishment, and its presence and impact in Portugal as well as in Brazil. I include examples of New Christian and Jewish figures and their contributions to early colonial Brazil. I also discuss the current situation of descendants of Jews and New Christians in modern Brazil today, and how they are interested in finding out about their old Jewish ancestral ties.

In Chapter 3, I highlight the lack of attention that Portuguese Jews and New Christians have received in the literature regarding navigation, science, and exploration in the fourteenth and fifteenth centuries—and the importance of the Convivência period (when the Iberian Peninsula was under Islamic rule). The goal here is not only to reflect on, and to highlight, the neglect of Portuguese Jews and New Christians, but also to underline the general ignorance of the Portuguese world in geographical literature and public spheres (vis-à-vis the Spanish world). This will dovetail with my point about the broader neglect—submerged memory—of the presence of Portuguese Jews and New Christians in Brazil. The last section includes a discussion of the first European arrivals in Brazil and the sources and accounts that are available from the sixteenth century.

In Chapter 4, I underline the salience of New World encounters with Indigenous populations and migration processes in the formation of Brazil's human geographies. First, I highlight the migration of New Christians and degredados (penal exiles) to Brazil, and the establishment of the first sugarcane industries in northeast Brazil, along with the first communities of Crypto-Jewish families (mostly in Pernambuco, Bahia, and Paraíba). Second, I provide an overview of the African diaspora through the transatlantic slave trade and the need to import slave labor since Brazil was the world's major sugar producer, and the diaspora of Portuguese Jews to Amsterdam, Hamburg, London, and Rouen, as well as to Suriname, and throughout Latin America, and the Caribbean.

In Chapter 5, I focus on Recife and Olinda, and the first official Jewish communities in the Americas in Recife and Dutch-controlled Brazil (northeast Brazil). I highlight the migration of Portuguese Jews from Amsterdam to Recife, the establishment of the first synagogues and Jewish cemetery in the Americas, the arrival of the first rabbis in the Americas, and how the

Dutch allowed Portuguese Jews to profess their religion in Brazil, which was the only time they could do so within 322 years, during colonial rule in Brazil. I also underline examples of many "firsts" in colonial Brazil, including the first Jewish settlement in the Americas. I describe the period in 1654 when the Dutch left Brazil, and as a result the Portuguese reoccupied the northeast, the economy suffered, and there was a major sugar slump (due to competition from the Dutch Antilles and the British West Indies). I look at the exodus of Portuguese Jews to the rest of Latin America, North America, and Europe, and how this "diaspora" out of Brazil led to the establishment of the first Jewish settlement in the rest of the Americas, and the subsequent introduction of the sugarcane industry in the Caribbean islands using the "Brazil system."

In Chapter 6, I provide the results from my examination of the Inquisition dossiers, looking at several new insights and the main places of arrests in Brazil at different points in time. I include graphs and tables, and a broad analysis of my observations gathered from Inquisition dossiers.

In the Conclusion, I have offered a summary of the major points in this book, and I also include my final thoughts and an overview of this book, followed by an Afterword, where I underline the legacy of Old World anti-Jewish sentiments and of modern anti-Semitism and its increased visibility in Brazil today. I point to the recent spike in neo-Nazi movements and the anti-Semitic political climate, which would prefer to keep this Jewish and New Christian legacy submerged and hidden.

CHAPTER ONE

The Portuguese New Christian "Uniqueness" in the New World

IN THE FIRST SECTION of this chapter, I highlight the early contributions of Portuguese New Christians in colonial Brazil. I address these questions: What roles did New Christians—Judaizers or not—play in colonial Brazil; how is this relevant here; and why does any of this matter? The second section of this chapter includes an important discussion on the contemporary anglophone regional and conceptual frameworks that have been used to understand Brazil, Latin America, and more broadly, the Atlantic world. I explain how Portuguese Jews and New Christians maintained ties to a widespread global and commercial network that self-identified as "gente da nação Portuguêsa," "people of the Portuguese Nation" (or simply, "gente da nação," "people of the nation").[1] Then I take a closer look at the predicaments of the anatomy of a geographical region known as "Latin America," a term that I discuss in great depth below. Thus, this chapter offers a broad overview of Spanish and Portuguese colonial differences and their respective legacies in the New World, and how these differences highlight the early developments during the colonial period in Brazil.

Gente da Nação: "People of the Nation"

After their conversions from Judaism to Christianity in Portugal (1496–1497)—voluntary, coerced, or forced, as explained in detail in Chapter 2—it is thought that many Portuguese New Christian families and their descendants retained a sense of continuity with their Jewish past, even if they were not Judaizers, becoming heirs to the professional occupations of their Jewish ancestors. They behaved as a community; as a largely autonomous and decentralized group (in today's vernacular, "transnational").[2] Keep in mind that while the Spanish Inquisition had been established in 1478, the Portuguese Inquisition was only implemented 56 years later, in 1536. Therefore, for over half a century New Christians in Portugal experienced different sociopolitical, cultural, and religious contexts than Spanish conversos. That is, for almost six decades New Christians in Portugal were allowed to retain closer ties to their past, if these had not been severed immediately, as was the case with conversos in Spain.[3] As David L. Graizbord explains, "Crypto-Judaism was a lingering reality among Portuguese New Christians long after Spanish Judaizing had withered under the cumulative impact of Inquisitorial persecution."[4] Thus, dynamic differences emerged between Portuguese and Spanish New Christians in the late fifteenth century and throughout the sixteenth century, particularly after 1580, as I explore ahead.[5]

Portuguese New Christians established several of their own important Portuguese-speaking communities, and business, mercantile, and kinship networks around the world, providing skilled labor capital—not only in Brazil, but also throughout the New World—remaining mobile and flexible. In Latin America alone, for example, their presence was significant in Potosí (Bolivia). In Lima (Peru) a street was named *Calle de los Lusitanos* ("Street of the Lusitanians/Portuguese") after their large presence, and during the first half of the seventeenth century, about a third of the population in Lima was thought to have been Portuguese New Christians, many of whom hailed from Brazil (known as *peruleiros*).[6] In Mexico City, an entire neighborhood was named *El barrio Portugués*.[7] In fact, in 1579 Portuguese-born Luis de Carabajal y de la Cueva (alias Luís de Carvajal), from a Portuguese New Christian family from Magadouro, Portugal (i.e,; formerly Jewish), became the governor of Nuevo León (Mexico today). However, because of "blood purity" laws the Inquisition unearthed his Jewish ancestry in his family genealogy. He was arrested and sent into exile for six years, and then had to attend an auto-da-fé ("act of faith," which involved a ritual of public penance) held in 1590 in Mexico City. He died awaiting his sentence in 1591.[8]

Such migrations, movements, and mobilities highlight their prominent role in colonial Brazil as well as throughout Latin America and the

Caribbean, as well as North America (as we shall see in detail later). As Daviken Studnicki-Gizbert points out, Portuguese New Christians maintained effective modes of trade through commercial and familial networks as "they could move French linens from Rouen, through Lisbon or Seville, then across to Cartagena, Lima, and up to the highland Peruvian town Arequipa: always staying within the Nation at every step."[9]

Presence, Prominence, and Contributions

As in other discussions in migration studies, a common question the researcher usually asks is: What were the contributions of these migrants and their descendants? In this case, there were many contributions in colonial Brazil as well as a long list of "firsts" and ironies.[10] We learn through their publications about the plight of New Christians and Crypto-Jews in Brazil, as well as the first and rare geographical descriptions of sixteenth-century Brazil. The following prominent Brazilian writers of Portuguese-Jewish origin were among the first to produce eminent literary work during Brazil's colonial period, including the first geographical essay of Brazil. For example: Bento Teixeira (1561–1600), Ambrósio Fernandes Brandão (1550?–1618), and Antônio José da Silva, known as "the Jew," "o judeu" (1705–1739). (Only Silva was born in Brazil; the other two were Portuguese immigrants.)[11]

Bento Teixeira stands out as Brazil's "first poet," and author of *Prosopopéia*—the first literary work produced in Brazil—which epitomized the experience of Crypto-Jews in Brazilian colonial literature. This became the first publication to illuminate the injustices of the New Christian condition in early colonial Brazil.[12] The son of New Christians, born in Porto, Portugal, in 1561, Bento Teixeira migrated with his family to Espírito Santo circa 1567, and studied at a Jesuit school there, later moving to Rio de Janeiro, to Bahia in 1579, and then shortly afterward to Olinda, Pernambuco.[13] He was arrested and accused of the "crime of Judaism," and later died in Portugal in his prison cell. In the Inquisition dossiers, Teixeira is listed as a New Christian, aged 35, and married to Filipa Raposo (allegedly, his adulterous wife). He was a grammar teacher (*mestre de gramática*), and had been living in Olinda, Pernambuco. His parents are both listed as New Christians: Manuel Álvares de Barros, a farmer, and Leonor Rodrigues (sister of another New

Christian, Fernão Rodrigues da Paz). Teixeira was arrested in Pernambuco on January 1, 1596. All his assets were confiscated, and he waited in prison for three years until he was sentenced to *hábito penitencial perpétuo* ("perpetual penitence") and an auto-da-fé, but on April 9, 1600, he died in his prison cell (processo 5206).

Another important figure, Ambrósio Fernandes Brandão, wrote the first geographical treatise of Brazil, *Diálogos das Grandezas do Brasil*, published circa 1618—a forgotten manuscript until the twentieth century, when it was rediscovered. *Diálogos* was created in the literary format of "five dialogues" between the fictional characters of Brandônio, an old-time resident of Brazil, and Alviano, a newcomer.[14] It is considered one of the most important geographical sources on early colonial Brazil and particularly of Brazil's northeast region. Little is known about Ambrósio Fernandes Brandão, but we do know that he left Portugal in 1583, lived in Pernambuco as a senhor de engenho ("sugarcane plantation owner"), and between 1597 and 1607 he went back and forth to Portugal, returning to Pernambuco, and then moving to Paraíba.[15] The importance of these fictional dialogues in his work is that we learn from them details about the geography, social life, Indigenous medicine, and politics of colonial Brazil, and they also highlight the prominence of sugar, cotton, timber, cattle, food crops, and the different types of trees native to Brazil. Brandão offers rare and rich insights as a knowleagable financier, economist, and businessman who was not only familiar with colonial operations, but with peninsular ones as well.[16] According to Brandão, there were five major economies in Brazil in the late sixteenth century, at that time known as *indústrias* ("industries"): that is, trade in general, sugar, brazilwood, cotton, and timber.[17]

Brandão had been living in Olinda. The territory at the time (capitania) was under the leadership of Duarte Coelho's son-in-law, Jorge de Albuquerque Coelho, and he worked as a tax collector (for the sugarcane trade and commerce). He became a wealthy senhor de engenho, and in 1585 he enlisted to serve in the military campaign against the French as captain of a brigade consisting of merchants led by Martim Leitão.[18] Brandão was denounced, arrested, and imprisoned by the Inquisition in 1591, accused as a Judaizer for attending an esnoga (an abbreviated term in Portuguese for "synagogue" or a Jewish prayer house) hidden in Camaragibe, Pernambuco.

After his release from prison, he died in 1618—about the same time *Diálogos* was published.[19]

I also found the dossiers of Antônio José da Silva (known as "o judeu") (processo 8027–1). This prominent Brazilian playwright, poet, and author of several comedies, operas, and plays such as *As Variedades de Proteu*, was born in Rio de Janeiro in 1705, and then lived in Lisbon where he had practiced law with his father, and was later imprisoned in 1737 for "relapsing into Judaism" (*relapsia em judaismo*) (processo 8027–1).[20] He was arrested, tortured, sentenced, and burned at the stake. The Inquisition tortured Silva with such intensity (through a method known as *polé*, explained in Chapter 2), that it left his wrists damaged. He was unable to sign his own name on the Inquisition's paperwork, and required a notary to sign for him.[21]

Silva's parents had been sentenced beforehand to an auto-da-fé in 1713, when he was eight years old. He had been raised in a household of Judaizers. He was married to Leonor Maria de Carvalho, and they had one daughter. In 1726, he was first imprisoned and sentenced to an auto-da-fé in Lisbon at age 21 for Judaizing and was freed. Later however, in 1737, at age 32, his mother's slave from Cape Verde denounced him, and he was sentenced to an auto in Lisbon where he met his fate at the stake (burned alive).[22]

Bandeirantes

During the seventeenth century, the Portuguese colonial enterprise prompted further territorial penetrations into the Brazilian hinterlands headed by the feared bandeirantes, meaning "frontiersmen," or literally "flag-carriers" (however, they were known at the time as *paulistas*, being from São Paulo, or *sertanistas*). Once they were lionized; today they are demonized in public discourses in Brazil. Bandeirantes were Portuguese colonists, who along with their mameluco offspring lived in the plateau of the Captaincy of São Vicente (today roughly the modern state of São Paulo). From there, they set out on exploration ventures to find gold and precious stones, and to capture and enslave Indians. They penetrated the hinterlands of Brazil, and eventually raided Jesuit missions and trespassed into Spanish domains in Paraguay (i.e., crossing the imaginary line of the Treaty of Tordesilhas that divided Spanish and Portuguese domains in the New World).[23] They mostly spoke the Tupi language, walked barefoot, learned survival strategies and trails from the Tupi tribes, walked extensively through Indigenous trails (i.e., the Peabiru trail that stemmed from São Paulo), and lived among the Tupi people and mamelucos. In 1603, in the will of bandeirante Martim Rodrigues, he declares, "I have a bastard daughter named Joana Rodrigues . . . I have two boys that I accept as my sons who are bastards that I had in the sertão."[24]

With their mameluco offspring, bandeirantes could automatically increase their internal group membership as well as strengthen their network of Indigenous allies through kinship relationships. One researcher claims that many bandeirantes were of Jewish origin (at least 60 names were identified).[25] Therefore, if this was indeed the case, then by implication it is also possible to assume that many of Brazil's mameluco population were also descendants of Jews. Notably, Brazilian historiography had not acknowledged bandeirantes' Jewish background until after the mid-twentieth century, and then only very rarely.

Historian Paulo Prado was the first scholar to mention the influence of Jews in sixteenth- and seventeenth-century São Paulo in *Retrato do Brasil*, published in 1928; however, it was José Gonçalves Salvador in the 1950s who was perhaps the first scholar to establish the Jewish heritage of the famous bandeirante, Rapôso Tavares.[26] Moreover, in 1958, historian Jaime Cortesão wrote about the tensions between bandeirantes and the Inquisition, and introduced the figure of Rapôso Tavares as a New Christian who challenged the oppression and theocracy of the Jesuits.[27] Notably, the Church saw bandeirantes as "subversives" who challenged Catholic orthodoxy.[28]

The most famous bandeirante, Antônio Rapôso Tavares, was from a Portuguese-Jewish family from Beja, Portugal, and conducted the first expedition of geographical reconnaissance throughout Brazil.[29] Rapôso Tavares was raised in a household of Judaizers, and his family members had been arrested by the Inquisition beforehand (he was familiar with Judaic ceremonies, as his stepmother revealed upon her arrest, and all the Judaic practices were followed within his household).[30] Between 1648 and 1652, Tavares, in his Bandeira campaign, "crossed the Chaco, skirted the Andes northwards, and followed the river system of the continent's interior to emerge at the mouth of the Amazon which was apparently commissioned by the crown and had a geopolitical purpose."[31] Other bandeirantes such as Pedro Vaz de

Barros, founder of São Roque, a town outside the city of São Paulo; and the Fernandes brothers, founders of Sorocaba, a municipality in the interior of today's state of São Paulo, were also of Jewish origin.[32]

Anti-Jewish and anti-Portuguese sentiments in Spanish America were spearheaded by the Spanish Jesuit priest Antônio Ruiz de Montoya, who according to Anita W. Novinsky "invented" crimes committed by bandeirantes, placing Rapôso Tavares as the leader of the destruction of the Jesuit missions in Paraguay.[33] Because many of the bandeirantes were New Christians, Anita W. Novinsky claims that the fear of the Inquisition produced a "culture of secret" in Brazil, as well as the "conspiracy of secrecy."[34]

Spanish Jesuits often described bandeirantes—their nemesis—as "Jewish banditti."[35] When the bandeirantes destroyed a Jesuit mission in 1632, a Jesuit priest, Antônio Rodrigues from the Mission of Guairá, asked them under what authority they worked, and the bandeirantes answered that it was under the "Law of Moses."[36] By stating that they followed the "Law of Moses," bandeirantes were also affirming that they did not recognize either the Spanish monarchy or the Roman Catholic Church as legitimate authorities over them, and at the same time, affirmed their ongoing identity with the "Hebrew Nation."

Moreover, in 1632, one Jesuit, Francisco Vesques Trujillo, a provincial of the Companhia de Jesus, wrote to Phillip IV, King of Spain, to say that the bandeirantes from São Paulo were "all masked Jews" (*judios encubiertos*).[37] The term "Jew" here could also have been used as an injurious insult thrown at bandeirantes (or perhaps more broadly, a Spanish insult to Portuguese people); keep in mind that the Jesuits were the "right hand" of the Inquisition during most of the sixteenth and seventeenth centuries. That is, Jesuits played an active and important role in terms of counseling, and in the process of implementing, expanding, and consolidating the Portuguese Inquisition in Portugal and in the New World, especially Brazil, and many Jesuits were preachers at sermons during seventeenth-century Portuguese autos-da-fé.[38]

Jesuits sent letters about their two major tasks in the New World which were: the Christian indoctrination of Indians, and "correcting licentious behavior of colonists."[39] As Claude B. Stuczynski explains, Jesuits were "instrumental in enforcing the exclusion of Christians of Jewish origin within the Society on ethnic grounds of 'purity of blood' . . . they were staunch supporters of the Holy Office in its fight against . . . Judaizers."⁴⁰ Moreover, Jesuits developed conspicuous pro-Spanish and anti-Portuguese tendencies especially after the 1640s.⁴¹

Ironically, one study found that many of the first Jesuit priests to arrive in Brazil in 1549 were the grandchildren of Jews.⁴² In fact, complaints had been made that there were too many New Christians within the Jesuit Order. For example, in 1533, Leonardo Nunes helped bring the well-known Jesuit priest José de Anchieta to Brazil—one of the founders of São Paulo, and considered the "Apostle of Brazil," (he was canonized by the Vatican in 2014).⁴³ The first Catholic Mass held in São Paulo de Piratininga, the birthplace of the city of São Paulo, was conducted by none other than José de Anchieta, a New Christian of Jewish ancestry on his maternal side (his great-grandfather was burned alive at the stake as a Judaizer).⁴⁴

Yet Jesuits used African and Indigenous slave labor in their engenhos ("sugarcane plantations") throughout Brazil, becoming a "veritable economic powerhouse," and they grew rich.⁴⁵ As Francisco Bethencourt states (rather charitably), "Jesuits were not entirely innocent."⁴⁶ Jesuits wanted to control access to Indigenous populations by using them for their own labor force within their own missions and sugar mills, which also used African slaves.⁴⁷ By the mid-eighteenth century, studies show that nobody and no institution at that time owned more slaves in Brazil than the Jesuits (e.g., by 1759 they owned slightly over 3,000 slaves in the province of Rio de Janeiro alone).⁴⁸

Notably, Jesuits were not only using slaves in Brazil, but they also enslaved blacks for 160 years in North America, starting in about 1700. As one scholar points out, Jesuits sold 272 slaves in Maryland in 1838 "to bolster the faltering finances of Georgetown University and shipped them to a plantation in Louisiana."⁴⁹

Religious orders established in Brazil, especially the Jesuits (supported by Portuguese royal subsidies, and by far the most influential of all religious orders in Brazil), had engaged in profitable agriculture and cattle-raising enterprises. For example, the Jesuit college of Bahia had acquired Engenho Sergipe in Bahia and Engenho Santana in Ilhéus, plantation farms that had belonged to Mem de Sá, governor-general of Brazil, in the latter 1500s. At the same time other religious orders, such as the Carmelites and Benedictines, also used Indigenous and African slave labor.⁵⁰

A report from Recife written on January 14, 1638, and signed by the leaders of Dutch rule at the time in Brazil—Johan Maurits, Count of Nassau, M. Van Ceullen, Adriaen van der Dussen, and S. Carpentier, Secretary—reveals the widespread involvement of the Jesuit Order in African and Indian slavery.[51] We also learn from this report that Benedictine monks also owned engenhos and slaves on the Barreiras Estate in Paraíba, and in Pernambuco, the large engenho Massurepê that had "extensive territory and is currently milling its sugar cane."[52] In addition to reporting on the ownership of religious orders and their engenhos that used slave labor, they continue, "there are also many clergy . . . [who] possess lands and incomes . . . they occupy themselves with their plantations, which they cultivate with their black [slaves]."[53] Furthermore, as Stuart B. Schwartz explains, "Indians in Jesuit-run villages could provide labor to the engenhos more efficiently," and by 1600, Jesuits had about 50,000 Indians under their control, working for them as laborers.[54] For perspective, here is a brief list provided in a Jesuit report written in 1702 showing the extent of how many individuals from local Indigenous villages in Brazil were under Jesuit control: 6,700 in Pernambuco; 900 in Bahia; 4,850 in Topayas in the interior of Bahia; 1,100 in Espírito Santo; 1,800 in Rio de Janeiro; and 15,450 in São Paulo.[55]

Loans and lines of credit were furnished by religious organizations, confraternities or "brotherhoods" (known as *misericórdias*), convents, and religious institutions that were engaged in loaning money, often at long-term high rates.[56] Therefore, the profitable enterprises and dividends earned by such religious orders from credit loans, cattle farms, and plantations using African and Indigenous slave labor, and for that matter their conspicuous involvement in slavery and the slave trade, sharply contradict their supposed altruistic and sanctimonious Christian stance of their "vows of poverty" and "Christian Brotherhood."[57] Moreover, Jesuits imposed catechism, coerced Christian conversions, practiced widespread proselytization, and introduced the concepts of Catholic "sins," forcing Indians to live in military-style barracks in Jesuit missions, such as those in Paraná and Rio Grande do Sul, instead of traditional villages (*malocas*). Eventually, hundreds of thousands of Indigenous peoples, such as the Guarani, Tupis, Guayrá, Carijós, and other tribes, saw their political autonomy, leading authorities (e.g., *pajés*, *caciques*), and religious and cultural heritage disappear under the right hand of the Inquisition—the Jesuits—and Catholic dogma.

However, it was not until the late eighteenth century that Portugal expelled the Jesuits from Brazil as well as from its other colonial acquisitions during the Pombaline reforms (see Chapter 5). Notably, this occurred at the same time that the easy wealth that had poured into Portugal from Brazil for most of the century was drying up, as gold production was tapering off. Portugal's Asian territorial acquisitions had long since been reduced to a very modest and largely non-remunerable few. Therefore, the now cash-strapped Portuguese state literally could no longer afford to tolerate a competing state-like organization operating within its borders that had realized great wealth for itself from such colonial goods as sugar, cotton, and cattle, all produced by slave labor—but they paid no taxes.

Unrecognized Contributions to Colonial Brazil

The case of Garcia Rodrigues Pais also stands out. Pais conceived and headed the construction of a shortened path from the older established trail, known as *caminho velho* ("the old trail"), which became known as the *caminho novo* ("new trail") or the *caminho do comércio* ("trail of commerce") that connected the ports of Rio de Janeiro with the town of Ouro Preto (today Minas Gerais).[58] The construction of this new trail in the southeast region was a milestone that significantly bolstered trade, internal and international migrations, and Brazil's economic transformation during the Age of Gold (ciclo do ouro). The caminho velho path was built upon a major old Indigenous path, the Peabiru, which went from the Paraíba Valley (today Guaratinguetá) through Vila Rica (today Ouro Preto) and Ribeirão do Carmo (today Mariana) in Minas Gerais, and went on to the ports of Paraty, and the beaches of Sepetiba (today the neighborhoods of Santa Cruz and Guaratiba, in the coastal southwest region of the state of Rio de Janeiro), finally ending in the heart of the city of Rio de Janeiro.[59]

After Pais conceived and built the milestone caminho novo that bolstered the transportation of Brazilian gold and diamonds, in 1710 he applied for admission into the prestigious Order of Christ and was refused entry because it was found that his maternal grandmother's side was "tainted" by Jewish ancestral blood (sangue infecto). Hence, despite being negotiable and fluid over time, the blood purity statutes in Brazil, nevertheless, lingered for generations, even after the first ancestor had long converted from Judaism to Christianity.[60]

Evidence in another study, however, shows that there were exceptions to such social restrictive mechanisms. For example, some New Christian doctors and engineers whose parents had been arrested for Judaism had graduated from the University of Coimbra in Portugal, evidently circumventing restrictions of pureza de sangue that would have prevented their entry into this institution, at least after the late sixteenth century when they were implemented in Portugal.[61] Therefore, it is also important to point out then that the statutes of pureza de sangue were also negotiable and fluid, were contingent on context, place, or time, and were applied with relatively less rigor in Brazil compared to Portugal.[62]

The discovery of Brazilian diamonds in the first quarter of the eighteenth century (more precisely between 1714 and 1728) occurred in the same regions where Brazilian gold was mined—mostly in Minas Gerais, but also in Mato Grosso and Goiás—soon flooding the European market by 1734, as Laura Jarnagin underlines in her new research.[63] Jarnagin explains that until then, diamonds sold in Europe came mostly from Golconda, Visapur, Bengala, and Goa, in India, through a transnational kinship network of Portuguese Jews (e.g., Francisco Salvador based in London). Jarnagin has also unearthed a web of commercial and kinship networks between English Protestant firms, especially Calvinists, and Portuguese-Jewish merchants who were involved in the production and marketing of Brazilian diamonds—I return to these commercial interrelationships in Chapter 3.[64]

The case of brothers Manuel and Thomas Beckman—sons of a German father and a Portuguese mother, both Jewish—also stands out. They helped to expel Jesuits and slave traders from Maranhão in the northern region of Brazil, and led the Revolta de Beckman, or "Beckman's Revolt," one of the first nativist political movements in Brazil that took place in 1684 in Maranhão.[65] One of the brothers, Manuel (a senhor de engenho), was eventually sentenced and executed in 1685 for the "crime of Judaism."[66] He was also known in Brazil by his "Brazilianized" name, Bequimão. Today an obelisk, Pirâmide de Beckman, stands in his honor in a public park, Parque 15 de

Novembro, in downtown São Luís, Maranhão. However, Brazilian public historiographies and popular spheres never refer to him as a New Christian, much less the son of Jews.

While clearly present and prominent in early colonial Brazilian society, however, as Frédéric Mauro points out, Portuguese Jews and New Christians "played an important part in this industry [of sugarcane], although public opinion often favored banning them from participating in it."[67] They were usually denied acceptance to prestigious orders, such as the Order of Christ (as we saw in the case of Garcia Rodrigues Pais); however, curiously, this was not the case with Brazilians of African and Indigenous ancestry.[68] For example, Antônio Felipe Camarão, an Indigenous Chieftain of the Potiguara tribe (raised by Jesuits and baptized a Catholic) who fought with the Portuguese against the Dutch during the *Insurreição Pernambucana* ("Pernambucan Insurrection") and the Battle of Guararapes (1648–1649), received the title of nobility granted by Portugal—and was accepted into the Order of Christ.[69] Henrique Dias, an Afro-Brazilian and the son of slaves, also fought for the Portuguese and received the title of "Governor" of all Brazilians of color (*governador dos crioulos, pretos e mulatos do Brasil*), and Camarão, who in addition to being accepted into the Order of Christ (*Comendador da Ordem de Cristo*), was granted the prestigious title of "Dom" and of "Governor of all Indians in Brazil."[70] Both Felipe Camarão and Henrique Dias are listed today as "Patriarchs of the Nation" in the official website of the Brazilian Ministry of Defense (Brazilian Armed Forces).[71]

Clearly, Catholicism was a prerequisite for any grantee to earn prestigious titles in colonial Brazil; however, it was not race alone ("color") or plebeian birth that automatically prevented entrée into those orders, national recognition, or being awarded noble titles. Quite simply, it was any trace of any "tainted Jewish blood" (*sangue infecto*) that became the explicit obstacle to be accepted into religious and social orders and receive prestigious accolades, which were based on public reputation, suppositions, and rumors (*fama pública*).[72] It was the formal demand that no Jew or New Christian would ever receive a knighthood, as Hebe Mattos puts it, "no matter how remote this 'stain of blood' was."[73]

One study of Bahian merchants and planters shows how New Christians "were formally excluded from membership in two of Bahia's . . . most prestigious lay brotherhoods (the Santa Casa da Misericórdia and the Third Order of St. Francis) and could not legally hold office in the municipal council."[74] This legacy of exclusion is seen to this day in Brazil. For example, recently an official Brazilian "Book of National Heroes" (*O Livro dos Heróis da Pátria*), etched as a steel plaque, was installed in 2007 at a monument in Brazil's capital city of Brasília (*Panteão da Pátria e da Liberdade Tancredo Neves*).[75] Among several names inscribed there are: Zumbi dos Palmares, a former slave and leader of the well-known maroon community of Palmares (i.e., Quilombo dos Palmares), as well as the Indian, Sepé Tiaraju—while not a single Jew or New Christian is listed.[76] Thus, here is a clear example of the paradoxes of absence and presence in this narrative of the Portuguese-Jewish and New Christian presence in colonial Brazil and within the broader idea of their insertion within the formation of Brazilian nationhood.

Notably, Edgar Samuel asserts that the underlying Portuguese anti-Jewish sentiment was largely based on the common belief that "every epidemic, famine or earth tremor in Portugal was due to divine vengeance for tolerating Judaism persisted over the centuries."[77] Therefore, if this was indeed the case, these folk, traditional, and universal anti-Jewish sentiments eventually would have transferred from Portugal to Brazil, most specifically after the late sixteenth century, which helps to explain why Luso-Brazilian Jewry was so despised in Portuguese territories, coupled with the commonly perceived stereotypical attributes of Jews, for example, "ritual abuse, black magic, bribery, swindling . . ."[78]

Popular Myths and Misconceptions

Popular myths currently circulating about Brazilian families who claim Portuguese-Jewish ancestry in the northeast region of Brazil underline a recent phenomenon of interest in public spheres today (I revisit this current interest in Chapter 2).[79] For example, when a family tradition avoids pork in their diet or follows Kosher-like rituals for killing animals or preparing food, it is commonly thought that this tradition must have stemmed from old Judaic roots. While avoiding pork and preparing foods in a Kosher ritual are indeed a part of Judaic practices, common sense also dictates that many families happen to also avoid pork as a personal preference. Several cultures in Brazil happen to also prepare food that may appear akin to Kosher rituals—however, these are not necessarily sole indicators that these families share a Jewish ancestry.

Another common myth that persists today (especially among some Luso-Brazilian genealogists), is that Portuguese surnames with the names of trees (e.g., Pereira, Macieira, Figueira, etc.) or of animals (e.g., Lobo, Carneiro, etc.) are de facto Jewish or New Christian surnames. However, they are not necessarily sole indicators of New Christian or Jewish ancestry, in the same way that family names such as Noronha, Sousa, or Menezes, for example, are not necessarily *fidalgos*—of "noble" ancestry—either ("Old Christian").[80] This is because New Christian last names were often the same as Old Christian Portuguese names, and New Christian family members from the same family often changed or had different last names from each other (discussed in Chapter 4).[81]

Another popular myth that has circulated widely is that all so-called "Sephardic Jews" from the Iberian Peninsula spoke *Ladino*. First, there are several forms of the Ladino dialect (e.g.; *Judeoespañol*). As Remy Attig explains, "not only is this language [Ladino] different from the various languages spoken by the Jews in medieval Spain, it has also evolved substantially in the last five centuries, though in different ways from Castilian."[82] Second, dialects of Ladino survive today only in Turkey and Israel, consisting of a core vocabulary of amalgamated languages—mostly old Spanish mixed with Turkish, Greek, Hebrew, and Arabic—and hence, many Jewish scholars and speakers of the language prefer the term "'Judeo-Spanish" or Judeoespañol.[83] It seems unlikely that it had been a spoken tradition in the Iberian Peninsula, since Ladino as a written language developed only in the early eighteenth century in the Balkans, Turkey, and Greece—as a result of the Spanish Jews migrating to the Ottoman Empire after they left Spain in 1492.[84] Therefore, Jews and New Christians who emigrated from Portugal held onto their cultural and linguistic ties to that nation and over time, they became a unique and de facto ethno-religious group, distinct from their Spanish converso brethren. The term "ethnic" (or "ethnicity"), from the Latin Christian *ethnicus* ("pagan" or "gentile"), is derived from the Greek *ethnos* ("nation" or "people")—and connotes otherness to describe a collective "identity."[85]

Many Portuguese Jews of the sixteenth and seventeenth centuries were often multilingual (e.g., in Portuguese, Spanish, Hebrew, and Dutch), and publications can be found written or translated from or into those languages. However, the Portuguese language was the official language and was spoken and used in the respective communities within the Portuguese-Jewish diaspora to Brazil and throughout Latin America, West Africa, and Europe (e.g., Amsterdam, London, Antwerp, Hamburg, Lima, Suriname, and Senegal). Portuguese (not Spanish, or Ladino) was the language of the "people of the nation."[86] For example, the word "esnoga" (Portuguese—short for *sinagoga*, "synagogue") is still in use today in Amsterdam's oldest Portuguese-Jewish community, Portugees-Israëlietische Gemeente ("the Portuguese-Jewish Congregation of Amsterdam") in the same way as it was used in Recife, Olinda, Matoim, and Camaragibe, and throughout northeast Brazil during the sixteenth and seventeenth centuries. Portuguese terms and abbreviations such as *officiantes*, *misvoteiros*, or *snogeiros* are also still used today in this same congregation in Amsterdam.[87] Moreover, to this day, "service announcements" are still made in the Portuguese language.[88]

Peter Mark and José da Silva Horta describe the Portuguese-Jewish diaspora and presence in West Africa, for example in Porto d'Ale, Joal, and Petite Côte, where most of the Portuguese inhabitants were of Jewish origin, and where most Jewish ceremonies were conducted in Portuguese or Hebrew.[89] Also, Jorun Poettering explains how the Portuguese-Jewish community in Hamburg, for example, continued to speak Portuguese at home and within their community, well into the eighteenth century.[90] At the Bevis Marks Congregation in London, Britain's oldest synagogue, services were still conducted in the Portuguese language (not Spanish) until the mid-1800s. Moreover, the Portuguese-Hebrew Register of Regulations and Decisions, Recife, Pernambuco, during Dutch rule (1630–1654), was also written in Portuguese.[91]

In 1766, an author by the name of Solomon Saruco explained that the specific purpose of writing in the Portuguese language in Amsterdam was to make the Jewish liturgical readings (Book of Proverbs and King Solomon's teachings) more accessible to those who could only read Portuguese, and not Hebrew, within the Portuguese community of Amsterdam.[92] The Portuguese language would then become symbolic of nationhood among Portuguese Jews and New Christians: of "people of the Portuguese Nation."

The linguistic importance of the Portuguese language is also clearly seen in the case of Suriname (although Suriname during the seventeenth century was not an administrative unit; rather, "Dutch Guiana" was a combined name for the Dutch colonies of Suriname, Essequebo, Berbice, Pomeroon, Demerary, and Cayenne).[93] For example, Torarica (meaning "opulent Torah" in Portuguese—*Tora*, meaning "Torah," and *rica* meaning "rich" or "opulent"), the original capital of Suriname, was established by Portuguese Jews in 1629. One of the many creole languages spoken in Suriname, *Djutongo* (from *dju*, "Jew," and *tongo*, "language,"—literally meaning "language of the Jews"), was used on sugarcane plantations owned by Portuguese Jews, whose primary language was Portuguese. Jacques Arends explains that Djutongo was a likely precursor of another creole language, Saramaccan, and that several Portuguese language elements are found in the Sranan lexicon (another creole language of Suriname)—these were creole languages that had stemmed from the planters who were mostly Portuguese-speaking Jews, and who were numerically the most important group of Europeans in Suriname.[94]

One clear connection shared by "people of the nation" in their global diasporas, plural connotations, ambivalence, and fluidity, therefore, was its strong ties to the Portuguese language and to Portugal (not Spain or the Spanish language or Ladino). Therefore, one common shared characteristic of Portuguese Jews and New Christians in their diasporic trajectory is that the Portuguese language became their lingua franca within these global networks and communities as gente da nação.[95]

The Predicaments of the Terms, "the Hispanic World" and "Jew"

Any study about this topic of Portuguese Jews and New Christians in colonial Brazil requires us to rethink and reframe two conceptualizations that are used widely in the social science literature that engage with ethnicity and "race"—which are arbitrary dimensions of study in and of themselves. That is, ethnicity and "race" are fluid and ambiguous sociopolitical constructs, not biological certainties, and the interpretation of their meanings is construed through different contexts.[96] The two significant and popular categorizations to consider here are: (1) The conceptualization of the geographical region known as "Latin America" in the geographical imagination; and (2) The term "Jew."

Let me begin this section by briefly discussing the predicament of the geographical imagination. This imagination has played an important role in anglophone popular and academic perceptions of Latin America as a geographical region. That is, popular geographical imaginations spill over into academia, and consequently they become increasingly problematic within scholarly investigations of a geographical realm.[97] In this case, the geographic imagination has become significant in anglophone academic literature as it often associates "Latin America" with Spain and Spanish-speaking countries—as seen in Walter D. Mignolo's *The Idea of Latin America*.[98] Mignolo admits, "Brazil has been . . . the stepchild in a 'Latin' America whose image was more 'Spanish' than 'Portuguese.'"[99] Thus, these academic contexts in which the study of Latin America has currently been framed, offer just brief glimpses of how ill-conceived geographical imaginations can lead to the broader neglect of Luso-Brazil, and the ignorance of Portuguese Jews and New Christians in colonial Brazil. As Lúcia Helena Costigan explains, "the majority of scholars who work in the field of Latin American studies approach it from a partial perspective centering almost exclusively on Spanish America and disregarding Brazil."[100]

Current anglophone scholarship uses a vernacular that often tends to lump all Latin Americans into the same category ("Hispanic/Latino" and more recently, under the latest political rubric, "Latinx") or designating the region of Latin America under the umbrella term, "Hispanic world," or "Hispanic Jews." In historical studies and archaeology, the term "pre-Hispanic period" is a good example—it means "of, relating to, or being the time prior to Spanish conquests in the western hemisphere."[101] Another example is the "Hispanic Reading Room, Area Studies, Hispanic Division" of the US Library of Congress (in Washington, D.C.), which covers the books and research on Latin America, Portugal, and Spain, as well as "Luso-Hispanic heritage." Again, the idea of a "Hispanic Division" here effectively means that Portugal and Luso-Brazil become de facto "footnotes" or "afterthoughts" by designation. Some scholars have used terms such as "Hispanic," "Hispano-Portuguese Jews," and "Sephardi" interchangeably, and ostensibly always place the word "Spanish" before "Portuguese," as in "Spanish *and* Portuguese Jews."[102]

The point I am making here is that the meanings of these terms used in current academic vernacular and their relationship to the geography of Latin America is exceptionally muddled (often with academic postmodern jargon). That is, they are terms which have been understood almost intuitively—without attention—and taken for granted, which in turn shows how powerful the geographical imagination is. However, this conceptualization of a regional construct in effect erases all non-Spanish speakers from Latin America (i.e., hundreds of Indigenous languages, Portuguese, French, Dutch, and English) as well as Latin American countries that do not share a Spanish colonial legacy (e.g., Brazil, Suriname, Guiana, French Guiana, Jamaica, or Haiti).[103]

The term "Latin America" is a nineteenth-century creation. As Leslie Bethell explains, "none of the Spanish American intellectuals and writers who first used 'América Latina,' nor their French or Spanish counterparts, thought that it included Brazil. 'América Latina' was simply another name for 'América Española' [Spanish America]"[104] The legacy of such a regional construct has long-lasting consequences to this day. Keeping Bethel's explanation in mind, consider that, to this day, the appellation "Latin America" is still treated in popular and academic spheres virtually as if it were a giant Spanish-speaking landmass—as if it were once all a colony of Spain.[105] Based on that framework of América Española, the modern US-based category "Hispanic/Latino" today is used to categorize populations and their descendants from "Latin America" and has become a main framework in most academic scholarship produced in the United States to address Latin America as a region, and Latin American populations.[106]

In summary, the terms "Iberia," "Hispanic," and "Latin America" have become umbrella terms that are virtually synonymous for Spain, the Spanish language, Spanish-colonial legacy, and Spanish-speaking countries. These terms have projected popular and academic geographical imaginations. While there will always be some flaws and contentions in the process of categorizing populations and geographical regions, the prevailing imaginary connotations today of those terms translate into the idea that all Latin Americans speak the same language (i.e., Spanish), share the same colonial legacy, look alike, and share the same ancestries and the same ancestral homeland.[107] Such conceptions leave out the salience of the Portuguese world, of Portuguese Jews and New Christians in the New World, and of

Luso-Brazil. However, the problem with pan-ethnic labeling is not relegated to language alone; it is also a geographical predicament.[108]

Geography as an academic discipline is not taught in most US public schools and universities (it falls today under the generic rubric of "social studies" or it is not taught at all in the United States).[109] Given these current circumstances, it is easy to see why the mistaken idea that Brazilians speak Spanish or that Brazil had been a colony of the Spanish empire is so common (as I have personally witnessed many times).[110] However, leaving Brazil out of Latin American discussions (the largest territory with the largest population in Latin America) would be tantamount to the absurd notion of leaving China out of Asian studies, or akin to the notion that all Chinese people speak Hindi, for example.[111] In addition, other misconceptions and myths also play a role in obfuscating distinctions between Portuguese and Spanish realms in the New World, and altogether contribute to the submerged topic here of the Portuguese world, and the presence of Portuguese Jews and New Christians in colonial Brazil. Therefore, a brief geographical and historical perspective is needed.

The Problem with the Terms "Jew" and "Sephardim"

Some scholars who write about the so-called "Sephardic diaspora," or use the term "Sephardim," tend to avoid making a clear distinction between Sephardim and Portuguese Jews (even when they specifically discuss Portuguese merchant family names, for example). In most of the English-speaking historiography, with some exceptions, the term "Iberian Jews" has become virtually synonymous with "Spanish Jews."[112]

To begin with, Portuguese Jews did not identify themselves as Sephardim/Sephardi (from *Sephar/Sepharad* meaning "Spain" in Hebrew). As I mentioned earlier, they self-identified as "gente da nação Portuguêsa" ("people of the Portuguese Nation), a term that identified "a community of outsiders seen to share a common place of birth."[113] Individuals of this group were also known as *homens da nação* ("men of the nation"). The term "Sephardic" then becomes a misleading and inadequate category to address Portuguese Jews.[114]

The term "Sephardic" (plural "Sephardim") was a "catch-all identity" used by "outsiders" to describe Jews from the Iberian Peninsula; however, it was unwelcomed from the inside and "first-generation émigrés did not embrace a shared 'Sephardi' identity."[115] As Talya Fishman explains, "Iberian Jews of the late fourteenth and the fifteenth centuries identified themselves not as Sephardim, but as Jews of a particular town or principality."[116]

Miriam Bodian also explains that Portuguese Jews never referred to themselves as Sephardim but as "Hebrews of the Portuguese Nation" since "Portuguese Jews never simply integrated into the Sephardi world," and they remained Portuguese.[117] Moreover, the Mediterrean Sephardim (from North Africa, Greece, or the Ottoman Empire) or the ancient Mizrahi Jews (e.g., from the modern countries of Yemen, Iraq, or Iran, for instance) did not experience the oppression of the Holy Office of the Inquisition tribunals, which became the defining self-image of Portuguese Jews.[118] Furthermore, in the words of E. M. Koen, "official bodies [in Amsterdam] used the words 'Portuguese Nation' and 'Jewish Nation' as synonyms," making no distinction between "Portuguese" and "Portuguese Jews."[119] Therefore, "Portuguese became synonymous with Jew."[120]

Some scholars discuss Spanish and Portuguese Jews and New Christians (i.e., "Sephardim" or "Iberian conversos") together as if they were one imagined monolithic community living cohesively together overseas.[121] However, Daviken Studnicki-Gizbert explains that Portuguese "people of the nation," unlike their Spanish converso brethren, belonged to a distinct ethno-religious group of Portuguese-speaking people (over time this group came to also integrate Jews and New Christians, as well as some Old Christians). Thus, Portuguese ancestry and "Judaism and the sense of belonging to a broader Jewish community were central to the experience of many members of the Portuguese Nation."[122] As we shall see later in Chapter 5, with the case of Jewish migrants from Recife, Pernambuco, who arrived in New Amsterdam in 1654 (New York today), they are never referred to, or self-identify in official documents as Sephardim, but categorically as "Portuguese Jews," "People of the Jewish nation in Brazil," or "People of the Hebrew Nation."

While such frameworks may give the impression of unity, Jorun Poettering is quick to point out that their "social backgrounds and cultural experiences were very diverse."[123] Nonetheless, Portuguese New Christians and

Jews made a sharp distinction between themselves and "Jews who were German or Polish in origin and therefore not, in their opinion, of their own people."[124] According to Yirmiyahu Yovel a common presumption was "that a Portuguese abroad must be a trader, and a trader was usually a New Christian (whom foreigners, too, kept calling 'Jew')."[125] At the same time, Jews and New Christians in both Spain and Portugal between the fourteenth and early sixteenth centuries, share a few distinct commonalities that differ sharply from the experience of Ashkenazi Jews from Eastern Europe. For example, both were either expelled or fled their nations of origin; they were converted to Catholicism (mostly by force); and both Spain and Portugal established inquisitorial tribunals and "blood purity" statutes.[126]

However, again, there were major differences. David L. Graizbord maintains that Portuguese New Christians were in fact a different "ethnic group," and explains how their livelihoods were shaped in a "chaotic ideational landscape, in which several ethnic, racial, religious, and economic conceptions of conversos' 'otherness' combined."[127] Graizbord highlights the emergence of new designations in Spain after 1580, such as: *gente del linaje* ("people of lineage"), *esta raza* ("this race"), *esta casta* ("this caste"), *esta nacion* ("this nation"), and *gente de la nacion* ("people of the nation"), where Portuguese New Christians "presented a challenge to the conversophobic imagination"; that is, they became "a dangerous group in their own right," and a "grave religious menace as much as it connoted a purely racial one."[128]

Therefore, the academic pitfall of lumping both Spanish and Portuguese Jews and New Christians together (i.e., Sephardic), without making a careful distinction among them, effectively obfuscates the importance of the Portuguese world, Luso-Brazil, and of Portuguese Jews and their importance in Brazil.[129] This lumping process can set in motion a series of problems in research studies about Brazil (and of a geographic realm, "Latin America"), in the narrative of New World encounters, and in the salience of the Portuguese-Jewish and New Christian diaspora to the Americas.

On Being "Portuguese"

While the process of separating who was "Portuguese" from who was "Spanish" in this context is a necessary and an important one to make in this narrative of the migration of New Christians and Jews to Brazil, without a careful historiographical context it also becomes a difficult task.[130] This is because, as Javier Castaño aptly explains, the importance of the mobility of both Portuguese and Spanish Jews in the Iberian Peninsula transcended political boundaries, particularly after the dramatic demographic changes that occurred after the pogroms of Spain in 1391, where a growing concentration of Jews had moved to the Spanish-Portuguese borderlands known as *La Raya* in Spanish, or *A Raia* in Portuguese, meaning "The Line." This is a region where families have intermarried across the border for centuries, even up to the nineteenth century (along the Duero, Guadiana, and Tajo Rivers, an area straddling west-central Portugal and east-central Spain in Extremadura).[131] I return to this discussion later in my examination in Chapter 6, as I show a geographical cluster along the borderlands of Portuguese-born people who were arrested in Brazil as Judaizers, and their places of origin. Notably in my examination here, all nine Spaniards arrested in Brazil for Judaism were from the Extremadura border region with Portugal.

Moreover, Javier Castaño claims that migratory trends within the Iberian Peninsula have still not been studied in detail, and "Jews were in parallel building an identity as a nation of their own, with borders too, that were determined by religious and/or ethnic parameters rather than territorial."[132] Cultural and kinship connections continued over centuries prior to the fifteenth century, and the pourous "border fluidity" between Spain and Portugal, especially in A Raia region, facilitated and sustained those connections. Hence, our modern understanding of nationality, with clear-cut modern notions of nation-state borders, presents a set of challenges in these contexts of nationhood and modern national boundaries. For example, at what point, from a genealogical point of view, did an individual or family become uniquely "Portuguese?" Moreover, is it even possible for us to transpose the geographical context from what it meant to be Portuguese centuries ago into our "modern" vernacular of a monolithic "nationality?" These are challenging questions to keep in mind. However, Javier Castaño states, "there remains . . . a pressing need to integrate the study of Portuguese Jewry within the general framework of Iberian Jewries, examining parallelisms and also differences."[133] Taking Castaño's recommendations to task, if we are indeed to effectively engage in this pressing need, as he argues, then we should address the contentious task of determining, at the most basic level, what makes Portuguese New Christians and Jews, "Portuguese."

A starting point would then be to reiterate a few identifiable commonalities. First, the common shared language spoken among the "people of the nation" in their diasporas would be the Portuguese language, as discussed above. Second: the common and archetypal Portuguese family names spelled in the Portuguese language and old orthography, which are also commonly found in Portugal and Brazil, as well as throughout the Portuguese global diaspora, despite the fact that Portuguese New Christians would also use pseudonyms or change them often (e.g., Henriques, Gomes, Pereira, Castro, Coutinho, Andrade, Prado, Gonçalves, etc.).

We must also consider the strong sense of belonging, and the ancestral, linguistic, and cultural ties with Portugal—since the "people of the nation" identified Portugal as their shared ancestral homeland (not Spain).[134] That is, they self-identified themselves as a group on their own terms ("gente da nação Portuguêsa") with a strong sense of shared common descent and homeland.[135] Daviken Studnicki-Gizbert explains that eventually about half of the "people of the nation" comprised New Christians and the other half Jews, yet "Judaism and the sense of belonging to a broader Jewish community were central to the experience of many members of the Portuguese Nation."[136] I have used these strategies in my discussions here to address these challenging questions posed above. This task then carries important implications in later discussions about early colonial Brazil and the framing of the first Portuguese New Christian and Jewish communities in the New World.

Another predicament merits attention (often overlooked in public and popular spheres). That is, how the stereotypical and universal perception of "Jew" often translates as "Ashkenazi Jew," as if they were synonymous with each other, and hence, they are often used interchangeably. The term "Ashkenazi" refers mostly to Jewish population clusters from central and eastern Europe (i.e., modern countries of Germany, and Russia and its neighbors, Poland, Latvia, Lithuania, etc.) who mostly spoke Yiddish—a combination of German and Hebrew—while the "Sephardim" (plural) is an oversimplified, ambiguous (and inappropriate) umbrella term for Jews from the Iberian Peninsula as well as Jews in North Africa, the Ottoman Empire, and sometimes, other Muslim territories. The experience of Portuguese New Christians and their descendants developed in a completely different historical and geographical context from that of the Ashkenazim.[137]

The salience of Portuguese Jews and New Christians in Brazil in academic spheres has been neglected to such a degree that even a respected historian infelicitously makes a conspicuous mistaken claim: "Most of the Jews [in Recife, Brazil] were Ashkenazi."[138] They were not Ashkenazi; they were Portuguese-Jews based in Amsterdam. In fact, all of the earliest Jewish congregations throughout the Americas—including in Recife, Pernambuco—recognized the Portuguese-Jewish Community of Amsterdam as their only religious authority.[139]

Therefore, for the sake of clarity, here I specifically refer to them as "Portuguese Jews and New Christians," instead of the commonly used terms, Sephardim, Sephardic, or Spanish *and* Portuguese Jews. At the outset then, I want to demythologize, at least briefly, some lingering impressions that seem to remain commonplace in public and academic spheres.

Some Brief Differences Between the Spanish and Portuguese in the New World

In this section, I will further clarify the differences between Spanish and Portuguese encounters in the New World.[140] Why? This discussion supports my claim that the examination of the New World's geography warrants caution. This will help to clarify the salience of the Portuguese role in New World encounters, and of the presence of Portuguese Jews and New Christians in Brazil.

While scholars have focused on the similarities between Portuguese and Spanish colonial systems—for example, the centralized authority in the crown of the "mother country" (regulatory control in colonies), rigid class systems, the Roman Catholic religion, and the pursuit of mercantilism (all types of monopoly) —there were far more differences than similarities that are commonly overlooked.[141] Colonial Brazil (1500–1821) would develop differently from the rest of Latin America as it remained intact, and as Marshall Eakin points out, "in contrast to the eventual fragmentation of the four South American viceroyalties into fifteen new countries by 1850."[142]

The Portuguese New Christian "Uniqueness" in the New World 63

Again, this discussion of Latin America appears to be a geographical challenge that emerges in this narrative and plays an inherent role in the obfuscation of the broader Portuguese world overseas and within the geography of the Atlantic world.[143] I want to provide a historical context of Brazil's changing geography, which emerged in a distinct manner from colonial Spanish America, and in which eventually Portuguese Jews and New Christians would play a vital role.[144]

Consider that the variations between Portugal and Spain amount to more than just mere differences in language or semantics, or knowing the difference between Diogo, and its Spanish equivalent, Diego; or between the Portuguese auto-da-fé and the Spanish auto-de-fé (with "de" instead of "da"); or between Mendonça and Mendoza; or between mestiço and the Spanish equivalent, *mestizo* (with a "z"); or the Spanish *criollo* (Spanish whites born in the Americas) and the Portuguese, *crioulo*, which means a completely different thing in Brazil; in fact, it is a derogatory term to describe Brazilian-born blacks of African ancestry.[145] Such differences between Luso-Brazil and Spanish-speaking colonies are completely ignored in the social science literature today. This neglect, as petty or irrelevant as it might seem on the surface, however, in effect projects the extent of an insufficient portrayal, and a myopic view, of Luso-Brazil.

There are other major differences in colonial policies and economic structures (e.g., in the Spanish colonies, *cabeceras*, *ajuntamiento*, and *encomiendas*), especially in their distinct encounters and interactions with Indigenous and African populations. The organization of Portugal's admnistrative structures in Brazil (or in other domains such as Angola and Goa, for instance) were very different from those in Spain's territories.[146] These major differences between Portugal and Spain's colonial policies impacted the distinct political, demographic, and cultural landscapes that emerged in their respective domains. These distinctions were further magnified after their respective demographic encounters (between Indigenous populations with Portuguese Old and New Christians, and later, with the influx of Africans via the transatlantic slave trade).[147]

In addition, important differences distinguished the Portuguese Inquisition from the Spanish Inquisition. For instance, the Portuguese Inquisition was far more invested in the surveillance and preoccupation of New Christian

Crypto-Jews, and its concern with the "Jewish problem," particularly after the seventeenth century when Judaism accounted for roughly 80 percent of the total of Portuguese tribunal dossiers, compared to the Spanish Inquisiton, which at that same time accounted for only about 10 percent of the cases concerning Judaism.[148] The Spanish Inquisition especially targeted Judaizers between 1483 and 1525. For example, between 1490 and 1500, 58 percent of those arrested by the Spanish Inquisition were sentenced by the Tribunal of Ávila to be burned at the stake; similarly, in Valencia: 45 percent (1484–1530), in Guadalupe: 80 percent (1485), and, in Belalcázar: 98 percent (1485).[149] That is, the preoccupation with Judaizers was most intense in Spain only from the 1480s to the 1520s; however, after the 1520s, their preoccupation turned to other heretics, and Judaizers made up only 10 percent of their trials between 1540 and 1700.[150]

Within the Spanish Empire in the fifteenth and sixteenth centuries, the word "Portuguese" became an epithet for "Jew."[151] A general perception emerged throughout the Old and New World that Portuguese immigrants and their descendants were former Jews, and the term "Portuguese" came to mean that they were de facto "secret Jews."[152] That is, Portuguese New Christians were far more likely to be Crypto-Jews and were thought to be far more resilient, in terms of retaining old Judaic practices, than Spanish conversos.[153] By the 1530s, Portugal's total and growing population of about a million and a half only exarcebated the pressure to search for more natural resources, especially since Portugal was constrained to a small political territory. As a result, Portugal was driven to build on its overseas expansion to find new land, territories, and natural resources. Fortuitously, the commercial possibilities emerged with the natural resources found in the New World.[154]

During the period known as the Reconquista, Portugal had expelled the Moors and established its borders (roughly akin to today's modern nation-state) by the mid-thirteenth century. Until then, it was under the rule of the Islamic Umayyad Caliphate; however, Spain managed to do the same only two centuries later, in 1492. Notably, until 1492, there was no "Spain" as such (in modern vernacular), but rather a loosely associated set of "dominions," whereas Portugal had already established a nation-state identity for two centuries by then.

Therefore, the idea of "conquest" was still fresh in Spanish memory by the time they arrived in the New World. For example, John Moffitt and Santiago Sebastián point out that the Spaniards were far more interested in a conquest of the New World conducted as *"milites Christi"* ("Knights of Christ"), "championing Christendom" and a "'holy War' (*guerra santa*)" against the infidel.[155] In Spain, the Muslim (*Musulmán*) had been the Spanish infidel (only expelled in 1492) and now in the New World, the infidel became the *índio* ("Indian"). Notably, the conquistador Hernán Cortés referred to Aztec monuments and temples as "mosques" (*mezquitas*).[156] In the Yucatan alone, Inga Clendinnen estimates that about 4,500 Indians were tortured, and explains that Diego de Landa, a Spanish Franciscan bishop, did not see the method of hoisting as "torture"; instead he perceived it as a viable "remedy" for local Indians to become true believers of the Christian faith and renounce their pagan beliefs.[157] As Ross Hassig summarized, "it was the Spanish greed for gold that sealed the Aztecs' fate."[158] In addition, their drive to gain social status played an equally important role.

Conversely, in Brazil, the Portuguese did not immediately try to conquer Indigenous populations.[159] There was no effort to "claim or Christianize indigenous peoples" either (at least not until 1532 when João III created the Mesa da Consciência).[160] When the Portuguese first arrived in Brazil, they found no gold or silver mines, or imposing monuments such as the Aztec and Maya pyramids. Compared to India, Brazil had little to offer the Portuguese; until the French threatened their trading posts there, the Crown did not worry too much about it, as there was little reason or interest to try to colonize Brazil. It was not until the last quarter of the sixteenth century when the sugar boom began to show dividends that Brazil emerged from neglect. Until then, Portugal had concentrated on its domains in India (known as the "crown jewel" of the empire) and Southeast Asia.[161]

Unlike Spanish America, most of the few European men who were living in Brazil during the sixteenth and seventeenth centuries quickly assimilated with local Indigenous groups by marrying Indian women. The Portuguese men in Brazil tended to intermarry with Indigenous groups as a method of Portuguese colonial geostrategy. As Alida Metcalf explains, "the alliances between European men and Indian women facilitated the transfer of knowledge about the new domestic animals, seeds, and foods."[162] For the

Portuguese in Brazil, sexual intercourse with Indigenous women and entering into marriage with them, was not considered taboo. In fact it was encouraged by the Portuguese Crown. The chronic absence of European women in Brazil for most of the sixteenth century warranted this rationale, and this practice was followed throughout Portuguese colonies and outposts in Asia and Africa as well.[163] Thus, the early Portuguese colonists would create an automatic entrée to local Indigenous tribes through miscegenation, as they expanded their kinship ties through connections to their new offspring, and at the same time, strengthened local tribal alliances.[164] The offspring of these relationships (whether consensual, coerced, or through rape) were known as mamelucos, a term used to describe the offspring of Portuguese men and Indigenous women, and which likely derives from the Arabic, *mamluk*, "to be possessed," which according to Alida Metcalf, "suggested slavery, military service, and 'white' slave."[165] As we shall see later, many mamelucos had Portuguese New Christian and Indigenous parentage, and they appear several times in the Inquisition dossiers.

This type of mestiçagem, a Brazilian phenomenon, became a prominent facet in Brazil's human geography. Thus, complex population categories emerged. It is also important to recognize that mestiçagem was not a benign phenomenon, as it may imply on the surface, since it also involved rape and sexual violence (of course, although male rape of Indians and blacks did not involve reproduction, it was prevalent in colonial Brazil).[166] Max Justo Guedes explains that by the 1550s, the lack of European women was so chronic in Brazil, that Jesuit priests had ordered Portuguese orphan girls to be sent to Bahia, "in order to quiet those who justified their sexual promiscuity with Indians on the grounds that there were no white women to be had."[167] Notably, out of 1,033 dossiers for all heresies examined in my sample, bigamy was the second largest cohort of arrests in Brazil, after Judaism (discussed later in Chapter 6). That is, many married men from Portugal who went to Brazil without their wives, would have had relationships considered "bigamous," by marrying Indigenous women.

Another major difference between the Portuguese and Spanish colonial encounters in the New World was that Portuguese relations with Indigenous tribes in Brazil had been relatively harmonious for the most part, until about 1534. According to John Hemming, the Tupi-speaking Indians (i.e., Tupiniquim and Tupinambá) had no problem with felling trees for brazilwood dye (in the Tupi language, Ibirapitanga) during the first quarter of the sixteenth century. However, the conflict began when the Portuguese forced them to work in the fields, in agriculture (which was considered "women's work") and they refused to be brutally treated, and among most Indigenous populations the idea of possessing a surplus was "repugnant."[168] Later, they were captured as slaves, and succumbed to diseases that had spread exponentially after 1555. Along with raids and attacks, forging alliances with certain tribes against hostile enemy tribes, over time, many Indigenous populations were forced or coerced to flee further into the Brazilian hinterlands, all of which facilitated the task for the Portuguese to "divide and conquer."[169]

Brazil had been largely ignored by the Portuguese Crown during the first half of the sixteenth century; on the other hand, the Spanish domains were already a great source of pride for Spain by the 1530s.[170] For context, the comparative differences between the Spanish in Mexico and the Portuguese in Brazil provide a good example here. That is, the Spanish introduced pears, peaches, nectarines, apples, quinces, pomegranates, oranges, limes, dates, figs, walnuts, roses, grapes, and ungulates such as cattle, horses, sheep, pigs, and goats into Mexico. As a result, by the 1530s its physical landscape was already greatly modified.[171] However, until the first half of the sixteenth century the landscapes of Brazil were barely modified by the Portuguese—mainly because the European population in Brazil had been so sparse until then.[172] Cattle, goats, and sheep were only brought to Brazil after the 1550s from Cape Verde and São Tomé.[173]

Dramatic social, economic, geographical, and political shifts quickly emerged in the Valle de Mezquital (e.g., the shift from horticulture to agropastoralism), all of which, in effect, changed and weakened the entire political and social elements of Indigenous lifestyles in Mexico. Sheep can double in size in less than a year, and their grazing and overgrazing had played a role in changing the Mezquital Valley to barren hills. This occurred because of extensive sheet erosion, slope wash deposition, road cuts, gullies, and stream sedimentation—only exacerbating its vulnerable ecology further, as Elinor G. K. Melville explains in *A Plague of Sheep*.[174] However, in Brazil, according to Alida Metcalf, "the introduction of European and African domestic animals did not immediately degrade the coastal forests," especially since the Portuguese did not immediately introduce foreign animals and plants in Brazil.[175]

Unlike Spanish America, the Portuguese in Brazil were concerned about the destruction of the rainforest as far back as the mid-sixteenth century. The first land grantee of the Captaincy of Pernambuco, Duarte Coelho (discussed in Chapter 4), became concerned about the destruction of timber in northeast Brazil, and in 1609, he ordered that special care be taken of timber and woods (used for firewood and construction).[176] Royal orders (*ordenações do reino*) to the municipal councils (*câmaras municipais*) and co-regents of the districts (*coregidores da comarca*) were instructed to support such environmental conservation. A law in 1652 delineated how to stop forest destruction in Brazil through a ruling (*regimento*). Later in 1769, a magistrate with the title of Juiz Conservador das Matas ("Forest Conservation Judge") was created. Thus, as Kempton E. Webb comments, "there was a conservation mindedness even in those days."[177] The Regimento da Relação do Brasil, in 1607, highlighted the need to take care of woods and timbers, and that if "people continue to slash and burn the forests. . . then in some captaincies there will be a locale of firewood and timber, and further in the future there will be even a greater scarcity," which would mean that engenhos would need to shut down their operations.[178] Despite these warnings and ecological concerns at the time, according to Cameron J. G. Dodge, "deforestation from the early decades of brazilwood harvesting and land clearance for sugar planting led to a decline in the supply of the dyewood."[179]

Estimates of Indigenous populations scattered throughout Brazil at the time of Portuguese arrivals were dramatically fewer than those in the Valley of Mexico alone, in terms of scale (as well as in other Spanish colonies) and are estimated to have been around two to four million, albeit in a territory that was vastly larger than the Valley of Mexico. By the 1570s, the European population living in Brazil was estimated at a mere 20,000.[180] Within three centuries, by 1800 the Indigenous population had been reduced by at least three quarters.[181] Unlike Brazil, the central region of Mexico was densely populated. There were more people living in the Valley of Mexico in the early sixteenth century than in the entire Iberian Peninsula (estimated at two to three million); however, diseases such as syphilis, smallpox, influenza, typhoid, and tuberculosis contributed to the decrease of the Indigenous population to about 70,000 people.[182]

According to Alida Metcalf, "unlike Spanish America, where epidemics accompanied colonization, the first epidemics that likely occurred in Brazil before 1550 did not destroy the political or social structure of independent indigenous groups."[183] After 1550, however, diseases became more severe and frequent in Brazil. In summary, the Spanish military "conquering" mentality differed from the Portuguese "colonizing" efforts.[184] Now that I have underlined the important distinctions between the two empires in the New World, I conclude that A. J. R. Russell-Wood could not have put it more succinctly:

> Labourers in the field of Latin American history are resigned to textbooks purporting to be histories of Spain and Portugal in the New World, only to discover that the Portuguese part has about the same ratio to the Spanish as has the visible part of an iceberg to the bulk under water, namely one ninth.[185]

The point I make here is not only to highlight the academic "footnote treatment" Luso-Brazil has received in the social science literature vis-à-vis the highlighted Spanish-speaking New World, but also to show how the ignorance of the Portuguese world has had a compounding effect in the underlying "submerged factor" discussed throughout this book. With rare exceptions in Latin American studies, there is little acknowledgment of such differences or of the salience of the Portuguese world and Brazil within the region of Latin America, and by implication, of the importance of Portuguese Jews and New Christians in Brazil and the Atlantic world.

The Impact of Being New Christian and Their Descendants in Brazil

A commemorative volume, *A Fênix ou O Eterno Retorno: 460 anos da presença Judaica em Pernambuco*, edited by Alberto Dines, Francisco Moreno-Carvalho, and Nachman Falbel and published in 2001 by the Brazilian Ministry of Culture, highlights the first Jewish presence in the Americas in Pernambuco, with several contributions by eminent Brazilian historians and researchers. Yet only recently has the official Brazilian census office ("The

Map 1. Brazil and Latin American neighbors today

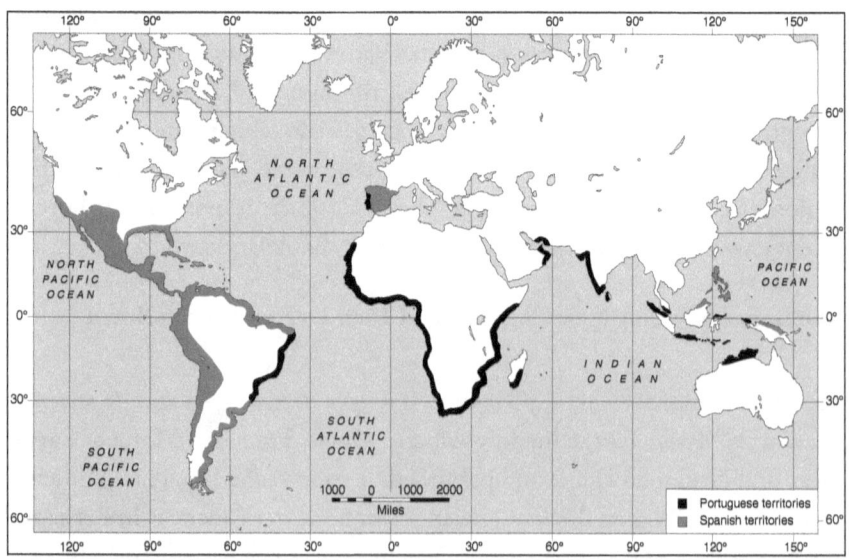

Map 2. Age of Exploration: Portuguese and Spanish territories in the late fifteenth and sixteenth centuries

Brazilian Institute of Geography and Statistics," Instituto Brasileiro de Geografia e Estatística/IBGE) acknowledged the significant presence and importance of New Christians in colonial Brazil in the context of Brazil's complex demography.[186] The underlining theme described by these recent publications is how Portuguese New Christians integrated socially and economically in colonial Brazil, especially in the sugar industries of the sixteenth and seventeenth centuries, often intermarrying with Indigenous, blacks, and Old Christians.[187] The IBGE furthermore underlines how their contributions have had far-reaching impacts in Brazil, ranging from politics, commerce, and trade to literature and science, in addition to providing insights into salient migration estimates for the first two centuries after the Portuguese arrived in Brazil.

For example, between 1500 and 1700, it is estimated that about 700,000 individuals left Portugal for Portuguese territories in Africa, Asia, and Brazil, of which an estimated 100,000 likely went to Brazil.[188] International migration was often forced through *degredo* ("penal exile") to address the deficiencies of scant populations throughout Portugal's territories. As a result, it is estimated that about 10 to 20 percent of the total white population of Bahia and Pernambuco were degradados, between 1500 and 1700.[189] During that same period the figures were far higher in peripheral regions, for instance in Maranhão, where degredados comprised about 80 to 90 percent of the total white population.[190] As we shall see ahead, many, if not most, degredados were New Christian (often educators and scientists). However, we should note that our modern concept of "whiteness" is an unreliable category for identifying New Christians in Brazil, Judaizers or not. That is, because of widespread miscegenation, many mamelucos, pardos, mestiços, and mulatos, were also considered New Christians by the Inquisition (as I show in Chapter 4 and Chapter 6). Whites had dispersed through rural areas of Brazil, unlike whites in Spanish America who preferred to settle in urban areas, and in this context, the Portuguese diaspora was notable.[191] Migration out of Portugal was so salient that some scholars claim that the diaspora of the Portuguese Jews and New Christians was the largest European diaspora of the early modern period.[192]

Between 1415 and 1800, it is estimated that slightly over 1.5 million people left Portugal (about 1,560,000. That is, 50,000 between 1415 and 1500; 280,000 between 1501 and 1580; 360,000 between 1581 and 1640; 150,000 between 1641 and 1700; 600,000 between 1701 and 1760; and 120,000 between 1761 and 1800).[193] Brazil became the major place of destination during the seventeenth century, and especially during the mid- to late eighteenth and early nineteenth centuries.[194] The discovery of gold and diamonds in Minas Gerais and Goiás precipitated migration to Brazil in the mid-eighteenth century.

Throughout the seventeenth century, one study estimated that three-fourths of the total population of Bahia consisted of New Christians, and almost all medical doctors there were of Jewish origin.[195] In my examination (Chapter 6), up to the early 1700s, the great majority of those individuals arrested in Brazil for the crime of Judaism (82 percent) were Portuguese immigrants mostly living in Pernambuco or Bahia (with one exception in Rio de Janeiro). One study on New Christians who lived in Bahia from 1620 to 1660 shows that 36 percent of New Christians were engaged in commerce, 20 percent in agriculture, and 12 percent in other professions, while 10 percent were artisans, and 10 percent held religious, civil, and military offices.[196] Conversely, my study here shows that most of those arrested for Judaism in Brazil actually worked in agriculture (accounting for 31 percent of all occupations)—mostly in sugarcane-related occupations in engenhos, followed by the occupation of merchant (14 percent) (for details see Chapter 6 here).

Marcos Chor Maio and Carlos Eduardo Calaça explain, "what differentiated Brazil from Portugal was the flexibility that enabled the New Christian to hide his origins."[197] This is especially important considering Brazil's vast geographical territory and its distance from Portugal, and hence, the genealogy of any individual who was unknown in Brazil would have been more difficult to reconstruct by the Inquisition tribunal than if that individual lived in Portugal.

It is also important to keep in mind that one characteristic of Portuguese New Christians in early colonial Brazil was their malleability, and their ability to integrate and mix in with local populations. As some scholars have shown, there were high levels of miscegenation between New Christians, Old Christians, and African and Indigenous populations; and the thriving sugarcane business and social interactions reflected a relatively lax attitude toward New Christians and Crypto-Jewry in the early stages of colonial Brazil—an attitude, however, that would not last for long. This environment illustrates the high levels of integration of New Christians in early colonial

Brazil, at least until the Inquisition's first visitation in 1591.[198] Nonetheless, as late as the 1620s, the governors of Portugal felt that New Christians still dominated that nation.[199]

The sites, situations, and scales of surveillance and socioeconomic circumscriptions prompted significant local and global mobilities and movements. For example, Portuguese New Christians in Brazil had access to global networks and connections that strengthened mercantile and kinship linkages around the world, as well as their malleability and mobility internally within Brazil. For example, Minas Gerais received New Christian internal migrants from Bahia, Pernambuco, and Rio de Janeiro, and prominent New Christians owned and lived simultaneously in residences in Bahia, Rio, and Minas Gerais. Many migrated to Goiás and São Paulo later. Many new immigrants from Portugal had settled in Vila Rica, Mariana, Serro Frio, and Cachoeiro, and the region of Rio das Mortes in Minas Gerais.[200] Mobility and movement became even more accentuated after 1654, as I show later, when several hundreds of Portuguese Jews and New Christians emigrated directly from Brazil to North America and to elsewhere in Latin America, the Caribbean (e.g., Barbados, Curaçao, and Jamaica), and Europe (e.g., Amsterdam, London, and Hamburg).

While Catholicism still dominates all sectors of sociocultural and even political interactions in most of Brazil today, it is ironic that the first synagogue in the Americas, Synagogue Kahal Zur Israel in Recife, Pernambuco, with the first official Jewish community, was established in Brazil (discussed in detail in Chapter 5). In the next chapter, I discuss the establishment of the Portuguese Inquisition and its impact in Portugal, and the resulting push-pull factors driving the migration of Portuguese New Christians to Brazil.

CHAPTER TWO

The Portuguese Inquisition and the Impact on Portuguese Jews and New Christians

NOW THAT I HAVE provided a few examples of the contributions of New Christians and Jews in early colonial Brazil, and a few misconceptions and differences between Spain and Portugal's colonies in the New World, in this chapter I will offer an overview of the implementation of the Portuguese Inquisition and its marked impacts on Portuguese Jewry and New Christians and their descendants. The existing dossiers of the Holy Office of the Inquisition Tribunal of Lisbon, *Tribunal do Santo Ofício da Inquisição de Lisboa*, offer rich documentation on New Christians and their families and descendants who were presumed to be Judaizers in Brazil (i.e., they specifically targeted New Christians and their descendants, even if they were not, in fact, "Judaizers," that is, practicing Judaism in secret). Thus, here I highlight how changing sociopolitical, cultural, political, and religious environments in Portugal affected important migration movements of former Jews and their descendants (newly baptized Christians) to Brazil. Eventually, we shall see how Portuguese anti-Jewish sentiments and the Inquisition's activities in Brazil transferred to the New World.

A Backdrop of the Portuguese Inquisition and Brazil

Three tribunals were created in Portugal between 1536 and 1821 in Lisbon, Évora, and Coimbra, and one in Goa, India, in 1560. However, no tribunal was established in Brazil. Nonetheless, the Portuguese Inquisition made visitations to Portugal's domains, such as Brazil and the islands of Cape Verde, Azores, and Madeira, where suspects were imprisoned and sent back to the Lisbon tribunal for sentencing and punishment.[1] Conversely, Spain had implemented its Inquisition much earlier, in 1478, and established three official tribunals in the Spanish New World: in Mexico (1571), Cartagena (1610), and Peru (1570).[2]

The Inquisition made three separate visitations to Brazil (there is also a likelihood that the Inquisition may have visited the south of Brazil; however its documentation was lost).[3] Dom Heitor Furtado de Mendonça, who went to Bahia from 1591 to 1593, and to Pernambuco from 1593 to 1595, headed the first Inquisition visitations. The second visitation went to Bahia between 1618 and 1620 under Dom Marcos Teixeira, and the third visitation to Grão Pará (roughly equivalent to the modern states of Amazonas and Pará today), under Dom Giraldo de Abranches, from 1763 to 1769.[4] Brazilian-based agents were also employed by the Inquisition to work within Brazil. For example, between 1613 and 1821, 1,046 Brazilian men applied to work for the Inquisition in the Captaincy of Pernambuco alone.[5]

Two main mechanisms of control were implemented in Brazil through visitations (*visitações*) and inquiries (*inquirições*)—which were far more impactful and were conducted continuously under the order of the Inquisition, led by bishops, priests, and local clergy, and were responsible for most arrests in Brazil. pastoral or episcopal visits (*visitas pastorais/episcopais*) were concerned with controlling thought, behavior, belief systems, and customs (mostly concerned with crimes such as witchcraft, bigamy, and sodomy, and usually targeted the poorer populations).[6] All Lisbon tribunals fell under the jurisdiction of the *Conselho Geral* ("General Council"), a forum consisting of at least three deputies who resolved disputes. There were three inquisitors on each tribunal who sat as judges (referred to as *Mesa*), and they were the ones who questioned witnesses, made accusations, and imposed sentencing with the assistance of prosecutors (*promotores*), bailiffs (*meirinhos*), wardens (*alcaides dos cárceres*), commissioners, and clerical officials of the Inquisition (*commisários*); censure officials (*qualificadores*); and lay officials (*familiares*). Only *comissários*, qualificadores, and familiares (the highest in the ranking) lived in Brazil.[7]

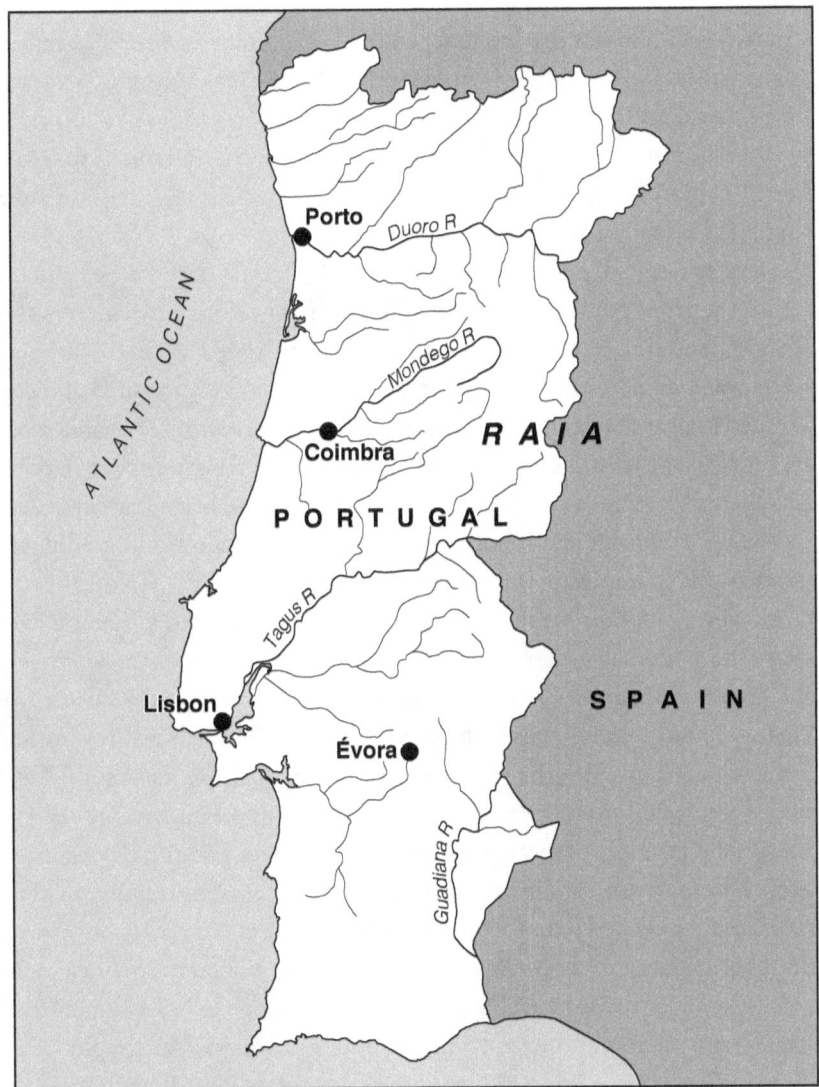

Map 3. Inquisition tribunals in Portugal

The historical roots of Iberian anti-Jewish sentiments were intrinsically tied to broadly held stereotypes and misconceptions of Jews and Jewry (i.e., "imagined Jews") to justify and legitimize the Inquisition's existence. This institution acted as a powerful agent in a joint venture with Crown and

Church, yet it did not operate independently of secular and ecclesial forces.[8] The term "Inquisition" derives from the Latin, *inquisitio*, meaning "to search for evidence" or "to investigate," and inquisitional procedure had its origins in Roman criminal and civil law in the fifth century (later used in Spain, Portugal, Rome, and Venice), and by the fifteenth century, inquisitors were appointed by the Pope.[9]

Despite popular portrayals and myths, the Inquisition did not circumscribe the legal system; inquisitors did not freely torture whomever they desired. Not all heretics were tortured and condemned to death (although many were, and New Christians were disproportionately tortured and condemned to death by the Portuguese Inquisition).[10] According to some scholars, images of the Inquisition which have circulated for a long time in popular spheres have reached mythical proportions that are often inaccurate, and according to those same scholars, some academic studies profoundly misdunderstand and misrepresent this institution.[11]

However, another camp of scholars point out that such a rhetoric overlooks the undeniable persecution, discrimination, oppression, repression, and cruelty inflicted on New Christians for almost 300 years—especially in Portugal and its territories, where almost all individuals who were condemned to be burned at the stake were New Christians (in the case of Brazil, they were exclusively New Christians).[12] More important here, the Portuguese were far more preoccupied with Crypto-Jewry and the "Jewish problem" than the Spanish, inflicting harsher punishments for those individuals sentenced for alleged Judaizers, with proportionally more executions than its neighboring nation.[13] According to Fernando G. P. Vieira, the political right-wing climate of the 1970s in Portugal and Spain propelled several politically conservative authors to revisit the legitimacy in the historiography of the Holy Office, emphasizing its "tolerance" offered to New Christians—this body of research was supported by the Vatican.[14] The Inquisition's sole purpose, as Marc Rosenstein explains, was to "purify the Church from heresy and insincere conversion. Jews were supposed to be Jews and Christians, Christians, each having a clear identity with a defined religious and social status."[15] In this case, Jews were outside the Inquisition's jurisdiction.[16]

The word "Judaizer" (judaizante), in the words of David L. Graizbord, "connoted a *Christian* who hereticized by performing Jewish (or Jewish-like) rites and holding 'Judaic' beliefs," and importantly, *pureza de fé* ('purity of faith') and pureza de sangue ('blood purity') became the two "pillars of inquisitorial thinking about conversos."[17] These "blood purity" statutes made any New Christian a suspect of heresy, and they were guilty a priori merely by virtue of their Jewish "ancestral blood," no matter how distant that genealogical Jewish ancestry was.[18]

The "blood purity" statutes were first established in Toledo, Spain, in 1449, implemented by Old Christians against New Christians who, as Francisco Bethencourt explains, were "accused of collusion with the king for raising undue taxes."[19] These statutes were implemented in Portugal only much later, after 1558, forbidding New Christians to enter some prestigious orders (e.g., the Order of Franciscans and the Order of Christ). It was only after the Iberian Union (1580–1640) that the blood purity statutes spread throughout Portugal and its territories. New Christians were not allowed access to royal jobs, universities, misericórdias (confraternities sponsored by the king), municipal councils, cathedral chapters, guilds, or religious orders.[20]

By the mid-sixteenth century, blood purity statues had been widely diffused throughout the Portuguese world in ecclesiastic and civil legislations, military orders, and religious orders and brotherhoods.[21] Over time, the concept of blood purity was built upon convenience, and was also negotiable, depending on the historical period or context.[22] There were also known cases of corrupt Inquisition officials in Brazil who sold bogus certificates of "blood purity" for a price.[23]

The statutes initially derived from outside the Inquisition, a mechanism that had been appropriated from local municipal (pre-existing) instruments of racial discrimination in Spain after the 1390s. Such blood statutes were only formally abolished in Spain well over four centuries later, between 1835 and 1870, and in Portugal in 1821.[24]

Some scholars claim that the Inquisition's motivations (alongside those of the Church and Crown) for targeting New Christians in Portugal were multifold. Marcos Chor Maio and Carlos Eduardo Calaça, for instance, have examined various scholarly tangents that have addressed the supposed objectives of the Portuguese Inquisition.[25] Jorun Poettering claims "there was no real conflict of interest between the New Christian businessmen and the higher nobility, the higher clergy, or the Crown." That is, Poettering claims that the economic decline was not necessarily the cause of emigration of many Portuguese New Christian merchants, but that emigration was a consequence of the nation's economic decline, rather than the cause.[26]

There is no doubt that Portugal had a significant, viable, commercially driven emerging class of some ilk, at least as of the fifteenth century (whether "businessmen," "bourgeoisie," or "middle class" in modern vernacular), well before much of the rest of Western Europe—a class that continued to expand thereafter. The relationship between the "New Christian social class" and the nobility had evolved and deteriorated over time. For example, Anita W. Novinsky claims that the Inquisition reacted against the growing New Christian mercantile "middle class" in Portugal who had become extremely mobile, entrepreneurial, and competitive, with an increasing financial power, and who therefore posed a threat to the autonomy of the aristocracy and their political and financial hegemony—and this was the case in Brazil in the seventeenth century with the discovery of gold and precious stones in Minas Gerais.[27] That is, this socioeconomic ascendancy of New Christians concerned clerical sectors and members of the Portuguese nobility who found this rise "repulsive," and resulted in the institutionalization of New Christian persecution motivated by anti-Jewish sentiments. According to Novinsky, the Inquisition had a specific goal of preventing the rise of this threatening and growing New Christian social class.[28]

New Christians—Judaizers or not—were placed under public and private surveillance. The methods of observation in various sites, spaces, and scales of surveillance were implemented by the Inquisition, and through mechanisms made available to the public through the process of denouncements and rumors or "public reputation," fama pública. That is, the scales of surveillance ranged from the local, to the national, to the global (e.g., Portuguese territories, Atlantic islands, Brazil, and Goa). They were under scrutiny and observation, being "watched" for an indication of any behavior that might reveal potential secret Judaic practices; for example, taking Saturdays off from work or the avoidance of certain foods such as pork or shellfish. They could always be denounced for any suspicious behavior. This ongoing search to find the "hidden Judaizer" altogether constitutes examples of the Judeophobic anxieties and imaginations that prompted the implementation of policies that legitimized persecution and discrimination that lingered for almost three centuries against Portuguese New Christians.

In order to clarify the sociopolitical and religious contingencies that unfolded in Portugal in the late fifteenth century, it is important to provide a brief geographical and historical context of the Iberian Peninsula and the influence of Spain's anti-Jewish policies upon its neighbor nation, Portugal—with dramatic consequences. The discussion in the following section begins by looking at Spain's anti-Jewish political and religious environment and the impact it had on its neighbor, Portugal. For the sake of clarity and simplicity, I have kept this discussion brief.

Migration: The Push-Pull Factors

By the end of the thirteenth century, Portugal was the first European monarchy to establish stable borders that have remained relatively unchanged since about 1250—the first in Europe—defeating the Moors much earlier than Spain (which they did not accomplish until 1492 with the conquest of Granada). The large proportion of Jews living in Spain and Portugal underlines the importance of Iberian Jewry; for example, during the late fifteenth century about one-third of the entire European Jewish population lived in the Iberian Peninsula.[29]

Historian Rita Costa-Gomes describes how eminent Jewish families (e.g., Abranavel, Latão, Palaçano, Negro) became important financiers, specialists in medicine or astrology, and judicial officials or mediators between king and communities in Portugal as far back as the 1370s, and in the courts of the Aviz dynasty, the chief rabbi played a salient role in the Portuguese courts.[30] Costa-Gomes also points out that during the late fourteenth century, Jews were held in high esteem, with their respected tailors, goldsmiths (i.e., dealing in silverware, liturgical plates, and ornamental jewelry), and armorers working in the Portuguese courts.[31] Conversely, there was little evidence of the presence of Moors within Portuguese courts, with few exceptions.[32]

Before the fifteenth century, Jewish farmers, artisans, tax collectors, peasants, shopkeepers, and small merchants lived side by side with Christians. The Black Death (1348–1349), for example, contributed to the rising anti-Jewish sentiment against Portuguese-Jewish tax collectors, and only exacerbated further public resentment directed against Jews (they were blamed for the Black Death).[33] At the end of the late fifteenth century, anti-Jewish sentiments gave way to a new and specific discrimination and persecution.[34]

It is estimated that at least one tenth of Portugal's population was Jewish at the time of the infamous pogroms of 1391 in Spain.[35] Alexandre Herculano estimated that about 100,000 Jews lived in Spain by 1391, and in that year alone, 5,000 Jews were assassinated. Similar pogroms spread throughout Spain, from Barcelona and Palma to Valencia and Toledo.[36] By 1481, 300 people in Seville were burned at the stake, and another 80 received life imprisonment, and within a ten-year period, Seville would see another 3,000 condemned and 400 burned alive. At Cadiz, 2,000 were burned at the stake, and 17,000 were condemned to various canonical punishments.[37]

In Portugal, the situation was different before the late fifteenth century. Most frictions between Christians and Jews in Portugal were motivated by personal or economic reasons rather than strictly religious ones, and unlike Spain, except for one registered attack in 1449, Portugal did not experience significant anti-Jewish attacks.[38] As Javier Castaño explains, "Lisbon's Jewish elite enjoyed a political centrality, an intellectual-religious prestige, and an economic dynamism that was attractive to other Jews" [outside of Portugal].[39] However, this relatively harmonious social, religious, ethnic, and political environment in Portugal would soon change.

The Iberian Peninsula Backdrop

On March 31, 1492, Jews and Muslims were ordered to leave Spain within a period of four months under penalty of death and confiscation of property (and the same punishment applied to anybody who gave refuge to them).[40] Most Muslims left for North Africa, the Ottoman Empire, or other Muslim territories. Converted Muslims, known as *mouriscos*, at that time comprised the majority of Spain's agricultural workers, estimated at about 300,000—most of whom also left for Muslim territories.[41] As a result, a mass exodus of Jews from Spain to Portugal ensued (due to Portugal's proximity and because it was known for its relative religious tolerance).[42]

Scholars have estimated that about 80,000 to 100,000 Spanish-Jewish exiles entered Portugal by 1493, and thus, the Jewish population in Portugal ballooned from an estimated 100,000 to 200,000 (about 10 to 20 percent of Portugal's total population at that time).[43] Spanish Jews migrated in droves across the borders to Portugal, mainly to Lisbon, Évora, Santarém, Coimbra, and Bragança.[44]

However, the situation in Portugal would soon change. This happened when Isabel of Spain (her godfather was none other than the infamous Tomás de Torquemada, the first Inquisitor-General of Castile), gave her husband-to-be and future king of Portugal, Dom Manuel I, an ultimatum. She told him that she would not marry him if there were any Jews living in Portugal (i.e., a marriage clause stipulated this condition).[45] Under pressure to marry Isabel, Dom Manuel went ahead and expelled Jews from the nation. Thus, Portugal would follow Spain's anti-Jewish policies in 1496, with a new royal edict of expulsion that gave Jews ten months (up to October 1497) to leave Portugal or convert to Christianity.[46] Consider the magnitude of this edict as it impacted Jews in Portugal, who accounted for about 10 or 20 percent of its total population in 1496.[47] Dom Manuel I's strategy backfired though, as Jews began to leave the nation in droves and arrived in the thousands at the port of Lisbon to board ships that were sailing overseas. So, Dom Manuel I took further drastic steps. In the spring of 1497, during the Jewish holiday of Passover, all Jewish children between the ages of 4 and 14 who remained in Portugal were snatched from their parents by royal decree and adopted by Christian adoptive parents, in the hopes that by being raised in a Christian household, they would forget any Judaic practice or their Jewish heritage.[48]

Yet another edict would transform Lusitanian Jewry dramatically, in effect annihilating the existence of Jews in Portugal (consider that to this day, the Jewish population in Portugal remains at about 0 percent). By October 1497, any remaining Jews living in Portugal who had resisted conversion were forced to convert to Christianity (*batizados em pé*, literally "baptized on foot" or "baptized standing up"), and a new category was created to ascribe those new converts and their descendants: "New Christian." This social category was now used to distinguish them from the portion of the population that had not been "tainted" by Jewish or Muslim "blood" (*sangue infecto*), thus making a clear distinction from "Old Christians." The sociopolitical marker of "New Christian" carried the negative stigma of "tainted blood," and this perception would linger for generations. Hence, New Christians (former Jews) were not defined solely by their religion; rather by their ancestry.

However, Arnold Wiznitzer points out how the Portuguese Crown "were unwilling to relinquish the benefits accruing to them from the wealth of the Jews, and their commercial and scientific skills."[49] Therefore, facing an imminent economic downturn in Portugal, former Jews who had held prominent occupations and roles in Portugal's economy (e.g., wealthy bankers, merchants, doctors, geographers, and scientists) were now leaving the country en masse. Portugal then decided to forbid New Christians from leaving the nation in 1499. However, in 1507, Portugal restored the right to emigrate, but again re-instated the law in 1532, and consequently, from then onward, New Christians could not legally leave the country (although many New Christians were able to migrate clandestinely).[50]

Jews had been expelled from England in 1290; from France in 1306; and later during the fifteenth century from all major German cities; from Spain in 1492; from Navarre in 1498; and by 1500, all of Europe had closed its doors to Jews except parts of Italy (they were eventually expelled from Naples in 1541).[51] Therefore, Jews in Europe had virtually no place to go.[52] Muslim territories were still open (many went to Morocco or the Ottoman Empire), and the historiography has shown that some New Christians returned to Portugal and Spain after a few years abroad.[53] Since 711, Jews found relative tolerance and freedom under Muslim rule in the Iberian Peninsula, as they did for the next eight centuries—a period also known as Convivência—an experience that would mark the Portuguese world overseas.[54] That is, although Jews lived separately in *aljamas* or *judarias* ("Jewish quarters")—designated residential spaces for Jews—they were treated as *dhimmis*, "People of the Book" (i.e., Jews and Christians), who were protected under Islamic law through the statute of *ahl al-dimma* ("people under protection" in Arabic).[55]

After the Moors left Portugal, these judarias, as Ronaldo Vainfas and Jacqueline Herman assert, became a "micro-society" inserted into the Christian universe, where they held the right to auto-govern themselves, with their own councils, tribunals, and rules.[56] Toward the end of the fifteenth century, official segregation restrictions were implemented in Portugal; for example, Jews were required to return to their quarters by sunset, and mixed marriages were forbidden.[57] They were also not allowed to touch food in the market or to bake in communal ovens, and Jews required a special authorization to use water from wells.[58]

For New Christians, costly royal licenses were required to travel abroad, and many could not afford them. Others secured arrangements to travel clandestinely to Muslim territories in North Africa and the Ottoman Empire. Some went to southwest France, to Pyrénées-Atlantiques and Les Landes, during the sixteenth and seventeenth centuries, a geographically viable route reachable by land (although Judaism had been forbidden in France since 1306, they seldom persecuted Judaizers).[59] Other Portuguese New Christians migrated to Palestine, returning to Judaism, while others went to Salonica (in the Ottoman Empire, today Greece), Constantinople, Adrianople, Cyprus, Egypt, or the Balkans.[60]

Those who managed to afford transportation costs and secure royal licenses, or make clandestine travel arrangements to migrate to Brazil, were offered new possibilities and the opportunity to live without repression, fear, and discrimination—a possible solution to the Portuguese New Christian plight. An estimated 70,000 former Jewish families fled Portugal, most of whom went to Brazil (others went to North Africa, France, Italy, or the Ottoman Empire). Anti-Jewish sentiments by this time had increased in Portugal, resulting in the Lisbon Massacre of 1506 where an estimated 2,000 New Christians were killed.[61]

As this environment intensified, likely instigated by envy of wealth and/or religious zealotry, it culminated in 1536 when the Portuguese Inquisition was implemented in Portugal with the papal bull *Cum ad nihil magis*.[62] Portugal replicated the model that had been used by the Spanish Inquisition.[63] King D. João III negotiated with Pope Paul III to establish the Portuguese Inquisition on May 23, 1536. The creation of the Inquisition within the framework wanted by the king was established in 1539, since Dom Diogo da Silva— who had originally been named by the Pope as *inquisidor-mor*—had renounced his position, and the monarch then nominated his brother, Dom Henrique, as Archbishop of Braga in 1539.[64]

Some scholars claim that between 1497 (with forced conversions) and 1536 (with the advent of the Portuguese Inquisition), it is still not clear if

Portuguese New Christians embraced Catholicism sincerely, and some data suggests the possibility that internal resistance to Christianization was "considerable."[65] While Portuguese New Christians had maintained strong ties to their Judaic past for a longer time than their Spanish converso brethren, at the same time, ironically, they were able to blend into Portuguese society—so much so that it was difficult to distinguish an Old Christian from a New Christian in Portugal.[66]

Dom Manuel died in 1521, and his son, Dom João, took over the Portuguese Crown (he was not even 24 years old)—and in the words of Alexandre Herculano, he was largely regarded as an "intellectual imbecile" who had a deep-seated hatred of the "Hebrew race."[67] Between 1580 and 1640, Portugal was annexed to Spain, known as the Iberian Union, when Dom Sebastião (1554–1578) never returned from the battle of Alcácer-Quibir (Morocco) in 1578, and with the death of his successor, Dom Henrique (1512–1580), his uncle, Dom Felipe II (1527–1598) king of Spain, assumed the Portuguese crown in 1580—a union which is often viewed by the Portuguese as a "foreign occupation."[68] This annexation also offered additional mobility to New Christians from Spain to cross into Portugal since national borders were eliminated for that period of 40 years.[69] Discrimination of New Christians through the Spanish "blood purity" statutes had spread after king Philip of Spain invaded Portugal with an army of 37,000 men, but notably he did not try to assimilate or acculturate the Portuguese, and in fact, Brazil remained under Portuguese control.[70] However, as David L. Graizbord explains, "Spanish Judeophobia now acquired a distinctly anti-'Portuguese' accent."[71]

An assembly (junta) in the city of Tomar, Portugal, took place in 1629, with twenty ecclesiastical, legal, and theological dignitaries who galvanized to discuss the "Jewish problem" in Portugal (more precisely, the problem of Crypto-Jews).[72] Jews were described repeatedly as "evil, iniquitous, malicious, provocative, perverse, perfidious"; and medical doctors asserted that the "Jewish condition is irremediable and incurable because the Jews are inherently unrepentant and incorrigible."[73] The final deliberations of the assembly were centered on the idea that the Portuguese Inquisition had ultimately failed. This was because they thought that New Christians, even after baptism, secretly held on to old Judaic practices, living as Crypto-Jews. Here we find an example of this type of obsession with the "imagined Jew" seemingly ever-present and "hidden." Jews were described as the embodiments of the "Anti-Christ" and "enemies of Christ," and Jews were "deserving of condign punishment."[74] This ideational landscape of the "imagined Jew" and of "Jewish perfidy" perpetuated through Jewish descendants who had been baptized and were living as New Christians, was widespread in Portugal. The coveted aspiration to find such secret Judaizers became an obsession for the Church, the Crown, and the Portuguese Inquisition.

Denunciation, Prison, and Autos-da-fé

For crimes of Judaism, the Inquisition questioned prisoners in sessions consisting of a genealogical interrogation, where they would ask about the accused's age; where they lived; their family background; their spouse; their children; their cousins, uncles, and aunts; and what they knew about their grandparents—and more important, if any of the prisoners had been sentenced to penitence by the Inquisition before.[75]

Any hint or suspicion of Jewish ancestry or Judaic practices (i.e., avoiding pork; not working on Saturdays), or of a Hebrew name—any Jewish ancestry found in somebody's family genealogy, for instance—could be enough motive for an individual to be denounced, no matter how devoutly Catholic they were.[76] Allied with the Church and Crown, the Inquisition used a mechanism of denunciation to identify any suspicious heretic behavior.[77] In colonial Brazil, according to James E. Wadsworth, "denunciation served as the primary mechanism for discovering religious and moral unorthodoxy."[78]

Denunciations could be made based on mere rumor or hearsay. If anyone failed to come forward to report a heresy and denounce others—including friends, neighbors, and family members—they were also liable to excommunication and to be prosecuted as a "promoter of heresy."[79] However, while anyone could denounce a New Christian (even slaves), a New Christian could not denounce an Old Christian.[80] Notably, if a blasphemous statement was uttered by a New Christian, it was far more likely that the accused would be prosecuted by the Inquisition than if it had been uttered by an Old Christian. As Stuart B. Schwartz aptly put it, "it was not the offense, but the origin of the accused that determined how and with what severity punishment was carried out."[81] My examination reflects this facet, and out of all arrests made in Brazil (1,033 individuals), New Christians and their descendants comprised over two-thirds of arrests (70 percent) for all heresies (see Chapter 6). Other studies have showed that New Christians represented somewhere between 60 and 80 percent of all victims in all Portuguese tribunals.[82]

The harshest sentences were always reserved for New Christians, and most sermons of the autos-da-fé "concentrated on the 'problem of Judaism,' even where no sentences related to Judaism were involved."[83] Ronaldo Vainfas and Zeb Tortorici comment, "the Holy Office literally thrived on seeing the defendant submissive, contrite, and humiliated in the face of the tribunal's authority."[84] In this case, the inquisitors appear to have experienced a sadistic and voyeuristic pleasure from their stance of power: of watching and observing defendants being imprisoned, tortured, humiliated, and submissively helpless or keeping them clueless about their accusation. It was through the "exercise of power" that the men of the Holy Office and their orthodoxy, propped by the Catholic Church, Pope, and Crown, "deprived others of the freedom to think, believe, and act."[85]

If prisoners of the Inquisition broke a limb or lost consciousness during torture sessions, the blame was theirs alone. Torture methods often consisted of the polé or *estrapada* ("pulley"), where victims were hoisted up by a rope with their feet pulled down by weights; or the *potro* ("rack"), where prisoners were positioned on a flat plank attached to chains or ropes by their ankles and wrists, and through a ratchet mechanism that rolled in opposite directions, it would snap their ligaments and bones.[86] Doctors were needed during Inquisition torture sessions to prevent the early death of any suspect during the process, although many did not survive or ended up dying in their prison cells.[87]

The Inquisition handed over the prisoners who were sentenced to death to be processed within the civil justice (a process known as *justiça relaxada*, "relaxation of the secular arm"); as Francisco Bethencourt explains, canon law "prohibited the clergy from pronouncing the death sentence (hence the expedience of handing the prisoner over to civil justice)."[88] If a suspect wished to die under the "Law of Christ" rather than the "Law of Moses," the condemned were offered the option to be killed first—strangled to death with an iron collar tightened by a screw, known as the "garrote"—and then their body would be delivered to the flames, and burned.[89] If the prisoner declined the offer, then they would be burned alive. Burning at the stake was the preferred method of extermination, as Francisco Bethencourt asserts, "because the burning of the body of the condemned could be equated with the eternal burning of their soul in Hell."[90]

Samuel Oppenheim describes the account of a witness in one of the autos in Lisbon in 1726, where Manoel Lopes da Carvalho from Bahia, aged 44, was burned alive as a Judaizer. Carvalho was told that he could "renounce his errors," and "own the Doctrines of the Inquisition" but he refused, saying, "The Inquisition were not Christians, but Idolators." The witness then reports that it took twenty minutes for the body to be entirely consumed by flames. The flames lasted overnight until his body was burned to ashes, as the witness describes: "His body was not burnt to ashes till nine in the morning although the execution began at half an hour after three [the day before]."[91]

Under the duress of interrogation or torture, prisoners accused of Judaism often denounced their neighbors, friends, and family members, and would say anything they thought the inquisitors wanted to hear. In this context, confessions obtained under such circumstances were highly questionable, and allegations held against others could also be interpreted as doubtful and would play a role in the perpetuation of the existence of the hidden and secret "imagined Jew."[92]

The auto-da-fé (literally, "act of faith" in Portuguese) systematically glorified the humiliation and punishment of those sentenced through public celebrations in Portugal in front of crowds often numbering in the tens of thousands. For example, in the first auto-da-fé of Lisbon on September 20, 1540, Antônio José Saraiva estimates the attendance of about 30,000 spectators.[93] Penitents were paraded in front of a crowd, wearing a penitential garment with a red St. Andrew's cross on it, or images of devils, dragons, or flames, and a yellow conical hat on their heads—the *capirote* (a pointed conical hat), worn for many years or indefinitely, in the case of the *hábito perpétuo* ("perpetual penance"). Together, the garment and hat became known as the *sanbenito*.[94] The effect of the sanbenitos emerged as a mechanism for maintaining social control and surveillance.[95] Furthermore, the sermons of the autos-da-fé were staunchly anti-Jewish in their rhetoric, giving continuity to both Catholic and medieval European anti-Jewish traditions.[96]

These autos became de facto "family picnics," where the headliner of the event was when individuals were burned at the stake in public plazas, with free huge banquet suppers served afterward to spectators.[97] In the words of Cecil Roth, "the smoke which went up, amid the popular jubilation, from the *quemaderos* [the places where New Christians were burned at the stake] defiled the pure skies at frequent intervals."[98] The autos also served as "instruments of instruction and theaters of power."[99] Francisco Bethencourt makes an important comment about the connections between the themes of memory and persecution:

> The memory of the auto-da-fé was kept alive by the spectacle of the enforcement of the lesser penalties pronounced by the inquisitors: the whipping of prisoners by the civil authorities two days after the auto on the public highway, the penitential garments that had to be worn for years on end and the detention of the reconciled in the college of faith to receive their religious instruction.[100]

One study shows that the majority of individuals (mostly from Rio de Janeiro, Bahia, Paraíba, and Pernambuco) who were arrested in Brazil and punished throughout the eighteenth century by autos were imprisoned for the crimes of Judaism and bigamy, respectively.[101] Sodomites were burned at the stake in very rare cases only, since "the principal theme was Jewish 'perfidy.'"[102] In fact, only thirteen individuals arrested for sodomy were ever executed during the entire history of the Portuguese Inquisition, that is, in almost 300 years (compared to almost 2,000 New Christians burned at the stake).[103] With rare exceptions, suspects arrested for Judaism accounted for virtually all individuals who were burned at the stake.

The Spanish Inquisition had considered sodomy a heretical crime in 1509, and the Portuguese Inquisition followed suit, starting in the 1550s.[104] The Inquisition prosecuted sodomites in the confessional just as they did with those accused of same-sex solicitation, which desecrated the sacrament. Ronaldo Vainfas and Zeb Tortorici have argued that sodomy in Portugal and colonial Brazil, like other crimes against Catholic morals, fell under the Holy Office's jurisdiction because it came to be associated with suspicions of heresy.[105] However, Maria Leônia Chaves de Resende and Rafael José de

Sousa point out that sodomy was not merely a "heretical crime"; and that the Inquisition considered it a crime based on the fact that sodomites had "erred in their desires."[106] Lamont Aidoo points out how same-sex sexual violence examined in the Inquisition dossiers, listing cases of male rape in Brazil between masters and their slaves, conspicuously show the complicit involvement of the Catholic Church "at the very least turning a blind eye to—sexual abuse inflicted on enslaved men and women. Sex was considered the duty of slaves or justifiable use by the master of property, and thus the church chose not to intervene."[107] Hence the cases of sodomy in the Inquisition dossiers often involved cases of rape that were overlooked; or else the blame and crime (a "sodomite") would often be placed on the person who was raped instead of the perpetrator.

Since confiscations of all assets were made upon sentencing, and expenses were paid by those arrested, targeting New Christians became a major source of income for the Inquisition.[108] All assets were confiscated from prisoners accused of Judaism (*confisco de bens*), and no secular tribunal could take cognizance of anything that concerned the Inquisition, which granted inquisitors immunity.[109] It is apparent, then, that the persecution of New Christians was also motivated by financial factors. For example, the permanent confiscation of assets provided a continual source of dividends, becoming a profitable means of filling the Inquisition's coffers—all of which helped sustain the institution for 285 years (from its inception in 1536, to its end in 1821).[110] These confiscations of assets turned out to be very lucrative for the Crown and Church.[111] Hence, the dividends earned by the Inquisition would have played a big role in the encouragement and motivation to increase the number of arrests—particularly of wealthy New Christians.

In total, about 750 autos-da-fé took place in Portugal over a span of 250 years.[112] The last three autos-da-fé to take place were held in Lisbon on October 11, 1778; in Coimbra on August 26, 1781; at Évora on September 16, 1781; and in Goa on February 7, 1773. As Antônio José Saraiva observes, "the ashes of the dead disappeared more quickly from collective memory than the auto-da-fé."[113]

There were plenty of reasons for New Christians to fear the Inquisition, especially at times when persecution was intense. Yet New Christians in Brazil integrated relatively well into Brazilian society until the first visitation of the Inquisition in the late sixteenth century. I am not suggesting that all New Christians lived in complete and permanent fear for 285 years, but at the same time, the ongoing surveillance, and the imminent fear and threat of denunciation, was still present and "real," as David L. Graizbord explains: "expressed in the allied (though not always concordant) ideologies of honor, purity of blood (*pureza de sangre*), and purity of faith (pureza de fé), a virulent phobia motivated attempts to stigmatize and isolate conversos."[114]

The first person from Brazil whom I found in my examination to have been burned alive at the stake was Gaspar Gomes, aged 30. Born in Arraiolos, Portugal, Gomes had been living in Bahia, and was listed as a shoemaker and soldier, and as one-quarter New Christian. His parents were Sebastião Gomes (an Old Christian) and Isabel Dias (half New Christian), both from Portugal. He was sentenced to an auto-da-fé, and in 1644, was burned alive at the stake (processo 5019).[115]

Addressing the Black Legend and the "Myth" of the Inquisition

The so-called "Black Legend myth" stems from a long tradition in Anglo-American historiography that demonized Catholicism and the Spanish Crown and their policies in the New World for political reasons. As Francisco Malta Romeiras explains, "even if the Black Legend did not stem directly from this portrait of the Spanish Inquisition, it was successfully incorporated in the general framework of Hispanophobia lending it further credence."[116] The Black Legend dates back to the sixteenth century, when Bartholomé de Las Casas, a Dominican friar, vehemently condemned the Spanish treatment of Amerindians and exposed the atrocities of Spanish cruelty and exploitation, pointing to the inhumane Amerindian demise. Historian Charles Gibson explains, "The Black Legend provides a gross but essentially accurate interpretation of relations between Spaniards and Indians."[117] The Black Legend has by tradition been perpetuated by Protestant Anglo-American historiographers and became part of apolitical effort to demonize the Spanish—since Spain was Britain's political and economic archenemy and rival. That is, this perception projected the Spanish as a "backward" people with a so-called "provincial Catholic mentality," magnified by the atrocities they committed in the New World.[118] Yet the same

Black Legend supporters willfully (and hypocritically) overlooked the actions of British Protestants in North America, Africa, and Australia, for example, or the intolerance of the English and the Puritans in New England where in 1692 alone, nineteen alleged witches were burned alive.[119] On the role of the Black Legend myth and the historiography of the Iberian Inquisition, James B. Wadsworth claims that they were "shrouded in myth, exaggeration, misrepresentation, and literary hyperbole."[120]

Therefore, conversely, the "White Legend" proponents view the "Black Legend" as an exaggeration based on anti-Spanish propaganda and perceive the Inquisition "as a positive movement which helped to unify the previously fractured kingdom," as Matthew Tracy comments: "unsurprisingly, some of the largest proponents of the 'White Legend' are members of the Catholic Church."[121] The rhetoric thus, circulating within this camp of scholars—particularly Catholic scholarship—has opposed the negative public imagery of the "Inquisition" traditionally portrayed. The position of such a camp of scholars insists that this institution has been historically portrayed in a stereotypical way—as an exaggeration—and that it was "not all that bad" a rhetoric that the Vatican has also taken.[122] Notably, in 2000, Pope John Paul II sought to apologize "for millennia of grievous violence and persecution—from the Inquisition to a wide range of sins against Jews, nonbelievers, and the indigenous people of colonized lands."[123] Despite the apology, the Vatican's position still greatly minimizes and downplays the extent of the Inquisition's persecution, maintaining to this day that the number of victims is much lower than previously thought.[124] What is important here, however, is that such discussions ignore Portugal and the Portuguese Inquisition, and instead have focused solely on Spain and the Spanish Inquisition. Furthermore, as Francisco Bethencourt puts it, "in the Portuguese case, the Inquisition played an even more important role in the long run when it came to the stigmatization of New Christians."[125]

Most of the scholarly focus on Spain or the Spanish Inquisition obfuscates Portugal and the Portuguese Inquisition, which was far more invested in its preoccupation with New Christian Crypto-Jews and the "Jewish problem," and executed far more New Christians than its Spanish counterpart. Therefore, most discussions on the polemic of the umbrella term "Inquisition" appear to focus solely on Spain. Discussions of the Black Legend focus on the rivalry between England and Spain, and consequently, Portugal is then left out of this historiographical framework of Black Legend discussions. Hence, problems emerge again in this scholarship that unwittingly lumps Spain and Portugal together without any attempt to separate the two and their respective differences.

Some scholars claim that the popular image of the Inquisition is flawed and exaggerates both the power and reach of the Inquisition as well as its repressive capacity, and more recently some scholars have ostensibly become more "attuned to the nuances of time and place" and show that the Inquisition was complex and was an institution with varying and diverse purposes.[126] For example, in *Agents of Orthodoxy*, James E. Wadsworth strives to understand how the Inquisition persisted for so long and showed that most people shared a negative view of its unorthodoxy yet many "benefited" from the Inquisition's exclusionary practices. In another book, *In Defense of the Faith*, Wadsworth claims that tolerance was more common in the Iberian world than the "bulk of the historical literature would have us believe."[127] In addition, in *All Can Be Saved*, Stuart B. Schwartz claims that the ideas of the Inquisition promoted a persistent upwelling of what he determines as "religious tolerance" throughout the Iberian world that has been long ignored or misunderstood.[128]

Some scholars go further, and claim that equating the Inquisition with Nazi Germany and the Holocaust (as Anita W. Novinsky has done) is inappropriate and historically inaccurate.[129] According to James E. Wadsworth in the case of Portugal, "certainly, nearly 1,200 executions is no small number, but it is not the rampant psychotic pyromania of the thirteenth century, nor the genocidal barbarism of Nazi Germany."[130] Moreover, Wadsworth claims that the activities of the Inquisition did not amount to genocide (in the modern sense of the definition). Wadsworth states, "at least in terms of scale, any comparisons of the Iberian Inquisitions with either Nazi Germany or Soviet Russia are inaccurate and inappropriate."[131] He concludes, "even combined, the Iberian and Latin American Inquisitions came nowhere near to an attempted genocide—"culturecide" perhaps, but certainly not genocide."[132] That is, if the Portuguese Inquisition had attempted a genocide of its Jewish population it would have killed far more than 1,175 people in 285 years. However, one big problem with this type of thinking is that the exact numbers for those who were executed are inaccurate and incomplete, especially since hundreds of Inquisition documents and dossiers did not survive, and in addition, prisoners who died in their cells or after torture were not counted in such death estimates.

While some of these scholars can argue that the numbers alone were relatively small (almost 2,000 were executed in Portugal; about 4 to 6 percent of all accusations), other scholars claim that to quantify and compare the number of deaths, even if they are inaccurate, downplays the outright loss of Jewish religion and culture, and the oppression, discrimination, cruelty, and human suffering inflicted on Portuguese New Christians for almost three centuries.[133] Even if the point of the Inquisition's approach was not to systematically "kill all Jews" (as in Nazi Germany), it was to reform Judaizers (Crypto-Jews) and readmit them to the body of the Church, and only those the Inquisition deemed relapsed or unwilling to confess and conform were burned. Yet consider that the official Jewish population in Portugal was reduced then to zero within a generation (and remains at virtually zero to this day), when in the late fifteenth century there were an estimated 100,000 to 200,000 Jews living in Portugal, possibly accounting for as much as 10 to 20 percent of the total population—in no other terms, Jewry was erased from Portugal in one fell swoop.[134]

For example, Marcos Chor Maio and Carlos Eduardo Calaça point out that any comparison in terms of numbers of deaths carried out by the Inquisition with other repressive institutions in other countries at different historical periods, does not take away the uniqueness of the Portuguese Inquisition that specialized in punishing New Christians, Judaizers or not.[135] That is, the Portuguese Crown, Church, and the Portuguese Inquisition employed a systematic strategy to target, persecute, discriminate, punish, control, and in many cases, torture and execute (specifically) New Christians in Portugal and throughout its territorial domains, including Brazil.[136] It is important to also underline that capital punishment was proportionally administered far more often by the Portuguese Inquisition in comparison to the Spanish Inquisition—with a focus on New Christians, and with far higher numbers of individuals accused of Judaism.[137] Moreover, as Francisco Bethencourt aptly states, "Judaism invariably emerges as the principal 'heresy' to be combated."[138]

The modern meaning of genocide includes the "deliberate and systematic extermination (or attempt to exterminate) an ethnic or national group."[139] Genocide, a combination of *geno*, "race," and *cide*, from the Latin, "killing," was first coined by Raphael Lemkin in 1944 in his publication, *Axis Rule in Occupied Europe*. According to the United Nations General Assembly Resolution 96 (I) the simplified definition of genocide is as follows:[140]

> Genocide is a denial of the right of existence of entire human groups, as homicide is the denial of the right to live of individual human beings; such denial of the right of existence shocks the conscience of mankind, results in great losses to humanity in the form of cultural and other contributions represented by these human groups and is contrary to moral law and to the spirit and aims of the United Nations. Many instances of such crimes of genocide have occurred when racial, religious, political and other groups have been destroyed, entirely or in part.[141]

There is a vast difference between genocide and long-standing policies of discrimination that harm a minority group; the two sometimes go hand in hand, and one can lead to the other, but they are not necessarily the same thing. However, Portuguese Jews experienced the destruction of their religion, culture, customs, and the purging and crushing of Jewish culture and religious practices that persisted among their baptized Christian descendants, as well as the systematic oppression and persecution of those descendants of converted Jews, stigmatized as New Christians, which lasted for almost three hundred years. That is, Jewish culture and Judaic religious practices were intentionally eradicated in a manner that went far beyond mere discriminatory policy. Therefore, what happened to Jews and New Christians in Portugal and its territories contradicts the claim made by some scholars, and what happened does in fact constitute genocide as much as cultural genocide or "culturecide."[142]

In this vein, under a recent resolution of the Portuguese Republic Assembly n.º 20/2020, the day of March 31 was proclaimed *Dia Nacional da Memória das Vítimas da Inquisição* ("National Day in Memory of the Victims of the Inquisition").[143] Perhaps this is a sentiment that translates to the Jewish perspective of תחית המתים, which is, "bringing back to life" the memories of those who perished.¹⁴⁴ Here I want to recognize and acknowledge their lives, their presence and experience, and their contributions in colonial Brazil and more broadly, the Atlantic world. As Bruno Feitler comments, "The conversion marked the end of the legal existence of Judaism in Portugal and the beginning of the troubled history of the descendants of these Portuguese Jews."¹⁴⁵ Feitler aptly concludes, "its impact on Portuguese society would be long lasting. Indeed, the shock waves of the conversion are still felt today."¹⁴⁶

It is also important not to forget all of the individuals in Brazil who were arrested and punished for other heresies by the Inquisition. For example, among the silent victims of the Inquisition in Brazil were also Africans and Indigenous populations and their descendants, many of whom held on to their own non-Christian ancestral belief systems and practices, as I point out later in Chapter 6, and consequently were considered heretics.¹⁴⁷

The Aftermath of the Portuguese Inquisition

Now that I have provided an overview of the Portuguese Inquisition and Portuguese Jewry, to better understand the broader sociocultural contexts in early colonial Brazil it is also necessary to contextualize the Portuguese amalgamated cultural elements deeply embedded in the Portuguese spirit that reflect the archetypal Portuguese melancholic sentiment. For example, the Portuguese word, *saudades* (untranslatable in any language, but loosely meaning "longing" or "missing"), reflected in "the longing for the past" and epitomized in Portuguese prose and poetry, such as in Luís de Camões's *Lusíadas*; or in *Canção de Exílio*, Exile Song, by Gonçalves Dias. Or, for example, the paradoxical sentimentality of "the happiness of sadness," and the "sadness of happiness"; of *angústia e sofrimento* ("anguish and suffering"); in the *estranha forma de vida* ("the strange form of life") expressed in Fado music—or in Baruch Spinoza's notion of *fluctuatio animi* ("floating soul")—that philosopher of Portuguese-Jewish ancestry. These musings of the lingering Portuguese spirit are also tied to Luso-Brazilian Jewry. These cultural elements in Portugal's collective memory diffused and spread to the New World.¹⁴⁸ With the destruction of their religion, and former Jewish sons and daughters taken for adoption, nostalgia set in, and the hope for a better future emerged among Portuguese New Christians.¹⁴⁹

As anthropologist Naomi Leite observes, "The vacillation between absence and presence, oblivion and memory, still defines Portugal's Jewish imaginary."[150] This is a salient commentary, since by the end of the fifteenth century it is estimated that Jews accounted for about 10 to 20 percent of Portugal's total population—yet today Portugal's Jewish population is close to zero.[151] In this context and on the recent phenomena of Portugal's tourist destination with visits to the old judarias ("Jewish quarters") celebrating Portuguese Jewry, Stuart B. Schwartz comments, "remembrance has become painfully selective and pragmatic."[152] With a significant proportion of Portugal's once-thriving Jewish population, subsequently victimized by the Inquisition for almost three centuries, that nation recently instituted a new law, "Right of Return," (*direito de retorno*) in 2013—similar to Israel's policy of the "right of return"—securing Portuguese citizenship for those families of Jewish ancestry who fled the Inquisition centuries ago.[153] The Portuguese Parliament approved a law effective in 2015, Decreto-Lei n.º 30-a/2015, which grants Portuguese nationality status to descendants of Jews who were expelled from Portugal starting in the fifteenth century.[154]

These immigration policies have also transferred to Brazil.[155] For example, the Israeli Syndicate of Communities of Victims of the Inquisitional Tribunals (*Hahistradut Hayisraelit Lekehilot Haanoussim*) opened applications for Brazilians who are descendants of Jews—giving them the right to immigrate to Israel, and the right to full Israeli Citizenship.[156] The return to Judaism has recently been discussed in the Knesset, Israel's Parliament, since under the Halakhah/Halachá (Judaic religious law) there is no spontaneous return to Judaism, and conversion is obligatory for those who were born to a non-Jewish mother. This debate has created significant tensions among those descendants in Brazil who were converted by force generations ago in Portugal, yet who now find themselves having to face a new tribunal of Jewish Rabbis for them to be considered fully Jewish.[157]

Notably, a newly created organization in Brazil, the Brazilian Association of Descendants of Jews from the Inquisition, *Associação Brasileira dos Descendentes de Judeus da Inquisição* (ABRADJIN), in Belo Horizonte, Minas Gerais, has inaugurated the first museum of the history of the Inquisition in Brazil, which also includes a public exhibit of replicas of the tools and methods of torture used by the Inquisition.[158] Another recent museum exhibit has highlighted 200 years of the end of the Portuguese Inquisition at the Jewish Museum in São Paulo.¹⁵⁹

In 2016, newspapers report that Brazilian Jews are migrating to Israel in unprecedented numbers.¹⁶⁰ Not only are they migrating to Israel in record numbers, but descendants of New Christians in Brazil are also converting to Judaism in unprecedented numbers. The *Times of Israel* reports that since 2015, "at least 400 people with Sephardic ["Portuguese-Jewish"] ancestry have undergone Orthodox conversions to Judaism in northern ["northeast"] Brazil . . . In Israel, the number of Brazilian immigrants has more than doubled."¹⁶¹ More recently in 2022, for the month of April alone, the number of Brazilians who claimed Jewish ancestry and who applied to gain Portuguese citizenship totaled 10,000 people.¹⁶²

Given this recent surge of interest in Brazilians with Jewish ancestry, the president of the Israelite Confederation of Brazil, *Confederação Israelita do Brasil*, Fernando Lottenberg, as well as the Consul of Portugal, General Consul of Israel, and eminent representatives of the local Brazilian Jewish community, publicly acknowledged the importance of New Christians in colonial Brazil, including Gaspar da Gama (translator on Cabral's first voyage to Brazil), Fernando de Noronha (who first introduced sugarcane production in Brazil), João Ramalho (first known non-Indigenous inhabitant of Brazil who was married to several Tupi tribeswomen), and Rapôso Tavares (Bandeirante) —all of whom are discussed in this book.¹⁶³ The growing interest in this Jewish legacy in Brazil has prompted research for any traces of Jewry lingering from colonial New Christian Crypto-Jews.¹⁶⁴ For example, researchers have found families living today in the isolated backlands of the Sertão in Brazil's interior semi-arid and desolate rural areas of the northeast region who still maintain Jewish traditions, such as lighting candles on Friday nights in their homes, as is tradition for the Jewish *Shabbat*, and avoiding pork and shellfish.¹⁶⁵ Yet, while some of these communities may be aware of their Jewish roots, many still do not know why these traditions have existed in their families for generations, nor are they clear about their Jewish roots.

The northeast region of Brazil was once considered by the Inquisition to be a haven for the earliest Judaizing New Christian communities in the sixteenth and seventeenth centuries, particularly in Recife, Olinda, Salvador,

Matoim, and throughout rural Pernambuco (e.g., Camaragibe) and the Sertão hinterlands of Rio Grande do Norte and Paraíba (e.g., Seridó, Patos, and Campina Grande).[166] Today some residents in parts of this region have also been observed to add the Magen David, the "Star of David" or "Shield of David" (the hexagram with two equilateral triangles, symbolic of Jewish people), to their folklore and cultural landscapes, even on local church steeples.[167] It is believed that the small town of Seridó, in the state of Paraíba in the hinterlands of the northeast, gained its namesake from a derivation of the Hebrew word *Sarid* ("survivor"), or a variation of *Serid*, with the "o" added (meaning "The one who escaped" or "in exile")—and named after those Crypto-Jews and New Christians who had found refuge in the backlands of the northeastern Sertão.[168] There are many parallels between the narrative of New Christians who fled the Iberian Inquisitions and found refuge in isolated geographies of the Brazilian Sertão, and of New Mexico in the United States. The parallels can also be seen in the story of their descendants today in New Mexico, many of whom are unaware of their Jewish ancestry, or the customs practiced at home in secret that have persisted for generations.[169]

According to Ricardo Berkiensztat, vice-president of the Israelite Federation of São Paulo (*Federação Israelita de São Paulo*), today there are about 100 synagogues throughout Brazil and about 120,000 Jews, most of whom live in São Paulo and Rio de Janeiro, respectively, representing only a tiny minority in Brazil (0.06 percent of the total population).[170] Yet some scholars, such as Anita W. Novinsky, claim that some of the oldest families in Brazil today are in fact descendants of former Portuguese Jews, especially those in northeastern Brazil. For example, among other prominent old Brazilian families, Bahia's famed contemporary singer-songwriter, Chico Buarque de Holanda, and his father, eminent Brazilian historian Sérgio Buarque de Holanda, author of the seminal historical study, *Raízes do Brazil* (published in 1956), are thought to be direct descendants of Portuguese Jews from a lineage of prominent Portuguese rabbis.[171] One recent genetic study found that about 30 percent of Brazilians today can trace their heritage to those Portuguese Jews who fled the Portuguese Inquisition, equivalent to about almost half a million Brazilians.[172] Other scholars have suggested that this number may be even higher—about a million Brazilians—which is probably unrealistic and unlikely, and which would questionably make Brazil the largest country in the world with Portuguese-Jewish ancestry (i.e., the descendants of Jews and New Christians who had fled the Inquisition).[173]

On a much larger scale for Latin America (including Brazil), a new genetic study claims that almost a quarter of Latin Americans (23 percent) share Jewish ancestry from Portugal and Spain.[174] This study is one of the most comprehensive genetic surveys taken from a sample of 6,500 individuals (from Chile, Colombia, Peru, Bolivia, Mexico, and Brazil), suggesting that New Christians fled the Inquisition to the Americas in significantly large numbers—much larger than previously thought. This study also noticed rare genetic diseases and mutations in Latin Americans that have been prevalent only in Jewish communities.[175] Jews and New Christians who fled the Inquisition evidently seem to have left prominent genetic markers throughout Latin America, including Brazil, reflecting an old presence in the Americas.

It is worthwhile pointing out that public and popular spheres can emphasize how some traces of centuries-old Portuguese Judaic cultural practices (albeit, most likely amalgamated and syncretic versions) in Brazil's northeast region may have continued to this day, although this is also a questionable phenomenon.[176] That is, cultural practices such as these may have many different origins, not just Jewish; and more documentation and analysis are needed to provide concrete scholarly evidence. Bruno Feitler cautions us about such findings and this recent phenomenon, since there is no concrete evidence available that would allow for these kinds of claims to be made—which remains a topic left for future research studies to explore.[177]

These recent ideas circulating in Brazil today seem to suggest that if someone discovers a Jewish ancestor, no matter how distant, then that person has a monolithic Jewish identity and faith, and can never "escape it." However, it is important to also point out that ethnicity and faith are not fixed identities; they are fluid, especially since New Christians straddled liminal forms of self-identification that changed over time, and involved complex, flexible, and even contradictory dimensions. Thus, a far more nuanced interpretation and serious research is required to address these complex, syncretic, and nebulous Crypto-Jewish phenomena appearing today in Brazil's northeast.[178]

Much earlier in Portugal, similar findings had been reported in small towns such as Belmonte, among other communities in Portugal, entirely made up of New Christians who had secretly survived for generations—a phenomenon that was first documented in a well-known study by Samuel Schwarz in 1925, *Os Cristãos-Novos em Portugal No Século XX*.[179] Schwartz explains that they were known to have observed the Sabbath, Jewish dietary laws, "The Feast of Queen Esther" or Purim, and avoidance of pork, for example, as they were relegated to live in a surreal paradoxical duality, betwixt and between.[180] Bruno Feitler alerts us that there are no accounts of Crypto-Jewish groups of Jewish origin that survived after the end of the eighteenth century in Brazil—contrary to those accounts of groups that survived, for instance, in Belmonte, Portugal—yet beginning in the 1970s, some groups in Brazil claimed Jewish-New Christian ancestry (starting in Natal, Rio Grande do Norte).[181]

It is a staggering commentary in the geography of the Atlantic world—one that is not an exaggeration or shrouded in myth, and one that speaks volumes about the themes of submerged legacy and memory, and the silencing of an imperative component of Brazilian geography—that for over three centuries (322 years to be exact), between 1500 and 1822, Jews were only allowed to profess their religion openly during a span of 24 years (1630–1654), and this occurred only when northeastern Brazil was under Dutch rule.[182] Former Jews or their converted descendants, New Christians, were subjected to persecution, targeted by the Inquisition, and marked by their social status categorization, carrying the perpetual "taint" of Jewish ancestry. Ironically, the contribution of Portuguese Jews and New Christians in colonial Brazil would become vital to its early nation-building, and to Brazil's demographic, economic, and ecological transformations and developments.

CHAPTER THREE

The Portuguese World and Portuguese-Jewish Diasporas

THE LATE HISTORIAN FROM Johns Hopkins University, Baltimore, Maryland, A. J. R. Russell-Wood, commented in 1992 on the prevailing ignorance concerning the Portuguese world. He asked, "how many would recognize his Portuguese name of Fernão de Magalhães?" (better known by his Anglicized name, Magellan—the "Strait of Magellan" is named after him).[1] Russell-Wood continues:

> How is it that every schoolboy of the English-speaking world can rattle off the names of Hernán Cortés, Francisco Pizarro, Hernando de Soto ... and others of their ilk? And yet, when questioned about the pantheon of Portuguese explorers, that selfsame schoolboy would be hard pressed to name one other than the anglicized and inappropriately named Henry "the Navigator."[2]

Remarkably, Russell-Wood's commentaries still ring true today over thirty years later. The complexities and varieties of the Portuguese experience in their encounters during more than a century in Africa, Asia, and the Americas, as Russell-Wood aptly points out, makes the "Spanish experience in the Americas and the Philippines pale by comparison."[3]

As geographer Kempton E. Webb stated, "if there were ever an area of Brazil where traditions have persisted, it is northeast Brazil. So, it is toward the early Portuguese experience there that we must look for enlightenment."[4] In this context of the historical geography of Brazil, as geographer Kempton

Webb had claimed, indeed it is important to look toward the early Portuguese experience.

As A. J. R. Russell-Wood aptly claimed, the Portuguese "heralded a new transcontinental, transoceanic, and transnational age of globalization which was to be characterized by interdependence, interaction, and exchange."[5] Moreover, the Portuguese were the first Europeans to discover two fundamental wind systems in the south and north Atlantic ("trade winds"), oceanic gyres, the determination of latitude, and the seasonal monsoon wind systems of the Indian Ocean, Arabian Sea, Bay of Bengal, Indonesia, and East Asia.[6] Therefore, this body of geographical knowledge enabled the Portuguese to find new oceanic pathways which extended from Africa and India, to China, Japan, and Southeast Asia—pathways unknown to Europeans until then.[7] Instead of obstacles, oceans became pathways, effectively acting as "superhighways" that connected one place to another. In addition, as Frédéric Mauro asserts, Portuguese Jews and New Christians became the "backbone of the Portuguese trading class in Europe and overseas."[8]

It is important to consider that the world had already long been globalized by the fifteenth century and these "new" lands that the Portuguese had reached by oceanic pathways were, of course, known beforehand by other local trade routes in the East.[9] However, what these new Portuguese voyages and explorations meant to Europeans now, was that commerce and trade intensified as more diverse commodities from various global regions were sold at a lower cost, with a far more effective and faster mode of transportation than land, with a vast geographic expansion by sea until then unknown to Europeans.

The objective here is not to convey yet another confirmation and old adage of "Western superiority" or of the "triumph of the West."[10] John Hobson explains the problem with the traditional view perpetuated in school and university textbooks in this imaginary division between West and East (i.e., the "Orientalist" and "Eurocentric" views): "Europeans spread outward conquering the East and Far West while simultaneously laying down the tracks of capitalism along which the whole world could be delivered from the jaws of deprivation and misery into the bright light of modernity."[11] In this vein, my intention in this chapter is not to callously aggrandize the Portuguese world and Portuguese Jews and New Christians, and merely trumpet their achievements. The point I make here is to give continuity to the theme of a "submerged" historiographical legacy of a neglected memory, yet at the same time, not to give credence to primacy theories (i.e., being the "first").

The general ignorance of the Portuguese world obscures the importance of Jews and New Christians within these global geographical explorations. The Portuguese Jews and New Christians were involved in all aspects of the Portuguese entrerpise of overseas exploration, including its financing, scientific innovations, and cartographic productions, which facilitated Portuguese prominence in the age of new global trans-oceanic navigations. In short, in the words of Patricia Seed, "Portuguese rulers initiated their claims to the New World through science, which had been created for them by Jewish astronomers based upon the heritage of the Islamic era."[12]

By the mid-sixteenth century, Portuguese territorial domains extended across the world, and as Daniel Banes explains, Lisbon became the "focal point of the scientific research needed to enhance instrument-aided navigation and to improve Portugal's trading advantages."[13] Consequently, because of these commercial and global networks, Portuguese Jews virtually controlled the economy in Portugal, and in the words of Cecil Roth, they "made fabulous fortunes as bankers and merchants."[14] The Portuguese were the first known people to land on the uninhabited Atlantic islands of Madeira (1419), the Azores (1427), Cape Verde (1456–1460), and Tristão da Cunha (1506), and by 1500, they had already landed in (albeit inhabited) Greenland, and part of which today forms and the province of Newfoundland and Labrador, Canada.[15] Labrador, was named after Portuguese explorer, João Fernandes (*o lavrador* meaning "the farmer" or "sharecropper" in Portuguese).[16] They were the first Europeans to establish commercial networks via oceanic pathways throughout the world. Gil Eannes rounded Cape Bojador (1434), opening the way to upper Niger, Senegal, and Guinea (in Africa); and Bartolomeu Dias rounded the Cape of Good Hope (1488).[17] Furthermore, they were the first Europeans to arrive by sea in the Clove Islands, Bandas, and Moluccas in Southeast Asia (1512), and the first European sea-based mission to arrive in Canton, China (1514), New Guinea (1525), and Japan (1542–1543).[18]

Behind these pioneer oceanic explorations, Portuguese maritime expansions were developed by the advent of new navigational instruments, tidal timetables, and overall geographic knowledge largely developed by

Portuguese Jews who "created the modern science of navigation."[19] Portugal's new scientific techonologies developed by Jewish scientists would lead to their arrival in Brazil, as Patricia Seed explains: "on the coast of Brazil Master John made the first accurate European depiction of the most famous constellation in all the new skies, the Southern Cross."[20]

Large tracts of forested lands in Europe, between the 1300s and 1500s, turned into pastures as a direct consequence of increased demand for food supply and increase in population growth for most of Europe.[21] As a result, Europeans were under pressure to find new lands overseas. In 1700, about 230 million hectares of forests existed in Europe, with about 190 million hectares of pasture, and 67 million hectares of croplands. By 1850, forest lands decreased to about 205 million, while pastures increased to 150 million, and croplands to 132 million hectares.[22] Hence, as environmental historian Carolyn Merchant claims, the pressure on arable lands increased at the same time as populations and towns grew. Merchant shows that within three hundred years, from 1000 to 1300, the European population grew from 36 million to about 80 million people. It increased to 200 million in 1800. Thus, as Merchant explains, "Mercantile capitalism cast America [the Americas] as a site of natural resources, [and] Africa as the source of enslaved human resources." That is, with this reshaping of the sixteenth-century landscapes in Europe, the phenomenon of a new European mercantile class of "bourgeois entrepreneurs" emerged with their arrival in the New World, and at the same time, an increased demand for human labor, which was supplied by Indigenous populations for a short period, and then by Africans, was subsequently met, in the Americas, through the transatlantic slave trade.[23]

The Omissions in the Literature of Geography

Most English-speaking encyclopedias, dictionaries, surveys, and college textbooks in geography ignore the importance of the Portuguese world, and neglect the role and contributions of Jews and New Christians in the acceleration of Portugal's geographical exploration, navigation, and the modern scientific method.[24]

With a unique exception in *The Geographical Tradition* by geographer David N. Livingstone, most of the anglophone pedagogical narrative of the history of the discipline of geography in the Western world is conveyed in the following standard progression. Starting with the developments of geographical knowledge by ancient Greek geographers (e.g., Eratosthenes, Strabo, etc.); the subsequent transmittal of this knowledge, and the contributions of Islamic/Arab geographers (e.g., Al Idrisi, Ibn Battuta, Ibn Khaldun, etc.); the voyage of Columbus and the Age of Navigation, and perhaps with a miserly and inadequate mention of "Henry the Navigator," with an emphasis ad nauseam of the Spanish Empire and the Spanish Conquistadors and the Spanish presence in the Americas; then finally on to discussions about Immanuel Kant, and the so-called "forefathers of modern geography" (e.g., Alexander von Humboldt and Carl Ritter)—and so on.[25]

This standard progression, repeated so many times, ignores the Portuguese world, the arrival of the Portuguese in the New World, and the scientific contribution of Portuguese Jews as well as their role in the prominence of Portugal's global explorations and transoceanic navigations. Their important role in the development of modern European science is notably absent in most of the annals of geography (as well as in most of anglophone social sciences).[26] This omission is a salient matter, especially in this narrative of Portuguese Jews and New Christians in colonial Brazil, as we shall see ahead.

These omissions are surprising, especially if we consider the important contributions of Portuguese-Jewish and New Christian cartographers, astronomers, mathematicians, scientists, and geographers such as Pedro Nunes, inventor of the nonius (a measuring tool used in navigation and astronomy), whose grandsons, Matias Pereira and Pedro Nunes Pereira, were imprisoned by the Inquisition as Judaizers.[27] Also, Garcia d'Orta, sometimes spelled, "da Orta," or "d'Horta" (1501–1568), pioneer scientist, who was the son of Jewish parents, and had been forcibly converted to Christianity in Portugal in 1497.[28] Timothy D. Walker's study of Garcia d'Orta notes that he became chief physician of the Estado da Índia during the mid-sixteenth century (his official title was "physician named by the king," *físico d'el Rei*).[29] He first arrived in Goa in 1534, and spent the next thirty years living in India, eventually in 1563 publishing a seminal book, *Colloquies on the Simples and Drugs and Medicinal Things of India*, the first systematic description of Asian medicine by a European. His extensive knowledge and his own garden of Indian medicinal plants was used to supply hospitals in Goa.[30] D'Orta had studied medicine in Salamanca, Spain, and returned to his native Portugal in 1523, to become a professor at Coimbra University. Garcia d'Orta then sailed for Goa, India, as a personal physician to Martim Afonso de Sousa, Captain Major of the Indian Ocean (1542–1545), and then governor of Portuguese India.[31] Sousa became the first land grantee, *donatário*, of the Captaincy of São Vicente, Brazil, was likely a New Christian himself, and became close friends with d'Orta.[32]

Garcia d'Orta had practiced Judaism with his family in secret, many of whom were arrested and sentenced by the Inquisition—for example, his sister Catarina d'Orta was burned at the stake in Goa, India.[33] Marcelo Bogaciovas claims that since d'Orta and Martim Afonso de Sousa were close friends and maintained close contact with each other, d'Orta would have been familiar with the New Christian flight to Brazil and their need to find a new home free of persecution. Thus, the settlement in São Vicente (southeast Brazil) might have been established specifically to anticipate a large-scale migration of New Christians to Brazil.[34]

Both Nunes and d'Orta were "exponents of the experimental method"—as well as other Jewish scientists such as Jacob Poel, Ismael Bonfil, and José Vizinho.[35] In addition, Yehuda Ibn Verga's important scientific publications written in Hebrew, *Kitzur ha-Mispar* (Abridged Arithmetic), *Keli ha-Ofek* (Instrument of the Horizon), and *L'dat Middoth Kol D'var* (Method for the Measurement of All Objects), also followed the experimental method.[36] Thus, the Portuguese Age of Exploration benefited from the mass migration of these Jewish scientists, astronomers, and geographers, for example, Abraham Cresques (born in Majorca), and wealthy families such as the Abravanel family, who had migrated from Spain after the pogroms of the 1390s and throughout the fifteenth century, especially since Portugal had traditionally welcomed Jewish geographers and astronomers and was known for its religious tolerance, at least until 1496.[37]

Jewish scientists, astronomers, geographers, and cartographers, such as José Vizinho and his brother, Moisés Vizinho, Master Rodrigo, and Abraham Zacuto (or Zakkut), all worked under King John II of Portugal.[38] For example, Zacuto, former professor of astronomy at the University of Saragossa, had incorporated Yehuda Ibn Verga's work into his treatise in Hebrew,

Ha-Hibbur ha-Godol (The Great Codex). Both Vasco da Gama and Pedro Álvares Cabral used the tables from Zacuto's *Perpetual Almanac* in their voyages.[39]

Abraham Zacuto had published *Rules for the Astrolabe* in 1473, which included "the mathematically correct prediction of the sun's seasonal position in relationship to the earth."[40] Furthermore, in 1497, Zacuto also created the first mariner's astrolabe, handing it personally to Vasco da Gama before his historic voyage to India and back.[41] I will return later to Zacuto's work, which would later play a role in the first Portuguese arrival in Brazil in 1500 when a former Jew, Mestre João, determined Brazil's geographic location through astronomy by establishing the location via the Southern Cross constellation.[42] Vizinho, Rodrigo, and Zacuto calculated new methods to observe latitude at sea.[43] Later, Vizinho was forced to convert to Christianity, and Zacuto fled to the Ottoman Empire.

Another scientific treatise was written by eminent physician and Portuguese Jew, Zacutus Lusitanus (Zacuto "the Portuguese," also known as Abraham Zacuto or Zacuth)—a descendant of Abraham Zacuto, mentioned above. Born in Lisbon with the name of Manuel Álvares Távora, he wrote *De Medicorum principum historia*, which provided a systematic description of all known diseases. It was published posthumously and became a fundamental treatise in medicine.[44] Notably, none of these names, inventions, or contributions are listed in the *Dictionary of the History of Science* published by the Princeton University Press.[45] Despite this ommission, Daniel Baines explains how the Jewish style of science practices in sixteenth-century Portugal "provided the template for English science."[46] Patricia Seed points out that omissions in the academic literature have most likely stemmed from language and scholarly (disciplinary) barriers in the historiography, among other interrelated reasons, ranging from the "innocuous" to blatantly anti-Semitic reasons.[47]

The modern science of navigation and geography developed in Portugal was intimately tied to Jews. Dom João I, Mestre de Avis (1357–1433), father of Dom Henrique ("Henry the Navigator"), employed Jews such as Abraão Cresques, mentioned earlier, of the Cresques family of cartographers (who had studied lunar cycles, ocean tides, and astronomical calculations in the Majorcan cartographic tradition)—and author of the famous atlas, *Atlas*

Catalão (1375).⁴⁸ This atlas was unique, as Francisco Bethencourt explains: it "represents a striking combination of sea chart and *mappamundi*, introducing the representation of human types in different parts of the world—an innovation later developed by the cartographers of Lisbon and Dieppe."⁴⁹

Cresques was also known by his Hebrew name, Elisha ben Abraham Cresques, and had produced "one of the most lavish Sefardi manuscripts, known as the 'Fardi Bible.'"⁵⁰ He had lived in Majorca from 1325 to 1387, and became a highly regarded cartographer. Before him, medieval world maps were circular; however, the maps that he created were unusual—a fusion of traditions, projected in a rectangular shape.⁵¹ Katrin Kogman-Appel claims that it was precisely Cresques's Jewish cultural background that allowed for the creation of the unusual features of his cartographic productions, and "provided him with access to a corpus of knowledge that was available in his vicinity . . . but was apparently less accessible or of less interest to his Christian colleagues in the mapmaking trade."⁵² Furthermore, renowned Portuguese explorers during the so-called Golden Age of Exploration, such as Pedro Álvares Cabral, Bartolomeu Dias, Vasco da Gama, Fernão de Magalhães (i.e., known by the Anglicized name of "Magellan"), and Christopher Columbus, among others, were all "indoctrinated in the scientific schools of Zacuto and Vizinho."⁵³

Salvador Madariaga's bibliography of Columbus from 1949, for example, had observed that cosmography, mapmaking, geography, and astronomy were exclusively Jewish occupations.⁵⁴ Jews were also involved in the financing of explorations.⁵⁵ However, the case that Christopher Columbus was Jewish, or part Jewish, or that he was Portuguese and not Italian (from Genoa), or that his real name was Salvador Fernandes Zarco, has not been proven and is not accepted by serious scholars.⁵⁶

In addition, research about the figure inadequately known as "Henry the Navigator" is also worthwhile clarifying. We know that he participated in the conquest of Ceuta (North Africa), and that he had sent his courtiers to the African coast to search for the source of African gold, and was deeply involved in the colonization of Madeira and the construction of the Atlantic islands' sugar economy. However, he was not a "navigator," nor did he establish the famed "School at Sagres" (the alleged first European institution devoted to cartographic and geographical exploration), and hence, the appellation of "Henry the Navigator" is inappropriate.[57] Moreover, most of the more remarkable Portuguese achievements in exploration occurred after Prince Henry died in 1460.[58]

Nonetheless, the contributions of Portuguese Jews and New Christians in the enterprise of Portuguese navigation, science, transoceanic explorations, and commerce, are clearly vital components to Lusitanian expansion worldwide—and provide us with a backdrop to their role in the development of early colonial Brazil.

Portuguese Jews and their Access to Scientific Bodies of Knowledge

As early as the thirteenth or fourteenth century, Genoese and Venetian communities had established important commercial networks in Lisbon, as they worked closely with Jewish mercantile communities.[59] Malyn Newitt explains the extent of their cartographic, commercial, and political influence on the Portuguese, as "it was the grafting of Italian commercial skills, technical expertise and spirit of enterprise onto fifteenth century Iberian society with its particular economic and political characteristic . . . that was to produce the powerful drive for overseas expansion."[60]

Furthermore, Patrick Manning and Abigail Owen edited a volume, *Knowledge in Translation: Global Patterns of Scientific Exchange, 1000–1800 CE*, that includes essays addressing the transmittance (or as geographers say, "diffusion") of this scientific body of knowledge.[61] They explain the salience of translations in the facilitation and advent of new scientific developments, and how scientific and geographical knowledge developed and was built upon previous work that was translated from one language to another (i.e., in a "snowball effect" over time). In this case, we learn here how the process of language translations became vital for the continuation, development, and expansion of scientific thought and geographic exploration.

As seen earlier, the Iberian Peninsula had been under Muslim rule (as of 711), where Muslims, Christians, and Jews lived side by side in relative political-social harmony during the period known as Convivência, and where Islamic caliphs treated Christians and Jews better than the previous Gothic and Visigoth kings in the peninsula had done (and certainly better than the Catholic monarchies of the late fifteenth century).[62] The overall environment during Convivência enabled intense cultural, intellectual, geographical, and scientific exchanges to occur, specifically between Muslim and Jewish scholars. Consequently, a significant corpus of the Arabic scientific literature in the Iberian Peninsula was written in Hebrew. That is, as A. J. R. Russell-Wood points out, "Convivência was a marked characteristic of the Portuguese overseas experience."[63] It is this style of Convivência that would come to characterize early Brazilian colonial society.

Jews facilitated the exploration of Portuguese navigators by furnishing them with scientific material, for example, as Guiseppi Marcocci explains: they used "trigonometry and the use of the astrolabe to chart the exact position of the *caravelas* [Portuguese sailing vessels] as they crossed the Atlantic, both of which they inherited from the Muslim world."[64] That is, Jewish scientists had been intimately familiar with the works of fellow Muslim astronomers, mathematicians, geographers, and cartographers, and had access to their work, since most Jewish scientists in Portugal were multilingual, speaking Arabic, Hebrew, and Portuguese. Patricia Seed explains, "their calculations and observations had originated in the astronomy, scientific observations, and trigonometry invented by Muslims and Jews during the Golden Age of Islamic Science."[65]

With the benefit of being multilingual and literate, Jews became primary sources of information for such translations, and those who worked at the Portuguese court "would translate these disciplines into the science of celestial navigation."[66] Moreover, as Patricia Seed explains, "Iberian Jewish astronomers composed at least fifteen known original treatises on instruments of observation and created the first scientific literature written in Hebrew."[67] However, Jewish astronomers and scientists were not merely vehicles for Islamic science; their corpus of scientific work became accepted into Islamic tradition.[68] Therefore, Portuguese Jews had inherited a significant body of navigational and cartographic knowledge from other traditions (e.g., Muslim, Venetian, and Genoese); for example, the positioning of a central rudder on the stern post of the keel, application of the magnetic needle and compass; the triangular lateen sail; and the portolan chart.[69] They also developed and invented legitimately new scientific innovations (e.g., the cross-staff, or the "cane of Jacob," for measuring the height of the sun and stars at sea; and a distinctive astrolabe with Hebrew characters).[70]

One motivation for the development of scientific studies among Portuguese Jews was religious. For example, in Judaism the first sighting of the new moon marks Tishrei, the first month of the Sabbath year and the start of the day for celebrating the Jewish New Year (Rosh Hashanah).[71] Forecasting the tidal timing of the oceans requires knowledge of lunar cycles, which was an expertise developed by Muslim and Jewish scientists to establish religious ritual dates.[72] Therefore, Jewish cartographers, such as Abraão (Abraham) Cresques, calculated the timing of ocean tides, and as a result this allowed him to construct the first tide tables of Europe. Another Jewish cartographer, Mestre Jaime (born in Mallorca), who was invited by Prince Henry to relocate and join his court in Portugal, produced newly created tide tables for the Portuguese coast and expanded his predictions for West African coastal tides.[73]

One popular myth also prompted explorations overseas: this was the search for Prester John, a legendary Christian king and partriarch (popular in medieval fantasy). An alleged letter stated that he was being held against his will by Muslims somewhere in a "glorious land filled with fortune" and was awaiting Christian rescue (it was believed that he was living in East Africa, probably Ethiopia, or Trabrobane, modern-day Sri Lanka). However, while there is no evidence the letter ever existed, the myth endured and eventually prompted several searches for him, and resulted in subsequent global explorations.[74] In this case, the myth component that inspired geographical explorations emerged from two major sources: the interest of the medieval tales written by Sir John Mandeville about "headless men and women with horseshoe mouths or kneelength ears," and, the hope to find Prester John's glorious utopia.[75] Portuguese Jews shared a common interest in finding the mythic lost Christian kingdom of Prester John, as Patricia Seed clarifies: "for Portuguese-Jewish folklore of the time held that a lost tribe of Israel—now sometimes identified as the Ethiopian Jews—was located in the same part of Africa as the Christian Kingdom of Prester John."[76] There are several references to Prester John in the chronicles of Vasco da Gama's voyage to India.[77] These Portuguese explorations and the involvement of Portuguese Jews, dovetail with the next section about the first Portuguese arrival in Brazil in 1500.

Hence, it was under these syncretic and dynamic interrelationships that scientific advancements were developed by Portuguese Jews who were employed by the Portuguese court, and who contributed to the once prominent role of Portuguese global navigation and exploration.

First Descriptions of Brazil

While Christopher Columbus has received most of the universal attention for his arrival in the Americas, ostensibly, Pedro Álvares Cabral, receives a backseat in this narrative of New World encounters (except, of course, in Brazil).[78] However, while Columbus had merely landed on a handful of Caribbean islands, the Spanish had no idea of the existence of the landmass of Mexico and beyond until Hernán Cortés arrived there in 1519, almost thirty years after Columbus arrived in the Caribbean.[79] Meanwhile, the Portuguese had already explored the north and south Atlantic and already knew about the existing landmasses in Latin America beforehand (i.e., with the explorations of Corte-Real and Gonçalo Coelho in 1501 and 1503, respectively).[80] Columbus died believing that he had landed in Japan or China.[81]

Pedro Álvares Cabral, today immortalized in Brazil as the European "discoverer" of Brazil in 1500, claimed the land of Brazil for Portugal, yet we shall see that his landing was hardly a "discovery."[82] Cabral sailed with an enormous fleet of about one thousand men (of which about seven hundred were soldiers) aboard thirteen vessels, with Bartolomeu Dias (the renowned Portuguese explorer), Diogo Dias, and Nicolau Coelho as captains.[83] While some of the documents survived, most documents about the early history of Brazil were lost when the Casa da India in Lisbon was destroyed by fire and the catastrophic earthquake of 1755.[84]

The first sighting of Brazil occurred on April 22, 1500, on Cabral's way to India (via Vasco da Gama's newly discovered route to India around the southern Cape of Africa, the Cape of Good Hope, *Cabo da Boa Esperança*)— allegedly by accident, while thrown off course. It is very likely that the Portuguese had previous knowledge about the existing land of Brazil, and this voyage was hardly accidental, but intentional.[85] It is also known that D. Manuel furnished secret verbal (or written) instructions to Cabral about his voyage trajectory.[86] Stuart B. Schwartz points out how the Portuguese had maintained a so-called "policy of secrecy or governmental control of information," and that there is speculation that the Portuguese already had made contact with Brazil beforehand but kept it a secret, which as Schwartz puts it, helps to explain Cabral's ostensibly "peculiar" voyage route when it landed in Brazil on its way to India.[87]

The imaginary line defined by the Treaty of Tordesilhas (1494) divided the two geographic regions between Spanish and Portuguese world dominions along the meridian line, 370 leagues west of the Cape Verde Islands. The Portuguese initially rejected the first proposed line of demarcation for the Treaty of Tordesilhas in 1493, which ran just to the east of Brazil. The final line of the treaty, as accepted by the Portuguese in 1494, just so happens to incorporate the northeast "hump" of Brazil (i.e., the northeast region). Given that the treaty was signed six years prior to Portuguese arrival in Brazil in 1500, therefore, it is likely that the Portuguese already had prior knowledge of the landmass of South America when they signed the treaty.[88]

A letter from the Portuguese chronicler on board, Pero Vaz de Caminha, describes Cabral's voyage to Brazil. On April 20, 1500, the crew observed plants known as *botelhas* and *rabo d'asno* floating in the sea, and birds known as *fura-buchos*, indicative of land nearby.[89] They spotted an elevated mount which they named Monte Pascoal ("Easter Mount") [today in the municipality of Prado, about 40 miles from Porto Seguro, Bahia].[90] On the morning of April 22, they came closer to land and first saw Brazil's Indigenous inhabitants. Nicolau Coelho and his men were ordered to further explore the adjacent river that flowed into the ocean, where about thirty naked Indigenous men with pierced lower lips waited for them on land, and they proceeded to exchange items in peace. The *degredado*, Afonso Ribeiro, was ordered to go out to learn the Indigenous language and customs at Cabrália Bay (today in Bahia).[91]

Pedro Álvares Cabral first named this land—believed to be an island—Ilha de Vera Cruz, "Island of the Holy Cross," which eventually changed to "Land of the Holy Cross," and then again in 1503 to "Land of Brazil," and finally to just "Brasil"—stemming from ambiguous etymological origins, likely from the redness of brazilwood (pau brasil, a tree used for its red dye, called Ibirapitanga in the Tupi language), as in the redness of burning coals (*brasa*), or improbably from an alleged mythical island, "Hy Brasil."[92]

A banner with the Order of the Knights of Christ was erected on the beach (a flag with a red "Maltese Cross" set in a white background)—similar to an order like the Knights Templars, to which virtually all Portuguese explorers belonged.[93] The act of inserting a Christian cross into new lands as an overt symbolism of Christianity in the New World epitomizes European colonialism in the New World par excellence—that is, colonialism and the proselytization of Christianity went hand in hand, one justifying the other.

The chronicler, Pêro Vaz de Caminha, reported, "the admiral named the mountain Easter Mount [Monte Pascoal] and the country, the Land of the True [Holy] Cross."[94] This letter became known as the first official announcement of Brazil, yet it had disappeared until it was rediscovered and published in 1817 by historian Aires de Casal, in *Corografia Brasilica*.[95] Caminha describes that on May 1, 1500, a Christian cross was erected at Porto Seguro near the margin of a river. Mass was conducted by Friar Henrique, with about Indigenous spectators, who were presented with small crucifixes after mass.[96]

The letter written by Mestre João that was sent back to Lisbon to D. Manuel (along with the other official letter about the discovery written by chronicler Pero Vaz de Caminha) is a document written between April 28 and May 1, 1500. It is here that we find the first known description that identified the Southern Cross (O Cruzeiro do Sul) as well as the mention of an ancient map belonging to Pero Vaz Bisagudo—which alludes to Portugal's possible previous knowledge about the land of Brazil, albeit it was thought to have been an island. Historian Francisco Adolfo de Varnhagen only found this letter centuries later at the National Archives at Torre do Tombo, in 1843.[97]

Considered one of the most important documents of the landing in Brazil, the letter to Dom Manuel from Caminha, a clerk of Cabral's Armada, is one of only three firsthand accounts of this encounter (the others were the letters by Mestre João and an anonymous pilot).[98] This excerpt is from the letter of Pero Vaz de Caminha to King Manuel, written from Porto Seguro (Bahia) on May 1, 1500:

> They were dark and entirely naked, without anything to cover their shame. They carried in their hands bows with their arrows. All came boldly towards the boat, and Nicolau Coelho made a sign to them that they should lay down their bows, and they laid them down.

They seem to me people of such innocence that, if one could understand them and they us, they would soon be Christians ... For it is certain this people is good and of pure simplicity, and there can easily be stamped upon them whatever belief we wish to give them.[99]

On that occasion, there were at least two former Jews on board Cabral's fleet that we know of, and they were multilingual and served as translators. They were Gaspar da Gama, a New Christian who had been hired as a translator on Vasco da Gama's explorations and later, on Cabral's. The other was Mestre João ("Master John," also known as João Faras), chief pilot of Cabral's fleet.[100]

Jews or former Jews were often taken along on Portuguese overseas voyages and expeditions, as we have seen before, since most were multilingual (e.g., speaking Portuguese, Hebrew, and Arabic), and they often served as translators.[101]

How were Portuguese Jews and New Christians involved in this epistle of the first Portuguese arrivals in Brazil? We learn from Patricia Seed's research that "the process of establishing latitudes thus became the principal technique the Portuguese would observe when encountering previously unknown territories and peoples."[102] This is exactly what Mestre João did in April of 1500—and here lies a salient component in this discussion.[103]

We already have seen how Abraham Zacuto had created innovative astronomy studies, "Rules for the Astrolabe" (*Regimento do astrolábio*), as discussed earlier, which established accurate latitudes any day of the year, anywhere. Mestre João consulted them when he arrived in Brazil and these rules also became the basis of Portuguese navigation that would influence later Dutch, Spanish, and English nautical enterprises.[104] We know this from a letter that was sent to King D. Manuel in 1500, as William B. Greenlee explains:

The height of the sun was taken with the astrolabe and indicated 56° on the 27th of April by the Julian Calendar. When this determination was made, Master John referred to his book of instructions for the use of the astrolabe and he found that the sun's declination at noon for that day was approximately 17° 0'. The latitude was thus 90°-56°-17°0' S ... this was probably based on the work of the eminent . . . astronomer Abraham Zacuto.[105]

Mestre João used Abraham Zacuto's rules of astronomy, and as Patricia Seed explains, "on the coast of Brazil, Master John made the first accurate European depiction of the most famous constellation in all the new skies, the Southern Cross."[106] Today, the Southern Cross appears conspicuously on the Brazilian national flag, O Cruzeiro do Sul. This constellation has become a symbol of nationhood to Brazilians today.[107] Yet in one recent book on the historical biography of Brazil, *Brazil: A Biography*, the authors refer to Mestre João merely as "the Spanish Astronomer."[108] Infelicitously the authors neglect to mention that he was a former Jew, and this omitted fact is important (he was likely to have been Galician by birth, and raised in Portugal).[109] We know that he was a New Christian steeped in the scientific and geographical traditions of Jews in Portugal.[110]

Gaspar da Gama, the other former Jew on board, was known as "Gaspar from India"; however, the kings and chroniclers continued to refer to him as "the Jew"—despite the fact that he had been converted.[111] He was the first Jew to land on Brazilian soil. As a child, he fled his native Poland with his family after 1444, lived in Alexandria and Jerusalem, and then worked with commerce in Angediva, on the west coast of India, where Vasco da Gama first met him. He was immediately imprisoned and taken to Portugal. Interestingly, on his way to Portugal, Vasco da Gama baptized him and renamed him, Gaspar da Gama. He then introduced him to Dom Manuel, and he was quickly accepted by the Portuguese courts and admired for his vast knowledge in geography and languages. He was also included in future Portuguese expeditions, and Cabral brought him along on his voyage because he was fluent in Arabic, Hebrew, and ten other languages, including languages spoken in West Africa (*lingua de Guiné*), and—as was the case with other explorers in the Americas—because they assumed that the Tupi-speaking tribes perhaps might understand one of those languages—which of course they did not. Along with Nicolau Coelho and two African slaves (one from Angola and the other from Guinea), Gaspar da Gama was likely the first Jew to set foot in Brazil, on April 23, 1500.[112]

This first encounter with Indigenous tribes characterizes the blended nature of early colonial Brazil, with new interactions between Indigenous peoples, Africans, Portuguese Old Christians, and Portuguese people with Jewish ancestry. A year later in 1501, Portugal sent three vessels headed by none other than Amerigo Vespucci (originally from Florence, now working for the Portuguese Crown), whose name lends itself to the appellation for the entire continent, "America."[113] They landed on Cape São Roque (Cabo São Roque today is about 51 km/31 miles from the city of Natal, capital of the modern state of Rio Grande do Norte).[114]

The Portuguese Crown was overtly leasing Brazilian territories to New Christians.[115] King Dom Manuel was actively pursuing the strategy of populating Brazil's territory with New Christians through subsidies that stipulated conditions such as expanding "discoveries," and contingencies regarding slavery and exports of pau brasil ("brazilwood" that produces the red dye "dyewood"). In the Tupi language, Ibirapitanga, known as "pau brasil" (*Paubrasilia echinate*), is native to Brazil.[116] Its trade during the sixteenth and seventeenth century was concentrated in the northeast region, more precisely on the coast of the modern states of Bahia and Pernambuco.[117] Notably, the Portuguese term for a "national" from Brazil, *brasileiro*, "Brazilian," had been an early reference to the commercial occupation of those individuals involved in the brazilwood enterprise, as in *carpinteiro* ("carpenter"), and not *brasiliano* (i.e., using the suffix "eiro" instead of "ano," as is commonly used for ascribing other nationals in the Portuguese language, for example, *mexicano*, *colombiano*, *venezuelano*, etc.).

An important yet mysterious figure who emerged during this period of early colonial Brazil and the exploration of pau brasil was João Ramalho, who appears in southeast Brazil. He had established alliances between Tupi tribes and the Portuguese and was especially important in the establishment of Vila de São Paulo de Piratininga (where the modern city of São Paulo was founded). He became the son-in-law of the famous tribal leader, Tibiriçá (from the Guianazes tribe). Ramalho did not know how to write.[118]

Little is known about Ramalho; however, we do know that he was born in Vouzela, in northern Portugal, in 1493.[119] Documents from Serafim Leite claim that Ramalho was the son of João Velho Maldonado and Catarina Afonso de Balbode, and eventually married Catharina Fernandes from Vacas. He left Portugal, never to return to his nation or family.[120] Some scholars believe that he arrived in Brazil as a degredado or else was marooned there, perhaps in 1515 (however, there is no registration or evidence of this), while other scholars have claimed that it is very likely that he was a New Christian.[121] However, there is some doubt cast on Ramalho's ancestry, and one scholar claims that he was related to a Jesuit priest, Manoel de Paiva, who was neither New Christian nor of Jewish ancestry.[122] João Fernando de Almeida Prado explains that since Ramalho's civil status in Brazil was deemed "irregular," and he was an ally of Indigenous tribes, Jesuits immediately suspected that Ramalho must have been a Jew, and an enemy of the Crown and Church, being a man "who wanted nothing with God."[123] Speculations have long been made that Ramalho was in fact Jewish, since he signed his name with a Hebrew "kaf" letter, despite being illiterate.[124]

In 1580, five people offered testimony. They would recall that Ramalho had already been living for ninety years in Brazil—evidently a typo in the reports, and an improbable scenario since that would mean that he had arrived in Brazil in 1490 before he was born; however, Ramalho had indeed already lived a long time in Brazil (probably for forty or fifty years, by that time).[125] He had abandoned Catholicism, and Jesuits considered him a "savage," and were horrified to find Ramalho walking around naked, and married to several Indian women (i.e., the concept of nakedness to Jesuits was akin to extreme poverty and being destitute).[126] In 1553, the first Provincial of the Society of Jesus in Brazil, Jesuit Manuel da Nóbrega, reported that Ramalho and his sons bore children with the sisters of their respective spouses and would participate in war with the tribe Ramalho was affiliated with, and attended their festivities—all naked—which was considered "scandalous" by the Jesuits.[127] Ultimately, Martim Afonso de Souza, first donatary of the Captaincy of São Vicente, realized that Ramalho was a major leader of the region (Planalto Paulista) who had great political influence with the allied Tupi-speaking tribes, and who became a helpful ally to the Portuguese.[128] He would have been the first known non-Indigenous inhabitant of Brazil (and if he was indeed a New Christian, he would have been the first person with Jewish ancestry to inhabit Brazil).[129]

However, after Cabral's arrival, there are very few detailed accounts of the encounters with Indigenous populations in Brazil during the early sixteenth century, with some exceptions described by Pero de Magalhães, Gabriel

Soares de Sousa, and two Jesuit priests, Manuel da Nóbrega and José de Anchieta. One of the earliest accounts, first published in 1557, was written by a German, Hans Staden, who was a captive of the Tupinambá tribe in southeast Brazil.[130] Other accounts of foreign captives by Indigenous tribes in Brazil were described by Frenchmen Jean de Léry and André Thevet.[131]

Hans Staden had been acting as a gunner for the Portuguese at a fort east of São Vicente (on the coast of the modern state of São Paulo) when he was captured. São Vicente was the first village to be established in Brazil by the Portuguese by Martim Afonso de Souza, who also introduced and implemented the first sugarcane plantations that would be used as a model in the rest of Brazil, later.[132] Before Staden's chronicles, only vague accounts of the Tupinambá and Tupiniquim were known through the letters of Pedro Vaz de Caminha and Amerigo Vespucci—although in very little detail.[133]

The French had been competing with the Portuguese since the 1520s for the brazilwood trade, and several attempts by the French were made to take over Brazil. For example, Nicolas Durand de Villegagnon first arrived in Brazil in 1555, and quickly established a French settlement known as *France Antarctique* in Guanabara Bay (in Rio de Janeiro).

Notably, the earliest Inquisition arrest in Brazil that I found in my study was of a Frenchman in 1564 named João/Jehovanan des Boulez, Senhor de Boulez/Boles, or Giovanni des Boulez, arrested for Lutheranism in Rio de Janeiro. He is listed as the "governor of the French in Brazil," *governador dos franceses no Brasil* (processo 1586).

Another detailed account of early Brazil, and of Indigenous populations, was published by an Englishman, Anthony Knivet (in today's vernacular perhaps these chronicles would be likely classified as an "ethnography"). In 1592, privateer Thomas Cavendish, with fifty men—among them Anthony Knivet—sailed to São Sebastião (north of Santos, modern-day state of São Paulo) and were abandoned onshore. As we have already seen, in 1580 Portugal was occupied by Spain until 1640, and England was at war with Spain (1580–1604); therefore, during this period, Brazilian coastal settlements were targeted by the English.[134]

There were several foreign British attacks in Brazil, for example, by Robert Withrington and Christopher Lister in Salvador, Bahia (in 1587); Thomas Cavendish in Santos, off the coast of São Paulo (1591); and, James Lancaster in Recife, Pernambuco (1595).[135] Thomas Cavendish, along with twenty-three Englishmen, looted the village of São Sebastião and burned five sugar mills, killing Brazilian men, women, and children, and also burned down the coastal town of São Vicente (today on the coast of the state of São Paulo), where many of Brazil's earliest deeds and documents stored there were lost forever.[136] Knivet's account was only published later, in 1625, and remains one of the few firsthand narratives of sixteenth-century Brazil (with some exceptions of Portuguese chroniclers, mostly Jesuit missionaries).[137]

Knivet became a servant to either Salvador Correia de Sá, or his son, Martim de Sá—the first Brazilian-born European to govern the Captaincy of Rio de Janeiro.[138] Salvador Correia de Sá was born into a prominent family and the great-grandson of Mem de Sá, third governor-general of Brazil (1557–1572). Another prominent family member was Estácio de Sá, the nephew of Mem de Sá—founder of modern Rio de Janeiro.[139] Together, Mem de Sá and Estacio de Sá successfully fought off the French in 1555. Interestingly, Martim de Sá, and his brother Gonçalo were born out of wedlock to a mother who had been accused and tried for Judaism by the Inquisition. She had been Salvador Correia de Sá's mistress.[140] I found other individuals under the last name of Sá in the dossiers who were persecuted by the Inquisition much later, although it is unknown if they were descendants of Salvador Correia de Sá. For example, Luís Mendes de Sá, aged 37, was burned at the stake after an auto-da-fé in 1739. He was from Coimbra, residing in Minas do Rio das Contas, Bahia, and was arrested in 1738. His father is listed as Salvador Mendes de Sá and his mother, Isabel Cardoso (processo 8015).

The Portuguese Diaspora, Migrations, and the Amsterdam Connection

The Dutch had been influenced by Portugal's navigational explorations. Wim Klooster claims, "the Netherlanders were emboldened by Portugal," and explains that many Dutch navigators "owed the expertise as mariners to their schooling on board Portuguese ships, while others had served Portugal ashore in India . . . Yet others had gathered information while in Portuguese captivity or during a stay in Brazil."[141] Klooster cites the case of Dierick Ruyters, who was imprisoned by the Portuguese in Rio de Janeiro in 1618, and who later became familiar with the Atlantic world as he "combined a variety of Portuguese and Dutch data in his influential navigational guide, *Toortse der Zeevaert* (1623)."[142] In addition, the Dutch borrowed not only the navigational expertise, naval tactics, commercial strategies, accounting practices, and capital from the Portuguese, but as Patricia See explains, they "also derived their right to rule as founded upon discovery and related claims to commercial monopolies."[143]

To further explore the connection between Brazil, Portuguese Jews, and the Dutch, it is necessary to first take a brief look at the historical backdrop, and the importance of Amsterdam. The establishment of the first (official) Jewish communities in the Western Hemisphere in Recife, and Olinda, Pernambuco, were rooted in Amsterdam's Portuguese-Jewish community, known as *Amstelredam galut*, a reference to the "Exile in Amsterdam."[144] Moreover, all the earliest Jewish congregations in the Americas—including in Recife—recognized the Jewish Portuguese Community of Amsterdam as their only religious authority.[145] That becomes an important fact here, as this group were not Ashkenazim just because they were from Amsterdam; they were Portuguese Jews who had migrated to Amsterdam with an important connection to Brazil, as we shall see ahead.

Evidence also shows that a significant number of Portuguese New Christians of European and African ancestry, "Eurafricans" (from West Africa, for example, Senegal), also migrated to Amsterdam and lived as Jews, as seen in the burial records of the Jewish cemetery there (at Beth Haim in Ouderkerk, established in 1614).[146] Here the importance of spatial and migration processes within geography reappears conspicuously. That is, we also gain a clearer understanding of the ties between Recife and Amsterdam, and of the Portuguese-Jewish residents of Amsterdam who migrated to Brazil during Dutch rule (1630–1654), and from there to the Caribbean and Suriname or back to Europe, for instance. Notably, as we shall see in Chapter 5, these sociocultural and ancestral ties to Portugal were clear, as "official bodies [in Amsterdam] used the words 'Portuguese Nation' and 'Jewish Nation' as synonyms," making no distinction between "Portuguese" and "Portuguese Jews."[147] "Jew" and "Portuguese" were virtually synonymous.[148] They were considered and self-identified as gente da nação ("people of the nation"), who were linked to global kinship and commercial networks. As

Francesca Trivellato explains, "Nação thus stood for the translocal identity (at the same time real and imagined)."[149]

Jessica Vance Roitman explains the long-lasting enterprises Portuguese New Christians conducted with the help of Dutch associates. Roitman uses Patrick Manning's concept of "cross-community migration" as a framework and shows that inter-cultural trade is among the innovations that emerged from these cross-community migrations.[150] Roitman explains the strong "sense of solidarity as a transnational group" among Portuguese New Christians and Jewish merchants.[151] Here we find another example of how Portuguese Jews and New Christians were attached to "place" and to their perception of a shared common homeland in Portugal (not Spain). Shared kinship and cultural connections to Portugal (even with Catholics from Portugal) rather than with Eastern European Ashkenazi immigrants, as Roitman explains, illustrate the "clear sense of ethnic identification that had little or nothing to do with religious belief and practice."[152]

The earliest Portuguese Jews arrived in Amsterdam probably around 1593, and shortly afterward the first Portuguese-Jewish congregation was established.[153] Judah Aryeh Modena, a Portuguese Jew from Venice, arrived in Amsterdam in 1616, becoming the rabbi of the Beit Ya'acov congregation, and after the unification of the first three Portuguese-Jewish communities in 1639, he was appointed as one of the four rabbis of the United Portuguese Congregation, Talmud Torah.[154] Ronaldo Vainfas refers to this newly established community of Portuguese Jews in Amsterdam as the "Jerusalem of the North."[155]

Among the prominent figures in the first congregations to be founded was José Pardo, a Portuguese Jew from Salonica, who had arrived in Amsterdam in 1608; Judah Vega became the first rabbi of the second congregation in Amsterdam, Neveh Shalom, established in 1608; Rabbi Saul Mortera arrived from Venice in 1616; and David Pardo, the son of José Pardo, became rabbi of the third congregation, Bet Israel, established in 1618.[156] Originally there were three separate Portuguese-Jewish congregations in Amsterdam: Neve Salom or Neveh Shalom (1608–1612), Bet Ya'acov or Bet Jacob (1610–1612), and Bet Israel (1618). However, in 1639 they merged under one name, Talmud Torah (which Cecil Roth refers to as K. K. Beth, "Kahal Kadosh"), better known as the Portuguese-Israelite Congregation of Amsterdam

(Portugees-Israëlietische Gemeente te Amsterdam)—today the oldest continuous Jewish congregation in the Netherlands.[157] The congregation of Kahal Kadosh of the Talmud later moved to the synagogue at the Houtgracht in 1670 (today located at Waterloo Square).[158]

According to historian Leonardo Dantes Silva, Jaime Lopes da Costa, born in 1544 in Porto, had migrated to Brazil and became a senhor de engenho ("sugarcane plantation owner") at Engenho da Várzea in Pernambuco.[159] He moved to Lisbon and later to Amsterdam in 1598, changing his name to Jacob Tirado, and established one of the first congregations of Portuguese Jews in Amsterdam, Bet Ya'akob or Bet Jacob ("House of Jacob")—named after him (mentioned above). In 1615, Jaime Lopes da Costa (aka, Jacob Tirado) and fifteen other Portuguese Jews established the Santa Companha de Dotar Orfãs e Donzelas ("Dotar"), which later added four new members, two of whom were still living in Pernambuco: João Luís Henriques and Francisco Gomes Pina.[160]

The "Dotar" society collected money on the Sunday following Purim as a dowry for the orphan girls and poor young daughters of Amsterdam's Portuguese-Jewish community. The regulations, or *haskamot*, of the "Dotar" society, were originally written in Portuguese between 1756 and 1825 (the society was founded in 1615).[161] The Kahal Kadosh Zur Israel congregation, established in 1640 in Recife (Pernambuco), continued operating this "Dotar" charity, raising funds in Brazil.[162]

The language used by the Portuguese-Israelite Congregation of Amsterdam (Portugees-Israëlietische Gemeente te Amsterdam) was Portuguese or Hebrew, and to this day, the service announcements at this congregation are still made in Portuguese. Notably, the term "esnoga" (Portuguese; short for "sinagoga," "synagogue") is also still in use today in Amsterdam, as it was used in Recife, Matoim, or Camaragibe and throughout northeast Brazil between the sixteenth and seventeenth centuries. In addition, Portuguese-Jewish terms, or abbreviations such as officiantes, misvoteiros, or snogeiros, are still used in that congregation in Amsterdam.[163]

The "Archive of the Municipality of Bet Jacob in Amsterdam," *Livro de Bet Haim do Kahal Kados de Bet Yahacob*, is written in Portuguese, and the congregation referred to themselves as *Nação Hebrea de Portuguezes* ("Portuguese Hebrew Nation").[164] This congregation is named after the former senhor de engenho from Pernambuco, Jacob Tirado—introduced earlier—who had moved from Brazil to Amsterdam. The register of this congregation contains regulations, decisions, and statements of income and expenditure of the Beth Haim cemetery in Ouderkerk aan de Amstel, and also served as a burial book and burial register between 1614 and 1630 of the Portuguese-Jewish Congregation of Amsterdam.[165]

During the seventeenth century, Amsterdam became one the world's foremost commercial entrepôts.[166] By the 1690s, it became the center of European Jewry, as Cecil Roth claims: "theology, philosophy, jurisprudence, mathematics, Oriental languages, physics, history, were all cultivated with eager enthusiasm."[167] This newly established center for Jewry was specifically tied to Portuguese Jews who had migrated there from Portugal and, later from Brazil.[168] In an important statement, Jonathan Israel explains, "it may be that overall immigration from Portugal was the single largest component in the making of Dutch Sephardic [i.e., Portuguese] Jewry."[169]

Migration processes are salient dimensions of interest here, particularly as we consider the ability of Portuguese Jews in their mobility, and who moved from Amsterdam to Brazil and back to Amsterdam, or to the Caribbean. For instance, in the late sixteenth century, Portuguese Jew, Diogo Dias Querido, moved from Bahia to Amsterdam, and formally converted back to Judaism, founding one of Amsterdam's first Jewish congregations. Other New Christian merchants and sugar exporters from Pernambuco moved from Brazil to Amsterdam as early as the 1610s, and converted back to Judaism, such as Manuel Carvalho, Tomás Fernandes, José Frazão, Gonçalo Nunes, David Ovale, Paulo Pinto, and Diogo Nunes Vitória.[170]

Benjamin E. Fisher examined the Portuguese-Jewish community in Amsterdam in the seventeenth century. Among the figures he examined is the narrative of (New Christian) banker Tomas Rodrigues Pereyra and his conversion back to Judaism when he moved to Amsterdam, changing his name to Abraham Israel Pereyra.[171] Therefore, as Daviken Studnicki-Gizbert claims, these migrations, marriage alliances, and global commercial networks forged "interlinked merchant houses based in dozens of expatriate Portuguese communities."[172] Furthermore, Portuguese Jews had settled in Hamburg, supplying sugar, tobacco, spices, and cotton through transnational trading connections with Spain, Portugal, and the Americas, following the Peace of

Westphalia that ended the Thirty Years' War in 1648. They also relocated to Livorno Antwerp, and especially Amsterdam.[173]

Within fifty years, the Jewish community in Amsterdam grew from two hundred in 1600, to almost three thousand in 1650.[174] Most of the newly formed Portuguese-Jewish communities in seventeenth-century Amsterdam had previously been living as New Christians in Portugal or in Brazil, and upon moving to that city, many had returned to Judaism openly.[175]

Portuguese Jews in Europe

Keep in mind that by the end of the fifteenth century, most if not all of the medical doctors and surgeons in Portugal were of Jewish ancestry, for example, Mestre Isaque Franco of Lisbon, Mestre Joane of Évora, and Mestre Rodrigo of Leiria, most of whom had fled that nation.[176] A long list of eminent Portuguese Jews and their descendants who held these occupations made their way to Amsterdam as well as to England. Among those names are Portuguese-Jewish business magnate Mendes da Costa, and his cousin, the renowned economist David Ricardo, who wrote *The Principles of Political Economy and Taxation* (1817), one of the pillars of modern theoretical economics and market principles—both of whom went to England.[177]

Portuguese Jews and New Christians did not simply migrate to one place and stay there. They often went back and forth or moved on to other destinations (in modern vernacular they epitomized what we now call "transnationalism"). They established several Jewish communities throughout Europe—a fact which also speaks volumes of the geographical extent of the Portuguese-Jewish and New Christian diaspora (gente da nação).

For instance, the first Jewish sites and cemeteries in Ireland, such as Ballybough cemetery in Dublin, for instance, were estbalished by Portuguese Jews in the late seventeenth century.[178] However, much earlier, the first Jewish mayors in Ireland were William Eannes (the grandson of Gil Anes from Belmonte, Portugal), in 1555, and a few years later, Francisco Eannes, both in Youghal, county Cork.[179] More importantly, the first Jewish cemetery and the first synagogue in Dublin were established by Portuguese Jews (not Spanish Jews) in the seventeenth and eighteenth centuries, respectively.[180] Abraham Machado de Sequeira, doctor of the Hebrá of the Portuguese-Jewish community of London, was the father of David Machado de Sequeira, an eighteenth-century writer and a leading member of the Jewish community of Dublin.[181]

In London, Portuguese Jews founded the Bevis Marks congregation in that city, Britain's oldest synagogue (services were still conducted in the Portuguese language until the mid-1800s).[182] The founder of Anglo-Jewry, Menasseh ben Israel (born under the name of Manuel Dias Soeiro), was a Portuguese Jew.[183] Furthermore, evidence shows that the first Crypto-Jews in the British Isles were Portuguese Jews who had fled Portugal much earlier—as early as 1497.[184] By 1720, London's Portuguese-Jewish community was estimated at about 1,050, increasing to over 2,000 by the 1730s, after new refugees from Portugal arrived.[185]

In Germany, the Portuguese-Jewish community in Hamburg increased from 100 in 1610 to 800 in 1670.[186] Jacob Curiel (or Duarte Nunes of Coimbra), for example, was considered one of the most influential merchants of the sixteenth century, brother of a horse trader in India, Fernão Nunes, and father of physician and renowned doctor, Dr Abraham Curiel (1545–1609) (also known as Dr Jeronimo Nunes Ramires).[187] In her study of Portuguese Jews and New Christians in Hamburg, Juron Poettering points out that the Portuguese-Jewish cemetery established in 1611 in Hamburg (Altona) was nominated for possible inclusion as a UNESCO World Heritage site.[188]

After their conversion and expulsion from Portugal, some Portuguese New Christians had also crossed into France (known as *Israélites Portugais*) via the Pyrenees and settled in Saint-Jean-de-Luz and Saint-Esprit-lès-Bayonne, as Francesca Trivellato points out: "in parts of the interior of the region (Bidache and Peyrehorade), and as far north as Bordeaux. A few families stopped in Nantes, and others established an enclave in Rouen."[189] They numbered about 300 in 1637, and by 1728, the community in Bayonne was estimated at 1,100, and in Bordeaux, 1,500 by the 1750s.[190]

Portuguese Jews throughout the Atlantic World

Portuguese Jews were the first non-Indigenous settlers in Suriname, establishing the unique agrarian self-ruled society (about fifty miles from Paramaribo) of Jodensavanne (meaning "Savanah of the Jews" in Dutch)—and by the mid-eighteenth century, this society became the largest self-governing Jewish agrarian community in the world.[191] It was in Jodensavanne that the first synagogue, Beracha ve Shalom (in Hebrew, "Blessings and Peace"), was built between 1665 and 1671. Wieke Vink explains that maroons (escaped slaves) were familiar with Portuguese-Jewish plantation owners' Judaic practices, as one of the most well-known attacks on Jodensavanne by maroons occurred during the Jewish religious holiday of Yom Kippur, in 1743.[192] As discussed earlier, several of the creole languages of Suriname were based on, or included, elements of the Portuguese language, due to the significant presence of Portuguese Jews there in the seventeenth and eighteenth centuries.

Thus, Portuguese Jews established their first communities in Antwerp, Amsterdam, Hamburg, Dublin, London, Bayonne, Bordeaux, and Rouen, as well as throughout the New World, West Africa (Senegal, Porto d'Ale, Joal, and Petite Côte), and the west coast of India (Goa).

They founded the first official Jewish community in North America, in New Amsterdam—today New York City—when twenty-three Portuguese-Jewish immigrants from Brazil arrived there in 1654 and established the first Jewish community in Newport, Rhode Island, between 1655 and 1658—as I discuss in detail in Chapter 5.[193] Portuguese Jews from Recife had also migrated to Guadeloupe and Martinique by 1664.[194] They established official Jewish communities throughout the Caribbean, for example in Curaçao, Aruba, Barbados, Tobago, Trinidad, and Jamaica (these were Portuguese Jews, not Spanish Jews).[195] Names of Portuguese Jews are mentioned in wills throughout the Caribbean British Islands.[196] Therefore, it is important to highlight here that during the mid-seventeenth century those Portuguese Jews who had fled Recife, Pernambuco, after the Dutch left, played an important role in establishing Jewish communities throughout the New World.[197]

They also established commercial and familial networks in Mexico City (Mexico), Lima (Peru), and Potosí (Bolivia), with direct connections that extended from Lisbon, Rouen, and Seville, to Cartagena, Recife, and Salvador, to Rio de Janeiro.[198] According to Michael Studemund-Halévy, Portuguese-Jewish family names such as Cohen, Belinfante, de Mercado, Na(h)mias, and Pacheco can be traced from Recife (Pernambuco), Barbados, Martinique, Antigua, and Saint Kitts and Nevis, to Boston, New York,

Newport, London, and Hamburg.[199] Therefore, some historians claim that the diaspora of the Portuguese Jews and New Christians was the largest European diaspora of the early modern period.[200]

It is also important to point out a few caveats. Christopher Ebert, for example, challenges the common assumption that Portuguese New Christians and Jews, viewed as a group, had exclusively monopolized the sugar trade: "viewing the international sugar trade as a Sephardic preserve is a position lacking in nuance," and, "scholars of Dutch-Portuguese trade have gone too far in privileging so-called 'Sephardic' networks in explaining sugar trade."[201] Ebert explains that there is little evidence to show that Portuguese New Christian business practices were any different from those of Old Christians, and that commercial networks were not exclusive or separated.[202]

The involvement of non-Portuguese New Christians and Jews in global sugar trade networks is indeed a dimension that warrants more attention. For instance, David Blackbourn points out that, despite their invisibility in the literature of colonial Brazil, there is ample evidence of the direct involvement of German banking and merchant houses financing sugar plantations in Pernambuco and São Vicente during the mid-sixteenth century. The well-known Fuggers of Augsburg, for example, who invested in Brazilian sugar through a local agent; or Erasmus Schetz, who bought an engenho ("sugarcane mill") in São Vicente; or Sebald Lins of Ulm and the Hoelscher family, who invested and financed an engenho in Pernambuco.[203]

David Grant Smith also points out how stereotypes of the New Christian or Jewish monopoly in the mercantile professions (i.e., merchants as Jew or Crypto-Jew) have endured in Luso-Brazilian history. That is, the association between *burguesia* and *cristãos-novos*.[204] However, Smith shows that this perception needs to be revised, since the mercantile class was not exclusively New Christian and appears to be "a heterogenous group of diverse social and geographic origin attracted to commerce as the surest path to wealth and social advancement."[205]

Thus, Portuguese Jews and New Christians were at the same time commercially connected to non-Jewish networks, including Protestant transnational commercial networks, and in some cases, especially Calvinist ones.[206] Laura Jarnagin's new research, for example, shows how the Dutch Antilles was integral to the Madeira-Azores commercial hub, which was linked to

Jewish and Calvinist merchants. Curaçao, for example, became one of the busiest ports in the Americas. Jarnagin highlights such connections to transnational commercial networks of Portuguese Jews from Amsterdam, for example the Crasto family members (Duarte and Miguel de Crasto).[207]

Port Jews

These interconnected Portuguese-Jewish and New Christian mercantile communities in the New World would eventually become vital and dynamic embryonic entrepôts especially within the seventeenth-century transatlantic networks of global mercantilism. For this reason many Portuguese Jews have been labeled by some scholars as "Port Jews" as they were international cross-cultural brokers at major Atlantic seaports. Richard L. Kagan and Philip D. Morgan edited a volume that includes essays of recent studies about these networks, linkages, and migrations in the New World. As the editors explain, "Port Jews epitomize the restlessly fluid, border-crossing, and culture-bridging qualities that characterize life in the Atlantic basin"; moreover, they were "in-between people, liminal individuals."[208] That is, as they claim, the "informal zones of market activity and social organization and culture" were a marked characteristic of the Portuguese-Jewish diaspora.[209] Furthermore, it is estimated that about 90 percent of all merchants in the New World during the late seventeenth and early eighteenth centuries were born in either Portugal, Brazil, or the Portuguese Atlantic islands (or were their descendants).[210]

Indeed, a new comprehensive genetic study has found that about a quarter of Latin Americans share Iberian-Jewish ancestry, suggesting that Jewish genetic markers found throughout Latin America are far more salient that previously thought, including in Brazil, and that migrations of former Jews fleeing the Inquisition to the Americas was significantly large.[211]

Now that I have offered examples of the scientific contributions of Portuguese Jews and New Christians, the omissions within geography, and the migration of "people of the nation" to the New World, I have thus established a framework to understand how the narrative of Portuguese Jews and New Christians in Brazil unfolds. I have also established a much-needed backdrop to this facet of a new human geography of Latin America and the

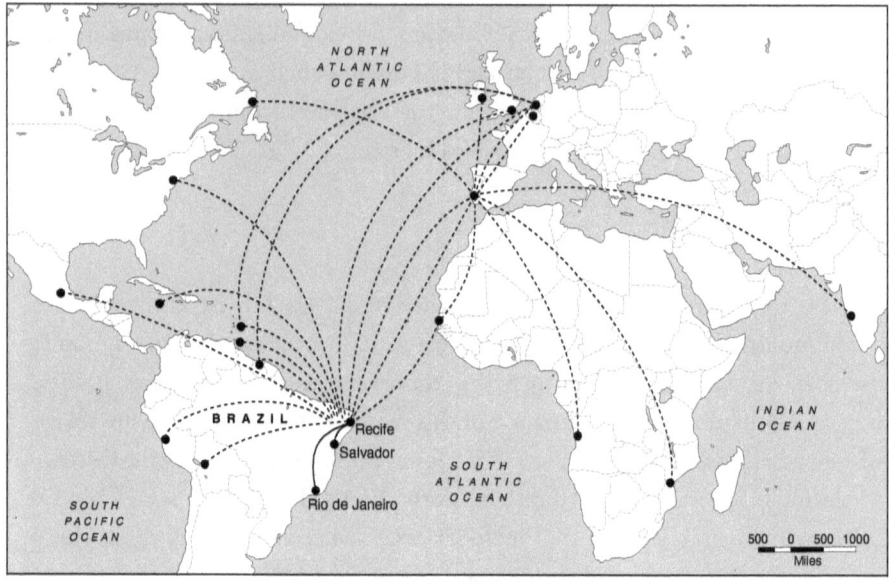

Map 4. Portuguese diasporas and exploration

Caribbean—a geography which in the past has neglected the inherent commercial, demographic, and sociocultural participation of Portuguese Jews and New Christians.

These transatlantic networks based on familial and commercial enterprises offer insights into the insertion of Jews within the Portuguese world and into the Portuguese-Jewish diasporas, and their first arrivals in Brazil, where migration again becomes a salient theme in this narrative. Among the push factors that prompted migration movements to Brazil were, for example, the subjugation, surveillance, restrictions, intimidation, and fear instilled upon "people of the nation" by the Portuguese Inquisition and the stifling economic policies imposed by the Church and Crown on New Christians. Conversely, the major pull factors included socioeconomic opportunities, religious freedom, living without fear of oppression, and perhaps adventure and curiosity, as there were few or no other options left.

Before I explore the story of the first official and openly Jewish communities in the Americas (in Recife, and then Olinda), I will next discuss the economic and social milieu in Brazil during the seventeenth and eighteenth

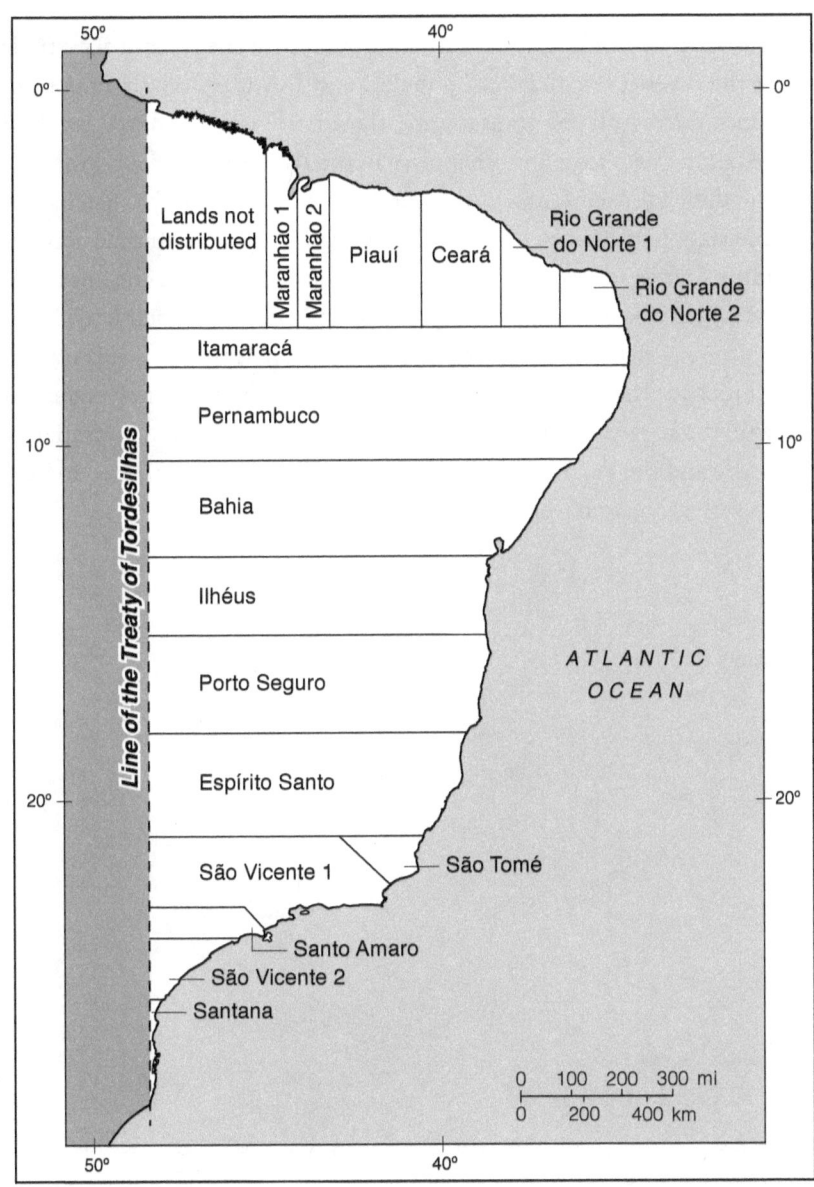

Map 5. *Capitanias* (Brazilian captaincies)

centuries. I also provide an overview of the salience of the African slave trade and of the diversity of Brazilian populations. This is especially important here since during all the transatlantic slave trade period, Brazil received more African slaves than any other place in the Americas.[212] Hence, we shall see how the vital need for an agricultural labor force drove the demand for the importation of African slaves, and at the same time, the chronic need for agricultural labor and expertise became a major pull factor for the migration of New Christians to Brazil, who were especially noted for their knowledge in sugarcane agriculture, cultivation, and industry, as well as mercantilism and commerce. The point of dovetailing this discussion of the first engenhos in Brazil, the sugarcane industry, and New Christians with the transatlantic slave trade and the Portuguese world, is that they are inherently tied to each other, as we shall see in the next chapter.

CHAPTER FOUR

Sugar and the First New Christians in Colonial Brazil

BY THE MID-SIXTEENTH CENTURY, the Brazilian northeast became an attractive region for Portuguese New Christians (i.e., a major "pull factor"). Potential economic opportunities were made available in the 1530s with captaincy governor Duarte Coelho who was especially receptive to New Christians, as he recognized their expertise in the sugar industry.[1] Coelho was the first land grantee, donatário, of Pernambuco (*Nova Lusitânia*, "New Lusitania" at the time), one of Brazil's most successful captaincies, along with São Vicente in the southeast region, in the sixteenth century.

Duarte Coelho's letters written in the 1540s reveal important aspects of daily life, and of the sugar industry in Pernambuco, where he also planted hemp and cotton, and where engenhos employed those with "special skills on the sugar plantations, in sugar production, in carpentry, in the forges, and in pottery; others are craftsmen in creating molds for the sugar."[2]

Brazilian historian Evaldo Cabral de Mello points out that Duarte Coelho's idea was to replicate a "New Portugal" in the New World, and that Coelho had named the region "Nova Lusitânia."[3] Only after Coelho's death in 1553, did the name change to Pernambuco ("Gap in the Sea" in Tupi), although the etymological roots of the word "Pernambuco" from the Tupi language are still disputed among Brazilian scholars.[4]

In 1535, Duarte Coelho received a large grant of land that extended from the mouth of the Santa Cruz River in the north, to the mouth of the São Francisco River to the south, where he moved in with his brother-in-law, wife, relatives, and friends.[5] Within fifteen years after his arrival in Brazil, he founded the towns of Igaraçu (or Igarassu) and Olinda, opened five sugar mills, and continued to struggle with the Caeté and Tabajara Indians. Duarte Coelho had encouraged single men in Brazil to marry local Indigenous women, given the chronic shortage of European women:

> Every day I succeed in getting some to marry, while I work constantly at persuading others to do so. This, Sire, is because we have such sound practices to populate the new territories which are far from the kingdom, which are as large as this and from which much profit is expected.[6]

This letter also offers an important insight into how Brazilian miscegenation was openly encouraged in the early colonial years, and how this phenomenon was very much inherent in Brazil's colonial human geography tied to New Christians. For instance, Coelho aggressively initiated the sugarcane industry in Brazil as he specifically recruited New Christians from Portugal and the Atlantic islands (e.g., Madeira, Azores). Evidence that the introduction of the sugarcane industry and sugar cultivation in Brazil was prompted by Portuguese New Christians is clear, as we shall see ahead. Coelho imported technicians who, as Manuel Correia de Andrade explains, were "almost always Jews . . . so large were the numbers of Jews [They would have been "New Christians" though], and such their importance in Pernambuco toward the end of the sixteenth century, that the captaincy of Duarte Coelho received a visit from the Holy Office of the Inquisition."[7] According to Andrade, those New Christians that Duarte Coelho had hired became "the first sugarmasters, boiler-room workers, sugar purgers, stokers, and box-makers of the colonial mills . . . they and the small farmers would eventually constitute the central nucleus of a rural middle-class."[8] Incidentally, these occupations tied to the sugarcane industry and sugar cultivation indeed overlap many of the occupations of those New Christians arrested for Judaism in Brazil (see Chapter 6 for a full discussion of my study of Inquisition dossiers). A year after Coelho died, Jerônimo de Albuquerque, his brother-in-law, took ownership over his lands in 1554.[9] He had constructed Pernambuco's first major sugarcane mill (known as "engenhos," explained in detail ahead), Engenho Nossa Senhora da Ajuda.[10]

The potential for upward social mobility was another pull factor that attracted New Christians to Brazil, given the nation's territorial vastness, and its geographical distance from Portugal and from the surveillance of the Portuguese Inquisition. During most of the sixteenth century, New Christians in Brazil were often able to circumvent discrimination with greater ease than in Portugal. Restrictions on their status as "New Christians" were imposed and enforced with relatively less rigor in Brazil, and they were able to integrate into early colonial Brazilian society. Most of them found relative religious and socioeconomic freedom from persecution, at least for the first half of the sixteenth century until the arrival of the Portuguese governor-general and the Jesuits in 1549, and later, with the introduction of the Portuguese Inquisition and its agents in Brazil.[11]

By 1570, there were already 60 sugarcane mills operating in Brazil, most of them in Pernambuco and Bahia, and by 1585, 120 engenhos were functioning in both these captaincies (other engenhos were established in Ilhéus, São Vicente, and Espírito Santo).[12] By 1590, the total Brazilian population was estimated at 100,000 (about 30,000 Portuguese, 28,000 Indians, and 42,000 Africans). The population cluster in the northeast (Bahia and Pernambuco) was due to the burgeoning sugar cultivation there, with a similar concentration of Africans and Indians who were used as slaves for labor in the sugar mills, the engenhos.[13]

The Backdrop of Geography, Agriculture, and Economy in Early Colonial Brazil

In 1534, the Portuguese created the system of captaincies (*capitanias*) in Brazil, where parallel imaginary lines divided twelve, and later, a total of fifteen land tracts along the eastern coastal belt of Brazil. These land tracts were divided into administrative units, some held by the Crown and some by the grantees (donatários), who were usually soldiers and bureaucrats, and who in turn, were also given the power to grant the practice of *sesmarias* (a form of land distribution established by the Portuguese in Brazil) within their own capitanias.[14] Only two captaincies were successful: in Pernambuco (under Duarte Coelho, discussed earlier), and in São Vicente (under Martim Afonso de Souza).[15]

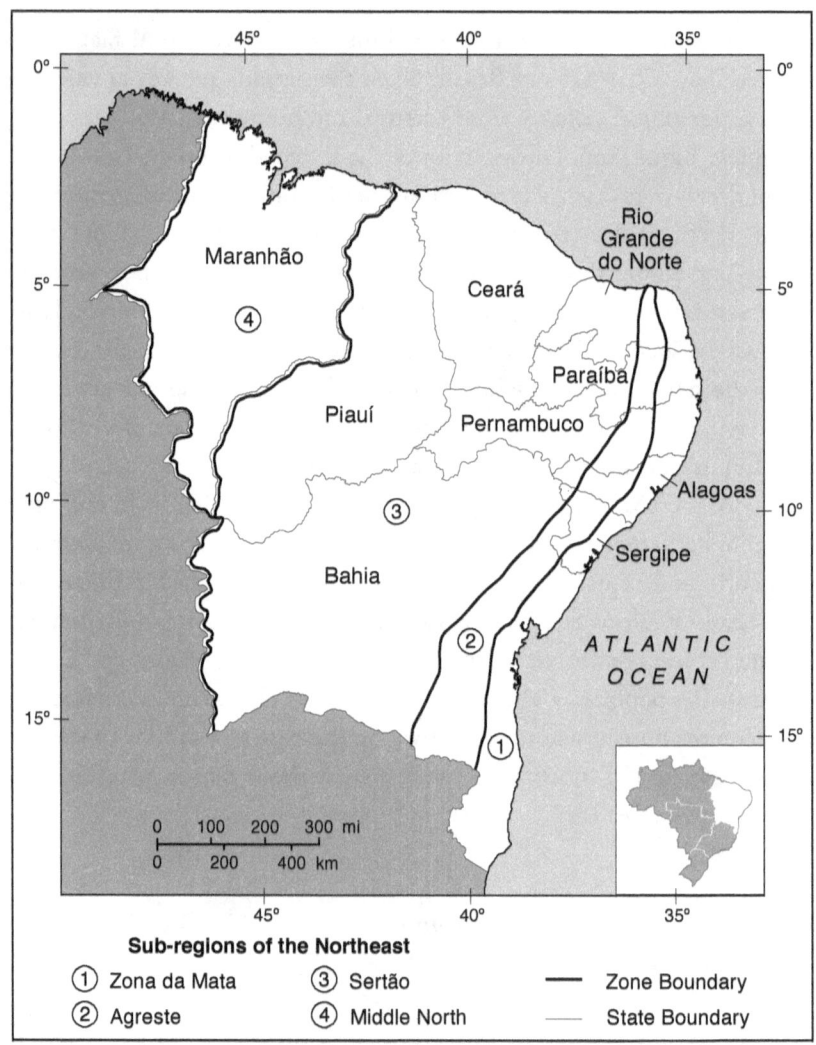

Map 6. Northeast sub-regions

In the early sixteenth century, Portugal's annual grain harvest had fallen short of its national basic needs, and this was compounded by large landholdings of unproductive land. As a result, its national population, the Portuguese, needed to search for new lands to populate and at the same time, they needed to increase the food supply. Timothy J. Coates explains how there was an uneven population distribution in Portugal at that time, with the largest density in Minho (northwest Portugal) while the eastern and southern interior had the least. For example, the city of Lisbon's population in 1527 was estimated at about 50,000 to 60,000, and Porto and Évora at about 15,000 each. By 1641, Lisbon had grown to about 165,000; however, remarkably, by 1864 Lisbon's population had only increased to 190,000—just a mere 25,000 increase in 250 years.[16] Portugal needed to find and increase the availability of manual labor as they faced a labor force scarcity.

The Indigenous people of Brazil were exceptional agriculturalists and planted a wide range of crops; however, eventually they refused to be brutally treated and coerced to perform agricultural work, and to be enslaved. Ultimately, many succumbed to diseases. Moreover, for the Tupimnambás, agriculture was considered "women's work," and they found it demeaning; therefore, they refused to work.[17] The principal problem in early colonial Brazil was a lack of manual labor (a major problem that lingered well into the late nineteenth century with the pending end of the institution of slavery in 1888).[18] Between 1580 and 1650, despite its sharp overall decrease in numbers, the Indigenous population still comprised a large percentage of the labor force, and Afro-Indigenous marriages and rape were also common, which would add to the diverse "racial" make-up of Brazil.[19]

Degredados and the Sugar Industry in Brazil

The chronic need for labor supply in Brazil fueled the growing transatlantic African slave trade, and African slaves were brought to Brazil for manual labor in the engenhos. The enslavement of Brazilian Indians was prohibited only in 1831, and Brazil was the last country in the Western Hemisphere to officially abolish the institution of slavery in 1888.[20]

The discussion ahead then highlights the importance of geography, for example with the salience of migrations, diasporas, population encounters, human-environment interactions, and how cultural and physical landscapes and ecologies were modified through various commodity booms. Moreover, this discussion here underlines how New Christians were deeply involved in the Brazilian colonial enterprise.

Between 1570 and 1650, Brazil became the world's largest producer of sugar. The adopted model for sugarcane cultivation was transferred from the Madeira Islands and implemented in Brazil, first consisting of small-scale production but then expanding to a larger enterprise with 80 to 100 slaves on each engenho, producing about 140 tons a year.[21]

In 1493, sugarcane was transferred by the Portuguese from the Madeira Islands to the island of São Tomé (off the west coast of Africa), where convicts and exiled Portuguese (former) Jews, degredados, were often sent.[22] Among those degredados was João Gonçalves Zarco (which was a well-known Jewish last name, and who was likely a New Christian), who had eventually became the established captain at Funchal, Madeira Islands in 1450.[23] The Portuguese first arrived on the islands of Porto Santo in 1418, and a year later, under the leadership of Tristão Vaz and Bartolomeu Perestrelo, on the islands of Madeira in 1419—named for its abundance of *madeira*, or "wood," in Portuguese.[24] By 1500, the Madeira Islands were the largest sugar producer in the world, and later it became a major exporter of degredados to Africa and Brazil—just in 1697 alone, one hundred degredados were sent to Maranhão, and two hundred to Angola.[25]

In the first decade of the sixteenth century, Fernão de Noronha, donatary captain and a New Christian, commanded the first group of settlers—comprised mostly of New Christians—to transfer the implementation of sugarcane production to Brazil. He originally spelled his name "Loronha," but changed it to "Noronha," likely to appear part of Portuguese nobility.[26] Notably, in an early map of Brazil created by a Piedmontese cartographer who worked in Venice and rose to the position of cosmographer of the Venetian Republic, Jacopo Gastaldi, the islands are labelled "Fernando Lorona" (and not "Fernão Noronha" or "Loronha").[27]

Today the archipelago consisting of 21 islands off the coast of northeast Brazil (360 km from Natal, Rio Grande do Norte, and 545 km from Recife, Pernambuco) carries Noronha's name (i.e., the island of Fernando de Noronha).[28] In 2001, UNESCO designated the islands as a World Heritage Site. The islands had allegedly first been sighted during an exploration in 1501 by Amerigo Vespucci, Gonçalo Coelho, and Fernão de Noronha.[29] They were subsequently donated by King Manuel to Fernão de Noronha as the grantee to an official hereditary possession, in 1504.[30] This system of donating hereditary captaincies was the first of its kind implemented in Brazil, and it was only thirty years later that the hereditary captaincies would be officially implemented throughout the colony (i.e., capitanias hereditárias).

Subsequent expeditions headed by Fernão de Noronha sailed all the way from Cabo Calcanhar in the northeast (today just north of Natal, Rio Grande do Norte), to Cabo Frio in the southeast (today just north of the city of Rio de Janeiro), and to Cananéia (today on the coast of São Paulo)—voyages upon which the famous Cantino map of 1502 were based (a forerunner of all other known maps of early Brazil).[31]

In 1503, Amerigo Vespucci—after whom the continent of "America" is named—had arrived at the harbor of Cananéia on this brief exploratory trip. As French geographer Élisée Reclus mentioned, "this port [Cananéia] marks the spot where Christovão Jacques and Amerigo Vespucci landed in 1503, and from the same place set out the first bandeira of eighty adventures in search of gold."[32] However, the Portuguese did not find gold or precious stones in Brazil until much later in the mid-seventeenth century. Noronha did not seem to have participated in the expedition of 1503; only Vespucci was on that expedition.[33]

John L. Vogt clarifies the process of the leasing of Brazil's lands to New Christians in the historiography, a venture headed by Fernão de Noronha, and tells how Pietro Rondinelli, a Genoese resident of Lisbon, accurately reported the first Brazilian voyages of 1501–1502, and the New Christian venture enterprise.[34] Rondinelli's letter was written on October 3, 1502, clearly outlining the expectations of New Christians in Brazil:

> The king of Portugal has leased the land which he discovered to certain New Christians, and they are obliged to send six ships to explore three hundred leagues of new coast each year, and to construct a fortress in this newly-discovered territory, maintaining it for three years; and in the first year nothing is paid (to the Crown); in the second, one sixth (of the products shipped from there), in the third, one fourth, and they have contracted to carry Brazilwood and slaves, and perhaps they will find other items of profits.[35]

Vespucci confirms the leasing of Brazilian lands to Portuguese New Christians in the letter, and that "Loronha dispatched six ships to Brazil in 1503, which returned with cargoes of dyewood logs."[36]

Yet despite Fernão de Noronha's unusually high social standing for a New Christian at that time, it did not prevent his son, Pêro (or Pedro) de Noronha, from being arrested. I found his purported son listed in the Inquisition dossiers as a merchant from Lisbon, a 45-year-old New Christian (married to Gracia Gomes), accused of the crime of Judaism. He was denounced as a Judaizer and imprisoned in Lisbon in 1541: Fernão de Noronha is named as his father (processo 8716).

By 1600, 120 sugar mills were in existence, most in Brazil's northeast, and at least five belonged to New Christians.[37] And by 1612, Brazil may have been producing 672,000 arrobas of sugar (9,871,680 kilograms) per year.[38] Again, it is important to reiterate that the sugar trade was not an exclusive New Christian or Jewish enterprise; neither was the slave trade. While the role of the British, French, and Dutch involvement in colonial Brazil have been abundantly available in the literature, the role of Germans is notably absent, as David Blackbourn claims.

That is, the great Upper German merchant houses also traded with the Portuguese (dealing in pepper, spices, pearls, precious stones, ivory, and the sugar industry). For example, German banking and merchant houses such as the Fuggers, Welsers, Höchstetters, Imhofs, Hirschvogels, and Herwarts played a substantial role in the economy of the Portuguese Atlantic world, especially the sugarcane plantation system; moreover, David Blackbourn points out, "the real prize was Brazil."[39] Examples of German investors in Pernambuco abound. For instance, the famous Fugger merchant House of Augsburg invested in Brazilian sugar plantations through a local agent (and this agent was none other than Fernão de Noronha), as well as Aachen merchant Erasmus Schetz, who operated mainly out of Antwerp, and as Blackbourn describes, "worked through his Lisbon-based nephew to buy a plantation and sugar mill in São Vicente. Sebald Lins of Ulm and the Hoelscher family invested in sugar plantations through the same Antwerp-Lisbon-Pernambuco axis."[40]

Degredados

One scholar mentions a study that degredados sent to Brazil represented about half of all exiles banished to all penal colonies in Portuguese territories (i.e., Magazão in Morroco, Cape Verde, Angola, São Tomé).⁴¹ For example, Tomé de Sousa, Brazil's first governor-general of the colony (1549–1553), established the first capital city of Salvador in Bahia. Sousa arrived along with one thousand soldiers, colonists, and six hundred degredados ("penal exiles") deported to Brazil, most of whom were New Christians.⁴²

While degredados were known mostly as criminals, deviants, heretics, prostitutes, or the poor who had been deported to Brazil, new research has found that degredados also included a large contingency of New Christian scientists, physicians, or educators from Portugal (i.e., former Jews or descendants of Jews).⁴³ Norman Simms, for example, points out that there may have been a conscious attempt by the Portuguese Crown to wipe out or downplay the important role of New Christians in the formation of early Brazilian nationhood.⁴⁴ That is, many New Christian degredados were actually educated, and were prominent members of Portuguese society. Here then, we find another example in this narrative of a subermerged legacy and memory in Brazil, being that even degredados, many if not most of whom were New Christians, were banished from Brazilian historiography.

Notably, Portuguese poet and playwright Gil Vicente compares the exile of degredados sent to Brazil akin to being sent to "Hell" in his *Auto da Barca do Purgatorio* (Act of the Ferry to Purgatory), one of his plays in the renowned trilogy, *Triologia das Barcas*, Trilogy of the Boats, written between 1516 and 1519.⁴⁵

Timothy Coates's research shows that sodomites were sent as exiles to Magazão (Morocco), Tangier, São Tomé, Príncipe, Angola, and Brazil.⁴⁶ Notably, Nova Mazagão ("New Mazagão"), in Amazonian Brazil, was named after this Portuguese colony in Morocco, now El Jadida, which the Portuguese abandoned in 1769 after some 250 years of occupation. Mazagão in Morocco had been one of the places where degredados were sent as punishment for their crimes; most were accused of sodomy or bigamy, but the crime of Judaism was also included. However, much later, in the early 1770s, its Portuguese inhabitants were evacuated from there after Portugal lost its territory, and about 340 families were sent to Brazil to a new location. Thus, a new settlement was established near the city of Belém in the Amazon region (today in the modern state of Pará), named Nova Mazagão.⁴⁷ The reference to Mazagão (in Morocco) appears often in the Inquisition dossiers.

In one study, out of a sample of those individuals who were degredados in Brazil, among other crimes that they were accused of, Judaism comprised a little over half of the majority (52.7 percent), followed by bigamy (14.9 percent), deceit (9.3 percent), witchcraft (7.3 percent), and sodomy (4.2 percent), and most of the degredados were sent to Brazil during the seventeenth century.[48] By 1535, the islands of São Tomé in the Gulf of Guinea, off the western equatorial coast of central Africa (today the Democratic Republic of São Tomé and Príncipe), was replaced by Brazil as the major destination of degredados. Thereafter, Brazil in turn began to export degredados to Angola between 1650 and 1700. Timothy Coates points out that most female degredados were destined for Brazil (62 percent of all female penal exiles were sent to Brazil), whereas only 23 percent of males were sent to Brazil, and the most common crime for women degredados sent to Brazil was Judaism, followed by heresy, witchcraft, and bigamy, respectively.[49]

Another migration movement to Brazil in the seventeenth century was state sponsored. Because of overpopulation in the Azores, as well as frequent earthquakes during the seventeenth century, Portuguese state-sponsored migration spurred the influx of new immigrants from those Atlantic islands to Maranhão and Pará (in north Brazil), and later, the Crown organized and paid Azorean couples to relocate to Ceará (in northeast Brazil).[50]

The Sugarcane Boom in Brazil's Northeast and Crypto-Jews

Brazil's northeast region today consists of the following modern states: Maranhão, Piauí, Ceará, Rio Grande do Norte, Paraíba, Pernambuco, Alagoas, Sergipe, and Bahia (comprising an area of about 1,500,000 square km).[51] However, during the mid-sixteenth century, this region was simply known *as capitanias de cima* ("captaincies above") comprising Bahia, Pernambuco, Itamaracá, and Paraíba.[52] They were also referred to as *norte*, the "north" ("captaincies of the north"), which included Bahia, Pernambuco, Itamaracá, Paraíba, and Rio Grande.[53] The term *"nordeste"* ("northeast") and *"norte"* ("north") were later often used interchangeably, and "nordeste" was only used exclusively after the 1930s.[54]

Today this northeast region is defined by its characteristics, made up of four geographical sub-regions: Zona da Mata, Agreste, Sertão, and Middle

North.[55] The Zona da Mata (in Portuguese, literally meaning "zone of the forest," connoting moist, fertile conditions) is the area where sugarcane agriculture still predominates; it is covered in dense, evergreen semideciduous forest and has a hot and humid climate, with two distinct seasons: rainy and dry. The Agreste is considered a transition zone—an intermediate area between the coastal humid Atlantic forests of the Zona da Mata, and the dry interior of Sertão, with small landholdings and mixed farming. It is characteristically rustic; hard to farm, with its dense thorn forest (Caatinga); and receives only 800–1200 millimeters of rainfall annually. The Sertão is characterized by its dry and hot climate where intense droughts have caused historical decimation of animals and have long prompted massive human migration movements, mostly to the southeast region.[56] The middle-north (*meio-norte*) region includes the modern state of Maranhão, and the intermediary sub-region between the lush Amazonian rainforest to its west, and the arid Sertão to its east, and is characterized by its cattle ranching.[57] The climate of the Atlantic rainforest resembles that of the Zona da Mata and includes a few characteristics of the dry Sertão.[58]

The Recôncavo Baiano is a geographically distinct region surrounding Salvador, and its surrounding towns around the Bay, Baia de Todos os Santos, in Bahia. Later in the seventeenth and eighteenth centuries, towns and villages in the Recôncavo Baiano, such as Cairú, Camurú, and Ilhéus, experienced the highest incidence of escaped slaves, and maroons established their own clandestine communities there, known as *quilombos*. The frontier nature of the Recôncavo Baiano was the most important contributing factor to the success of these quilombos.[59]

Sugarcane was successfully productive in the region's rich, reddish-dark *massapé* soils (dark heavy clay, impermeable soils), for example, those found in the *várzeas* (flood plains and riverside lowlands) of Pernambuco along the Capibaribe, Ipojuca, and Jabotão Rivers.[60] In the *massapé* soils of northeast Brazil, sugarcane could be cut for seven to ten years without replanting.[61] These *massapé* soils, with their high content of minerals such as calcium, phosphorous, magnesium, and potassium, originated in the "fine sediments in low, flooded fields or lake beds that dry up during summer: it is a morass of clayey mud in the winter rainy season, and is covered by sun-baked mud cracks in summer [summer would be late December to April in the Southern

Hemisphere]."[62] To preserve the soil's fertility, workers in cane fields used a system of land rotation, and as geographer Kempton E. Webb states, "sugarcane and its sugarcane culture continued to dominate the Zona da Mata as much in the twentieth century as in the sixteenth and seventeenth centuries."[63]

Sugarcane cultivation developed in the eastern Mediterranean, and basically marched through to the western Mediterranean (from Sicily and southern Spain, to Morocco and the Algarve), and then to Madeira and Cabo Verde. Sugarcane wears out soils quickly; therefore there was always a need to find new lands for it, and in Brazil, Pernambuco and Bahia became other such sites.[64] Notably, to this day, Brazil's northeast is the world's largest producer of sugarcane.

Coastal northeast Brazil was ideal for sugarcane plantation with its ideal "location, climate, soils, water, rainforests to supply firewood and other supplies," particularly in the várzeas of Pernambuco, which had the right amount of rainfall for sugarcane (between one and two millimeters a year) and was never subject to freezing temperatures.[65] Rivers such as the Capiberibe, Ipojuca, and Beberibe Rivers in Pernambuco, and in Bahia, the Subaé, Cotegipe and Sergimirim Rivers—supplied water transportation and powered the mills.[66]

These northeastern regions offered a geographical advantage, with a proximity to seaports that reduced the transportation costs of machinery and tools; rivers and streams that irrigated fields and powered the mills; and nearby forests, which furnished game, firewood for furnaces, and wood for housing.[67] Christopher Ebert points out that Brazilian sugar was more than just one product—it in fact included three separate products in a range of purity: branco ("white"), the refined sugar (refined in Amsterdam); *moscovado*, a light-brown sugar; and *panela*, a dark brown sugar.[68] Pernambuco merits attention here as a place where sugarcane methods were developed, learned, and disseminated to other places, particularly in the Caribbean, such as Barbados—introduced by Portuguese New Christians. As Charles R. Boxer explains, "improved methods of sugar-manufacture which were introduced into Barbados about the years 1636–1650 were due to island planters who had gone to Pernambuco to study Brazilian methods and conditions."[69]

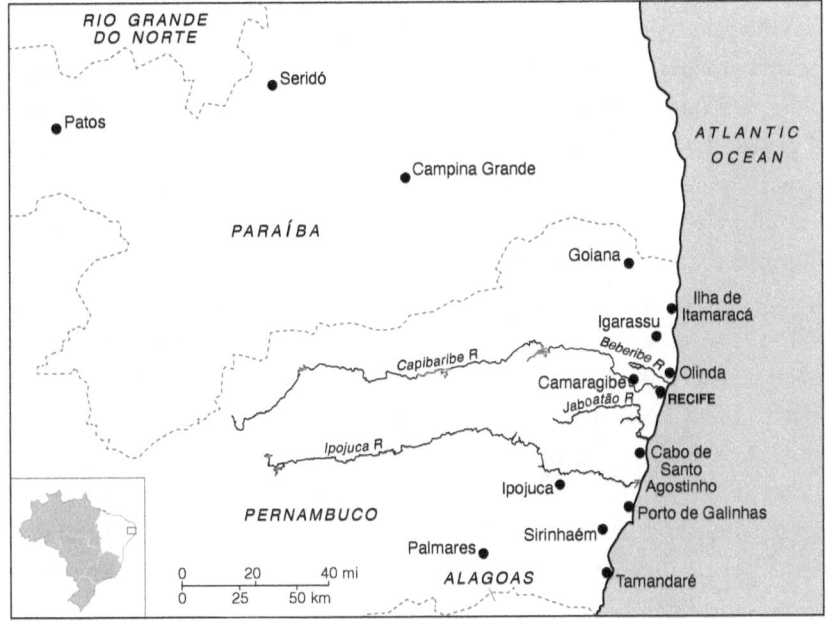

Map 7. Map of Sertão, Pernambuco

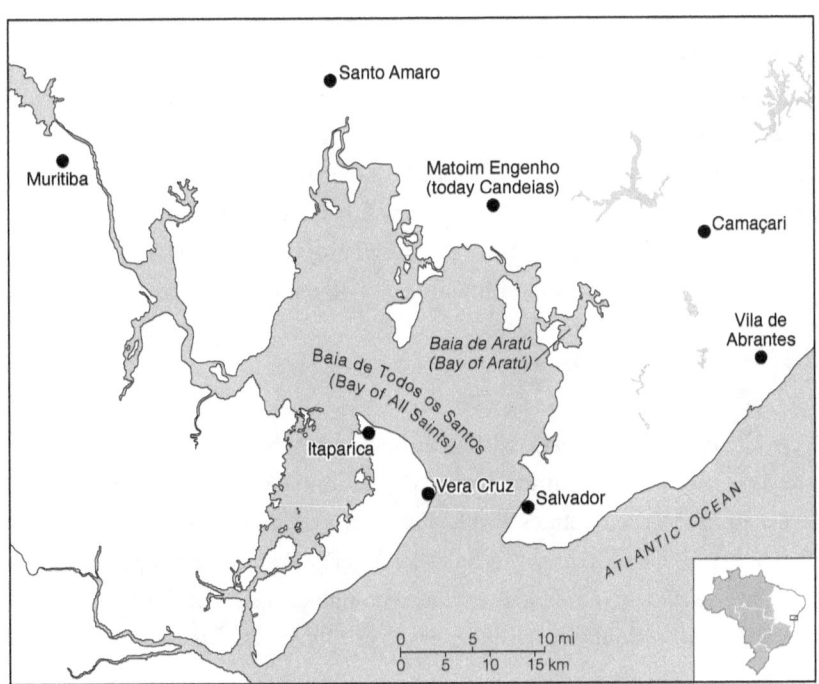

Map 8. Map of Bahia (Recôncavo Baiano)

By the mid-sixteenth century, the *região açucareira* ("sugarcane region"), the first productive *engenhos de açucar* ("sugarcane mill plantations"), emerged in Brazil's northeast, consisting of a monocrop, large-scale export, slave labor-based economy. This region emerged more precisely in the Zona da Mata in Pernambuco (e.g., the Engenho Camaragibe, about 5.6 miles/9 km from Recife), and the Recôncavo Baiano in Bahia (e.g., the Engenho Matoim, today the municipality of Candeias, near the city of Salvador located on the Baía of Aratú, along the Baía de Todos os Santos).[70]

The first known clandestine New Christian Judaizing communities in Brazil (and also at the same time, in the New World) formed in these regions of Bahia and Pernambuco simultaneously with Brazil's northeast sugar boom, by the mid-sixteenth century. As I show in Chapter 6, in my study, almost all arrests for Judaism that occurred before 1600 in Brazil were either in Pernambuco or Bahia. We shall also observe the importance of the first New Christian communities in this region which retained old Judaic practices clandestinely.

These Judaic practices and the presence of New Christians in colonial Brazil impacted local livelihoods, particularly in the northeast region. Many confessions given to inquisitors revealed how some northeastern family customs maintained Judaic practices, such as throwing out a household's water after the passing of a family member, or the preparation or avoidance of certain foods. Yet at the same time, those individuals who were accused claimed they were unaware of those "condemnable origins."[71] The contact and intermixture between Old and New Christians was significant enough where even Old Christians had been unwittingly practicing Crypto-Judaic customs, thus leaving them vulnerable also to denouncements.[72]

The Maccabees of Matoim

New Christians in Bahia had been affected by the Inquisition visitations after 1591, and it was common knowledge among local children to be fearful of revealing their real names and Jewish ancestries in public. For example, in one study of New Christians in Bahia, a description stands out about a Jesuit priest in the mid-seventeenth century who had asked a child what his name was, at a Jesuit school. The child responded: *Qual deles, o de dentro ou de fora?*,

"Which one of them, the one from inside or outside?" (i.e., in other words, "my domestic/private or my public name?").[73] This indicates that a public name was designated to prevent any suspicion or potential denunciations. The fear of the Inquisition in the Old World had transferred to the New World, and new communities of New Christian Judaizers emerged in Bahia.

There is abundant evidence of the emergence of New Christian Judaizers in Bahia by the mid-sixteenth century. Günter Böhm, for example, explains that Manuel Brás in Bahia reported that "Jews met to 'make esnoga,'" that is, to hold Judaic practices at the home of Diogo Ilhôa, while another group kept watch outside the house for any suspicious persons conducting surveillance who could denounce them to inquisitors, and that there had been a private synagogue inside the house of Heitor Antunes in Matoim (Bahia).[74] The Engenho Matoim (today the municipality of Candeias) was one of the most productive engenhos in Bahia, about 46 km/26 miles from Salvador (today the capital of the state of Bahia). It was there where Heitor Antunes and his wife, Ana Rodrigues, lived. They were known to have held on to Judaic practices in secret at the *"casinha separada,"* (literally, "separate little house"), yet continued to live as Catholics in public.[75] The term "casinha separada" was a separate building used as an improvised or informal synagogue (known as "esnoga").

According to Angelo Adriano Faria de Assis, Heitor Antunes was a second cousin of his wife, Ana Rodrigues. They had seven children together, and arrived in Brazil in 1557, along with Mem de Sá, the third governor-general of Brazil (an eighth child had died in Portugal before they left for Brazil).[76] Assis explains that Heitor Antunes claimed to be a descendant of the Hebrew Maccabean family line, and while he eventually achieved the prestigious status of senhor de engenho, he was never able to enter Portuguese nobility or social orders because of his Jewish ancestry, and became known instead as the "Maccabean gentleman/cavalier," *"cavaleiro macabeu,"* or as the "Matoim Maccabean," *Macabeu de Matoim*, who adored the *"toura"* ("Torah").[77]

Heitor Antunes died sometime between 1575 and 1577, and was buried according to Judaic tradition. He was denounced during the Inquisition visitation to Bahia as a Judaizer, after his death.[78] The Inquisition visitation, upon its first arrival in Bahia in 1591, declared in a public statement that inquisitors had been informed that some men, as well as some women, had been perpetrating crimes of heresy against the Catholic faith, and had been following the Law of Moses, and other Jewish rites, practices, and ceremonies.[79] The inquisitors announced that anyone who "hears, sees, or knows" about these persons who are committing these heretical crimes, should come forward and denounce them. As Angelo Adriano Faria de Assis explains, they stated that locals should be aware about any person taking Saturdays off work, or wearing festive clothes on Judaic holidays, or cleaning the house on Fridays, or lighting candles on Friday evenings, or if they do anything that may be "Judaic" in nature such as not eating at Queen Esther's ceremony, or follow Jewish customs and avoid food such as shellfish, pork, rabbits, squid, or drowned birds, or doing "things forbidden to Jews in the 'Old Law'": "*item que não comem toucinho, nem lebre, nem Coelho, ne aves afogadas, nem inguia, polvo nem congro, nem arraya, nem pescado, que não tenha escama, nem outras cousas prohibidas aos judeos na ley velha.*"[80]

After Heitor Antunes died, it was his wife Ana Rodrigues who ran the family sugarcane business and family affairs, and continued to teach her children the Judaic faith. Ronaldo Vainfas and Angelo A. F. Assis explain how the local population in Bahia was scandalized and thereafter named Ana and her daughters pejoratively, "the Maccabees: Judaizers of the Recôncavo" (*Macabéias, judaizantes do Recôncavo*).[81] She had learned Judaic practices early in life in Portugal and passed them on to her offspring in Brazil, but when the Inquisition arrested her, she claimed that she was a "good Christian."[82] Ana Rodrigues was pressed by the Inquisition head during his visitation to Brazil in 1591, D. Heitor Furtado, who asked her how and when she had become knowledgeable in Judaism and when she had "abandoned the faith of Our Lord Jesus Christ," and when she had taught her daughters the "Laws of Moses."[83] She originally claimed she was eighty years old; however she was probably one hundred, as she once admitted, and it is likely that she may have been among the first generation of children to be forcibly converted and baptized (*batizado em pé*) in Portugal by D. Manuel in 1496–1497.[84]

The case of Ana Rodrigues, as Ronaldo Vainfas and Angelo A. F. Assis point out, offers an example of how strong kinship ties facilitated the diffusion and transmission of old Judaic practices from Portugal to Brazil, from the Old to the New World, and at the same time, show how the role of women was instrumental for this Judaic transmission to occur.[85] The fact that Rodrigues opened the first school for girls in Brazil is significant here, given that illiteracy rates were dramatically high in colonial Brazil for both men and women. Consider that nearly 90 percent of all women throughout Brazil were still illiterate centuries later, in 1872.[86]

I found the Inquisition dossiers for Ana Rodrigues. She was arrested in 1593 in Bahia and was sent to Lisbon for sentencing, where she died in a prison cell a few months later, awaiting her sentence (processo 11680). She is listed as a New Christian born in Covilhã, Portugal, and living in Bahia, and as an eighty-year-old as well (despite her admission that she was twenty years older); and as the wife of Heitor Antunes, a New Christian and merchant. Ten years after her death in 1604, she was sentenced to be burned in effigy. Her bones were unearthed from the Christian cemetery she had been buried in and then thrown into a fire.[87]

Most of the daughters and granddaughters of Ana Rodrigues and Heitor Antunes were also imprisoned and sentenced by the Inquisition as Judaizers. Therefore, with the ongoing persecution of their family members, the descendants of Ana Rodrigues and Heitor Antunes eventually changed their last names to avoid further persecution by incorporating eminent Old Christian family names, for example, Ferreira, Bethencourt, Moniz Barreto, or Faria, and encouraged their daughters and sons to marry conspicuously Old Christian family members in Brazil.[88] In fact, all their children (except one, Nuno, who remained single) eventually married into Old Christian families to foil suspicions about their Christian sincerity.[89]

Ana Rodrigues was among the earliest arrests for Judaism in Brazil in 1593 (processo 11680). She was also one of the two oldest individuals arrested for Judaism along with Ines Aires, aged 80 (widow of André de Barros, merchant), who was arrested much later in Rio de Janeiro in 1713 (processo 13099).

I found the following information in the Inquisition dossiers about their daughters and one son, who were arrested for Judaizing. Violante Antunes, from Matoim, Bahia (married to Diogo Vaz de Escobar, an Old Christian), was arrested in 1593, and died in prison (processo 12926). Leonor Rodrigues (listed just as "D. Leonor") was arrested twice, once in 1592 and then in 1593, and was married to Henrique Muniz Teles, an Old Christian (processos 5509 and 10716). Beatriz Antunes, aged 55, born in Lisbon, married to Sebastião Faria, was arrested later in 1601, and sent to prison and sentenced to an auto in 1603 (processo 8991). Lastly, there was one son, Nuno Fernandes, the only child who did not marry, aged 30, arrested in 1593, and the process of investigation took place at the house of inquisitor, D. Heitor Furtado de Mendonça, during his visitation to Salvador, Bahia. In this case, the inquisitor was clearly focused on his mother, Ana Rodrigues, and asked how she may have passed on Judaic practices to other family members (processo 12936). The Inquisition continued to persecute New Christians in Matoim. For example, in 1605, D. Ana Alcoforada from Matoim Engenho, Bahia, aged 27, was arrested for Judaism. She was listed as half New Christian, and her parents were Isabel Antunes (from the Antunes family) and Antonio Alcoforado, listed as an Old Christian (processo 11618).

Notably, centuries later in 1943, the old Engenho Matoim was listed as a Brazilian national heritage site by the Brazilian Historical and Artistic Institute of Patrimony, IPHAN, *Instituto do Patrimônio Histórico e Artístico Nacional*, for its contribution to the sugarcane industry; however, there is no mention of the earliest New Christian or Crypto-Jewish community that spawned this engenho.[90]

The Camaragibe Judaizing Community of Pernambuco

By the mid- to late sixteenth century, Pernambuco became the epicenter of Brazil's first sugarcane plantation mills (with at least sixty-six sugar mills in existence then). During Brazil's subsequent sugarcane commodity boom, Diogo Fernandes and his wife, Branca Dias, established the *comunidade Camaragibe* ("Camaragibe community") making available an esnoga and a Torah to its members.[91] Denouncements to the inquisitors in 1593 claimed that members of the community in Camaragibe gathered to celebrate the Jewish holiday of Yom Kippur.[92] Along with Matoim in Bahia, these were likely the earliest (and earliest documented) settlements of Crypto-Jews in the New World.

Branca Dias left Portugal clandestinely and arrived in Recife, Pernambuco, as a New Christian and a fugitive from the Inquisition, and Diogo

Fernandes had arrived likely as a degredado.[93] With the ongoing intimidation of Portuguese Inquisition visitations to Pernambuco from 1593 to 1595, Diogo Fernandes and Branca Dias moved with their family to Olinda (north of Recife), where Diogo became the administrator of the Bento Dias Santiago Engenho in Camaragibe, and one of the first New Christian specialists in the sugar industry in Brazil. Branca Dias would establish a well-known local school for girls (similar to the case of Ana Rodrigues, who also founded and taught at a school for girls in Bahia).

Branca Dias was arrested in 1543, denounced by her own mother and sister, Isabel (both had been arrested earlier as Judaizers). She came from a long line of family members (five generations) who had been arrested for Judaizing beginning with her grandmother, Violante Dias, and ending with her grandchildren.[94] After both Branca Dias and Diogo Fernandes died, their children and grandchildren continued to be persecuted by the Inquisition. When Branca died (similar to the case of Ana Rodrigues in Matoim, Bahia), she was sentenced postmortem to be burned in effigy.[95]

The children of Branca Dias and Diogo Fernandes who were still alive in 1595 were: Jorge Dias da Paz (living in Paraíba), Andresa Jorge, Beatriz Fernandes, and another daughter, Briolanja Fernandes, from an adulterous affair Diogo Fernandes had had with a maid, although she was still raised in the Antunes family household. Another daughter, Beatriz Fernandes was imprisoned in 1595 and sent to the prison at the Estaus (at the Palace of the Inquisition) in Lisbon.[96] She had physical and mental health issues (hence her nickname, *alcorcovada*) and confessed under pressure in 1598 and was sentenced to an auto in 1599, which resulted in all her assets being confiscated.[97] She was not burned at the stake, and still lived in Lisbon in 1604. Because of her confession, her siblings, and other grandchildren of Branca Dias and Diogo Fernandes, were also targeted in northeast Brazil. For example, her sister Andressa Jorge was arrested and sent to prison in Lisbon in 1599 with her daughter, Beatriz de Souza, and two nieces, the daughters of Filipa Paz (Ana Costa Arruda and Catarina Favela, who was just 17 years old).[98]

I found Diogo Fernandes's daughters, who were arrested for Judaism, listed in the Inquisition dossiers. One daughter, Beatriz Fernandes, was single, aged 54, and arrested in 1596. Born in Viana de Caminha (northwest

Portugal) and arrested in Pernambuco, she was sentenced to an auto-da-fé in 1599 and all her assets were confiscated (she had to wait the customary three to five years in prison until sentencing). Her parents are listed as Branca Dias and Diogo Fernandes (a senhor de engenho) (processo 4580).

The other daughter mentioned earlier, Briolanja Fernandes, aged 60, listed as "half New Christian" and widow of André Gonçalves Pinto—an Old Christian and carpenter—was arrested on December 16, 1599, in Pernambuco. However, while her father was listed as Diogo Fernandes, she had a different mother than her sister, Beatriz Fernandes: a mother by the name of Madalena Gonçalves, an Old Christian—keeping in mind that she was the offspring of her father's adulterous affair (mentioned above). The fact that she had been married to an Old Christian did not matter, and carried no weight or bearing on her arrest, as in other cases for Judaism. She was also sentenced to an auto-da-fé in 1603 (processo 9417).[99]

Another daughter, Andressa Jorge, aged 43, listed as half New Christian, married to Fernão Sousa, a New Christian, was arrested in 1599 in Olinda, Pernambuco, and sentenced to pay the expenses of the Inquisition and an auto-da-fé in 1603 (processo 6321).[100] Andressa's own daughter (this would be Branca Dias's granddaughter), Beatriz de Sousa, aged 14, born in Olinda, was also arrested in 1599 and sentenced to an auto-da-fé in 1603 (processo 4273). Clearly, the families and descendants of Heitor Antunes and Ana Rodrigues in Bahia, and Diogo Fernandes and Branca Dias in Pernambuco, reflect the vigor and extent to which New Christian family members in Brazil were persecuted, suppressed, interrogated, and sentenced by the Inquisition, especially the women.

As Angelo Adriano Faria de Assis points out, Judaic practices had then transformed into an indoor "household religion" through the education diffusion offered by women. In this case, Judaism saw its propagation in private homes, a result of attempts to avoid denouncements and public suspicion. Women therefore received a special status in their role for the survival of Judaic practices and customs, especially since men were often absent in the household. This important responsibility evidently concerned the inquisitors, and New Christian women were often the focus of denouncements and arrests for Judaism (as seen with the cases of the matriarchs, Branca Dias and Ana Rodrigues and their descendants).[101]

During the late sixteenth century and early seventeenth century, most arrests for Judaism in Brazil up to then either took place in Bahia or Pernambuco (as I show in my examination in Chapter 6)—mainly because those were the sites of major population clusters during the sixteenth century. I found only one New Christian who was imprisoned in Rio de Janeiro during the sixteenth century: this was a merchant, Diogo Lopes, aged 43, in 1596 (processo 12364).[102] The next arrest in Rio only occurred in 1620 (João Nunes, aged 15, processo 9326), and, one other arrest in 1617 in Espírito Santo, of Francisco Ramires, aged 17, listed as half New Christian (processo 1847). Otherwise, all other arrests for Judaism in Brazil in the sixteenth century occurred in Pernambuco or Bahia. These productive and lucrative sugarcane regions in Brazil caught the attention of the Inquisition, which considered that region as a haven for Crypto-Jews. The Inquisition considered Camaragibe, Pernambuco, to be a community of "secret Jews."[103]

Among the most common occupations among New Christians accused of Judaism in Brazil, I found that individuals working in agriculture comprised the majority; that is, lavradores ("farmers" or "sharecroppers"), *lavradores de cana* ("sugarcane planters") and *senhores de engenho* ("sugarcane plantation owners"). The second most common occupation comprised of *mercadores* ("merchants"). (See full results in Chapter 6.) The term "lavrador" could mean any "sharecropper" or "farmer"; however, the term "lavrador de cana" referred to an agricultural elite, a step below the status of senhor de engenho. Being a senhor de engenho in Brazil was equivalent to the title of nobility in Portugal.[104]

New Christians were deeply involved in the sugarcane industry in Brazil as "mill owners, farmers, technicians and skilled workers as well as merchants."[105] The New Christian connection to sugarcane agriculture in the northeast is corroborated in another study by Bruno Feitler, who documented communities and families of Crypto-Jews significantly present in the rural northeast region, such as in Goiana, Paraíba, Recife, Olinda, Penedo, Itamaracá, and Ipojuca—and around the engenhos and sugarcane regions.[106] For instance, according to Feitler, in Paraíba, in the proximity of the Poxim River (by the Engenho do Meio, Engenho Novo, and Engenho Velho), it was well known that families of New Christians gathered for Judaic practices. This was where Ambrósio Vieira (born around 1587) and his wife and three daughters lived. One of their daughters, Maria, would marry Baltazar da Fonseca, and the couple were known to gather with other Crypto-Jews in Recife (before the official Jewish congregation and synagogue were established there during Dutch rule, discussed in Chapter 5).[107] Notably, Evaldo Cabral de Mello asserts that religious orthodoxy, racial purity ("non-Jewish ancestry"), and the absence of peasant origins, emerged as measures of rank and status in Pernambuco during colonial rule in Brazil; nevertheless, New Christians in Pernambuco's original sugar aristocracy and their descendants often tried to disguise that they had Jewish ancestry.[108]

As we have seen, the connection between Portuguese Jews and New Christians in Brazil with the communities they established in the Caribbean becomes increasingly important from the mid-seventeenth century on, as we notice the large-scale migration after Jews left the Brazilian northeast for the Caribbean islands (to Curaçao and Aruba for example), establishing other Jewish communities and sugarcane plantations.[109]

Regional Population Dynamics

By 1570, the total white population (i.e., non-Indigenous, non-African) in Brazil was estimated to be at about 20,760, and according to H. B. Johnson's study, this cohort was mostly living in the following Brazilian captaincies: Pernambuco (Olinda, Igaraçu): 6,000; Bahia (Salvador, Vila Velha): 6,500; Itamaracá: 600; Ilhéus (São Jorge): 1,200; Porto Seguro (Santa Cruz, Santo Amaro): 1,320; Espírito Santo (Vitória, Vila Velha): 1,200; Rio de Janeiro (São Sebastião): 840; and São Vicente (Santos, Santo Amaro, Itanhaém, São Paulo): 3,000.[110]

By the last quarter of the sixteenth century, about sixteen or seventeen major settlements were established along the Brazilian coast, and within a span of fifteen years, the white population increased slightly (from 20,760 in 1570 to about 29,400 in 1585), and the total number of engenhos in the northeast increased significantly (they more than doubled during this time period) as a direct result of the late sixteenth-century sugar boom.[111]

By the 1630s, New Christians in Brazil grew in prominence and became major financiers and exporters of sugar, and Brazil became the world's leading exporter between 1600 and 1650, when sugar accounted for up to 95 percent of its exports.¹¹² Rae Flory and David Grant Smith point out in their study that, during most of the seventeenth century, the "mercantile profession in the Luso-Brazilian world had become so thoroughly associated with the descendants of forcibly converted Jews that the terms 'New Christian' and 'homem de negócio' ["merchant"] were often used as synonyms."¹¹³ In their study they explain how Salvador, Bahia, was a major Brazilian trading center for the export of sugar, tobacco, brazilwood, and hides, and the importation of dry goods, iron, and food staples from Portugal. However, unlike Lisbon, where the great majority of merchants were New Christians, a little over half of the merchants of Bahia (of those examined in their study) during the seventeenth century were, in fact, Old Christians.¹¹⁴

By the mid-seventeenth century, according to A. J. R. Russell-Wood, the white population in Brazil increased to an estimated 50,000, and by the 1680s, an additional 2,000 European immigrants each year arrived in Brazil, mostly from the Atlantic islands and Portugal.¹¹⁵ Yet by the 1700s, whites still accounted for only about 25 percent of the total population in Brazil, and the remaining population consisted of 30 percent "mixed race" (pardos, mulatos, including Indians), and 45 percent black.¹¹⁶

Salvador's population (in Bahia) increased from 14,000 in 1585 to 25,000 in 1724, and, to 40,000 by 1750 (about half were black); and Olinda (Pernambuco) had grown from 4,000 in 1630 to 8,000 in 1654.¹¹⁷ As a result, of the New Christian population influx to towns and cities in Pernambuco, Bahia, Rio de Janeiro, and especially Minas Gerais in the late seventeenth to mid-eighteenth centuries, the proportion of New Christians engaged in ecclesiastical occupations became a matter of concern in the Jesuit Order. For example, in 1603, the Board of Conscience of Lisbon ordered the Bishop of Brazil to appoint only Old Christians in Pernambuco since they were concerned when they found out that most ecclesiastic occupations at that time in Pernambuco comprised New Christians.¹¹⁸

Rio's white population grew exponentially with the ciclo do ouro—and with the new forging of roads, connecting the interior of Minas Gerais to the city of Rio de Janeiro (the opening of roads built by New Christian, Garcia Pais, mentioned earlier)—and at the same time, those towns in Minas Gerais and the city of Rio also became major ecclesiastical and civil centers.¹¹⁹ Neusa Fernandes points out how the activities of the Portuguese

Inquisition intensified in Minas Gerais with the discovery of gold and diamonds there, and the subsequent migration of New Christians. During the first quarter of the eighteenth century, political, religious, and economic repression also intensified in Brazil, as "blood statutes" became more rigorous and the number of familiares increased.[120] For example, in their study, Maria Leônia Chaves de Resende and Rafael José de Sousa point out the significant increase in arrests for Judaism in Minas Gerais throughout the eighteenth century and early nineteenth century (e.g., in towns and hamlets such as Rio das Mortes, Rio das Velhas, Serro do Frio, and Vila Rica). They highlight the salient participation of New Christians in the demarcations of routes and the development of hamlets, villages, and towns, and their role in the discovery of gold in Minas Gerais (e.g., Antônio Rodrigues de Arzão known as the *entrante*, "the "incomer" or "entering person", a reference to a person making inroads into the hinterlands).[121]

Due to the discovery of gold and diamonds in Minas Gerais, immigrant arrivals in Brazil increased from approximately five thousand to six thousand every year between 1700 and 1720.[122] In 1800, the total population was estimated at about 3.2 million (of which blacks comprised the significant majority).[123]

The *Engenhos* in Brazil's Northeast

The senhor de engenho in northeast Brazil often owned around one hundred slaves, and for tobacco growing, about fifteen or twenty slaves, but for manioc growers, who were mostly pardos, mestiços, and free blacks, they typically owned two to four slaves.[124] There was less social prestige or political power in growing tobacco (*fumo*) than planting sugarcane. After sugar, tobacco was the most important crop in Brazil, mostly grown in Pará, Maranhão, and Pernambuco, but it was most successful in Bahia (which accounted for about 90 percent of Brazil's total tobacco exports).[125]

Stuart B. Schwartz explains that engenhos were "agro-industrial enterprises," which involved "planting, growing, cutting, milling, cooking, cooling, crystallizing, sorting, packing, shipping," and "seemed to foreshadow the modern factory."[126] Therefore, the sugar industry helped to shape the high demand for labor, skill, and experience. Notably, the term "plantation" was never used during this period in Brazil.[127]

The term "engenho" initially only referred to the mill for grinding the sugarcane; however, over time, it came to refer to the entire sugarcane production, structure, and system: it was both farm and factory, including its administration, its slaves, and its diverse economic system.[128] As Stuart B. Schwartz explains, engenhos needed to be efficient and profitable with a typical twenty-four-hour work cycle, virtually never stopping (akin to a "factory" in the modern sense). The engenho employed a diverse labor force, ranging from manual workers to skilled labor that included "skilled blacksmiths, carpenters, masons, and technicians."[129] Sugarcane had to be processed within 48 hours; if not, it would dry up. Engenhos in Brazil typically operated 270 to 300 days a year (compared to the Caribbean Islands, which typically operated 120 to 180 days a year), and cane took 14 to 18 months to mature after first planting, and then another 9 to 10 months for second growth.[130]

In the 1590s, it was commonplace for some New Christian senhores de engenho to make slaves take Saturdays off, a sign of the Jewish observance of the Sabbath.[131] Manuel Correia de Andrade claims, "the slaves belonging to Jews [i.e., "New Christians"] had more leisure time, inasmuch as they, for religious motives, observed Saturdays, and for fear of the authorities, also observed Sundays."[132] The new mercantile class of sugarcane plantation owners, sugarcane industry experts, and sugarcane farmers of the northeast region, were mostly of Jewish ancestry.[133]

Consequently, these engenhos became places of interest to Portuguese inquisitors. I found a significant number of arrests for Judaism, particularly in Pernambuco, Paraíba, and Bahia under "place of birth" in the following engenhos: (1) Five individuals born at Engenho Velho, city of Paraíba, Bispate of Pernambuco; (2) Four born at Engenho Matoim, São Salvador da Baía de Todos os Santos, Bahia; (3) Two at Engenho Novo, District of Paraíba, Bispate of Pernambuco; (4) Two at Engenho da Pindoba (Ipojuca), Pernambuco; (5) Two at Engenho de Inhohim/Inhobim, Paraíba, Bispate of Pernambuco; (6) One at Engenho de Santo André, Pernambuco; (7) One at Engenho do Meio, Paraíba, Bispate of Pernambuco; and (8) One at Engenho do Meio, Rio de Janeiro.

Jonathan Schorsch points out that while both blacks and New Christians were marginalized and persecuted, albeit in different ways, many slaves and servants in Latin America denounced their employers and owners.[134] The Inquisition used slaves as spies to monitor their slave-owner's domestic practices (e.g., maids who cooked certain kosher foods; not eating pork; or refraining from working on Saturdays).[135] Many slaves in Spanish America denounced their plantation owners, where the motivation may have been to appear as "good Christians"—at least in the eyes of the Inquisition—or for revenge. However, Schorsch also suggests that the case in Brazil may have been different, since some slaves in the Brazilian isolated regions of the interior of the Sertão became familiar (and even sympathetic) with Judaic practices of their New Christian Crypto-Jewish senhores de engenho. Some slaves may have adopted Crypto-Jewish practices; however, there is little evidence that this was the case with most Brazilian engenhos (it was probably unlikely that this occurred in the same way as it did in Senegal or Suriname).[136] The orthodoxy of the Christian religion affected labor relations, and three-quarters of the days of the sugar season were taken off for Christian religious holidays.[137] Brazilian slaves had the right to take 32 days off a year, and in addition an extra day off on Saturdays (influenced by Judaizing families). This was a system taken to the Caribbean, known as the "Brazilian system."[138]

The context of Portuguese Jews and their communities in seventeenth-century West Africa are worthwhile bringing up. Peter Mark and José da Silva Horta point out how African or Eurafrican women who migrated to Amsterdam "would then have transmitted their Jewish identity to their children born in Amsterdam" through their paternal side.[139] They discuss the cases of Portuguese-Jewish merchants such as Diogo Dias Querido (also known as David Querido)—mentioned earlier—and Diogo Nunes Belmonte (or Jacob Israel Belmonte), "who were among the wealthiest members of the Amsterdam community and leaders of the Bet Jacob congregation," and who were actively involved in the West African trade with the Dutch.[140] Many merchants, such as Querido and Belmonte, brought African household servants to Amsterdam, who were converted to Judaism there, while others had been converted in Senegal (by Portuguese Jews living there); however, unlike the case in Suriname, no evidence shows that "Eurafrican Jews of Joal and

Porto d'Ale were in any way relegated to lower status."[141] Notably, in Brazil, African and Indigenous-based religious belief systems and practices were considered heresies, such as witchcraft and sorcery, and were often confused with Judaism (whether they were in fact Judaizers or not). Consequently, the surveillance on those populations was particularly acute in the northeast region in Bahia and Pernambuco (for more details see Chapter 6).

Engenhos and African Slavery

We learn several important geographical and social insights about early seventeenth-century Brazil from author Ambrósio Fernandes Brandão through one of his fictional characters, Brandônio, in the literary forms of "dialogues." He was introduced earlier in Chapter 1, and had been arrested as a Judaizer. He was the author of the first geographical treatise on Brazil. Brandônio explains, "in Brazil a new Guinea has been created, with so much multitude of slaves coming from there that one feels they are there, so much that in some captaincies there are more Negroes than local Indians."[142] Thus, a constant supply of African slaves was needed for the engenho enterprises to remain effective and profitable. Here we find another salient and parallel narrative of migration processes to Brazil—albeit a macabre forced migration via the transatlantic slave trade.

Philip D. Curtin's seminal book published in 1969, *The Atlantic Slave Trade: A Census*, remains the authoritative study on the transatlantic slave trade. In addition, to understand the full extent and scope of this enterprise, the recently published *Atlas of the Transatlantic Slave Trade*, by David Eltis and David Richardson, offers a new array of cartographic representations of the vast slave trade to all the Americas.[143] The Slave Voyages data set, also supervised by David Eltis had documented 27,000 slave voyages across the Atlantic, but we learn that by 2010, the actual number of documented voyages had risen to 35,000, and the number of 4.4 million African slaves brought to Brazil, from data compiled in 1999, also rose to 5.6 million.[144] Luís de Alencastro explains how Portuguese and Spanish New and Old Christians, as well as Jesuits, had both established a wide web of network contacts in Africa that facilitated slave trade networks in the New World.[145] To reiterate, Jesuits used not only African, but also Indigenous slave labor in the profitable engenhos and properties they owned throughout the northeast of Brazil, as discussed in Chapter 1.

The Portuguese were the only Europeans who took advantage of the southern winds and Atlantic currents, and most African captives were taken from the Bight of Benin, the Gold Coast, the Bight of Biafra, and West and Central Africa (the largest region of all African captives).[146] Notably, the earliest ports of departure of slave captives taken from Africa on record were to Brazil.[147]

Recife became the first Brazilian-based traffic port around 1560, and it became the base of the Dutch slave trade from 1630 to 1654 (when northeast Brazil was under Dutch Rule). During the seventeenth and eighteenth centuries, most slave voyages were organized at the Port of Salvador, more than at any other Atlantic port in the Americas, showing a strong link with the Bight of Benin (as the Portuguese were taking advantage of two main southern Atlantic currents), and by the early nineteenth century (due to a high demand with the coffee boom), Rio de Janeiro became the major outfitting center in the Americas for slave voyages.[148] The Portuguese had taken over Angola in 1575, and after 1629, Luanda supplied more captives to the Americas than any other location in sub-Saharan Africa, and almost all captives taken from Quilimane, Mozambique—also under the Portuguese—went to Brazil.[149] Between 1500 and 1867, vessels from Brazil, England, France, Portugal, and the Netherlands carried off about 90 percent of all transatlantic captives removed from Africa; and the Caribbean and Brazil accounted for 95 percent of all slaves arriving in the Americas, where the major destinations in Brazil were Pernambuco, Bahia, and Rio de Janeiro.[150]

Between 1501 and 1867, of all vessels transporting slaves across the Atlantic, Portugal and Brazil carried the most African captives, followed by Great Britain.[151] By 1808, Denmark, the United States, and Britain made it illegal to engage in the transatlantic slave trade, while the Portuguese and Spanish continued with the trade, accounting for 80 percent of all traffic to the Americas.[152] Between 1696 and 1790, the major ports of slave voyages arrived in Salvador, Rio, and Recife. Between 1791 and 1856, illegal slave voyages continued, yet now the points of arrival moved to other minor Brazilian ports to avoid detection (e.g., in the southeast: Santos, Ilha das Palmas, São Sebastião, Ilha Grande, Mangaratiba, Cabo Frio, Búzios, and Macaé; and in the northeast: Taipú, Ponta Negra, Ilha de Itamaracá, Catuamo, and Maria Farinha; and to other ports in Maranhão and Paraíba).[153] Manuel Correia de Andrade describes the conditions of black slaves: "living like veritable animals in loathsome quarters, poorly fed, without rights or comforts, the slaves, for more than three centuries, were the mainstay of the Northeast's sugar economy."[154]

Overall, during the transatlantic slave trade period, more Africans were brought to Brazil than to any other country in the world (over 40 percent during the entire transatlantic slave trade period)—an estimated 5.6 million.[155] As a result, by 1817 over two-thirds (2,887, 500) of the total Brazilian population (3,617, 900) was black, and less than one-fourth was "white" (843,000).[156]

Jews, New Christians, and the Slave Trade

There is some tension in the historiography about the involvement of New Christians in the transatlantic slave trade to Brazil (not of slave ownership). For example, while historian José Gonçalves Salvador stated that most slave traders were New Christians, Anita W. Novinsky claims that he presented no concrete evidence of their involvement in the trade per se.[157] Salvador's conclusions, according to Novinsky, were merely based on the identification of the most common surnames of New Christians, which Novinsky refutes, as she asserts this would be an impossible task to undertake.[158] That is, surnames that are commonly thought to be New Christian were also commonly found among Old Christian names. Novinsky claims that the cases of New Christians who profited as "contractors" using their own ships to bring slaves to Brazil were extremely rare, and that New Christians, as with all colonists in Brazil, were integrated into a socioeconomic society grounded in slavery. Novinsky claims that most New Christians were not specifically slave-trade magnates who profited from the slave trade.[159]

However, James C. Boyajian paints a polar opposite picture to Novinsky's take, and claims that Portuguese New Christians actively participated in the slave trade.[160] Nevertheless, it is important to clarify that most scholarship has shown that the bulk of the slave trade during the first two hundred years was monopolized by the Portuguese and Spanish—whether Old or New

Christians.[161] In some studies, very few Portuguese New Christians were conspicuously and clearly identified as slave traffickers, while other studies have shown that members of religious orders (e.g., Santa Casa de Misericórdia), Jesuits, and agents of the Church and the Inquisition were just as actively and conspicuously involved in the transatlantic slave trade as New Christians or Portuguese Old Christians.[162] Peter Mark and José da Silva Horta aptly comment on the role of New Christians in slave trade networks, and that some sources "exaggerate the role of New Christians while omitting the role of *cristãos-velhos* [Old Christians] in a manner that is misleading to the historian."[163]

The methods that are often used to identify New Christian names in the slave trade can present serious problems. A common mistake made by genealogists and scholars is to assume that all surnames named after trees or animals are New Christian names (e.g., Figueira, Carvalho, Lobo, etc.), in the same manner that names such as Noronha, Sousa, and Menezes, for example, are not necessarily fidalgos—of "noble" ancestry—either ("Old Christian").[164] One study found that the most common New Christian last names found were surnames based on Portuguese villages and towns, such as Miranda, Chaves, Bragança, Oliveira, Santarém, and Castelo Branco.[165] Yet New Christians also adopted surnames that referred to animals: Leon ("lion"), Carneiro ("sheep"), Lobo ("wolf"), Raposo ("fox"), and Coelho ("rabbit"); or trees: Pinheiro ("pine tree"), Carvalho ("oak tree"), Pereira ("pear tree"), and Oliveira ("olive tree"); or physical characteristics, such as Moreno ("dark skin"), Negro ("black"), or Branco ("white"); or geographical features: Serra ("mountain range"), Monte ("mount"), Rios ("rivers"), and Vales ("valleys").[166]

In my examination (discussed in Chapter 6), the most common last names of individuals arrested for Judaism in Brazil were: Henriques, Silva, Costa, Nunes, Paredes, Miranda, Coutinho, Gomes, Pereira, Rodrigues, and Fonseca. Many, if not most of New Christian last names, however, were no different from most common Old Christian Portuguese names. One reason to explain this phenomenon is that "there was a strong admixture of Jewish blood in many Portuguese families."[167] In her study, Angela Maria Vieira Maia showed that New Christians integrated well in early colonial society in Brazil, and that there were considerable intermarriages between Old and

New Christians.[168] Many confessions to the Inquisition revealed family customs relating to Judaic practices such as throwing out a household's water after the passing of a family member, or the preparation or avoidance of certain foods, yet at the same time claiming they were unaware of those "condemnable origins." Therefore, the contact and intermixture between Old and New Christians was commonplace in colonial Brazil.[169]

One major commonality among New Christians is that the same family members often adopted different last names from each other.[170] Furthermore, to add to this inconsistency, New Christians sometimes changed their first names, adopting Hebrew first names, but they frequently maintained their Portuguese surnames, for example, Luís Dormido became Daniel Dormido; Simão Franco Drago adopted the name of Isaac Franco Drago; Francisco de Faria was named Jacob de Faria; João de La Faye became Aron de la Faye; Gaspar Rodriguez became Abraão Rodrigues.[171] However, what is certain is that the concept of colonialism went hand-in-hand with profits, and to achieve profits, slave labor was required. That meant that colonists—whether Jesuits, or Old or New Christians—enslaved Indigenous and African populations and used their slave labor in the sugarcane and tobacco plantations and later, for the mining of precious stones and gold. This mechanism of both profit and colonialism resulted in the largest and most repugnant phenomenon in humanity where an estimated five million Africans were enslaved and taken to Brazil.

The Sugar Industry and the Dutch in the Seventeenth Century

Sugar was the world's prized Brazilian commodity, and the Dutch were lured by its profits, prompting them to invade northeast Brazil in 1630. However, the sugar boom in Brazil entered a period of decline by the end of the seventeenth century due to competition and lower prices from sugar produced in the West Indies and the Dutch Antilles.[172] By the 1640s, Brazil's sugarcane industry began to fall to the competition, which came mostly from Barbados, Jamaica, Suriname, the French Caribbean islands, and the Dutch Antilles, and by 1670, sugarcane supplied to London fell from 80 percent to 40 percent.[173] Another factor accounting for this economic slump in Brazil was that the Dutch had destroyed many Portuguese-owned engenhos and sugarcane fields in the northeast after their arrival in 1630, as I discuss in the next chapter.[174]

From a Dutch official report written in 1638, when the Dutch ruled northeast Brazil, we learn, "those from Africa come from Angola or from other places where the Company [West India Company] has dealings ... however, those that the Company acquires on the Ardra coast [Dahomey, today Benin, West Africa] are slow-moving, obstinate, and disinclined to work."[175] Furthermore, the same report states, "It is impossible to achieve anything in Brazil without slaves. Without them, the mills cannot crush the cane, nor can the fields be tilled."[176] This report written by the Dutch rulers in Brazil also offers important insights into the Dutch position (i.e., the Dutch West India Company), as far as the slave trade with Brazil went, and the profits from the institution of slavery (i.e., since slaves were needed to labor on engenhos to provide profits from the sugarcane industry):

> It is most important that every means possible is brought to bear to ensure the traffic along the coast of Africa. The Company has the greatest interest in this matter because, apart from selling them at a good profit, the Company receives annually one third of the work of each black, so that the black works not only for his master but also for the Company.[177]

With the profitable sugar boom in Brazil, the stakes for the Portuguese to fend off the oncoming Dutch and French raids and attacks were high. Eventually the Dutch attacked the northeastern coast of Brazil, first in Bahia where they were unsuccessful in 1624, and then again in Pernambuco in 1630, as I explore in the following chapter. During the first half of the seventeenth century, the Dutch consolidated their economic power by eliminating Portuguese and Spanish competition.[178] Once the Dutch established themselves in northeast Brazil in 1630, they initiated the slave trade with Africa in an unprecedented systematic manner until 1803, where more than half a million Africans were transported to the New World on board Dutch ships.[179] The transatlantic slave trade was a major source of profit for the Dutch West India Company.[180]

The next chapter underlines the theme of migration again and illustrates how the status of New Christian was fluid and not static, and their condition as migrants was in constant flux. For example, many living in northeast Brazil reverted to their Judaic faith, as they were allowed to profess their Jewish religion for twenty-four years during Dutch rule. However, once the Dutch left Brazil and Portugal recovered their territory, many of those who had reverted to being Jewish returned to their status as New Christians while many others migrated yet again, either to the Caribbean islands, Suriname, North America, or back to Europe.

Notably, as we shall see in the next chapter, the exodus of Portuguese Jews from Dutch Brazil after 1654, "accelerated the establishment of Jewish communities in other parts of the New World," and were especially vital within the Dutch and English trading and sugar-producing colonies in the Caribbean, such as Barbados, Jamaica, and Curaçao, as well as Suriname.[181]

This is the twenty-four-year period when Jews could profess their religion openly for the first and only time in colonial Brazil, and when Jews established the first Jewish community in the Americas in Recife. The Dutch began a new sociocultural and religious experiment in Brazil that would only last from 1630 to 1654.

CHAPTER FIVE

The First Jewish Settlement in the Americas

IN 1630, THE DUTCH successfully took over Pernambuco and Brazil's northeast region after a failed takeover in Bahia six years earlier. Dutch-controlled Brazil included the provinces of Paraíba, Pernambuco, Alagoas, and Sergipe, all the way north to Rio Grande [do Norte], Ceará, and Maranhão.[1] Since Portugal was occupied by the Spanish from 1580 to 1640, Brazil, as well as other Portuguese territories, became a prime target for the Dutch. The Dutch West India Company, *West-Indische Compagnie* (from here on, WIC), was formed in 1621 by individuals in rebellious Dutch provinces in the struggle against the Spanish Hapsburg Crown.[2] Similar to the Dutch East India Company, founded in 1602, the governing body of the United Provinces of the Netherlands (the States General) granted the WIC a twenty-four-year monopoly on all trade by Dutch merchants and inhabitants in the Americas and West Africa.[3] Notably, many of the major shareholders of the WIC were prominent members of the Portuguese-Jewish community of Amsterdam, as we shall see ahead.

The experience in Brazil during Dutch rule opened an unprecedented gamut of religious options, whereby the Protestant Dutch allowed Jews to profess their religion for the first time in Catholic Brazil. Jewish life during Dutch rule in Brazil was unique for the "people of the nation," *gente da nação*.[4]

As we already saw in Chapter 4, sugarcane was successfully productive in the rich reddish-dark *massapé* soils of Pernambuco, and the Dutch were eager to capitalize on the profitable sugarcane industry. Brazil's northeast would become a coveted location for the Dutch takeover. Michiel van Groesen argues that Dutch Brazil was an integral part of Atlantic history, and the "possession of northeast Brazil enabled the West India Company to transform the sugar market . . . and . . . it looked to set to dominate the transatlantic slave trade as well."[5] Van Groesen explains how scholars have commonly distinguished between the northern Atlantic, Spanish Atlantic, and Portuguese Atlantic spheres, whereas only after the late seventeenth and eighteenth centuries did these three separate spheres effectively merge.[6]

Wim Klooster fittingly points out, in *The Dutch Moment*, that Brazil should be placed "front and center" in Dutch Atlantic studies, and that few scholars acknowledge that most of northeast Brazil was under Dutch control between 1630 and 1654. Dutch Brazil had a long-lasting socioeconomic impact on the Atlantic world, and most studies focus on New Netherland which, in Klooster's opinion, was marginal compared to Brazil.[7]

An abundant scholarship available today has addressed this period of Dutch rule in Brazil.[8] Notably, Blanche T. Ebeling-Koning translated into English, Caspar van Baerle's *The History of Brazil Under the Governorship of Count Johan Maurits of Nassau, 1636–1644*. However, this body of scholarship has focused on one single period, and the purpose of this chapter is to give continuity to the theme of this book: the memory and legacy of New Christians and Jews *throughout* colonial Brazil and beyond, throughout the Americas. This was when the first official Jewish community emerged in the New World, with its first synagogues, rabbis, calligraphers, and first poems written in the New World in Hebrew (written in and about Recife).

The official Jewish communities in Recife and Olinda recognized the Portuguese-Jewish community of Amsterdam as their only religious authority, since they had been established by Jews who had migrated to Brazil from Amsterdam, from the established Portuguese-Jewish community (they were not Spanish, Sephardic, or Ashkenazi, but Portuguese Jews).[9] However, this topic has been ignored in anglophone academia to such an extent that even one respected historian infelicitously makes the mistaken claim, "most of the Jews [in Recife, Brazil] were Ashkenazi."[10] These communities in Pernambuco were comprised of Portuguese Jews (not Ashkenazi or Sephardic or Spanish)—either New Christian Brazilian locals who had reverted to Judaism, or members of the Portuguese-Jewish community from Amsterdam who had migrated directly from Amsterdam.[11] As Dutch humanist Caspar van Baerle describes:

> Most of the Jewish inhabitants came here from the Dutch Republic. Some, who were originally Portuguese, pretended to convert to Christianity during the Spanish king's reign, but freed from the fear of persecution under a more indulgent ruler, they now freely associate with the Jews. This proves clearly that such hypocrisy was the result of fear of persecution, induced by the worshippers of the purple rather than by God.[12]

Dutch rule in Brazil would become a new experiment of religious tolerance and economic inclusion in the Atlantic world, albeit one that was relatively short-lived. A report from Recife written on January 14, 1638, signed by Dutch rulers at the time, Johan Maurits, Count of Nassau, M. Van Ceullen, Adriaen vander Dussen, and S. Carpentier, Secretary, states:

> There are, among the settlers in this land, many Jews and people with Jewish tendencies. Formerly, for fear of justice or the Inquisition, they concealed their beliefs and pretended to be Christians. After the conquest, however, they began to make public their religion. They joined the Jews who have come from the Netherlands and accompany them in their superstitious practices.[13]

In 1629, on the eve of their occupation of Pernambuco, the Dutch had already issued a pledge of religious tolerance, and this tolerance toward Jews was unprecedented in Brazil. The same report states, "the Portuguese, who are Old Christians, are scandalized with the freedom granted to Jews."[14] As a result, many local Brazilian residents who were once New Christian Crypto-Jews returned to openly practicing Judaism as bona fide Jews (i.e., "New Jews"). Tolerance of Judaism by Johan Maurits, the governor-general of Dutch Brazil who ironically detested Jews personally, as Jonathan Israel explains, "was clearly not the result of the Governor-General's personal benevolence or any intrinsic preference for, or disposition toward, toleration on the part of the WIC, but rather the consequence of sheer, straightforward necessity."[15] Despite some complaints about Dutch bailiffs and sheriffs (*shouten*) abusing power, according to Charles R. Boxer, a greater degree of religious freedom and tolerance emerged in Dutch Brazil during Maurits's rule than anywhere else in the Western world at that time.[16] This religious tolerance, however, did not include Jesuits though (which was anathema to Protestants, especially to Calvinists), and the Dutch deported all Jesuits they could find in northeast Brazil.[17]

A common notion in past historiographies held that Brazilian New Christians, "simply threw off their masks and joined their Jewish brethren" after the Dutch arrived.[18] However, contrary to this notion, several local New Christians remained loyal to the Portuguese Crown during the Dutch occupation of Brazil perhaps for financial, social, or political reasons, and despite popular belief, several doubted the freedom to practice Judaism in Brazil would last, and did not convert back to Judaism, maintaining their Catholic identities.[19] Norman Simms points out that many Brazilian local New Christians did not want to associate themselves with their "faded Jewish ancestry" since they were not "Judaizing" and did not engage in any Judaic practices, and it put them at risk of being denounced to Portuguese inquisitors. They remained cautious about publicly revealing their Jewish ancestry, if they knew about it, and many feared that these new religious tolerance policies toward Jews would not last long.[20]

Bruno Feitler cautions us that we should avoid the static view of the Jewish experience during this period of Dutch rule in Brazil, especially since there was as much freedom as there were restrictions, and economic and social downturns.[21] Evidence of existing antagonism against Jews and anti-Jewish sentiments had been expressed by some Dutch Calvinists and directed against Jews in Recife, although most of it was driven by rivalry and competition.[22] For example, some members of the Dutch Protestant clergy were quite vocal about the intermarriages between Jews and Calvinists in Recife, and often cited the restrictions on Jews elsewhere as a reason to impose them in Brazil as well. At the same time, as Daniela Levy points out, a Catholic friar, Manoel Calado do Salvador from the Congregation of Serra d'Ossa of the Order of Saint Paul, disseminated virulent anti-Jewish sentiments during the period of Dutch rule in Brazil, publishing *O Valoroso Lucidero e o Trinfo da Liberdade*, where he accused Jews in Brazil of corruption, rape, and greed, stating that Recife had become "a Sodom and Gomorrah."[23] More importantly, despite the attention given to the general sense of freedom during Dutch rule, there were restrictions imposed on Jews that are often overlooked during this period, as Caspar van Baerle explains:

> There were restrictions imposed on the Jews. No new synagogues could be built. A Jew was not permitted to marry a Christian woman or to have a Christian concubine. No one could be converted from Christianity to Judaism, or be called from the freedom of the Scriptures to the burden of the Law of Moses, from the light to the darkness. Jews were forbidden to curse the sacred name of Jesus Christ. A broker's fee could not exceed a third part of the total. No one could be defrauded in commercial transactions. At the death of the parents, children born of a Jew and a Christian had to be given to the Christian relatives to be educated.[24]

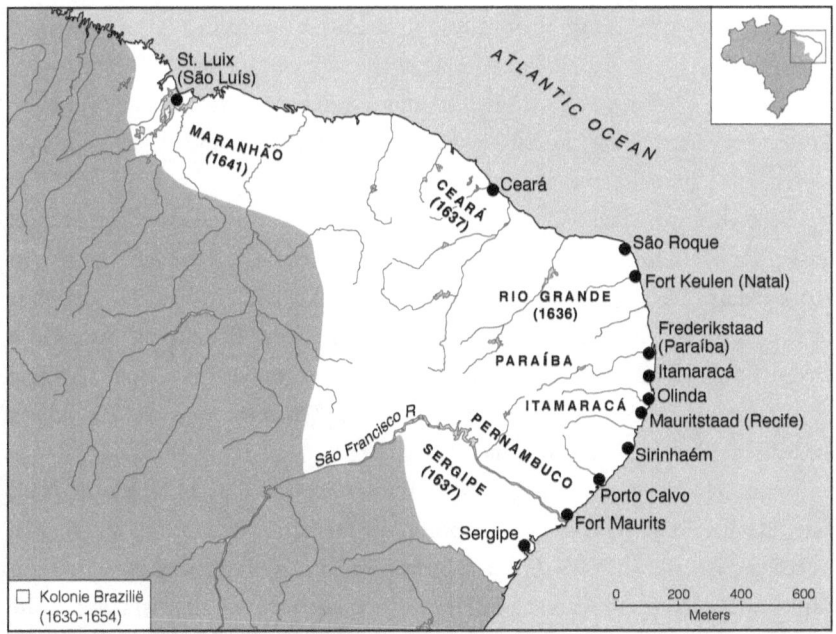

Map 9. Dutch Brazil. Dutch Brazil (1630–1654)—Kolonie Brazilië. Rio Real, Sergipe, Fort Maurits, Porto Calvo, Mauritstaad (Recife), Olinda, Itamaracá, Frederikstaad (Paraíba), Fort Keulen (Natal), São Roque, Ceará, St. Luix (São Luís) (Sergipe, Pernambuco, Itamaracá, Paraíba, Rio Grande, Ceará, Maranhão)

Brazil's Northeast under Dutch Rule

On February 14, 1630, the Dutch arrived in Brazil with about 7,180 soldiers and sailors in 56 ships off Recife, Pernambuco, where 3,000 of them landed at "the beach of Pão Amarello [sic]"[25] However, Arnold Wiznitzer's reference to *Pão Amarelo* ("Yellow Bread Beach") is likely a typo or misspelling of *Praia do Pau Amarelo* ("Yellow Wood Beach"), just north of Olinda.

The WIC divided Dutch citizens in Brazil into *vrijburghers* (free citizens, artisans, and merchants) and *dienaaren* (WIC employees: public servants, bureaucrats, sailors, and soldiers).[26] The soldiers and sailors comprised mostly Dutch, Germans, Norwegians, Scots, and Portuguese Jews. The latter group stood out since they were instrumental intermediaries and acted as guides for the Dutch in Brazil, as they tended to be multilingual and literate.[27] That is, they served as important interpreters for the Dutch and were often fluent in Dutch, Portuguese, and Hebrew.[28] Only the Portuguese Jews from Amsterdam were "both Portuguese and Dutch-speaking, and combined these skills with an expert knowledge of the sugar industry."[29] The language barrier gave Portuguese Jews an advantage in the retail trade, since very few Dutch ever learned the Portuguese language in Brazil, and most "people of the nation" knew both Portuguese and Dutch.[30]

According to Mark Ponte, some Afro-Brazilians sided with the Dutch, and when the Dutch left Brazil in 1654, they went back with them to live in Amsterdam. Hence, not all Afro-Brazilian blacks living in Brazil's northeast during Dutch rule were slaves, and there were Afro-Brazilians among the soldiers and sailors working for the Dutch; for example, Francisco d'Angola or "Francijcks of Angola," who left Brazil for Amsterdam after 1654, where he later died in 1659, and was buried there.[31]

Johan Maurits van Nassau-Siegen, known in Brazil as Maurício de Nassau ("Maurício of Nassau") was appointed governor of the Dutch territory in northeast Brazil by the WIC.[32] He arrived in Recife in 1637 and brought with him Dutch geographers, cartographers, administrators, scientists, and writers such as Elias Herckmans, author of *Generale Beschrjvinge van de Capitania Paraíba* ("General Description of the Captaincy of Paraíba"); eminent painters such as Abraham Willaerts, Frans Post, and Albert Eckhout; and philosophers and historians such as Caspar van Baerle, who wrote a landmark historical narrative of Brazil and published it in Latin ("The History of Brazil under the Governorship of Count Johan Maurits of Nassau, 1636–1644").³³ Van Baerle also wrote *Rerum per octennium in Brasilia et alibi nuper gestarum, sub praefectura illustrissimi Comiti I. Mauritii Historia* ("History of the Recent Activities in Brazil and Elsewhere over a Period of Eight Years under the Governorship of Count Johan Maurits"), during the period of 1636–1644. Caspar van Baerle, known in scholarly circles as Barlaeus, was a professor of classical philology and philosophy at the Athenaeum Illustre, an academy in Amsterdam. Maurits also brought to Brazil Johannes de Laet, who wrote *Historie ofte Iaerlyck verhael van de verrichtingen der Geoctroyeerde West-Indische Compagnie* ("History, or Annual Report of the Activities of the Chartered West-India Company"), written in Dutch and published in 1644.³⁴

In 1631, a new map of Brazil was created by Willem Blaeu (1571–1638), the founder of a famous Dutch mapmaking dynasty and the appointed mapmaker of the Dutch East India Company.³⁵ Blaeu had established his own mapmaking studio in Amsterdam, and in 1635, together with his sons Joan and Cornelis, he published the *Atlas Novus* ("New Atlas"), 11 volumes consisting of 594 maps of the Americas.³⁶ The book, *Historia Naturalis Brasiliae*, written by Willem Piso and Georg Marcgraf, with observations by Johannes de Laet, and published in 1648, was dedicated to Maurits.³⁷ This publication was the first detailed scientific study of flora and fauna of Brazil, with meticulous rainfall records, notes on geography, an ethnographical survey of the local Indigenous population, illustrations, and woodcuts of plants, animals, birds, insects, and fishes, most of which had never been described before by Europeans.³⁸ The Dutch expressed a great deal of interest in the physical/natural features of Brazil, including its fruits and food:

> They have excellent fruit, such as oranges, lemons, melons, watermelons, two varieties of bananas, pineapples, potatoes, two varieties of passion-fruit [*maracujá*], custard-apples, and the most delicious of all fruits, mangaba plums [*mangabeira*]. They also east sundry legumes, as well as maize, rice, and other crops from which they make a variety of sweet dishes."³⁹

Hence, because of the abundance of fruit and flowers that grew on the island of Antônio Vaz, Recife, Maurits named it Vrijburg (meaning loosely "independence" or "freedom" in Dutch). On the lands of Vrijburg, Maurits built a palace named Friburgum Palace ("Castle of Freedom") or, in Portuguese, Palácio de Friburgo—which eventually fell into disrepair and was demolished soon after the Dutch left Recife. Under the directive of Maurits, the Dutch also built canals, a botanical garden, a zoo, and the first astronomical observatory in the Americas.[40]

Jewish architect Baltazar da Fonseca built a bridge connecting Recife to the island of Antônio Vaz in the mid-1630s (today the neighborhood of Santo Antônio in Recife)—the first bridge of its size in Brazil and today, the country's oldest functioning bridge. This same bridge is still named Ponte Maurício de Nassau ("Mauricio Nassau Bridge").[41] Thus, the Dutch and Portuguese Jews of Amsterdam together brought with them to Brazil their intellectual skills in science, engineering, architecture, philosophy, literature, and medicine as well as their vast network contacts and understanding of international trade and commerce.[42] A pamphlet published in 1642, *Wel-vaert van de West-Indische Compagnie* ("Prosperity of the West India Company"), detailed meticulous sums of costs and profits outlined by the Dutch. These were proposals to increase profits benefiting its shareholders that relate to Brazil and the sugar trade, and to transatlantic slavery.[43]

One of the leaders in the Dutch conquest of Pernambuco was Antônio Vaz Henriques, alias Moses Cohen, a Portuguese Jew from Amsterdam.[44] In fact, the island of Antônio Vaz, the Dutch capital in Brazil in Recife (today comprising the neighborhoods of Santo Antônio, São José, Cabanga, and Ilha Joana Bezerra), was likely named after him.

One of the four companies of the Dutch militia was entirely Jewish. A guard house in a fort called "guard-house of the Jews," referred to as *excubiae Iudaeorum*, located between Recife and Olinda, was recorded in a map produced by Cornelis Goliath in 1648 with the name *Jodenwacht*, "Jewish guard."[45] Notably, Moyses (Moisés or Moses) Navarro, Antônio Manuel, and David Testa are the first known Jewish soldiers in the Americas.[46]

Navarro, one of those Jewish soldiers, gained permission to remain in Brazil as a *vrijeluijden* ("free civilian"). He had arrived in Brazil as an *adelborst* ("naval cadet"), and after he asked to be a freeman in 1635, he secured a broker's license, and two years later he became a senhor de engenho ("sugarcane plantation owner") in Jurisseca, Pernambuco. Navarro eventually returned to Amsterdam, and his brothers Jacob and Aaaron later moved to Barbados.[47]

The Dutch built a major fort in Recife (which became the capital of Dutch Brazil) called "Fredrik Hendrik," known in Portuguese as *Forte das Cinco Pontas* ("Fort of the Five Points"), since it was built as a pentagon. The Portuguese later destroyed it and rebuilt the fort with four points, yet the structure today is still known by the same name, *Cinco Pontas*.[48] A Dutch report describes the fort: "Fort Frederik Hendrik [also] known as the Fort das Cinco Pontas . . . From there can be seen all the ships at anchor in Recife's harbor . . . it also protects the waterholes, which are the only ones that provide water to Recife and Antonio Vaz [the island mentioned earlier, adjacent to Recife] in times of necessity and siege"[49] We learn from original Dutch reports that other forts were built throughout Brazil's northeast, from Pernambuco, Itamaracá, and Paraíba, to Rio Grande do Norte, Ceará, and Fort Maurits, in Penedo (today in Alagoas, on the north bank of River São Francisco), "about twenty-five miles from the sea. It is a pentagonal fort and is perched on a rocky escarpment, eighty feet above the river."[50] According to the same report, Recife became the Dutch headquarters in Brazil, and "the members of the High and Secret Council, as well as the Political Counsellors, all reside there. It constitutes the main port for all major shipping throughout the captaincy of Pernambuco. It is there that all the general warehouses lock away all foodstuffs, artillery, military supplies, and merchandise."[51]

Other forts included Fort Ghijselin, Fort Prince Willem in Afogados to the west of Antônio Vaz Island, which was quadrangular (today a neighborhood in the eastern part of Recife), Porto Calvo, Pontal, Cabo Santo Agostinho, Fort Ernestus, Fort Waedenburgh, and Fort Emilia (on the island of Santo Antônio).[52] The name Fort Brum was a corrupted version of "Bruyne", as in Fort Bruyne, and Fort Schoonenborch was built by Mathias Beck (by the Pajeú River), yet after the Dutch left, the Portuguese renamed it Fortaleza de Nossa Senhora da Assunção ("Fortress of Our Lady of Asuncion"), where the modern city of Fortaleza stood (capital of today's state of Ceará).[53] Descriptions of members of Catholic religious orders are abundant, as outlined by Caspar van Baerle:

The Catholic population is granted free exercise of religion, although not without objections and grumbling by some. Their ministers are either clergy or monks, known as presbyters and priests, who are subject to their vicar; they celebrate mass and assist with the sick. The monks are Franciscans, Carmelites, and Benedictines, according to their order. The Franciscan order is the largest, housed in six convents distinguished for their beautiful architecture. The first one is in Frederica, the second in Iguaraçu, the third in Olinda, the fourth in Ipojuca, the fifth on the island of Antonio Vaz, and the sixth in Serinhaím.[54]

The dichotomy of being officially a Jew and a New Christian would remain vague, and there are examples of ambiguous and contradictory cases.[55] For example, indecision and internal identity conflicts were seen in the case of Manoel Gomes Chacão from Trancoso, Portugal, who had migrated to Itamaracá and returned to Judaism in 1642 with the legalization of Jewry during Dutch rule. However, a year later he decided to return to Catholicism, underlining this internal as well as external conflict of identity and the sociological perception of being stigmatized as Jewish.[56] As Bruno Feitler points out, this was also the case of a New Christian who had returned to Judaism, Simão (Isaac Franco) Drago. He migrated to Amsterdam and died as a Jew there in 1662. In another case, Manuel Rodrigues (Moisés Moreno), born in Portugal and a resident of Pernambuco, moved to Amsterdam as a Jew in 1636.[57]

However, not all New Christians and Jews in Brazil and Amsterdam would have straddled religions—voluntarily switching from one religion to another—because of deeper religious reasons or internal existential struggles alone. There are many factors that we do not know about, which may have had nothing to do with those reasons; for example, love, marriage, fleeing a crime, debt, or procuring higher social status and practical socioeconomic opportunities. There are some common parallels seen in the decision-making process of migrants in general who move from one place to another. For example, people migrate for multiple reasons and factors, and not economic reasons alone. Many of those factors involve non-economic reasons, which sometimes are interrelated (e.g., adventure, curiosity, geographical imagination, love, marriage, or to join family).[58] The complex reasoning for New

Christian "reversal conversions" to Judaism, or voluntary conversions from Judaism to Christianity, for example, were complex and multifold. Therefore, these processes of reversal conversions may have involved many unknown factors that are not necessarily driven by persecution or economic factors alone.

The First Synagogues in the Americas

The first synagogue in the Americas, Kahal Kadosh Zur Israel, was established in 1640 in Recife, Pernambuco, located at *Rua dos Judeus* ("Street of the Jews"). Beforehand, in 1636, that location had already been a gathering place for local Jews who were known to have met for Judaic practices at a rented house there.[59] Evidence also shows that a pre-existing local Brazilian New Christian population in Recife with a "robust Judaizing subculture" existed prior to the establishment of this synagogue—and prior to the arrival of the Dutch when Judaizing was forbidden.[60]

A secondary synagogue, Kahal Kadosh Magen, founded by Rabbi Mosseh Rafael de Aguilar, functioned independently between 1637 and 1649 in Olinda, about 10 km/6 miles north of Recife.[61] However, the Dutch did not allow the establishment of any other synagogue. The Jewish community in Pernambuco maintained its own charity societies, schools, *mikveh*, and cemeteries as well as its close ties to the Portuguese-Jewish community in Amsterdam.[62] Two Jewish religious schools were created in Recife (Talmud Torah and Etz Hayim), and a Jewish cemetery was established on the banks of the Capiberibe River.[63] This Jewish cemetery first appears on record in 1639, identified in a map as *De Jodse Begraef Plaets* ("The Jewish Cemetery"), as cartographer Cornelis Bastaanz Goliath had marked it as "Joden Kerckhof" ("Jewish Churchyard").[64] However, the Bethaym ("cemetery") had already existed prior to 1630—although details about its origin are still unknown.[65] The Jewish cemetery, named Sítio dos Coelhos, was located in an old map, in the neighborhood of Boa Vista, about two kilometers from the main synagogue in Recife (today a *favela*, "slum," named Favela dos Coelhos).[66]

The Register of Regulations and Decisions of the Portuguese-Jewish community in Recife, Pernambuco (5409–5414), 1648–1654, includes the names of its prominent members during the Jewish year of 5409, such as: Jaacob [Jacob] Drago, Abraham de Azerredo, Jacob Navarro, David Diaz, Ishac [Isaac] Atias, Abrahao Israel, Jacob Valverde, and Benjamin de Pina. In this register, statements are made clear about the role of the community's charitable contributions through the charity "Dotar") and the assistance to the poor and orphans in Amsterdam or any part of Brazil, Paraíba, "Resiphe" [Recife], or the island of Antonio Vaz.[67] This register was written in Portuguese and underlines the significance of the Portuguese language and cultural component—a thread that is weaved throughout this book.[68]

The "Dotar" was not restricted to only Jews in Amsterdam or Recife, but to all people across global regions. This flexibility is understandable since Jews were not allowed to declare themselves openly in most parts of the world, which allowed the charity to reach those who wished to remain anonymous as New Christians receiving help from a Jewish charity without creating a public stir and fear of potential denouncements that could ensue thereafter.[69]

During Dutch rule, the street of the main synagogue in Recife was named *Bockestraet*; however, after the Dutch left Brazil in 1654, the Portuguese renamed it *Rua da Cruz* ("Street of the Cross"), and later the name changed again to *Rua do Bom Jesus* ("Street of the Good Jesus").[70] José Antônio Gonsalves de Mello points out that this street was also popularly known as *Rua do Bode* ("Street of the Goat"); most likely this name emerged as an injurious local reference to the Jewish community living there.[71]

The name changes of this street here marks yet another example of the geographical process of palimpsest discussed earlier in the Introduction, and of the silencing of Luso-Brazilian Jewry and a submerged memory in colonial Brazil.[72] In this concept of "place" an accumulation of subsequent cultural "layers" are metaphorically stacked upon each other, yet ultimately become submerged like a medieval palimpsest. Alberto Dines describes that this synagogue in Recife had been submerged in time yet never forgotten.[73]

When the Dutch left Brazil in 1654, and Judaism was forbidden again, the building where the main synagogue in Recife was located was then given to João Fernandes Vieira (for his participation and role in the Portuguese successful insurrection against the Dutch), and eventually donated to a Catholic congregation, Congregação do Oratório de São Felipe de Neri, in 1679.

The building deteriorated significantly over time and eventually it was demolished, and two row houses were built in its place, which then passed over to a charitable health and social assistance organization (Casa da Misericórdia do Recife). In the late eighteenth century, it was transformed again, this time into a chapel, Capela do Senhor Bom Jesus das Portas, which was eventually demolished in 1850.[74]

Today a commemorative plaque is placed at the old location of the main synagogue in Recife. The name of the street where it is located reads, *Rua do Bom Jesus antiga/Rua dos Judeus 1636–1654* ("Old Street of the Good Jesus/Street of the Jews 1636–1654"); however, the official street name is still Rua do Bom Jesus.

Restoration and archaeological verification contributed to its status of a Brazilian national monument and heritage site through Brazilian legislation in 1998.[75] Archaeological evidence has also found old *mikvahs* (Jewish ritual "baths") and prayer rooms there.[76] Today a cultural center is located where Kahal Kadosh Zur Israel in Recife once stood.[77] In 2000, it was declared a national heritage site by the Brazilian Historical and Artistic Institute of Patrimony (IPHAN) (Instituto do Patrimônio Histórico e Artístico Nacional)—the Brazilian federal agency dedicated to the preservation of historic sites in Brazil, and, in 2002, the building was restored, and the day of March 18 was declared "National Day of Jewish Immigration."[78]

The Jewish Cultural Center of Pernambuco was inaugurated in 2001 on the premises of the old synagogue in Recife and has become a historic monument to the Jewish legacy in Brazil. It can be visited by tourists today. The location of this old synagogue also serves as the "Jewish Center of Pernambuco," *Centro Judaico de Pernambuco*. About two hundred local Brazilians who self-identify as *B'nei Anussim* (from the Hebrew, "children of the coerced ones") and claim Portuguese-Jewish ancestry with those who were forcibly converted by decree of the Crown and the Inquisition, annually gather in front of the old synagogue in Recife to listen to readings of Meguilat Esther, the "Book of Esther."[79]

It is worthwhile to point out that the cemetery at Bet Haim in Curaçao is considered a UNESCO World Heritage site and Jodensavanne in Suriname is next on the UNESCO list for consideration as a World Heritage site.[80] Although the city of Olinda, Pernambuco, was declared a UNESCO World

Heritage site, the first Portuguese-Jewish synagogue founded in the Americas in Recife has not yet received such international recognition or attention.

The Importance of Jewry in the Northeast Region

So, how did Recife benefit from having two synagogues? In addition to being a vital gathering place and a sacred space to worship for Jews, they became centralized places in which the Jewish community could organize itself socially and politically, adding to their cohesive economic and social influence (especially in the urban city of Recife).[81] Judaic life was centered mainly around the synagogue in urban Recife and around institutions tied to a traditional Jewish community.[82] The secondary synagogue in Olinda, located about 10 km/6 miles from Recife, was also a coastal town but not as large as Recife; however, both Recife and Olinda were far away from main agricultural clusters in the hinterlands.

Due to the geographical distance from those coastal and urban synagogues, a few esnogas became meeting places and "informal synagogues" where local Jews and Judaizers could gather in rural regions in the interior of the northeast—in the Sertão. Bruno Feitler's study shows that in rural Paraíba, for instance, Pedro da Costa Caminha participated in Judaic ceremonies at the house of Jacob Nunes, David Paredes, and Isaac Serrano around the Engenho São João.[83] Local Jews (and New Christians) would also gather to celebrate the Jewish Sabbath at the house of Moisés Peixoto, where prayers were conducted in Hebrew.[84] They gathered in a "large living room" for Judaic ceremonies; however, they were not *Yahidim* (i.e., from the term "*Yahid*," meaning an official member of a Jewish congregation, and registered according to the congregation rules and regulations, the Ascamot).[85] Bruno Feitler explains that Ambrósio Vieira, a senhor de engenho in Paraíba, participated in these gatherings, and would donate a small quantity of sugarcane to impoverished Portuguese-Jews in Amsterdam. Other rural esnogas operated throughout the rural outskirts in the Brazilian northeast, for example in Itamaracá, Olinda, Ipojuca (e.g., the Valença Caminha family, south of Pernambuco), and Penedo, where Samuel Israel acted as the local rabbi.[86] Hence, while traditional Jewish community life centered around the urban synagogues, especially in Recife, there were examples of the dispersion of

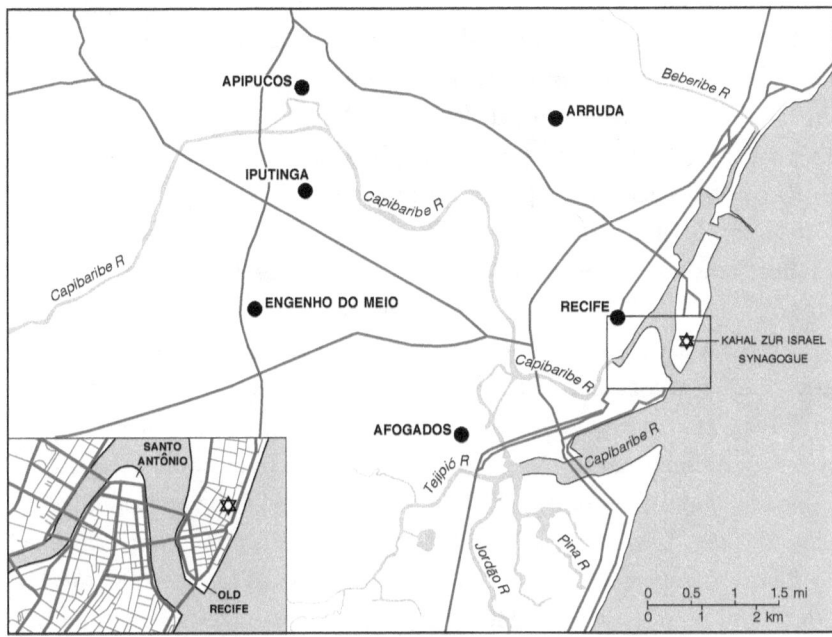

Map 10. Synagogue in Recife

Jewry and Jewish practices throughout the northeast hinterlands, the Sertão, attended by several members, ranging from senhores de engenho to "peddlers," known as *mascates*.⁸⁷ After the Dutch left in 1654, there is some indication that their descendants may have fled further into other areas of the Sertão in Rio Grande do Norte and Ceará.⁸⁸

Portuguese-Jewish Immigrants from Amsterdam

By 1642, another two hundred Portuguese Jews arrived in Recife from Amsterdam along with Rabbi Aguilar, who became the rabbi of the secondary synagogue in Olinda.⁸⁹ Among those who arrived was Aguilar's nephew, Isaac de Castro, also known as José (Joseph) de Lis (his baptized Christian name), who was born in Tartas, France, and who went to Recife with his uncle. However, soon after arriving in Brazil, he was accused of murder and fled to neighboring Bahia to avoid prosecution (Bahia was still under Portuguese rule).[90] I found the Inquisition dossier for Joseph de Lis (alias Isaac de Castro), aged 20, arrested in 1645 (processo 11071). His parents were listed as Agostinho de Paredes, a New Christian and a tailor (the Paredes family was clearly targeted by the Inquisition half a century later in Rio, as I discuss in Chapter 6), and his mother was Violante da Costa, also New Christian (listed as from "vila de Tartáz, província de Gascunha, França," and living in Salvador da Baía de Todos os Santos) (processo 11071).

Isaac de Castro was quickly denounced as a Judaizer as he had been seen attending an esnoga in Recife. Witnesses alleged that Castro's real mission in Bahia was to teach Judaism to local Brazilian New Christians, and he was considered a subversive by local authorities and the Inquisition.[91] Castro was imprisoned and then sent to Lisbon and sentenced to be burned alive for choosing the "Law of Moses," and at the age of 22 his body was consumed by flames. The crowd that witnessed his death heard his screams, "*Shema, Israel!*" ("Listen, Israel!").[92] However, Arnold Wiznitzer claims that it is more likely that he died exclaiming the words "*Ely, Adonai, Sabohot!*" (roughly "Our Lord of armies") as recorded by an alleged eyewitness.[93] Embracing the "Law of Moses," Isaac de Castro died as a martyr.[94]

As the number of Jews in Recife increased steadily from 1630 on, Arnold Wiznitzer estimates that the number grew to about 1,450 Jews in 1645—that is, over half the population of Recife was estimated to be Jewish.[95] This was a significant proportion of the populace since the total population of Recife in that year was estimated at about 2,899 (other historians estimate the unlikely figure of 5,000 Jews at that time, while José Lúcio de Azevedo estimates 600 Jews, and Isaac S. Emmanuel about 1,000).[96] Gilberto Freyre mentions that the chanting of the melancholic *piyyutim* was often heard in public places around Recife—these were Hebrew liturgical poems, usually sung, chanted, or recited during religious services in a repeated rhythmic pattern (also known as the Hazaj meter in epic poetry also used in Arabic, Persian, Turkish, and Urdu poetry).[97]

Whilst these estimated numbers of Jews vary greatly, the influx of Portuguese Jews from Amsterdam to Recife increased substantially, as seen by the increase in complaints made by the Dutch that "Brazil was being flooded by Jews arriving on every boat."[98] One traveller who visited Recife in 1640 wrote, "among the free inhabitants of Brazil . . . those of the Jewish nation were the most considerable in number . . . They had a vast traffic beyond the rest, they purchased sugarmills and built stately houses in the Recife."[99]

By 1638, the number of sugar plantations was listed in a Dutch report, with 408 engenhos: 108 in Pernambuco; 20 in Itamaracá; 20 in Paraíba; and 260 in Rio Grande [do Norte].[100] A year later, of the 166 engenhos in existence in Pernambuco, 60 percent were Portuguese-owned, 34 percent were Dutch, and 6 percent were owned by known Jews.[101] Other than Moyses Navarro, other major Jewish senhores de engenho during Dutch rule, for example, included Duarte Saraiva, Fernão do Vale, and Pedro Lopes de Vera.[102]

Despite being forbidden by law, intermixing between Catholics, Old and New Christians, Dutch, blacks, and Indigenous populations was widespread. However, descriptions of sexual activity may not have always been consensual, as the prevalence of rampant unpunished rape is documented in reports. Descriptions suggested that "fornication" with blacks (slaves or not) and prostitution were commonplace. As Caspar van Baerle describes:

> Jews were permitted to hold their services and celebrate their feast days within a private space, but not in public areas; the Council would attempt to restrain the illicit sexual activities of female Negroes, of fornication, and of prostitution, the ultimate companions of good fortune turned bad.[103]

Important Figures During Dutch Rule in Brazil

Rabbi Isaac Aboab da Fonseca, born in Portugal and raised in Amsterdam, moved to Recife as the rabbi at the synagogue Kahal Kadosh Zur Israel, becoming the first rabbi in the New World.[104] Fonseca was the author of the first poem written in Hebrew in the Americas, written in 1646, *Zekher asiti lenifloat El* ("I erect a memorial to the miracles of God"), where he refers to the Portuguese Jews in exile and the Dutch siege of Recife.[105] Born in 1605 in Castro Daire, Viseu (Beira Alta), Portugal, he was the son of David Aboab and Isabel da Fonseca and had migrated to Amsterdam with his family when he was young.[106] After leaving Recife, Aboab da Fonseca returned

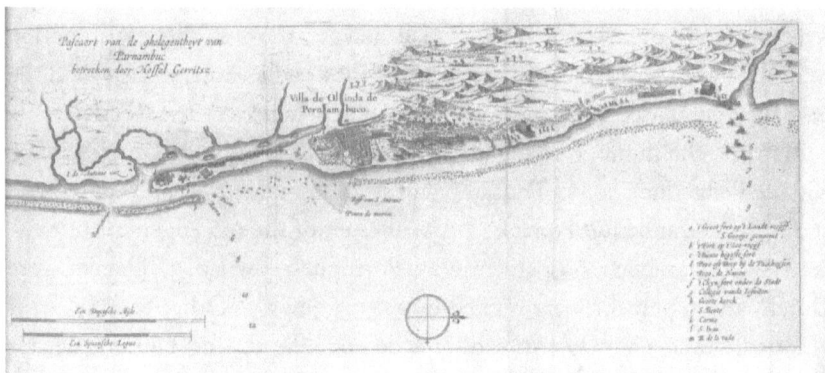

Figure 5.1. Map of Olinda. "A true relation of the vanquishing of the towne Olinda, cituated in the captiania of Phernambuco . . ." Bird's-eye view of the settlement of Olinda, Pernambuco, Brazil, including the Island of Antônio Vaz and Recife. Created by Henrik Cornelis Lancq, b. 1568. Published by Jan Frederickszoon Stam, 1630. Courtesy of the John Carter Brown Library (call number 585 E96t).

Figure 5.2. Maurício de Nassau. *Mauritius Nassauieae & Comes, Brazilae preaefectus, Qua patet orbi. Th. Matham*. Created by Franciscus Plante. Title: *Mauritiados libri xvii. Francisci Plante Brugensis Mauritiodos libri xvii*. Published by Ex Officina Ioannis Maire, 1647. Courtesy of the John Carter Brown Library (call number F647 P713f/2-Size.

Figure 5.3. Map of Recife, known as Mauritsstadt. "A plan of Recife, Mauritsstadt, Pernambuco, sea banks or shoals, and fortifications." Created by Pierre Moreau, fl. 1651–1652. Title: *Histoire des derniers troubles du Brésil entre Hollandais et les Portugais.* Published by Jan Hendriksz, Jan Riuwertz, 1652. Courtesy of the John Carter Brown Library (call number E652 M837k).

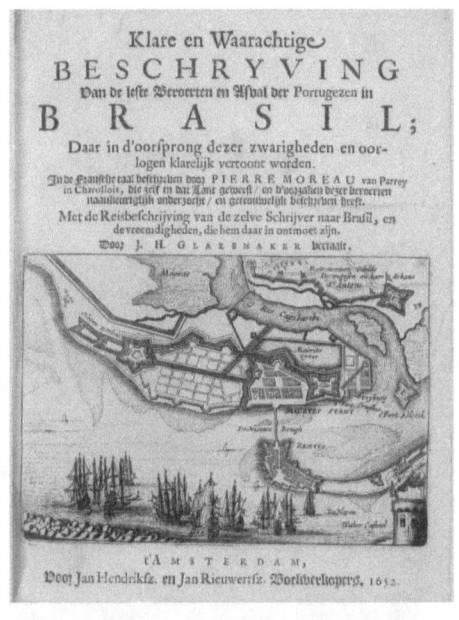

Figure 5.4. Portrait of the first rabbi in the Americas: Isaac Aboab da Fonseca (1605–1693). Created by Aernout Naghtgael, Amsterdam, 5441 (i,e. 1681). Title: *Parafrasis comentado sobre el Pentateuco.* Doctissimo y Clarissimo Senor H. H. Yshack Aboab. Rabino del K. K. de Amsterdam. Published by Estampado en caza de Iaacob de Cordova. Courtesy of the John Carter Brown Library (call number FA681 F676p/ 1-Size).

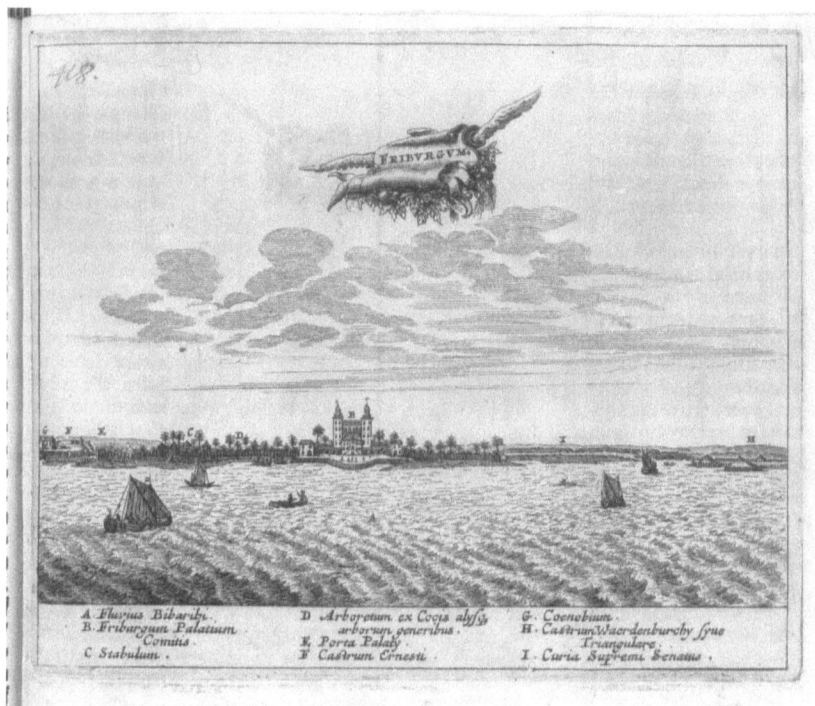

Figure 5.5. Map of Friburgum Palace, Recife, Brazil, 1656. Created by Caspar van Baerle. Rerum per octennium in Brasilia et alibi nuper gestarum historia. Brasilianische Geschichte. Johan Maurits van Nassau-Siegen (1604–1679), colonial governor of the Brazilian colony of the Dutch West India Company, built the Friburgum Palace or "Castle of Freedom" at Vrijburg. This image is derived from the author's Rerum per octennium in Brasilia, Amsterdam, 1647. Published by Tobias Silberling. Courtesy of the John Carter Brown Library (call number F659, record number 01597–006).

to Amsterdam in 1656, where he was elected head of the Talmudic Academy, and served as the Haham at the Portuguese-Jewish Congregation of Amsterdam until his death in 1693 at age 88. He is buried at Ouderkerk, on the banks of the Amstel River, beside his wife, Esther, and had belonged to the Rabbinical tribunal that excommunicated eminent Portuguese-Jewish philosopher Baruch Spinoza in Amsterdam in 1656—he was the person who read Spinoza's sentence.[107]

Rabbi Fonseca was an associate of another prominent Portuguese Jew from Amsterdam, the founder of Anglo-Jewry, Menasseh Ben Israel (his Portuguese name was Manoel Dias Soeiro).[108] Menasseh's brother, Ephraim Soeiro, had been dispatched to Recife to watch over joint commercial interests of their brother-in-law, Jonas Abrabanel.[109] Menasseh, in turn, was in close contact with Padre Antônio de Vieira (1608–1680), known as "The Apostle of Brazil."[110]

Vieira famously supported the integration of New Christians into Portuguese society, actively criticized the local Inquisition for "fabricating Jews" out of many "innocent" Catholics, addressed numerous letters to kings and popes on behalf of the New Christians, and reputedly authored influential tracts against the Portuguese Holy Office, such as the *Notícias recônditas* and *Gravamina*.[111] Vieira commented in his letters about the importance of Portuguese New Christians and their successful commercial activities and entrepreneurial skills.[112] Vieira claimed that New Christians were vital to Portugal's economy and called for a reform to Portugal's harsh and biased Inquisition.[113] Since Vieira was the only voice in the seventeenth century among Catholics to defend the rights of Jews, New Christians, and Judaism, the Inquisition thought that his work "smelled of Judaism."[114]

Vieira was also a defender of Indigenous populations in the Americas, and argued that they should not be captured as slaves and treated with such brutality, which was interpreted as an affront to the Inquisition.[115] He accused the Inquisition of acting as a "factory of Jews" that sought out Jewry only to "reproduce" Jews artificially by increasing the number of arrests (in his publication, *Esperanças de Portugal*, which was largely inspired by Menasseh Ben Israel's *Esperanza de Israel*, published in 1650).[116] When Vieira was arrested and imprisoned by the Inquisition (1663–1667) he maintained that Jews could convert to the Catholic faith without unnecessary coercion.[117]

I found Vieira's dossiers in my examination of the Inquisition (along with hundreds of additional documents). He was arrested in 1663 and sentenced to a private auto-da-fé in 1667, and was forbidden to preach or write again (processo 01664). However, Pope Clement X granted him a pardon, and in 1668 he went to Rome, and then returned to Brazil where he died in Salvador, Bahia, in 1697.[118]

Jews and the Dutch in the Tropics

Jews living in Brazil under Dutch rule were allowed to own shops and participate in wholesale and retail trade and commerce, which resulted in a new type of experiment of a Jewish society in the New World, and which, as Jonathan Israel explains, was "based on a wide range of trade and finance linked to tropical agriculture."[119] Jewish shop owners and small business owners included merchants such as Jacob Valverde, Moses Netto, Moses Zacutto, Jacob Fundão, Moses Navarro, David Atias, Benjamin de Pinah, Abraham de Azevedo, Fernão Martins, and David Brandão.[120] Moisés Orfali claims that Abraham de Mercado was the first Jewish doctor and pharmacist in the New World, described by Menasseh ben Israel as one of the most distinguished leaders of the Jewish community in Recife.[121]

Yehudah Machabeu became the first professional calligrapher in the Americas (who used all kinds of scripts, such as *Letra Redondilla*, *Letra Grifa*, and *Letra Ynglesa*). He was also known as Louis Nunes do Vale, a member of the Portuguese-Jewish Congregation of Amsterdam. Between 1646 and 1654 he lived in Recife, and after the Dutch left Brazil in 1654 he moved to France—living in La Rochelle for three years before returning to Amsterdam.[122]

Notably, two events instigated by a vilified Jew known as Jacob Rabbi (born in Waldeck, Germany) and who was working with the Dutch, are still discussed to this day. At São Gonçalo do Amarante (in Rio Grande do Norte) stands a new monument to the "martyrs" whom Jacob Rabbi allegedly assassinated over three centuries ago. Jacob Rabbi would become doubly vilified in Brazilian public and popular spheres, both as a Jew and as an ally of the Calvinist Dutch and Janduis tribe. The polemic figure of Jacob Rabbi stems from his participation in the events on July 15, 1645, when allegedly, seventy Catholics were praying at a local chapel in Canguaretama, Capela de Nossa Senhora das Candeias, at the Engenho Canhaú (Rio Grande do Norte). Dutch soldiers and Janduis and Potiguares allies, led by Jacob Rabbi, locked the chapel doors and purportedly proceeded to kill all of them.[123] Another eighty people were allegedly killed on the banks of the Rio Uruaçú that same year in October.

Jacob Rabbi had arrived in Brazil on January 23, 1637, along with the

Dutch, and soon married a woman from the local Janduis tribe named Domingas, and served as interpreter for the Dutch and Indigenous allies in northeast Brazil. Eventually he came to own land in Rio Grande do Norte; however, he was assassinated in 1646.[124] He was blamed for the two massacres, providing fodder for anti-Semitic historiography. Brazilian scholar Luís Câmara Cascudo is clear about his opinion on Jacob:

> A Jew of classic legends, without scruples, mean, a thief, a coward. He is a mentor of the Janduis [tribe] ... a Jewish merchant who craves profit ... buying low and confiscating assets from Portuguese. The useless killings brought him profits. Rabbi never lost the opportunity to negotiate well.[125]

Hence, Cascudo placed responsibility solely on Jacob Rabbi, without mentioning any Dutch administrative blame or Dutch orders. Today, the Vatican claims that those who were killed there were massacred for refusing to convert to Calvinism. Therefore, on December 21 in 1998, Pope John II canonized them, and the Vatican considers them "martyrs" at the "Massacres at Cunhaú and Uruaçú," although only thirty of those killed were identified.[126] The ceremony took place at the Vatican on March 5, 2000.[127]

The Aftermath of Dutch Rule

Tensions between Jews and Old Christians began to increase. Local Portuguese merchants had written a letter to the governor protesting, "poor Jews had come to the colony and enriched themselves at the Christians' expense."[128] As Herbert I. Bloom claims, it is likely that most of those same Christians who protested against Jews (perhaps because of resentment, jealousy, or business rivalry) may well have been New Christians themselves. These complaints and anti-Jewish sentiments held no sway, and the Supreme Council of the WIC decided to treat Jews as if they were Dutch.[129] However, the Dutch rule proved to be a brief interlude for Jewry in Brazil. The twenty-four years of occupation and wars culminated in the Dutch defeat by the Portuguese forces in 1654.

The grassroots Brazilian movement to fight against the Dutch occupation in Brazil was known as Insurreição Pernambucana ("Pernambucan Insurrection"). As early as 1648, at the Engenho of São João, Portuguese-born men in Brazil rallied other Brazilians to fight against Dutch control and reoccupy Brazil's northeast using small, organized ambushes, known as *campanhias de emboscadas*. The main cities of Dutch-controlled Brazil were Mauritsstad (Recife, the capital until then), Frederikstad (João Pessoa, today in Paraíba), and Nieuw Amsterdam (Natal, today in Rio Grande do Norte). André Vidal de Negreiros, João Fernandes Vieira, Henrique Dias, a former slave "governor of people of color in Brazil," and Filipe Camarão, a Potiguar Indian Chief (both Camarão and Dias are mentioned in Chapter 1), would lead Portuguese military troops against Dutch forces.[130] At the Battle of Guararapes, the Portuguese troops, under the command of Francisco Barreto de Meneses, later known as the "Restorer of Pernambuco," won two battles against the Dutch in two subsequent confrontations—in 1648, and then in 1649 at the Morro dos Guararapes, Pernambuco (today Jaboatão dos Guararapes, in the municipality of the metropolitan region of Recife). The Portuguese troops in Brazil consisted mostly of Portuguese-born men, former black slaves, and Indigenous men.

The situation for the Dutch was not good. Food had become scarce, and more important, the Dutch warned in their report, "we are unable to assemble a force of more than three thousand to three thousand, three hundred men. Consequently, we are starting to feel that our forces are insufficient."[131] Finally, after ongoing precarious living conditions, the Dutch were defeated.

The Dutch signed the Treaty of Taborda, in front of the Forte das Cinco Pontas in Recife (today the neighborhood of São José, Recife). This agreement meant the Dutch had lost control of Recife and would abandon all possessions in Brazil because all their troops left the colony in January 1654. A final treaty that confirmed the agreement was signed seven years later in 1661, known as the Treaty of the Hague (Tratado de Haia), whereby the Dutch formally agreed to return possession of all Brazilian territory for 4 million cruzados (estimated to be equivalent to about 4.5 tons of gold at the time).[132]

The local sugar economy suffered because of the conflict between the Dutch and Portuguese, and especially because of the destruction of many engenhos and sugarcane fields—from Pernambuco, Paraíba, to Rio Grande do Norte.¹³³ The Dutch failed to secure control in the hinterlands in the Sertão, since most of the time during their twenty-four-year rule in northeast Brazil was spent battling the Portuguese.¹³⁴ Stuart B. Schwartz explains how the impacts of the Dutch in Brazil were "long lasting and set into motion a series of processes with great influence over the remainder of the seventeenth century and beyond."¹³⁵ One of those legacies, as Schwartz claims, was the multiracial nativist collaboration (or its myth) which aimed to fight the Dutch, and which became the "basis of early Brazilian nationalism."¹³⁶

When the Portuguese re-established their political power in 1654, they reinstated anti-Jewish statutes and restrictions.¹³⁷ At that time, because the legal freedoms of Jews and Judaic practices were again disallowed, hundreds left Brazil for Amsterdam, Suriname, or the Caribbean islands, and twenty-three of them went to New Amsterdam (today New York City), and some to Newport (Rhode Island).¹³⁸ Again, the themes of migration, mobility, and spatial processes emerge as central themes in this narrative.

The WIC suffered significant financial losses with the defeat of Recife and northeast Brazil. The focus of the WIC would from now on rest on the potential in New Netherland, established in 1614 as the first Dutch colony in North America, spanning parts of what is now New York, New Jersey, Pennsylvania, Maryland, Connecticut, and Delaware (and New Amsterdam corresponds to roughly where Manhattan is today).¹³⁹ Most of the financial support that had once been directed to Brazil, was now directed to New Netherland.¹⁴⁰

Jews from Brazil Migrate to North America

In 1654, twenty-three Brazilian Jews from Recife became the first Jewish immigrants to arrive in North America. These Brazilian immigrants were directly linked to the first synagogue built in the Americas in Recife, Brazil—that is, the first Jewish immigrants to arrive in North America were from Brazil, a fact that remains unknown in most public and academic spheres.¹⁴¹ They arrived on the Dutch caravel *Valck* (Falcon), captained by Jan Craeck.¹⁴² Shortly thereafter, they established the first Jewish settlement in North America—Congregation Kahal Kadosh Shearith Israel, which became the only synagogue in New York City from 1654 until 1825 (today located on 2 West 70th Street in Manhattan).[143] Twenty-three Jews embarked from Recife to New Amsterdam on the *St. Catarina*, commanded by Jaques De La Motthe. According to Isaac Markens, they included: Abram de Lucena, David Israel, Moses Ambrasias, Abram De LaSimon, Salvador D'Andrada, Joseph da Costa, David Fiera, Jacob C. Henrique, Isaac Mesa, and Isaac Levy.[144]

Other Jews from Brazil arrived in Newport (Rhode Island). The names of some of the families arriving in Newport in 1658 include Portuguese Jews who had arrived via Barbados: Aboab; Pacheco, spelled "Pacheckoe"; and Campanall, spelled "Camperwell."[145] The Jeshuat Israel congregation in Newport dates back to the year they arrived, 1658, and the Touro Synagogue (or Congregation Jeshuat Israel), which was built later in 1763, is considered to be the old synagogue building still standing in the United States.

As Samuel Oppenheim points out, the connection between Amsterdam, Recife, and Newport is an interesting one. For instance, Isack Abof (a possible transliteration of the Hebrew, Isaac Aboab), who was in Barbados in 1680 and then went to Newport, is likely a descendant of Rabbi Isaac Aboab Fonseca (mentioned earlier, the rabbi at the main synagogue in Recife).[146]

The migration of Portuguese Jews from Brazil to North America in 1654 is tied to a polemic figure, Peter (or Petrus) Stuyvesant, director of the Dutch West India Company in New Netherland, who had connections to Brazil and the Caribbean. He had been appointed in the 1630s as a commercial agent in Fernando de Noronha, off the coast of Pernambuco (mentioned in Chapter 3), then in Curaçao where he was acting governor of the colony, and then in Aruba and Bonaire. After his positions in Brazil and the Dutch Antilles he was appointed director of the WIC in New Netherland from 1647 until 1664, when the British took it over. Stuyvesant vehemently opposed religious plurality, and personally loathed Jews.[147]

Members of the "people of the nation" wrote a petition letter to Stuyvesant, and according to Samuel Oppenheim, this petition letter seeking asylum in New Amsterdam is "undoubtedly one of the most important documents we have in relation to the settlement of the Jews in this country [United States]."[148] The original petition addressed to Stuyvesant, dated September 22, 1654, had never been published until Samuel Oppenheim translated it from Dutch into English and published it in 1909.[149] Here is an extract from the original letter:

> 1655, January, To the Honorable Lords, Directors of the Chartered West India Company, Chamber of the Jewish Nation. City of Amsterdam ... There are many of the nation who have lost their possessions at Pernambuco and have arrived from there in great poverty, and part of them have been dispersed here and there. So that your petitioners had to expend large sums of money for their necessaries of life, and through lack of opportunity all cannot remain here to live. It is well known to your Honors that the Jewish nation in Brazil have at all times been faithful and have striven to guard and maintain that place, risking for that purpose their possessions and their blood. Your Honors should also please consider that many of the Jewish nation are principal shareholders in the Company. They have always striven their best for the Company, and many of their nation have lost immense and great capital in its shares and obligations ... The English also consent at the present time that the Portuguese and Jewish nation may go from London and settle at Barbados, whither also some have gone. As foreign nations consent that the Jewish nation may go to live and trade in their territories, how can your Honors forbid the same and refuse transportation to this Portuguese nation who reside here and have been settled here well on to about sixty years, many also being born here and confirmed burghers, and this to a land that needs people for its increase?[150]

In the only surviving copy of this petition letter, the signatures do not appear, so we do not know who the petitioners were. We learn from this letter how the "Jewish Nation in Brazil" had lost their properties in Pernambuco after the Dutch were defeated, and the petitioners point out that "many of the Jewish nation are principal shareholders in the Company." Note that in these correspondence letters from the WIC, Jews are never referred to as "Spanish *and* Portuguese Jews" or "Sephardim," but categorically as "Portuguese Jews," "People of the Jewish nation in Brazil," or "People of the Hebrew Nation."

After this letter of petition was received, Stuyvesant replied to the board of the WIC. He attempted to have Jews "in a friendly way to depart" the colony. He referred to Jews as "repugnant," "a deceitful race," "hateful enemies and blasphemers of Christ," and "usurers." He refused their entry to the colony; however, he soon rescinded his decision after pressure from the directors of the company, many of whom were major shareholders in the WIC and prominent members of the Portuguese-Jewish community in Amsterdam. As a result, Jewish immigrants were allowed to stay in the colony. This is an extract of the reply from a letter written by Stuyvesant in 1655, also translated and published by Samuel Oppenheim:

> The Jews who have arrived would nearly all like to remain here, but learning that they (with their customary usury and deceitful trading with the Christians) were very repugnant to the inferior magistrates, as also to the people having the most affection for you; the Deaconry also fearing that owing to their present indigence they might become a charge in the coming winter, we have, for the benefit of this weak and newly developing place and the land in general, deemed it useful to require them in a friendly way to depart; praying also most seriously in this connection, for ourselves as also for the general community of your worships, that the deceitful race—such hateful enemies and blasphemers of the name of Christ—be not allowed further to infect and trouble this new colony, to the detraction of your worships and the dissatisfaction of your worships most affectionate subjects.[151]

Thus, under pressure, Stuyvesant retracted his initial refusal to allow those Jews from Recife into New Amsterdam. The shareholders of the Dutch West India Company were divided into two classes: chief shareholders (*Hooftparticipanten*) and minor shareholders (*minder participanien*).[152] Oppenheim's studies report several lists of WIC shareholders; most were Portuguese-Jewish names.[153] Oppenheim also points out that Joseph [José] d'Acosta [da Costa] appears as one of the principal WIC shareholders, one of the first Jews to arrive in New Amsterdam. He was the son of Bento da Costa and brother of Uriel da Costa—who had left Recife, Pernambuco—and by 1655 became a prominent merchant in New Amsterdam.[154]

Peter Stuyvesant would not allow Jews to build a synagogue, forcing them to worship instead at a private house. In 1655, three Portuguese Jews, Abraham de Lucena, Salvador Dandrada ["de Andrade"] and Jacob Cohen, wrote to Stuyvesant and WIC to petition on behalf of the "people of the nation" for a burial ground for Jews, which was later granted.[155] Therefore, Portuguese Jews played an imperative role not only in the founding of the first congregations and synagogues in Recife and Olinda, Brazil, Suriname, and throughout the Caribbean, but also in the establishment of the first Jewish communities in North America. They were active participants and migrants within the colonial period throughout the Americas. More importantly here, they were important participants in colonial Brazil.

Migrations After the Dutch Left Brazil

Brazil would come to suffer economically after the migration of several hundreds of Jews who left Recife in 1654 after the Dutch defeat.[156] Portuguese general Francisco Barreto de Menezes explains that any Dutch citizen from the WIC who was unable to procure passage out of Brazil would still be welcome to stay; however, Jews who remained were not welcomed, and would be swiftly prosecuted by the Inquisition.[157] Therefore, this shift in Brazil's northeast authority and anti-Jewish policy prompted another exodus to London, Amsterdam, North America, and the Caribbean islands.

Among other names of those who left Brazil from the Jewish community in Recife were a few of its prominent members, such as Isaac D'Aguillar, David Rodrigues, Abraham Jacob Rodrigues (and his wife Serafina), Joseph Abenaca, Jacob Serrana, Abraham Ferera, and Abraham Redondo.[158]

Some migrants who left Recife went to England. For example, Samuel da Veiga, a member of the synagogue in Recife, migrated to London and became a prominent banker and jeweler, and one of the elders of Congregation Sha'ar ha-Shamayim in London—he was the first Jew to be admitted as a Freeman of the City of London (he died a victim of the plague in 1665).[159] There is an indication that Portuguese Jews were fleeing to England earlier—before the Dutch left Brazil. For example, a letter from the WIC on February 7, 1646, reports, "A ship from Brazil has been wrecked near the Island of Wight. It carried 148 people, mostly Jews, only 28 have been saved."[160] Another eight Portuguese-Jewish families from Brazil also migrated to

London and joined the Bevis Marks Synagogue (established by Portuguese Jews) in the mid-seventeenth century.[161]

Aron, or Arão ("Abraham") Abravanel Dormido and Solomon Dormido moved to London in 1647. Jacob Navarro moved to Amsterdam; his one brother, Isaac Navarro, moved to Curaçao in 1659, and his other brother, Arão (Abraham) Navarro, moved to Amsterdam—later settling in Barbados, where he died in 1685.[162] Noah L. Gelfand has studied the dispersion of Portuguese Jews from Recife to the Caribbean, and aptly states, ". . . the career of Aaron Navarro . . . provides an excellent example . . . of the types of commercial endeavors, trading networks, and religious activities that characterized Jewish involvement in the Caribbean in the aftermath of the loss of Dutch Brazil."[163]

Abraham de Mercado (the New World's first physician and pharmacist, mentioned earlier) had left Recife for Amsterdam in 1654, and from there went to London. In 1655, he obtained from Oliver Cromwell a passport to Barbados where he was offered a quasi-official position.[164] Joseph Jesurum Mendes, who lived in Recife—the son of David Mendes—also left for Amsterdam in 1654, and from there went to Barbados, where he died in 1699, and was buried in Bridgetown.[165]

One of the oldest Jewish communities in the Caribbean in Bridgetown, Barbados, Kahal Kadosh Nidhe Israel, was established by Portuguese Jews around 1661. As N. Darnell Davis explains, "The Portuguese Jews came to us, either directly from the Brazils, or through Surinam when possessed by us, or on its final evacuation by us to the Dutch, 1667."[166] As Davis points out, the oldest Jewish tombstones in Barbados are of Aron De Mercado (d. 1660) and David Raphael de Mercado (d. 1685): "a Hebrew inscription on the tomb corresponds with these."[167]

A Portuguese Jew, Jacob Joshua Bueno Enriques of the "Hebrew Nation," requested that he and his brothers Joseph and Moses, living in Jamaica, "may use their own law and hold synagogues" in Barbados.[168] The synagogue in Bridgetown was established between 1654 and 1655 by Joseph Jesurun Mendes (alias Luís Dias) and Abraham de Mercado, who was active in the Jewish community of Recife.[169] There were about thirty Portuguese-Jewish families who had moved from Brazil to Barbados, including Abraham de Mercado, and by 1689 more would arrive, totaling about fifty-four families, most of whom lived on "Jew Street" in Bridgetown. Arão Burgos moved from Brazil to Barbados, then later settled in Newport, Rhode Island, in 1679.[170] Gilberto Freyre claims that Barbados became so similar to Brazil that it was virtually a "piece of Northeastern Brazil."[171] From Barbados the sugarcane industry (and the "Brazilian system") was introduced to Jamaica. Although it had been introduced earlier, it only began to flourish with the arrival of Jews from Brazil after the mid-seventeenth century.[172]

Another outcome from these migrations (and another connection to Portuguese Jews) can be seen in the linguistic connection that arose with the influx of Portuguese Jews who migrated from Brazil to Curaçao. The creation of the local patois, Papiamentu, spoken in Curaçao, was allegedly tied to the first wave of Portuguese-speaking Jewish immigrants from Brazil.[173] Abraham Drago was among the first Portuguese-Jewish settlers in Curaçao in 1651, with the Portuguese-Jewish community established shortly afterward in 1659, and the synagogue, Mikvé Israel-Emanuel, built in 1732.[174]

In another case, Portuguese Jews had first arrived in Suriname, in about 1651, along the Pomeroon River near the region of the Essequibo.[175] Prominent Portuguese-Jewish family members, such as Medina (e.g., Francisco Medina), and Pinto families (e.g., Paulo Jacomo Pinto, and Abraham or David Pinto, who were active in the Jewish community of Rotterdam and Amsterdam) acted as representatives in Amsterdam for Jews who migrated from Recife to Suriname, making the necessary arrangements for them to travel, and also as bondsmen for them, when required.[176] Evidence shows that David Nassy would have left Recife and taken his slaves directly to Cayenne and Essequibo (1658–1659), at "Jew's Savannah," up the river from today's Paramaribo.[177] Dutch Guiana at that time was not a single "nation"; rather, it was a combined name for the Dutch colonies of Suriname, Essequibo, Berbice, Pomeroon, Demerary, and Cayenne.[178] In the Portuguese-Jewish colony on the Pomeroon River, in the region of Essequibo (today British Guyana) and the Jewish colony in Cayenne (today French Guiana), synagogues were only established between 1651 and 1664, and the first mention of a synagogue in Suriname is found in the grant of the British governor, dated August 17, 1665.[179]

Some Dutch Calvinists also migrated to the Caribbean (as they followed their assigned professional appointments with the WIC). For example,

Mathias Beck, vice-director of the WIC, left Ceará, went to Tobago, and then moved to Barbados before going to Curaçao, where he lived until his death in 1668.[180] Beck had lived in Brazil since 1636—first in Itamaracá, and then in Rio Grande do Norte at the Engenho Cunhaú, after which he went to Ceará. He had introduced sugarcane cultivation in Barbados and Curaçao, with the commercial and technical knowledge he had acquired in Brazil (in Dutch "Brazilië").[181]

All these earliest Portuguese-Jewish congregations, synagogues, and cemeteries mentioned above—for instance in New York City, Rhode Island, and London, and throughout the Caribbean—were clearly founded by Portuguese Jews (specifically), yet today they are known as "Sephardic" sites or infelicitously as "Spanish *and* Portuguese"—but not as "Portuguese-Jewish sites," which would be more appropriate and accurate.

The End of the Inquisition and Independence from Portugal

As the new gold boom emerged in Brazil's center-west regions of Minas Gerais and Goiás (1690–1750s), known in Brazil as ciclo do ouro (as mentioned earlier), this region received a new influx of foreign immigrants as well as internal migrants—especially New Christians. Their arrests in the first quarter of the eighteenth century increased significantly in Minas Gerais, particularly in the hamlets of Vila Rica, Sêrro Frio, Mariana, Pinhal, and Paracatu—simultaenously with the emergence of the Age of Gold.[182] One study retells the story of Miguel Teles da Costa, a New Christian from Minas Gerais, who was arrested by the Inquisition in 1713 for the crime of Judaism.[183] He had been appointed as captain (*capitão-mor*) of the vilas de Itanhaém, Iha Grande de Paraty, and had owned land in Nossa Senhora do Carmo, being one of the first settlers of the region. He was accused of being a part of a secret society of New Christians, mostly merchants and miners of Rio das Mortes, and was imprisoned for the crime of Judaism, and taken to Lisbon. There, he was sentenced to an auto-da-fé, all his assets were confiscated, and eventually he went mad and died indigent.[184]

During the eighteenth century, the population density shifted from the northeast region to the southeast, mainly to Rio de Janeiro. In my examination I found that most of the arrests by the Inqusition in Brazil after the 1700s occurred in Rio de Janeiro, and of the 444 total arrests for Judaism in Brazil, 272 were made in Rio alone during that period (see details of results in Chapter 6). By the early eighteenth century, the city and population of Rio de Janeiro began to grow, and the Inquisition targeted its New Christian residents suspected of Judaizing, most of them doctors, lawyers, sugarcane industry experts, and merchants.[185] By the late seventeenth century, a large proportion of the New Christian population was already living in Rio de Janeiro, and made up about two-thirds of the total "white" population there.[186] Moreover, by the early eighteenth century, out of a total population of twenty thousand free whites living in Rio, an estimated two thousand were New Christians (10 percent).[187] New Christians living in Rio de Janeiro increasingly came under the surveillance of the Inquisition, resulting in hundreds of arrests in the early eighteenth century.[188] A French traveller once described Rio as "a den of Jews," *um antro de Judeus*.[189]

However, by the mid-eighteenth century, as Stuart Schwartz puts it, "the cultural and religious distinctiveness of the new Christians faded away."[190] Yet it was only much later in 1773 that the category of New Christian was removed with the new reformas Pombalinas ("Pombaline reforms") issued by the Marquês de Pombal.[191]

This tumultuous period of the mid- to late eighteenth century coincides with the expulsion of all Jesuits from Brazil in 1759. As discussed in Chapter 1, the presence of Jesuits in colonial Brazil had been mired with accusations that they had been callously profiting from sugar, cotton, cattle, using African and Indigenous slave labor, and avoiding taxes, and it took over two centuries for the Portuguese to finally expel all Jesuits throughout Brazil.

Sebastião José de Carvalho e Melo (1699–1782), the Marquês de Pombal (the Marquis of Pombal) and minister to the king, José I of Portugal, implemented new economic and political reforms (*reformas Pombalinas*) which enabled him to finally expel all Jesuits from the entire Portuguese Empire in 1759. Notably, he also eliminated the category of "New Christian"—a sociocultural marker almost two centuries old, that carried a distinct form of discrimination with long-lasting impacts on Portuguese populations of Jewish ancestry, no matter how distant.[192] However, I found an example of a

New Christian who was arrested and imprisoned after this date in Brazil for the crime of Judaism: José Ricardo de Morais, born in Meia Ponte, Rio de Janeiro, listed as a lavrador, and living in Vila Boa de Goiás. He was arrested in 1778 for Judaism.[193] It is unknown whether the date for this arrest is incorrect or whether the Pombaline Reforms were ignored or delayed in Brazil, as seen in this particular case. In addition. Ademir Schetini Júnior points out the case of Dona Luiza Correia de Souza and her family living in the Freguesia de Nossa Senhora do Rosário da Vila de Cachoeira, Recôncavo Baiano. They were accused of Judaizing as late as the 1790s, twenty years after the implementation of the Pombaline Reforms.[194]

During the period between 1760 and 1791, Portuguese migration to colonial Brazil increased significantly—especially from the region of Minho, comprising immigrants who were mostly poor and/or unemployed. Between 1808 and 1817, wealthy immigrants arrived in Brazil along with ten to fifteen thousand other Portuguese migrants, most of whom belonged in the court of D. João VI (who had transferred Portugal's royal court to Rio).[195]

Brazil had entered a new phase of political and economic change, with the arrival of the royal family to Rio in 1808 (who were fleeing the Napoleonic war) and the development of new infrastructure in that city, along with newspapers, and the opening of foreign trade. By 1818, the total population of Brazil was estimated at 3.8 million.[196] D. João, Prince Regent of Portugal, returned to Europe, and his son D. Pedro I, left behind in Brazil, declared independence from Portugal in 1822—a year after the institution of the Portuguese Inquisition was abolished.

In the first quarter of the eighteenth century prior to independence, Brazil went through a series of political and economic upheavals. Rio had suffered two French invasions—the city was ransacked in the second invasion, and New Christians in Rio were targeted aggressively during the first quarter of the eighteenth century. Due to the suspicion of other European intrusions and attacks, Brazil had entered a period of isolation akin only to Japan and China at that time, and the Portuguese king decided to issue an edict expelling all foreigners from Brazil.[197]

The official end of the Inquisition on April 5, 1821, came about as the institution failed to continuously produce honor and prestige, and began its slow decay, as James E. Wadsworth explains: "the symbolic capital used to purchase prestige, honor, and power began to lose its social value."[198] The new constitution of the empire in 1822, created with Brazil's declared independence from Portugal (by D. Pedro I, by the Ipiranga River in São Paulo), produced and implemented a new commercial treaty signed between England and Portugal, finally offering Protestants and Jews the freedom to profess their faiths in Brazil.

Brazilian newspapers in the early nineteenth century reported on the impact of the Inquisition (when the Portuguese Inquisition was still active), and their reports offer glimpses of how the Inquisition may have been perceived in some public spheres. For example, in 1808 the *Correio Braziliense: Ou Armazém Literário* called it "the shame of humanity" ("*vergonha da humanidade*").[199] In 1821, the year the Inquisition ended, the *Gazeta do Rio de Janeiro* called it "barbaric and stupid," reporting that a total of 23,068 individuals had been penitent, and 1,554 had been burned at the stake by the end of the Inquisition in March, 1821.[200] However, these figures are likely to be inaccurate, nor does the newspaper article reveal its source, and it is likely that about a total of 1,175 were executed.[201]

In 1830, nine years after the end of the Inquisition, the newspaper, *O Cruzeiro*, stated that the Inquisition was "a Tribunal of fire and blood invented in the name of religion of a God of peace" ("*Hum Tribunal de fogo, e sangue inventado à bem da Religião de hum Deus de paz*").[202] In that same year, the *Diário de Pernambuco* commented, "The Holy Tribunal Office ... burned people like mosquitos" ("*O Evangélico Tribunal do Santo Ofício, que queimou gente como mosquitos*").[203] Therefore, despite the continuation of anti-Jewish sentiments in colonial Brazil, ostensibly the overall perception of the Portuguese Inquisition in Brazil appeared to be overwhelmingly negative in public spheres, at least toward the end of its demise.

In the next chapter, I discuss my examination of the Inquisition processos, and show that the Inquisition especially targeted New Christians for the crime of Judaism in Brazil; however, they also arrested and sentenced individuals from all over Brazil for all crimes of heresy, starting in 1564, and ending with the last processo that I found in Brazil in 1778. The charges of heresy, in addition to Judaism, varied vastly; for example: bigamy, sodomy, bestiality, witchcraft, sorcery, superstition, perjury, blasphemy, Freemasonry, Protestantism, false visions of God, revolutionary ideas, heretical propositions, and several other accusations listed in the Appendix. The occupations of those accused were equally varied, and the locations of arrests also varied by region. Arrests occurred throughout Brazil from its extreme north to south regions, and its center-west, northeast, and southeast regions.

CHAPTER SIX

Results from the Examination of the Portuguese Inquisition Dossiers in Brazil

THIS CHAPTER WILL FOCUS on an examination of the sample of digitized dossiers made available online by the Arquivo Nacional, Torre do Tombo, Portugal. The discussion of these original results discussed here only reflect the arrests made by the Portuguese Inquisition in Brazil, focused on New Christians accused of Judaizing ("crime of Judaism," crime de judaismo). These results are not meant to be interpreted as a statistical representation, nor to project a numerical analysis of New Christians or Crypto-Jews living in colonial Brazil, especially since the goal of the Inquisition was not to gather statistical data.

A total of 1,033 individuals were arrested in Brazil, of which a little over two-fifths (43 percent), 449 individuals, were arrested for the crime of Judaism. Over the period of almost 300 years this figure may seem relatively small; however, in terms of context and proportion, they tell a different story. That is, out of all arrests for any heresy—not only for Judaism—over two-thirds (70 percent) comprised New Christians and their descendants, while Old Christians comprised merely 15 percent of total arrests. This significant proportion of arrests illustrates how the Inquisition targeted New Christians in Brazil, and how this institution took denunciations of those individuals with "tainted blood" (sangue infecto) more seriously than those accusations against Old Christians.

The largest single cohort of heretical crimes I found was Judaism (with

449 arrests) accounting for 43 percent of the total, followed by bigamy (223 arrests) accounting for 21.5 percent. Other crimes accounting for less than 1 percent of the total were: heretical propositions (78 arrests), sodomy (46), blasphemy (39), superstitions, sorcery, and witchcraft (30), heresy (25), sacrilege (24), solicitation (18), perjury (16), Lutheranism (14), idolatry (7), polyandry (4), polygamy (2), possession of a forbidden book (2), Islam (2), and other miscellaneous heresies (See Appendix for full list).

The clusters of European-born populations living in Brazil during the sixteenth century (non-Indigenous, non-African) were pointedly low. Consider, for example, that the total European population in all of Brazil in 1570 was estimated at just about 20,760. Urban population clusters during most of the sixteenth and seventeenth centuries were concentrated in the coastal northeast region (especially in Bahia and Pernambuco), and it was not until the early eighteenth century that the population in Rio de Janeiro began to grow (i.e., in 1570, the white population in Rio alone was estimated at just 840). By the 1570s, European population estimates in the following early settlements in Brazil were as follows: Pernambuco (Olinda, Igaraçu), 6,000; Bahia (Salvador, Vila Velha), 6,500; Itamaracá, 600; Ilhéus (São Jorge), 1,200; Porto Seguro (Santa Cruz, Santo Amaro), 1,320; Espírito Santo (Vitória, Vila Velha), 1,200; Rio de Janeiro (São Sebastião), 840; and São Vicente (Santos, Santo Amaro, Itanhaém, São Paulo), 3,000.[1]

Again, to highlight the scale of the Portuguese diaspora, during a period of two hundred years (1500–1700) it is estimated that about 700,000 individuals left Portugal, mostly for Portuguese territories (i.e., in the Atlantic islands or in Africa, Asia, and Brazil), of which an estimated 100,000 went to Brazil. Most were men, a fact which contributed to the chronic sex-ratio imbalance in that nation.[2] By all indications, a significantly much larger number of New Christians lived throughout colonial Brazil than the number of these arrests by the Inquisition reflect.

No tribunals of the Portuguese Inquisition were established in Brazil, and the Inquisition's tribunal of Lisbon oversaw all arrests made in Brazil. Those individuals who were arrested in Brazil were shipped to Lisbon for sentencing, only to wait in their prison cells an average of three to six years, and as a result, many died in their cells awaiting their sentence.[3] The Inquisition's concern with the "Jewish problem" thus focused on New Christians who were nominally Catholic in public yet who were allegedly practicing Judaism in secret ("Judaizers")—hence this was the cohort that most concerned the Inquisition, Church, and Crown.

The first arrest in Brazil was that of a Frenchman named João, or Jehovanan des Boulez (Senhor de Boulez/Boles, Giovanni des Boulez), in 1564. He was arrested for "Lutheranism" in Rio de Janeiro, and listed as the "governor of the French in Brazil," governador dos franceses no Brasil (processo 1586). The first accusation of a person for Judaism, which only occurred later in 1591, was that of a man named Salvador Maia—a merchant, aged 40. He was born in Lisbon, was living in Ilhéus, Bahia, and had murdered his wife—an Old Christian, Domingas Aires—for adultery (processo 2320). His father was Manuel da Maia (a New Christian), and his mother, Branca Rodrigues (an Old Christian). He was later absolved and released from prison a year later in 1592.[4]

The first arrest for Judaism in Rio de Janeiro was that of Diogo Lopes in 1596: a merchant, aged 43; also born in Lisbon, and living in Rio (processo 12364). This was one of the rare arrests for Judaism in Rio at that time, since most arrests until 1700 were in the northeast region (mostly Pernambuco or Bahia). Places of birth for those individuals arrested, other than Brazil or Portugal, included: France, Italy (Florence), Belgium (Flandres), England, Netherlands, Spain, and Algeria.

The last person accused of Judaism in Brazil was José Ricardo de Morais—born in Meia Ponte, Rio, living in Vila Boa de Goiás (modern state of Goiás), and lavrador—in 1778 (processo 16953). Curiously, his arrest for Judaism was made after the implementation of the Leis Pombalinas, which eliminated the social status (estatuto social) of "New Christian." It is unknown why this arrest was made after the status of New Christian had been eliminated in Portuguese territories (as the arrest was made in 1778). Although I did not conduct a study on arrests made in Portugal, the very last arrest that I could find by the Portuguese Inquisition was of Antônio José de Miranda from Lisbon, for the crime of bigamy in 1816. He was sent to prison in Castro Marim for three years (processo 14654).

The places of origin (place of birth) of those accused by the Inquisition, varied widely. Among all of the arrests that I found, both in Portugal and Brazil, there were individuals from places as varied as: France, Ireland,

Germany, Belgium, Italy, Poland, India (from Goa or Cochim), England, Scotland, the Netherlands, Spain, Morocco, Algeria, Malta, Angola, Azores, Cape Verde, Madeira, Palestine, Ceuta, Ceylon, Kingdom of Sicily, Switzerland, China (Macau), Turkey, and Greece (Corfu).[5]

There is a notable difference between "place of origin" and the place where those individuals were living (morada). That is, out of all the 76 arrests by the end of the seventeenth century, only nine individuals were born in Brazil (i.e., those who were Brazilian-born accounted for only 8 percent of the total during that period). Most of those individuals arrested up to 1700 were immigrants from Portugal, although other immigrants from Spain, France, and the Netherlands were also arrested. However, by the early eighteenth century, arrests for Brazilian-born individuals increased to the point where most of those individuals arrested for Judaism by then were born in Brazil, mostly in Rio de Janeiro.

Overall, the places of birth of those arrested in Brazil for all heresies were as follows: 62.5 percent were born in Brazil (mostly in Rio de Janeiro, Pernambuco, Bahia, Paraíba, and São Paulo); 33.8 percent were born in Portugal; 2.2 percent in Spain; and less than 1 percent in the Atlantic Islands (Azores and Madeira), France, and the Netherlands (Amsterdam). We should also remain cautious about this interpretation of birthplace category, especially if we consider that Lisbon and Porto were major ports of exit. That is, we should account for any potential inaccuracies or confusion in the dossier listings between birthplace and ports of exit from which immigrants may have departed Portugal.

In the category "place of birth" for those individuals arrested for Judaism in Brazil up to the late seventeenth century, an interesting pattern emerges (See Table 1). That is, an observable geographic cluster showing up for towns or villages in Portugal on the eastern border of Portugal with western Spain appear in a region known as A Raia (in Portuguese for "the line") or La Raya (in Spanish), along the Duero, Guadiana, and Tajo Rivers, where families have intermarried across borders for centuries. This is because after the Spanish pogroms of 1390, many Spanish Jews migrated to Portugal, and to this region on the borderlands with Spain, as discussed in Chapter 2. Curiously, out of the nine Spaniards who were arrested in Brazil for Judaism, all of them hailed from the Spanish western region along the borderlands with

Portugal (most were from Extremadura). This new finding here about those arrested in Brazil corroborates Javier Castaño's discussion about the porous region of A Raia between Portugal and Spain, and the concentration of Spanish Jews who had flocked to that region in a dramatic demographic movement from Spain to Portugal after the Spanish pogroms of 1390 (discussed in detail in Chapter 1). Notably, several battles have been fought in this region up to the nineteenth century, and it remains one of the poorest and sparsest populated regions in the Iberian Peninsula.[6]

The engenhos ("sugarcane plantations") in the Brazilian northeast region were also clearly places of interest for inquisitors' activities, since New Christians held many of the occupations there, and many of them were thought to have been Judaizers. I found arrests for Judaism in the following engenhos, mostly in the northeast region (particularly Pernambuco, Paraíba, and Bahia, as well as in Rio de Janeiro) where sugar cultivation thrived: five individuals in Engenho Velho, the city of Paraíba, Bispate of Pernambuco; four in Engenho Matoim, Salvador da Baía de Todos os Santos, Bahia; two in Engenho Novo, District of Paraíba, Bispate of Pernambuco; and two also in Engenho de Inhohim, Engenho de Santo André, Paraíba, Bispate of Pernambuco, among others, such as Engenho da Pindoba; Engenho do Meio, Paraíba, Bispate of Pernambuco; and Engenho do Meio, Rio de Janeiro.

Out of all prisoners in Portugal and Brazil that I came across, I found individuals who were as young as 10 and as old as 100 years old. Among the youngest prisoners were Juliana de Oliveira from Leiria, arrested in 1629; and Maria de Mesas from Lisbon, in 1654—both were just 10 years old. Four were aged 11, and ten of them were 12 years old. For example, Ana da Trindade, aged 11, imprisoned in 1735 and accused of the crime of Judaism, had all her assets confiscated (from her family) and was forced to pay 40,000 reis for expenses incurred by the Inquisition (processo 201). There were several individuals aged 13; for example, among them, D. Ana Maria Nogueira from Lisbon, aged 13, who was burned at the stake in 1704. Among the oldest I found were Simão Dias from Faro, Portugal—aged 100, arrested in 1567 (processo 8351), and sentenced and burned at the stake—and Joana de Franca from Vila Viçosa, Portugal, aged 100 (processo 10438), and arrested in 1669. Both of them had been accused of Judaism. All the youngest individuals

Table 6.1. Immigrants from Portugal Arrested for Judaism in Brazil: Place of Origin*

PLACE OF ORIGIN	#	PERCENTAGE OF IMMIGRANTS
Lisbon	25	16.7
Almeida	11	7.3
Idanha-a-Nova	9	6
Porto	7	4.7
Covilhã	5	3.3
Celorico da Beira	4	2.7
Castelo Rodrigo	4	2.7
Vila Real	4	2.7
Évora	3	2
Coimbra	3	2
Castro Daire	3	2
Arraiolos	3	2
São Vicente da Beira	3	2
Sabugal	3	2
Pinhel	3	2
Freixedas	3	2
Buarcos	2	1.3
Guarda	2	1.3
Vila do Mogadouro	2	1.3
Vila Nova de Foz Côa	2	1.3
Travaço	2	1.3
Fronteira	2	1.3
Freixo de Numão	2	1.3
Other places*	42	28
Total	149	Approx.100%

(Total of 149 out of total of 449 arrests = 33%)

Source: Arquivos Torre do Tombo, Portugal, Inquisição de Lisboa online, http://antt.dglab.gov.pt/exposicoes-virtuais-2/inquisicao-de-lisboa-online/.

*Other places in Portugal = one individual: Fundão, Estremoz, Alentejo, Elvas, Cucaú, Rio Formoso, Crato, Coruche, Chaves, Bragança, Basto, Azevo, Pinhel, Alcains, Castelo Branco, Alameida, Favaios, freguesia de Santa Justa, Freixo de Espada à Cinta, Leiria, Maçal do Chão, Vilar Torpim, Maçal do Chão, Manteigas, Monforte, Montemor-o-Velho, Moura, Olivença, Portimão, Sardoal, Setúbal, Tomar, Torre de Moncorvo, Torres Novas, Trancoso, Viana, Viana de Caminha, Viana do Minho, vila de Campo Maior, Vila de Graçu, Vila Nova de Portimão.

Table 6.2. The Youngest Individuals Imprisoned by the Portuguese Inquisition in Lisbon (All Except Three for the Crime of Judaism)

NAME	AGE	CITY/TOWN	YEAR	PROCESSO #
Juliana de Oliveira	10	Leiria	1629	11820
Maria de Mesas	10	Lisbon	1654	11923
Ana da Trindade	11	Guarda	1735	201
Maria Soares da Rosa	11	Lisbon	1654	11922
Jerónima Vaz	11	Lamego	1733	8016
Afonso	11	Arronches	1582	7458
Antônia Soares	12	Avis, Évora	1741	1118
Nicolau Rodrigues	12	Lisbon	1606	10588
Beatriz Lopes	12	Lisbon	1548	8532
Helena da Cruz	12	Rio de Janeiro	1718	8200
Pedro Chales [Charles]	12	Lisbon	1593	6110
Antônia Nunes	12	Lisbon	1597	4588
Ana Rodrigues	12	Beira	1646	3802
Joaquim Álvares da Costa	12	Lisbon	1741	3761
Isabel da Cunha	12	Guarda	1621	1052
Leonôr de Fontes	12	Leiria	1633	4399

Source: Arquivos Torre do Tombo, Portugal, Inquisição de Lisboa online, http://antt.dglab.gov.pt/exposicoes-virtuais-2/inquisicao-de-lisboa-online/.

arrested, except for three, had been arrested for crimes of Judaism. The exceptions were Afonso (accused of heresy), Pedro Chales [Charles] (accused of Anglicanism and originally from England), and Joaquim Álvares da Costa (for the crime of superstition).

Among the youngest arrested in Brazil was Helena da Cruz from Rio de Janeiro, aged 12, arrested in 1718 (processo 8200). She is listed as "part New Christian" since her father, Alexandre Freire, was an Old Christian, and her mother, Helena de Azevedo, was "half New Christian." She was sentenced to an auto-da-fé in 1720 (she spent two years in prison awaiting her punishment), and "perpetual penitence," and was instructed in "the mysteries of faith and spiritual penitence." She was forced to pay 10 cruzados to cover

Inquisition expenses, and later the inquisitors allowed her to return to Rio de Janeiro—by then she was already 15 years old.[7]

Judaism accounted for 74 percent of crimes in the youngest cohort of those arrested, that is, fourteen of the nineteen youngest individuals arrested (ranging from 12 to 16 in age) were for the crime of Judaism (see Table 2). The oldest individuals arrested for Judaism in Brazil were Ines Aires, aged 80 (widow of André de Barros, merchant), born in Rio de Janeiro and arrested there in 1713 (processo 13099), and Ana Rodrigues, aged 80 (wife of Heitor Antunes, a New Christian and merchant, discussed in Chapter 4), born in Portugal, and arrested in 1593 in Bahia (processo 11680).

Social Status and "Race"

Under the category of estatuto social ("social status") entries would vary, for example, from "Old Christian" and "New Christian" to varying gradations, such as one-eighth, one-fourth, three-quarters, or one-half or part New Christian. Since the concern of the Inquisition's activities in Brazil were focused on all heresies, it cast a wide net on heretics and was geographically spread out. Thus, the entries for estatuto social of those accused was equally diverse, for example: *negro/a* or preto/a ("black"); *preto crioulo* ("Brazilian-born black person"); *preto/a forro/a* ("free black person"), *escravo/a* ("slave"); *índio/a* ("Indian," Indigenous from Brazil, not from India); mulato/a ("half black and half white"); pardo/a (undefined mixed ancestry, loosely, "brown"); *mouro/a* ("Arab" or "Muslim" from North Africa, India, or the Ottoman Empire); *mourisco/a cativo* ("Arab convert slave"); mameluco/a ("half Indigenous and half black"); mestiço/a ("mixed ancestry"); *mestiço/a forro/a* ("free and mixed ancestry"); cigano/a ("Gypsy/Roma").[8]

Several individuals accused and arrested for Judaism had mothers who were listed as "black slave" or "captive black" (e.g., *escrava preta*, or *negra cativa*); as "free blacks" (*preta forra*); or as the offspring of a combination of Indigenous, black, and/or white parentage, that is, either: mestiço/a, pardo/a, or mameluco/a. These categorizations demonstrate the extent of mestiçagem in colonial Brazil (i.e., racial and ethnic hybridity and miscegenation). Moreover, these arrests also show that the Inquisition did not follow the Judaic law of maternal descent (i.e., where Jewish ancestry is passed down through the mother's side). That is, dozens of New Christians arrested for Judaism in Brazil had "mixed-race" parentage, and in some cases, parents who were fully African or Indigenous. Due to the chronic shortage of European women in early colonial Brazil, miscegenation was practiced and encouraged by Portuguese colonialists (earlier we saw evidence of this in Duarte Coelho's letter in Chapter 4) as a geo-strategic approach for occupation and territorial annexation, and at the same time, it created ties with Indigenous tribes through kinship relationships. Sexual intercourse between Portuguese men and Indigenous and African women was not taboo; to the contrary, it was promoted.[9] In fact, one recent genetic study shows that today most Brazilian "whites" share 60 percent of Indigenous and African matrilineal mitochondrial DNA, and the remaining proportion of European DNA on the patrilineal side. That is, the genetic evidence shows that most of the miscegenation that occurred during colonial rule in Brazil was unilinear, consisting of European men (Old and New Christians) and Indigenous and African women.[10]

I found thirty-six individuals arrested for the crime of Judaism in Brazil whose parentage (mostly mothers) were non-European (See full list in the Appendix). For example: *descendente de dois pretos da Guiné* ("descendant of two blacks from the Guinea Coast"—West Africa); *escrava preta* ("black slave"); *mulher negra* ("black woman"); *preta forra/preto forro* ("free black person"); *índia/índio* ("Brazilian Indian"); *mameluca* ("mixed-race," Portuguese and Indian); or *mulher parda* ("mixed-race woman," African and Portuguese). What is noticeable here, is that about one-third of the fathers were listed as *homem branco* ("white man") and were agriculturalists (mostly involved in sugarcane cultivation).

For instance, in one case we observe that several of the Paredes family members had intermarried with Indigenous and African populations in Brazil (See Table 6.3). Most arrests for Judaism for these family members occurred in Rio de Janeiro between 1713 and 1716.

In 1715, Ana de Paredes was arrested in Rio de Janeiro (processo 4944). Aged 40 and a widow, her parents were listed as descendants of "two blacks from Guinea" (West Africa), *descendente de dois pretos da Guiné*. Another member of the Paredes family, Leonor Mendes, aged 50, was arrested in 1713 (processo 9985). Her father was Rodrigo Mendes de Paredes, and her mother is listed by her first name only, Ursula, *escrava preta* ("black slave"). Gabriel

Table 6.3. Members of the Paredes Family Arrested in Rio de Janeiro

NAME	AGE	YEAR OF ARREST	DOSSIER #
Ana de Paredes	40	1715	4871
Ines de Paredes	40	1715	7135
Gabriel de Paredes	43	1715	3127
Isabel de Paredes	40	1715	2700
Isabel de Paredes	30	1715	3972
D. Brites de Paredes	39	1714	11666
Rodrigo Mendes de Paredes	27	1712	11677
Agostinho de Paredes	56	1714	8573
Manuel de Paredes	18	1712	9668
Agostinho Correia de Paredes	29	1731	6997
Padre Francisco de Paredes	40	1716	7949
Guimar de Paredes	52	1712	12224
Ines de Paredes	18	1719	9919-1
Francisco de Paredes	28	1723	7352
Luis de Paredes	22	1724	3648
José Gomes de Paredes	22	1721	7839

Source: Arquivos Torre do Tombo, Portugal, Inquisição de Lisboa online, http://antt.dglab.gov.pt/exposicoes-virtuais-2/inquisicao-de-lisboa-online/.

de Paredes, aged 43, a carpenter, is listed as "half New Christian," and was arrested in 1714. His father was Rodrigo Mendes de Paredes, a New Christian and lavrador, and his mother was Francisca, a *mulher preta* ("black woman") (processo 7966). Felipe de Mendonça, aged 60, arrested in 1716, was listed as "half New Christian." His parents were Luís Paredes, and Marta, a *escrava preta* ("black slave") (processo 11591). Isabel de Paredes, aged 40, was arrested in 1712 (processo 2700). Her parents were listed simply as Robertim, *índio* ("Brazilian Indian"), and Micaela, *índia*. Lastly, Dona Isabel de Lucena, aged 40—whose husband was Agostinho de Paredes, a lawyer and senhor de engenho—was arrested in 1714 (processo 11206). Her father was Jerónimo de Albuquerque, an Old Christian, and her mother was simply listed as Maria, *índia forra* ("free Indian").

I found further evidence of the substantive intermarriage between New Christians, blacks, and Indians. For instance, Teodoro Pereira da Costa, a medical doctor, aged 34, was arrested for Judaism in 1716. His father was Baltazar da Costa, and his mother, Branca, *a mulher negra* ("black woman") (processo 2222). João da Cruz, aged 40, a tailor, is listed as one-quarter New Christian, and was arrested in 1716. His parents were Bento Cardoso (half New Christian) and Esperança, *a mulher negra* ("black woman") (processo 2219). Manuel Rodrigues Coutinho, aged 43, unemployed and single, was arrested in 1713 (processo 9989). His parents were Baltazar Rodrigues Coutinho, New Christian and *senhor do engenho*, and Jerónima de Sequeira, *a mulher parda* ("mixed-race woman"). Lastly, Mariana Peres, aged 55, and arrested in 1714, was the widow of João da Silva, *lavrador de cana*, whose parents were António Peres Caldeira, part New Christian and also *a lavrador de cana*, and Marta Gomes, *a mulher parda* ("mixed race woman") (processo 7980).

The Inquisition did not follow Judaic law of matrilineal descent for an individual to be considered a "Judaizer." That is, any New Christian could be a potential Crypto-Jew regardless of whether their Jewish ancestry was traced from their father or mother's genealogical side—or whether they had any Jewish ancestry, for that matter. Noticeably, as seen above, several of the Paredes family members arrested for Judaism appear conspicuously here, as they had intermarried with Afro-Indigenous women (*parda, mameluca, mestiça forra, preta forra, escrava negra,* or *índia*).[11] This also evidently shows the high degree of hybridity and miscegenation in Brazil, and that the Inquisition aggressively targeted New Christian families, particularly in the early 1700s in Rio de Janeiro.

Hence, based on these examples, intermarriages between New Christians in Brazil, especially sharecroppers or farmers (lavradores), sugarcane plantation owners (*senhores de engenho*), and the sugarcane farming elite (lavradores de cana) with African and Indigenous women, were widespread. At the same time, several men with African and Indigenous ancestry had also intermarried with New Christian women. Miscegenation continued in Brazil when Judaism was allowed in Brazil during Dutch rule (1630–1654), where many residents who were officially and openly Jews had intermarried with African slaves or their descendants, or with local Indigenous women. By inference, the number of descendants of New Christians and Afro-Indigenous couples in Brazil would have likewise been significantly high during colonial rule in Brazil. Therefore, it is also likely that there are far more Brazilians today living in Brazil with Jewish ancestry than previously thought.

Entries Examined: Results

Occupations varied widely, ranging from nuns, priests, friars, and professors (mestre), to slaves, peasants, merchants, lawyers, doctors, sailors, fishermen ("men of the sea," "homem do mar"), bankers, soldiers, agricultural workers—sugarcane, manioc, corn, or tobacco farmers or sharecroppers (lavrador)—hairdressers, chocolatiers, painters, shoemakers, bakers, construction workers (pedreiro), and tailors, for instance.

The most common occupation for those arrested for Judaism in Brazil was "merchant," followed by lavrador and lavrador de cana, soldier, miner, unemployed, student, lawyer, doctor, carpenter, sailor, clergyman, professor, clerk, musician, tailor, cobbler, and pharmacist respectively, among other miscellaneous occupations. However, when all the occupations that involved agriculture are lumped together, they account for the largest cohort for all occupations, accounting for almost 31 percent of all arrests for Judaism in Brazil. Thus, I have lumped together such occupations under the broader category of "agriculturalists," which include: lavrador ("farmer" or "sharecropper" of tobacco, sugarcane, or manioc), lavrador de cana ("sugarcane planter/sharecropper"), senhores de engenho ("sugarcane plantation owner"), and other miscellaneous engenho occupations such as: *caldeireiro, aguardenteiro, caxeiro, comboieiro, curtidor, dizimeiro, latoeiro, ourives, almoxarife,* or *sirgueiro* (which loosely correspond to clerks, boiler-room workers, sugar purgers, and stokers).

The number of all New Christians and their descendants arrested in Brazil represent over two-thirds (70 percent) of all arrests in Brazil—not only for crimes of Judaism but for all heresies. In comparison, Old Christians accounted for just 15 percent of the total arrests. Clearly, New Christians were specifically targeted by the Inquisition in Brazil. I lumped all New Christians and their descendants together (i.e., of "Jewish ancestry"), ranging from half New Christian, part New Christian, and one-quarter New Christian, to three-quarters New Christian.

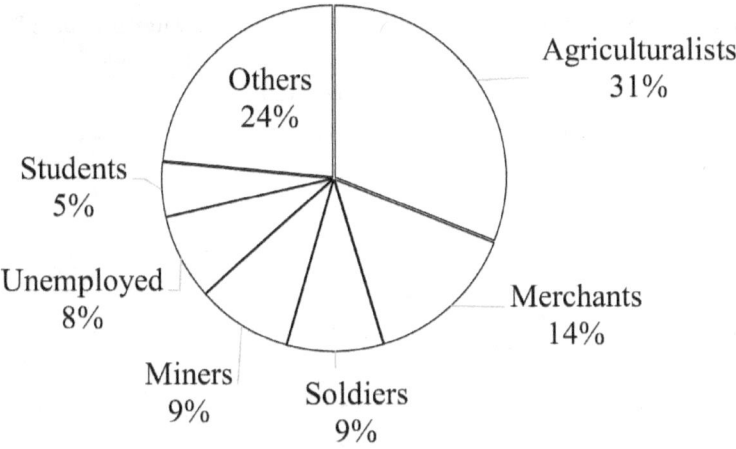

Figure 6.1. Occupations for those arrested for Judaism

The itemized breakdown under the category of "social status" for all arrests for all heresies include New Christians and their descendants, with a total of 444 individuals (accounting for 70 percent); 98 Old Christians (15 percent); 26 pardos (4 percent); 19 mamelucos (3 percent); 17 índio (3 percent); 14 black slaves (2 percent); 12 free blacks 12 (2 percent); and less than 1 percent (Gypsy, Jew, mulato).[12] There were 635 entries that included the category of "social status," and 393 entries for social status were missing in the digitized dossiers.

Indigenous and Black Populations

For all heresies that did not include the crime of Judaism, New Christians still appear as a significantly important cohort. Overall, Old Christians (38.5 percent) were the single majority under social status for those arrests for non-Judaic heresies, followed by pardo (14.5 percent); New Christian and descendants (12 percent); mameluco (10.5 percent); índio (9.5 percent); slave (5.5 percent); "free blacks" (5.5 percent); Gypsy (1.5 percent); and less than 1 percent: mulato slave, mulato, mestiço, and black.

Indigenous and Afro-Brazilian populations were significantly affected by the Inquisition's activities in Brazil. The Inquisition was obsessed with searching for, and finding the "hidden Jew" or the "imagined Jew," where

Table 6.4. Breakdown for Social Status in Arrests for All Heresies in Brazil

SOCIAL STATUS	TOTALS
New Christian	281
Part New Christian	106
Old Christian	98
½ New Christian	40
Pardo	26
Mameluco	19
Índio	17
¼ New Christian	14
Black Slaves	14
Free Blacks	12
¾ New Christian	3
Gypsy	3
Jew	1
Mulato	1
Total	635*

Source: Arquivos Torre do Tombo, Portugal, Inquisição de Lisboa online, http://antt.dglab.gov.pt/exposicoes-virtuais-2/inquisicao-de-lisboa-online/.

* There were 635 entries that included the category of "social status," and 398 entries for social status were missing in the digitized dossiers.

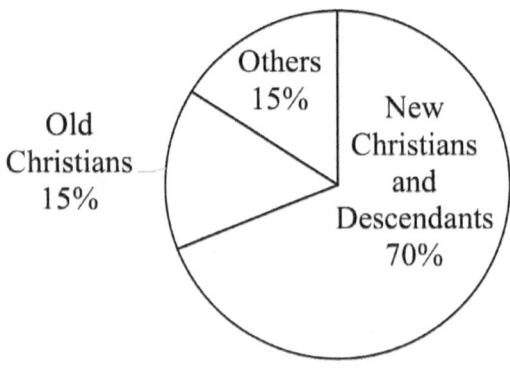

Figure 6.2. Breakdown of social status for arrests for all heresies in Brazil

Judaic practices were often being mistaken for Indigenous or African cultures and belief systems, as discussed ahead. The Portuguese Inquisition did not merely single out individuals because of their physical appearance (in today's popular vernacular, "racial profiling"); they were obsessed with the search for the "secret" and "imagined Jew"; that is, any individual who was secretly practicing Judaism, even if they were in fact not practicing Judaism. In the Inquisition dossiers, for example, I found 36 individuals arrested for Judaism who had Indigenous or African parents or who were Brazilian Indians or African slaves, which reflects the Inquisition's obsession with surveillance and punishment.

The breadth of accusations and crimes other than Judaizing also varied. Other crimes included: bigamy, sodomy, witchcraft, sorcery, superstition (*bruxaria, feitiço, superstição*), heresy, heretical propositions, disrespect, Protestantism (Anglican, Lutheran, Calvinist), Islamism, obstruction, false vision of God, revolutionary ideas, blasphemy, perjury, receiving mass after lunch, Freemansonry (*maçonaria*, or *pedreiro livre*), polyandry, polygamy, solicitation, bestiality, or the possession of a forbidden book (See Appendix for full list of miscellaneous accusations). For example in 1591, Paula de Sequeira, aged 40, and imprisoned in Salvador, Bahia, was accused of the crime of sodomy—one of the very rare cases of female sodomy—and also for having in her possession a book deemed forbidden by the Inquisition, "Diana" (*The Seven Books of Diana*, in Spanish: *Los siete libros de la Diana* published in 1559), by Portuguese author Jorge de Monte Maior or Montemayor ("*Ter em seu poder e ler o livro defeso, proibido pelo inquisidor geral do reino: Diana de Jorge de Monte Maior*") (processo 3306).[13] Those accused of sodomy were usually sent as exiles, degredados, to Portuguese territories and outposts such as Angola, São Tomé, Principe, Magazão in Morocco, or Castro Marim. The following thirteen New Christians were arrested for Judaism in Brazil and were burned alive at the stake as "Judaizers" (the last one being in 1748):

GASPAR GOMES, aged 30, born in Arraiolos, Portugal, living in Bahia, one-quarter New Christian, shoemaker, and soldier. His parents were: Sebastião Gomes (Old Christian) and Isabel Dias (half New Christian). He was sentenced to the auto-da-fé in 1644, and burned at the stake (processo 5019).

MANUEL RODRIGUES MONSANTO, born in Pernambuco and arrested in Pernambuco, and listed as a merchant. He was burned at the stake after the auto-da-fé in 1644 (processo 4044).

JOSEPH DE LIS, also known as Isaac de Castro, aged 20, born in France, living in Salvador, Bahia, arrested in 1645. His parents were: Cristovão Luís and Isabel da Paz. He was burned at the stake after the auto-da-fé of 1647 (processo 11550).

TEOTÔNIO DA COSTA, aged 23, born in Lisbon, living in Vila de São Paulo, married to Ana Vidigal (Old Christian), arrested in 1683. His parents were: Gaspar da Costa de Mesquita (banker) and Ines Gomes—both New Christians. He was burned at the stake after the auto-da-fé of 1686 (processo 2816).

TERÊSA PAIS DE JESUS, aged 64, born and living in Rio de Janeiro, part New Christian, married to Francisco Mendes Simões, teacher, arrested in 1718. Her parents were: João Godinho Leite (part New Christian) and Romana Pais (Old Christian). She was burned at the stake after the auto-da-fé of 1720 (processo 2218).

MATEUS DE MOURA FOGAÇA, aged 47, accused of "relapse of Judaism," born in Rio de Janeiro and living there also, part New Christian, miner, widower of Antónia de Barros (New Christian), arrested in 1722. His parents were: Manuel de Moura Fogaça, senhor de engenho (part New Christian), and Catarina Machado (Old Christian). He was burned at the stake after the auto-da-fé of 1723 (processo 2040–1).

FELIX NUNES DE MIRANDA, aged 59, arrested in 1729 for "relapse in Judaism," born in Almeida Lamego, Portugal, living in Bahia. Listed as a businessman, married to Gracia Rodrigues (New Christian). His parents were: Manuel Nunes de Almeida (New Christian), clerk, and Leonor Rodrigues (New Christian). He was burned at the stake after the auto-da-fé of 1731 (processo 2293–1).

MIGUEL DE MENDONÇA VALADOLID, aged 43, born in Valladolid, Kingdom of Castile (Spain), living in Sítio de Nossa Senhora de Penha de Franca São Paulo, Bispate of Rio (modern state of Goiás), married to Maria Nogueira Falcão, and arrested in 1729. His parents were: João de Castro de Mendonça and Ana Maria de Castro. He was burned at the stake after the auto-da-fé of 1731 (processo 9973).

DIOGO CORREIA DO VALE, aged 58, born in Seville, Castille (Spain), living in Minas Gerais, doctor and widower, arrested in 1730. His father was Luís Correia, married to Violante de Mesquita (New Christian). He was burned after the auto-da-fé of 1731. He was not the biological son of his mother (she had adopted him) (processo 821).

DOMINGOS NUNES, aged 38, born in Viseu, Portugal, living in Minas Gerais, arrested in 1730. His parents were: António Rodrigues, merchant, and Maria Mendes. He was burned at the stake after the auto-da-fé of 1732 (processo 1779).

LUÍS MIGUEL CORREIA, aged 26, born in Viseu, Portugal, living in Vila Rica, Minas Gerais, farmer, arrested in 1730. His father was Diogo Correia do Vale (doctor). He was burned at the stake after the auto-da-fé of 1732 (processo 9249).

LUÍS MENDES DE SÁ, aged 37, born in Coimbra, Portugal, living in Minas do Rio das Contas, Bahia, arrested in 1738. His parents were: Salvador Mendes de Sá and Isabel Cardoso. He was burned at the stake after the auto-da-fé of 1739 (processo 8015).

JOÃO HENRIQUES, aged 27, born in São Vicente da Beira, Portugal, living in Minas de Paracatú, modern state of Minas Gerais. A pharmacist by trade, and arrested in 1747. His parents were: João Henriques, also a pharmacist, and Maria Gomes. He was burned at the stake after the auto-da-fé of 1748 (processo 8378).

Individuals from Brazil living in the following places (equivalent to modern states in Brazil today) were burned alive: Minas Gerais (4); Bahia (4); São Paulo (1); Goias (1); Rio (2); and Pernambuco (1). Seven of the thirteen were born in Portugal; three in Brazil; two in Spain; and one in France. The following three individuals arrested in Brazil were sentenced to be burned in effigy as "Judaizers"—post-mortem (two were living in Rio de Janeiro, and one in Bahia):

ANA RODRIGUES (introduced earlier), aged 80 (more likely to have been 100), born in Covilhã, Portugal, and living in Bahia, New Christian, married to Heitor Antunes, a New Christian and merchant. She was imprisoned in 1593. She was burned in effigy in 1600 (processo 12142).

ANDRÉ DE BARROS, born and living in Rio de Janeiro, a miner and mining contractor, arrested in 1713. His father was José Gomes Silva (senhor de engenho and contractor) and his mother, Maria de Barros. He ran away from prison and was burned in effigy in 1714 (processo 8752). BRÁS GOMES DE SEQUEIRA, born in Rio de Janeiro, living in Espírito Santo (then part of the Bispate of Rio de Janeiro), part New Christian, merchant, and married to Teodósia de Oliveira, arrested in 1718. His father was Luís Gomes Pereira (no occupation), and his mother, Inês do Rosario. He died in prison and his bones were burned in effigy after the auto of 1729 (processo 9655).

The first arrests for the crime of Judaism were made in 1591 in Bahia and Pernambuco. Of the 1,033 individuals arrested in Brazil, 449 were accused of Judaism, and 584 for other crimes. Two men were arrested for being Muslim, *Islamismo* ("Islamism"), in Pernambuco and Maranhão, in 1592 and 1646, respectively. Half of the eighteen arrests for solicitation were members of the clergy. The last individual arrested for Judaism was José Ricardo de Morais in 1778, in Vila Boa de Goiás, Goiás, originally from Meia Ponte, Rio de Janeiro, listed as "lavrador" (processo 16953). See Map 11 below for the full breakdown of arrests of Judaism by century and state in Brazil.

Between 1591 and 1599, there were 33 arrests for Judaism in Brazil, almost all in either Pernambuco or Bahia (17 in Pernambuco, 14 in Bahia, and 1 in Rio de Janeiro, and another was just listed as "Brasil"). Throughout the seventeenth century, there were a total of 42 arrests for Judaism, twice as many in Bahia (20) than in Pernambuco (10), and we can observe how arrests for Judaism have spread across different regions, from Maranhão in the north, to Espírito Santo, São Paulo in the southeast. However, during most of the eighteenth century, until the last arrest made for Judaism in 1778, most arrests by far were made in Rio de Janeiro, followed by Bahia, Minas Gerais, Paraíba, and Pernambuco. New arrests for Judaism in Minas Gerais and Goiás coincide with the discovery of gold and diamonds in the center-west region of Brazil.

The fact that Rio de Janeiro appears with the largest proportion of arrests for Judaism is somewhat misleading since this proportion may lead to the conclusion that overall, there were more Judaizers living in Rio than in

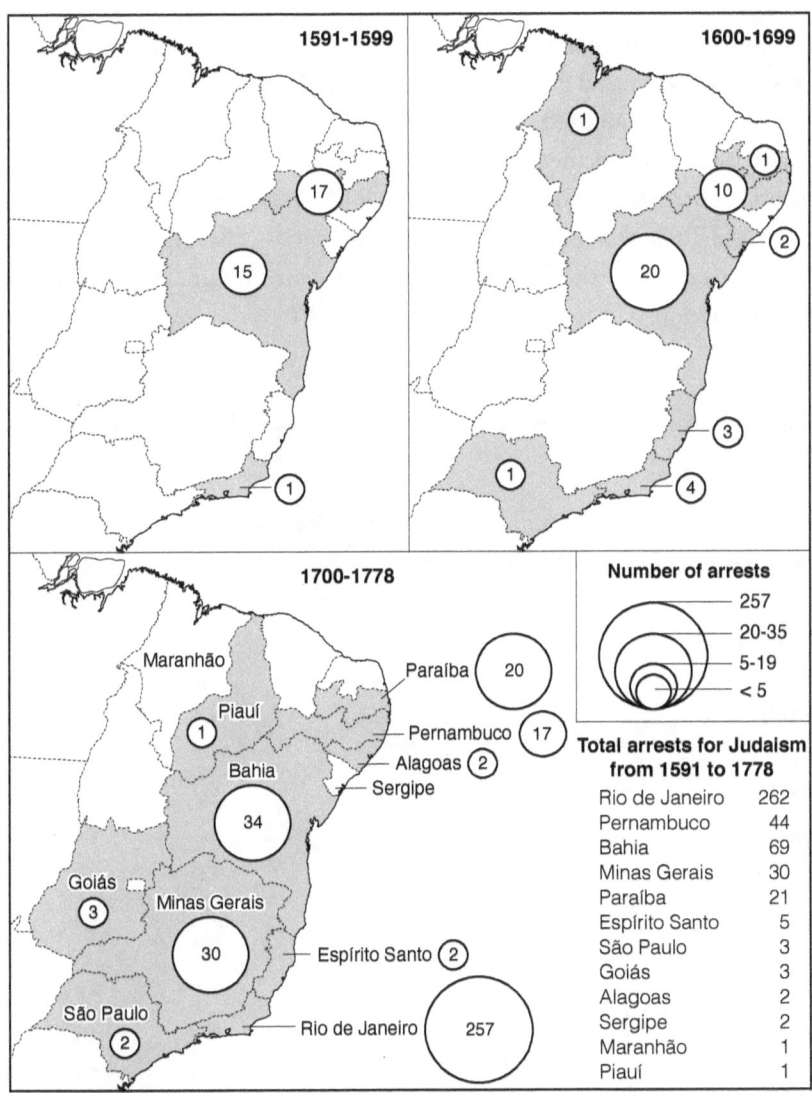

Map 11. Breakdown of results: arrests of Judaism by century and state in Brazil

Pernambuco or Bahia, for example. That is, as mentioned earlier, most of the arrests in Rio occurred during the first quarter of the eighteenth century, and for virtually one hundred and fifty years, the Inquisition had concentrated its activities in the northeast region (e.g., Pernambuco and Bahia). Moreover, the proportions shown here illustrate the location according to only modern states (See Table 5). For example, the modern states of Sergipe, Paraíba, and Alagoas were under the jurisdiction of the bispate of Pernambuco or Bahia at different points in time.

Table 6.5. Location of Arrests for All Heresies in Colonial Brazil (Equivalent Modern States)

EQUIVALENT MODERN STATES	TOTAL ARRESTS FOR JUDAISM	TOTAL FOR OTHER HERESIES	TOTAL	PERCENTAGE OF TOTAL
Rio de Janeiro	263	84	347	33.5
Pernambuco	46	175	221	21
Bahia	67	136	203	19.6
Minas Gerais	30	46	76	7.4
Pará	0	49	49	4.7
Paraíba	24	10	34	3
Maranhão	1	27	28	2.7
São Paulo	3	23	26	2.5
Espírito Santo	5	5	10	< 1
Goiás	3	2	5	< 1
Sergipe	2	4	6	< 1
Alagoas	2	4	6	< 1
Piauí	1	2	3	< 1
Undetermined	2	1	3	< 1
Amazonas (Grão-Pará)	0	5	5	< 1
Ceará	0	4	4	< 1
Mato Grosso	0	4	4	< 1
Rio Grande do Sul	0	3	3	< 1

Source: Arquivos Torre do Tombo, Portugal, Inquisição de Lisboa online, http://antt.dglab.gov.pt/exposicoes-virtuais-2/inquisicao-de-lisboa-online/.

Judaism in Rio de Janeiro accounted for 76 percent of all arrests for all heresies, followed by Paraíba (71 percent), Espírito Santo (50 percent), and Goiás (60 percent). Judaism accounted for 39 percent of all crimes in Minas Gerais, 33 percent in Bahia, and 21 percent in Pernambuco. Notably, Bahia and Pernambuco, were well known for their Crypto-Jewish communities, despite overall low proportions of total arrests for Judaism. Again, just because, for example, these locations accounted for a small or large proportion of arrests for Judaism over different periods, does not necessarily mean that there were more Crypto-Jews living there than in other locations throughout the period between 1500 and 1821. It is important to underline that the disproportionally high number of arrests for Judaism made in Rio de Janeiro were only made mostly between 1700 and 1730. Thus, the top places for all arrests (Judaism and non-Judaism) were in Rio de Janeiro (33 percent), Pernambuco (21 percent), Bahia (20 percent), Minas Gerais (7 percent), Pará (5 percent), and Paraíba (3 percent).

Anita W. Novinsky conducted a study in 2002 and found slightly more arrests of individuals in Brazil—a total of 1,076—however, she included Brazilians who were also living in Portugal (which I did not include in my study), and which might help explain the slightly higher totals than in my examination.[14] She found slightly fewer arrests for Judaism, that is, 322 (accounting for 41 percent of total arrests) where I found 449; and she found different totals for places of arrests, for example, with more arrests in Bahia (345 arrests) than in Rio de Janeiro (249), Pernambuco (135), and Minas Gerais (60).[15] In summary, my results here roughly corroborate Novinsky's results.

By far, the decade in which most arrests for all heretical crimes occurred was the first half of the eighteenth century (58 percent of all imprisonments occurred during the 1700s). The following breakdown illustrates the percentage of all arrests by century: 1564 to 1600, 29 percent; 1600 to 1700, 13 percent; and 1700 to 1807, 58 percent.

Arrests for Judaism alone during the period between 1700 to 1778 were accentuated in the first twenty-five years, with a great majority of arrests occurring during that quarter (82 percent), while the seventeenth century accounted for only 9 percent and the sixteenth century for only 7 percent of arrests for Judaism.

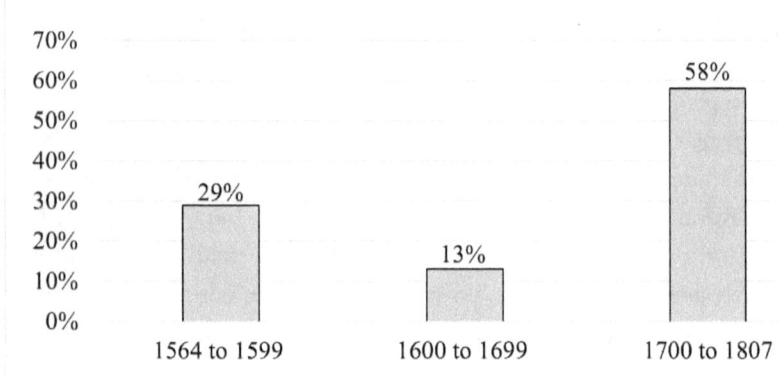

Figure 6.3. Totals for all arrests in Brazil by century

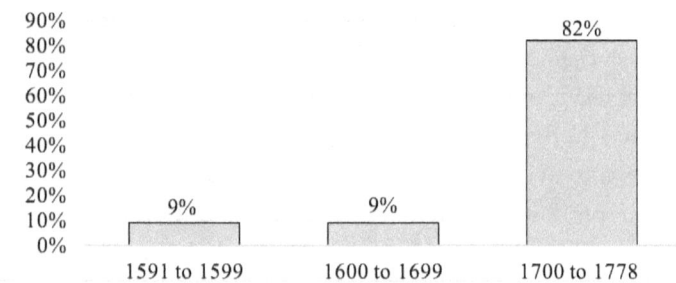

Figure 6.4. Total arrests only for the crime of Judaism by century

However, if we look closely at the breakdown for half-century periods instead, the results are telling, especially for the eighteenth century. For example, from 1500 to 1549, there were no arrests reported for Judaism; from 1550 to 1599, 33 arrests; from 1600 to 1650, 21 arrests; and from 1651 to 1699, 21 arrests. Yet from 1700 to 1750 the number of arrests ballooned to a total of 374 arrests, but from 1751 to 1799, only 6 arrests were made. Notably, the period of the first half of the eighteenth century is marked by the discovery of gold and diamonds, known as the ciclo do ouro (i.e., in the region of Minas Gerais and Goiás, with a transportation route tied directly to the ports of Rio de Janeiro through a route known as the caminho novo, as discussed in Chapter 1). Most New Christians arrested by that time (1690–1750) were involved in the gold and diamond trade, and several were merchants or medical doctors.

By the last half of the eighteenth century only six individuals were arrested for Judaism, signaling the decline of the ciclo do ouro. Evidently, the number of arrests for Judaism overlap with the location of profitable enterprises and elite families from Minas Gerais and Goiás to Rio, who eventually lost all their assets by virtue of forced confiscations made by the Inquisition. Knowing that all assets were confiscated from those New Christians accused of Judaism, the Portuguese Crown, Church, and Inquisition had found an easy source of acquiring assets and a steady profitable activity resulting from these arrests. With the decline of the Age of Gold, the Inquisition made significantly fewer arrests for New Christians (only six individuals). Of course, many factors went into who was targeted for arrest, so one cannot assume an economic cycle alone can explain everything; however, the discernable trend and pattern clearly appear during this period.

New Christian Names

The most common last names that I found for individuals arrested for Judaism in Brazil were as follows: Henriques (18 individuals), Silva (17), Costa (16), Nunes (16), Paredes (16), Miranda (15), Coutinho (13), Gomes (12), Pereira (12), Rodrigues (12), Fonseca (11), Jesus (10), Mendes (9), Sousa (9), Azevedo (8), Cardoso (8), Andrade (6), Barros (6), Carvalho (6), Correia (6), Leão (6), Mesquita (6), Vale (6), Cruz (5), Lopes (5), Lucena (5), Oliveira (5), Paz (5), Sanches (5), Álvares (4), Fernandes (4), Montarroio (4), Rego (4), Sequiera (4), and Ximenes (4). Curiously, there were ten individuals arrested for Judaism with the last name "Jesus," and five with the last name Cruz ("Cross")—perhaps an overt effort on the part of New Christians and their descendants to divert public suspicions of Judaic ancestry and avoid possible denunciation.

There were three individuals for each of the following last names: Baptista, Barreto, Caminha, Dias, Dique, Ferreira, Fogaça, Guterres, Machado, Morais, Palhana, Peres, Rangel, Simões, Tomás, Valença, and Viseu; and two individuals for each of the following ones: Aires, Azeredo, Antunes,

Bernal, Bezerra, Caldeira, Campos, Chaves, Doria, Fidalgo, Flores, Freire, Lemos, Maria, Matos, Moeda, Pina, Sliveira, Soares, and Sucesso.

Other last names include (one person for each last name): Abreu, Aguilar, Alcoforada, Almeida, Alves, Ávila, Barbalha, Barretta, Bragança, Bravo, Brum, Calaça, Castro, Castanho, Castro e Lara, Chacão, Coelho, Diamante, Dinis, Diniz, Dourado, Duarte, Faria, Favela, Ferrão, Figueiroa, França, Frances, Furtado, Garcia, Gramacha, Ilhôa, Inacia, Inacio, Isidoro, Jorge, Lara, Leite, Lima, Lis, Madalena, Maia, Mariz, Mendanha, Mendonça, Moeda, Monforte, Morão, Moreira, Penteado, Pilar, Pinto, Ramires, Ribeiro, Rosa, Sá, Sá de Almeida, Sotomaior, Teixeira, Valadolid, Vaz, Valente, Velho, Vila, and Xavier.

Overall, it appears that most of New Christian last names were not different from most common "Old Christian" Portuguese names. Many, if not most, of those individuals had last names that were different from that of their parents or fathers. I found an overlap with a few of the last names determined by the Portuguese Parliament that approved a law effective in 2015, *Decreto-Lei n.º 30-a/2015* (Lei Orgânica nº 1/2013, on July 29), which grants Portuguese nationality status to Jewish descendants who can claim their ancestors were expelled from Portugal starting in the late fifteenth century. The last names of Jewish origin mentioned in this Portuguese law are used as guidelines to determine Portuguese-Jewish ancestry.[16]

Arrests for Non-Judaic Crimes

African and Indigenous belief systems and customs were often considered and (mis)understood as Judaism or as other heresies, and the geographic locations of those arrests were widespread across Brazil. Yet I noticed a pattern in these arrests for Indigenous belief systems and practices. Common Brazilian Indigenous tribal traditions, for instance, were then considered heresy and anathema to Catholic moral orthodoxy (e.g., they were considered crimes of bigamy, sorcery, witchcraft, sacrilege, or superstition). Most arrests in these cases occurred mostly in the north region (Grão-Pará—today overlapping a good portion of the Amazonian region, roughly in the modern states of Pará and Amazonas). This region mostly comprised a local Indigenous population.

Most arrests for African belief systems that would have been considered crimes, for instance, sorcery, witchcraft, sacrilege, or superstition, occurred mostly in the northeast region (Pernambuco or Bahia)—perhaps attributed to the fact that the region had the largest cohort of African slaves and African descendants in Brazil (to this day that region comprises the largest number of African descendants in Brazil).[17] Laura de Mello e Souza has explored how blacks and Indians were traditionally local "healers," using methods known as *calundus*, *beberagens*, or *benzeduras*, and they were in fact locally respected and feared, at the same time, for their excellent knowledge of plants used in healing.[18] Those individuals who continued to practice their ancestral customs and belief systems, and did not adhere to Catholic orthodoxy, were swiftly arrested and punished. This was the case with Custódio da Silva, aged 28, listed as a *índio forra* ("free Indian" from Brazil), who was arrested for the crime of bigamy at Aldeia do Menino Jesus do Igrapé Grande, Pará, roça do Marajó, Pará, in 1745 (processo 11178). It was common practice for Indigenous tribes to practice communal polygamy and polyandry. His penitence was an auto-da-fé in 1745; receiving a public whipping; and being sent to the galleys to work as a degredado for five years—in addition to spiritual penitence. He was also obligated to pay for Inquisition expenses.[19]

The case of a man listed by his first name only, José, aged 30, who was arrested in Pernambuco in 1595, stands out. He is listed as being an *escravo mulato*, the "mulatto slave" of an Old Christian named Fernão Soares, and he was arrested for "relapse of blasphemy" (relapsia em blasfémias) (processo 2556–1). His punishment was to walk barefoot with a wooden pole across his mouth and a rope around his neck, at an auto-da-fé. He was publicly whipped, sent to the galleys for four years, and was required to pay Inquisition expenses. The process took place in Olinda, Pernambuco, at the house of Heitor Furtado de Mendonça, during his visitation to Brazil as head of the Inquisition.[20]

In another case, for example, Rosa Maria Egipcíaca, aged 45, was arrested for witchcraft and sorcery, in 1763. She is listed as a *preta forra*, a "free black person," and a servant of a Catholic priest, Francisco Gonçalves Lopes, living Rio de Janeiro. She was born in West Africa ("Coast of Judah," *Costa de Judá*) (processo 9065). As late as 1771, Francisco da Costa Xavier, aged 23, was arrested for the crime of sacrilege. A shoemaker, born in Bahia and living in Grão-Pará, he is listed as a "Brazilian-born black slave," *escravo crioulo*. His punishment was to receive a public whipping, do forced labor in the galleys for ten years, receive instructions on the Catholic faith, perform spiritual penitence, and pay for Inquisition expenses (processo 719).[21] Even later in 1785, a woman listed as Gracia, aged 30, a black slave born in Angola (listed as a slave of an Old Christian named Manuel da Costa), was arrested for the sin of "sacrilege" at Freguesia de Nossa Senhora do Amparo de Marica, Rio de Janeiro (processo 3641). She died in her prison cell waiting to be sent to Lisbon.[22]

I found other non-Judaic heresies listed under the crimes, for instance, of Lutheranism, Islamism, and Calvinism—for example, João Bono, aged 20, from Anvers [Antwerp], Flandres (Belgium), and a servant of Nicolau Mendes. He was living in Salvador, Bahia, and was arrested in 1591 for the crime of Lutheranism (processo 2558). The trial and sentencing took place at the house of Heitor Furtado de Mendonça in Salvador, Bahia. João Bono's penitence sentence was to walk barefoot and hold a candle in his hand at an auto-da-fé in 1591.[23] Also, a man by the name of Paulo de Brito, aged 40, was arrested for the crime of Islamism in 1595. Born in North Africa, *"Argel"* (roughly modern Algeria), he was living in São Lourenço, Pernambuco, and was married to Vitória, a Brazilian Indian, and slave of António Fernandes de Barros (processo 11113). His father is listed as *turco* ("Turk," or from the Ottoman Empire), his mother, as a *moura* ("Arab"), and he, as a mourisco ("a converted Muslim"). He was sentenced to an auto-da-fé in 1595.

Final Considerations

The results of the Inquisition dossiers here represent a wide range of places of arrests, places of birth, occupations, ages, social status, and ancestries found in the arrests made by the Inquisition. These results also reflect the impact on New Christians living in colonial Brazil who were targeted by the Inquisition, and who were deeply involved in the colonial enterprise.

The activities of the Inquisition in Brazil also reflect how the coercion of Catholic moral orthodoxy de facto eliminated local Indigeneity, as local Indigenous customs, cultural practices, and belief systems were considered anathema and heresy. Consequently, local Indigenous tribes and their children were Christianized as the result of widespread missions, proselytization, and conversions, over time, conducted by priests and members of the clergy from religious orders throughout Brazil, including in the hinterlands, especially Jesuits. Descendants of Indigenous populations who were "mixed-race" (e.g., caboclo, mameluco, cafuzo) also fell under the Inquisition's surveillance and Catholic dogma. Moreover, African slaves and their descendants received severe punishments for varied sins (including what was perceived as "Judaizing"), even if they were victims of rape or sexual abuse or violence.[24]

In summary, these results project the scale, tactics, surveillance, and power of the Portuguese Inquisition, Crown, and Catholic Church in the Brazilian colonial enterprise. Using Christian orthodoxy as a violent method to annihilate other cultures, languages, and religions, committing blatant "culturecide" that impacted not only Portuguese New Christians, Jews, and Judaism, but also crushed local Indigenous and African belief systems and cultures, this powerful strategy of coercion projected intimidation and oppression on a large geographical scale.

The Inquisition, along with the Crown and Catholic Church (with the full support of the Pope), intentionally eradicated non-Christian religions, including Indigenous, African, and Jewish ones. However, it specifically targeted New Christians in a manner that went far beyond mere discriminatory policy. To reiterate Francisco Bethencourt's statement of the Portuguese Inquisition's investment in seeking out Judaizers, "Judaism invariably emerges as the principal 'heresy' to be combated."[25] This preoccupation with Judaism also explains the Portuguese Inquisition's obsession with surveillance, searching, finding, arresting, and punishing the "imagined Jew" in Brazil. While one of the goals of the Inquisition was to readmit heretics into the body of the Church, and only those the Inquisition had deemed relapsed or unwilling to confess and conform were burned, again consider that an estimated 100,000 to 200,000 Jews were once living in Portugal before 1497, accounting for as much as 10 to 20 percent of Portugal's total population, yet they disappeared in one fell swoop (and today the Jewish population in Portugal continues to be virtually zero, as discussed earlier in Chapter 2). The majority of their descendants, estimated in the several thousands, went to live in Brazil sometimes as penal exiles, only to be targeted again by the Inquisition. They represent the bulk of individuals arrested by the Inquisition throughout the colonial period, Judaizers or not.

Conclusion

THE CONSTELLATION OF THE Southern Cross, O Cruzeiro do Sul, which today covers Brazil's national flag and became an iconic Brazilian image within Brazilian nationhood, merits attention here. It was a former Jew (a New Christian) by the name of Mestre João who is credited as being the first (European) astronomer to depict and record it correctly during his first arrival on Brazil's shores of Bahia, along with Cabral's fleet, in 1500[1]—a fact that remains largely omitted in the historiography of Brazil and Latin American geography. In one sense, it is the perfect metaphor for Brazil: a constellation recorded by a former Jewish astronomer-turned-New Christian that was given a name that invokes the overtly symbol of the Christian cross. Its discoverer's true origins, however, remain obscured, just as the true origins of those who were at the forefront of much of Brazil's colonial development have been largely omitted in Brazil's historiography and public discourse. The symbol of the Southern Cross might be understood as a paradox—an inextricable fusion of that which is Jewish and that which is Christian. Yet the symbol is clearly one where the Christian element has been overly exalted at the cost of neglecting the contributions and achievements of former Jews, Jewish descendants, and New Christians in the "making of Brazil."

The constellation of the Southern Cross would eventually become a Brazilian symbol of nationhood. Not only is it emboldened across Brazil's national flag today, but the symbology of this constellation takes its namesake from the National Order of the Southern Cross, the prestigious Brazilian Order of chivalry, *Ordem Nacional do Cruzeiro do Sul*, founded by Brazil's emperor, Dom Pedro I, in 1822, the year Brazil declared independence from Portugal. In such epistles under Brazilian skies, the Christian cross projects the contested and tense unfolding of the colonial enterprise in Brazil.

From that moment in 1500 onward when Mestre João identified the Southern Cross, Brazil became a major destination for Portuguese immigrants, especially New Christians fleeing persecution from the Portuguese Crown, Catholic Church, and the Inquisition. Portuguese New Christians had been specifically recruited by the Crown to exploit Brazil's first economic boom, brazilwood. They had also been hired to expand Brazil's sugarcane cultivation and industry. They were recruited for their sugarcane cultivation expertise to establish the sugar industry in the dark, fertile *massapé* soils in Brazil's northeast region, mostly in Pernambuco and Bahia. Consequently, Brazil became the world's largest sugar producer and exporter.

The Christian crucifix became a powerful and influential symbol, in terms of scale and scope, and had an enormous impact in Brazil and throughout the Americas. Moreover, Christianity and European colonialism in the Americas go hand in hand, (Christianity justifying colonialism). The symbology of the crucifix, literally planted into the soil of the Americas since the first arrival of Columbus in 1492, and Cabral in Brazil in 1500, would forecast the subsequent coercion of Christian and European colonial enterprises that would follow. This broader relationship between religion and colonialism shows how the proselytization of Christianity spread throughout the Americas through forced and coerced conversions, and through the elimination of non-Christian religions, belief systems, practices, customs, languages, and cultures. Today, Christianity is by far the most prevalent religion in Brazil (with the largest Catholic population in the world today) and throughout the Americas, with some of the staunchest adherents in the world. The image and role of the crucifix in the Americas became more than just a religious symbol; it emerged as a major force in the projection of empire, colonialism, geopolitics, and geographical expansion.

In this case, there are two notable juxtapositions that stand out as Brazil's best-known iconographies today, a nation the Portuguese had originally named "Land of the Holy Cross" (Terra da Santa Cruz). First, the constellation of the Southern Cross, discussed above; and second, the iconic statue of "Christ the Redeemer" (*Cristo redentor*), which towers over Guanabara Bay in Rio de Janeiro—a statue depicting the figure of Jesus Christ with open arms. Placed on the peak of Mount Corcovado (700 meters/2,300 feet high), the statue is 28 meters/92 feet wide, and stands 30 meters/98 feet high. Built in the 1920s, the statue has become a cultural icon of Christianity throughout Brazil and the world. It is a historical representation and reminder of the Christian colonial orthodoxy implanted in Brazil from the Old World. The statue oversees all of the city of Rio, an inescapable image wherever *cariocas* look (local residents of Rio). The statue of "Christ the Redeemer" silently overlooks the narrative of former Portuguese Jews and their descendants in a land they arrived in centuries ago, as well as that of Brazilian Indigenous and African peoples, cultures, and religious belief systems that were annihilated over five hundred years ago.[2] It overlooks a land of extreme contradictions, with its geography of violence, sadness, silence. intolerance, and its façade of a land better known for the samba, carnaval, joy, and happiness ("*alegria, alegria!*").

I have explored such narratives, offering examples of human-environment interactions in colonial Brazil. I have included discussions of geography and spatial mobility, leading up to Dutch rule from 1630 to 1654, when Jews were allowed to profess their religion for the only time ever during the colonial period (a forbidden religion in Brazil from 1500 until the end of the Inquisition in 1821). I have also discussed the first official Jewish communities that spawned in Recife and Olinda, with the establishment of the first synagogues in the New World. During Dutch rule (1630–1654), many Portuguese Jews from Amsterdam migrated to Brazil and continued industry of sugarcane cultivation. Portuguese Jews would have comprised about half the population of the city of Recife during that period. Some Jewish families who stayed in Brazil after the Dutch had left, reverted to being New Christian, and eventually their descendants converted and became Catholic Brazilians. Over time, those descendants became completely unaware of their Jewish ancestral roots.

The role of Portuguese Jews and New Christians who had once thrived in Recife during Dutch rule is a salient one, related to various sites and scales of global commercial networks, movement, and migration. For example, when the Dutch left Brazil, many Portuguese sugarcane experts left as well. This movement out of northeast Brazil, implemented in Barbados, Jamaica, and Curaçao, for example, overlapped with the end of the sugar boom in Brazil, and with the diffusion of the sugarcane industry to the Caribbean Islands and the Dutch Antilles.

This diffusion coincided, at the same time, with the founding of the first official Jewish communities throughout the Caribbean. Notably, twenty-three Brazilian Jews who migrated from Recife to New Amsterdam (today New York City) established the first Jewish communities in North America, while others went to Newport (Rhode Island). In summary, they founded the first Jewish communities in the Western Hemisphere, as a result of the migration from the Jewish community in Recife, Brazil.

On this note, more research is needed to establish a link between descendants of Jews and New Christians and the well-known and old established Portuguese immigrant communities living today in the United States in Rhode Island (Newport, Pawtucket, Providence) and Massachusetts (New Bedford, Fall River, Taunton, Nantucket, Providence), who are the descendants of immigrants from the Atlantic Islands of Azores or Cape Verde, as well as mainland Portugal.

Over time, Anti-Jewish sentiments lingered in colonial Brazil, as New Christians continued to be persecuted and arrested by the Inquisition for being "potential Judaizers." The Portuguese Inquisition only ended in 1821, a year before Brazil's independence from Portugal in 1822. Except for 24 years during Dutch rule (albeit in the northeast region only), Jews were not allowed to "exist" or practice their faith in colonial Brazil for a period of 321 years. Even after being baptized and receiving the appellation of "New Christians," Jewish descendants continued to be discriminated against and persecuted. Yet New Christians migrated in droves to Brazil and imagined a better life there. Their story within colonial Brazil merits attention and recognition. Given that the diaspora of the Portuguese Jews and New Christians is considered one of the largest European diasporas of the early modern period (most went to Brazil), their migration movement should be placed front and center within the biography of Brazil.[3]

I have pointed out that these Jewish communities have received recognition in some public spheres in Brazil, and have been extensively studied by historians, mostly lusophone scholars. So, how is this narrative submerged? How is it that, despite the importance of this topic, it has been so widely ommited and neglected within anglophone social sciences, Latin American studies, and especially in geography? I have outlined seven important and possible interrelated explanations in the Introduction, which I have weaved throughout this book. Again, while the topics that I have discussed here may be familiar to a Brazilian audience, they are not to an anglophone one, and other points may be unfamiliar to both. There are many nuances found in the historiography, as much as contradictions, within the livelihoods of Portuguese Jews and New Christians—Judaizers or not. Some New Christians were forcibly sent to Brazil as degredados (penal exiles) while others went voluntarily (and/or clandestinely), searching for freedom of religion and socioeconomic opportunities, and perhaps, adventure or curiosity prompted by the geographical imagination. Many New Christian family members intermarried with Old Christians, Africans, and Indians in Brazil, yet the marker of "New Christian" still carried on over to their descendants as a symbol of the "taint" of Jewish ancestry (sangue infecto).

New Christians sought freedom and socioeconomic opportunities by migrating to Brazil. Most of them (especially after the sixteenth century) were restricted, and were therefore prevented from holding public office or entering prestigious social and religious Orders. Most remained stigmatized by their status and ancestry and were thus prone to suspicion, denunciations, and arrests.[4] Anti-Jewish sentiments and the fear of the Inquisition from the Old World transferred to the New World, and thus sociocultural anti-Jewish legacies were transferred to Brazil (i.e., sangue infecto, and fama pública).

There are no records of organized violent acts against New Christians in colonial Brazil as there were in Spain and Portugal, other than the presence and activities of the Portuguese Inquisition visitations beginning in 1591.[5] Such contradictions and nuances, as well as the ancestral ambiguity in early Portuguese families in Brazil, are salient considerations to keep in mind here, as their important roles in Brazil's early nation-making are often obfuscated.[6]

I have examined the Inquisition's concerns with New Christian presence and prominence in Brazil. Ironically, the documentation of dossiers left behind by the inquisitors underlines the concern of the Crown, Church, and Inquisition regarding the "infamous" presence of New Christian Judaizers in the colony, the number of which was undoubtedly far higher than that reflected in these arrests. Without their inclusion in the biography of colonial Brazil, the geography of Brazil is incomplete, and their presence, prominence, and experience merit more attention and recognition within the geography of colonial Brazil, and more broadly, within that of Latin America.

The perceptions gained here, then, offer unique insights into a new version of the complex and diverse human geographies and national demographics that emerged in Brazil. The movement of Portuguese Jews and New Christians and their participation in Brazilian colonial society was characterized by an ongoing tension—often pushing and pulling them somewhere between the Star of David and the Christian cross. This important legacy and memory of Brazil's colonial period is inherently tied to this "new" geography of Brazil and the Atlantic world.

Afterword

Since I have only addressed the Brazilian colonial period in this book, at this juncture the reader might be asking if anti-Jewish sentiments are still prevalent today; do they even exist and if so, how are they manifested in modern Brazilian society? Has modern anti-Semitism also contributed to the submerged memory and legacy that exists in the historiography of Jews and New Christians in colonial Brazil? These are broad and complex questions, and I do not intend to answer them in the same depth as other scholars have aptly done elsewhere.[1] However, it is worthwhile to offer brief insights that will suffice for this purpose here. That is, there is a clear undercurrent of anti-Semitism in modern Brazil which has gained increased public visibility today.

A Brazilian law enacted in 1989, named *Lei Caó* (Lei 7.716, Article 140 of the Brazilian penal code) after Carlos Alberto de Oliveira, *deputado* ("state representative") and activist of the Movimento Negro, "Black Movement," includes *injúria racial*, or "racial slurs." Therefore, it is unlawful to offend anybody in reference to race, color, ethnicity, religion, or origin. The Delegacia de Crimes Raciais e Delitos de Intolerância ("Police Station of Racial Crimes and Crimes of Intolerance"), created in São Paulo, for example, is a police station that deals specifically with racial crimes and intolerance, including homophobia.[2] Despite these preventative measures and the legislation implemented, altogether they have not foiled the recent spike in anti-Semitism in Brazil.

In 2017, an article published in *The Financial Times* (and re-printed by the Brazilian newspaper, *Folha de São Paulo*) reported: "the rise of neo-Nazis in Brazil has challenged a popular myth that racism, at least the overt variety on display in the US and other western countries, does not exist there."[3] This is referring to the popular and well-known "Brazilian myth" that has circulated for a long time, claiming that the problem in Brazil is "social," and not "racial." Another common myth perpetuated in Brazil is that anti-Semitism is not the same as it is in Europe or the United States, for instance, or that religious and racial discrimination do not exist in Brazil (commonly repeated by many Brazilian politicians). This is evidently a fallacy, considering that neo-Nazi groups in Brazil have grown by 170 percent, increasing from 7,600 to 20,502 between the years of 2002 and 2009.[4] The Brazilian national newspaper *O Globo* reported recently that anti-Semitism and attacks on Jews have risen dramatically in Brazil since 2020.[5]

The BBC News reported an even more glaring recent perspective: "the number of neo-Nazi cells in Brazil rose from 75 to 530 between 2015 and 2021 . . . the number of investigations launched into alleged Nazi apologisms has also shot up with federal police figures suggesting it rose by 900% between 2011 and 2020."[6] As of August 2022, neo-Nazi groups in Brazil continue to increase significantly under the presidency of Jair Bolsanaro.[7]

These cases of anti-Semitism in Brazil are not relegated to just fringe radical groups or movements; they have also entered the mainstream and political spheres as well. For example, in 2020, politician Roberto Jefferson, head of a majority Brazilian political party and a conservative Christian and Evangelical (Labor Party PTB, now a supporter of Brazil's current president, Jair Bolsanaro, a conservative, militant Christian-based politician) stated, "Baal, a Satanic deity that Canaanites and Jews sacrificed children to, to receive their sympathy"—thus reflecting how banal medieval anti-Jewish sentiments are still perpetuated today, even among prominent Brazilian politicians.[8] Notably, Brazil's Minister of Culture, Roberto Alvim, delivered a nationally televised public speech in 2019 in which he quoted, word for word (and translated into Portuguese), a speech from Adolf Hitler's associate and Third Reich's Minister of Propaganda, Joseph Goebbels. After a public uproar, he was eventually fired from his position.[9]

Episodes of anti-Semitism in Brazil also abound in public spheres. Recently, for example in February 2022, a popular Brazilian podcaster went on air to claim that Brazil should have its own national Nazi party, saying, "if someone wants to be anti-Jewish, I think he has a right to be."[10] In another recent case in 2021, The Israelite Confederation of Brazil, CONIB (Confederação Israelita do Brasil), expressed solidarity toward a popular television presenter who was attacked on social media for being

Jewish—although he is only part Jewish on his father's side. These attacks unleashed a barrage of grotesque anti-Semitic comments on Brazilian social media. One online commenter, for example, said, "For money . . . [he] (a Jew) loves even pork," and another commenter wrote that the presenter was "profiting like a good Jew. How I loathe this filthy race."[11]

Another recent account stands out. In 2019, Brazil's armed forces decided to posthumously honor a former member of the German Nazi Party and major in the Wehrmacht, Eduard Ernest Thilo Otto Maximilian von Westernhagen (who had been personally promoted in rank by Adolf Hitler). At the end of WWII, Westernhagen fled to Argentina, and then went to Brazil—in a similar trajectory made by hundreds of other Nazi war criminals through the so-called "ratlines" to South America and Brazil, many with the help of the Vatican and the Red Cross (e.g., Adolf Eichmann, Klaus Barbie, Josef Mengele, Walter Rauff, Franz Stangl, Eric Priebke).[12] Brazil became a haven for fugitive former Nazis, especially in the south and southeast regions (e.g.; Rio de Janeiro, São Paulo, Santa Catarina, Paraná, and Rio Grande do Sul).[13]

Westernhagen eventually enrolled and attended the Brazilian army's elite commando school, Escola de Comando e Estado-Maior do Exército (ECEME), in Rio de Janeiro. Later in 1968, he was killed by members of the Brazilian left-wing guerilla organization, Comando de Libertação Nacional (COLINA), who had mistaken him for Gary Prado (responsible for the death of Ernesto "Che" Guevara in Bolivia). Today, a message posted conspicuously on the official website of Brazil's armed forces states that Westernhagen was "assassinated by an act of terrorism." Furthermore, the armed forces of Brazil claim, "Major Otto was determined to show the world the value of the German Army, in an attempt to change Germany's negative image from WWII" (*O Major Otto também tinha a missão de apresentar ao mundo o valor do Exército da Alemanha, tentando desfazer a imagem negativa deixada na 2ª Guerra Mundial*).[14] Deplorably, a classroom at that same military school (ECEME, in Urca, Rio de Janeiro), was dedicated in 2019 to this former Nazi, with his name appearing on a bronze plaque in his honor.[15] This gesture by the Brazilian Army to honor the former Nazi received swift condemnation by the Israelite Confederation of Brazil; however, their complaints were unsuccessful, and the plaque has not been removed.[16]

While these fragmented vignettes reflect mere snippets of many examples in public spheres today, the academic literature on anti-Semitism in Brazil is broad.[17] During the 1930s the Brazilian state expressed strong anti-Semitic sentiments, as a large influx of Ashkenazi Jews who were fleeing Europe arrived in Brazil.[18] Brazilian politician and historian Gustavo Barroso, one of the main producers of that wave of anti-Semitism during the 1930s, produced and distributed a document which alluded to an imminent attack on Brazil by the so-called "Jewish international communist movement," allegedly foiled by the Brazilian armed forces, and known as Plano Cohen ("Cohen Plan").[19] The purported inherent connection between communism and Jews only exacerbated anti-Semitic public sentiments later, during the Brazilian right-wing military dictatorship (1964–1985), because of the communists' alleged association with a perceived global Jewish conspiracy akin to the *Protocols of the Elders of Zion*.[20] The Brazilian military went on to crush institutions or imprison people with any connections to Marxist-oriented thought. Therefore, given the close association made between Jews and communism, a major political effort by right-wing politicians emerged to combat communism in Brazil during the post-WWII period and during the military dictatorship. Altogether these imagined associations increasingly fanned anti-Semitic anxieties in Brazil.

Odilon Caldeira Neto has discussed the idea of collective memory, drawing attention to Michael Pollak's constructs of "memory, omission, and silence" in light of the Holocaust in WWII.[21] The process of reconstructing an official or legitimate historiography and memory of nationhood is mired in controversy. Caldeira Neto examined the context of Holocaust deniers in Brazil such as Siegfried Ellwanger, owner and founder of the publishing press, Editora Revisão, which focused on anti-Semitic literature, and writer of the most notorious Holocaust denial publication in Brazil, *Holocausto: Judeu ou Alemão? Nos bastidores da mentira do século* ("Holocaust: Jew or German? The background of the Lie of the Century"), published in 1987. Ellwanger, born in Candelária, Rio Grande do Sul, of German ancestry, often wrote under the pseudonym of S. E. Castan—according to him, in order to escape "Zionist persecution."[22] The Editora Revisão press also published, and became the Brazilian distributor of other notorious anti-Semitic publications authored by Henry Ford, David Duke, Gustavo Barroso, Sérgio

Oliveira, and Louis Marschalko, and was the national distributor in Brazil for the *Protocols of the Elders of Zion*.[23] Ellwanger's rhetoric was forged as an academic enterprise centered on virulent racist and anti-Semite hatred; and a long controversial legal case that centered on the injurious illegality of his book, *Holocausto: Judeu ou Alemão?*, ended up in the Brazilian Supreme Court—a legal case that lasted until 2003. Historian Caldeira Neto explains how Moreira Alves, minister and president of Brazil's Supreme Court (Supremo Tribunal Federal), claimed that the case was not valid because Jews could not be considered a "race"; therefore, Ellwanger's publication was not "racist." Another minister and Chief Justice of Brazil, Carlos Britto, agreed, claiming that Ellwanger's book was a result of historic research with the goal of "rehabilitating the image of the German people."[24]

However, in 2003 the legal case ended, and Ellwanger was found guilty of disseminating racist rhetoric—which is against Brazilian law—and he was sentenced to two years of community service. As Caldeira Neto points out, such episodes and available publications contribute to the ever-growing neo-Nazi dissemination and Holocaust deniers in Brazil today (as seen in a recent case of neo-Nazis who physically attacked a group of Brazilian Jews in the streets of Porto Alegre. Police found Nazi propaganda and materials published by Ellwanger's Editora Revisão in their possession).[25]

It is here that we also find a connection to Brazilian politician Daniela Cristina Reinehr, who is currently vice-governor of the state of Santa Catarina and the daughter of publicly overt anti-Semite, Altair Reinehr, a retired history teacher in Santa Catarina. Altair Reinehr is an outspoken admirer of Adolf Hitler and also a Holocaust denier (he had spoken for years about denying the veracity of the Holocaust to his students in public schools in Santa Catarina). Altair Reinehr was also a close associate of Siegfried Ellwanger, and had published various publications for Editora Revisão. When vice-governor Daniela Reinehr was asked if she was a Holocaust denier like her father, and also about her views on the rise of neo-Nazism in Brazil, she refused to answer, and instead responded that she "respected all people's individual rights and liberties." Despite a lukewarm retraction a few days later, she received swift condemnation from the Jewish community in Brazil, and from around the world.[26] Anti-Semitism is especially acute in the states of Santa Catarina, Paraná, and Rio Grande do Sul, where an overwhelming proportion of its population claims German ancestry, many of whom were overtly supportive of the Third Reich during WWII and affiliated to Germany's Nazi Party (with the largest Nazi Party membership outside of Germany during that time).[27]

Clearly, while Brazil's perceived joie de vivre may tantalize much of the world with its geographical imaginations, Brazil is a country still rife with medieval anti-Jewish and modern anti-Semitic sentiments, as seen in the examples above. Historical Old World and universal anti-Jewish sentiments lingering from the colonial period have ostensibly left a deep mark to this day, morphing into modern anti-Semitism, since to be a "Jew" today still carries a strong negative social stigma in Brazil. Therefore, a combination of the ancient universal anti-Jewish sentiments with modern racialized anti-Semitism, exacerbated by modern neo-Nazi movements, altogether emerge as significant forces in the omission of the Portuguese-Jewish and New Christian legacy and memory in colonial Brazil.

To reiterate Stuart B. Schwartz's commentary, "the early infamy of Brazil as a colony settled by New Christians . . . began to fade somewhat as the colony became profitable and the origins of the first settlers were forgotten."[28] Evidently, because of this "infamous legacy," modern anti-Semitic ideations articulated by prominent public, political, military, religious, and academic figures would prefer to exclude, and thereby silence, the important legacy of Jews and New Christians and their descendants from the narrative of Brazilian historiography and from the construct of Brazilian nationhood.

Appendix

Part I

All miscellaneous arrests by the Portuguese Inquisition are listed below in Portuguese along with the equivalent translation into English (translated by author):

Abuso da ordem do sacramento: "abuse of order of sacrament"
Acusado de impedir o recto mistério do Santo Oficio e de corrupção: "accused of obstructing the ministry of the Holy Office, and of corruption"
Atentado contra a moral cristã: "offense against Christian morals"
Celebrar missas tendo só a ordem da epístola: "celebrating mass only with order of epistle" (following a particular order as stated in the epistle)
Comer carne em dias defesos: "eating meat on holy days"
Cumplicidade de judaísmo: "accomplice in Judaism"
Cumplicidade em bigamia: "accomplice in bigamy"
Cumplicidade em embustes, blasfémias, bruxaria e feitiçaria: "accomplice/complicit in scams, blasphemy, witchcraft, and sorcery"
Desacato: "disrespect"
Desacato ao Santissímo Sacramento da Eucaristia: "disrespect to the Eucharistic Sacrament"
Desacatos a uma imagem do Senhor crucificado: "disrespect to the Lord Crucified"
Desrespeito ao Santo Ofício: "disrespect to the Holy Office"
Divulgar um segredo do Santo Oficio: "divulging secrets of the Holy Office"
Dizer missa e confessar, sem ter ainda ordem de missa: "giving a Mass sermon without orders"

Dizer missa, sem que tivesse sido ordenado: "giving a Mass sermon without being ordained"
Embustes e fingimentos: "scams and pretending"
Falso sacerdote jesuíta: "false Jesuit priest"
Fazer-se passar por comissário do Santo Ofício: "pretending to be an officer of the Holy Office"
Fazer-se passar por sacerdote, celebrar missa e confessor: "pretending to be a priest and celebrating Mass and confessions"
Fingimento de visões: "pretending to have visions"
Heresia por comer carne na Quaresma: "heresy for eating meat during Passover"
Impedir o recto ministério do Santo Oficio: "obstruction of the Holy Office"
Não entregar os despachos na Mesa da Visitação: "not forwarding reports of Inquisition Visitation"
Ofender e perturbar o recto ministério do Santo Ofício: "offending and disturbing the Holy Office"
Ofensas ao Santíssimo Sacramento: "offenses to the Holy Sacrament"
Pacto com o demónio: "pact with the Devil"
Pedreiro-livre, maçon: "Freemasonry"
Possuir livros proibidos: "possession of forbidden books"
Prejúrio: "perjury"
Receber a comunhão depois de ter almoçado: "receiving communion after eating lunch"
Revelações: "revelations"
Solicitação: "solicitation"
Usurpação de poderes eclesiásticos: "abuse of ecclesiastical powers"
Violação das Ordens: "violation of orders"
Violação do celibato: "violation of celibacy"

Part II

Place of birth for those arrested for the crime of Judaism in Brazil:

PORTUGAL (TOTAL OF 147)
    Fundão

Travaço, termo de Armamar
Alameida
Alcains, Castelo Branco
Almeida, bispado de Lamego (11)
Arraiolos (3)
Azevo, Pinhel, bispado de Lamego
Basto, arcebispado de Braga
Bispado de Lamego
Bragança
Buarcos, bispado de Coimbra (2)
Castelo Rodrigo, bispado de Lamego (4)
Castro Daire, bispado de Lamego (3)
Celorico da Beira, bispado da Guarda (4)
Chaves, arcebispado de Braga
Coimbra (3)
Coruche, arcebispado de Évora
Covilhã, bispado da Guarda (5)
Crato
Cucaú, Rio Formoso
Elvas
Estremoz, Alentejo
Évora (3)
Favaios, Comarca de Lamego
freguesia de Santa Justa, Lisboa
Freixadas, termo de Pinhel, bispado de Viseu
Freixedas, Pinhel, bispado de Viseu
Freixedas, termo de Pinhel, bispado de Viseu
Freixo de Espada à Cinta
Freixo de Numão
Fronteira
Fronteira, comarca de Évora
Guarda (2)
Idanha-a-Nova, bispado da Guarda (8)
Leiria
Lisbon (24)
lugar de Maçal do Chão

lugar de Vilar Torpim, Castelo Rodrigo
Maçal do Chão, bispado da Guarda
Manteigas, bispado da Guarda
Monforte, termo de Castelo Branco, bispado da Guarda
Montemor-o-Velho
Moura, arcebispado de Évora
Olivença
Pinhel, bispado de Viseu (2)
Portimao,
Porto (7)
São Vicente da Beira, Guarda (3)
Sabugal, bispado de Lamego (3)
Sardoal, bispado da Guarda
Setúbal
Tomar
Torre de Moncorvo
Torres Novas
Trancoso
Travaço, termo de Armamar
Viana
Viana de Caminha
Viana do Minho
vila de Campo Maior
vila de Freixo de Numão, bispado de Lamego
vila de Graçu
vila de Idanha-a-Nova, bispado da Guarda
vila do Mogadouro, arcebispado de Braga (2)
Vila Nova de Foz Côa, bispado de Lamego (2)
Vila Nova de Portimão
Vila Real, arcebispado de Braga (4)

BRAZIL (275 TOTAL)

Bahia (4)
Other places in Bahia:
Matoim, S. Salvador da Baía de Todos os Santos (4)
Porto Seguro

sítio do Serinhém, Bahia
Pernambuco (6)
Other places in Pernambuco:
Rio das Marés, termo de Paraíba, bispado de Pernambuco
Ebiribeira, termo de Paraiba, bispado de Pernambuco
Engenho da Pindoba
Engenho de Inhohim
Engenho de Santo André, Paraíba, bispado de Pernambuco
Engenho do Inhobim, capitania de Paraíba, bispado de Pernambuco
Engenho Novo, Distrito de Paraíba, Bispado de Pernambuco (2)
Engenho Velho, cidade de Paraíba, bispado de Pernambuco (4)
freguesia de Porto Calvo do Bom Jesus, termo de Olinda
freguesia de Santiago, sítio do Poxim, termo da cidade de Paraíba, bispado de Pernambuco
Goiana
Ipojuca
Olinda (2)
Poxim, termo de Paraíba, bispado de Pernambuco
Santo António do Cabo, bispado de Pernambuco
Serinhais, Pernambuco
Terras do Engenho Velho, Paraiba, bispado de Pernambuco
Sítio do Pochim—freguesia Nossa Senhora da Guia, Paraíba, bispado de Pernambuco (2)
Xirinem (likely, "Sirinhaém," south of Recife)

PARAÍBA (5)
Other places in Paraíba:
Emberibeira, distrito de Paraíba
Engenho do Meio, distrito de Paraíba
Paraíba, Rio das Marés
Sertão de Manguapé, Paraíba
terras de Poxim, termo de Paraíba

RIO DE JANEIRO (210)
Other places in Rio de Janeiro:
Jaraguá

Meia Ponte, bispado do Rio de Janeiro
Campinho, freguesia de Irajá, termo do Rio de Janeiro (2)
Freguesia de Irajá, distrito do Rio de Janeiro
Engenho do Meio, Rio de Janeiro
freguesia de São João Baptista, Itaboraí, Rio de Janeiro
Santos, bispado do Rio de Janeiro (3)
sítio dos Campinhos

SÃO PAULO
Santos, São Paulo (2)
Vila de São Paulo

SPAIN (9 TOTAL)
Sevilha
Valladolid
Sauzelhe
Medina del Campo
Lombardes
Ayamonte
Mérida
Antequera, Andaluzia
Cantalapiedra, Salamanca

FRANCE (3 TOTAL)
vila de Tartáz, província de Gascunha
vila de Vidaxe
lugar de Vidage

ATLANTIC ISLANDS (3 TOTAL)
Funchal, Ilha da Madeira (2)
Ponta Delgada, the Azores

THE NETHERLANDS (1 TOTAL)
Amsterdam

Appendix 251

New Christians (or Part New Christians) Arrested in Brazil for the Crime of Judaism with Non-European Parentage (Found under the Column Either of Mother's or Father's Name/Social Status)

NAME	AGE	OCCUPATION	FATHER'S NAME/ SOCIAL STATUS	MOTHER'S NAME/ SOCIAL STATUS	YEAR OF ARREST	DOSSIER #
Teodoro Pereira da Costa	34	Doctor	Baltazar da Costa	Branca, *mulher negra*	1716	2222
João da Cruz	40	Tailor	Bento Cardoso	Esperança, *mulher negra*	1716	2219
...na de Paredes	40	Widow	*descendente de dois pretos da Guiné**	*descendente de dois pretos da Guiné*	1715	4944
Leonor Mendes	50	N/A	Rodrigo Mendes de Paredes	Ursula *escrava preta*	1713	9985
Manuel Rodrigues Coutinho	43	Unemployed	Baltazar Rodrigues Coutinho, *senhor do engenho*	Jerónima de Sequeira, *mulher parda*	1713	9989
Padre João ...res Caldeira	60	Priest	António Peres Caldeira	Marta Gomes, *mulher parda*	1714	7893
Gabriel de ...edes	43	Carpenter	Rodrigo Mendes de Paredes, *lavrador*	Francisca, *mulher preta*	1714	7966
...riana Peres	55	Widow of João da Silva, *lavrador de cana*	António Peres Caldeira, *lavrador de cana*	Marta Gomes, *mulher parda*	1714	7980
...rança de ...eira	24	N/A	Inácio de Sousa	Úrsula de Oliveira, *mulher parda*	1714	11202

Appendix

NAME	AGE	OCCUPATION	FATHER'S NAME/ SOCIAL STATUS	MOTHER'S NAME/ SOCIAL STATUS	YEAR OF ARREST	DOSSIER #
Sebastião da Silva	18	Tailor, slave	João Rodrigues de Andrade, *lavrador*	Micaela Pedrosa, *mulher parda*	1715	7974
Felipe de Mendonça	60	N/A	Luís Paredes	Marta, *preta escrava*	1716	11591
Andresa Jorge	43	Married to Fernão de Sousa	Manuel Carvalho Serra, *homem branco, lavrador*, from Rio Douro, Portugal	Ana Barbosa, *preta forra*	1599	1078
Ana da Fonseca	50	Single	Francisco Luís, *homem branco*	Bárbara, *escrava negra*	1729	5546
Catarina da Paz	45	married to António de Miranda	Baltazar da Costa, Clergyman, Nossa Senhora do Carmo	Branca, *mulher negra*	1714	2222
Micaela Matos	30	married to Luís de Matos Coutinho, fisherman	Manuel Soares, fisherman	Luzia, *mulher preta, escrava*	1675	7762
Teresa Barbalha de Jesus	52	Single	Fernão Gonçalves, *homem branco, lavrador*	Antónia Brasília, *escrava*	1731	17762
Isabel Gomes da Costa	23	married to João Nunes Viseu, doctor	António Eanes, *homem branco, lavrador*	Catarina Martins, *mameluca*	1710	5534

Appendix 253

AME	AGE	OCCUPATION	FATHER'S NAME/ SOCIAL STATUS	MOTHER'S NAME/ SOCIAL STATUS	YEAR OF ARREST	DOSSIER #
rtoleza	20	N/A	N/A	Catarina, *negra*	1710	17809
gela do Vale Mesquita	20	married to Domingos Rodrigues, *lavrador*	Manuel Lopes de Morais, clerk	Guiomar Nunes, *mulher parda*	1710	9137
ariana Correia	20	N/A	João Correia, slave of João Rodrigues Santiago	*preta forra*	1714	1134
ria do Bom esso	20	N/A	Caetano da Costa Bravo, slave	Rosa Maria do Rosário, *escrava*	1716	719
pa Mendes	23	N/A	Diogo Leandro, *índio* and *infiel*	*índia*	1733	225
el Cardoso	74	N/A	Filipe Monteiro, *índio*	Teresa da Conceição, *índia*	1712	2693
el de des	40	N/A	Robertim, *índio*	Micaela, *índia*	1712	2700
s da Paz	15	N/A	Francisco Rodrigues, clerk	Isabel Rodrigues, *índia*	1712	10714
l Correia usa	33	N/A	Mateus de Sousa Madeira, tailor	Luísa Maria, *índia*	1714	2696
Correia nes	30	N/A	Pedro Afonso, clergyman	Francisca Coelho, *mestiça forra*	1714	2550
bel de a	40	married to Agostinho de Paredes, lawyer and *senhor de engenho*	Jerónimo de Albuquerque	Maria, *índia forra*	1714	11206

NAME	AGE	OCCUPATION	FATHER'S NAME/ SOCIAL STATUS	MOTHER'S NAME/ SOCIAL STATUS	YEAR OF ARREST	DOSSIER
Ana Peres de Jesus	25	married to António da Silva, unemployed	Inácio de Bulhões, *homem pardo*	Francisca, *índia do Brasil*	1714	7950
Maria Bernar de Miranda	40	N/A	Gregório Brandão	Leonor da Costa, *mulher parda*	1730	8198
Amaro de Miranda Coutinho	30	N/A	Baltazar Rodrigues Coutinho, New Christian, *senhor do engenho*,	Jerónima de Sequeira, *mulher parda*	1710	9989
Luís de Matos Coutinho	44	*lavrador*	Belchior, *pardo forro*	Antónia Barbosa, *parda forra*	1675	3382
Helena do Vale	37	single	António Peres Caldeira, merchant, *lavrador de cana*	Marta Gomes, *mulher parda*	1734	7908
Diogo de Avila Henriques	26	N/A	Miguel Henriques, merchant	Maria Leitão, *mameluca*	1729	6349
Henrique Frois Muniz	37	N/A	António Peres Caldeira, merchant	Marta Gomes, *mulher parda*	1734	7893
Pedro Dias Pereira	N/A	N/A	José de Castro, *escravo preto*	Jacinta de Andrade Nogueira, *preta forra*	1709	1131

Source: Arquivos Torre do Tombo, Portugal, Inquisição de Lisboa online, http://antt.dglab.go exposicoes-virtuais-2/inquisicao-de-lisboa-online/.

Part III

Top Occupations for Those Arrested for Judaism in Brazil

Occupation	Count
Merchants	25
Lavrador	20
Lavrador de cana	20
Soldiers	16
Miners	15
Unemployed	14
Students	9
Senhores de engenho	7
Lawyers	6
Doctors	6
Carpenters	5
Sailors	5
Clergymen	4
Lavrador de mandioca	4
Lavrador de roça	3
Professors	3
Clerks	3
Musicians	2
Lavrador de tabaco	2
Tailors	2
Cobblers	2
Pharmacist	1
*Others	10
**Total	180

Source: Arquivos Torre do Tombo, Portugal, Inquisição de Lisboa online, http://antt.dglab.gov.pt/exposicoes-virtuais-2/inquisicao-de-lisboa-online/.

*Others include miscellaneous occupations: *caldeireiro, aguardenteiro, caxeiro, comboieiro, curtidor, dizimeiro, latoeiro, ourives, almoxarife, sirgueiro*—all of these were occupations that loosely correspond to: cashiers, clerks, boiler-room workers, sugar purgers, and stokers.

** 214 occupations were not listed in the dossiers here examined.

Part IV

List of Last Names for Individuals Arrested for Judaism in Brazil

NAME (LAST)	# FOR EACH NAME
Henriques	18
Silva	17
Costa	16
Nunes	16
Paredes	16
Miranda	15
Coutinho	13
Gomes	12
Pereira	12
Rodrigues	12
Fonseca	11
Jesus	10
Mendes	9
Sousa	9
Azevedo	8
Cardoso	8
Andrade	6
Barros	6
Carvalho	6
Correia	6
Leão	6
Mesquita	6
Vale	6
Cruz	5
Lopes	5
Lucena	5
Oliveira	5
Paz	5
Sanches	5
Álvares	4
Fernandes	4
Montarroio	4
Rego	4
Sequeira	4
Ximenes	4
Baptista	3

NAME (LAST)	# FOR EACH NAME
Barreto	3
Caminha	3
Dias	3
Dique	3
Ferreira	3
Fogaça	3
Guterres	3
Machado	3
Morais	3
Palhana	3
Peres	3
Rangel	3
Simões	3
Tomás	3
Valença	3
Viseu	3
Aires	2
Azeredo	2
Antunes	2
Bernal	2
Bezerra	2
Caldeira	2
Campos	2
Chaves	2
Dória	2
Fidalgo	2
Flores	2
Freire	2
Lemos	2
Maria	2
Matos	2
Moeda	2
Pina	2
Silveira	2
Soares	2
Sucesso	2
Abreu	1

NAME (LAST)	# FOR EACH NAME
Aguilar	1
Alcoforada	1
Almeida	1
Alves	1
Ávila	1
Barbalha	1
Barreta	1
Bragança	1
Bravo	1
Brum	1
Calaça	1
Castro	1
Castanho	1
Castro e Lara	1
Chacão	1
Coelho	1
Diamante	1
Dinis	1
Diniz	1
Dourado	1
Duarte	1
Faria	1
Favela	1
Ferrão	1
Figueiroa	1
Franca	1
Francês	1
Furtado	1
Garcia	1
Gramacha	1
Ilhôa	1
Inácia	1
Inácio	1
Isidoro	1
Jorge	1
Lara	1
Leite	1

NAME (LAST)	# FOR EACH NAME
Lima	1
Lis	1
Madalena	1
Maia	1
Mariz	1
Mendanha	1
Mendonça	1
Moeda	1
Monforte	1
Monsanto	1
Morão	1
Moreira	1
Penteado	1
Pilar	1
Pinto	1
Ramires	1
Ribeiro	1
Rosa	1
Sá	1
Sá de Almeida	1
Santos	1
Sotomaior	1
Teixeira	1
Valadolid	1
Vaz	1
Valente	1
Velho	1
Vila	1
Xavier	1

Source: Arquivos Torre do Tombo, Portugal, Inquisição de Lisboa online, http://antt.dglab.gov.pt/exposicoes-virtuais-2/inquisicao-de-lisboa-online/.

Glossary

All translations by author

bruxaria: witchcraft
caboclo: "half Indigenous/half white"
cafuzo: "half Indigenous/half African"
crioulo: person of African descent born in Brazil (a pejorative term today)
cristão-novo: New Christian
degredado: penal exile
engenho de açucar or Engenho: sugarcane mill and plantation
escravo preto: black African slave
esnoga: small and informal synagogue (short for "sinagoga")
fama pública: public opinion or reputation
feitiçaria: sorcery
feitiço: spell
freira: nun
homem pardo: "mixed-race" man
homem preto: black man
índio or indígena: indigenous or "Native of Brazil"
índio escravo: Brazilian-Indigenous slave
judaizante: somebody who followed Jewish religious practices in secret, clandestinely ("Crypto-Jew")
lavrador: farm worker or sharecropper (generic)
lavrador de cana: sugarcane farmer or sharecropper
maçonaria or pedreiro livre: Freemasonry/Freemason
mameluco: "half Indigenous/half white"
mercador: merchant
mercador de loja: shop owner
mestiçagem: miscegenation
mestiço: "mixed-race"

mestre de açúcar: sugarcane industry specialist
mourisco: converted Muslim/Arab
mouro: Moor/Arab/descendant of Moors
mulato: "half black/half white" ("mulatto")
mulher parda: "mixed-race" woman
mulher preta: black woman
pardo: "mixed-race" (loosely meaning "brown")
Padre: priest
paulista: a person born in São Paulo in southeast Brazil (province or modern state)
preto forro: free black person
pureza de sangue: blood purity
sangue infecto: "tainted blood" ("non-Christian")
Santo Ofício: Holy Office (i.e., the Inquisition)
senhores de engenho: sugarcane plantation owners
superstição: superstition
região açucareira: sugarcane cultivation region
For additional translation of miscellaneous heresies and accusations, see Appendix.

Notes

Preface

1. Skidmore, *Brazil: Five Centuries of Changes*, xiii.
2. It was a New Christian, Ambrósio Fernandes Brandão, who wrote the first known geographical treatise on Brazil, *Diálogos das Grandezas do Brasil*—discussed in Chapter 1. He was denounced for being a Judaizer and for attending an *esnoga* (an abbreviated term in Portuguese for "synagogue" or a Jewish prayer house) in Camaragibe, Pernambuco, in Brazil's northeast region, and therafter, arrested and imprisoned by the Inquisition in 1591. See Falbel, *Judeus no Brasil*, 100–104.
3. For example, see Marcus, "(Re)Creating Places and Spaces in Two Countries: Brazilian Transnational Migration Processes"; Marcus, "Brazilian Immigration to the United States and the Geographical Imagination"; and Marcus, *Confederate Exodus*.
4. Sometimes even educated people have asked me whether Brazilians spoke Spanish!
5. As I explain later in Chapter 1, Portuguese Jews did not self-identify as Sephardim but as "People of the Portuguese Nation."
6. Lester, *The Fourth Part of the World*, 320.
7. Nor is this rhetoric an outdated adage of the "triumph of the West" or "Western superiority." See Hobson, *The Eastern Origins of Western Civilization*, 3–7.
8. For example, see Hemming, *Red Gold*; and Mann, *1491*.
9. See Brubaker, "Ethnicity without Groups," 50–77.

Introduction

1. Brazil was virtually all Catholic by 1872, but Catholic membership began to decline a century later. In 1970 it decreased to 90 percent, and then went down to 70 percent in 2010, and today it accounts for about 65 percent of the total population, due to the rapid rise of staunch Protestant Evangelicals and Pentecostals (known as *evangélicos*). See *Instituto Brasileiro de Geografia e Estatística*, IBGE, 2010. May 13, 2022, https://biblioteca.ibge.gov.br/visualizacao/periodicos/94/cd_2010_religiao_deficiencia.pdf.
2. As early as 1560, there were already at least ten New Christian families living in Rio de Janeiro, and in São Vicente (today São Paulo), where their presence was noted as well. See Salvador, "Os cristãos-novos: o povoamento e a conquista do solo brasileiro," 550–551.

3. Quoted in Salvador, "Os cristãos-novos: o povoamento e a conquista do solo brasileiro," 550.
4. Salvador, "Os cristãos-novos: o povoamento e a conquista do solo brasileiro," 550.
5. Assis, "Inquisição, religiosidade e transformações culturais: a sinagoga das mulheres e a sobrevivência do judaísmo feminino no Brasil colonial – Nordeste, séculos XVI–XVII," 49.
6. Notably, they were among the New World's first geographers, playwrights, poets, writers, medical doctors, pharmacists, merchants, mill owners, farm technicians, skilled workers, rabbis, calligraphists, and sugarcane industry experts. See Schwartz, "A Commonwealth in Itself. The Early Brazilian Sugar Industry, 1550–1670," 174.
7. For studies about the presence in modern Brazil and of Jews in Brazil after 1822 (post-Independence period), see for example Grinberg, *Os Judeus no Brasil*; Falbel, *Judeus no Brasil*; and Lewin, *Judaísmo e Globalizacão*. [Although all of these three publications have also included essays on Jews and New Christians in colonial Brazil in their volumes]. For scholarship on studies of contemporary Jewry in Brazil, see Lesser, Jeffrey. *Welcoming the Undesirables*; Lesser, "Continuity and Change within an Immigrant Community: The Jews of São Paulo, 1924–1945"; Lesser, "Jewish Brazilians or Brazilian Jews? A Reflection of Brazilian Ethnicity"; Lesser, "How the Jews Became Japanese and Other Stories of Nation and Ethnicity"; Levine, "Brazil's Jews during the Vargas Era and After"; Klein, *Kosher Feijoada*; and Zwerling, *Os Judeus na História do Brasil*.
8. For instance, Afro-Brazilian religions (i.e., Candomblé, Umbanda) and the African diaspora to Brazil have long been the subject of interest across international popular spheres and academic literature, given that the African diaspora during the transatlantic slave trade was the largest in the world (with about 5 million Africans enslaved and taken to Brazil). More recently, the US tourism industry has catered to the rising interest among African Americans who travel to Brazil to visit important Afro-Brazilian cultural and heritage sites. See Pinho, *Mapping Diaspora*. Yet the important legacy and memory of Portuguese Jewry and Portuguese New Christians (particularly their legacy in Brazil's northeast) is virtually unknown to the rest of the world and has not received similar international attention.
9. Schwartz, *All Can Be Saved*, 178.
10. For details, see Poettering, *Migrating Merchants*, 103.
11. For more details on the diaspora of Portuguese Jews, for example, see Poettering, *Migrating Merchants*; Mello, *Gente da Nação*; Graizbord, *Souls in Dispute*; also see maps of global networks of "Portuguese People of the Nation" in Studnicki-Gizbert, *A Nation Upon the Ocean Sea*, 38 and 106.
12. For example, see the current work of geographers such as Case Watkins (e.g., *Palm Oil Diaspora*, 2021) and Andrew Sluyter (e.g., *Colonialism and Landscape*, 2001; *Black Ranching Frontiers*, 2012; *Hispanic and Latino New Orleans*, 2015), among others.
13. This is a digitized catalogue with 19,775 descriptive dossiers (processos) and 2,392,997 digitized images. Arquivos Torre do Tombo, Portugal, Inquisição de

Lisboa online, http://antt.dglab.gov.pt/exposicoes-virtuais-2/inquisicao-de-lisboa-online/.
14. Arquivo Nacional, Torre do Tombo. "National Archives at Torre do Tombo." See catalogue: http://antt.dglab.gov.pt/exposicoes-virtuais-2/inquisicao-de-lisboa-online/.
15. See, Novinsky, "Prisioneiros no Brasil," 16.
16. Although I did not conduct a study on arrests made in Portugal, the very last arrest I could find made by the Portuguese Inquisition was that of Antônio José de Miranda from Lisbon, for the crime of bigamy, in 1816. He was sent to prison in Castro Marim for three years (processo 14654).
17. For a detailed study on the crime of solicitation and the Portuguese Inquisition in colonial Brazil, see Lima, *Confissão pelo avesso*. For details on sodomy and sexuality in colonial Latin America, see Tortorici, *Sexuality and the Unnatural in Colonial Latin America*; Vainfas and Tortorici, "Female Homoeroticism, Heresy, and the Holy Office in Colonial Brazil," 77–94; and Vainfas, *Trópico dos pecados*.
18. Novinsky, *Inquisição: prisioneiros do Brasil*, 22–43.
19. Novinsky, *Inquisição: prisioneiros do Brasil*, 22–43. Also see Novinsky, "Prisioneiros no Brasil," 10–18.
20. For example, for publications in Portuguese: *A Fênix ou O Eterno Retorno*, edited by Alberto Dines, Francisco Moreno-Carvalho, and Nachman Falbel; *Os Judeus no Brasil*, edited by Keila Grinberg; *Judeus no Brasil*, by Nachman Falbel; *Identidade e cidadania*, edited by Helena Lewin; *Vultos Judaicos no Brasil* by Kurt Loewenstamm; and *Os Judeus que Construíram o Brasil* by Anita W. Novinsky, Daniela Levy, E. Ribeiro, and Lina Gorenstein; and Lira Neto, *Arrancados da Terra*. They are all written by historians, are in Portuguese, and have not been translated into the English language.
21. The Inquisition's purpose was not to create a statistical and numerical analysis of how many New Christians existed; therefore, the Inquisition dossiers should not be interpreted as a statistical database.
22. For more details on Mestre João, see Valentim, "Uma Família de Cristãos-Novos do Entre Douro e Minho: Os Paz. Reprodução Familiar, Formas de Mobildade Social, Mecancia e Poder." Occasionally known as João Emenslau, he was of Jewish descent. Also see Hill, "Alvise Cadamosto, Mestre João Faras and the Controversial History of Early European Mapping of the Southern Cross." 138.
23. Silverblatt, "The Heresies and Colonial Geopolitics," 65.
24. Studnicki-Gizbert, *A Nation Upon the Ocean Sea: Portugal's Atlantic Diaspora and the Crisis of the Spanish Empire, 1492–1640*, 4.
25. Studnicki-Gizbert, *A Nation Upon the Ocean Sea*, 95–96.
26. Trivellato, *The Familiarity of Strangers*, 44–45.
27. Falbel, "Sobre a Presença dos Cristãos Novos na Capitania de São Vicente e a Formação da Etnia Paulista," 114.
28. Webb, *The Changing Face of Northeast Brazil*, 8.
29. For a recent study on Brazil's northeast, see Blake, *The Vigorous Core of Our Nationality*.

30. Webb, *The Changing Face of Northeast Brazil*, 89.
31. An approach that is used effectively by other geographers today, such as Andrew Sluyter, for example, to study the relationship between colonial legacies and landscapes, and Case Watkins, to study palm oil in northeast Brazil. See Sluyter, *Landscape and Colonialism*; and Watkins, *Palm Oil*.
32. Webb, *The Changing Face of Northeast Brazil*, 89.
33. Schwartz, Stuart B. "The Uncourted Menina: Brazil's Portuguese Heritage," 12; and Coates, *Convicts and Orphans*, 10.
34. Quoted in Klein, "The Atlantic Slave Trade to 1650," 203. Also see Bethencourt, *Racisms*.
35. Coates, *Convicts and Orphans*, 45–46.
36. See, Bogaciovas, *Tribulações do Povo de Israel na São Paulo Colonial*, 238. Also, on the Portuguese cultural impact in Southeast Asia, see, Jarnagin, *The Making of the Luso-Asian World*; and in India, see Faria, "Todos desterrados & espalhados pelo mundo: A perseguição inquisitorial de judeus e de cristãos-novos na India Portuguesa (séculos XVI e XVII)"; and Fischel, "Leading Jews in the Service of Portuguese India."
37. Notably, as Ernst Pijning has pointed out, race and Jewishness were "negotiable"—he claims that for "mulatto," we can read "New Christian." Pijning, "New Christians as Sugar Cultivators and Traders in the Portuguese Atlantic, 1450–1800," 498.
38. Newitt, *A History of Portuguese Overseas Expansion 1400–1668*, 99.
39. See Sauer, "The Morphology of Landscape."
40. Marvell and Simm, "Unravelling the Geographical Palimpsest Through Fieldwork," 126.
41. Marvell and Simm, "Unravelling the Geographical Palimpsest Through Fieldwork," 126.
42. Cresswell, *In Place/Out of Place*, 13.
43. Cresswell, *In Place/Out of Place*, 13.
44. See Tuan, *Topophilia*; and Tuan, "Humanistic Geography."
45. See Tuan, *Topophilia*; and Tuan, "Humanistic Geography."
46. Klein, *Kosher Feijoada*, 16.
47. Also, for a discussion on place and sense of place, see Buttimer, "Grasping the Dynamism of Lifeworld," 277.
48. Graizbord, *Souls in Dispute*, 98.
49. Gould, *The Mismeasure of Man*, 22.
50. For a detailed discussion of place, sense of place, and a pedagogical insight into place-making, see Marcus, "Using 'Autogeography,' sense of place and place-based approaches in the pedagogy of geographic thought."
51. Morrill, "A Theoretical Imperative," 536–537.
52. For another study looking at migration processes of Jews in Europe, see Poettering, *Migrating Merchants*, 103.
53. As pointed out by Maio and Calaça, "New Christians and Jews in Brazil: Migrations and Antisemitism," 75.
54. See *Instituto Brasileiro de Geografia e Estatística*. IBGE 2021, https://brasil500anos.

ibge.gov.br/territorio-brasileiro-e-povoamento/portugueses/imigracao-restrita-1500-1700.html.
55. Bethencourt, *Racisms*, 183.
56. Quoted in Bogaciovas, *Tribulações do Povo de Israel na São Paulo Colonial*, 13.
57. Another genetic study claims that about a quarter of Latin Americans today, including Brazilians, share Iberian Jewish genetic ancestry, suggesting that they are descendants of Jews who had fled persecution by the Inquisition, and that they migrated in far greater numbers than previously thought. See Chacón-Duque et al., "Latin Americans show wide-spread Converso ancestry and imprint of local Native ancestry on physical appearance."
58. See Bethencourt, *Racisms*, 183–189. For a detailed list of Indigenous tribes in Brazil, see Vasconcelos, *Selecta Brasiliense ou noticias, descobertas, observações, factos e curiosidades em relação aos homens á historia e cousas do Brasil*, 181–212.
59. See Greyerz, "Portuguese conversos on the Upper Rhine and the converso Community of Sixteenth-Century Europe"; Häberlein, *The Fuggers of Augsburg*; and Poettering, *Migrating Merchants*. Although, in the case of Portuguese New Christians, there are serious doubts that most Portuguese New Christians in Antwerp and Hamburg were in fact, Judaizers, as Israel Revah had claimed. Greyerz, "Portuguese conversos on the Upper Rhine and the converso Community of Sixteenth-Century Europe," 77.
60. "Push-pull" terminologies were first heralded by late nineteenth-century geographer Ernst Georg Ravenstein, who had first formulated the well-known theory of "laws of migration." See Ravenstein, "The Laws of Migration." Notably, another side of Ravenstein's scholarship, perhaps overshadowed by his renowned work on migration, is that he also translated publications about Portuguese explorations, including a translation and discussion of Vasco da Gama's first voyage to India. See Ravenstein, "Vasco da Gama's First Voyage."
61. See Marcus, "Brazilian Immigration to the United States and the Geographical Imagination."
62. See Novinsky, "Jewish Heresy in the Light of New Documents," 114.
63. Maio and Calaça, "New Christians and Jews in Brazil: Migrations and Antisemitism," 75.
64. Maio and Calaça, "New Christians and Jews in Brazil: Migrations and Antisemitism," 75.
65. Mark and Horta, *The Forgotten Diaspora*, 63
66. Mark and Horta, *The Forgotten Diaspora*, 57.
67. Mark and Horta, *The Forgotten Diaspora*, 62.
68. Mark and Horta, *The Forgotten Diaspora*, 64.
69. Freyre became the first historian to place the African Brazilian within the formation of Brazilian collective identity. Stuczynski, "Preconceitos de uma hibridação: judeus e cristãos-novos em Casa-Grande & Senzala," 118.
70. For example, see Maio, "'Estoque semita': A presença dos judeus em Casa-Grande & Senzala."

71. Freyre, *The Masters and the Slaves*, 9. His milestone book, *Casa Grande e Senzala*, first published in 1933, was later translated into English as *The Masters and the Slaves*.
72. Freyre, *Sobrados e Mocambos*, 328–329.
73. Freyre, *The Masters and the Slaves*, 10. For a detailed discussion, see Maio, "'Estoque semita': A presença dos judeus em Casa-Grande & Senzala."
74. Freyre, *The Masters and the Slaves*, 231–232.
75. Freyre, *The Masters and the Slaves*, xi.
76. Shohat and Stam, "Genealogies of Orientalism and Occidentalism: Sephardi Jews, Muslims, and the Americas," 24. For a detailed discussion, see Maio, "'Estoque semita': A presença dos judeus em Casa-Grande & Senzala."
77. See, Freyre, *The Masters and the Slaves*.
78. This notion would be known as the *imaginário nacional* ("national imaginary"), as explained in Roberto da Matta's "*fábula das três raças*" ("myth of the three races"). Marshall C. Eakin calls it the "myth of mestiçagem" ("miscegenation") that had been built on Gilberto Freyre's idea of a narrative of *brasilidade* ("Brazilianness"). Eakin, *Becoming Brazilians*, 1–4.
79. Eakin, *Becoming Brazilians*, 1–4.
80. See Eakin, *Becoming Brazilians*, 24.
81. Aidoo, *Slavery Unseen*, 4.
82. Nascimento, *O Genocídio Do Negro Brasileiro*, 38. Also see Nobles, *Shades of Citizenship*.
83. Freyre, *The Masters and the Slaves*, 85.
84. Skidmore, *Black into White*, xii.
85. For a detailed discussion on Gilberto Freyre and his viewpoints, see Eakin, *Becoming Brazilians*, 43–78.
86. For example, Claude B. Stuczynski claims that Freyre was criticized for portraying Jews and New Christians (without making the distinction between the two) within classical anti-Semitic stereotypes, saying that Jews had an alleged "propensity for commerce and usury." Stuczynski, "Preconceitos de uma hibridação: judeus e cristaos-novos em Casa-Grande & Senzala," 121. Marcos Chor Maio, however, refutes this dominant idea of the presence of anti-Semitism in Freyre's work. Maio, "'Estoque semita': A presença dos judeus em Casa-Grande & Senzala."
87. See Maio and Calaça. "Um balanço da bibliografia sobre o anti-semitismo no Brasil," 446–447.
88. Bethencourt, *Racisms*, 1.
89. Metcalf, *Go-betweens and the Colonization of Brazil*, 129.
90. See, for example, Marcus, "Sex, Color, and Geography: Racialized Relations in Brazil and Its Predicaments," and Marcus, *Confederate Exodus*.
91. Blake, *The Vigorous Core of Our Nationality*, ix.
92. In Brazil's first national census survey in 1872, there were two options for "slave population": either black or pardo. For the free population, the options were: white, black, pardo, and caboclo. By 1891, the options changed by eliminating the slave

population section, and including the option *mestiço*. The official "color" categories used by the Brazilian census today are: *branco* ("white"), *preto* ("black"), *amarelo* ("yellow" a category used for Asians), pardo (loosely translated as "brown" or "mixed"), and a separate category for *indígena* ("Indigenous")—which was only created in the Brazilian census of 1991. For details, see Nobles, *Shades of Citizenship*. Also see Marcus, *Confederate Exodus*; and Marcus, "Sex, Color, and Geography: Racialized Relations in Brazil and Its Predicaments."

93. Bethencourt, *Racisms*, 173.
94. Bethencourt, *Racisms*, 17.
95. Bethencourt, *Racisms*, 190.
96. For a broader discussion about "race," see Bethencourt, *Racisms*. This US-based "racial" optic then becomes problematic in the process of examining "race" in colonial Brazil. Various Brazilian historical categorizations were not based on physical appearance alone, but they were tied to socioeconomic, religious, and/or occupational status as well. The process of examining "race" in the way it was used in colonial Brazil and the way it is used today in the United States, therefore, is mired with historical and geographical predicaments and contingencies.
97. That is, sentiments publicly voiced by a new type of political militant right-wing Christian nationalist cohort that is increasingly Evangelical and white, as I discuss in the Afterword later.
98. Graizbord, *Souls in Dispute*, 3.
99. Graizbord, *Souls in Dispute*, 2.
100. Kaplan, "The Portuguese Jews in Amsterdam. From Forced Conversion to a Return to Judaism," 38.
101. Saraiva, *The Marrano Factory*, xvi; and Bethencourt, *Racisms*, 145.
102. Also, for another discussion on the absence of the usage of Marrano, see Wiznitzer, "Isaac de Castro, Brazilian Jewish Martyr," 63.
103. For example, here are some names among the many priests (*padres*) and nuns (*freiras*) that I found in my examination, and who were accused by the Inquisition of Judaism in Brazil: Padre Gaspar de Mesquita, aged 44, arrested in 1630 (processo 183); Padre Antonio do Amaral, arrested in 1735 (processo 598); and, among the nuns: Freira Leonora da Encarnação, aged 54, half New Christian, arrested in 1638 (processo 329); Freira Ana Pinta Pereira, aged 35, one-quarter New Christian, arrested in 1623, who died in jail in 1629 (processo 2487); and Freira Mariana de Jesus, aged 25, part New Christian, arrested in 1623 (processo 4928).
104. Wadsworth, *Agents of Orthodoxy*, 59.
105. Wadsworth, *Agents of Orthodoxy*, 59.
106. See, Paim, "Anita Novinsky—Inquisição. Prisioneiros do Brasil (Séculos XVI a XIX)."
107. After the earthquake on November 1, 1755, the Inquisition dossiers were temporarily stored in a wooden shelter at the Praça de Armas, and then transferred to the Monastery of São Bento da Saúde. Arquivos Torre do Tombo, "Identificação Institucional," https://digitarq.arquivos.pt/details?id=1457733.

108. For example, the case of António José da Silva (also known as *o judeu*—"the Jew"), aged 32, was born in Rio de Janeiro and was living in Lisbon when he was imprisoned in 1737 and sentenced to be burned at the stake. Arquivo Nacional, Torre do Tombo, processo 8027–1.
109. This is a digitized catalogue with 19,775 descriptive dossiers (processos) and 2,392,997 digitized images. Arquivos Torre do Tombo, Portugal, Inquisição de Lisboa online, http://antt.dglab.gov.pt/exposicoes-virtuais-2/inquisicao-de-lisboa-online/.
110. Archive of Amsterdam (Archief Amsterdam), the Portuguese-Hebrew Register of Regulations and Decisions (5409–5414), 1648–1654 (Recife, Pernambuco), Inventaris van het Archief van de Portugees-Israëlietische Gemeente, https://archief.amsterdam/inventarissen/scans/334/7.2.1.1/start/0/limit/10/highlight/8.
111. Archival Collection at the Ets Haim Bibliotheek Library Amsterdam (Livraria Montezinos), https://jck.nl/en/node/1210; for their collection of manuscripts, see http://etshaimmanuscripts.nl/collection/manuscripts/#.
112. The Portuguese-Jewish Congregation in Amsterdam (De Portugees-Israëlietische Gemeente te Amsterdam), https://www.esnoga.com/geschiedenis-van-de-gemeente/.
113. Coates, "The Early Modern Portuguese Empire: A Commentary on Recent Studies," 84. For example, the English translation of *The Chronicle of Discovery and Conquest of Guinea* by Portuguese chronicler Gomes Eannes Zurara, published by the Hakluyt Society (1896–1899), remains the only complete version of the work of a fifteenth-century Portuguese historian available in English. Costa-Gomes, "Zurara and the Empire: Reconsidering Fifteenth-Century Portuguese Historiography," 57. For a few examples on the Portuguese Empire, see Newitt, *A History of Portuguese Overseas Expansion*; Coates, *Convicts and Orphans*; Costa-Gomes, "Zurara and the Empire: Reconsidering Fifteenth-Century Portuguese Historiography"; Alden, *The Making of an Enterprise*; Jarnagin, *The Making of the Luso-Asian World*; Schwartz, *Tropical Babylons*; and Villeirs, *Portuguese Encounters with the World in the Age of the Discoveries*.
114. See Herculano, *History of the Origin and Establishment of the Inquisition in Portugal*; and Moreira, *História dos principais actos e procedimentos da Inquisição em Portugal*.
115. Southey, *A History of Brazil Vol 1*, 463.
116. Southey, *A History of Brazil Vol 1*, 646.
117. For example, Roth, *A Life of Menasseh Ben Israel*; Roth, "The Middle Period of Anglo-Jewish History (1290–1655) Reconsidered," and Oppenheim, "The Early History of the Jews in New York, 1654–1664. Some New Matter on the Subject."
118. Olival, "The Portuguese Inquisition in the Historical Writing of J. Romero Magalhães," 125. Also see Marcocci, "Forgers and Martyrs: Conflicting Histories of the Portuguese Inquisition (1598–1647)," 53–54.
119. For example, by Brazilian and Portuguese scholars who first seriously studied this topic, such as Francisco A. Varnhagen (1845); Antônio Baião (1907); João Lucio Azevedo (1922); and Capistrano de Abreu (1935). For more details, see Marcocci,

"Forgers and Martyrs: Conflicting Histories of the Portuguese Inquisition (1598–1647)," 53. For early scholarship, see Varnhagen, "Brasileiros no auto-de-fé de 1711–1767"; Azevedo, "Notas sobre o judaísmo e a Inquisição no Brasil"; Baião, *A Inquisição em Portugal e no Brasil*; and Abreu, "Prefácio a Primeira Visitação do Santo Ofício às partes do Brasil, pelo licenciado Heitor Furtado de Mendonça." The Spanish had burned most of their Inquisition dossiers, and instead kept documents known as *"Relaciones de Causas,"* a summary of the original dossiers, to facilitate the work of Spanish inquisitors (i.e., a documentation of judicial dossiers). However, the Portuguese kept most of their processos from the Inquisition.

120. For example, historians Arnold Wiznitzer, José Gonçalves Salvador, José Antônio Gonsalves de Mello, Egon and Frieda Wolff, and Anita W. Novinsky pioneered the studies of Jews, New Christians, and the Portuguese Inquisition in colonial Brazil. Rifka Berezin, Zipora Rubinstein, and Gisele Beiguelman provide a synopsis of this scholarship, which had been published before 1985. See Berezin, Rifka, Zipora Rubinstein, and Gisele Beiguelman, "Research on Jews in Brazil—Present Stage." Notably, it was only in 1988 that Maria do Carmo Jasmins Dias Farinha made a big difference for future scholarship about the Portuguese Inquisition, since her watershed publication, *Os Arquivos da Inquisição*, carefully classified and organized the vast documentation and material from the dossiers of the Portuguese Inquisition that had been unorganized until then. Farinha, *Os Arquivos da Inquisição*.

121. Novinsky, "Jewish Heresy in the Light of New Documents," 111.
122. Novinsky, "Marranos and Marranism—a New Approach," 6.
123. Novinsky, "Marranos and Marranism—a New Approach," 6.
124. The list is far too extensive to do it justice. However, for a few examples, see Berezin et. al., "Research on Jews in Brazil—Present Stage;" Cascudo, *Mouros, Francêses e Judeus;* Loewenstamm, *Vultos Judaicos no Brasil*; Mello, *Gente da Nação*; Gorenstein, *Heréticos e impuros*; Mello, *Tempo dos Flamengos*; Mello, *Gente da Nação*; Novinsky, "A Historical Bias: The New Christian Collaboration with the Dutch Invaders of Brazil (17th Century)"; Novinsky, "Jewish Heresy in the Light of New Documents"; Novinsky, "Padre Antonio Vieira, the Inquisition, and the Jews"; Novinsky, "The Inquisition and the Mythic World of a Portuguese Kabbalist in the Eighteenth Century"; Novinsky, "A Catholic Priest and his Fight for Justice for the Jews: Father Antonio Vieira"; Wolff and Wolff, "Mistaken Identities of Signatories of the Congregation Zur Israel, Recife"; Wolff and Wolff, "The Problem of the First Jewish Settlers in New Amsterdam, 1654"; Novinsky and Carneiro, eds., *Inquisição: Estudos sobre Mentalidade, Heresias, e Arte*; Wiznitzer, "The Synagogue and Cemetery of the Jewish Community in Recife, Brazil (1630–1654)"; and Wiznitzer, "The Members of the Brazilian Jewish Community (1648–1653)."
125. Notably by scholars such as Lúcia Helena Costigan, Roberto Bachman, Bruno Feitler, Lina Gorenstein, Keila Grinberg, Tania. N. Kaufman, Daniela Levy, Elias Lipiner, Marcos Chor Maio and Carlos Eduardo Calaça, Evaldo Cabral de Mello, Nachman Falbel, Sônia A. Siqueira, Stuart B. Schwartz, Ronaldo Vainfas, James E. Wadsworth, and Uri Zwerling, among others. For example, see Bogaciovas,

Tribulações do Povo de Israel na São Paulo Colonial; Costigan, *Diálogos da Conversão*; Falbel, *Judeus no Brasil: estudos e notas*; Feitler, "Ofícios e estratégias de acumulação: o caso do despenseiro da Inquisição de Lisboa Antonio Gonçalves Prego (1650–1720)"; Oliveira, *Inquisição e Cristãos-Novos no Rio de Janeiro*; Cabral de Mello, *O Nome e o Sangue*; Calaça, "A confissão como dilema: cristãos-novos letrados do Rio de Janeiro—século XVIII"; Gorenstein, "Um Brasil subterrâneo: cristãos-novos no Brasil XVIII"; Gorenstein, *Heréticos e impuros*; Feitler, "Four Chapters in the History of Crypto-Judaism in Brazil: The Case of the Northeastern New Christians (17th–21st centuries)"; Grinberg, *Os Judeus no Brasil*; Kaufman, *Passos perdidos, história recuperada*; Levy, *De Recife para Manhattan;* Lipiner, *Os judaizantes nas capitanias de cima*; Lipiner, *Izaque de Castro*; Vainfas, *Trópico dos Pecados*; Schorsch, "Cristãos-novos, Judaísmo, Negros e Cristianismo nos Primórdios do Mundo Atlântico Moderno"; Vainfas, *Santo Ofício da Inquisição de Lisboa*; Pieroni, *Os Excluídos do Reino*; Scwartz, *All Can be Saved*; Siqueira, "O Poder da Inquisição e a Inquisição como Poder"; Wadsworth, "Children of the Inquisition: Minors as Familiares of the Inquisition in Pernambuco, Brazil, 1613–1821"; Wadsworth, "In the Name of the Inquisition: The Portuguese Inquisition and Delegated Authority in Colonial Pernambuco, Brazil"; Wadsworth, *Agents of Orthodoxy*; and Zwerling, *Os Judeus na História do Brasil*.

126. See López-Salazar, "Marcocci, Giuseppe & Paiva, José Pedro: História da Inquisição Portuguesa. (1536–1821), Lisboa: A Esfera dos Livros, 2013."
127. See López-Salazar, "Marcocci, Giuseppe & Paiva, José Pedro: História da Inquisição Portuguesa. (1536–1821), Lisboa: A Esfera dos Livros, 2013."
128. The work of Daviken Studnicki-Gizbert, Francisco Bethencourt, Wim Klooster, Paolo Bernardini, Norman Fiering, Juron Poettering, and Patricia Seed, for example, provide important information on the roles of the migration of Portuguese Jews and of New Christians to the New World. They also offer vital insights into the salience, participation, and contributions of Portuguese Jews in the development of science, the forging of networks throughout the Atlantic world, and the first Portuguese global exploration and navigation enterprises by sea. See Klooster, "Communities of Port Jews and Their Contacts in the Dutch Atlantic World"; Klooster, "Networks of Colonial Entrepreneurs: The Founders of the Jewish Settlements in Dutch America, 1650s and 1660s"; Bernadini and Fiering, *The Jews and the Expansion of Europe to the West, 1450–1800*; Poettering, *Migrating Merchants*; and Seed, *Ceremonies of Possession in Europe's Conquest of the New World, 1492–1640*. Also, for a recent volume on Portuguese Jews, see Stuczynski and Feitler (Eds.), *Portuguese Jews, New Christians, and "New Jews."*
129. For example, geographers Arthur Davies and Karl W. Butzer have written about the early science and New World encounters, yet they focus on Spain's contributions, and not a word is said about the Portuguese world or Portuguese Jews and New Christians and their contribution to the science of that time and the New World, or about their presence in Brazil. See Butzer, "The Americas before and after 1492: An Introduction to Current Geographical Research";" Butzer, "From

Columbus to Acosta: Science, Geography, and the New World"; and Davies, "Prince Henry the Navigator."

130. Omissions abound in Latin American geography college texts and surveys. For example, there is nothing written about the Jewish and New Christian presence in the Americas in: Jackiewicz and Bosco, *Placing Latin America: Contemporary Themes in Geography*; Kent, *Latin America: Regions and People*; Blouet and Blouet, *Latin America and the Caribbean: A Systematic and Regional Survey*; or Clawson, *Latin America and the Caribbean*. Some Brazilian scholars have also claimed that the insertion of Jews and New Christians is absent from the Brazilian pedagogy in the biography of Brazil, and that their presence is omitted in school and university surveys and texts. Blay, *O Brasil como Destino*, 1–2. The only brief mention of the Jewish presence in Brazil's northeast is found in the work of Brazilian geographer Manuel Correia de Andrade's *The Land and People of Northeast Brazil* (translated by Dennis V. Johnson, originally published in Portuguese in 1980 as *A Terra e o Homem no Nordeste*).

131. For instance, in anglophone academic readers, surveys, encyclopedias, dictionaries, and college textbooks. In Thomas E. Skidmore's well-known *Brazil: Five Centuries of Change*, the eminent Brazilianist never once mentions the presence of Portuguese or Brazilian Jews and New Christians in colonial Brazil; and in his role as one of the co-editors of *The Cambridge Encyclopedia of Latin America and the Caribbean, Second Edition*, this is the same: not a word about Portuguese Jews or New Christians in colonial Brazil (or anywhere else in Latin America for that matter). In a recently published reader, *The Brazil Reader: History, Culture, Politics*, the editors left out the vital involvement of Portuguese New Christians in colonial Brazil, and barely discuss them at all—remarkably, even in the section devoted to the Inquisition in Brazil (where, very briefly, they discuss sexual crimes instead). The same omission is visible in Stanley E. Blake's *The Vigorous Core of Our Nationality*, where the historical importance of New Christians and Jews in Brazil's northeast region is conspicuously absent. In another example, in its entries, *The Cambridge Dictionary of Judaism and Jewish Culture* neglects to mention any of the first Jewish settlements in Brazil, or the first synagogues in the Americas in Recife and Olinda. The importance and presence of Portuguese Jews and New Christians in colonial Brazil are barely mentioned in Lilia M. Schwarcz and Heloísa M. Starling's recent publication, *Brazil: A Biography*. In fact, they are brought up merely three times in the book, in passing and without further examination or context, yet their presence was inherently tied to the "biography of Brazil."

132. For example, Sauer, *Sixteenth-Century North America*; Sauer, *Northern Mists*; and Sauer, *The Early Spanish Main*.

133. Levine, "Research on Brazilian Jewry: An Overview," 30.

134. See Lesser, *Negotiating National Identity*, 44. For more details on this Jewish community, and also Carneiro, "Judeus-caboclos da Amazônia."

135. Lesser, *Negotiating National Identity*, 45. Also see Carneiro, "Judeus-caboclos da Amazônia."

136. For examples of this type of monolithic framing of Latin American Jewry exclusively tied to Spanish-speaking countries and "Sephardim" from Spain that overtly neglect Portugal and Portuguese Jews in colonial Brazil, see Agosín, *Memory, Oblivion, and Jewish Culture in Latin America*; Perelis, *Narratives from the Sephardic Atlantic*; Stavans, *The Seventh Heaven*; Stillman and Stillman, *From Iberia to Diaspora*; Zucker and Stillman, *New Horizons in Sephardic Studies*; Rein et al., *The New Ethnic Studies in Latin America* (while one chapter examines contemporary Brazil, the rest of the volume clearly focuses on Spanish-speaking Latin America); and Harel et al., *Jews and Jewish Identities in Latin America* (the editors include two chapters on Jews in Brazil; however, the focus is on modern Brazil). Also see a recent publication, Rac and Valerio, *Jewish Experiences Across the Americas*, where the editors have clearly focused their central arguments on the idea of "Hispanicity," and on the history of Spain and Spanish-speaking America, as a euphemism for the "Americas." Despite the mountain of scholarship produced by Brazilian historians, they are omitted in the sources. One of the contributing authors, José C. Moya, has aptly outlined the importance of Luso-Brazil in the colonial period, and the salience of Portuguese New Christians in the Americas; however, the other chapters in this volume that discuss Brazil all focus on the modern period.

137. For a detailed discussion, see Seed, "Celestial Navigation"; Seed, "Jewish Scientists and the Origin of Modern Navigation"; and Seed, *Ceremonies of Possession in Europe's Conquest of the New World, 1492–1640*.

138. See Gade, "North American Reflections on Latin Americanist Geography," 11.

139. BRASA Report 2005. *Conference on the Future of Brazilian Studies in the U.S.*, 5–7.

140. See Young, "Teaching Brazil in U.S. Universities," 54; and BRASA Report 2005. *Conference on the Future of Brazilian Studies in the U.S.*, 5–7.

141. See Seed, "Celestial Navigation"; Seed, "Jewish Scientists and the Origin of Modern Navigation"; and Russell-Wood, *The Portuguese Empire*. For a discussion on the neglect of Brazil and Brazilian studies within geography, see Marcus, "Rethinking Brazil's Place within Latin Americanist Geography."

142. As Lúcia Helena Costigan aptly comments, "the majority of scholars who work in the field of Latin American studies approach it from a partial perspective centering almost exclusively on Spanish America and disregarding Brazil." Costigan, "The Invisible Giant: The Place of Brazil in (Latin) American Studies: An NEH Summer Institute," 644.

143. Davies, "Milton Santos: The Conceptual Geographer and the Philosophy of Technics," 585.

144. See Graizbord, *Souls in Dispute*, 4.

145. See Pijning, "New Christians as Sugar Cultivators and Traders in the Portuguese Atlantic, 1450–1800," 497–478.

146. See Cabral de Mello, *O Nome e o Sangue*.

147. Pijning, "New Christians as Sugar Cultivators and Traders in the Portuguese Atlantic, 1450–1800," 498. Also see Wadsworth, *Agents of Orthodoxy*, for details on genealogical fraud.

148. Dines, "Do Documento ao Monumento, A História como Canteiro," 19.
149. Dines, "Do Documento ao Monumento, A História como Canteiro," 19.
150. Sarenbrenick, *Breve história dos judeus no Brasil*, 9–12; See Falbel, *Judeus no Brasil*, 23–25.
151. Sarenbrenick, *Breve história dos judeus no Brasil*, 9–12. I have excluded insights on the period's post-colonial phase after 1822 in the Conclusion. Also see *Instituto Brasileiro de Geografia e Estatística*. IBGE 2021, https://brasil500anos.ibge.gov.br/territorio-brasileiro-e-povoamento/construcao-do-territorio/extensao-territorial-atual.html.
152. Schwartz, *All Can Be Saved*, 9.
153. Novinsky, *Inquisição: prisioneiros do Brasil*, 22–43.
154. See Wadsworth, "Agents of Orthodoxy," 2–4.
155. See Wadsworth, "Agents of Orthodoxy," 9.

Chapter One

1. See Mello, *Gente da Nação*.
2. See Graizbord, *Souls in Dispute*, 52. Also see maps of global networks of "Portuguese People of the Nation" in Studnicki-Gizbert, *A Nation Upon the Ocean Sea*, 38 and 106.
3. See Graizbord, *Souls in Dispute*, 52–53.
4. Graizbord, *Souls in Dispute*, 50.
5. For example, one study that focused on sixteenth-century publications written by Spaniards about Portuguese New Christians reflected the levels of ongoing anti-Portuguese rhetoric, often coupled with comparisons to Indigenous populations in the New World, referring to those groups as "cowards," "corrupt," "superstitious," and notably, collectively as "Jews." This type of rhetoric reflects the extent to which the "imagined Jew" reached in the New World, even if that meant arresting individuals for Judaism who were, in fact, adherents of Indigenous or African belief systems. See Costigan, "Judeus e Cristãos-novos nos escritos de letrados do Barroco Espanhol e de Antonio Vieira e Menasseh Ben Israel," 124–132.
6. See Alencastro, *O trato dos viventes*, 25; also see Novinsky et al., *Os Judeus Que Construiram of Brasil*, 180; and Green, "Pluralism, Violence and Empire: The Portuguese New Christians in the Atlantic World."
7. See Studnicki-Gizbert, "*La Nación* among the Nations: Portuguese and Other Maritime Trading Diasporas in the Atlantic, Sixteenth to Eighteenth Centuries," 88; and Green, "Pluralism, Violence and Empire: The Portuguese New Christians in the Atlantic World." Also see maps of these networks, Studnicki-Gizbert, *A Nation Upon the Ocean Sea*, 38 and 106.
8. See Temkin, *Luis de Carvajal*.
9. Studnicki-Gizbert, "*La Nación* among the Nations: Portuguese and Other Maritime Trading Diasporas in the Atlantic, Sixteenth to Eighteenth Centuries," 95. Also see Studnicki-Gizbert, *A Nation Upon the Ocean Sea*.

10. While some scholars have alluded to Tiradentes's Jewish origins, this speculation remains nebulous. In 1789, Joaquim José da Silva Xavier, known as Tiradentes (literally "tooth-extractor" in Portuguese—a reference to his profession as a dentist), was a leader of Inconfidência Mineira, one of the first separatist movements seeking independence from Portugal because of taxes levied on gold in Minas Gerais. He was denounced, imprisoned in Rio, and then hanged on April 21, 1792. Afterward, his body was butchered, and the body parts were sent to Vila Rica, Minas Gerais. However, most of his peers who were involved in the movement were exiled, not executed—Tiradentes was the only one who was executed. Tiradentes's political rhetoric resonated with the plight of New Christians in Brazil seeking to end persecution and discrimination from the Inquisition, Crown, and Church, which also suggests he may have been a New Christian. Moreover, his mother's name was Antônia de Encarnação Xavier Colaço—Colaço being a common New Christian name—and she subsequently changed it to Maria Antônia da Encarnação Xavier. However, I could not find enough convincing and concrete evidence to assert that Tiradentes indeed had Jewish ancestry, and maybe future research will shed more light on this topic. See Goldberg, *Psicologia e reflexões do inconsciente*, 54; Loewenstamm, *Vultos Judaicos no Brasil*; and Hubner, "Mártires: De Rabi Akiva a Tiradentes: uma aproximação," 13–14.
11. See Igel, "Escritores Judeus Brasileiros: Um Percurso em Andamento," 326. Also see Siqueira, "O cristão novo Bento Teixeira. Cripto-judaismo no Brasil Colônia."
12. See Mordoch, "Um cristão-novo nos trópicos: expansão imperial e identidade religiosa nos Diálogos das grandezas do Brasil de Ambrósio Fernandes Brandão," 202–203; Also see Siqueira, "O cristão novo Bento Teixeira. Cripto-judaismo no Brasil Colônia."
13. See Falbel, *Judeus no Brasil: estudos e notas*, 103.
14. For a detailed discussion, see Mordoch, "Um cristão-novo nos trópicos: expansão imperial e identidade religiosa nos Diálogos das grandezas do Brasil de Ambrósio Fernandes Brandão." Also see Falbel, *Judeus no Brasil*, 100–104.
15. See Falbel, *Judeus no Brasil: estudos e notas*, 103.
16. See Schwartz, *Early Brazil*, 205; and *Ambrósio Fernandes Brandão, Dialogues on the Great Things of Brazil*, translated and annotated by Hall, Harrison, and Welker, 131–153.
17. See Dodge, "A Forgotten Century of Brazilwood: The Brazilwood Trade from the Mid-Sixteenth to Mid-Seventeenth Century," 23.
18. Mordoch, "Um cristão-novo nos trópicos: expansão imperial e identidade religiosa nos Diálogos das grandezas do Brasil de Ambrósio Fernandes Brandão," 202.
19. Falbel, *Judeus no Brasil*, 100–104.
20. Other celebrated plays, operas, and comedies that Silva wrote included, for example, *A vida do Grande Dom Quixote de la Mancha e do gordo Sancho Pança* (1733); *Esopaida, ou a vida de Esopo* (1734); *Encantos de Medeia* (1735); *Anfitrião, ou Júpiter e Alcmena* (1736); *Labirinto de Creta* (1736); *Guerras do Alecrim e da Manjerona* (1737); and *Precipício de Faetonte* (1738). See Pereira, "O tribunal do Santo Ofício nas óperas de Antônio José da Silva, o Judeu," 2.

21. See Pereira, "O tribunal do Santo Ofício nas óperas de Antônio José da Silva, o Judeu" 2. Also see Vasconcelos, *Selecta Brasiliense ou noticias, descobertas, observações, factos e curiosidades em relação aos homens á historia e cousas do Brasil*, 16–17.
22. See Vainfas, "Santo Ofício em terra Fluminense—Cristão-novos e Inquisição no Rio de Janeiro colonial," 42. Also see Vasconcelos, *Selecta Brasiliense ou noticias, descobertas, observações, factos e curiosidades em relação aos homens á historia e cousas do Brasil*, 16–17.
23. Schwartz, *Early Brazil*, 192.
24. Arquivo do Estado de São Paulo, 1920–1977, Vol. 2 [1920], 5–107. Also see Schwartz, *Early Brazil*, 193.
25. Bogaciovas, *Tribulações do Povo de Israel na São Paulo Colonial*, 82.
26. See Bogaciovas, *Tribulações do Povo de Israel na São Paulo Colonial*.
27. For a detailed discussion, see Novinsky, "A 'Conspiração do Silêncio.' Uma História Desconhecida sobre os Bandeirantes Judeus no Brasil."
28. See Bogaciovas, *Tribulações do Povo de Israel na São Paulo Colonial*.
29. Novinsky et al., *Os Judeus Que Construíram o Brasil*, 215–244. Gorenstein, "Um Brasil subterrâneo: cristãos-novos no século XVIII," 142–143.
30. See Novinsky, "A 'Conspiração do Silêncio.' Uma História Desconhecida sobre os Bandeirantes Judeus no Brasil."
31. Schwartz, "Plantations and peripheries, c.1580–c.1750," 116.
32. Novinsky et al., *Os Judeus Que Construíram o Brasil*, 156–157.
33. See Novinsky, "A 'Conspiração do Silêncio.' Uma História Desconhecida sobre os Bandeirantes Judeus no Brasil."
34. See Novinsky, "A 'Conspiração do Silêncio.' Uma História Desconhecida sobre os Bandeirantes Judeus no Brasil." Historians from the city of São Paulo, such as Anita W. Novinsky (paulistas, meaning someone from São Paulo), however, tend to aggrandize bandeirantes as paulista "heroes," to the extent where they become symbolic of Brazilian nationhood, and who contributed to the territorial expansion of Brazil. Yet at the same time, those same paulista historians also appear to overlook the documented massacres on Indians perpetuated by bandeirantes, or the fact that they were Indian slave-hunters and captured hundreds of thousands of Indians, transporting them to São Paulo to be sold as slaves, and in the process had enslaved hundreds for themselves. It was only later in the late seventeenth century that bandeirantes abandoned hunting Indians to be sold as slaves. Instead, they concentrated their efforts on finding gold and precious stones and became known as *caçadores de esmeraldas*, or "emerald hunters" (such as Borba Gato).
35. Boxer, *The Golden Age of Brazil*, 33.
36. Quoted in Bogaciovas, *Tribulações do Povo de Israel na São Paulo Colonial*, 60.
37. Quoted in Bogaciovas, *Tribulações do Povo de Israel na São Paulo Colonial*, 80.
38. Franco and Tavares, "Cristãos-novos, Jesuítas e Inquisição: uma relação controversa em Portugal (séculos XVI e XVII)," 51; Stuczynski, "Negotiated Relationships: Jesuits and Portuguese Conversos—A Reassessment," 47.
39. From private notices received between 1551 and 1552 from Jesuit priests, "*Avisi particolari delle Indie di Portugallo Ricevuti in questi doi Anni del 1551 e 1552, da li*

Reverendi Padre de la campagnia de Iesu . . ." Quoted in Guedes, "Portugal-Brazil: The Encounter between Two Worlds," 196. For original letters sent by Jesuits in Brazil between 1550 and 1568, see *Cartas Avulsas de Jesuitas (1550–1568)*. Many of the concerns center on Indigenous attacks, cannibalism, naked women, and the much-needed proselytization to baptize as many Indians as possible.

40. Stuczynski, "Negotiated Relationships: Jesuits and Portuguese Conversos—A Reassessment," 43.
41. Stuczynski, "Negotiated Relationships: Jesuits and Portuguese Conversos—A Reassessment," 46.
42. See Bogaciovas, *Tribulações do Povo de Israel na São Paulo Colonial*.
43. Bogaciovas, *Tribulações do Povo de Israel na São Paulo Colonial*, 60.
44. Bogaciovas, *Tribulações do Povo de Israel na São Paulo Colonial*, 58.
45. Schwarcz and Starling, *Brazil*, 27–28.
46. Bethencourt, *Racisms*, 209.
47. Bethencourt, *Racisms*, 209.
48. Londoño, "A Historiografia dos Séculos XX e XXI Sobre os Jesuítas no Periodo Colonial. Conferindo Sentidos a uma Presença: Do Nascimento do Brasil à Globalização," 14.
49. Aidoo, *Slavery Unseen*, 43.
50. Schwartz, "A Commonwealth in Itself. The Early Brazilian Sugar Industry, 1550–1670," 180–181. Also see Seraphim Leite, *História da Companhia de Jesus no Brasil*.
51. See Schwartz, *Early Brazil*, 234; English translation of Mello, *Fontes para a história do Brasil holandês*, 96–129.
52. See Schwartz, *Early Brazil*, 238; English translation of Mello, *Fontes para a história do Brasil holandês*, 96–129.
53. Schwartz, *Early Brazil*, 238; English translation of Mello, *Fontes para a história do Brasil holandês*, 96–129.
54. Schwartz, "A Commonwealth in Itself. The Early Brazilian Sugar Industry, 1550–1670," 188.
55. Schwartz, *Early Brazil*, 283; English translation of Vainfas, *Santo Ofício da Inquisição de Lisboa: Confissões da Bahia*, 144–149.
56. Schwartz, "A Commonwealth in Itself. The Early Brazilian Sugar Industry, 1550–1670," 191.
57. For a discussion on the perception in the historiography of Jesuits in Brazil, see Londoño, "A Historiografia dos Séculos XX e XXI Sobre os Jesuítas no Periodo Colonial. Conferindo Sentidos a uma Presença: Do Nascimento do Brasil à Globalização."
58. See Novinsky, "Ser Marrano em Minas Colonial."
59. See Vainfas, "Santo Ofício em terra Fluminense—Cristão-novos e Inquisição no Rio de Janeiro colonial," 20.
60. See Novinsky. "Ser Marrano em Minas Colonial."
61. Vainfas, "Santo Ofício em terra Fluminense—Cristão-novos e Inquisição no Rio de Janeiro colonial," 33.

62. Novinsky, "Marranos and the Inquisition: On the Gold Route in Minas Gerais, Brazil," 215–249.
63. Laura Jarnagin, *Research work in progress/preparation*, 2021.
64. Laura Jarnagin, *Research work in progress/preparation*, 2021.
65. See Novinsky et al., *Os Judeus Que Construíram o Brasil*, 177.
66. For details on Beckman as senhor de engenho, see Schwartz, "Plantations and peripheries, c.1580–c.1750," 134. Also see Vasconcelos, *Selecta Brasiliense ou noticias, descobertas, observações, factos e curiosidades em relação aos homens á historia e cousas do Brasil*, 134. Vasconcelos had claimed that Beckman was decapitated.
67. Mauro, Frederic. "Political and economic structures of empire," 57.
68. The Order of Christ (*Ordo Militae Jesu Christi*) was established by the Papal bull, *ad ea ex quibus* by Pope John XXII in 1319. Arquivos Torre do Tombo, Expocisões Virtuais, "Ordem de Cristo," http://antt.dglab.gov.pt/exposicoes-virtuais-2/ordem-de-cristo/.
69. See Fagundes, "Felipe Camarão, um cavaleiro potiguar a serviço del Rei: memória, história e identidade nas guerras pernambucanas, século XVII," 204. Also see Boxer, *The Dutch in Brazil, 1624–1654*, 52 and 63.
70. See Mattos, "'Pretos' and 'Pardos' between the Cross and the Sword: Racial Categories in Seventeenth-Century Brazil," 45; and Fagundes, "Felipe Camarão, um cavaleiro potiguar a serviço del Rei: memória, história e identidade nas guerras pernambucanas, século XVII," 204.
71. "Patriarcas da Força Terrestre." Ministério da Defesa, Exército Brasileiro. Also see Boxer, *The Dutch in Brazil, 1624–1654*, 52 and 63.
72. While this may seem like an oversimplification, achieved status could be rewarded with reclassification, but in most cases, these exceptions proved the rule and reinforced the system of discrimination because those who accepted the reclassification had to accept the legitimacy of their previous exclusion.
73. Mattos, "'Pretos' and 'Pardos' between the Cross and the Sword: Racial Categories in Seventeenth-Century Brazil," 47.
74. Flory and Smith, "Bahian Merchants and Planters in the Seventeenth and Early Eighteenth Centuries," 586.
75. "Patriarcas da Força Terrestre." Ministério da Defesa, Exército Brasileiro.
76. "Patriarcas da Força Terrestre." Ministério da Defesa, Exército Brasileiro.
77. Samuel, "Some Eighteenth-Century Refugees from Brazil," 89.
78. Graizbord, *Souls in Dispute*, 135.
79. See Feitler, "Four Chapters in the History of Crypto-Judaism in Brazil: The Case of the Northeastern New Christians (17th–21st centuries)," 219–222.
80. See Bogaciovas, *Tribulações do Povo de Israel na São Paulo Colonial*, 41.
81. See Novinsky, "The Myth of the Marrano Names."
82. Attig, "Did the Sephardic Jews Speak Ladino?," 9. I return to this discussion in Chapter 4.
83. See Wexler, "Ascertaining the position of Judezmo within Ibero-Romance," 163; and Attig, "Did the Sephardic Jews Speak Ladino?," 6. Also see Asher, "Teaching

'Ladino Language and Culture' and 'Aspects of the Sephardic Tradition': Hopes, Fruits, Experiences."
84. Wexler, "Ascertaining the position of Judezmo within Ibero-Romance," 163; and Attig, "Did the Sephardic Jews Speak Ladino?," 6. Also see Asher, "Teaching 'Ladino Language and Culture' and 'Aspects of the Sephardic Tradition:' Hopes, Fruits, Experiences."
85. Bethencourt, *Racisms*, 7.
86. For example, among other publications found, see "Sermon on Deuteronomy XIII: 18," delivered by Isaac de Eliah Cohen Belinfante, Amsterdam 1768, written in Portuguese with excerpts in Hebrew. *Sermão do Labirinto pregado no K[ahal] K[ados] de T[almud] T[orah] em Sabath reé, R[os] H[odes] Elul a° 5528 em Amsterdam Is. de Eliau Cohen Belinfante*. The Archival Collection at the Ets Haim Library in Amsterdam (Ets Haim Livraria Montezinos), http://etshaimmanuscripts.nl/items/eh-47-b-04-07/.
87. Portuguese-Jewish community of Amsterdam, De Portugees-Israëlietische Gemeente, https://www.esnoga.com/traditie/.
88. See Portuguese Israelite community of Amsterdam, Portugees- Israëlietische Gemeente te Amsterdam, https://www.esnoga.com/schatten-van-de-snoge/.
89. Mark and Horta, *The Forgotten Diaspora*, 22–29.
90. Poettering, *Migrating Merchants*, 126. Also see Martins, *Os judeus portugueses de Hamburgo*.
91. For example, as seen in the register of regulations of the congregation of Portuguese Jews in Amsterdam and in Brazil. See Archive of Amsterdam (Archief Amsterdam) of the Portuguese-Hebrew Register of Regulations and Decisions (5409–5414), 1648–1654 (Recife, Pernambuco), *Inventaris van het Archief van de Portugees-Israëlietische Gemeente*, https://archief.amsterdam/inventarissen/scans/334/7.2.1.1/start/0/limit/10/highlight/8; and https://archief.amsterdam/inventarissen/scans/334/7.2.1.1/start/0/limit/10/highlight/3. Also see Leite, *Unorthodox Kin*, 50. Also see Zeman, "The Amazing Career of Doctor Rodrigo Lopez (?–1594)"; Wolf, "Crypto-Jews Under the Commonwealth"; Wolf, "The First English Jew"; and Samuel, "Jews in Jacobean London."
92. "Proverbios de Selomoh. [Provérbios de Selomoh comentado por Selomoh Saruco, Hazan e More Din de K.K. Honen Dal Na Haya, Anno 5526]." *A commentary on the Proverbs by Solomon Saruco, The Hague 1766*. The Archival Collection at the Ets Haim Library in Amsterdam (Ets Haim Livraria Montezinos), http://etshaimmanuscripts.nl/items/eh-48-b-09/.
93. For more details, see Dutch National Archives, *Nationaal Archief*, https://www.nationaalarchief.nl/onderzoeken/zoekhulpen/overzicht-van-archieven-over-guyana-guiana#collapse-6535.
94. Arends, *Language and Slavery*, 9–12. Also see Vink, *Creole Jews*, 112.
95. Notably, in 1656, six Portuguese merchants petitioned Oliver Cromwell (head of state of England), as David Cesarani explains, "asserting that they were Portuguese 'of the Hebrew nation' and not Spanish. They sought to preempt measures against

their conduct in trade and obtain permission to live and worship in London as Portuguese Jews." That is, since Spain was at war with England, Portuguese New Christians had emphasized their identification as "Portuguese" and not Spanish, knowing the respective trading and political advantages attached to that identity. See Cesarani, "The Forgotten Port Jews of London: Court Jews Who Were Also Port Jews," 111–123. Also see Cesarani, *Port Jews*.

96. Notably, the word "ethnicity" was not found in the Oxford English Dictionary until 1933. See Kaplan, *Navigating Ethnicity*, 1.
97. Geographical imaginations are not relegated to mere benign apolitical musings; they are mired in political deliberations that can lead to the implementations of policy—as I have commented elsewhere. See Marcus, "The Dangers of the Geographical Imagination in the U.S. Eugenics Movement."
98. For a counter-argument that points out the problems with this type of myopic thinking and bias, see, for example, Marcus, "Rethinking Brazil's Place within Latin Americanist Geography"; Marcus, "Where is the Geography? The Geographical Predicaments of the Panethnic terms, 'Hispanic' and 'Latino.'"
99. Mignolo, *The Idea of Latin America*, 93.
100. Costigan, "The Invisible Giant: The Place of Brazil in (Latin) American Studies: An NEH Summer Institute," 644.
101. "Pre-Hispanic." *Merriam-Webster.com Dictionary*, Merriam-Webster, https://www.merriam-webster.com/dictionary/pre-Hispanic, Accessed May 4, 2022.
102. For example, see Serrano, "Plural Identities: The Portuguese New Christians," 140.
103. See, for example, the map of Latin America. Jamaica (among other islands in the Caribbean), the Guianas, and Haiti are left blank since according to the author, they do not share an Iberian colonial legacy and therefore do not qualify to be a part of the geography of Latin America; Kent, *Latin America: Regions and People*, 13.
104. Bethell, "Brazil and 'Latin America,'" 460.
105. Despite the unification of Spain and Portugal between 1580 and 1640, Brazil remained under Portuguese control and Portugal was never "assimilated" by the Spanish during that time. I return to this discussion later.
106. This modern category of "Hispanic/Latino" (in official US census surveys) specifically states that this category does not include Brazilians because they do not speak Spanish. This modern category was originally created to designate Spanish-speaking Latin Americans, mostly Mexicans and Mexican-Americans, Puerto Ricans, and Central Americans, living *in the United States*—that is, it only has any meaning *in that country*, yet one that still maintains a powerful hold on academic and public geographical imaginations of Latin America (and in public spheres, past and present). For a discussion on this problem, see Marcus, "Where is the Geography? The Geographical Predicaments of the Panethnic terms, 'Hispanic' and 'Latino.'" As Suzanne Oboler explains, modern pan-ethnic labeling has become "a political strategizing tool within the United States to re-assert identity and political empowerment." Oboler, *Ethnic Labels, Latino Lives*, xvi.
107. See, for example, Mignolo, *The Idea of Latin America*. Notably, the term "Hispanic"

derives from *Hispania*, the ancient Roman name given to the Iberian Peninsula; however, Spaniards were certainly not ethnically homogeneous, as implied by "Spanish descent." For many centuries, Basques, Castilians, Aragonese, Catalans, Celts, Jews, and Arabs coinhabited Spain. See Marcus, "Rethinking Brazil's Place within Latin Americanist Geography."

108. For example, Earl Fitz points out that Brazilian literature continues to be "ignored or relegated to an afterthought, even by established scholars of what they themselves term 'Latin American' literature." Fitz, "Internationalizing the Literature of the Portuguese-Speaking World," 440.

109. Albeit geology or geosciences programs are found in US universities, any brief online searches through US Ivy League universities will show the conspicuous absence of any geography program. After Harvard eliminated its geography program in 1947, other Ivy League institutions followed suit. Eventually, most other US universities and colleges, as well as public schools, did the same. The result is that today geography is no longer taught in most US public schools, and the overall pedagogy of geography and geographical literacy in the United States is abysmal. See Smith, "'Academic War over the Field of Geography': The Elimination of Geography at Harvard, 1947–1951," and Lewis, "Global Ignorance."

110. One in every three individuals in South America today speaks Portuguese, and approximately two-thirds of South America today is occupied by Brazilian national territory. Yet I have not yet seen one US college world regional geography textbook or survey that does not use solely Spanish words to describe Latin American geographical features (e.g., *tierra caliente, tierra fria, tierra gelada*). See Marcus, "Rethinking Brazil's Place within Latin Americanist Geography."

111. It is important to consider the influence of Tupi-Guarani, unique to Brazilian Portuguese (making it unlike continental Portuguese). Its influence is considerable, especially in words with Brazilian toponyms, or which refer to botany, plants, and animals. See Bueno, *Vocabulário Tupi-Guarani*.

112. There are exceptions. One of them is Juron Poettering, who examined the Portuguese and New Christians in Hamburg and explicitly affirms the usage of "Portuguese Jews and New Christians" in her work, instead of Sephardim or Iberian Jews. See Poettering, *Migrating Merchants*.

113. Studnicki-Gizbert, *A Nation Upon the Ocean Sea*, 9.

114. For details on how Portuguese Jews were different from Spanish Jews, see Graizbord, *Souls in Dispute*.

115. Fishman, "Introduction," 1.

116. Fishman, "Introduction," 1.

117. Bodian, "Hebrews of the Portuguese Nation: The Ambiguous Boundaries of Self-Definition," 72. Also see Bodian, *Hebrews of the Portuguese Nation*.

118. Adler, "Lea on the Inquisition of Spain and Herein of Spanish and Portuguese Jews and Marranos," 551; Bodian, "Hebrews of the Portuguese Nation: The Ambiguous Boundaries of Self-Definition," 72; and see Bodian, *Hebrews of the Portuguese Nation*.

119. Koen, "The Earliest Sources Relating to the Portuguese Jews in the Municipal Archives of Amsterdam up to 1620," 25.
120. Adler, "Lea on the Inquisition of Spain and Herein of Spanish and Portuguese Jews and Marranos," 551; Bodian, "Hebrews of the Portuguese Nation: The Ambiguous Boundaries of Self-Definition," 72; and see Bodian, *Hebrews of the Portuguese Nation*.
121. See Serrano, "Plural Identities: The Portuguese New Christians," 140.
122. Studnicki-Gizbert, *A Nation Upon the Ocean Sea*, 10–11.
123. Poettering, *Migrating Merchants*, 103.
124. Poettering, *Migrating Merchants*, 126.
125. Yovel, *The Other Within*, 213.
126. Bodian, "Review of The Canonization of a Myth: Portugal's 'Jewish Problem' and the Assembly of Tomar 1629. Martin A. Cohen, Hebrew Union College Annual Supplements 5. Cincinnati, Ohio: Hebrew Union College Press, 2002."
127. Graizbord, *Souls in Dispute*, 53.
128. Graizbord, *Souls in Dispute*, 53. Also, for the uniqueness of Portuguese Jews in the fifteenth to seventeenth centuries, see Seed, "Jewish Scientists and the Origin of Modern Navigation"; Seed, "Celestial Navigation"; and Seed, *Ceremonies of Possession in Europe's Conquest of the New World, 1492–1640*.
129. For examples in this type of monolithic and myopic framing of Latin American Jewry exclusively tied to Spanish-speaking countries (i.e., "Sephardim"), see Agosín, *Memory, Oblivion, and Jewish Culture in Latin America*; Perelis, *Narratives from the Sephardic Atlantic*; Stavans, *The Seventh Heaven*; Stillman and Stillman, *From Iberia to Diaspora*; Zucker and Stillman, *New Horizons in Sephardic Studies*; and Rein et al., *The New Ethnic Studies in Latin America* (while one chapter examines contemporary Brazil, the rest of the volume clearly focuses on Spanish-speaking Latin America). In Harel et al., *Jews and Jewish Identities in Latin America*, the editors included two chapters on Jews, however, in modern Brazil.
130. As Francesca Trivellato points out in the case of "Sephardic" Jews in Livorno, it is not always possible to distinguish between (and among) Sephardic Jews. Trivellato, *The Familiarity of Strangers*, ix.
131. See Castaño, "The Peninsula as a Borderless Space: Towards a Mobility 'Turn' in the Study of Fifteenth-Century Iberian Jewries," 317. That is, the region of La Raya (along the Duero River), Idanha-a-Velha (the Roman Egitânia), the birthplace of Visigothic kings, curiously a major place of origin in the Inquisition arrests in Brazil. Portuguese towns and small villages along the Portuguese-Spanish borderlands (Extremadura), include Monsanto, Évora, Castelo de Vide (which still maintains an ancient Jewish quarter), Castelo Branco, Arronches, and Elvas, for example. Notably, most of the explorers and conquistadors of Spanish America hailed from the Extremadura region. Also, for centuries, this region has traditionally been sparsely populated and synonymous with battlefields.
132. Castaño, "The Peninsula as a Borderless Space: Towards a Mobility 'Turn' in the Study of Fifteenth-Century Iberian Jewries," 317–319.

133. Castaño, "The Peninsula as a Borderless Space: Towards a Mobility 'Turn' in the Study of Fifteenth-Century Iberian Jewries," 331.
134. For example, see Roitman, *The Same But Different?*, 52–54. For a discussion on "ethnic" and "ethnicity," see Bethencourt, *Racisms*, 7.
135. For more details on the "people of the nation," see Studnicki-Gizbert, *A Nation Upon the Ocean Sea*.
136. Studnicki-Gizbert, *A Nation Upon the Ocean Sea*, 11.
137. Misha Klein aptly explains, "defining who is a Jew is a central and irresoluble question, posing a variety of historical, practical, methodological, religious, genetic, and even philosophical difficulties." Klein, *Kosher Feijoada*, 11.
138. Disney, *A History of Portugal and the Portuguese Empire*, 222–223.
139. Böhm, "The First Sephardic Synagogues in South America and in the Caribbean Area," 14.
140. Also, for more details in this context of the age-old differences between Portuguese and Spanish, see, Berdichevsky, "The Age-Old Iberian Rivalry and the Jews."
141. See Webb, *The Geography of Latin America*, 24–25.
142. Eakin, *Becoming Brazilians*, 44.
143. For a discussion of the Portuguese cultural influence reaching Asia, for example, see Jarnagin, *The Making of the Luso-Asian World*.
144. The territory of Brazil—the largest in Latin America today—occupies about two-thirds of the South American continent, with a national territory size slightly larger than the continental United States. Roughly two-thirds of South Americans speak Portuguese.
145. For additional differences between Spanish and Portuguese Inquisitions, see Bethencourt, *The Inquisition*, 137 and 145; and Graizbord, *Souls in Dispute*.
146. For example, see Russell-Wood, *The Portuguese Empire, 1415–1808*. Also see Jarnagin, *The Making of the Luso-Asian World*.
147. See, for example, Clendinnen, *Ambivalent Conquests*; Stern, *Peru's Indian Peoples and the Challenge of Spanish Conquest*; Gibson, *The Aztecs Under Spanish Rule*; and Hassig, *Mexico and the Spanish Conquest*.
148. See Schwartz, *All Can Be Saved*, 23; and, Bethencourt, *The Inquisition*.
149. Quoted in Vainfas and Herman, "Judeus e conversos na Ibéria no século XV: sefardismo, heresia, messianismo," 26.
150. See Schwartz, *All Can Be Saved*, 95.
151. Lockhart and Schwartz, *Early Latin America*, 225.
152. Graizbord, *Souls in Dispute*, 50.
153. For further discussion, see Gitlitz, *Secrecy and Deceit*, 505–551.
154. See Johnson, "Portuguese Settlement, 1500–1580," 16.
155. Moffitt and Sebastian, *O Brave New People*, 272.
156. Moffitt and Sebastian, *O Brave New People*, 272.
157. Clendinnen, *Ambivalent Conquests*, 100.
158. Hassig, *Mexico and the Spanish Conquest*, 53.
159. See Metcalf, *Go-betweens and the Colonization of Brazil*, 124.

160. Seed, *Ceremonies of Possession in Europe's Conquest of the New World, 1492–1640*, 134.
161. For more details, see Schwartz, "A Commonwealth in Itself. The Early Brazilian Sugar Industry, 1550–1670"; Schwartz, *Tropical Babylons*; and Jarnagin, *Portuguese and Luso-Asian Legacies in Southeast Asia, 1511–2011*.
162. Metcalf, *Go-betweens and the Colonization of Brazil*, 130.
163. For a broader discussion, see Metcalf, *Go-betweens and the Colonization of Brazil*.
164. See Marcus, "Sex, Color, and Geography: Racialized Relations in Brazil and Its Predicaments."
165. Metcalf, *Go-betweens and the Colonization of Brazil*, 95.
166. See Aidoo, *Unseen Slavery*.
167. Guedes, "Portugal-Brazil: The Encounter between Two Worlds," 198.
168. Hemming, *Red Gold*, 156. For a detailed discussion on Indigenous tribes in Brazil, see Vasconcelos, *Selecta Brasiliense ou noticias, descobertas, observações, factos e curiosidades em relação aos homens á historia e cousas do Brasil*, 181–212.
169. Johnson, "Portuguese Settlement, 1500–1580," 17–19.
170. See Schwartz, *Early Brazil*; and Hemming, *Red Gold*.
171. See Melville, *Plague of Sheep*, 47.
172. See Metcalf, *Go-betweens and the Colonization of Brazil*, 120–124.
173. See Vasconcelos, *Selecta Brasiliense ou noticias, descobertas, observações, factos e curiosidades em relação aos homens á historia e cousas do Brasil*, 240.
174. Melville, *Plague of Sheep*, 56.
175. Metcalf, *Go-betweens and the Colonization of Brazil*, 120–124.
176. See Webb, *The Changing Face of Northeast Brazil*, 8.
177. Webb, *The Changing Face of Northeast Brazil*, 8 and 91.
178. Webb, *The Changing Face of Northeast Brazil*, 90.
179. Dodge, "A Forgotten Century of Brazilwood: The Brazilwood Trade from the Mid-Sixteenth to Mid-Seventeenth Century," 3.
180. See Hemming, *Red Gold*; and Johnson, "Portuguese Settlement, 1500–1580," 31.
181. Hemming, *Red Gold*, 492–501. Today the Indigenous population represents less than 0.5 percent of the total Brazilian population, as opposed to Indigenous populations and their descendants today in parts of Bolivia, Peru, Ecuador, Mexico, or Guatemala, for instance, comprising a much higher proportion, ranging from 20 percent to even 50 percent of the total population, in some cases. In addition, see *Instituto Brasileiro de Geografia e Estatística*, IBGE, 2000, *Ministério do Planejamento, Orçamento e Gestão, Brasil: 500 anos de Povoamento*. Rio de Janeiro, http://www.ibge.gov.br/brasil500/index2.html.
182. See Gibson, *The Aztecs Under Spanish Rule*, 5–7.
183. Metcalf, *Go-betweens and the Colonization of Brazil*, 120. It is well established now among scholars that at least five diseases arrived in the Americas after the Europeans first arrived: smallpox, measles, influenza, scarlet fever, and yellow fever, and probably half of them were carried to the Americas by animal hosts (insects and animals) that were onboard European sailing vessels. See Metcalf, *Go-betweens and the Colonization of Brazil*, 121.

184. For more details, see Burns, *A History of Brazil*, 9–10.
185. Russell-Wood, *The Portuguese Empire, 1415–1808*, 4.
186. *Instituto Brasileiro de Geografia e Estatística*. IBGE 2021, https://brasil500anos.ibge.gov.br/territorio-brasileiro-e-povoamento/judeus/cristaos-novos-no-brasil-colonia.html.
187. *Instituto Brasileiro de Geografia e Estatística*. IBGE 2021, https://brasil500anos.ibge.gov.br/territorio-brasileiro-e-povoamento/judeus/cristaos-novos-no-brasil-colonia.html.
188. *Instituto Brasileiro de Geografia e Estatística*. IBGE 2021, https://brasil500anos.ibge.gov.br/territorio-brasileiro-e-povoamento/portugueses/imigracao-restrita-1500-1700.html.
189. See *Instituto Brasileiro de Geografia e Estatística*. IBGE 2021, https://brasil500anos.ibge.gov.br/territorio-brasileiro-e-povoamento/portugueses/imigracao-restrita-1500-1700.html.
190. See *Instituto Brasileiro de Geografia e Estatística*. IBGE 2021, https://brasil500anos.ibge.gov.br/territorio-brasileiro-e-povoamento/portugueses/imigracao-restrita-1500-1700.html.
191. See Bethencourt, *Racisms*, 183.
192. See Poettering. *Migrating Merchants*, 103.
193. Quoted in Bethencourt, *Racisms*, 183.
194. See Bethencourt, *Racisms*, 183.
195. See Samuel, "Some Eighteenth-Century Refugees from Brazil," 89; and Novinsky et al., *Os Judeus Que Construíram of Brasil*, 123–124.
196. See Novinsky, *Cristãos novos na Bahia*, 176.
197. Maio and Calaça, "New Christians and Jews in Brazil: Migrations and Antisemitism," 78.
198. See Novinsky, *Cristãos novos na Bahia*, 58; and Vainfas and Assis, "A esnoga da Bahia: cristãos-novos e criptojudaísmo no Brasil quinhentista," 48.
199. See Schwartz, *All Can Be Saved*, 190.
200. For a discussion on internal migration patterns of New Christians within Brazil, see Gorenstein, "Um Brasil subterrâneo: cristãos-novos no século XVIII," 143.

Chapter Two

1. The islands of Madeira and Azores, Brazil, and the Portuguese territories on the west coast of Africa responded to the tribunal of Lisbon, and those territories on the east coast of Africa, to the tribunal of Goa. See Arquivo Torre do Tombo, "Tribunal Santo Oficio," http://antt.dglab.gov.pt/wp-content/uploads/sites/17/2021/03/Tribunal-Santo-Oficio-1.pdf.
2. See Novinsky et al., *Os Judeus Que Construiram of Brasil*, 180.
3. See Vainfas, "Santo Ofício em terra Fluminense—Cristão-novos e Inquisição no Rio de Janeiro colonial," 14.
4. See Wadsworth, *Agents of Orthodoxy*, 22.

5. See Wadsworth, *Agents of Orthodoxy*, 2.
6. For more details, see Novinsky, "Prisioneiros no Brasil," 12; and Wadsworth, *In Defense of the Faith*.
7. See Wadsworth. *In Defense of the Faith*, 11.
8. For more details, for example, see Feitler, *The Imaginary Synagogue*. Take, for instance, when New Christians were blamed for Lisbon's earthquake of 1531; or when the church of Odivelas was robbed, and two hundred New Christians were rounded up and imprisoned: eighteen were executed, yet they were all innocent—as the real perpetrator would confess to the robbery later. Vieira, "Os Calaças: Quatro Gerações de uma Família de Cristãos-Novos na Inquisição (Séculos XVII–XVIII)," 104.
9. See Peters, *Inquisition*, 12, and 2–4.
10. See, for example, Matthew Tracy, "Busting the Inquisitorial Myths," Special Faculty of Theology, Radboud University, the Netherlands, January 29, 2022, https://www.ru.nl/theology/society/imagining-the-inquisition/inquisition-history/busting-inquisitorial-myths/.
11. See, for example, Wadsworth, *In Defense of the Faith*, 7.
12. That is, under the category of heresy against the Catholic Church, it was the "perfidy" of Jewishness that was central. Even after baptism, New Christians carried the "taint of Jewish blood" that lingered generation after generation for a period that lasted almost three centuries, until the category of "New Christian" was eliminated in 1773. See, for example, Novinsky et al., *Os Judeus Que Construiram of Brasil*.
13. For a detailed discussion on the Spanish Inquisition, see Peters, *Inquisition*, 98. An important strategy, therefore, is to escape the narrow tunnel vision of the Inquisition and the categories it created, as we cannot easily replicate them in a modern context. Moreover, the Inquisition is not a statistical source—and should not be used as one—for example, it was not their purpose to count how many New Christians existed; the goal was to enforce religious conformity based on social mechanisms, surveillance, and control.
14. See Vieira, "Os Calaças: Quatro Gerações de uma Família de Cristãos-Novos na Inquisição (Séculos XVII–XVIII)," 23 and 84; Sam Jones, "Spain Fights to Dispel Legend of Inquisition and Imperial Atrocities," *The Guardian*, April 29, 2018, https://www.theguardian.com/world/2018/apr/29/spain-black-legend-inquisition-conquistadors; Kamen, *Inquisition and Society in Spain in the Sixteenth and Seventeenth Centuries*; Wadsworth, *Agents of Orthodoxy*; and Peters, *Inquisition*. This rhetoric has also received attention in newspaper reports, for example, "Historians say Inquisition wasn't that bad," *The Guardian*, June 16, 2004, https://www.theguardian.com/world/2004/jun/16/artsandhumanities.internationaleducationnews; and also, the BBC News reported from the Vatican, that according "to the 800-page report, the Inquisition ... did not use execution or torture to anything like the extent history would have us believe." Verity Murphy, *BBC News Online*, Tuesday, June 15, 2004, "Vatican 'Dispels Inquisition Myths,'" http://news.bbc.co.uk/2/hi/europe/3809983.stm.

15. Rosenstein, *Turning Points in Jewish History*, 198.
16. Feitler, *The Imaginary Synagogue*, 80.
17. For more details, see Graizbord, *Souls in Dispute*, 118.
18. See Vieira, "Os Calaças: Quatro Gerações de uma Família de Cristãos-Novos na Inquisição (Séculos XVII–XVIII)," 23 and 84.
19. Bethencourt, *Racisms*, 30.
20. See Bethencourt, *Racisms*, 149.
21. See Feitler, "A circulação de obras antijudaicas e anti-semitas no Brasil colonial."
22. For a further discussion, see Kamen, *Inquisition and Society in Spain in the Sixteenth and Seventeenth Centuries*.
23. Novinsky, "Marranos and the Inquisition: On the Gold Route in Minas Gerais, Brazil," 215–249.
24. Bethencourt, *Racisms*, 150.
25. Maio and Calaça, "Um balanço da bibliografia sobre o anti-semitismo no Brasil," 430–431.
26. Poettering, *Migrating Merchants*, 86.
27. Novinsky, "Marranos and the Inquisition: On the Gold Route in Minas Gerais, Brazil," 216–217.
28. Novinsky, "Marranos and the Inquisition: On the Gold Route in Minas Gerais, Brazil," 216–217.
29. See Berdichevsky, "The Age-Old Iberian Rivalry and the Jews," 41. Also see Prado, *Primeiros Povoadores do Brasil, 1500–1530*, 99.
30. Costa-Gomes, *The Making of a Court Society*, 169 and 199.
31. Costa-Gomes, *The Making of a Court Society*, 200.
32. Costa-Gomes, *The Making of a Court Society*, 200.
33. For a detailed discussion, see Peters, *Inquisition*, 81.
34. See Peters, *Inquisition*, 84. It was through this type of ethno-religious hostility toward New Christians that the doctrine of limpeza de sangue ("blood purity") emerged.
35. Feitler, "O Catolicismo como Ideal. Produção Literária Anitjudaica no Mundo Portugueses da Idade Moderna," 139. Also see Wolff, "The 1391 Pogrom in Spain. Social Crisis or Not?"
36. Adler, "Lea on the Inquisition of Spain and Herein of Spanish and Portuguese Jews and Marranos," 516.
37. Herculano, *History of the Origin and Establishment of the Inquisition in Portugal*, 223–332.
38. See Vainfas and Herman, "Judeus e conversos na Ibéria no século XV: sefardismo, heresia, messianismo," 31–32.
39. Castaño, "The Peninsula as a Borderless Space: Towards a Mobility 'Turn' in the Study of Fifteenth-Century Iberian Jewries," 318.
40. See Herculano, *History of the Origin and Establishment of the Inquisition in Portugal*, 234.
41. Quoted in Graizbord, *Souls in Dispute*, 28.

42. For further discussion, see Vainfas and Herman, "Judeus e conversos na Ibéria no século XV: sefardismo, heresia, messianismo," 33.
43. See Herculano, *History of the Origin and Establishment of the Inquisition in Portugal*, 234. Also see Leite, *Unorthodox Kin*, 41, and Prado, *Primeiros Povoadores do Brasil, 1500–1530*, 99. For a long time Portugal became the home of thousands of Jewish immigrants from Spain who would come to form part of the Portuguese cultural fabric, joining the existing local Portuguese-Jewish communities and altogether helping to forge the broader segment of "the Portuguese Nation." Furthermore, during the Iberian Union (1580–1640), Spain did not try to assimilate the Portuguese (i.e., language, culture) and Brazil remained under Portugal's jurisdiction.
44. See Vainfas and Herman, "Judeus e conversos na Ibéria no século XV: sefardismo, heresia, messianismo," 19.
45. See Herculano, *History of the Origin and Establishment of the Inquisition in Portugal*, 247.
46. See Feitler, "O Catolicismo como Ideal. Produção Literária Anitjudaica no Mundo Portugueses da Idade Moderna," 137.
47. Quoted in Wiznitzer, *Jews in Colonial Brazil*, 1. Other scholars have recently estimated much lower numbers: about 30,000 entered Portugal from Spain in 1492, and the estimated total of Jews in Portugal was 30,000, comprising 60,000 Jews—perhaps reaching 80,000 Jews—who would have been living in Portugal at that time (about 8 percent of Portugal's total population). See Bethencourt, *Racisms*, 146.
48. See Roth, *A Life of Menasseh Ben Israel*, 2. Also see Saraiva, *The Marrano Factory*, 11–12.
49. Wiznitzer, *Jews in Colonial Brazil*, 1.
50. See Wiznitzer, *Jews in Colonial Brazil*, 2.
51. Yerushalmi, "Between Amsterdam and New Amsterdam: The Place of Curaçao and the Caribbean in Early Modern Jewish History," 173.
52. Although Muslim territories were still open, and many returned to Portugal and Spain after a few years abroad. Several New Christians returned to the Iberian Peninsula. For more details, see Graizbord, *Souls in Dispute*.
53. See Graizbord, *Souls in Dispute*, 118.
54. In fact, it is a well-known fact today that anybody who speaks Portuguese knows that words used in common vernacular are derived from Arabic, for example: *alface* (lettuce), *armazém* (store), *azeite* (olive oil), *açúcar* (sugar), and *álcool* (alcohol)—all of which can be traced back to the Convivência period.
55. Barros, "The Muslim Minority in the Portuguese Kingdom (1170–1496): Identity and Writing," 22–23.
56. Vainfas and Herman, "Judeus e conversos na Ibéria no século XV: sefardismo, heresia, messianismo," 31–32, and 21.
57. See Vainfas and Herman, "Judeus e conversos na Ibéria no século XV: sefardismo, heresia, messianismo," 30.
58. Bethencourt, *Racisms*, 148.
59. For more details, see Graizbord, *Souls in Dispute*, 118.

60. See Greyerz, "Portuguese conversos on the Upper Rhine and the converso Community of Sixteenth-Century Europe," 62.
61. Quoted in Leite, *Unorthodox Kin*, 48.
62. See Bethencourt, *The Inquisition*, 44.
63. This is important to highlight since until the late fifteenth century, Portugal had been very different from its neighbors in southern Europe. For example, Jews in Portugal received ample state and civil protection by special public laws and civil laws, as well as the liberty to follow their own religion and publicly to practice customs and worship in synagogues. Although, they were still obliged to wear a six-pointed star sown on their clothing, were not allowed to have Christian servants, and could not leave the Jewish quarters, judarias, at night. See Herculano, *History of the Origin and Establishment of the Inquisition in Portugal*, 236–239.
64. Arquivo Nacional, Torre do Tombo, "Tribunal Santo Oficio," http://antt.dglab.gov.pt/wp-content/uploads/sites/17/2021/03/Tribunal-Santo-Oficio-1.pdf.
65. See, for example, Graizbord, *Souls in Dispute*, 51.
66. For further details, see Gitlitz, *Secrecy and Deceit*, 505–551; and Graizbord, *Souls in Dispute*, 51–52. It is important to highlight this uniqueness here in the context of the migration of Portuguese Jews and New Christians to Brazil, as it is different from the plight of Spanish Jews or conversos, or broadly the Sephardim, and of course, from the Ashkenazim.
67. Quoted in Herculano, *History of the Origin and Establishment of the Inquisition in Portugal*, 275–278.
68. Mordoch, "Um cristão-novo nos trópicos: expansão imperial e identidade religiosa nos Diálogos das grandezas do Brasil de Ambrósio Fernandes Brandão," 201.
69. See, Mordoch "Um cristão-novo nos trópicos: expansão imperial e identidade religiosa nos Diálogos das grandezas do Brasil de Ambrósio Fernandes Brandão," 201.
70. Graizbord, *Souls in Dispute*, 21.
71. Graizbord, *Souls in Dispute*, 21.
72. See, Cohen *The Canonization of a Myth*, 11–12.
73. Quoted in Cohen, *The Canonization of a Myth*, 24.
74. Quoted in Cohen, *The Canonization of a Myth*, 24.
75. See Vainfas, "Santo Oficio em terra Fluminense—Cristão-novos e Inquisição no Rio de Janeiro colonial," 24.
76. Many times, however, denouncements were also driven by revenge, jealously, or envy. For more details, for example, see Wadsworth, *Agents of Orthodoxy*.
77. Schetini Júnior, "Cristãs-novas e criptojudaismo na Bahia setecentista," 40.
78. Wadsworth, *Agents of Orthodoxy*, 42.
79. Saraiva, *The Marrano Factory*, 47. Ronaldo Vainfas and Zeb Tortorici explain that "heresy" and "sin" meant different things, and that "heresy" (which implied the abandonment of Christianity to embrace another religion) was different from "apostasy," which meant the abandonment of Christianity to embrace another religion—but the heretic remained a Catholic. See Vainfas and Tortorici, "Female Homoeroticism, Heresy, and the Holy Office in Colonial Brazil," 78.

80. See Bethencourt, *The Inquisition*, 373.
81. Schwartz, *All Can Be Saved*, 96.
82. See, for example, Bethencourt, *Racisms*, 148.
83. Bethencourt, *Racisms*, 147.
84. Vainfas and Tortorici, "Female Homoeroticism, Heresy, and the Holy Office in Colonial Brazil," 89.
85. Siqueira, "O Poder da Inquisição e a Inquisição como Poder," 87.
86. For further details on torture methods, see Saraiva, *The Marrano Factory*, 51–54. For photographs of replicas of the instruments of torture, see Museu da Inquisição, Minas Gerais, http://www.museudainquisicao.org.br/acervo/potro/.
87. Saraiva, *The Marrano Factory*, 51–54. For photographs of replicas of the instruments of torture, see Museu da Inquisição, Minas Gerais, http://www.museudainquisicao.org.br/acervo/potro/.
88. Bethencourt, *The Inquisition*, 301.
89. See Wiznitzer, "Isaac de Castro, Brazilian Jewish Martyr," 69.
90. Bethencourt, *The Inquisition*, 303. Also see page 89 for Bethencourt's explanation of memory of infamy, the annihilation of the body by fire. Adding to that the well-known Biblical notion that "the wages of sin is death."
91. Quoted in Oppenheim, "A Newspaper Account of an Auto Da Fe in Lisbon in 1726, in Which a Jew, a Native of Bahia, South America, Was Burnt," 181–182.
92. In R. Warren Anderson's study, he notes that "incarceration, exile, banishment, the galleys, confiscation and whipping were all commonly used to deter deviant behaviors." A sentence of working in the galleys mostly meant performing slave work instead of rowing on ships. See Anderson, "Inquisitorial Punishments in Lisbon and Évora," 2.
93. Saraiva, *The Marrano Factory*, 37.
94. Roth, *A Life of Menasseh Ben Israel*, 12; and Anderson, "Inquisitorial Punishments in Lisbon and Évora," 22.
95. See Bethencourt, *The Inquisition*, 288.
96. See Bethencourt, *The Inquisition*, 274.
97. Novinsky et al., *O Brasil Que os Judeus Construíram*, 44–46.
98. Roth, *A Life of Menasseh Ben Israel*, 7.
99. Schwartz, *All Can Be Saved*, 19.
100. Bethencourt, *The Inquisition*, 286.
101. Wadsworth, *Agents of Orthodoxy*, 46.
102. Bethencourt, *The Inquisition*, 286.
103. See Vainfas and Tortorici. "Female Homoeroticism, Heresy, and the Holy Office in Colonial Brazil," 79. Also see Vainfas, "Homoerotismo feminino e o Santo Ofício." As Ronaldo Vainfas and Zeb Tortorici explain, "the Inquisition certainly would prosecute sodomites, but mainly because of religious reasons (such as same-sex solicitation in the confessional, which desecrated the sacrament)." Vainfas and Tortorici, "Female Homoeroticism, Heresy, and the Holy Office in Colonial Brazil," 80. For more details on the Portuguese Inquisition's concepts of sodomy and

sexuality and their arrests in colonial Brazil, see Aidoo, *Slavery Unseen*, 33; Vainfas, *Trópico dos pecados*, 212; and Novinsky, *Prisioneiros do Brasil*, 46.

104. For a detailed description on sodomy and the Inquisition, see Vainfas and Tortorici, "Female Homoeroticism, Heresy, and the Holy Office in Colonial Brazil," 79. See Vainfas, "Homoerotismo feminino e o Santo Ofício," and Aidoo, *Slavery Unseen*, 33.

105. Vainfas and Tortorici. "Female Homoeroticism, Heresy, and the Holy Office in Colonial Brazil," 80. See Vainfas, "Homoerotismo feminino e o Santo Ofício,"

106. Resende and Sousa, "Por temer o Santo Ofício" As denúncias de Minas Gerais no Tribunal da Inquisição (século XVIII)," 217. Also see Lima, *A Confissão Pelo Avesso*.

107. For a detailed discussion on rape and sexual violence, the Inquisition, and the Church, see Aidoo, *Slavery Unseen*, 33.

108. See Schwartz, *All Can Be Saved*, 101.

109. See Adler, "Lea on the Inquisition of Spain and Herein of Spanish and Portuguese Jews and Marranos," 540.

110. Notably, the verb, *judiar* and the noun, *judiação* in Brazil are thought to have stemmed from the Portuguese word, "judeu" ("Jew"), and are commonly used in popular Brazilian vernacular (e.g., *que judiação!*, "what cruelty!"; or *judiaram do cachorro*, "they inflicted cruelty on a dog"), and which meanings "evoke unfair and censurable victimization of an innocent." See Shohat and Stam, "Genealogies of Orientalism and Occidentalism: Sephardi Jews, Muslims, and the Americas," 32.

111. See Lopes, "As Contas da Inquisição Portuguesa: O Exemplo dos Tribunais de Évora e Lisboa (1701–1755)."

112. See Leite, *Unorthodox Kin*, 50–51.

113. Saraiva, *The Marrano Factory*, 115, and 113–114.

114. Graizbord, *Souls in Dispute*, 2.

115. While Ronaldo Vainfas asserts that Ana Rodrigues from Engenho Matoim, Bahia, was the first person from Brazil to be burned at the stake in 1593, she was, however, burned "in effigy" after she died at the age of 80 (or 100), which they discovered when they unearthed her bones. Vainfas, "Santo Ofício em terra Fluminense—Cristão-novos e Inquisição no Rio de Janeiro colonial," 39.

116. Romeiras, "The Inquisition and the Censorship of Science in Early Modern Europe: Introduction," 1–9.

117. Gibson, *The Aztecs Under Spanish Rule*, 402.

118. For example, see Romeiras, "The Inquisition and the Censorship of Science in Early Modern Europe: Introduction," 1–9.

119. See Nash, *The Conquest of Brazil*, 128.

120. Wadsworth, *Agents of Orthodoxy*, 12.

121. Matthew Tracy, "The Black and White Legends," Special Faculty of Theology, Radboud University, the Netherlands, January 29, 2022, https://www.ru.nl/theology/society/imagining-the-inquisition/inquisition-history/black-white-legends/. Also see Sam Jones, "Spain Fights to Dispel Legend of Inquisition and Imperial Atrocities," *The Guardian*, April 29, 2018, https://www.theguardian.com/world/2018/apr/29/spain-black-legend-inquisition-conquistadors.

122. See Kamen, *Inquisition and Society in Spain in the Sixteenth and Seventeenth Centuries*; Wadsworth, *Agents of Orthodoxy*; and Peters, *Inquisition*. Also, for a discussion of scholars who found the Inquisition to be "not that cruel," see Vieira, "Os Calaças: Quatro Gerações de uma Família de Cristãos-Novos na Inquisição (Séculos XVII–XVIII)," 116–118. In public spheres, this rhetoric has also received the attention of newspaper reports, for example, "Historians say Inquisition wasn't that bad," *The Guardian*, June 16, 2004, https://www.theguardian.com/world/2004/jun/16/artsandhumanities.internationaleducationnews; and also, the BBC News reported from the Vatican, that according "to the 800-page report, the Inquisition . . . did not use execution or torture to anything like the extent history would have us believe." Also see Verity Murphy, *BBC News Online*, Tuesday, June 15, 2004, "Vatican 'Dispels Inquisition Myths,'" http://news.bbc.co.uk/2/hi/europe/3809983.stm.
123. Benjamin Soloway, *Foreign Policy*, July 10, 2015, https://foreignpolicy.com/2015/07/10/pope-francis-apologizes-for-churchs-colonial-sins/.
124. See Bogaciovas, *Tribulações do Povo de Israel na São Paulo Colonial*, 255.
125. Bethencourt, *Racisms*, 147–148.
126. See Bodian, "Review of The Canonization of a Myth: Portugal's 'Jewish Problem' and the Assembly of Tomar 1629. Martin A. Cohen, Hebrew Union College Annual Supplements 5. Cincinnati, Ohio: Hebrew Union College Press, 2002."
127. Wadsworth, *In Defense of the Faith*, 9.
128. For example, Wadsworth, *Agents of Orthodoxy*; Schwartz, *All Can Be Saved*; and Yovel, *The Other Within*.
129. Wadsworth, *Agents of Orthodoxy*, 12. For a discussion on the comparisons between the Inquisition and the Nazi Holocaust, see Novinsky, *Viver nos Tempos da Inquisição*.
130. Wadsworth, *Agents of Orthodoxy*, 12.
131. Wadsworth, *Agents of Orthodoxy*, 10.
132. Wadsworth, *Agents of Orthodoxy*, 10.
133. See Novinsky, *Viver nos Tempos da Inquisição*.
134. Although some other figures have been unrealistic, an estimate of the number of Jews who were living in Portugal by the late fifteenth century was as high as 800,000. For more details, see Herculano, *History of the Origin and Establishment of the Inquisition in Portugal*, 234–235.
135. Maio and Calaça, "Um balanço da bibliografia sobre o anti-semitismo no Brasil," 430.
136. For more information, see Feitler, "Ofícios e estratégias de acumulação: o caso do despenseiro da Inquisição de Lisboa Antonio Gonçalves Prego (1650–1720)."
137. Peters, *Inquisition*, 98.
138. Bethencourt, *The Inquisition*, 305.
139. Bethencourt, *Racisms*, 8.
140. See United Nations, 2022. "United Nations Office on Genocide Prevention and the Responsibility to Protect," https://www.un.org/en/genocideprevention/documents/publications-and-resources/GuidanceNote-When%20to%20refer%20to%20a%20situation%20as%20genocide.pdf.

141. "United Nations General Assembly Resolution 96 (I): The Crime of Genocide," *United Nations*, 11 December, 1946; June 18, 2021, 188–189. https://documents-dds-ny.un.org/doc/RESOLUTION/GEN/NR0/033/47/IMG/NR003347.pdf?OpenElement.
142. Perhaps in the same way that there are "Holocaust deniers," there are also "Inquisition deniers" or "minimizers."
143. Arquivo Nacional, Torre do Tombo, Portugal, "Dia Nacional da Memória das Vítimas da Inquisição," http://antt.dglab.gov.pt/exposicoes-virtuais-2/dia-nacional-da-memoria-das-vitimas-da-inquisicao-31-de-marco/.
144. I want to thank Dr. David Marcus, Professor Emeritus at the Jewish Theological Seminary of America, for pointing this out and for offering the correct spelling in Hebrew.
145. Feitler, *The Imaginary Synagogue*, 1.
146. Feitler, *The Imaginary Synagogue*, 1.
147. For example, a man simply named José, aged 30, who was arrested in Pernambuco, stands out. In 1595 he was listed as *escravo mulato* ("mulatto slave") of Fernão Soares and arrested for "relapse of blasphemy" (*relapsia em blasfémias*). His punishment was to walk barefoot at an auto-da-fé with a pole across his mouth and a rope around his neck. He was harshly whipped in public, was sent to the galleys for four years, and was required to pay Inquisition expenses (processo 2556–1).
148. See Schwartz, Stuart B. "The Uncourted Menina: Brazil's Portuguese Heritage."
149. See Vainfas and Herman, "Judeus e conversos na Ibéria no século XV: sefardismo, heresia, messianismo," 36.
150. Leite, *Unorthodox Kin*, 52.
151. Quoted in Leite, *Unorthodox Kin*, 41. There were already about 30,000 to 50,000 Jews living in Portugal by that time (Portugal was considered a safe haven for Jews after Spain's pogroms in 1391, and before the late fifteenth century), and after Spain expelled all its Jews, the influx into Portugal is estimated to have ranged from 100,000 to 120,000. Therefore, about 150,000 to 200,000 Jews were living in Portugal by the end of the fifteenth century when its total population was estimated at about 1 million.
152. Schwartz, *All Can Be Saved*, 47. Also, for a discussion of the return to Judaism in Portugal, see Mucznik, "Portugal e o resurgimento judaico: Uma herança de continuidade e ruptura," 591.
153. See *Comunidade Israelita de Lisboa*, "Concessão da Nacionalidade Portuguesa para Judeus Sefarditas Decreto Lei nº 30-A/2015 de 27 de Fevereiro," https://cilisboa.org/concess%C3%A3o-da-nacionalidade-portuguesa/. Also see Leite, *Unorthodox Kin*, 161.
154. Curiously, last names of Jewish origin were mentioned as guidelines to help determine if those candidates had any Jewish ancestry, even though those names were in effect a highly ambiguous way of determining Jewish ancestry, especially since Jews and New Christians changed their names frequently, depending on geography and context. For example: Abrantes, Aguilar, Andrade, Brandão, Brito, Bueno,

Cardoso, Carvalho, Castro, Costa, Coutinho, Dourado, Fonseca, Furtado, Gomes, Gouveia, Granjo, Henriques, Lara, Marques, Melo e Prado, Mesquita, Mendes, Neto, Nunes, Pereira, Pinheiro, Rodrigues, Rosa, Sarmento, Silva, Soares, Teixeira e Teles, Almeida, Avelar, Bravo, Carvajal, Crespo, Duarte, Ferreira, Franco, Gato, Gonçalves, Guerreiro, Leão, Lopes, Leiria, Lobo, Lousada, Machorro, Martins, Montesino, Moreno, Mota, Macias, Miranda, Oliveira, Osório, Pardo, Pina, Pinto, Pimentel, Pizarro, Querido, Rei, Ribeiro, Salvador, Torres e Viana, Amorim, Azevedo, Álvares, Barros, Basto, Belmonte, Cáceres, Caetano, Campos, Carneiro, Cruz, Dias, Duarte, Elias, Estrela, Gaiola, Josué, Lemos, Lombroso, Lopes, Machado, Mascarenhas, Mattos, Meira, Mello e Canto, Mendes da Costa, Miranda, Morão, Morões, Mota, Moucada, Negro, Oliveira, Osório (or Ozório), Paiva, Pilão, Pinto, Pessoa, Preto, Souza, Vaz, Vargas. Consulate of Portugal in Porto Alegre, Brazil, "Aquisição de Nacionalidade Derivada. Nacionalidade portuguesa para judeus sefarditas de origem portuguesa," https://www.consuladoportugalportoalegre.com/nacionalidade-judeus-sefardita.
155. For a discussion of the Portuguese return to Judaism, see Mucznik, "Portugal e o resurgimento judaico: Uma herança de continuidade e ruptura," 591.
156. *Diario do Nordeste*, "Nordestino pode Virar Cidadão Israelense," October 13, 2005, https://diariodonordeste.verdesmares.com.br/metro/nordestino-pode-virar-cidadao-israelense-1.304876.
157. See, for example, Felipe Goifman, *National Geographic Brasil*, 2017, "Retorno do Nordeste Brasileiro ao Judaísmo. Séculos depois da Inquisição e da Conversão Forçada dos Cristãos-Novos, Nordestinos Buscam suas Raízes Judaicas," https://www.nationalgeographicbrasil.com/fotografia/2017/11/o-retorno-do-nordeste-brasileiro-ao-judaismo, November 23, 2017.
158. Associação Brasileira dos Descendentes de Judeus da Inquisição (ABRADJIN), http://anussim.org.br/quem-somos/.
159. "Inquisição e cristãos novos no Brasil, 2021–2022," Museu Judaico, https://museujudaicosp.org.br/exposicoes/inquisicao/, May 24, 2022.
160. Steve Linde, "What is Behind the Significant Rise in Aliya from Brazil to Israel?" *Jerusalem Post*, November 20, 2016, https://www.jpost.com/Israel-News/Jewish-Agency-notes-spike-in-aliya-from-Brazil-473082. Also see *Diario do Nordeste*, "Nordestino pode Virar Cidadão Israelense," October 13, 2005, https://diariodonordeste.verdesmares.com.br/metro/nordestino-pode-virar-cidadao-israelense-1.304876.
161. Cnaan Liphshiz, "Sephardic converts give northern Brazil's dwindling Jewish communities new life," *Times of Israel*, December 29, 2018, https://www.timesofisrael.com/sephardic-converts-give-northern-brazils-dwindling-jewish-communities-new-life/.
162. Giuliana Miranda, "Decedentes de judeus, correm por nacionalidade lusa antes de nova regra," *Folha de São Paulo*, May 6, 2022, https://www1.folha.uol.com.br/mundo/2022/05/descendentes-de-judeus-sefarditas-correm-por-nacionalidade-em-portugal-antes-de-nova-regra.shtml.

163. Confederação Israelita do Brasil, "Presidente da Conib fala sobre "Herança Judaica" em evento na Hebraica," June 13, 2019, https://www.conib.org.br/presidente-da-conib-fala-sobre-heranca-judaica-em-evento-na-hebraica/.
164. The interest on the topic of Jews in Latin America, broadly speaking, has increased as well. For example, Raanan Rein and Jeffrey Lesser delivered a joint lecture at the Library of Congress, discussing how Latin-American Jewish studies has become an increasingly popular area of academic inquiry, with a growing number of institutions offering classes in related subjects. *Jewish-Latin American Historiography: The Challenges Ahead*. 2010. Video. https://www.loc.gov/item/webcast-4929/.
165. For a nuanced interpretation of these findings, see Feitler, "Four Chapters in the History of Crypto-Judaism in Brazil: The Case of the Northeastern New Christians (17th–21st centuries)," 219–222. Also see Braga, *Da Arte de se Tornar Judeu*; Kaufman, "Novos personagens. Novas identidades. O marranismo contemporâneo em Pernambuco"; and Simms, "Being Crypto-Jewish in Colonial Brazil (1500–1822): Brushing History Against the Grain."
166. Simms, "Being Crypto-Jewish in Colonial Brazil (1500–1822): Brushing History Against the Grain," 449. This includes the presence and movement of New Christians into the hinterlands of Ceará; see Almeida, "Cristãos-novos e seus descendentes no Ceará Grande: a inquisição nos sertões de fora." Also see Braga, *Da Arte de se Tornar Judeu*; and Kaufman, "Novos personagens. Novas identidades. O marranismo contemporâneo em Pernambuco." These cultural practices were also featured in a documentary film, *A Estrela Oculta do Sertão* (The Occult Star of the Sertão) directed by Elaine Eiger and Louise Valente (2005), and, in addition, described in a report published in 2017 by *National Geographic Brasil*. Felipe Goifman, *National Geographic Brasil*, "Retorno do Nordeste Brasileiro ao Judaísmo. Séculos depois da Inquisição e da Conversão Forçada dos Cristãos-Novos, Nordestinos Buscam suas Raízes Judaicas," November 23, 2017, https://www.nationalgeographicbrasil.com/fotografia/2017/11/o-retorno-do-nordeste-brasileiro-ao-judaismo. Also, other than Brazil, for a context on the rest of Latin America, see Rich Tenorio, *The Times of Israel*, "How Jews expelled from Spain forged a diaspora with ties to 25 percent of Latin America: Film 'Children of the Inquisition' examines forced conversion of Sephardim from the Iberian Peninsula 500 years ago and why their descendants still feel ripple effects," October 6, 2019, https://www.timesofisrael.com/how-jews-expelled-from-spain-forged-a-diaspora-with-ties-to-25-of-latin-america/.
167. See Feitler, "Four Chapters in the History of Crypto-Judaism in Brazil: The Case of the Northeastern New Christians (17th–21st centuries)," 219–222. Also see Novinsky et al., *Os Judeus Que Construiram o Brasil*, 253–257.
168. Jane de Glasman, *E-Sefarad: Noticias del Mundo Sefaradí*, "Presença Judaica na Língua Portuguesa Expressões e Dizeres Populares em Português de Origem Cristã-Nova ou Marrana," *E-Sepharad, Noticias do Mundo Sephardi*, https://esefarad.com/?p=26210. Also see Leite, *História dos judeus : no Seridó do RN, no sertão da Paraíba, na Serra da Borborema*.
169. For example, see Hordes, *To the End of the Earth*.

170. Among them comprise prominent figures and heads of firms and companies such as Samuel Klein (Casas Bahia), José Safra (Banco Safra), Hans Stern (H. Stern Jewelers), Silvio Santos (SBT television network), and Roberto Civita (Abril Publications). See Simone Kafruni, "Judaísmo rende cifras bilionárias com indústrias literária e cinematográfica. No Brasil, são aproximadamente 120 mil judeus, sendo que 70 percent praticam a religião de alguma forma," *Estado de Minas, Economia*, February 1, 2014, https://www.em.com.br/app/noticia/economia/2014/02/01/internas_economia,493944/judaismo-rende-cifras-bilionarias-com-industrias-literaria-e-cinematografica.shtml.
171. On Chico Buarque de Holanda's Jewish ancestry, see Jaimes Fuchs Bar, July 27, 2013, "Uma Princesa Cristã-Nova na Genealogia de Chico Buarque," *Judaísmo Humanista* https://judaismohumanista.ning.com/group/marranismo-anussim/forum/topics/uma-princesa-crista-nova-na-genealogia-de-chico-buarque-paulo-val.
172. Quoted in Bogaciovas, *Tribulações do Povo de Israel na São Paulo Colonial*, 13.
173. See Klein, *Kosher Feijoada*, 25.
174. Chacón-Duque et al., "Latin Americans show wide-spread Converso ancestry and imprint of local Native ancestry on physical appearance."
175. Chacón-Duque et al., "Latin Americans show wide-spread Converso ancestry and imprint of local Native ancestry on physical appearance."
176. See Feitler, "Four Chapters in the History of Crypto-Judaism in Brazil: The Case of the Northeastern New Christians (17th–21st centuries)," 219–222.
177. For details, see Feitler, "Four Chapters in the History of Crypto-Judaism in Brazil: The Case of the Northeastern New Christians (17th–21st centuries)," 219–222.
178. New research indicating that there are no more descendants from the first Jewish community in Recife have gained national attention; see Gustavo Chacra, "O Brasil nao tem mais descendentes do grupo de judeus de Recife," *Estado de Sao Paulo*, July 14, 2012, https://brasil.estadao.com.br/noticias/geral,brasil-nao-tem-mais-descendente-do-grupo-de-judeus-do-recife,900310.
179. Schwarz, *Os Cristãos-Novos em Portugal No Século XX*.
180. Schwarz, *Os Cristãos-Novos em Portugal No Século XX*. In addition, similar findings in Portugal were published in newspapers articles, such as an article in *The Jewish Daily Bulletin* in 1927, reporting, "The movement to return to Judaism is spreading in various Marrano centers. A kehillah has been established in Bragança that has a population of approximately 800 Crypto-Jews. In Bilarinho where nearly all of the 500 inhabitants are Marranos, the community has formed a kehillah." "Marranos In Portugal Returning to Judaism," *Jewish Daily Bulletin*, December 18, 1927, 947, 409, 4.
181. Feitler, "Four Chapters in the History of Crypto-Judaism in Brazil: The Case of the Northeastern New Christians (17th–21st centuries)," 219. New research indicating that there are no more descendants from the first Jewish community in Recife have gained national attention; see Gustavo Chacra, "O Brasil nao tem mais descendentes do grupo de judeus de Recife," *Estado de Sao Paulo*, July 14, 2012,

https://brasil.estadao.com.br/noticias/geral,brasil-nao-tem-mais-descendente-do-grupo-de-judeus-do-recife,900310.

182. See Wiznitzer, "The Minute Book of Congregations Zur Israel of Recife and Magen Abraham of Mauricia, Brazil," 217.

Chapter Three

1. Russell-Wood, *The Portuguese Empire, 1415–1808*, 5.
2. Russell-Wood, *The Portuguese Empire, 1415–1808*, 5.
3. Russell-Wood, *The Portuguese Empire, 1415–1808*, 10.
4. Webb, *The Changing Face of Northeast Brazil*, 89.
5. Russell-Wood, *The Portuguese Empire, 1415–1808*, xiv. Also see Jarnagin, *The Making of the Luso-Asian World*, vols. 1 and 2, and Albuquerque, "The Art of Astronomical Navigation."
6. Russell-Wood, *The Portuguese Empire, 1415–1808*, xiv. Also see Jarnagin, *The Making of the Luso-Asian World*, vols. 1 and 2.
7. For example, the following names are merely a few examples of many renowned Portuguese navigators between the fifteenth and sixth centuries: João Gonçalves Zarco, Gil Eanes, Diogo Gomes, Fernão Gomes, Lopo Gonçalves, Diogo Cão, Bartolomeu Dias, Pêro de Covilha, João Fernandes Lavrador, Vasco da Gama, Gaspar Côrte-Real, Pedro Álvares Cabral, Diogo Zeimoto, Francisco Joséde Lacerda e Almeida, Henrique Augusto Dias de Carvalho, and Tristão da Cunha. For more information, see Albuquerque, "The Art of Astronomical Navigation," and Newitt, *A History of Portuguese Overseas Expansion 1400–1668*. See Jarnagin, *The Making of the Luso-Asian World*, vols. 1 and 2
8. Mauro, "Political and economic structures of empire," 40.
9. See Hobson, *The Eastern Origins of Western Civilization*; and Seed, *Ceremonies of Possession in Europe's Conquest of the New World, 1492–1640*.
10. See, for example, a discussion of the "West," Hobson, *The Eastern Origins of Western Civilization*, 5.
11. Orientalism and Eurocentrism are worldviews that assert the inherent superiority of the West (Europe) over the East, where "the imagined values of the inferior East were set up as the antithesis of rational (Western) values." Hobson, *The Eastern Origins of Western Civilization*, 7.
12. Seed, *Ceremonies of Possession in Europe's Conquest of the New World, 1492–1640*, 135.
13. Banes, "The Portuguese Voyages of Discovery and the Emergence of Modern Science." 53.
14. Roth, *A Life of Menasseh Ben Israel*, 6.
15. For a detailed discussion on Portuguese navigation, see Russell-Wood, *The Portuguese Empire, 1415–1808*, 9–10. Also see Albuquerque, "The Art of Astronomical Navigation."
16. See Newitt, *A History of Portuguese Overseas Expansion 1400–1668*, 93.
17. For further details, see Mauro, "Political and economic structures of empire," 39.

Keep in mind that the Portuguese held Hormuz and Muscat in 1507, and Aden in 1513 (and the island of Socotra, off the coast of Yemen, which was abandoned by them after five years). They renamed the fortress of Suk on Socotra to São Miguel, as well as the small mosque to Nossa Senhora da Vitória ("Our Lady of Victory"). Andreu Martínez d'Alòs-Moner explains that King Dom Manuel I of Portugal (1495–1526) had "eschatological dreams" of material profits, prompting the Portuguese to go toward the Red Sea. The Portuguese also dominated the Indian Ocean, taking Mallaca in 1511; Timor in 1512; Damão/Daman in 1531; Saisette, Bombay/Mumbai, and Baçaim/Vasai in 1534; and Diu in 1535—all by sea, thus establishing important trade network links between its other domains (Brazil, Angola, São Tomé, Príncipe, Cape Verde, and Mozambique), territories, and feitorias (trading post forts) around the world. For more details, see d'Alòs-Moner, "Conquistadores, Mercenaries, and Missionaries: The Failed Portuguese Dominion of the Red Sea"; Livingstone, *The Geographical Tradition*; and Banes, "The Portuguese Voyages of Discovery and the Emergence of Modern Science."

18. Russell-Wood, *The Portuguese Empire, 1415–1808*, 9–10. Also see Jarnagin, *The Making of the Luso-Asian World*, vols. 1 and 2, and Albuquerque, "The Art of Astronomical Navigation."
19. Seed, "Jewish Scientists and the Origin of Modern Navigation," 76.
20. Seed, *Ceremonies of Possession in Europe's Conquest of the New World, 1492–1640*, 104. However, we must also consider that, as Alberta Frances Hill points out, "the question of when, and by whom, the first European depiction of the asterism now known as the Southern Cross was produced is both complex and thorny." 133. Hill, "Alvise Cadamosto, Mestre João Faras and the Controversial History of Early European Mapping of the Southern Cross," 138.
21. See Merchant, *Reinventing Eden*, 66–67.
22. See Merchant, *Reinventing Eden*, 66–67.
23. Merchant, *Reinventing Eden*, 93.
24. For examples of such omissions of the Portuguese world in anglophone textbooks, dictionaries, and surveys in geography, see Cresswell, *Geographic Thought*; James and Martin, *All Possible Worlds*; and Holt-Jensen, *Geography*. Although only a brief reference is found in an entry in Gregory et al., *Dictionary of Human Geography*, there is nothing in geography textbooks and surveys about the Portuguese world or on Portuguese-Jewish scientific and geographical achievements.
25. For blatant omissions of the Portuguese world and Portuguese contributions to early global navigation, see Cresswell, *Geographic Thought*; James and Martin, *All Possible Worlds*; and Holt-Jensen, *Geography*.
26. While geographers Arthur Davies and Karl W. Butzer have written about science and encounters in the New World, their emphasis is on Spain's contributions, and not a word is said about the Portuguese world, or about Portuguese Jews and New Christians and their contribution to the science of that time. For instance, in Butzer's articles, nothing is said about the Portuguese in the New World and their contribution in Brazil. See, for example, Butzer, "The Americas before and after

1492: An Introduction to Current Geographical Research"; Butzer, "From Columbus to Acosta: Science, Geography, and the New World"; and Davies, "Henry the Navigator."
27. Novinsky, *Os Judeus Que Construíram o Brasil*, 32.
28. Russell-Wood, *The Portuguese Empire, 1415–1808*, 83.
29. Walker, "Supplying Simples for the Royal Hospital: An Indo-Portuguese Medicinal Garden in Goa (1520–1830)," 26.
30. See Walker, "Supplying Simples for the Royal Hospital: An Indo-Portuguese Medicinal Garden in Goa (1520–1830)," 26–27.
31. See Albuquerque, "The Art of Astronomical Navigation."
32. See Russell-Wood, *The Portuguese Empire, 1415–1808*, 83.
33. See Russell-Wood, *The Portuguese Empire, 1415–1808*, 83.
34. See Bogaciovas, *Tribulações do Povo de Israel na São Paulo Colonial*, 55–56.
35. Saraiva, *The Marrano Factory*, 5.
36. For a detailed discussion on modern science and Portuguese Jews, see Banes, "The Portuguese Voyages of Discovery and the Emergence of Modern Science." 50.
37. See Seed, *Ceremonies of Possession in Europe's Conquest of the New World, 1492–1640*, 118–119. Also see Albuquerque, "The Art of Astronomical Navigation."
38. See Bachmann, "Judeus e Globalizacão," 581–582.
39. Seed, "Celestial Navigation," 285. Also see Seed, "Jewish Scientists and the Origin of Modern Navigation," and, Seed, *Ceremonies of Possession in Europe's Conquest of the New World, 1492–1640*.
40. Seed, "Jewish Scientists and the Origin of Modern Navigation," 79. Also see Albuquerque, "The Art of Astronomical Navigation."
41. See Seed, "Jewish Scientists and the Origin of Modern Navigation," 80. Also see Albuquerque, "The Art of Astronomical Navigation."
42. For more details on Mestre João, see Valentim, "Uma Família de Cristãos-Novos do Entre Douro e Minho: Os Paz. Reprodução Familiar, Formas de Mobildade Social, Mecancia e Poder."
43. See Banes, "The Portuguese Voyages of Discovery and the Emergence of Modern Science," 50.
44. See Roth, *A Life of Menasseh Ben Israel*, 109–111.
45. Bynum et al., *Dictionary of the History of Science*. Despite the omission in this dictionary, some scholars have claimed that without the scientific development produced by Jews, it is likely that the Portuguese global presence and its advancements in world navigation and exploration would not have occurred, or at least, they would have been significantly delayed. See Margarido, *Le rôle des juifs dans l'expansion européenne*, 218.
46. Quoted in Livingstone, *The Geographical Tradition*, 61. For a list of names of eminent Portuguese-Jewish philosophers, doctors, and scientists who left Portugal by the end of the fifteenth century, see Bachmann, "Judeus e Globalizacão," 581–582.
47. Seed, "Jewish Scientists and the Origin of Modern Navigation," 81–82.
48. See Novinsky et al., *Os Judeus Que Construíram o Brasil*, 30.

49. Bethencourt, *Racisms*, 54.
50. Kogman-Appel, "The Geographical Concept of the Catalan *mappamundi*," 19.
51. Kogman-Appel, "The Geographical Concept of the Catalan *mappamundi*," 20. Also see Albuquerque, "The Art of Astronomical Navigation."
52. Kogman-Appel, "The Geographical Concept of the Catalan *mappamundi*," 29.
53. Banes, "The Portuguese Voyages of Discovery and the Emergence of Modern Science," 51.
54. Quoted in Banes, "The Portuguese Voyages of Discovery and the Emergence of Modern Science," 52.
55. For example, a cousin of Luís de Santagel (who was burned at the stake by the Inquisition), Rabbi Azarias Ginillo, had advanced Queen Isabel 16,000 ducats to help fund Columbus's voyage. Adler, "Lea on the Inquisition of Spain and Herein of Spanish and Portuguese Jews and Marranos," 535.
56. For a detailed clarification, see Bronner, "Portugal and Columbus: Old Drives in New Discoveries." Also see Berdichevsky, "The Age-Old Iberian Rivalry and the Jews," 38–39; and Bernadini, "A Milder Colonization: Jewish Expansion to the New World, and the New World in the Jewish Consciousness of the Early Modern Era," 2.
57. See Randles, "The Alleged Nautical School Founded in the Fifteenth Century at Sagres by Prince Henry of Portugal. Called the 'Navigator.'" Also see Guedes and Lombardi, *Portugal Brazil: The Age of Atlantic Discoveries*.
58. See Newitt, *A History of Portuguese Overseas Expansion, 1400–1668*, 29; and Bronner, "Portugal and Columbus: Old Drives in New Discoveries," 58. Also see Randles, "The Alleged Nautical School Founded in the Fifteenth Century at Sagres by Prince Henry of Portugal. Called the 'Navigator.'"
59. Newitt, *A History of Portuguese Overseas Expansion, 1400–1668*, 6. For example, Fred Bronner dates the Genoese-Portuguese connection to 1317. Bronner, "Portugal and Columbus: Old Drives in New Discoveries," 56. Also see Guedes and Lombardi, *Portugal Brazil: The Age of Atlantic Discoveries*.
60. Newitt, *A History of Portuguese Overseas Expansion, 1400–1668*, 8.
61. Manning and Owen, *Knowledge in Translation*.
62. See Adler, "Lea on the Inquisition of Spain and Herein of Spanish and Portuguese Jews and Marranos," 513.
63. Russell-Wood, *The Portuguese Empire, 1415–1808*, xxi.
64. Marcocci, "Toward a History of the Portuguese Inquisition Trends in Modern Historiography (1974–2009)," 23.
65. Seed, "Celestial Navigation," 275.
66. Seed, "Celestial Navigation," 276.
67. Seed, *Ceremonies of Possession in Europe's Conquest of the New World, 1492–1640*, 117.
68. Seed, *Ceremonies of Possession in Europe's Conquest of the New World, 1492–1640*, 117.
69. For more details, see Russell-Wood, *The Portuguese Empire, 1415–1808*, 17.
70. For a detailed discussion, see Guedes and Lombardi, *Portugal Brazil: The Age of Atlantic Discoveries*; and Albuquerque, "The Art of Astronomical Navigation."

71. For more details, see Seed, "Celestial Navigation," 282. I want to thank Dr. David. Marcus, Professor Emeritus, Jewish Theological Seminary of America, for pointing out to me that Tishrei is on the first month of the Sabbath year.
72. Seed, "Celestial Navigation," 280; and Seed, *Ceremonies of Possession in Europe's Conquest of the New World, 1492–1640*, 117.
73. Seed, "Celestial Navigation," 280.
74. In fact, Columbus believed that he had found the "garden of delight" in the New World when he stood under a waterfall (in Venezuela). See Livingstone, *The Geographic Tradition*, 36. For more historical details on Prester John, see Matteo, "The Ethiopian Age of Exploration: Prester John's Discovery of Europe, 1306–1458."
75. See Matteo, "The Ethiopian Age of Exploration: Prester John's Discovery of Europe, 1306–1458." Also see Livingstone, *The Geographic Tradition*, 36.
76. Seed, "Celestial Navigation," 284.
77. See Ravenstein, "Vasco da Gama's First Voyage," 14–15.
78. For further details, see Guedes and Lombardi, *Portugal Brazil*. Columbus, as well as the Spanish Empire, receive most of the popular and academic attention at the expense of neglecting the Portuguese world. For further details, see Guedes and Lombardi, *Portugal Brazil*.
79. See Seed, "Jewish Scientists and the Origin of Modern Navigation," 74.
80. See Seed, "Jewish Scientists and the Origin of Modern Navigation," 74.
81. See Braga, "Centenário da Descoberta da América," 17–18.
82. See, for example, Schwartz, *Early Brazil*; Cortesão, *A política de sigílo nos descobrimentos*; Castro, *A Carta de Pero Vaz de Caminha*; and Hue, *Primeiras Cartas do Brasil, 1551–1555*. Moreover, the Eurocentric term "discovery" alone annihilates the existence of Indigeneity and the Indigenous populations and cultures that already lived in Brazil prior to the arrival of Europeans.
83. See Schwarcz and Starling, *Brazil*, 6. Also see Guedes, "Portugal-Brazil: The Encounter between Two Worlds," 164.
84. Vogt, "Fernão de Loronha and the Rental of Brazil in 1502: A New Chronology," 154.
85. See, for this discussion, Schwartz, *Early Brazil*, ix. See Cortesão, *A política de sigílo nos descobrimentos*; Castro, *A Carta de Pero Vaz de Caminha*; and Hue, *Primeiras Cartas do Brasil, 1551–1555*.
86. See Aragão, "Breve Notícia sobre o Descobrimento da América. Pedro Alvares Cabral e o Brasil," 43.
87. See Schwartz, *Early Brazil*, ix. Also see Cortesão, *A política de sigílo nos descobrimentos*; Castro, *A Carta de Pero Vaz de Caminha*; and Hue, *Primeiras Cartas do Brasil, 1551–1555*.
88. See *Instituto Brasileiro de Geografia e Estatística*. IBGE 2021, https://brasil500anos.ibge.gov.br/territorio-brasileiro-e-povoamento/construcao-do-territorio/territorio-legalizado-os-tratados.html.
89. See Aragão, "Breve Notícia sobre o Descobrimento da América. Pedro Alvares Cabral e o Brasil," 38.

90. See Aragão, "Breve Notícia sobre o Descobrimento da América. Pedro Alvares Cabral e o Brasil," 38.
91. See Aragão, "Breve Notícia sobre o Descobrimento da América. Pedro Alvares Cabral e o Brasil," 38.
92. See Schwartz, *Early Brazil*, ix. Also see Guedes, "Portugal-Brazil: The Encounter between Two Worlds," 168. Also, Christian myths, such as that of sixth-century Saint Brendan and the imaginary islands named after him, attracted adventurers toward the Atlantic in a similar way that they were attracted to Ethiopia and India by the myths of Prester John. Braga, "Centenário da Descoberta da América," 10. Greenlee, "The Captaincy of the Second Portuguese Voyage to Brazil, 1501–1502," (footnote) 7.
93. See Ley, "The Discovery of Brazil. Letter of Pedro Vaz de Caminha, written in Porto Seguro of Vera Cruz on the First Day of May in the Year 1500," 48.
94. Quoted in Ley, "The Discovery of Brazil. Letter of Pedro Vaz de Caminha, written in Porto Seguro of Vera Cruz on the First Day of May in the Year 1500," 42.
95. Schwartz, *Early Brazil*, 1; and Ley, "The Discovery of Brazil. Letter of Pedro Vaz de Caminha, written in Porto Seguro of Vera Cruz on the First Day of May in the Year 1500," 48. Also see Castro, *A Carta de Pero Vaz de Caminha*.
96. Aragão, "Breve Notícia sobre o Descobrimento da América. Pedro Alvares Cabral e o Brasil," 41.
97. Varnhagen, "Carta de Mestre Joao Physico d'el-rei, para o mesmo senhor, De Vera Cruz ao 1 de Maio de 1500," 342–344.
98. Guedes, "Portugal-Brazil: The Encounter between Two Worlds," 164.
99. "Letter of Pero Vaz de Caminha to King Manuel, written from Porto Seguro (Bahia) May 1, 1500," Quoted in Guedes, "Portugal-Brazil: The Encounter between Two Worlds," 162.
100. See Seed, "Celestial Navigation," 289; Falbel, "Sobre a Presença dos Cristãos Novos na Capitania de São Vicente e a Formação da Etnia Paulista," 112; and Falbel, *Judeus no Brasil: estudos e notas*, 67. For more details on the Jewish background of Mestre João, see Valentim, "Uma Família de Cristãos-Novos do Entre Douro e Minho: Os Paz. Reprodução Familiar, Formas de Mobildade Social, Mecancia e Poder."
101. Morison, *The Great Explorers*, 388. Also see Lipiner, *Gaspar da Gama*, 112.
102. Seed, *Ceremonies of Possession in Europe's Conquest of the New World, 1492–1640*, 115.
103. For more details on the Jewish background of Mestre João, see Valentim, "Uma Família de Cristãos-Novos do Entre Douro e Minho: Os Paz. Reprodução Familiar, Formas de Mobildade Social, Mecancia e Poder."
104. See Seed, *Ceremonies of Possession in Europe's Conquest of the New World, 1492–1640*, 125–126, and 136. Also see Albuquerque, "The Art of Astronomical Navigation."
105. From the translation of "The Letter of Master John to King Manuel, 1 May 1500," in Greenlee, *The Voyage of Pedro Álvares Cabral to Brazil and India*, 36.
106. Seed, *Ceremonies of Possession in Europe's Conquest of the New World, 1492–1640*, 104.

107. See Valentim, "Uma Família de Cristãos-Novos do Entre Douro e Minho: Os Paz. Reprodução Familiar, Formas de Mobildade Social, Mecancia e Poder."
108. Schwarcz and Starling, *Brazil*, 10.
109. See the omissions in Schwarcz and Starling, *Brazil*, 10.
110. See Falbel, *Judeus no Brasil: estudos e notas*, 67.
111. See Wiznitzer, *Jews in Colonial Brazil*, 3. Also see Lipiner, *Gaspar da Gama*, 112.
112. See Wiznitzer, *Jews in Colonial Brazil*, 5; and Valentim, "Uma Família de Cristãos-Novos do Entre Douro e Minho: Os Paz. Reprodução Familiar, Formas de Mobildade Social, Mecancia e Poder."
113. The Waldseemüller map was the first map to include the "new" continent "America" in a world map. See Waldseemüller, Martin, cartographer; Johann Schöner, and Jay I. Kislak Collection. *Manuscript copy of sheet 6 of Waldseemüller's Carta marina*. [Saint Dié, France: Johann Schöner, ?, 1516] Map. https://www.loc.gov/item/2016586443/.
114. Wiznitzer, *Jews in Colonial Brazil*, 5.
115. See Vogt, "Fernão de Loronha and the Rental of Brazil in 1502: A New Chronology," 155. Translation from Gugliemo Bercher, "Fonti italiane per la scoperta del Nuovo Mondo," Raccolta colombiana [Rome], ser.3, vol. 2, 121, 1893. Also see Wiznitzer, *Jews in Colonial Brazil*, Appendix.
116. *Ibirapitanga*, see Bueno, *Vocabulário Tupi-Guarani*, 156.
117. Dodge, "A Forgotten Century of Brazilwood: The Brazilwood Trade from the Mid-Sixteenth to Mid-Seventeenth Century," 2–3.
118. See Vasconcelos, *Selecta Brasiliense ou noticias, descobertas, observações, factos e curiosidades em relação aos homens á historia e cousas do Brasil*, 86–87.
119. See Garcia, "O 'bárbaro' que salvou São Paulo."
120. See Prado, *Primeiros Povoadores do Brasil, 1500–1530*, 99–100.
121. See Bogaciovas, *Tribulações do Povo de Israel na São Paulo Colonial*, 51. Also see Garcia, "O 'bárbaro' que salvou São Paulo."
122. See Prado, *Primeiros Povoadores do Brasil, 1500–1530*, 99.
123. Quoted in Prado, *Primeiros Povoadores do Brasil, 1500–1530*, 100–101.
124. Carvalho, *O kaf. De João Ramalho*.
125. See Aragão. "Breve Notícia sobre o Descobrimento da América. Pedro Alvares Cabral e o Brasil," 53.
126. Garcia "O 'bárbaro' que salvou São Paulo."
127. Quoted in Garcia, "O 'bárbaro' que salvou São Paulo."
128. See Garcia, "O 'bárbaro' que salvou São Paulo."
129. See Garcia, "O 'bárbaro' que salvou São Paulo."
130. See Whitehead and Harbsmeier, *Hans Staden's True History*, ix–xvi.
131. Whitehead and Harbsmeier, *Hans Staden's True History*, xxxii. See Thevet, André, *Les singvlaritez de la France antarctiqve, avtrement nommée Amerique: & de plusieurs terres & isles decouuertes de nostre temps*. A Paris: Chez les heritiers de Maurice de la Porte, 1557. pdf. https://www.loc.gov/item/07009857/.
132. *Instituto Brasileiro de Geografia e Estatística*. IBGE 2021IBGE, 2021, https://

brasil500anos.ibge.gov.br/territorio-brasileiro-e-povoamento/construcao-do-territorio/territorio-legalizado-os-tratados.html.
133. Whitehead and Harbsmeier, *Hans Staden's True History*, xxii.
134. Whitehead and Harbsmeier, *Hans Staden's True History*, 29.
135. See Sá, *The Admirable Adventures and Strange Fortunes of Master Anthony Knivet*, 29–31.
136. Sá, *The Admirable Adventures and Strange Fortunes of Master Anthony Knivet*, 33–50.
137. See Sá, *The Admirable Adventures and Strange Fortunes of Master Anthony Knivet*, 2–3.
138. See Sá, *The Admirable Adventures and Strange Fortunes of Master Anthony Knivet*, 1.
139. See Johnson, "Portuguese Settlement, 1500–1580," 27.
140. See Sá, *The Admirable Adventures and Strange Fortunes of Master Anthony Knivet*, 89.
141. Klooster, *The Dutch Moment*, 19.
142. Klooster, *The Dutch Moment*, 19.
143. Seed, *Ceremonies of Possession in Europe's Conquest of the New World, 1492–1640*, 150.
144. See Vainfas, *Jerusalém Colonial*.
145. Böhm, "The First Sephardic Synagogues in South America and in the Caribbean Area," 14.
146. Mark and Horta, *The Forgotten Diaspora*, 70.
147. Koen, "The Earliest Sources Relating to the Portuguese Jews in the Municipal Archives of Amsterdam up to 1620," 25.
148. Boxer, *The Dutch in Brazil, 1624–1654*, 101.
149. Trivellato, *The Familiarity of Strangers*, 44–45.
150. Roitman, *The Same But Different?*, 3.
151. Roitman, *The Same But Different?*, 52–54.
152. Roitman, *The Same But Different?*, 52–54.
153. Roth, *A Life of Menasseh Ben Israel*, 16–17.
154. De Portugees-Israëlietische Gemeente, https://www.esnoga.com/geschiedenis-van-de-gemeente/. See *Kol Tefilah ve-Kol Zimrah, Quartetos Na Celebração do Estreamento da Esnoga de T[almud] T[orah] na União das Quehilot*. Portuguese poetry for the Union of the three congregations in Amsterdam, 1639. This is a collection of prayers and poetry recited in the Portuguese synagogues of Amsterdam from 1597 to 1782. Collected and copied by David Franco Mendes, Amsterdam, 1792, and includes a speech of Menasseh ben Israel at the occasion of the visit of Queen Henrietta Maria of England and Prince Frederik Hendrik of Orange in the Sephardic synagogue of Amsterdam, 1642, where he refers to Parnassim and *regentes* ("regents") members of the Amsterdam KK congregation: Abraham Ferrar, Aharon A. Cohen, Moises de Mesquita, Jacob Cohen Henrinques, and Abraham Franco. The Archival Collection at Ets Haim Library in Amsterdam (Ets Haim Livraria Montezinos), http://etshaimmanuscripts.nl/items/eh-47-e-05/.
155. See Vainfas, *Jerusalém Colonial*.
156. See Vainfas, *Jerusalém Colonial*.

157. De Portugees-Israëlietische Gemeente, https://www.esnoga.com/geschiedenis-van-de-gemeente/. See *Kol Tefilah ve-Kol Zimrah, Quartetos Na Celebração do Estreamento da Esnoga de T[almud] T[orah] na União das Quehilot*. Portuguese poetry for the Union of the three congregations in Amsterdam, 1639. This is a collection of prayers and poetry recited in the Portuguese synagogues of Amsterdam from 1597 to 1782. Collected and copied by David Franco Mendes, Amsterdam, 1792, this includes a speech of Menasseh ben Israel at the occasion of the visit of Queen Henrietta Maria of England and Prince Frederik Hendrik of Orange in the Portuguese synagogue of Amsterdam, 1642, where he refers to Parnassim and regentes ("regents") members of the Amsterdam KK congregation: Abraham Ferrar, Aharon A. Cohen, Moises de Mesquita, Jacob Cohen Henrinques, and Abraham Franco. The Archival Collection at Ets Haim Library in Amsterdam (Ets Haim Livraria Montezinos), http://www.etshaimmanuscripts.nl/ajaxzoom/single.php?zoomDir=/pic/zoom/EH_47_E_05; and http://etshaimmanuscripts.nl/items/eh-47-e-05/.
158. The Archival Collection at The Ets Haim Library in Amsterdam (Ets Haim Livraria Montezinos), http://etshaimmanuscripts.nl/items/eh-48-a-26/.
159. Silva, *A Primeira comunidade Judaica do Novo Mundo*, 29. Also see Silva, *Primeira Visitação do Santo Ofício às partes do Brasil*.
160. Silva, *A Primeira comunidade Judaica do Novo Mundo*, 29. Also see Silva, *Primeira Visitação do Santo Ofício às partes do Brasil*.
161. See "Reglementen. Dutch translation of the regulations (haskamot) of the Dotar society." Originally written in Portuguese between 1756 and 1825, reference to many of the well-known Jewish-Portuguese names in the history of Amsterdam (Sarfaty, Da Costa, Spinoza, Senior Coronel) can be found here. The Archival Collection at the Ets Haim Library in Amsterdam (Ets Haim Livraria Montezinos), http://etshaimmanuscripts.nl/items/eh-48-a-25/.
162. See Archive of Amsterdam (Archief Amsterdam), the Portuguese-Hebrew Register of Regulations and Decisions (5409–5414), 1648–1654 (Recife, Pernambuco), Inventaris van het Archief van de Portugees-Israëlietische Gemeente, https://archief.amsterdam/inventarissen/scans/334/7.2.1.1/start/0/limit/10/highlight/8.
163. De Portugees-Israëlietische Gemeente, https://www.esnoga.com/traditie/.
164. Archief Amsterdam, https://archief.amsterdam/inventarissen/scans/334/1.1/start/0/limit/10/highlight/2.
165. Archief Amsterdam, "Livro de Bet Haim do Kahal Kados de Bet Yahacob," https://archief.amsterdam/inventarissen/scans/334/1.1/start/0/limit/10/highlight/3.
166. For further details, see Israel, "Sephardic Immigration into the Dutch Republic, 1595–1672," 45.
167. Roth, *A Life of Menasseh Ben Israel*, 140.
168. See Kaplan, "The Portuguese Jews in Amsterdam. From Forced Conversion to a Return to Judaism." Also see Fisher, *Amsterdam's People of the Book*.
169. Israel, "Sephardic Immigration into the Dutch Republic, 1595–1672," 53.
170. For further details, see Klooster, "Communities of Port Jews and Their Contacts

in the Dutch Atlantic World," 133. Also see Klooster, "Networks of Colonial Entrepreneurs: The Founders of the Jewish Settlements in Dutch America, 1650s and 1660s."

171. Fisher, *Amsterdam's People of the Book*, 4. Also see a discussion of Abraham Pereyra in Kaplan, "The Portuguese Jews in Amsterdam. From Forced Conversion to a Return to Judaism," 40.

172. Studnicki-Gizbert, "*La Nación* among the Nations: Portuguese and Other Maritime Trading Diasporas in the Atlantic, Sixteenth to Eighteenth Centuries," 75. Also see Studnicki-Gizbert, *A Nation Upon the Sea*.

173. Aaslestad, *Places and Politics*, 50–51; Israel, *Diasporas within a Diaspora*, 236; Martins, "Women and Communal Discipline in the Portuguese Nation of Hamburg during the Seventeenth Century"; and Martins, *Os judeus portugueses de Hamburgo*.

174. See Leite, *Unorthodox Kin*, 50.

175. See Kaplan, "The Portuguese Jews in Amsterdam. From Forced Conversion to a Return to Judaism," 27.

176. Bachmann, "Judeus e Globalizacão," 581–582 [also see the list of names he provides of Portuguese Jews in Europe].

177. For more details, see Bachmann, "Judeus e Globalizacão," 581–582 [also see the list of names he provides of Portuguese Jews in Europe].

178. See Hyman, *The Jews of Ireland: From Earliest Times to the Year 1910*; and Shillman and Wolf, "The Jewish Cemetery at Ballybough in Dublin."

179. Shillman and Wolf, "The Jewish Cemetery at Ballybough in Dublin"; Wolf, "Note on the Early History of the Dublin Hebrew Congregation"; Dawson, "Crane Lane to Ballybough"; and Hiney, "5618 and All That: The Jewish Cemetery Fairview Strand." Also see Bernard Shillman. *The Jewish Gazette*, "The Jewish Cemetery at Ballybough," 18:1933. We also find other evidence of Crypto-Jews in Ireland, as Cecil Roth informs us, "Thomas Fernandes, of Viana [Portugal], who was arrested in the Low Countries in 1540 as a Judaiser, informed the authorities there that he was the son of the late Master Fernandes, a physician, born in Ireland." Roth, "The Middle Period of Anglo-Jewish History (1290–1655) Reconsidered," 3.

180. Shillman and Wolf, "The Jewish Cemetery at Ballybough in Dublin"; Wolf, "Note on the Early History of the Dublin Hebrew Congregation"; Dawson, "Crane Lane to Ballybough"; and Hiney, "5618 and All That: The Jewish Cemetery Fairview Strand." Also see Bernard Shillman, *The Jewish Gazette*, "The Jewish Cemetery at Ballybough," 18:1933; and Roth, "The Middle Period of Anglo-Jewish History (1290–1655) Reconsidered," 3.

181. Wolf, "Note on the Early History of the Dublin Hebrew Congregation"; also see *Reposta do Dr. Sequeira Vezinho de Londres, ao Libro Ititulado (sic!) dialogos Theologicos, que compós hum autor anonimo, cristão para reduzir aos Judeos, ao Cristianismo*, The Archival Collection Ets Haim Library Amsterdam (Ets Haim Bibliotheek Livraria Montezinos), http://etshaimmanuscripts.nl/items/eh-49-b-16/.

182. For example, see Leite, *Unorthodox Kin*, 50. Also, for evidence that Portuguese Jews were the first Jews in England, see Zeman, "The Amazing Career of Doctor

Rodrigo Lopez (?–1594)"; Wolf, "Crypto-Jews Under the Commonwealth"; Wolf, "The First English Jew"; and Samuel, "Jews in Jacobean London."
183. Roth, *A Life of Menasseh Ben Israel*, xi. Also see Wolf, "Jews in Elizabethan England"; Wolf, "Crypto-Jews Under the Commonwealth"; and Samuel, "Jews in Jacobean London."
184. Roth, "The Middle Period of Anglo-Jewish History (1290–1655) Reconsidered," 3. Also see Wolf, "Crypto-Jews Under the Commonwealth"; Wolf, "The First English Jew"; and Samuel, "Jews in Jacobean London."
185. Trivellato, *The Familiarity of Strangers*, 57.
186. Martins, "Women and Communal Discipline in the Portuguese Nation of Hamburg during the Seventeenth Century," 23–25. For more details on Portuguese Jews and New Christians in Hamburg, see Poettering. *Migrating Merchants*.
187. Israel, "Duarte Nunes da Costa (Jacob Curiel), of Hamburg, Sephardi Nobleman and Communal Leader (1585–1664)," 14.
188. Poettering. *Migrating Merchants*, 2.
189. Trivellato. *The Familiarity of Strangers*, 47.
190. Quoted in Trivellato, *The Familiarity of Strangers*, 57.
191. See Ben-Ur, "A Matriarchal Matter: Slavery, Conversion, and Upward Mobility in Suriname's Jewish Community," 152 and 168. For more details on Portuguese in Suriname, see Israel, "Jews in Dutch America"; and Frankel, "Antecedents and Remnants of Jodensavanne: The Synagogues and Cemeteries of the First Permanent Plantation Settlement of the New World Jews."
192. See Vink, *Creole Jews*, 116 (footnote 12). Also, for details about Portuguese Jews in Suriname, see Ben-Ur, "A Matriarchal Matter: Slavery, Conversion, and Upward Mobility in Suriname's Jewish Community," 152–168; Israel, "Jews in Dutch America"; and Frankel, "Antecedents and Remnants of Jodensavanne: The Synagogues and Cemeteries of the First Permanent Plantation Settlement of the New World Jews."
193. See Oppenheim, "The First Settlement of the Jews in Newport: Some New Matter on the Subject," 3.
194. Oppenheim, "The Early History of the Jews in New York, 1654–1664. Some New Matter on the Subject," 17. See Gelfand, "A Caribbean Wind: An Overview of the Jewish Dispersal from Dutch Brazil."
195. For example, evidence shows the extent of widespread early migrations of Portuguese Jews to the New World to Curaçao, for example, see Kaplan, "The Curaçao and Amsterdam Jewish Communities in the 17th and 18th Centuries"; to Tobago, see Arbell, "The Failure of the Jewish Settlement in the Island of Tobago"; to Suriname, see Roitman, "Portuguese Jews, Amerindians, and the Frontiers of Encounter in Colonial Suriname"; and to Peru, see Liebman, "The Great Conspiracy in Peru." To the Caribbean in general, see Merrill, "The Role of Sephardic Jews in the British Caribbean Area during the Seventeenth Century"; and more broadly within Latin America, see Elkin, *The Jews of Latin America*. The scholarship extends to other regions as well; for example in the Dutch domains, see Fisher, *Amsterdam's*

People of the Book; Israel, "Sephardic Immigration into the Dutch Republic, 1595–1672"; Kaplan, "The Portuguese Jews in Amsterdam. From Forced Conversion to a Return to Judaism"; and Yerushalmi, "Between Amsterdam and New Amsterdam: The Place of Curaçao and the Caribbean in Early Modern Jewish History"; and in England, see Hyamson, *The Sephardim of England*; and Ireland, Shillman, *A Short History of the Jews in Ireland*; and in Portuguese India, see Faria, "Todos desterrados, & espalhados pelo mundo: A perseguição inquisitorial de judeus e de cristãos-novos na India Portuguesa (séculos XVI e XVII)"; and Fischel, "Leading Jews in the Service of Portuguese India."

196. Oppenheim, "List of Wills of Jews in the British West Indies Prior to 1800."
197. See Feitler, "Jews and New Christians in Dutch Brazil, 1630–1654," 123, and Oppenheim, "An Early Jewish Colony Western Guiana, 1658–1666: And Its Relation to the Jews in Surinam, Cayenne and Tobago."
198. See Studnicki-Gizbert. *A Nation Upon the Sea*, and Studnicki-Gizbert, "*La Nación* among the Nations: Portuguese and Other Maritime Trading Diasporas in the Atlantic, Sixteenth to Eighteenth Centuries," 88. For details on Portuguese New Christians in Lima, Peru, see Green, "Pluralism, Violence and Empire: The Portuguese New Christians in the Atlantic World."
199. Studemund-Halévy, "Sea is History, Sea is Witness: The Creation of a Prosopographical Database for the Sephardic Atlantic," 488–490. Also see Studnicki-Gizbert, *A Nation Upon the Sea*, and Poettering, *Migrating Merchants*.
200. See Poettering, *Migrating Merchants*, 103.
201. Ebert, *Between Empires*, 7.
202. Ebert, *Between Empires*, 7.
203. See Blackbourn, "Germans Abroad and 'Auslandsdeutsche': Places, Networks and Experiences from the Sixteenth to the Twentieth Century," 329–330. Also see Häberlein, *The Fuggers of Augsburg*.
204. Smith, "Old Christian Merchants and the Foundation of the Brazil Company, 1649," 232.
205. Smith, "Old Christian Merchants and the Foundation of the Brazil Company, 1649," 259.
206. For a detailed discussion of the trading networks between Portuguese Jews and non-Jews and strangers, see Trivellato. *The Familiarity of Strangers*.
207. See, Jarnagin. *Research work in progress/preparation 2021*.
208. Kagan and Morgan, "Preface," viii.
209. Studnicki-Gizbert, "*La Nación* among the Nations: Portuguese and Other Maritime Trading Diasporas in the Atlantic, Sixteenth to Eighteenth Centuries," 98.
210. Quoted in Pijning, "New Christians as Sugar Cultivators and Traders in the Portuguese Atlantic, 1450–1800," 488.
211. See Chacón-Duque et al., "Latin Americans show wide-spread Converso ancestry and imprint of local Native ancestry on physical appearance."
212. See Alencastro, *Trade in the Living*, xviii.

Chapter Four

1. See Mordoch, "Um cristão-novo nos trópicos: expansão imperial e identidade religiosa nos Diálogos das grandezas do Brasil de Ambrósio Fernandes Brandão," 202.
2. Schwartz, *Early Brazil*, 18; an English translation of José Antônio Gonsalves de Mello and Xavier de Albuquerque, *Cartas de Duarte Coelho a el Rei*, 85–91.
3. "Charter of donation of the Captaincy of Pernambuco to Duarte Coelho, March 10, 1534." Quoted in Guedes, "Portugal-Brazil: The Encounter between Two Worlds," 173, and Mello, *A Ferida de Narciso*, 10.
4. For the Tupi translation of "Pernambuco," see Bueno, *Vocabulário Tupi-Guarani*, 269. For a discussion on the etymological disputes of the word "Pernambuco," see Mello, *A Ferida de Narciso*, 10.
5. Andrade, *The Land and People of Northeast Brazil*, 42–43.
6. Schwartz, *Early Brazil*, 32, an English translation of José Antônio Gonsalves de Mello and Xavier de Albuquerque, *Cartas de Duarte Coelho a el Rei*, 85–91.
7. Andrade, *The Land and People of Northeast Brazil*, 47.
8. Andrade, *The Land and People of Northeast Brazil*, 48.
9. Andrade, *The Land and People of Northeast Brazil*, 42–43.
10. See Schwartz, "A Commonwealth in Itself. The Early Brazilian Sugar Industry, 1550–1670," 160.
11. See Leite, *História da Companhia de Jesus no Brasil*.
12. Quoted in Schwartz, "A Commonwealth in Itself. The Early Brazilian Sugar Industry, 1550–1670," 161.
13. See Bethencourt, *Racisms*, 189.
14. See Johnson, "Portuguese Settlement, 1500–1580," 15.
15. For an in-depth discussion, see Boxer, *The Golden Age of Brazil, 1695–1750*, 227–228; and Bethel, *Brazil: Empire and Republic, 1822–1930*, 9–10. However, the system of *capitanias* left a long-lasting legacy in Brazil, and it is worth speculating that this legacy continues to this day in Brazil, such as in the Brazilian tradition of clientelism, unproductive *latifúndios*, and absentee land ownership of large lands.
16. Quoted in Coates, *Convicts and Orphans*, 5–9.
17. For details, see Schwartz, "A Commonwealth in Itself. The Early Brazilian Sugar Industry, 1550–1670," 188; and Hemming, *Red Gold*, 156.
18. See, for example, Alencastro, *O trato dos viventes*; Bethell, *Colonial Brazil*; and Marcus, *Confederate Exodus*.
19. Schwartz, *Slaves, Peasants and Rebels*, 111. Also see Mauro, "Political and economic structures of empire."
20. See Andrade, *The Land and People of Northeast Brazil*, 46.
21. For details, see Schwartz, "Introduction," in *Tropical Babylons*, 12.
22. See Wiznitzer, "The Jews in the Sugar Industry of Colonial Brazil," 189.
23. See Vieira, "Sugar Islands. The Sugar Economy of Madeira and the Canaries, 1450–1650," 42. For more details on the sugarcane industry in the Americas, see Schwartz, *Tropical Babylons*.

24. Arquivo Nacional, Torre do Tombo, "Descobrimento das Ilhas de Madeira e Porto Santo," http://antt.dglab.gov.pt/exposicoes-virtuais-2/descobrimento-das-ilhas-da-madeira-e-porto-santo/.
25. See Coates, *Convicts and Orphans*, 60 and 77.
26. The name of Noronha (instead of Loronha) was perhaps given to him when he was baptized as a Christian; he became a *cavaleiro* of the court of Dom Manuel and was granted a coat of arms—unusual for converted Jews. Greenlee, "The Captaincy of the Second Portuguese Voyage to Brazil, 1501–1502," footnote 8.
27. Gastaldi produced maps and illustrations for parts of Delle Navigationi et Viaggi (Travels and voyages), a compilation of travel writings by the Venetian diplomat and geographer Giovanni Battista Ramusio (1485–1557). Ramusio's work contained more than fifty memoirs, including the writings of Marco Polo. Gastaldi, Giacomo, 1500?–1565? Cartographer, and Giovanni Battista Ramusio. *Brazil*. [Venice, Italy: publisher not identified, 1565] Map. https://www.loc.gov/item/2021668321/.
28. Curiously, it is well known that the first name given for the shoals between Mozambique and Madagascar, "Baixo da Judia" ("Jewess Shoals"), was given due to Fernão de Noronha's Jewish ancestry, after Portuguese ships ran into them in 1506.
29. See Greenlee, *The Voyage of Pedro Álvares Cabral to Brazil and India: From Contemporary Documents and Narratives*, 11.
30. See Vogt, "Fernão de Loronha and the Rental of Brazil in 1502: A New Chronology," 156.
31. See Vogt, "Fernão de Loronha and the Rental of Brazil in 1502: A New Chronology," 153, and Guedes, "Portugal-Brazil: The Encounter between Two Worlds," 164. *Padrões* or *Marcos* (stone markers) still exist in Cabo Sao Roque, Sao Vicente, and Cananéia. See Greenlee, "The Captaincy of the Second Portuguese Voyage to Brazil, 1501–1502," (footnote) 6.
32. Reclus, *The Earth and Its Inhabitants*, 226.
33. See Greenlee, "The Captaincy of the Second Portuguese Voyage to Brazil, 1501–1502," 10.
34. Vogt, "Fernão de Loronha and the Rental of Brazil in 1502: A New Chronology," 154.
35. Quoted in Vogt, "Fernão de Loronha and the Rental of Brazil in 1502: A New Chronology," 155. Translation from Gugliemo Bercher, "Fonti italiane per la scoperta del Nuovo Mondo," Raccolta colombiana [Rome], ser. 3, vol. 2, 121, 1893.
36. Vogt, "Fernão de Loronha and the Rental of Brazil in 1502: A New Chronology," 156.
37. See Wiznitzer, "The Jews in the Sugar Industry of Colonial Brazil," 191.
38. Quoted in Ebert, *Between Empires*, 3.
39. Blackbourn, "Germans Abroad and 'Auslandsdeutsche': Places, Networks and Experiences from the Sixteenth to the Twentieth Century," 329–330.
40. Blackbourn, "Germans Abroad and 'Auslandsdeutsche': Places, Networks and Experiences from the Sixteenth to the Twentieth Century," 330.
41. See Wadsworth, *Agents of Orthodoxy*, 46.

42. See Russell-Wood, *The Portuguese Empire, 1415–1808*, 106.
43. See Simms, "Being Crypto-Jewish in Colonial Brazil (1500–1822): Brushing History Against the Grain," 424.
44. Simms, "Being Crypto-Jewish in Colonial Brazil (1500–1822): Brushing History Against the Grain," 424.
45. Guedes, "Portugal-Brazil: The Encounter between Two Worlds," 171.
46. Coates, *Convicts and Orphans*, 28.
47. For details, see *Brasil Arqueológico: Site da Equipe do Laboratório de Arqueologia da Universidade Federal de Pernambuco UFPE*, "Arqueologia de Magazão Velho: Sonho Luso-Marroquino," February 12, 2022, https://www.brasilarqueologico.com.br/arqueologia-mazagao-velho.php.
48. Quoted in Pieroni, "Outcasts from the Kingdom: The Inquisition and the Banishment of New Christians to Brazil," 246.
49. See Coates, *Convicts and Orphans*, 78–85.
50. See Coates, *Convicts and Orphans*, 78–85.
51. See Andrade, *The Land and People of Northeast Brazil*, 7.
52. See Lipiner, *Judaizantes nas Capitanias de Cima*.
53. See Vainfas, "Santo Oficio em terra Fluminense—Cristão-novos e Inquisição no Rio de Janeiro colonial," 12.
54. See Blake, *The Vigorous Core of Our Nationality*, 6.
55. See Andrade, *The Land and People of Northeast Brazil*, 9.
56. See Webb, *The Changing Face of Northeast Brazil*, 11–12.
57. See Andrade, *The Land and People of Northeast Brazil*, 9–13. Also see Webb, *The Changing Face of Northeast Brazil*.
58. See Webb, *The Changing Face of Northeast Brazil*.
59. The largest quilombo named "Palmares" (1605–1694), where 20,000 people resided in the modern state of Alagoas, just south of Pernambuco. *Quilombo* is an Mbundu word for "war camp," and *mocambo* means "Hideout." The word *kilombo* refers to a male-initiation society circumcision camp in West-Central Africa, where young men prepared to become warriors. For more details, see Schwartz, *Slaves, Peasants and Rebels*, 49 and 111–126.
60. Schwartz, "Plantations and peripheries, c.1580–c.1750," 69.
61. Schwartz, "A Commonwealth in Itself. The Early Brazilian Sugar Industry, 1550–1670," 159.
62. Webb, *The Changing Face of Northeast Brazil*, 63.
63. Webb, *The Changing Face of Northeast Brazil*, 80.
64. For more details, see Schwartz, *Tropical Babylons*, and Schwartz, "A Commonwealth in Itself. The Early Brazilian Sugar Industry, 1550–1670,"
65. See Schwartz, "A Commonwealth in Itself. The Early Brazilian Sugar Industry, 1550–1670," 159.
66. See Schwartz, "A Commonwealth in Itself. The Early Brazilian Sugar Industry, 1550–1670," 159.
67. See Andrade, *The Land and People of Northeast Brazil*, 43.

68. See Ebert, *Between Empires*, 3.
69. Boxer, *The Dutch in Brazil, 1624–1654*, 143.
70. In the late sixteenth century, Brazil's northeast was known as the "North" ("captaincies of the North"), which included Bahia, Pernambuco, Itamaracá, Paraíba, and Rio Grande. See Vainfas, "Santo Ofício em terra Fluminense—Cristão-novos e Inquisição no Rio de Janeiro colonial," 12.
71. Assis, "Inquisição, religiosidade e transformações culturais: a sinagoga das mulheres e a sobrevivência do judaísmo feminino no Brasil colonial—Nordeste, séculos XVI–XVII," 49.
72. See Assis, "Inquisição, religiosidade e transformações culturais: a sinagoga das mulheres e a sobrevivência do judaísmo feminino no Brasil colonial—Nordeste, séculos XVI–XVII," 49.
73. Quoted in Novinsky, *Cristãos-novos na Bahia*, 61–62.
74. Quoted in Böhm, "The First Sephardic Synagogues in South America and in the Caribbean Area," 1. For an excellent discussion of Ana Rodrigues and Heitor Antunes, her husband, see Vainfas and Assis, "A esnoga da Bahia: cristãos-novos e criptojudaísmo no Brasil quinhentista." Also see Assis, "Um Israel possível na Bahia colonial: sobre mulheres e resistência judaica em tempos de perseguição."
75. See Vainfas and Assis, "A esnoga da Bahia: cristãos-novos e criptojudaísmo no Brasil quinhentista," 59–61.
76. See Assis, "A Inquisição portuguesa e o processo contra Heitor Antunes, cavaleiro d'el Rey e Macabeu do Recôncavo: um (cripto) rabino na Bahia quinhentista," 356; and Abreu, *Um visitador do Santo Ofício*, 21.
77. Quoted in Assis, "A Inquisição portuguesa e o processo contra Heitor Antunes, cavaleiro d'el Rey e Macabeu do Recôncavo: um (cripto) rabino na Bahia quinhentista," 358.
78. See Assis, "A Inquisição portuguesa e o processo contra Heitor Antunes, cavaleiro d'el Rey e Macabeu do Recôncavo: um (cripto) rabino na Bahia quinhentista," 358.
79. Abreu, *Um visitador do Santo Ofício*, 39.
80. Quoted in Abreu, *Um visitador do Santo Ofício*, 40.
81. Assis, "A Inquisição portuguesa e o processo contra Heitor Antunes, cavaleiro d'el Rey e Macabeu do Recôncavo: um (cripto) rabino na Bahia quinhentista," 358.
82. Vainfas and Assis, "A esnoga da Bahia: cristãos-novos e criptojudaísmo no Brasil quinhentista," 59–61.
83. Vainfas and Assis, "A esnoga da Bahia: cristãos-novos e criptojudaísmo no Brasil quinhentista," 59–61.
84. Vainfas and Assis, "A esnoga da Bahia: cristãos-novos e criptojudaísmo no Brasil quinhentista," 59–61.
85. Vainfas and Assis, "A esnoga da Bahia: cristãos-novos e criptojudaísmo no Brasil quinhentista," 59–61. Notably, as Stuart Schwartz points out, some of the wealthiest slave owners in the Recôncavo Baiano (particularly in the region of Santo Amaro and São Francisco do Conde) during the late eighteenth and early nineteenth centuries were women. Schwartz, *Segredos internos: engenhos e escravos na sociedade*

colonial, 1550–1835, 242–243. Also see Schetini Júnior, "Cristãs-novas e criptojudaísmo na Bahia setecentista," and Assis, "Um Israel possível na Bahia colonial: sobre mulheres e resistência judaica em tempos de perseguição."
86. Quoted in Marcus, *Confederate Exodus*, 116.
87. See Vainfas and Assis, "A esnoga da Bahia: cristãos-novos e criptojudaísmo no Brasil quinhentista," 59–61.
88. See Vainfas and Assis, "A esnoga da Bahia: cristãos-novos e criptojudaísmo no Brasil quinhentista," 61.
89. Assis, "A Inquisição portuguesa e o processo contra Heitor Antunes, cavaleiro d'el Rey e Macabeu do Recôncavo: um (cripto) rabino na Bahia quinhentista," 357.
90. IPHAN, Instituto do Patrimônio Histórico e Artístico Nacional, May 8, 2022, http://portal.iphan.gov.br/galeria/detalhes/457.
91. See Novinsky et al., *Os Judeus Que Construíram o Brasil*, 87–88. Also see Braga, Mirella de Almeida, *Da Arte de se Tornar Judeu*.
92. See Assis, "Inquisição, religiosidade e transformações culturais: a sinagoga das mulheres e a sobrevivência do judaísmo feminino no Brasil colonial—Nordeste, séculos XVI–XVII," 56–57.
93. See Falbel, *Judeus no Brasil: estudos e notas*, 98.
94. See Falbel, *Judeus no Brasil: estudos e notas*, 98.
95. For more details on Branca Dias and Crypto-Jews, see Braga, Mirella de Almeida, *Da Arte de se Tornar Judeu*.
96. The location of the Palace of the Inquisition in Lisbon, Estaus, was at the Largo do Rossio (today by the Praça D. Pedro IV, D. João da Câmara, Rua 1 de Dezembro—in front of the Teatro Maria I.). Silva, *A Primeira comunidade Judaica do Novo Mundo*, 34
97. See Silva, *A Primeira comunidade Judaica do Novo Mundo*, 32–34. Also see Mello, *Gente da Nação*, 552; and Silva, *Primeira Visitação do Santo Ofício às partes do Brasil*.
98. Silva, *A Primeira comunidade Judaica do Novo Mundo*, 32–34. Also see Mello, *Gente da Nação*, 552; and Silva, ed. *Primeira Visitação do Santo Ofício às partes do Brasil*.
99. Another successful senhor de engenho in Pernambuco, and an associate of Diogo Fernandes, was Diogo Nunes, who had also been arrested as a Judaizer. Wiznitzer, "The Jews in the Sugar Industry of Colonial Brazil," 192.
100. The full sentence in Portuguese: "*auto-da-fé de 03/08/1603. Ir ao auto-da-fé com vela acesa na mão, abjuração de veemente, cárcere a arbítrio dos inquisidores, instrução na fé católica, penitências espirituais, pagamento de custas.*"
101. See Assis, "Inquisição, religiosidade e transformações culturais: a sinagoga das mulheres e a sobrevivência do judaísmo feminino no Brasil colonial—Nordeste, séculos XVI–XVII," 56–57.
102. For more information on New Christians arrested in Rio, see Vainfas, "Santo Ofício em terra Fluminense—Cristão-novos e Inquisição no Rio de Janeiro colonial."
103. Novinsky et al., *Os Judeus Que Construíram o Brasil*, 87–88. Also see Braga, Mirella de Almeida, *Da Arte de se Tornar Judeu*.
104. See Schwartz, "A Commonwealth in Itself. The Early Brazilian Sugar Industry, 1550–1670," 183 and 192.

105. Schwartz, "A Commonwealth in Itself. The Early Brazilian Sugar Industry, 1550–1670," 174.
106. See Feitler, "Jews and New Christians in Dutch Brazil, 1630–1654."
107. Feitler, *Cristãos-Novos na Paraíba*, 147.
108. See Cabral de Mello, *O Nome e o Sangue*.
109. See Kaplan, "The Curaçao and Amsterdam Jewish Communities in the 17th and 18th Centuries"; and Yerushalmi, "Between Amsterdam and New Amsterdam: The Place of Curaçao and the Caribbean in Early Modern Jewish History"; in Tobago, see Arbell, "The Failure of the Jewish Settlement in the Island of Tobago"; in Suriname, see Roitman, "Portuguese Jews, Amerindians, and the Frontiers of Encounter in Colonial Suriname"; and in the Caribbean in general, see Merrill, "The Role of Sephardic Jews in the British Caribbean Area during the Seventeenth Century."
110. Quoted in Johnson, "Portuguese Settlement, 1500–1580," 31. Also see Orfali, "The Dutch Occupation and Defense of Brazil: The Question of the Support of Jews and Conversos," 132.
111. Quoted in Johnson, "Portuguese Settlement, 1500–1580," 31. Also see Orfali, "The Dutch Occupation and Defense of Brazil: The Question of the Support of Jews and Conversos," 132.
112. Skidmore, *Brazil*, 19.
113. Flory and Smith, "Bahian Merchants and Planters in the Seventeenth and Early Eighteenth Centuries," 585.
114. Flory and Smith, "Bahian Merchants and Planters in the Seventeenth and Early Eighteenth Centuries," 585.
115. Russell-Wood, *The Portuguese Empire, 1415–1808*, 61.
116. Quoted in Bethencourt, *Racisms*, 189.
117. Quoted in Schwartz, "Plantations and peripheries, c.1580–c.1750," 139.
118. See Schwartz, "Plantations and peripheries, c.1580–c.1750," 139.
119. See Schwartz, "Plantations and peripheries, c.1580–c.1750," 128 and 139.
120. Fernandes, *A Inquisição em Minas Gerais no século XVIII*, 108.
121. Resende and Sousa, "Por temer o Santo Oficio" As denúncias de Minas Gerais no Tribunal da Inquisição (século XVIII)," 212.
122. See Russell-Wood, *The Portuguese Empire, 1415–1808*, 61.
123. *Instituto Brasileiro de Geografia e Estatística*. IBGE 2021, https://brasil500anos.ibge.gov.br/estatisticas-do-povoamento/evolucao-da-populacao-brasileira.html.
124. Schwartz, "Plantations and peripheries, c.1580–c.1750," 100–102.
125. Schwartz, "Plantations and peripheries, c.1580–c.1750," 100–102.
126. Schwartz, "Introduction," 3.
127. Johnson, "Portuguese Settlement, 1500–1580," 30. Also, for more details on the sugarcane industry in Latin America, see Schwartz, *Tropical Babylons*.
128. See Schwartz, "Plantations and peripheries, c.1580–c.1750," 76–81.
129. Schwartz, "Plantations and peripheries, c.1580–c.1750," 77.
130. For more details, see Schwartz, "A Commonwealth in Itself. The Early Brazilian Sugar Industry, 1550–1670," 177.

131. Schwartz, "A Commonwealth in Itself. The Early Brazilian Sugar Industry, 1550–1670," 197.
132. Andrade, *The Land and People of Northeast Brazil*, 55.
133. Cabral de Mello, *A Ferida de Narciso*, 16–17.
134. See Schorsch. *Swimming the Christian Atlantic*.
135. Schorsch, "Cristâos-novos, Judaísmo, Negros e Cristianismo nos Primórdios do Mundo Atlântico Moderno," 158. For more details on slaves, holidays, and Judaizers in colonial Brazil, see Wolff, "Judeus, Judaizantes e seus escravos."
136. See Schorsch. "Cristâos-novos, Judaísmo, Negros e Cristianismo nos Primórdios do Mundo Atlântico Moderno," 171; and for more detailed perspectives on New Christians, Afroiberians, and Amerindians, see Schorsch, *Swimming the Christian Atlantic*. For details about Jewish "Eurafricans" in Suriname and Senegal, see Mark and Horta, *The Forgotten Diaspora*, 64.
137. Schwartz, *Slaves, Peasants and Rebels*, 17 and 44. Also see Wolff, "Judeus, Judaizantes e seus escravos."
138. Wolff, "Judeus, Judaizantes e seus escravos," 119.
139. Mark and Horta, *The Forgotten Diaspora*, 71.
140. Mark and Horta, *The Forgotten Diaspora*, 75.
141. Mark and Horta, *The Forgotten Diaspora*, 72.
142. Quoted in Andrade, *The Land and People of Northeast Brazil*, 47.
143. Also, a vast collection of studies and maps are available in an expertly set up website: https://www.slavevoyages.org/.
144. Alencastro, *Trade in the Living*, x
145. Alencastro, *O trato dos viventes*, 28–37.
146. Eltis and Richardson, *Atlas of the Transatlantic Slave Trade*, 2–5.
147. Eltis and Richardson, *Atlas of the Transatlantic Slave Trade*, 46.
148. Eltis and Richardson, *Atlas of the Transatlantic Slave Trade*, 66–69.
149. Eltis and Richardson, *Atlas of the Transatlantic Slave Trade*, 143–158.
150. Eltis and Richardson, *Atlas of the Transatlantic Slave Trade*, 13–17.
151. Eltis and Richardson, *Atlas of the Transatlantic Slave Trade*, 23–26.
152. Eltis and Richardson, *Atlas of the Transatlantic Slave Trade*, 23–26.
153. Eltis and Richardson, *Atlas of the Transatlantic Slave Trade*, 259–261. Frédéric Mauro explains that African slaves were brought to Brazil from two major regions in Africa. The first wave was from West Africans known inappropriately as "Sudanese." The term, "Sudanese" was not a reference to slaves from Sudan proper; rather it was an "umbrella term" used to describe slaves from West Africa, mostly Wolof, Mandingo, Songhai, Mossi, Hausa, and Peul, and included many Muslims and herdsmen,. The other major region was central and Equatorial Africa, which included men from Bantu-speaking tribes, who were mostly animists. Mauro, "Political and economic structures of empire," 53.
154. Andrade, *The Land and People of Northeast Brazil*, 69.
155. Alencastro, *Trade in the Living*, x.
156. Tannenbaum, *Slave and Citizen*, 5. Notably, even some slaves were literate. For

instance, Hausa and Yoruba slaves in Brazil who were Muslim and were sufficiently literate in Arabic to read religious scripture, were involved in the Muslim *Malê* uprising—the first and only Muslim revolt in the New World in Salvador, Bahia in 1835—a decade and a half after Brazil's independence. See Kent, "Revolt in Bahia: 24–25, January 1835," 341.

157. See Salvador, *Os cristãos-Novos em Minas Gerais durante o Ciclo do Ouro*, and Novinsky, "Ser marrano em Minas Colonial."

158. See Novinsky, "Ser marrano em Minas Colonial."

159. Novinsky, "Prisioneiros no Brasil," 18.

160. Boyajian, "New Christians and Jews in the Sugar Trade, 1550–1750: Two Centuries of Development of the Atlantic Economy," 476–477.

161. See Studnicki-Gizbert, *A Nation Upon the Ocean Sea: Portugal's Atlantic Diaspora and the Crisis of the Spanish Empire, 1492–1640*, 35–37.

162. Schetini Júnior, "Cristãs-novas e criptojudaismo na Bahia setecentista," 80–81. Also see Souza, "'Perseguidores da espécie humana': capitães negreiros da Cidade da Bahia na primeira metade do século XVIII."

163. Mark and Horta, *The Forgotten Diaspora*, 11.

164. See Bogaciovas, *Tribulações do Povo de Israel na São Paulo Colonial*, 41

165. See Novinsky, "The Myth of the Marrano Names," 2.

166. Novinsky, "The Myth of the Marrano Names," 2.

167. Boxer, *The Golden Age of Brazil*, 107.

168. Maia, *À sombra do medo*, 111–114.

169. Assis, "Inquisição, religiosidade e transformações culturais: a sinagoga das mulheres e a sobrevivência do judaísmo feminino no Brasil colonial—Nordeste, séculos XVI–XVII," 49.

170. See Novinsky, "The Myth of the Marrano Names," 3.

171. Quoted in Novinsky, "The Myth of the Marrano Names," 10.

172. Mauro, "Political and economic structures of empire," 55–56.

173. Quoted in Schwartz, "A Commonwealth in Itself. The Early Brazilian Sugar Industry, 1550–1670," 166.

174. Schwartz, "A Commonwealth in Itself. The Early Brazilian Sugar Industry, 1550–1670," 166.

175. Schwartz, *Early Brazil*, 244, English translation of José Antônio Gonsalves de Mello, *Fontes para a história do Brasil holandês*, 96–129.

176. Schwartz, *Early Brazil*, 245, English translation of José Antônio Gonsalves de Mello, *Fontes para a história do Brasil holandês*, 96–129.

177. Schwartz, *Early Brazil*, 245, English translation of José Antônio Gonsalves de Mello, *Fontes para a história do Brasil holandês*, 96–129.

178. See Orfali, "The Dutch Occupation and Defense of Brazil: The Question of the Support of Jews and Conversos," 129.

179. See Klooster, *The Dutch Moment*, 8.

180. Boxer, *The Dutch in Brazil, 1624–1654*, 138.

181. See Vink, *Creole Jews*, 24.

Chapter Five

1. As seen in a map, "Depiction of the conquest of the city of Olinda. Capture of the Portuguese city of Olinda (16 February), the capital of the captaincy of Pernambuco (East Brazil), by forces of the Dutch West India Company under the command of Hendrik Corneliszoon Lonck, and the subsequent surrender of the forts of Recife on 3 March 1630." Hauslab, Franz, Dlc, Collector. *Entwerffung von Eroberung der Stadt Olinda so in der Hauptmansschaft Pharnambuco gelegen, vnd durch den Edlen Gestrengen vnd Manhafften Herrn Heinrich Cornelius Lonck, Generaln zu Wasser vnd Herrn Colonell Wartenburg zu Land eingenommen, Welche Eygentlich abgebildet vnd mit dem Jagd Schiff, der Braeck genannt überschicket worden*. Brazil Pernambuco Olinda, 1630. [Germany: Publisher not identified, ?] Photograph. https://www.loc.gov/item/02030037/. Also see Bloom, "A Study of Brazilian Jewish History 1623–1624, Based Chiefly Upon the Findings of the Late Samuel Oppenheim." 59.
2. For a detailed discussion, see Schwartz, *Early Brazil*.
3. Candele, P. Le Author. *Prosperity of the West India Company*. [Madrid, Spain: publisher not identified, 1642] Pdf. https://www.loc.gov/item/2021666729/.
4. See Feitler, "'Gentes' da Nação: judeus e cristãos-novos no Brasil holandês," 77–83.
5. Groesen, "Introduction: The Legacy of an Interlude," 1.
6. Groesen, "Introduction: The Legacy of an Interlude, 4.
7. Klooster, *The Dutch Moment*, 5–8.
8. A few examples of this scholarship stand out, notably, José Antônio Gonsalves de Mello's *Tempo dos Flamengos*; Charles R. Boxer's *The Dutch in Brazil, 1624–1654*; Evaldo Cabral de Mello's *Rubro veio: O imaginário da restauração pernambucana*; Evaldo Cabral de Mello's *Olinda Restaurada*, and *O Negócio do Brasil*; and more recently, Jonathan Israel and Stuart B. Schwartz's *Expansion of Tolerance: Religion in Dutch Brazil (1624–1654)*; Bruno Feitler's book chapter, "Jews and New Christians in Dutch Brazil, 1630–1654"; and a volume edited by Michiel van Groesen, *The Legacy of Dutch Brazil*.
9. Böhm, "The First Sephardic Synagogues in South America and in the Caribbean Area," 14. See Boxer, *The Dutch in Brazil, 1624–1654*, 133.
10. Disney, *A History of Portugal and the Portuguese Empire*, 222–223.
11. Feitler, "Jews and New Christians in Dutch Brazil, 1630–1654," 123.
12. Baerle and Koning. *The History of Brazil Under the Governorship of Count Johan Maurits of Nassau, 1636–1644*, 128.
13. Quoted in Schwartz, *Early Brazil*, 238, English translation of José Antônio Gonsalves de Mello, *Fontes para a história do Brasil holandês*, 96–129.
14. Quoted in Schwartz, *Early Brazil*, 238, English translation of José Antônio Gonsalves de Mello, *Fontes para a história do Brasil holandês*, 96–129.
15. Israel, "Religious Toleration in Dutch Brazil (1624–1654)," 24.
16. Boxer, *The Dutch in Brazil, 1624–1654*, 124.
17. Boxer, *The Dutch in Brazil, 1624–1654*, 57.

18. Southey, *A History of Brazil* vol. 1, 646.
19. See Simms, "Being Crypto-Jewish in Colonial Brazil (1500–1822): Brushing History Against the Grain," 422–435.
20. Simms, "Being Crypto-Jewish in Colonial Brazil (1500–1822): Brushing History Against the Grain," 422–435.
21. Feitler, "'Gentes' da Nação: judeus e cristãos-novos no Brasil holandês," 74.
22. Levy, "Anti-Jewish 'Propaganda' in Brazil under Dutch Occupation," 320.
23. Quoted in Levy, "Anti-Jewish 'Propaganda' in Brazil under Dutch Occupation," 320.
24. Baerle and Koning, *The History of Brazil Under the Governorship of Count Johan Maurits of Nassau, 1636–1644*, 295–296.
25. Wiznitzer, "Jewish Soldiers in Dutch Brazil (1630–1654)," 40.
26. See Boxer, *The Dutch in Brazil, 1624–1654*, 131.
27. See Southey, *A History of Brazil* vol. 1, 646.
28. See Cabral de Mello, *A Ferida de Narciso*, 32.
29. Israel, "Religious Toleration in Dutch Brazil (1624–1654)," 24.
30. See Boxer, *The Dutch in Brazil, 1624–1654*, 134.
31. Ponte, "'Al de swarten die hier ter stede comen': Een Afro-Atlantische gemeenschap in zeventiende-eeuws Amsterdam." Also see Mark Ponte, "Dossies, histórias da nova holanda, a afro-brasileira Juliana em amsterdã," http://bndigital.bn.gov.br/dossies/historias-da-nova-holanda/a-afro-brasileira-juliana-em-amsterda/. See burial registration for Francijcks of Angola in Amsterdam, Archief Amsterdam, https://archief.amsterdam/indexen/deeds/ba7f1bff-e64e-48a1-ba2a-513aaf6a9d33?person=99e87e12-7962-2bb2-e053-b784100a6a2e. For details on Brazilian blacks and mulatos buried in Amsterdam with Jewish mothers, see Wolff, "Judeus, Judaizantes e seus escravos," 118–121.
32. A detailed archival collection of the WIC experience in Brazil is available at the Inventaris van het archief van de Oude West-Indische Compagnie (Oude WIC) ["1.05.01.01 Inventory of the archives of the Old West India Company (Old WIC), 1621–1674 (1711)"]. Dutch National Archive, Nationaal Archief, https://www.nationaalarchief.nl/onderzoeken/archief/1.05.01.01/invnr/%40D..~D.4.~49-67~64~95.
33. Baerle, Caspar Van, *Nederlandsch Brazilië onder het bewind van Johan Maurits, grave van Nassau, -1644: historisch, geographisch, ethnographisch, naar de Latijnsche uitgave van 1647 voor het eerst in het Nederlandsch bewerkt*. 's-Gravenhage, M. Nijhoff, 1923. Pdf. https://www.loc.gov/item/24004248/. Also see Freyre, *Sobrados e Mocambos*, 320.
34. Baerle and Koning, *The History of Brazil Under the Governorship of Count Johan Maurits of Nassau, 1636–1644*, ix.
35. Blaeu, Joan, Cartographer. *Brazil: of the Noble Class, of Loves, and of Letters*. [Amsterdam, Holland: publisher not identified, 1640] Map. https://www.loc.gov/item/2021668367/.
36. Blaeu, Willem Janszoon, Cartographer. *New Image of Brazil*. [Amsterdam, Holland: publisher not identified, 1631] Map. https://www.loc.gov/item/2021668368/.

37. See Freyre, *Sobrados e Mocambos*, 320.
38. Boxer, *The Dutch in Brazil, 1624–1654*, 151.
39. Schwartz, *Early Brazil*, 246, English translation of José Antônio Gonsalves de Mello, *Fontes para a história do Brasil holandês*, 96–129.
40. See Freyre, *Sobrados e Mocambos*, 5 and 320.
41. Novinsky et al., *Os Judeus Que Construíram of Brasil*, 135–136; and Franca, *Monumentos do Recife*, 382.
42. See Freyre, *Sobrados e Mocambos*, 327–328.
43. Candele, P. Le Author. *Prosperity of the West India Company*. [Madrid, Spain: publisher not identified, 1642] Pdf. https://www.loc.gov/item/2021666729/.
44. Bloom, "A Study of Brazilian Jewish History 1623–1624, Based Chiefly Upon the Findings of the Late Samuel Oppenheim," 53–54.
45. See Orfali, "The Dutch Occupation and Defense of Brazil: The Question of the Support of Jews and Conversos," 136; and Wiznitzer, "Jewish Soldiers in Dutch Brazil (1630–1654)," 40–42.
46. Wiznitzer, "Jewish Soldiers in Dutch Brazil (1630–1654)," 40–42.
47. Wiznitzer, "Jewish Soldiers in Dutch Brazil (1630–1654)." 41–42.
48. Governo Brasileiro. *Histórias da Nova Holanda*, http://bndigital.bn.gov.br/dossies/historias-da-nova-holanda/.
49. Schwartz, *Early Brazil*, 253–254, English translation of José Antônio Gonsalves de Mello, *Fontes para a história do Brasil holandês*, 96–129.
50. Schwartz, *Early Brazil*, 250, English translation of José Antônio Gonsalves de Mello, *Fontes para a história do Brasil holandês*, 96–129.
51. Schwartz, *Early Brazil*, 254, English translation of José Antônio Gonsalves de Mello, *Fontes para a história do Brasil holandês*, 96–129.
52. Schwartz, *Early Brazil*, 250–254, English translation of José Antônio Gonsalves de Mello, *Fontes para a história do Brasil holandês*, 96–129.
53. See Xavier, "A Experiência Colonial Neerlandesa no Brasil (1630–1654). Anais do II Encontro International de História Colonial," 3–9. Also, for details on Ceará and the interaction between the Dutch and Indigenous tribes, see Meuwese, "From Dutch Allies to Portuguese Vassals. Indigenous Peoples in the Aftermath of Dutch Brazil," 63–64.
54. Baerle and Koning, *The History of Brazil Under the Governorship of Count Johan Maurits of Nassau, 1636–1644*, 128.
55. See Feitler, "'Gentes' da Nação: judeus e cristãos-novos no Brasil holandês," 67.
56. Feitler, "'Gentes' da Nação: judeus e cristãos-novos no Brasil holandês," 78–79.
57. Feitler, "'Gentes' da Nação: judeus e cristãos-novos no Brasil holandês," 80.
58. For example, for details about modern migration decision processes and decisions on why Brazilian immigrants migrate, see Marcus, "Brazilian Immigration to the United States and the Geographical Imagination."
59. Feitler, "'Gentes' da Nação: judeus e cristãos-novos no Brasil holandês," 69.
60. Feitler, "Four Chapters in the History of Crypto-Judaism in Brazil: The Case of the Northeastern New Christians (17th–21st centuries)," 211.

61. Bloom, "A Study of Brazilian Jewish History 1623–1624, Based Chiefly Upon the Findings of the Late Samuel Oppenheim," 55.
62. Glasman, "O início da literature Judaíca nas Americas," 2. Also see Silva, *Rabi Aboab da Fonseca*; and Santos, *Entre Meandros da Tolerância*.
63. Novinsky et al., *Os Judeus Que Construíram of Brasil*, 136.
64. See Böhm, "The First Sephardic Synagogues in South America and in the Caribbean Area," 3; See Mello, *Gente da Nação*.
65. See Wiznitzer, "The Synagogue and Cemetery of the Jewish Community in Recife, Brazil (1630–1654)," 128.
66. Glasman, "O início da literature Judaíca nas Americas," 2. Also see Silva, *Rabi Aboab da Fonseca*; and Santos, *Entre Meandros da Tolerância*.
67. Archive of Amsterdam (Archief Amsterdam), of the Portuguese-Hebrew Register of Regulations and Decisions (5409–5414), 1648–1654 (Recife, Pernambuco), *Inventaris van het Archief van de Portugees-Israëlietische Gemeente*, https://archief.amsterdam/inventarissen/scans/334/7.2.1.1/start/0/limit/10/highlight/8; and https://archief.amsterdam/inventarissen/scans/334/7.2.1.1/start/0/limit/10/highlight/3.
68. See "Reglementen. Dutch translation of the regulations (haskamot) of the Dotar society." This is a Dutch translation of the regulations or haskamot of the "Dotar" society, originally written in Portuguese between 1756 and 1825, with reference to many eminent names of the Jewish-Portuguese community in Amsterdam (Sarfaty, Da Costa, Spinoza, Senior Coronel). The Archival Collection at the Ets Haim Library in Amsterdam (Ets Haim Livraria Montezinos), http://etshaimmanuscripts.nl/items/eh-48-a-25/.
69. Feitler, "'Gentes' da Nação: judeus e cristãos-novos no Brasil holandês," 76.
70. Wiznitzer, "The Synagogue and Cemetery of the Jewish Community in Recife, Brazil (1630–1654)," 129. Also see Silva, *Rabi Aboab da Fonseca*.
71. Mello, *Gente da Nação*. 111.
72. New archaeological research of this synagogue in Recife received international public attention in 2000 in the *New York Times*, which reported on its important role within Recife. Larry Rohter, "Recife Journal; A Brazilian City Resurrects Its Buried Jewish Past," *New York Times*, May 19, 2000, https://www.nytimes.com/2000/05/19/world/recife-journal-a-brazilian-city-resurrects-its-buried-jewish-past.html.
73. Dines, "Do Documento ao Monumento, A História como Canteiro," 19.
74. Silva, *A Primeira comunidade Judaica do Novo Mundo*, 64–69. See Mello, *Gente da Nação*, 552, and Kaufman, "Da Península Ibérica para Pernambuco . . . Eles vieram para ficar," 14.
75. Silva, *A Primeira comunidade Judaica do Novo Mundo*, 64–69. See Mello, *Gente da Nação*, 552. Through the research work conducted by historian José Antônio Gonsalves de Mello, José Luiz Mota Menezes, and the Instituto Arqueológico, Histórico e Geográfico Pernambucano ("The Archaeological, Historical and Geographical Institute of Pernambuco") along with the Mayor's Office of the city of Recife.

76. For example, see Albuquerque and Lucena, "Sinagoga Kahal Zur Israel Retornando à Vida do Recife."
77. Federação Israelita de Pernambuco Confederação Israelita do Brasil, May 10, 2021, https://www.conib.org.br/comunidades/fipe-federacao-israelita-de-pernambuco/. Also see Brasil Arqueológico, "Arqueologia Sinagoga Kahal Zur Israel," May 10, 2021, https://www.brasilarqueologico.com.br/arqueologia-sinagoga-kahal-zur-israel.php.
78. Federação Israelita de Pernambuco, Confederação Israelita do Brasil, May 10, 2021, https://www.conib.org.br/comunidades/fipe-federacao-israelita-de-pernambuco/. Also see Brasil Arqueológico, "Arqueologia Sinagoga Kahal Zur Israel," May 10, 2021, https://www.brasilarqueologico.com.br/arqueologia-sinagoga-kahal-zur-israel.php.
79. See Felipe Goifman, *National Geographic Brasil*, 2017. "Retorno do Nordeste Brasileiro ao Judaísmo. Séculos depois da Inquisição e da Conversão Forçada dos Cristãos-Novos, Nordestinos Buscam suas Raízes Judaicas," November 23, 2017, https://www.nationalgeographicbrasil.com/fotografia/2017/11/o-retorno-do-nordeste-brasileiro-ao-judaismo.
80. See Studemund-Halévy, "Sea is History, Sea is Witness: The Creation of a Prosopographical Database for the Sephardic Atlantic," 493.
81. See Mello, *Gente da Nação*, 111. Also see Feitler, "'Gentes' da Nação: judeus e cristãos-novos no Brasil holandês," 69.
82. Feitler, "'Gentes' da Nação: judeus e cristãos-novos no Brasil holandês," 69.
83. Feitler, *Cristãos-Novos na Paraíba*, 141–143.
84. Feitler, "'Gentes' da Nação: judeus e cristãos-novos no Brasil holandês," 72–73, and 81.
85. Feitler, *Cristãos-Novos na Paraíba*, 147.
86. See Feitler, "'Gentes' da Nação: judeus e cristãos-novos no Brasil holandês," 72–73, and 81.
87. Feitler, "'Gentes' da Nação: judeus e cristãos-novos no Brasil holandês," 73.
88. See Feitler, *Cristãos-Novos na Paraíba*, 147.
89. Bloom, "A Study of Brazilian Jewish History 1623–1624, Based Chiefly Upon the Findings of the Late Samuel Oppenheim," 55.
90. For further discussion, see Wiznitzer, "Isaac de Castro, Brazilian Jewish Martyr," 64; Lipiner, *Izaque de Castro: o mancebo que veio preso do Brasil*; and Santos, *Entre Meandros da Tolerância*.
91. See Wiznitzer, "Isaac de Castro, Brazilian Jewish Martyr," 64.
92. Quoted in Novinsky et al., *Os Judeus Que Construíram o Brasil*, 129.
93. See Wiznitzer, "Isaac de Castro, Brazilian Jewish Martyr," 71.
94. Bodian, *Dying in the Law of Moses*, 192.
95. Wiznitzer, "The Number of Jews in Dutch Brazil (1630–1654)," 107. However, estimates of the Jewish population have varied widely. See Mello, "The Dutch Calvinists and Religious Toleration in Portuguese America," 487.
96. Wiznitzer, "The Number of Jews in Dutch Brazil (1630–1654)," 107. See discussion in Falbel, *Judeus no Brasil: estudos e notas*, 110.
97. Freyre, *Sobrados e Mocambos*, 321.

98. Quoted in Wiznitzer, "The Number of Jews in Dutch Brazil (1630–1654)," 109.
99. Quoted in Bloom, "A Study of Brazilian Jewish History 1623–1624, Based Chiefly Upon the Findings of the Late Samuel Oppenheim," 62–63. Also see Böhm, "The First Sephardic Synagogues in South America and in the Caribbean Area," 3.
100. Schwartz, *Early Brazil*, 260–261, English translation of José Antônio Gonsalves de Mello, *Fontes para a história do Brasil holandês*, 96–129.
101. Quoted in Wiznitzer, "The Jews in the Sugar Industry of Colonial Brazil," 83–84.
102. Quoted in Wiznitzer, "The Jews in the Sugar Industry of Colonial Brazil," 195–196.
103. Baerle and Koning, *The History of Brazil Under the Governorship of Count Johan Maurits of Nassau, 1636–1644*, 68. For details on the intensified relationships between Jews and blacks, see Wolff, "Judeus, Judaizantes e seus escravos," 119.
104. See Wiznitzer, "The Number of Jews in Dutch Brazil (1630–1654)," 218.
105. See "Three works by Isaac Aboab (1605–1693) copied by David Franco Mendes. Amsterdam, 1728." The Archival Collection at Ets Haim Library in Amsterdam (Ets Haim Livraria Montezinos), http://etshaimmanuscripts.nl/items/eh-47-c-12/. Also see Novinsky et al., *Os Judeus Que Construíram of Brasil*, 136; and Wiznitzer, "Jewish Soldiers in Dutch Brazil (1630–1654)," 44.
106. See Glasman, "O início da literatura Judaíca nas Americas," 3. For a list of eminent Portuguese-Jewish figures during that time, see Santos, *Entre Meandros da Tolerância*.
107. See Glasman, "O início da literatura Judaíca nas Americas," 7–8.
108. See Roth, *A Life of Menasseh Ben Israel*, 26. For a full list of the congregation, see Wiznitzer, *Jews in Colonial Brazil*, 137.
109. Roth, *A Life of Menasseh Ben Israel*, 52.
110. Glasman, "O início da literatura Judaíca nas Americas," 9. Today the bibliography on Padre Vieira is vast. A recent publication by Alcyr Pécora offers a good overview of who is working in the field. See Pécora, *Sermões*, vol. 1. Also see Azevedo, *Cartas do Padre António Vieira coordenadas e anotadas por J. Lúcio d'Azevedo* (Volume II).
111. Quoted in Stuczynski, *The Jesuit António Vieira on Paul's Judeo-Gentile Universalism and Jewish Resiliency*, 250–252. Also see Pécora, *Sermões*, vol. 1.
112. Quoted in Stuczynski, *The Jesuit António Vieira on Paul's Judeo-Gentile Universalism and Jewish Resiliency*, 254.
113. Stuczynski, *The Jesuit António Vieira on Paul's Judeo-Gentile Universalism and Jewish Resiliency*, 254–255.
114. Quoted in Novinsky, "A Catholic Priest and his Fight for Justice for the Jews: Father Antonio Vieira," 35.
115. Costigan, "Judeus e Cristãos-novos nos escritos de letrados do Barroco Espanhol e de Antonio Vieira e Menasseh Ben Israel," 140. Also see Pécora, *Sermões*, vol. 1.
116. Costigan, "Judeus e Cristãos-novos nos escritos de letrados do Barroco Espanhol e de Antonio Vieira e Menasseh Ben Israel," 141–142.
117. Roth, *A Life of Menasseh Ben Israel*, 162–164. Also see Muhana, "António Vieira: A Jesuit Missionary to the Portuguese Jews of Amsterdam."
118. See Costigan, "Judeus e Cristãos-novos nos escritos de letrados do Barroco Espanhol e de Antonio Vieira e Menasseh Ben Israel," 142.

119. Israel, "Religious Toleration in Dutch Brazil (1624–1654)," 27.
120. See Wiznitzer, "The Jews in the Sugar Industry of Colonial Brazil," 83–84.
121. See Orfali, "The Dutch Occupation and Defense of Brazil: The Question of the Support of Jews and Conversos," 137.
122. See "Shema ha'kol Yehudah." Portfolio of the Dutch master scribe Yehudah Machabeu. Probably Amsterdam, second half 17th century. The Archival Collection at the Ets Haim Library in Amsterdam (Ets Haim Livraria Montezinos), http://etshaimmanuscripts.nl/items/eh-48-a-24/.
123. See details in *Vatican News*. 2017, "Canonizations," http://www.vatican.va/news_services/liturgy/libretti/2017/20171015-libretto-canonizzazione.pdf; and Renata Moura. *BBC Brasil in London*. "O massacre holandês há 372 anos que levou o papa Francisco a decretar a santidade de 30 brasileiros," October 14, 2017, https://www.bbc.com/portuguese/brasil-41568388.
124. See Cascudo, "O Brasão Holandês do Rio Grande do Norte."
125. Cascudo, "O Brasão Holandês do Rio Grande do Norte," 91 [Translation by author].
126. *Vatican News*. 2017, "Canonizations," http://www.vatican.va/news_services/liturgy/libretti/2017/20171015-libretto-canonizzazione.pdf; and Renata Moura. *BBC Brasil in London*. "O massacre holandês há 372 anos que levou o papa Francisco a decretar a santidade de 30 brasileiros," October 14, 2017, https://www.bbc.com/portuguese/brasil-41568388.
127. *Vatican News*. 2017, "Canonizations," http://www.vatican.va/news_services/liturgy/libretti/2017/20171015-libretto-canonizzazione.pdf; and Renata Moura. *BBC Brasil in London*. "O massacre holandês há 372 anos que levou o papa Francisco a decretar a santidade de 30 brasileiros," October 14, 2017, https://www.bbc.com/portuguese/brasil-41568388.
128. Quoted in Bloom, "A Study of Brazilian Jewish History 1623–1624, Based Chiefly Upon the Findings of the Late Samuel Oppenheim," 74.
129. Bloom, "A Study of Brazilian Jewish History 1623–1624, Based Chiefly Upon the Findings of the Late Samuel Oppenheim," 75.
130. Moreau, Pierre, Active. *Klare en waarachtige beschryving van de leste beroerten en afval der Portugezen in Brasil; daar in d'oorsprong dezer zwarigheden en oorlogen klarelijk vertoont worden*. t'Amsterdam: J. Hendriksz. en J. Rieuwertsz, 1652. Pdf. https://www.loc.gov/item/02016591/.
131. Schwartz, *Early Brazil*, 258, English translation of José Antônio Gonsalves de Mello, *Fontes para a história do Brasil holandês*, 96–129.
132. See Boxer, *The Dutch in Brazil, 1624–1654*, 160–258; Santiago, *História da guerra de Pernambuco: e feitos memoráveis do mestre de campo, João Fernandes Vieira, herói digno de eterna memória, primeiro aclamador da Guerra. Volume 5 de Série 350 anos. Restauração pernambucana*; Gândavo, *Tratado da Terra do Brasil; História da Província Santa Cruz*; Cabral de Melo, *O Negócio do Brasil: Portugal, os Países Baixos e o Nordeste 1641–1669*; and Xavier, "A Experiência Colonial Neerlandesa no Brasil (1630–1654). Anais do II Encontro International de História Colonial."
133. Cabral de Mello, *A Ferida de Narciso*, 42.

134. See Boxer, *The Dutch in Brazil, 1624–1654*, 144.
135. Schwartz, "Looking for a New Brazil: Crisis and Rebirth in the Atlantic World after the Fall of Pernambuco," 41.
136. Schwartz, "Looking for a New Brazil: Crisis and Rebirth in the Atlantic World after the Fall of Pernambuco," 41.
137. See Feitler, "Four Chapters in the History of Crypto-Judaism in Brazil: The Case of the Northeastern New Christians (17th–21st centuries)," 216.
138. Wiznitzer, "The Exodus from Brazil, and Arrival in New Amsterdam of the Jewish Pilgrim Fathers, 1654," 85.
139. See Gehring, *Correspondence, 1654–1658*.
140. Gehring, *Correspondence, 1654–1658*, xiii.
141. See, for example, Kayserling, "The Colonization of America by Jews"; Stern, "The First Jewish Settlers in America: Their Struggle for Religious Freedom"; and Levy, *De Recife para Manhattan*.
142. Wiznitzer, "The Exodus from Brazil, and Arrival in New Amsterdam of the Jewish Pilgrim Fathers, 1654," 90.
143. See Salomon, "K. K. Shearith Israel's First Language: Portuguese," and Levy, *De Recife para Manhattan: Os Judeus na Formação de Nova York*.
144. Quoted in Markens, *The Hebrews in America*, 3.
145. Oppenheim, "The First Settlement of the Jews in Newport: Some New Matter on the Subject," 3.
146. See Oppenheim, "The First Settlement of the Jews in Newport: Some New Matter on the Subject," 8.
147. See Oppenheim, "The Early History of the Jews in New York, 1654–1664. Some New Matter on the Subject," and Gehring, *Correspondence, 1654–1658*. Notably, because of his virulent and overt anti-Semitism, amid recent removals of Confederate and Columbus monuments and statues in the United States, an Israeli NGO has now called to remove all memorials of Peter Stuyvesant. Ben Sales, "Should New York City remove statues of its anti-Semitic Dutch governor?" *Times of Israel*, August 23, 2017, https://www.timesofisrael.com/should-new-york-city-remove-statues-of-its-anti-semitic-dutch-governor/.
148. Oppenheim, "The Early History of the Jews in New York, 1654–1664. Some New Matter on the Subject," 8.
149. Oppenheim, "The Early History of the Jews in New York, 1654–1664. Some New Matter on the Subject," 9–11.
150. Quoted in Oppenheim, "The Early History of the Jews in New York, 1654–1664. Some New Matter on the Subject," 9–11.
151. Quoted in Oppenheim, "The Early History of the Jews in New York, 1654–1664. Some New Matter on the Subject," 4–5.
152. See Oppenheim, "The Early History of the Jews in New York, 1654–1664. Some New Matter on the Subject," 14.
153. For example, the following list of shareholders of the Amsterdam Chamber for 1656 include several prominent members of the Portuguese "people of the nation,"

for instance: Abram Isaac Perera, Andres Cristof Nunes, Abram Isaac Bueno, Bento Osorio, Joseph d'Acosta, Louys [Luís] Bodrigues [Rodrigues] de Sousa, and Ferdinando Dias de Britto. For 1658: Abraen Ysaac [Abraham Isaac] Pereira, André Nunnes, Isaac Bueno, Bentto Osorio, Fernando Dias de Britto, Joseph Da Costa, Symon and Louis [Luís] de Sousa, and Louys [Luís] Bodrigues [Rodrigues] de Sousa. And for 1658: Francisco Yaz de Crasto, Francisco Lopo Henriques, Balth'r [Balthazar] Alvares Naugera [Nogueira], Josepho [José] de los Bios, Buij Gommes Frontiera, Aron Chamis Vaz, Dionis Jennis, and Diego Yaz de Sousa. For 1671, the following names are under the heading of "Hebreen," or "Hebrews": Abraham and Isaac Perera, Simon and Louis Bodrigues [Rodrigues] de Souza, Aron Chamiz Vaz, Jacob de Pinto, Jeronimo Nunes da Costa, Jacomo and Fernando Ozorio, and Abraham Cohen. Oppenheim, "The Early History of the Jews in New York, 1654–1664. Some New Matter on the Subject," 15.

154. Oppenheim, "The Early History of the Jews in New York, 1654–1664. Some New Matter on the Subject," 15.
155. "Abraham deLucena, Salvador Dandrada and Jacob Cohen, Jews, in the name of the others, petition the Honorable Director General this day to be permitted to purchase a burying place for their nation, which being reported to the meeting and voted on, it was agreed to give them the answer that inasmuch as they did not wish to bury their dead (of which as yet there was no need) in the common burying ground, there would be granted them when the need and occasion therefor arose." Oppenheim, "The Early History of the Jews in New York, 1654–1664. Some New Matter on the Subject," Appendix, (Translation of N. Y. Col . MSS., vol. 6, 285, in New York State Library). In correspondence regarding the cargo manifest of a ship, *Nieuw Amsterdam*, David Fereira and Abraham de Lucena are again mentioned (relating to brandy shipments). According to the bills of lading, boxes of brandy were supposed to be delivered "to David Fereira or in his absence, to Abram de Lucena." Gehring, *Correspondence, 1654–1658*, 100–101.
156. See, for example, Mello, *Gente da Nação*.
157. See Gelfand, "A Caribbean Wind: An Overview of the Jewish Dispersal from Dutch Brazil," 49.
158. Quoted in Bloom, "A Study of Brazilian Jewish History 1623–1624, Based Chiefly Upon the Findings of the Late Samuel Oppenheim," 87.
159. See Wiznitzer, *Jews in Colonial Brazil*, 172.
160. Quoted in Bloom, "A Study of Brazilian Jewish History 1623–1624, Based Chiefly Upon the Findings of the Late Samuel Oppenheim," 87.
161. Samuel, "Some Eighteenth-Century Refugees from Brazil," 89.
162. Klooster, "Networks of Colonial Entrepreneurs: The Founders of the Jewish Settlements in Dutch America, 1650s and 1660s," 37–40.
163. Gelfand, "A Caribbean Wind: An Overview of the Jewish Dispersal from Dutch Brazil," 51.
164. Wiznitzer, *Jews in Colonial Brazil*, 174.
165. Wiznitzer, *Jews in Colonial Brazil*, 174.

166. Davis, "Notes on the History of the Jews in Barbados," 129.
167. Davis, "Notes on the History of the Jews in Barbados," 148
168. Quoted in Böhm, "The First Sephardic Synagogues in South America and in the Caribbean Area," 11.
169. See Gelfand, "A Caribbean Wind: An Overview of the Jewish Dispersal from Dutch Brazil," 50.
170. See Klooster, "Networks of Colonial Entrepreneurs: The Founders of the Jewish Settlements in Dutch America, 1650s and 1660s," 37–40.
171. Quoted in Wolff, "Judeus, Judaizantes e seus escravos," 119.
172. Wolff, "Judeus, Judaizantes e seus escravos," 120
173. See Schaumloeffel, "Papiamentu and the Brazilian Connection Established through the Sephardic Jews." Also see Gelfand, "A Caribbean Wind: An Overview of the Jewish Dispersal from Dutch Brazil."
174. See Klooster, "Networks of Colonial Entrepreneurs: The Founders of the Jewish Settlements in Dutch America, 1650s and 1660s," 37–40. Also see Gelfand, "A Caribbean Wind: An Overview of the Jewish Dispersal from Dutch Brazil."
175. Böhm, "The First Sephardic Synagogues in South America and in the Caribbean Area," 7.
176. See Oppenheim, "An Early Jewish Colony Western Guiana, 1658–1666: And Its Relation to the Jews in Surinam, Cayenne and Tobago," 103–104.
177. See Oppenheim, "An Early Jewish Colony Western Guiana, 1658–1666: And Its Relation to the Jews in Surinam, Cayenne and Tobago," 99 and 103.
178. For more details on the Guianas, see Dutch National Archives, Nationaal Archief, https://www.nationaalarchief.nl/onderzoeken/zoekhulpen/overzicht-van-archieven-over-guyana-guiana#collapse-6535.
179. See Böhm, "The First Sephardic Synagogues in South America and in the Caribbean Area," 7–8.
180. See Gehring, *Correspondence, 1654–1658*, xvii.
181. See Xavier, "A Experiência Colonial Neerlandesa no Brasil (1630–1654). Anais do II Encontro International de História Colonial," 9, and Xavier, "A Experiência Colonial Neerlandesa no Brasil (1630–1654). Anais do II Encontro International de História Colonial," 2–3. Also see Fatah-Black, "Paramaribo as Dutch and Atlantic Nodal Point, 1650–1795," 58.
182. For example, in 1726: Diogo Henriques (in Vila Rica), José da Cruz Henriques (in Mariana), and David Mendes da Silva (Serro Frio). In 1735: João Rodrigues de Morais (Vila Rica), José Nunes (Sêrro Frio), and Helena do Vale (Ouro Preto). In 1732: Manuel de Albuquerque e Aguiar (Ouro Preto), Antônio Fernandes Pereira (Aracuaí), and Domingos Nunes (Pinhal). In 1748: Antônio Sanches (Paracatu), and João Henriqurs (Ouro Preto). In 1733: Antônio Rodrigues Garcia (Pinhal), Miguel Nunes Sanches (Paracatu), and Antônio Ribeiro Furtado (Sêrro Frio); and in 1739: Manuel Gomes de Carvalho (Vila Rica). Freyre, *Sobrados e Mocambos*, 328–329.
183. See Novinsky, "Ser marrano em Minas Colonial."

184. Novinsky, "Ser marrano em Minas Colonial."
185. For details on the first families in Rio, see Fragoso et al., *O Antigo Regime nos trópicos*, 33.
186. See Samuel, "Some Eighteenth-Century Refugees from Brazil," 89; and Novinsky et al., *Os Judeus Que Construíram of Brasil*, 123–124.
187. See Gorenstein, *Heréticos e impuros: a Inquisição e os cristão-novos no Rio de Janeiro—século XVIII*, 41.
188. For example, see Oliveira, *Inquisição e Cristãos-Novos no Rio de Janeiro*; Calaça, "A confissão como dilema: cristãos-novos letrados do Rio de Janeiro—século XVIII"; and, for details on the first families in Rio, see Fragoso et al., *O Antigo Regime nos trópicos*, 33.
189. Quoted in Freyre, *The Masters and The Slaves*, 95. For more information on New Christians in Rio de Janeiro, see Gorenstein, *Heréticos e impuros: a Inquisição e os cristão-novos no Rio de Janeiro—século XVIII*; Oliveira, *Inquisição e Cristãos-Novos no Rio de Janeiro*; and Calaça, "A confissão como dilema: cristãos-novos letrados do Rio de Janeiro—século XVIII."
190. Schwartz, "Plantations and peripheries, c.1580–c.1750," 141.
191. For a detailed discussion, see Falbel, *Judeus no Brasil: estudos e notas*, 147.
192. See Wadsworth, *Agents of Orthodoxy*, 216. For a more detailed description of the expulsion of the Jesuits in Brazil, see the special edition devoted to the topic in *Revista Intituto Histórico e Geográfico Brasileiro*, Rio de Janeiro, (170) 443, 9–332, (April-June), 2009.
193. Arquivo Nacional, Torre do Tombo, Processo 16953.
194. See Schetini Júnior, "Cristãs-novas e criptojudaismo na Bahia setecentista," 26.
195. *Instituto Brasileiro de Geografia e Estatística*, território brasileiro e povoamento, portugueses, IBGE 2021, https://brasil500anos.ibge.gov.br/territorio-brasileiro-e-povoamento/portugueses.html.
196. Quoted in Russell-Wood, *The Portuguese Empire, 1415–1808*, 62.
197. See Pijning, "New Christians as Sugar Cultivators and Traders in the Portuguese Atlantic, 1450–1800," 496.
198. Wadsworth, *Agents of Orthodoxy*, 209–216.
199. *Correio Braziliense: Ou Armazem Literário*, 1808, (1) 8, 123–124.
200. *Gazeta do Rio de Janeiro*, May 5, 1821, 36, 2.
201. See Wadsworth, *Agents of Orthodoxy*, 12 and 46.
202. *O Cruzeiro*, January 12, 1830, 193, 2.
203. *Diário de Pernambuco*, March 30, 1830, 348 1.

Chapter Six

1. Quoted in Johnson, "Portuguese Settlement, 1500–1580," 31. Also see Orfali, "The Dutch Occupation and Defense of Brazil: The Question of the Support of Jews and Conversos," 132.
2. See Brazilian Census Bureau, IBGE 2021, https://brasil500anos.ibge.gov.br/

territorio-brasileiro-e-povoamento/portugueses/imigracao-restrita-1500-1700.html.

3. See Vainfas, "Santo Ofício em terra Fluminense—Cristão-novos e Inquisição no Rio de Janeiro colonial," 14. The first visitation headed by D. Heitor Furtado de Mendonça, went to Bahia from 1591 to 1593, and to Pernambuco from 1593 to 1595. The second visitation to Bahia between 1618 and 1620 was headed by D. Marcos Teixeira; and the third visitation to Grão Pará (roughly equivalent to the modern states of Amazonas and Pará today), was headed by D. Giraldo de Abranches from 1763 to 1769 (a period when most arrests for Indigenous individuals were made, occurring in the Amazon region). Notably, most of the arrests for Judaism were made in Rio de Janeiro during the first quarter of the eighteenth century; however, these arrests were not made during official Inquisition visitations but through denunciations and, for example, familiares, who worked for the Inquisition and lived in Brazil. Only commissioners and clerical officials of the Inquisition (*commisários*), censure officials (qualificadores), and lay officials (familiares) lived in Brazil. See Wadsworth, *In Defense of the Faith*, 11.

4. Full sentence given by the Inquisition: "*Confisco de bens, abjuração em forma, cárcere e hábito penitencial, instrução na fé católica, penitências espirituais, pagamento de custas. O réu foi casado com Domingas Aires, cristã-velha, a qual assassinou por cometer adultério. Por despacho de 06/10/1592, o réu foi absolvido e solto.*" His sentence was a mandatory auto-da-fé, the confiscation of all his assets, penitence, and instruction of the Catholic faith. He was later absolved and released from prison.

5. I noticed many individuals who hailed from Ireland who were living in Lisbon at the time of their arrest (i.e., for the crimes of Lutheranism, Anglicanism, or solicitation). On that note, the livelihoods of the Irish-born living in Portugal who were imprisoned by the Inquisition is a topic that future researchers might want to take up.

6. See Castaño, "The Peninsula as a Borderless Space: Towards a Mobility 'Turn' in the Study of Fifteenth-Century Iberian Jewries," 317.

7. Original Inquisition unedited sentence in Portuguese: "*auto-da-fé de 16/06/1720. Abjuração em forma, cárcere e hábito penitencial perpétuo, instruída nos mistérios da fé, penitências espirituais. Por apontamento na capa do processo é referido que a Mesa a 06/08/1720 deu licença para que a ré fosse para o Rio de Janeiro.*"

8. Note that the term "crioulo" in Brazil is a pejorative term (i.e., a black person of African ancestry born in Brazil) and means something completely different in Spanish-speaking colonies in Latin America (i.e., A European born in the Americas of Spanish ancestry); see explanation in Chapter 1.

9. For more details, see Marcus, "Sex, Color, and Geography: Racialized Relations in Brazil and Its Predicaments"; and Metcalf, *Go-betweens and the Colonization of Brazil, 1500–1600*.

10. See Pena et al., "Retrato Molecular."

11. Also, for a discussion on the Paredes family members, see Calaça, "A confissão como dilema: cristãos-novos letrados do Rio de Janeiro—século XVIII."

12. For New Christians and their descendants, the breakdown was as follows: 281 New Christian (43 percent); 106 part New Christian (16 percent); 98 Old Christian (15 percent); 40 half New Christian (6 percent); 14 one-quarter New Christian (2 percent); and 3 three-quarters New Christian (1 percent).
13. For more information on sodomy and solicitation in colonial Brazil, see Vainfas, *Trópico dos pecados*. Also see Lima, *Confissão pelo avesso*; Tortorici, *Sexuality and the Unnatural in Colonial Latin America*; Vainfas and Tortorici, "Female Homoeroticism, Heresy, and the Holy Office in Colonial Brazil," 77–94; and Aido, *Unseen Slavery*.
14. The differences stem from a number of interrelated reasons, one of them being that the dossiers I examined were from the dossiers available online, and hers were conducted in situ at Torre do Tombo ("hard copies"). Novinsky, *Inquisição: prisioneiros do Brasil*, 22–43.
15. Novinsky, *Inquisição: prisioneiros do Brasil*, 22–43.
16. For example: Abrantes, Aguilar, Andrade, Brandão, Brito, Bueno, Cardoso, Carvalho, Castro, Costa, Coutinho, Dourado, Fonseca, Furtado, Gomes, Gouveia, Granjo, Henriques, Lara, Marques, Melo e Prado, Mesquita, Mendes, Neto, Nunes, Pereira, Pinheiro, Rodrigues, Rosa, Sarmento, Silva, Soares, Teixeira e Teles, Almeida, Avelar, Bravo, Carvajal, Crespo, Duarte, Ferreira, Franco, Gato, Gonçalves, Guerreiro, Leão, Lopes, Leiria, Lobo, Lousada, Machorro, Martins, Montesino, Moreno, Mota, Macias, Miranda, Oliveira, Osório, Pardo, Pina, Pinto, Pimentel, Pizarro, Querido, Rei, Ribeiro, Salvador, Torres e Viana, Amorim, Azevedo, Álvares, Barros, Basto, Belmonte, Cáceres, Caetano, Campos, Carneiro, Cruz, Dias, Duarte, Elias, Estrela, Gaiola, Josué, Lemos, Lombroso, Lopes, Machado, Mascarenhas, Mattos, Meira, Mello e Canto, Mendes da Costa, Miranda, Morão, Morões, Mota, Moucada, Negro, Oliveira, Osório (or Ozório), Paiva, Pilão, Pinto, Pessoa, Preto, Souza, Vaz, Vargas. Consulate of Portugal in Porto Alegre, Brazil. "Aquisição de Nacionalidade Derivada. Nacionalidade portuguesa para judeus sefarditas de origem portuguesa," https://www.consuladoportugalportoalegre.com/nacionalidade-judeus-sefardita.
17. For example, see Marcus, "Sex, Color, and Geography: Racialized Relations in Brazil and Its Predicaments."
18. Souza, *O diabo e a terra de Santa Cruz*. For a discussion of the use of Indigenous healing and plants by Jesuits in Portuguese Goa and Brazil, see Walker, "Supplying Simples for the Royal Hospital: An Indo-Portuguese Medicinal Garden in Goa (1520–1830)."
19. Original punishment sentenced in Portuguese: "*Abjuração de leve, açoitado publicamente, degredo por cinco anos para as galés, penitências espirituais, pagamento das custas.*"
20. Original punishment sentenced in Portuguese: "*Auto-da-fé privado de 11/10/1595. Ir à igreja com vela acesa na mão, descalço, baraço ao pescoço, vara atravessada na boca e carocha infame na cabeça, açoitado publicamente, abjuração de leve, degredo para as galés, por quatro anos, algumas penitências espirituais, pagamento de custas.*"

O réu era escravo de Fernão Soares. O processo decorreu na casa da morada de Heitor Furtado de Mendonça, visitador do Santo Ofício da vila de Olinda, da capitania de Pernambuco."

21. Original punishment sentenced in Portuguese: *"Auto-da-fé privado de 28/09/1771. Abjuração de veemente, açoitado publicamente, degredo para as galés, por dez anos, instrução na fé católica, penitências espirituais, pagamento de custas."*
22. Original punishment sentenced in Portuguese: *"A ré, que se encontrava recolhida na cadeia da Relação no Rio de Janeiro, faleceu a 14/12/1785, tendo sido sepultada na Santa Casa da Misericórdia, antes de ser enviada para o cárcere de Lisboa."*
23. Original punishment sentenced in Portuguese: *"Auto-da-fé privado de 25/10/1591. Ir à igreja descalço, com a cabeça descoberta e vela acesa na mão, abjuração de leve, instrução na fé católica, pagamento de custas. O processo decorreu na casa da morada de Heitor Furtado de Mendonça, visitador do Santo Ofício da cidade de Salvador, da capitania da Baía de Todos os Santos. O réu era criado de Nicolau Mendes)."*
24. For details, see Aidoo, *Slavery Unseen*. Aidoo also explains the involvement of the Catholic Church choosing not to intervene in the cases of rape and sexual abuse and violence in Brazil.
25. Bethencourt, *The Inquisition*, 305.

Conclusion

1. For more details on Mestre João, see Valentim, "Uma Família de Cristãos-Novos do Entre Douro e Minho: Os Paz. Reprodução Familiar, Formas de Mobildade Social, Mecancia e Poder."
2. However, Catholic membership is rapidly declining due to the rapid rise of the Protestant Evangelical and Pentecostal churches (evangélicos), with a membership that accounts for over 20 percent of Brazilians. In one hundred years, Brazil shifted from being virtually 100 percent Catholic in 1872, to being 90 percent in 1970, 70 percent in 2010, and today about 65 percent. Most of this Catholic membership decline is due to the rapid rise of Evangelicals. See *Instituto Brasileiro de Geografia e Estatística*, IBGE, 2010. May 13, 2022, https://biblioteca.ibge.gov.br/visualizacao/periodicos/94/cd_2010_religiao_deficiencia.pdf.
3. For a discussion of Portuguese New Christian diasporas, for example, see Poettering, *Migrating Merchants*, 103.
4. See Bethencourt, *Racisms*, 149.
5. See Maio and Calaça, "Um balanço da bibliografia sobre o anti-semitismo no Brasil," 432.
6. Their interpretations of the historiography have been discussed and highlighted before by Marcos Chor Maio and Carlos Eduardo Calaça, and by Bruno Feitler. See Maio and Calaça, "New Christians and Jews in Brazil: Migrations and Antisemitism," 75–79; and Feitler, "Four Chapters in the History of Crypto-Judaism in Brazil: The Case of the Northeastern New Christians (17th–21st centuries)."

Afterword

1. For a historical perspective of twentieth-century Jewish refugees in Brazil and Nazis in southern Brazil, see Mello, *Travessias da Terra Vermelha*. Marcos Chor Maio and Carlos Eduardo Calaça have shown that the literature on antisemitism in Brazil has traditionally focused on two periods: the sixteenth and eighteenth centuries, with the advent of the Portuguese Inquisition; and the 1930s. Maio and Calaça, "Um balanço da bibliografia sobre o anti-semitismo no Brasil." Joe Leahy, "Brazil Neo-Nazi Claim Challenges Myth of Nation's Racial Harmony," *The Financial Times, Folha de Sao Paulo*, January 1, 2017, https://www1.folha.uol.com.br/internacional/en/brazil/2017/01/1848562-brazil-neo-nazi-claim-challenges-myth-of-nations-racial-harmony.shtml.
2. See Governo do Brasil, 2018, "Cidadania e Justiça. Consciência Negra. Racismo é crime. Saiba o que é e como denunciar," Governo do Brasil, August 15, 2018, http://www.brasil.gov.br/cidadania-e-justica/2015/11/racismo-e-crime-saiba-o-que-e-e-como-denunciar.
3. Joe Leahy, "Brazil Neo-Nazi Claim Challenges Myth of Nation's Racial Harmony," *The Financial Times, Folha de Sao Paulo*, January 1, 2017, https://www1.folha.uol.com.br/internacional/en/brazil/2017/01/1848562-brazil-neo-nazi-claim-challenges-myth-of-nations-racial-harmony.shtml.
4. Léo Rodrigues, "Mapa da intolerância: região sul concentra maioria dos grupos neonazistas no Brasil," Empresa Brasil de Comunicacao EBC, November 4, 2013, https://memoria.ebc.com.br/noticias/brasil/2013/04/mapa-da-intolerancia-regiao-sul-concentra-maioria-dos-grupos-neonazistas [translated into English by author]. Also, for a historical perspective of twentieth-century Jewish refugees in Brazil and Nazis in southern Brazil, see Mello, *Travessias da Terra Vermelha*.
5. Carolina Mazzi, "Aumentam Denuncias de Antissemitismo no Brasil e Pandemia Acentua Tendencia, Aponta Relatorio," *O Globo*, November 7, 2020, https://oglobo.globo.com/sociedade/aumentam-denuncias-de-antissemitismo-no-brasil-pandemia-acentua-tendencia-aponta-relatorio-24538816. Guilherme Magalhaes, "Exercito Brasileiro Homenagia Major Alemao Condecorado por Hitler," *Folha de Sao Paulo*, July 1, 2019, https://www1.folha.uol.com.br/poder/2019/07/exercito-brasileiro-homenageia-major-alemao-condecorado-por-hitler.shtml.
6. "Bruno Aiub: Podcaster fired over call for Brazilian Nazi party," *BBC News World: Latin America*, February 9, 2022, https://www.bbc.com/news/world-latin-america-60317432.
7. Mônica Bergamo, "Episódios neonazistas no Brasil crescem ano a ano sob Bolsonaro, diz observatório judaico. Entidade já contabilizou 114 eventos desse tipo desde 2019," *Folha de Sao Paulo*, August 14, 2022, https://www1.folha.uol.com.br/colunas/monicabergamo/2022/08/episodios-neonazistas-no-brasil-crescem-ano-a-ano-sob-bolsonaro-diz-observatorio-judaico.shtml.
8. Carolina Mazzi, "Aumentam Denuncias de Antissemitismo no Brasil e Pandemia Acentua Tendencia, Aponta Relatorio," *O Globo*, November 7, 2020, https://

oglobo.globo.com/sociedade/aumentam-denuncias-de-antissemitismo-no-brasil-pandemia-acentua-tendencia-aponta-relatorio-24538816.

9. Carolina Mazzi, "Aumentam Denuncias de Antissemitismo no Brasil e Pandemia Acentua Tendencia, Aponta Relatorio," *O Globo*, November 7, 2020, https://oglobo.globo.com/sociedade/aumentam-denuncias-de-antissemitismo-no-brasil-pandemia-acentua-tendencia-aponta-relatorio-24538816.

10. "Bruno Aiub: Podcaster fired over call for Brazilian Nazi party," *BBC News World: Latin America*, February 9, 2022, https://www.bbc.com/news/world-latin-america-60317432.

11. "Tiago Leifert sofre ataques racistas por ser judeu após briga com Ícaro Silva," *Veja Abril*, December 21, 2021, https://vejasp.abril.com.br/coluna/pop/tiago-leifert-sofre-ataques-racistas-por-ser-judeu-apos-briga-com-icaro/.

12. For more details on the role of the Vatican and the Red Cross in the escape of Nazis to South America, see Steinacher, *Humanitarians at War*.

13. See Maio and Calaça, "New Christians and Jews in Brazil: Migrations and Antisemitism," 73; and Maio and Calaça, "Um balanço da bibliografia sobre o antisemitismo no Brasil." Also, for details on Jewish refugees in the 1930s and 1940s, and Nazis in southern Brazil, see Mello, *A Travessia da Terra Vermelha*, and Lesser, *Welcoming the Undesirables*.

14. Ministério da Defesa, Exercito Brasileiro, "Tributo Ao Major Eduard Ernest Thilo Otto Maximilian von Westernhagen, Oficial Alemão Assasinado no Brasil por um Ato Terrorista em 1968," May 7, 2021, https://www2.eb.mil.br/web/noticias/noticiario-do-exercito/-/asset_publisher/U3X7kX8FkEXD/content/id/10113044.

15. Ministério da Defesa, Exercito Brasileiro, "Tributo Ao Major Eduard Ernest Thilo Otto Maximilian von Westernhagen, Oficial Alemão Assasinado no Brasil por um Ato Terrorista em 1968," May 7, 2021, https://www2.eb.mil.br/web/noticias/noticiario-do-exercito/-/asset_publisher/U3X7kX8FkEXD/content/id/10113044.

16. Guilherme Magalhães, "Exercito Brasileiro Homenagia Major Alemao Condecorado por Hitler," *Folha de São Paulo*, July 1, 2019, https://www1.folha.uol.com.br/poder/2019/07/exercito-brasileiro-homenageia-major-alemao-condecorado-por-hitler.shtml.

17. For example, see Grinberg, *Os Judeus no Brasil*; Falbel, *Judeus no Brasil*; Lewin, *Judaísmo e Globalizacão*; Lesser, Jeffrey, *Welcoming the Undesirables*; Lesser, "Continuity and Change within an Immigrant Community: The Jews of São Paulo, 1924–1945"; Lesser, "Jewish Brazilians or Brazilian Jews? A Reflection of Brazilian Ethnicity"; Lesser, "How the Jews Became Japanese and Other Stories of Nation and Ethnicity"; Levine, "Brazil's Jews during the Vargas Era and After"; Klein, *Kosher Feijoada*; and Zwerling, *Os Judeus na História do Brasil*.

18. See Maio and Calaça, "New Christians and Jews in Brazil: Migrations and Antisemitism," 73; and Maio and Calaça, "Um balanço da bibliografia sobre o antisemitismo no Brasil." Also, for details on Jewish refugees in the 1930s and 1940s,

and Nazis in southern Brazil, see Mello, *A Travessia da Terra Vermelha*; and Lesser, *Welcoming the Undesirables*.

19. See Dantas, "Palimpsesto Antissemita: Deconstruindo o Plano Cohen," 130–134.
20. A notorious anti-Jewish text, which today is publicly known to have been a hoax; a plagiarized text elaborated in 1897 by the secret police during the regime of Czar Alexander III of Russia used to propagate anti-Semitism.
21. See Caldeira Neto, "Memória e justiça: o negacionismo e a falsificação da história," 1113–1114.
22. Caldeira Neto, "Memória e justiça: o negacionismo e a falsificação da história," 1109–1110.
23. See Caldeira Neto, "Memória e justiça: o negacionismo e a falsificação da história," 1113–1114.
24. Caldeira Neto, "Memória e justiça: o negacionismo e a falsificação da história," 1115.
25. See Caldeira Neto, "Memória e justiça: o negacionismo e a falsificação da história," 1115.
26. Folha de São Paulo, "Governadora de SC se recusa a responder se concorda com ideas neonazistas e negacionistas sobre holocaust," October 2020, https://www1.folha.uol.com.br/poder/2020/10/governadora-de-sc-se-recusa-a-responder-se-concorda-com-ideias-neonazistas-e-negacionistas-sobre-holocausto.shtml. Also see Thomas Traumann. "A governadora neonazista. Ao não negar as ideias racistas do pai, Daniela Reinehr mostrou-se indigna de permanecer no cargo," October 28, 2020, https://veja.abril.com.br/coluna/thomas-traumann/a-governadora-neonazista/.
27. See Caldeira Neto, "Memória e justiça: o negacionismo e a falsificação da história," Several of these communities still publish their own German-language newspapers in Brazil, which began as early as the 1850s (e.g., *Der Kolonist*; *Der Deutsche Einwanderer*; *Kolonie Zeitung*; *Der Deutsche Beobachter*; *Allgemeine Deutsche Zeitung für Brasilien*; and *Der Deutsche Kolonist*). In addition, Nazi sympathies and anti-Semitism still abound also within the German immigrant community in São Paulo (as I personally witnessed several times). With the strong support from this German community, well-known Nazi war criminal fugitives such as Josef Mengele (harbored by the German community in São Paulo, and who eventually drowned at a beach in Bertioga), Franz Stangl (who had been working for Volkswagen in São Bernardo do Campo on the outskirts of São Paulo), and Gustav Wagner (living in São Paulo under the false name of Günther Mendel), among many more, were able to continue to live anonymously in Brazil for so long after WWII.
28. Schwartz, *All Can Be Saved*, 178.

References

Aaslestad, Katherine. *Places and Politics: Local Identity, Civic Culture, and German Nationalism in North Germany during the Revolutionary Era.* Leiden: Brill, 2005.
Abreu, João Capistrano de. "Prefácio a Primeira Visitação do Santo Ofício às partes do Brasil, pelo licenciado Heitor Furtado de Mendonça." In *Confissões da Bahia, 1591–1592.* Rio de Janeiro: F. Briguet, 1935.
———. *Um visitador do Santo Ofício: à cidade do Salvador e ao Reconcavo da Bahia de Todos os Santos (1591–1592).* Typ. do Jornal do Commercio de Rodrigues & C., 1922.
Adler, Elkan N. "Lea on the Inquisition of Spain and Herein of Spanish and Portuguese Jews and Marranos." *The Jewish Quarterly Review* 20, no. 3 (1908): 509–571.
Agosín, Marjorie, ed. *Memory, Oblivion, and Jewish Culture in Latin America.* Austin: University of Texas Press, 2005.
Aidoo, Lamonte. *Slavery Unseen: Sex, Power, and Violence in Brazilian History.* Durham and London: Duke University Press, 2018.
Albuquerque, Luís de. "The Art of Astronomical Navigation." In *Portugal Brazil: The Age of Atlantic Discoveries,* edited by Max Justo Guedes and Gerald Lombardi, 23–64. Lisbon, Milan, and New York: Bertrand Editora, Franco Maria Ricci, and Brazilian Cultural Foundation, 1990.
Albuquerque, Marcos and Veleda Lucena. "Sinagoga Kahal Zur Israel Retornando à Vida do Recife." *Revista de Arqueología Americana, Arqueologia Histórica* 22 (2003): 63–79.
Alencastro, Luiz Felipe de. *O trato dos viventes: formação do Brasil no Atlântico sul (séculos XVI e XVII).* São Paulo: Companhia das Letras, 2000.
———. *Trade in the Living: The Formation of Brazil in the South Atlantic, Sixteenth to Seventeenth Centuries.* Translated by Gavin Adams and Luiz Felipe de Alencastro. Revised by Michael Wolfers and Dale Tomich. Fernand Braudel Center Studies in Historical Social Science. Albany: State University of New York Press, 2018.
Almeida, Nilton Melo. "Cristãos-novos e seus descendentes no Ceará Grande: a inquisição nos sertões de fora." Doctoral Dissertation, Department of History. School of Social Sciences and Humanities of the Universidade Nova de Lisboa, Portugal. 2016.
Anderson, R. Warren. "Inquisitorial Punishments in Lisbon and Évora." *E-Journal of Portuguese History* 10, no. 1 (Summer 2012): 1–18.

Andrade, Manuel Correia de. *The Land and People of Northeast Brazil*. Translated by Dennis V. Johnson. Albuquerque: University of New Mexico Press, 1980.
Aragão, Augusto C. Teixeira de. "Breve Noticia sobre o Descobrimento da America. Pedro Alvares Cabral e o Brasil." In *Centenário do Descobrimento da America: Memórias da Commissão Portugueza*, 37–60. Lisbon: Typographia da Academia Real das Sciencias, 1892.
Arbell, Mordechai. "The Failure of the Jewish Settlement in the Island of Tobago." *Proceedings of the World Congress of Jewish Studies*, Vol. Division B (1993): 303–310.
Arends, Jacques. *Language and Slavery: A Social and Linguistic History of the Suriname Creole*. Amsterdam and Philadelphia: John Benjamins Publishing Company, 2017.
Ascher, Gloria J. "Teaching 'Ladino Language and Culture' and 'Aspects of the Sephardic Tradition': Hopes, Fruits, Experiences." *Shofar: An Interdisciplinary Journal of Jewish Studies* 19, no. 4 (2001): 77–84.
Assis, Angelo Adriano Faria de. "A Inquisição portuguesa e o processo contra Heitor Antunes, cavaleiro d'el Rey e Macabeu do Recôncavo: um (cripto) rabino na Bahia quinhentista." *Cadernos de Estudos Sefarditas* 10–11 (2011): 351–372.
———. "Inquisição, religiosidade e transformações culturais: a sinagoga das mulheres e a sobrevivência do judaísmo feminino no Brasil colonial—Nordeste, séculos XVI-XVII." *Revista Brasileira de História*. 22, no. 43, São Paulo, (2002): 47–66.
———. "Um Israel possível na Bahia colonial: sobre mulheres e resistência judaica em tempos de perseguição." *Arquivo Maaravi: Revista Digital de Estudos Judaicos da UFMG* 7, no. 12 (March, 2013).
Attig, Remy. "Did the Sephardic Jews Speak Ladino?" *Bulletin of Spanish Studies: Hispanic Studies and Research on Spain, Portugal and Latin America* 89, no. 6 (2012).
Azevedo, João Lúcio de. *Cartas do Padre António Vieira coordenadas e anotadas por J. Lúcio d'Azevedo*. Vol. 2. Coimbra: Imprensa da Universidade, 1926.
———. *História dos cristãos novos portugueses*. Lisbon: Livraria Clássica [1921], 1975.
———. "Notas sobre o judaísmo e a Inquisição no Brasil." *Revista do Instituto Histórico e Geográfico Brasileiro* 91 (1922): 679–697.
Bachmann, Roberto. "Judeus e Globalização." In *Judaísmo e Globalização: Espaços e Temporalidades*, edited by Helena Lewin, 580–587. Rio de Janeiro: Programa de Estudos Judaicos, Viveiros de Castro Editora Ldta., 2010.
Baerle, Caspar van, and Blanche T. van Berckel-Ebeling-Koning. *The History of Brazil Under the Governorship of Count Johan Maurits of Nassau, 1636–1644*. Translated, with notes and an Introduction, by Blanche T. van Berckel-Ebeling Koning. Gainesville: University Press of Florida, 2011.
Baião, Antônio. *A Inquisição em Portugal e no Brasil: Subsídios para a sua história Lisboa*. Arquivo Histórico Português, 1907.
Banes, Daniel. "The Portuguese Voyages of Discovery and the Emergence of Modern Science." *Journal of the Washington Academy of Sciences* 78, no. 1 (1988): 47–58.
Barros, Maria Filomena Lopes de. "The Muslim Minority in the Portuguese Kingdom

(1170–1496): Identity and Writing." *E-Journal of Portuguese History* 13, no. 2 (December 2015): 18–32.
Baskin, Judith R, ed. *The Cambridge Dictionary of Judaism and Jewish Culture*. Cambridge: Cambridge University Press, 2011.
Ben-Ur, Aviva. "A Matriarchal Matter: Slavery, Conversion, and Upward Mobility in Suriname's Jewish Community." In *Atlantic Diaspora: Jews, Conversos, and Crypto-Jews in the Age of Mercantilism, 1500–1800*, edited by Richard L. Kagan and Philip D. Morgan, 152–169. Baltimore: The Johns Hopkins University Press, 2009.
Bentley, Jerry H. *Old World Encounters: Cross-Cultural Contacts and Exchanges in Pre-Modern Times*. New York and Oxford: Oxford University Press, 1993.
Berezin, Rifka, Zipora Rubinstein, and Gisele Beiguelman. "Research on Jews in Brazil—Present Stage." *Proceedings of the World Congress of Jewish Studies*, Vol. Division B, no. 3 (1985): 353–360.
Berdichevsky, Norman. "The Age-Old Iberian Rivalry and the Jews." *Jewish Political Studies Review* 16, no. 1–2 (2004): 35–49.
Bernardini, Paolo. "A Milder Colonization: Jewish Expansion to the New World, and the New World in the Jewish Consciousness of the Early Modern Era," 1–21. In *The Jews and the Expansion of Europe to the West, 1450–1800*, edited by Paolo Bernardini and Norman Fiering. New York and Oxford: Berghahn Books, 2001.
Bernardini, Paolo and Norman Fiering, eds. *The Jews and the Expansion of Europe to the West, 1450–1800*. New York and Oxford: Berghahn Books, 2001.
Bethell, Leslie, ed. "Brazil and 'Latin America.'" *Journal of Latin American Studies* 42, no. 3 (2010): 457–85.
———. *Colonial Brazil*. Cambridge: Cambridge University Press, [1984] 1991.
Bethencourt, Francisco. *The Inquisition: A Global History, 1478–1834*. Translated by Jean Birrell. Cambridge, UK: Cambridge University Press, 1995.
———. *Racisms: From the Crusades to the Twentieth Century*. Princeton and Oxford: Princeton University Press, 2013.
Blackbourn, David. "Germans Abroad and 'Auslandsdeutsche': Places, Networks and Experiences from the Sixteenth to the Twentieth Century." *Geschichte Und Gesellschaft* 41, no. 2 (2015): 321–346.
Blake, Stanley E. *The Vigorous Core of Our Nationality: Race and Regional Identity in Northeastern Brazil*. Pittsburgh: University of Pittsburgh Press, 2011.
Blay, Eva Alterman. *O Brasil como Destino: Raízes da imigração Judaica contemporânea para São Paulo*. São Paulo: UNESP, 2013.
Bloom, Herbert I. "A Study of Brazilian Jewish History 1623–1624, Based Chiefly Upon the Findings of the Late Samuel Oppenheim." *Publications of the American Jewish Historical Society* 33 (1951): 43–125.
Blouet, Brian W. and Olwyn M. Blouet. *Latin America and the Caribbean: A Systematic and Regional Survey*. 5th ed. Hoboken, NJ: John Wiley & Sons, Inc., 2006.
Bodian, Miriam. *Dying in the Law of Moses: Crypto-Jewish Martyrdom in the Iberian World*. Bloomington and Indianapolis: Indiana University Press, 2000.

———. *Hebrews of the Portuguese Nation: Conversos and Community in Early Modern Amsterdam*. Bloomington: Indiana University Press, 1997.

———. "Hebrews of the Portuguese Nation: The Ambiguous Boundaries of Self-Definition." *Jewish Social Studies* 15, no. 1 (2008): 66–80.

———. "Review of The Canonization of a Myth: Portugal's 'Jewish Problem' and the Assembly of Tomar 1629. Martin A. Cohen, Hebrew Union College Annual Supplements 5. Cincinnati, Ohio: Hebrew Union College Press, 2002." *The Jewish Quarterly Review* 95, no. 4 (2005): 738–741.

Bogaciovas, Marcelo Meira Amaral. *Tribulações do Povo de Israel na São Paulo Colonial*. Master's Thesis. Programa de Pós-Graduação em História Social do Departamento de História, Faculdade de Filosofia, Letras e Ciências Humanas da Universidade de São Paulo, 2006.

Böhm, Günter. "The First Sephardic Synagogues in South America and in the Caribbean Area." *Studia Rosenthaliana* 22, no. 1 (1988): 1–14.

Boxer, Charles R. *The Dutch in Brazil, 1624–1654*. Oxford: Clarendon Press, 1957.

———. *The Golden Age of Brazil, 1695–1750*. Fourth Printing. Berkeley: University of California, 1973 [1962].

Boyajian, James C. "New Christians and Jews in the Sugar Trade, 1550–1750: Two Centuries of Development of the Atlantic Economy." In *The Jews and the Expansion of Europe to the West, 1450–1800*, 471–484, edited by Paolo Bernardini and Norman Fiering. New York and Oxford: Berghahn Book, 2001.

Braga, Mirella de Almeida. *Da Arte de se Tornar Judeu: Interpretando Estratégias Identitárias Vivenciadas por Comunidades Judáicas em Campina Grande, Paraíba*. Universidade Federal da Paraíba, Programa de Pós-Graduação em Antropologia, Mestrado em Antropologia, 2016.

Braga, Theophilo. "Centenario da Descoberta da America." In *Centenario do Descobrimento da America: Memorias da Commissao Portugueza*, 3–19. Lisbon: Typographia da Academia Real das Sciencias, 1892.

Brandão, Ambrósio Fernandes. *Dialogues on the Great Things of Brazil*. Translated and annotated by Hall, Frederick Holden, William F. Harrison, and Dorothy Winters Welker. Albuquerque: University of New Mexico Press, 1987.

BRASA Report 2005. *Conference on the Future of Brazilian Studies in the U.S.* Brown University, Providence, RI, September 30–October 1, 2005, report accessed online: http://www.brasa.org/about/future. Accessed September 2018, 2005.

Bronner, Fred. "Portugal and Columbus: Old Drives in New Discoveries." *Mediterranean Studies* 6 (1996): 51–66.

Brubaker, Rogers. "Ethnicity without Groups." In *Ethnicity, Nationalism, and Minorities*, edited by May, Stephen, Tariq Modood, and Judith Squires, 55–77. Cambridge: Cambridge University Press, 2004.

Bueno, Francisco da Silveira. *Vocabulário Tupi-Guarani Português*. São Paulo: Éfeta Editora, 1998.

Buttimer, Anne. "Grasping the Dynamism of Lifeworld." *Annals of the Association of American Geographers* 66 (1976): 277–292.

Butzer, Karl W. "The Americas before and after 1492: An Introduction to Current Geographical Research," *Annals of the Association of American Geographers* 82, no. 3 (1992): 345–368.

———. "From Columbus to Acosta: Science, Geography, and the New World," *Annals of the Association of American Geographers* 82, no. 3 (1992): 543–565.

Bynum, William F., E. Janet Browne, and Roy Porter. *Dictionary of the History of Science*. New Jersey: Princeton University Press, 1984.

Cabral de Mello, Evaldo. *A Ferida de Narciso: Ensaio de história regional*. Sao Paulo: Editôra SENAC, 2001.

———. *O Negócio do Brasil: Portugal, os Países Baixos e o Nordeste 1641–1669*. Rio de Janeiro: Topbooks, 1998.

———. *O Nome e o Sangue: Uma fraude genealógica no Pernambuco colonial*. São Paulo: Companhia das Letras, 1989.

Calaça, Carlos Eduardo. "A confissão como dilema: cristãos-novos letrados do Rio de Janeiro—século XVIII" (The confession as a dilemma: new-Christian scholars of Rio de Janeiro—XVIII century). *Antíteses* 1, no. 2 (July–December, 2008): 305–323.

Caldeira Neto, Odilon. "Memória e justiça: o negacionismo e a falsificação da história." *Antíteses* 2, no. 4 (2009): 1097–1123.

Carneiro, Maria Luiza Tucci. "Judeus-caboclos da Amazônia." *Arquivo Maaravi: Revista Digital de Estudos Judaicos da UFMG*. Belo Horizonte 15, no. 29 (2021): 60–87.

Cartas Avulsas de Jesuitas (1550–1568). Materiaes e achêgas para Historia e Geographia do Brasil. Publicados por ordem do Ministerio da Fazenda. Rio de Janeiro: Imprensa Nacional, 1887.

Cascudo, Luís da Câmara. *Mouros, Francêses e Judeus—Três presenças no Brasil*. São Paulo: Editôra Perspectiva, 1986.

———. "O Brasão Holandês do Rio Grande do Norte." *Revista do Instituto Histórico e Geográfico do Rio Grande do Norte*. Natal, vols. 35–37, 1938–1940. Natal, Brazil: Typ. Santo Antônio, 1941.

Castro, Sílvio. *A Carta de Pero Vaz de Caminha: O Descobrimento do Brasil*. Porto Alegre, Brazil: L&PM Editores, 1985.

Carvalho, Horácio de. *O kaf, de João Ramalho*. São Paulo: Typographia do Diario Oficial, 1903.

Centenario do Descobrimento da America: Memorias da Commissao Portugueza. Lisbon: Typographia da Academia Real das Sciencias, 1892.

Cesarani, David. "The Forgotten Port Jews of London: Court Jews who were Also Port Jews." In *Port Jews: Jewish Communities in Cosmopolitan Maritime Trading Centres: 1550–1950*, 111–124, edited by D. Cesarani. New York and London: Routledge, 2013 [First published by Frank Cass Ltda., 2002].

———. *Port Jews: Jewish Communities in Cosmopolitan Maritime Trading Centres: 1550–1950*. New York and London: Routledge, 2013 [First published by Frank Cass Ltda., 2002].

Chacón-Duque, J. C., K. Adhikari, M. Fuentes-Guajardo, et al. "Latin Americans show wide-spread Converso ancestry and imprint of local Native ancestry on physical appearance." *Nature Communications* 9, no. 5388 (2018).

Clawson, David L. *Latin America and the Caribbean*. 5th ed. Oxford and New York: Oxford University Press, 2012.

Clendinnen, Inga. *Ambivalent Conquests: Maya and Spaniard in Yucatan, 1517–1570*. 2nd ed. Cambridge University Press, UK, 2003.

Coates, Timothy J., *Convicts and Orphans: Forced and State-Sponsored Colonizers in the Portuguese Empire, 1550–1755*. Stanford, CA: Stanford University Press, 2001.

———. "The Early Modern Portuguese Empire: A Commentary on Recent Studies." *The Sixteenth Century Journal* 37, no. 1 (Spring 2006): 83–90.

Collier, Simon, Thomas E. Skidmore, and Harold Blakemore, eds. *The Cambridge Encyclopedia of Latin America and the Caribbean*. 2nd ed. New York: Cambridge University Press, 1992.

Cortesão, Jaime. *A política de sigílo nos descobrimentos*. Lisbon: Centenary Publication, 1960.

Costa-Gomes, Rita. *The Making of a Court Society: Kings and Nobles in Late Medieval Portugal*. Translated by Alison Aiken. Cambridge; Cambridge University Press, 2003.

———. "Zurara and the Empire: Reconsidering Fifteenth-Century Portuguese Historiography." *Storia della Storiografia* 47 (2005): 56–89.

Costigan, Lúcia Helena, ed. *Diálogos da Conversão: Missionários, Índios, Negros e Judeus no Contexto Ibero-Americano do Período Barroco*. Campinas, Brazil: Universidade de Campinas, 2005.

———. "The Invisible Giant: The Place of Brazil in (Latin) American Studies: An NEH Summer Institute." *Hispania* 85, no. 3 (2002): 644–648.

———. "Judeus e Cristãos-novos nos escritos de letrados do Barroco Espanhol e de Antonio Vieira e Menasseh Ben Israel," 133–154. In *Diálogos da Conversão: Missionários, Índios, Negros e Judeus no Contexto Ibero-Americano do Período Barroco*. Edited by Lúcia Helena Costigan. Campinas, Brazil: Universidade de Campinas, 2005.

Cresswell, Tim. *Geographic Thought*. Malden, MA: Wiley-Blackwell, 2013.

———. *In Place/Out of Place: Geography, Ideology, and Transgression*. Minneapolis: University of Minnesota Press, 1996.

Curtin, Philip D. *The Atlantic Slave Trade: A Census*. Madison: The University of Wisconsin Press, 1969.

d'Alòs-Moner, Andreu Martínez. "Conquistadores, Mercenaries, and Missionaries: The Failed Portuguese Dominion of the Red Sea." *Northeast African Studies* 12, no. 1 (2012): 1–28.

Dantas, Elynaldo Goncalves. "Palimpsesto Antissemita: Desconstruindo o Plano Cohen." *Escritas* 6, no. 1 (2014): 126–143.

Davies, Archie. "Milton Santos: The conceptual geographer and the philosophy of technics." *Progress in Human Geography* 43, no. 3 (2019): 584–591.

Davies, Arthur. "Prince Henry the Navigator." *Transactions and Papers Institute of British Geographers* 35 (1964): 119–127.
Davis, N. Darnell. "Notes on the History of the Jews in Barbados." (18) 129–148. *American Jewish Historical Society*. 1909.
Dawson, Timothy. "Crane Lane to Ballybough," *Dublin Historical Record* 27, no. 4 (1974): 131–145.
Dines, Alberto. "Do Documento ao Monumento, A História como Canteiro," 19–22. In *A Fênix ou O Eterno Retorno: 460 anos da presença Judaíca em Pernambuco*, edited by Alberto Dines, Francisco Moreno-Carvalho, and Nachman Falbel. Brasília, Brazil: Ministério da Cultura, Programa Monumenta, 2001.
Dines, Alberto, Francisco Moreno-Carvalho, and Nachman Falbel, eds. *A Fênix ou O Eterno Retorno: 460 anos da presença Judaíca em Pernambuco*. Brasília, Brazil: Ministério da Cultura, Programa Monumenta, 2001.
Disney, A. R. *A History of Portugal and the Portuguese Empire: Volume 2, The Portuguese Empire: From Beginnings to 1807*. Cambridge: Cambridge University Press, 2009.
Dodge, Cameron J. G. "A Forgotten Century of Brazilwood: The Brazilwood Trade from the Mid-Sixteenth to Mid-Seventeenth Century." *E-Journal of Portuguese History* 16, no. 1 (June 2018): 1–27.
Eakin, Marshall C. *Becoming Brazilians: Race and National Identity in Twentieth-Century Brazil*. UK: Cambridge University Press, 2017.
Ebert, Christopher. *Between Empires: Brazilian Sugar in the Early Atlantic Economy, 1550–1630*. Leiden: Brill, 2008.
Eiger, Elaine and Luize Valente (directors). *A estrela oculta do Sertão, documentário sobre a vida de comunidades de origem judaica no sertão nordestino* (The hidden star of the backlands, documentary about the life of communities of Jewish origin in the northeastern backland), 2005.
Elkin, Judith Laikin. *The Jews of Latin America*. 3rd ed. Boulder and London: Lynne Rienner Publishers, 2014.
Eltis, David, and David Richardson. *Atlas of the Transatlantic Slave Trade*. With a Foreword by David Brion Davis, and Afterword by David W. Blight. New Haven and London: Yale University Press, 2010.
Fagundes, Igor Pereira. "Felipe Camarão, um cavaleiro potiguar a serviço del Rei: memória, história e identidade nas guerras pernambucanas, século XVII." *Revista 7 Mares* 5 (October 2015): 200–212.
Falbel, Nachman. *Judeus no Brasil: estudos e notas*. São Paulo: Editora da Universidade de São Paulo, 2008.
———. "Sobre a Presença dos Cristãos Novos na Capitania de São Vicente e a Formação da Etnia Paulista." *Revista USP* 41 (March/May 1999): 112–119.
Faria, Patricia Souza de. "Todos desterrados & espalhados pelo mundo: A perseguição inquisitorial de judeus e de cristãos-novos na India Portuguesa (séculos XVI e XVII)." *Antíteses* 1, no. 2 (2008): 283–304.
Farinha, Maria do Carmo Jasmins Dias. *Os Arquivos da Inquisição*. Lisboa, Arquivo Nacional da Torre do Tombo, 1990.

Fatah-Black, Karwan. "Paramaribo as Dutch and Atlantic Nodal Point, 1650–1795." In *Dutch Atlantic Connections, 1680–1800: Linking Empires, Bridging Borders*, edited by Gert Oostindie and Jessica V. Roitman, 52–71. Brill, 2014.

Feitler, Bruno. "A circulação de obras antijudaicas e anti-semitas no Brasil colonial." *Cultura. Revista de História e Teoria de Ideas* 24, 55–74, https://journals.openedition.org/cultura/810, 2007.

———. "Four Chapters in the History of Crypto-Judaism in Brazil: The Case of the Northeastern New Christians (17th—21st centuries)." Translated from Portuguese by David Graizbord. *Jewish History* 25, no. 2 (2011): 207–227.

———. "'Gentes' da Nação: judeus e cristãos-novos no Brasil holandês." In *Os Judeus no Brasil: Inquisição, imigração e identidade*, edited by Keila Grinberg, 65–86. Rio de Janeiro: Civilização Brasileira, 2005.

———. *The Imaginary Synagogue: Anti-Jewish Literature in the Portuguese Early Modern World (16th–18th Centuries)*. Leiden and Boston: Brill, 2015.

———. *Inquisition, juifs et nouveux-chréstiens au Brésil: Le Nordeste XVIIe-XVIIIe siècles*. Louvain: Presses Universitaires de Louvain, 2003.

———. "Jews and New Christians in Dutch Brazil, 1630–1654." In *Atlantic Diaspora: Jews, Conversos, and Crypto-Jews in the Age of Mercantilism, 1500–1800*, edited by Richard L. Kagan and Philip D. Morgan, 123–151. Baltimore: The Johns Hopkins University Press, 2009.

———. "O Catolicismo como Ideal. Produção Literária Anitjudaica no Mundo Português da Idade Moderna." *Novos Estudos* 1, no. 72 (2005): 137–158.

———. "Ofícios e estratégias de acumulação: o caso do despenseiro da Inquisição de Lisboa Antonio Gonçalves Prego (1650–1720)." *Topoi* (Rio de Janeiro) 17, no. 33 (July–December, 2016): 468–489.

Fernandes, Neusa. *A Inquisição em Minas Gerais no século XVIII*. Rio de Janeiro: EDUERJ, 2000.

Fischel, Walter. J. "Leading Jews in the Service of Portuguese India." *The Jewish Quarterly Review* 47, no. 1 (1956): 37–57.

Fisher, Benjamin E. *Amsterdam's People of the Book: Jewish Society and the Turn to Scripture in the Seventeenth Century*. Cincinnati, Ohio: Hebrew Union College Press, 2020.

Fishman, Talya. "Introduction," 1–19. In *Regional Identities and Cultures of Medieval Jews*, edited by Javier Castaño, Talya Fishman, and Ephraim Kanarfogel. UK: Liverpool University Press, Littman Library of Jewish Civilization, 2018.

Fitz, Earl. "Internationalizing the Literature of the Portuguese-Speaking World." *Hispania* 85, no. 3 (2002): 439–448.

Flory, Rae, and David Grant Smith. "Bahian Merchants and Planters in the Seventeenth and Early Eighteenth Centuries." *The Hispanic American Historical Review* 58, no. 4 (1978): 571–594.

Fragoso, João, Maria Fernanda Bicalho, and Maria de Fátima Gouvêa, eds. *O Antigo Regime nos trópicos: A dinâmica imperial portuguêsa (séculos XVI-XVIII)*. Rio de Janeiro: Civilização Brasileira.

Franca, Rubem. *Monumentos do Recife: estátuas e bustos, igrejas e prédios, lápides, placas e inscrições históricas do Recife.* Recife: Secretaria de Educação e Cultura, 1977.

Franco, José Eduardo, and Célia Tavares. "Cristãos-novos, Jesuítas e Inquisição: uma relação controversa em Portugal (séculos XVI e XVII)." *Navegações* 9, no. 1 (January–June, 2016): 48–58.

Frankel, Rachel. "Antecedents and Remnants of Jodensavanne: The Synagogues and Cemeteries of the First Permanent Plantation Settlement of the New World Jews." In *The Jews and the Expansion of Europe to the West, 1450–1800*, edited by Paolo Bernardini and Norman Fiering, 394–436. New York and Oxford: Berghahn Books, 2001.

Freyre, Gilberto. *The Masters and The Slaves: A Study in the Development of Brazilian Civilization.* Translation by Samuel Putnam. 2nd ed. (English-language). Berkeley and Los Angeles, CA: University of California Press, [1933] 1986.

———. *Sobrados e Mocambos. Decadência do Patriarcado Rural e Desenvolvimento do Urbano.* 4th ed. Rio de Janeiro: Livraria José Olympio Editôra, [1936] 1968.

Gade, Daniel. W. "North American Reflections on Latin Americanist Geography." In *Latin America in the 21st Century: Challenges and Solutions*, edited by G. Knapp, 1–45. Conference of Latin Americanist Geographers. University of Texas, Austin, 2002.

Gândavo, Pero de Magalhães. *Tratado da Terra do Brasil; História da Província Santa Cruz*, Belo Horizonte: Itatiaia, 1980.

Garcia, Rodrigo. "O 'bárbaro' que salvou São Paulo," *Apartes: Revista da Camara Municipal de São Paulo.* June 20, 2016, https://www.saopaulo.sp.leg.br/apartes-anteriores/revista-apartes/numero-20/perfil-joao-ramalho/, 2016.

Gehring, Charles T., trans. and ed. *Correspondence, 1654–1658.* Syracuse, NY: Syracuse University Press, 2003.

Gibson, Charles. *The Aztecs Under Spanish Rule: A History of the Indians of the Valley of Mexico, 1519–1810.* Stanford University Press, CA, 1964.

Gitlitz, David Martin. *Secrecy and Deceit: The Religion of The Crypto-Jews.* Albuquerque: University Of New Mexico Press, 2002.

Glasman, Jane Bichmacher de. "O início da literature Judaíca nas Americas." *Arquivo Maaravi: Revista Digital de Estudos Judaícos da UFMG* 5, no. 9 (2011): 1–11.

Goldberg, Jacob Pinheiro. *Psicologia e reflexões do inconsciente.* São Paulo: Associação OINA do Brasil, 1978.

Gorenstein, Lina. *Heréticos e impuros: a Inquisição e os cristão-novos no Rio de Janeiro—século XVIII.* Rio de Janeiro: Secretaria Municipal de Cultura, 1995.

———. "Um Brasil subterrâneo: cristãos-novos no Brasil XVIII." In *Os Judeus no Brasil: Inquisição, imigração e identidade*, edited by Keila Grinberg, 137–160. Rio de Janeiro: Civilzação Brasileira, 2005.

Gould, Stephen Jay. *The Mismeasure of Man.* New York: W. W. Norton, 1981.

Graizbord, David L. *Souls in Dispute: Converso Identities in Iberia and the Jewish Diaspora, 1580–1700.* Philadelphia: University of Pennsylvania Press, 2004.

Green, James N., Victoria Langland, and Lilia Moritz Schwarcz, eds. *The Brazil*

Reader: History, Culture, Politics. 2nd ed. Revised and updated. Durham and London: Duke University Press, 2019.

Green, Toby. "Pluralism, Violence and Empire: The Portuguese New Christians in the Atlantic World." In *Cosmopolitanism in the Portuguese-Speaking World*, edited by Francisco Bethencourt, 40–58. Leiden: Brill, 2017.

Greenlee, William B. "The Captaincy of the Second Portuguese Voyage to Brazil, 1501–1502." *The Americas* 2, no. 1 (July 1945): 3–12.

———. *The Voyage of Pedro Álvares Cabral to Brazil and India : From Contemporary Documents and Narratives*. Ashgate/Routledge, 2010 [originally published by the Council of the Hakluyt Society, 1937].

Gregory, Derek, Ron Johnston, Geraldine Pratt, Michael J. Watts, and Sarah Whatmore, eds. *Dictionary of Human Geography*, London: Wiley-Blackwell, 2009.

Greyerz, Kaspar von. "Portuguese conversos on the Upper Rhine and the converso Community of Sixteenth-Century Europe." *Social History* 14, no. 1 (1989): 59–82.

Grinberg, Keila, ed. *Os Judeus no Brasil: Inquisição, imigração e identidade*. Rio de Janeiro: Civilzação Brasileira, 2005.

Groesen, Michiel van, ed. "Introduction: The Legacy of an Interlude." In *The Legacy of Dutch Brazil*, edited by Michiel van Groesen, 1–24. New York: Cambridge University Press, 2014.

———. *The Legacy of Dutch Brazil*. New York: Cambridge University Press, 2014.

Guedes, Max Justo. "Portugal-Brazil: The Encounter between Two Worlds." In *Portugal Brazil: The Age of Atlantic Discoveries*, edited by Max Justo Guedes and Gerald Lombardi, 161–234. Lisbon, Milan, and New York: Bertrand Editora, Franco Maria Ricci, and Brazilian Cultural Foundation, 1990.

Guedes, Max Justo and Gerald Lombardi, eds. *Portugal Brazil: The Age of Atlantic Discoveries*. Lisbon, Milan, and New York: Bertrand Editora, Franco Maria Ricci, and Brazilian Cultural Foundation, 1990.

Häberlein, Mark. *The Fuggers of Augsburg: Pursuing Wealth and Honor in Renaissance Germany*. Charlottesville and London: University of Virginia Press, 2012.

Harel, Yaron, Margalit Bejarano, Marta Francisca Topel, and Margalit Yosifon, eds. *Jews and Jewish Identities in Latin America: Historical, Cultural, and Literary Perspectives*. Boston: MA, Academic Studies Press, 2017.

Hassig, Ross. *Mexico and the Spanish Conquest*. UK: Addison Wesley Longman Limited, 1994.

Hemming, John. *Red Gold: The Conquest of the Brazilian Indians, 1500–1760*. Cambridge: Harvard University Press, 1978.

Herculano, Alexandre. *History of the Origin and Establishment of the Inquisition in Portugal*. Translated by John C. Branner. California: Stanford University Press, [1852] 1926.

Hill, Alberta Frances. "Alvise Cadamosto, Mestre João Faras and the Controversial History of Early European Mapping of the Southern Cross. In *Navegação no Atlântico/Atlantic Navigation: XVIII Reunião Internacional de História da Náutica*, 133–146. Coordinated by Francisco Contente Domingues and Susana Serpa Silva. Nova Gráfica, Ltda, São Miguel, Azores, 2019.

Hiney, Diarmuid G. "5618 and All That: The Jewish Cemetery Fairview Strand." *Dublin Historical Record* 50, no. 2 (1997): 119–129.
Hobson, John. *The Eastern Origins of Western Civilization*. Cambridge: Cambridge University Press, 2004.
Holt-Jensen, Arild. *Geography: Its History & Concepts*. Totowa, New Jersey: Barnes & Noble Books [1980] 1982.
Hordes, Stanley M. *To the End of the Earth: A History of the Crypto-Jews of New Mexico*. NY: Columbia University Press. 2005.
Hubner, Manu Marcus. "Mártires: De Rabi Akiva a Tiradentes: uma aproximação." *Arquivo Maaravi: Revista Digital de Estudos Judaicos da UFMG, Belo Horizonte* (15) 28, May 2021.
Hue, Sheila Moura (Tradução, Introdução, e Notas). *Primeiras Cartas do Brasil, 1551–1555: Introdução e notas*. Rio de Janeiro: Jorge Zahar Editor, 2006.
Hyamson, Albert M. *The Sephardim of England: A History of the Spanish and Portuguese Jewish Community 1492–1951*. London: Methuen & Co., 1951.
Hyman, Louis. *The Jews of Ireland: From Earliest Times to the Year 1910*. Shannon, Ireland: Irish University Press, 1972
Igel, Regina. "Escritores Judeus Brasileiros: Um Percurso em Andamento." *Revista Iberoamericana* 66, no. 191 (2000): 325–338.
Instituto Brasileiro de Geografia e Estatística (IBGE) *Brasil: 500 anos de povoamento*. Rio de Janeiro, 2000.
Israel, Jonathan. *Diasporas within a Diaspora: Jews, Crypto-Jews and the World Maritime Empires (1540–1740)*. Leiden: Brill, 2002.
———. "Duarte Nunes da Costa (Jacob Curiel), of Hamburg, Sephardi Nobleman and Communal Leader (1585–1664)." *Studia Rosenthaliana* 21, no. 1 (1987): 14–34.
———. "Jews in Dutch America." In *The Jews and the Expansion of Europe to the West, 1450–1800*, edited by Paolo Bernardini and Norman Fiering, 335–349. New York and Oxford: Berghahn Books, 2001.
———. "Religious Toleration in Dutch Brazil (1624–1654)." In *Expansion of Tolerance: Religion in Dutch Brazil (1624–1654)*, edited by Jonathan Israel and Stuart B. Schwartz, Introduction by Michiel van Groesen, 13–34. Amsterdam: Amsterdam University Press, 2007.
———. "Sephardic Immigration into the Dutch Republic, 1595–1672." *Studia Rosenthalia* 23 (Fall 1989): 45–53.
Israel, Jonathan and Stuart B. Schwartz, eds. *Expansion of Tolerance: Religion in Dutch Brazil (1624–1654)*. Amsterdam: Amsterdam University Press, 2007.
Jackiewicz, Edward L. and Fernando J. Bosco, eds. *Placing Latin America: Contemporary Themes in Geography*. 4th edition. London: Rowman & Littlefield, 2020.
James, Preston E., and Geoffrey J. Martin. *All Possible Worlds: A History of Geographical Ideas*. 2nd ed. New York: John Wiley & Sons, Inc., [1972] 1981.
Jarnagin, Laura, ed. *Portuguese and Luso-Asian Legacies in Southeast Asia, 1511–2011: The Making of the Luso-Asian World*. Vols. 1 and 2. Singapore: Institute of Southeast Asian Studies, 2011.

Johnson, H. B. "Portuguese Settlement, 1500–1580." In *Colonial Brazil*, edited by Leslie Bethell, 1–39. University of Cambridge Press, [1984] 1991.

Kagan, Richard L., and Philip D. Morgan, eds. *Atlantic Diaspora: Jews, Conversos, and Crypto-Jews in the Age of Mercantilism, 1500–1800*. Baltimore: The Johns Hopkins University Press, 2009.

———. "Preface." In *Atlantic Diaspora: Jews, Conversos, and Crypto-Jews in the Age of Mercantilism, 1500–1800*, edited by Richard L. Kagan and Philip D. Morgan, vii–xvii. Baltimore: The Johns Hopkins University Press, 2009.

Kamen, Henry. *Inquisition and Society in Spain in the Sixteenth and Seventeenth Centuries*. London: Weidenfeld and Nicolson, 1985

Kaplan, David. H. *Navigating Ethnicity: Segregation, Placemaking, and Difference*. Lanham, MD: Rowman & Littlefield, 2018.

Kaplan, Yosef. "The Curaçao and Amsterdam Jewish Communities in the 17th and 18th Centuries." *American Jewish History* 72, no. 2 (1982): 193–211.

———. "The Portuguese Jews in Amsterdam. From Forced Conversion to a Return to Judaism." *Studia Rosenthalia* 15, no. 1 (1981): 37–51.

Kaufman, Tânia Neumann. "Da Península Ibérica para Pernambuco ... Eles vieram para ficar." In *Identidade e cidadania: como se expressa o judaísmo brasileiro*, edited by Helena Lewin, 9–20. Rio de Janeiro: Centro Edelstein de Pesquisas Sociais, 2009.

———. "Novos personagens. Novas identidades. O marranismo contemporâneo em Pernambuco." In Lewin, H., coordinator. *Judaísmo e modernidade:* suas múltiplas inter-relações [online], 133–146. Rio de Janeiro: Centro Edelstein de Pesquisas Sociais, 2009.

———. *Passos perdidos, história recuperada: A presença judaica em Pernambuco*. Recife: Editôra Bagaço, 2000.

Kayserling, Meyer. "The Colonization of America by Jews." *Publications of the American Jewish Historical Society* 2 (1894): 73–76.

Kent, R. K. "Revolt in Bahia: 24–25, January 1835." *Journal of Social History* 3, no. 4 (1970): 334–356.

Kent, Robert B. *Latin America: Regions and People*. New York: Guilford Press, 2006.

Klein, Misha. *Kosher Feijoada and Other Paradoxes of Jewish Life in São Paulo*. Gainesville: University of Florida Press, 2016.

Klooster, Wim. "Communities of Port Jews and Their Contacts in the Dutch Atlantic World." *Jewish History* 20, no. 2 (2006): 129–145.

———. *The Dutch Moment. War, Trade, and Settlement in the Seventeenth-Century Atlantic World*. Ithaca and London: Cornell University Press, 2016.

———. "Networks of Colonial Entrepreneurs: The Founders of the Jewish Settlements in Dutch America, 1650s and 1660s." In *Atlantic Diaspora: Jews, Conversos, and Crypto-Jews in the Age of Mercantilism, 1500–1800*, edited by Richard L. Kagan and Philip D. Morgan, 33–49. Baltimore: The Johns Hopkins University Press, 2009.

Knivet, Anthony. *The Admirable Adventures and Strange Fortunes of Master Anthony*

Knivet: An English Pirate in Sixteenth-Century Brazil, edited by Vivien Kogut Lessa de Sá. New York: Cambridge University Press, 2015.

Koen, E. M. "The Earliest Sources Relating to the Portuguese Jews in the Municipal Archives of Amsterdam up to 1620." *Studia Rosenthaliana* 4, no. 1 (1970): 25–42.

Kogman-Appel, Katrin. "The Geographical Concept of the Catalan mappamundi." In *Knowledge in Translation: Global Patterns of Scientific Exchange, 1000–1800 CE*, edited by Patrick Manning and Abigail Owen, 19–40. University of Pittsburgh, PA: Pittsburgh Press, 2018.

Largman, Esther Regina, and Robert M. Levine. "Jews in the Tropics. Bahian Jews in the Early Twentieth Century." *The Americas* 43, no. 2 (1986): 159–170.

Leite, Humberto Ferreira. *História dos judeus: no Seridó do RN, no sertão da Paraíba, na Serra da Borborema*. Natal, História e Arqueologia, Universidade Federal do Rio Grande do Norte, UFRN, 2011.

Leite, Naomi. *Unorthodox Kin: Portuguese Marranos and the Global Search for Belonging*. Oakland: University of California Press, 2017.

Lesser, Jeffrey. "Continuity and Change within an Immigrant Community: The Jews of São Paulo, 1924–1945." *Luso-Brazilian Review* 25 no. 2 (1988): 45–58.

———. "Jewish Brazilians or Brazilian Jews? A Reflection of Brazilian Ethnicity." *Shofar* 19, no. 3 (2001): 65–72.

———. "How the Jews Became Japanese and Other Stories of Nation and Ethnicity." *Jewish History* 18, no. 1 (2004): 7–17.

———. *Negotiating National Identity: Immigrants, Minorities, and the Struggle for Ethnicity in Brazil*. Durham: Duke University Press, 1999.

———. *Welcoming the Undesirables: Brazil and the Jewish Question*. Berkeley and Los Angeles: University of California Press, 1995.

Lester, Toby. *The Fourth Part of the World: The Race to the Ends of the Earth, and the Epic Story of the Map that Gave America its Name*. New York: Free Press, 2009.

Levine, Robert M. "Brazil's Jews during the Vargas Era and After." *Luso-Brazilian Review* 5, no. 1 (1968): 45–58.

———. "Research on Brazilian Jewry: An Overview." *Canadian Journal of Latin American and Caribbean Studies* 20, no. 39 (1995): 227–237.

Levy, Daniela. "Anti-Jewish 'Propaganda' in Brazil under Dutch Occupation." In *Global Antisemitism: A Crisis of Modernity*, edited by Charles Asher Small, 319–326. Leiden: Netherlands: Brill, 2013.

———. *De Recife para Manhattan: Os Judeus na Formação de Nova York*. São Paulo: Editora Planeta do Brasil, 2018.

Lewin, Helena, ed. *Identidade e cidadania: como se expressa o judaísmo brasileiro*. Rio de Janeiro: Centro Edelstein de Pesquisas Sociais, 2009.

———. *Judaísmo e Globalização: Espaços e Temporalidades*. Rio de Janeiro: Programa de Estudos Judaicos, Viveiros de Castro Editora Ldta., 2010.

Lewis, Martin W. "Global Ignorance." *Geographical Review* 90, no. 4 (2000): 603–28.

Ley, Charles David. "The Discovery of Brazil. Letter of Pedro Vaz de Caminha, written in Porto Seguro of Vera Cruz on the First Day of May in the Year 1500." In

Portuguese Voyages, 1498–1663: Tales from the Great Age of Discovery, 39–60. London: Phoenix Press, [1947] 2000.

———, ed. *Portuguese Voyages, 1498–1663: Tales from the Great Age of Discovery*. London: Phoenix Press, [1947] 2000.

Library of Congress. "The Portuguese Role in Exploring and Mapping the New World," https://www.loc.gov/rr/hispanic/portam/role.html, accessed January 2022.

Liebman, Seymour. B. "The Great Conspiracy in Peru." *The Americas* 28, no. 2 (1971): 176–190.

Lima, Lana Lage da Gama. *Confissão pelo avesso: o crime de solicitação no Brasil Colonial*. Doctoral Dissertation. Universidade de São Paulo, São Paulo, 1991.

Lipiner, Elias. *Gaspar da Gama, um Converso na Frota de Cabral*. Rio de Janeiro, Nova Fronteira, 1987.

———. *Izaque de Castro: o mancebo que veio preso do Brasil*. Recife: FUNDAJ, Editora Massangana, 1992.

———. *Os judaizantes nas capitanias de cima*. São Paulo: Brasiliense, 1969.

Livingstone, David N. *The Geographical Tradition: Episodes in the History of a Contested Enterprise*. Malden: Blackwell Press, 1992.

Lockhart, James, and Stuart B. Schwartz. *Early Latin America: A History of colonial Spanish America and Brazil*. U.K.: Cambridge University Press, [1983] 1984.

Loewenstamm, Kurt. *Vultos Judaicos no Brasil: uma contribuição à história dos judeus no Brasil*. Rio de Janeiro: Livraria Editora A Noite, 1949.

Londoño, Fernando Torres. "A Historiografia dos Séculos XX e XXI Sobre os Jesuítas no Período Colonial. Conferindo Sentidos a uma Presença: Do Nascimento do Brasil à Globalização. *Projeto História, São Paulo* 64 (January–April 2019): 10–40.

Lopes, Bruno. "As Contas da Inquisição Portuguesa: O Exemplo dos Tribunais de Évora e Lisboa (1701–1755)," *Revista de História da Sociedade e da Cultura* 16, no. 195 (2016): 201–210.

López-Salazar, Ana Isabel. "Marcocci, Giuseppe & Paiva, José Pedro: História da Inquisição Portuguesa. (1536–1821), Lisboa: A Esfera dos Livros, 2013." *E-Journal of Portuguese History* 11, no. 2 (Winter 2013): 127–137.

Maia, Angela Maria Vieira. *À sombra do medo: Cristãos velhos e cristãos novos nas capitanias do açúcar*. Rio de Janeiro: Oficina Cadernos de Poesia, 1995.

Maio, Marcos Chor. "'Estoque semita': A presença dos judeus em Casa-Grande & Senzala." *Luso-Brazilian Review* 36, no. 1 (1995): 95–110.

Maio, Marcos Chor and Carlos Eduardo Calaça. "Um balanço da bibliografia sobre o anti-semitismo no Brasil." In *Os Judeus no Brasil: Inquisição, imigração e identidade*, edited by Keila Grinberg, 423–470. Rio de Janeiro: Civlzação Brasileira, 2005.

Maio, Marcos Chor, Carlos Eduardo Calaça, and Nelson H. Vieira. "New Christians and Jews in Brazil: Migrations and Antisemitism," translated by Nelson H. Vieira. *Shofar. Special Issue: The Jewish Diaspora of Latin America* 19, no. 3 (2001): 73–85.

Mann, Charles C. *1491: New Revelations of the Americas Before Columbus*. New York: Vintage Books, 2006.

Manning, Patrick, and Abigail Owen, eds. *Knowledge in Translation: Global Patterns of Scientific Exchange, 1000–1800 CE*. University of Pittsburgh, PA: Pittsburgh Press, 2018.

Marcocci, Giuseppe. "Forgers and Martyrs: Conflicting Histories of the Portuguese Inquisition (1598–1647)." *The Journal of Baroque Studies* 1, no. 2 (2017): 51–64.

———. "Toward a History of the Portuguese Inquisition Trends in Modern Historiography (1974–2009)." *Revue de l'histoire des religions* 3 (2010): 355–393.

Marcus, Alan P. "Brazilian Immigration to the United States and the Geographical Imagination." *Geographical Review* 99, no. 4 (2009b): 481–498.

———. *Confederate Exodus: Environmental and Social Forces in the Migration of U.S. Southerners to Brazil*. Lincoln: University of Nebraska Press, 2021.

———. "The Dangers of the Geographical Imagination in the U.S. Eugenics Movement." *Geographical Review* 1, no. 111 (2021): 36–56.

———. "(Re)Creating Places and Spaces in Two Countries: Brazilian Transnational Migration Processes." *Journal of Cultural Geography* 26, no. 2 (2009a): 173–198.

———. "Rethinking Brazil's Place within Latin Americanist Geography." *Journal of Latin American Geography* 10, no. 1 (2011a): 129–147.

———. "Sex, Color, and Geography: Racialized Relations in Brazil and Its Predicaments." *Annals of the Association of American Geographers* 103, no. 5 (2013): 1282–1299.

———. Using "Autogeography," sense of place and place-based approaches in the pedagogy of geographic thought, *Journal of Geography in Higher Education* 47, no. 1 (2023): 71–84.

———. "Where is the Geography? The Geographical Predicaments of the Panethnic terms, "Hispanic" and "Latino." *Journal of Latin American Geography* 19, no. 2 (2020): 170–190.

Margarido, Alfredo. *Le rôle des juifs dans l'expansion européenne*. Andorra: Universitat d'Estiui Tardor d'Andorra, 1984.

Mark, Peter, and José da Silva Horta. *The Forgotten Diaspora: Jewish Communities in West Africa and the Making of the Atlantic World*. NY: Cambridge University Press. 2011.

Markens, Isaac. *The Hebrews in America*. New York, Pub. by the author, 1888. Image. Retrieved from the Library of Congress, www.loc.gov/item/03004959/.

Marks, Robert B. *The Origins of the Modern World: A Global and Ecological Narrative*. Lanham, Maryland, Rowman & Littlefield, 2002.

Martins, Hugo. *Os judeus portugueses de Hamburgo: a história de uma comunidade mercantil no século XVII*. Firenze, Italy: Firenze University Press, 2021.

———. "Women and Communal Discipline in the Portuguese Nation of Hamburg during the Seventeenth Century." *E-Journal of Portuguese History* 18, no. 2 (December 2020): 22–42.

Marvell, Alan and David Simm. "Unravelling the Geographical Palimpsest Through Fieldwork." *Geography* 101, no. 3 (2016): 125–136.

Matteo, Salvadore. "The Ethiopian Age of Exploration: Prester John's Discovery of Europe, 1306–1458." *Journal of World History* 21, no. 4 (2010): 593–627.

Mattos, Hebe. "'Pretos' and 'Pardos' between the Cross and the Sword: Racial Categories in Seventeenth Century Brazil". *Revista Europea de Estudios Latinoamericanos y del Caribe* 80 (April 2006): 43–55.

Mauro, Frédéric. "Political and economic structures of empire." In *Colonial Brazil*, edited by Leslie Bethell, 39–67. University of Cambridge Press, [1984] 1991.

Mello, José Antônio Gonsalves de. "The Dutch Calvinists and Religious Toleration in Portuguese America." *The Americas* 14, no. 4 (1958): 485–488.

———, ed. *Fontes para a história do Brasil holandês: A economia açucareira*. Recife: MEC/SPHAN, 1981.

———. *Gente da Nação: Cristãos e judeus em Pernambuco, 1542–1654*. 2nd ed. Recife: Fundação Joaquim Nabuco, 1996.

———. *Tempo dos Flamengos*. Rio de Janeiro: J. Olympio Editores, 1947.

Mello, José Antônio Gonsalves de, and Cleonir Xavier de Albuquerque, eds. *Cartas de Duarte Coelho a el Rei*. Recife: Fundação Joaquim Nabuco, Editora Masanga, 1967.

Mello, Lucius de. *A Travessia da Terra Vermelha: Uma Saga dos Refugiados Judeus no Brasil*. São Paulo: Novo Século Editôra, 2007.

Melville, Elinor G. K. *A Plague of Sheep: Environmental Consequences in the Conquest of Mexico*. UK: Cambridge University Press, 1994.

Merchant, Carolyn. *Reinventing Eden: The Fate of Nature in Western Culture*. New York: Routledge, 2004

Merrill, Gordon. "The Role of Sephardic Jews in the British Caribbean Area during the Seventeenth Century." *Caribbean Studies* 4, no. 3 (1964): 32–49.

Metcalf, Alida C. *Go-betweens and the Colonization of Brazil, 1500–1600*. Austin: University of Texas Press, 2005.

Meuwese, Mark. "From Dutch Allies to Portuguese Vassals. Indigenous Peoples in the Aftermath of Dutch Brazil." In *The Legacy of Dutch Brazil*, edited by Michiel van Groesen, 59–76. New York: Cambridge University Press, 2014.

Mignolo, Walter D. *The Idea of Latin America*. Malden, MA: Blackwell Publishing, 2005.

Ministério da Defesa, Exército Brasileiro, "Patriarcas da Força Terrestre," http://www.eb.mil.br/exercito-brasileiro?p_p_id=101&p_p_lifecycle=0&p_p_state=maximized&p_p_mode=view&_101_struts_action=%2Fasset_publisher%2Fview_content&_101_assetEntryId=1360479&_101_type=content&_101_urlTitle=patriarcas-da-forca-terrestre&_101_redirect=http%3A%2F%2Fwww.eb.mil.br%2Fexercito-brasileiro%3Fp_p_id%3D3%26p_p_lifecycle%3D0%26p_p_state%3Dmaximized%26p_p_mode%3Dview%26_3_cur%3D115%26_3_keywords%3Dcampo%2Bgrande%26_3_advancedSearch%3Dfalse%26_3_groupId%3D0%26_3_delta%3D20%26_3_resetCur%3Dfalse%26_3_andOperator%3Dtrue%26_3_struts_action%3D%252Fsearch%252Fsearch&inheritRedirect=true, Accessed January 2021.

Moffitt, John F., and Santiago Sebastián. *O Brave New People: The European Invention of the American Indian*. Albuquerque: University of New Mexico Press, 1996.
Mordoch, Gabriel. "Um cristão-novo nos trópicos: expansão imperial e identidade religiosa nos Diálogos das grandezas do Brasil de Ambrósio Fernandes Brandão." *Colonial Latin American Review* 25, no. 2 (2016): 200–219.
Moreira, António Joaquim. *História dos principais actos e procedimentos da Inquisição em Portugal*. Lisbon: Impresnsa Nacional, [1845] 1980.
Morison, Samuel Eliot. *The Great Explorers: The European Discovery of America. Abridgement of the European Discovery of America: The Northern Voyages and the Southern Voyages*. New York and Oxford: Oxford University Press, 1978.
Moritz Schwarcz, Lilia. *O Espetáculo das Raças: Cientistas, Instituições e a Questão Racial no Brasil 1870–1930*. Editôra Schwartz, São Paulo, Brazil, 1993.
Morrill, Richard L. "A Theoretical Imperative." *Annals of Association of American Geographers* 77, no. 4 (1987): 535–541.
Mucznik, Esther. "Portugal e o resurgimento judaico: Uma heranca de continuidade e ruptura." In *Judaísmo e Globalizacão: Espaços e Temporalidades*, edited by Helena Lewin, 588–598. Rio de Janeiro: Programa de Estudos Judaicos, Viveiros de Castro Editora Ldta., 2010.
Muhana, Adma. "António Vieira: A Jesuit Missionary to the Portuguese Jews of Amsterdam." *Journal of Jesuit Studies* 8, no. 2 (2021): 233–249.
Nascimento, Abdias do. *O Genocídio Do Negro Brasileiro: Processo de Racismo Mascarado*. Editora Paz e Terra, Rio de Janeiro, Brazil, 1978.
Nash, Roy. *The Conquest of Brazil*. New York: AMS Press, [1926] 1969.
Newitt, Malyn. *A History of Portuguese Overseas Expansion, 1400–1668*. London and New York: Routledge, 2005.
Nobles, Melissa. *Shades of Citizenship: Race and the Census in Modern Politics*. Stanford: Stanford University Press, 2000.
Novinsky, Anita Waingort. "A 'Conspiração do Silêncio.' Uma História Desconhecida sobre os Bandeirantes Judeus no Brasil," May 8, 2021, https://congresojudio.org/ed-n-20-a-conspiracao-do-silencio/.
———. "Marranos and the Inquisition: On the Gold Route in Minas Gerais, Brazil." 215–241. In *The Jews and the Expansion of Europe to the West, 1450–1800*, edited by Paolo Bernardini and Norman Fiering. New York and Oxford: Berghahn Books, 2001.
———. "Marranos e a Inquisição: sobre a Rota do Ouro em Minas Gerais." In *Os Judeus no Brasil: Inquisição, imigração e identidade*, edited by Keila Grinberg, 161–196. Rio de Janeiro: Civilzação Brasileira, 2005.
———. "Prisioneiros no Brasil." In *Populações (Con)Vivência e (In)Tolerância*, edited by Eni de Mesquita Samara, 10–18. São Paulo: Universidade de São Paulo, Humanitas, 2004.
———. *Viver nos Tempos da Inquisição*. Perspectiva. São Paulo, 2018.
Novinsky, Anita W. "A Catholic Priest and his Fight for Justice for the Jews: Father Antonio Vieira." *Iggud: Selected Essays in Jewish Studies* 2 (2005): 33–39.

———. *Cristãos-novos na Bahia*. São Paulo: Perspectiva, 1972.

———. "A Historical Bias: The New Christian Collaboration with the Dutch Invaders of Brazil (17th Century)." *Proceedings of the World Congress of Jewish Studies* 2 (1969): 141–154.

———. *Inquisição: prisioneiros do Brasil*. São Paulo: Editôra Expressão e Cultura, 2002.

———. *Inquisição: Prisioneiros do Brasil, Séculos XVI—XIX*. São Paulo: Perspectiva, 2009.

———. "The Inquisition and the Mythic World of a Portuguese Kabbalist in the Eighteenth Century." *Proceedings of the World Congress of Jewish Studies*, Vol. Division B (1993): 115–122.

———. "Jewish Heresy in the Light of New Documents." *Proceedings of the World Congress of Jewish Studies* 2 (August 13–19, 1973): 111–121.

———. "The Last Marranos. Anita Novinsky and Amilcar Paulo's diary from a recent visit to Portugal," *Commentary Magazine*, May 1967, https://www.commentary.org/articles/anita-novinsky/the-last-marranos/

———. "Marranos and Marranism—a New Approach." *Jewish Studies* 40 (2000): 5–20.

———. "The Myth of the Marrano Names," *Revue des Études Juives* 165, no. 3–4 (2006): 445–456.

———. "Padre Antonio Vieira, the Inquisition, and the Jews." *Jewish History* 6, no. 1–2 (1992): 151–162.

———. "Ser Marrano em Minas Colonial." *Revista Brasileira de História* 21, no. 40, São Paulo, February 22, 2021, https://www.scielo.br/j/rbh/a/m9BHw96SxvjbjZwVbkvfpqr/?format=pdf&lang=pt, 2001.

Novinsky, Anita W., Daniela Levy, E. Ribeiro, and L. Gorenstein. *Os Judeus que Construíram o Brasil: Fontes Inéditas para Uma Nova Visão da História*. São Paulo: Editôra Planeta do Brasil, 2016.

Oboler, Suzanne. *Ethnic Labels, Latino Lives: Identity and the Politics of (Re)Presentation in the United States*. Minneapolis MN: University of Minneapolis Press, 1995.

Olival, Fernanda. "The Portuguese Inquisition in the Historical Writing of J. Romero Magalhães." *E-Journal of Portuguese History* 17, no. 1 (June 2019): 124–135.

Oliveira, Monique Silva de. *Inquisição e Cristãos-Novos no Rio de Janeiro: O Caso da Família Azeredo (c.1701–1720)*. Universidade Federal Fluminense, Instituto de Ciências Humanas e Filosofia, Program de Pós-Graduacao em História, Disertação, Mestrado em História, 2016.

Oppenheim, Samuel. "The Early History of the Jews in New York, 1654–1664. Some New Matter on the Subject." *Publications of the American Jewish Historical Society* 18 (1909): 1–91.

———. "An Early Jewish Colony Western Guiana, 1658–1666: And Its Relation to the Jews in Surinam, Cayenne and Tobago." *Publications of the American Jewish Historical Society* 16 (1907): 95–186.

———. "The First Settlement of the Jews in Newport: Some New Matter on the Subject." *Publications of the American Jewish Historical Society* 34 (1937): 1–10.

———. "List of Wills of Jews in the British West Indies Prior to 1800." *Publications of the American Jewish Historical Society* 32 (1931): 55–64.

———. "A Newspaper Account of an Auto Da Fe in Lisbon in 1726, in Which a Jew, a Native of Bahia, South America, Was Burnt." *Publications of the American Jewish Historical Society* 22 (1914): 180–82.

Orfali, Moisés. "The Dutch Occupation and Defense of Brazil: The Question of the Support of Jews and Conversos." *Journal of Levantine Studies* 6 (Summer/Winter, 2016): 129–152.

Paim, Antonio. "Anita Novinsky—Inquisição. Prisioneiros do Brasil (Séculos XVI a XIX)." *Resenha* 2, no. 7 (January–March): 2010.

Pécora, Alcyr, and Antônio Vieira. *Sermões*. Vol. 1. São Paulo: Hedra Editora, 2003.

Pena, Sérgio D. J., Denise R. Carvalho-Silva, Vânia F. Prado, and Fabrício R. Santos. "Retrato Molecular." *Ciência Hoje* 27, no. 159 (2010): 16–25.

Pereira, Kenia Maria de Almeida. "O tribunal do Santo Ofício nas óperas de Antônio José da Silva, o Judeu." *Arquivo Maaravi: Revista Digital de Estudos Judaicos da UFMG* 15, no. 28 (May 2021).

Perelis, Ronnie. *Narratives from the Sephardic Atlantic: Blood and Faith*. Bloomington: Indiana University Press, 2016.

Peters, Edward. *Inquisition*. Berkeley and Los Angeles: University of California Press, [1988] 1989.

Pieroni, Geraldo. "Outcasts from the Kingdom: The Inquisition and the Banishment of New Christians to Brazil." In *The Jews and the Expansion of Europe to the West, 1450–1800*, edited by Paolo Bernardini and Norman Fiering, 242–251. New York and Oxford: Berghahn Books, 2001.

Pijning, Ernst. "New Christians as Sugar Cultivators and Traders in the Portuguese Atlantic, 1450–1800." In *The Jews and the Expansion of Europe to the West, 1450–1800*, edited by Paolo Bernardini and Norman Fiering, 485–500. New York and Oxford: Berghahn Books, 2001.

Pinho, Patricia de Santana. *Mapping Diaspora: African American Roots Tourism in Brazil*. Chapel Hill: The University of North Carolina Press, 2018.

Poettering, Jorun. *Migrating Merchants: Trade, Nation, and Religion in Seventeenth-Century Hamburg and Portugal*, translated by Kenneth Kronenburg. Berlin and Boston: Walter de Gruyter Oldenbourg, 2019.

Pomeranz, Kenneth, and Steven Topik. *The World that Trade Created: Society, Culture, and the World Economy, 1400 to the Present*. New York and London: M. E. Sharpe, 1999.

Ponte, Mark. "'Al de swarten die hier ter stede comen': Een Afro-Atlantische gemeenschap in zeventiende-eeuws Amsterdam." *Tijdschrift voor Sociale en Economische Geschiedenis* 15, no. 4 (2019): 33–62.

Prado, João Fernando de Almeida. *Primeiros Povoadores do Brasil, 1500–1530*. São Paulo and Rio de Janeiro: Companhia Editora Nacional, 1939.

Prado, Paulo. *Retrato do Brasil: Ensaio sobre a tristeza brasileira*. Rio de Janeiro: Livraria José Olympio, 1962.

Rac, Katalin Franciska, and Lenny A. Ureña Valerio, eds. *Jewish Experiences Across the Americas: Local Histories through Global Lenses.* Gainesville: University of Florida, 2022.

Randles, W. G. L. "The Alleged Nautical School Founded in the Fifteenth Century at Sagres by Prince Henry of Portugal. Called the 'Navigator.'" *Imago Mundi* 45, no. 1 (1993): 20–28.

Ravenstein, Ernest George. "The Laws of Migration." *Journal of the Royal Statistical Society* 48, no. 2 (1885): 167–227.

———. "Vasco da Gama's First Voyage." Translation of *Roteiro da viagem que em discobrimento da India pelo Cabo da Boa Esperança fez Dom Vasco da Gama.* F. R. G. S., Hakluyt Society, 1898. In *Portuguese Voyages, 1498–1663. Tales from the Great Age of Discovery*, edited by Charles D. Ley. London: Phoenix Press, [1947] 2000.

Reclus, Élisée. *The Earth and Its Inhabitants: South America*, edited by A. H. Keane. Vol. 2, *Amazonia and La Plata.* New York: D. Appleton and Company, 1893.

Rein, Raanan, Stefan H. Rinke, and Nadia Zysman, eds. *The New Ethnic Studies in Latin America.* Leiden and Boston: Brill, 2017.

Resende, Maria Leônia Chaves de, and Rafael José de Sousa. "Por temer o Santo Ofício." As denúncias de Minas Gerais no Tribunal da Inquisição (século XVIII)." *Varia Historia, Belo Horizonte* 32, no. 58 (2016): 203–224.

Roitman, Jessica Vance. "Portuguese Jews, Amerindians, and the Frontiers of Encounter in Colonial Suriname." *New West Indian Guide/Nieuwe West-Indische Gids* 88, no. 1–2 (2014): 18–52.

Romeiras, Francisco Malta. "The Inquisition and the Censorship of Science in Early Modern Europe: Introduction." *Annals of Science* 77, no. 1 (2020): 1–9.

Rosenstein, Marc, J. *Turning Points in Jewish History.* University of Nebraska Press, Jewish Publication Society, 2018.

Roth, Cecil. *A Life of Menasseh Ben Israel: Rabbi, Printer, and Diplomat.* Philadelphia: The Jewish Publication Society of America, 1934.

———. "The Middle Period of Anglo-Jewish History (1290–1655) Reconsidered." *Transactions (Jewish Historical Society of England)* 19 (1955–1959): 1–12.

Russell-Wood, A. J. R. "The Gold Cycle circa 1690–1750." In *Colonial Brazil*, edited by Leslie Bethell, 190–243. Cambridge University Press, UK, 1987.

———. *The Portuguese Empire, 1415–1808: A World on the Move.* Baltimore and London: The Johns Hopkins University Press, [1992] 1998.

Sá, Vivien Kogut Lessa de, ed. *The Admirable Adventures and Strange Fortunes of Master Anthony Knivet: An English Pirate in Sixteenth-Century Brazil.* New York: Cambridge University Press, 2015.

Salomon, Herman P. "K. K. Shearith Israel's First Language: Portuguese." *Tradition: A Journal of Orthodox Jewish Thought* 30, no. 1 (1995): 74–84.

Salvador, José Gonçalves. *Os cristãos-Novos em Minas Gerais durante o Ciclo do Ouro.* São Paulo: Pioneira, 1992.

———. "Os *cristãos-novos*: o *povoamento* e a *conquista* do *solo brasileiro*." *Revista de História* 54, no. 108 (December 1976): 549–553.

———. *Cristãos novos, jesuítas e Inquisição*. São Paulo: Pioneira, 1969.
Samara, Eni de Mesquita. *Populações (Con)Vivência e (In)Tolerância*. São Paulo: Universidade de São Paulo, Humanitas, 2004.
Samuel, Edgar. "Some Eighteenth-Century Refugees from Brazil." *Jewish Historical Studies* 43 (2011): 89–96.
Samuel, Edgar Roy. "Jews in Jacobean London." *Transactions (Jewish Historical Society of England)* 18 (1953–1955): 171–230.
Santiago, Diogo Lopes. *História da guerra de Pernambuco: e feitos memoráveis do mestre de campo, João Fernandes Vieira, herói digno de eterna memória, primeiro aclamador da Guerra*. Série 350 Anos, vol. 5, *Restauração pernambucana*. Governo de Pernambuco, Secretaria de Turismo, Cultura e Esportes, Fundação do Patrimônio Histórico e Artístico Pernambuco, Diretoria de Assuntos Culturais, 1984.
Santos, Nelson Santana. *Entre Meandros da Tolerância: Cristãos-Novos, Judeus e as Especifidades da Institucionalização do Judaísmo no Contexto Inter-Religioso do Brasil Holandês (1630–1654)*. Universidade Federal de Sergipe, Programa de Pós-Graduação em Ciências da Religião, Mestrado em Ciências da Religião. Master's Thesis. São Cristovão, Sergipe, 2017.
Saraiva, Antônio José. *The Marrano Factory: The Portuguese Inquisition and Its New Christians 1536–1765*, translated, revised, and augmented by H. P. Salomon and I. S. D. Sassoon. Leiden, Netherlands: Brill, [1969] 2001.
Sarenbrenick, Salomão. *Breve história dos judeus no Brasil*. Rio de Janeiro: Editora Biblos, 1962.
Sauer, Carl O. *The Early Spanish Main*. Berkeley and Los Angeles: University of California Press, [1966] 1969.
———. "The Morphology of Landscape." *University of California Publications in Geography* 2, no. 2 (1925): 19–53.
———. *Northern Mists*. San Francisco, California: Turtle Island Foundation, [1968] 1973.
———. *Sixteenth-Century North America: The Land and the People as Seen by Europeans*. Berkeley and Los Angeles: University of California Press, 1971.
Schaumloeffel, Marco. A. "Papiamentu and the Brazilian Connection Established through the Sephardic Jews." *LETRAS* 67 (2020): 75–89.
Schetini Júnior, Ademir. "Cristãs-novas e criptojudaismo na Bahia setecentista." Masters's thesis, Universidade Federal Fluminenese, Instituto de História, Programa de Pós-Graduação em História, Niterói, Rio de Janeiro, 2018.
Schorsch, Jonathan. " Cristâos-novos, Judaísmo, Negros e Cristianismo nos Primórdios do Mundo Atlântico Moderno. Uma Visão Segundo Fontes Inquisitoriais." In *Diálogos da Conversão: Missionários, Índios, Negros e Judeus no Contexto Ibero-Americano do Período Barroco*, edited by Lúcia Helena Costigan, 155–184. Campinas: Universidade de Campinas, 2005.
———. *Swimming the Christian Atlantic: Judeoconversos, Afroiberians and Amerindians in the Seventeenth Century*. Leiden and Boston: Brill, 2009.

Schwarcz, Lilia M., and Heloisa M. Starling. *Brazil: A Biography*. Translated from the Portuguese. New York: Farrar, Straus and Giroux, [2015] 2018.

Schwartz, Stuart B. *All Can Be Saved: Religious Tolerance and Salvation in the Iberian Atlantic World*. New Haven and London: Yale University Press, 2008.

———. "A Commonwealth in Itself. The Early Brazilian Sugar Industry, 1550–1670." In *Tropical Babylons: Sugar and the Making of the Atlantic World, 1450–1680*, edited by Stuart B. Schwartz, 158–200. Chapel Hill: University of North Carolina, 2004.

———, ed. *Early Brazil: A Documentary Collection to 1700*. Translated by Clive Willis and Stuart B. Schwartz. Cambridge and New York: University of Cambridge Press, 2010.

———. "Introduction." In *Tropical Babylons: Sugar and the Making of the Atlantic World, 1450–1680*, edited by Stuart B. Schwartz, 1–26. Chapel Hill: University of North Carolina, 2004.

———. "Looking for a New Brazil: Crisis and Rebirth in the Atlantic World after the Fall of Pernambuco." In *The Legacy of Dutch Brazil*, edited by Michiel van Groesen, 41–58. New York: Cambridge University Press, 2014.

———. *Os Cristãos-Novos em Portugal No Século XX*. Lisbon: Emprêsa Portuguesa de Livros, Ltda, 1925.

———. "Plantations and peripheries, c.1580–c.1750." In *Colonial Brazil*, edited by Leslie Bethell, 67–145. University of Cambridge Press, [1984] 1991.

———. *Segredos internos: engenhos e escravos na sociedade colonial, 1550–1835*. São Paulo: Companhia das Letras, 1988.

———. *Slaves, Peasants and Rebels: Reconsidering Brazilian Slavery*. University of Illinois Press: Urbana and Chicago, 1992.

———. *Tropical Babylons: Sugar and the Making of the Atlantic World, 1450–1680*. Chapel Hill: University of North Carolina, 2004.

———. "The Uncourted Menina: Brazil's Portuguese Heritage." *Luso-Brazilian Review* 2, no.1 (1965): 67–81.

Seed, Patricia. "Celestial Navigation." In *Knowledge in Translation: Global Patterns of Scientific Exchange, 1000–1800 CE*, edited by Patrick Manning and Abigail Owen, 262–175. University of Pittsburgh, PA: Pittsburgh Press, 2018.

———. *Ceremonies of Possession in Europe's Conquest of the New World, 1492–1640*. 14th ed. New York: Cambridge University Press [1995] 2010.

———. "Jewish Scientists and the Origin of Modern Navigation." In *The Jews and the Expansion of Europe to the West, 1450–1800*, edited by Paolo Bernardini and Norman Fiering, 73–85. New York and Oxford: Berghahn Books, 2001.

Serafim Leite, S. J., ed. *História da Companhia de Jesus no Brasil*. Vol. 5. Rio de Janeiro and Lisbon: Civilização Brasileira, 1945.

Serrano, Juan Ignacio Pulido. "Plural Identities: The Portuguese New Christians." *Jewish History* 25, no. 2 (2011): 129–151.

Shillman, Bernard. *A Short History of the Jews in Ireland*. Cahill & Co. Ltd. Dublin: Parkgate Printing Works, 1960.

Shillman, Bernard, and Lucien Wolf. "The Jewish Cemetery at Ballybough in Dublin." *Transactions Jewish Historical Society of England* 11, no. 11 (1924): 143–167.
Shohat, Ella, and Robert Stam. "Genealogies of Orientalism and Occidentalism: Sephardi Jews, Muslims, and the Americas." *Studies in American Jewish Literature* 35, no. 1 (2016): 13–32Silva, Leonardo Dantas. *Rabi Aboab da Fonseca*. São Paulo: Morashá, 2001.
Silva, Leonardo Dantas. *A Primeira comunidade Judaica do Novo Mundo*. In *A Fênix ou O Eterno Retorno: 460 anos da presença Judaica em Pernambuco*, 27–81. Brasília: Ministério da Cultura, Programa Monumenta, 2001.
———, ed. *Primeira Visitação do Santo Ofício às partes do Brasil: Confissões e denunciações de Pernambuco, 1593–1595*. Preface by José Antonio Gonsalves de Mello (coleção Pernambucana segunda fase. Vol. 14). Recife: FUNDARPE, diretoria de assuntos culturais, 1984.
Silverblatt, Irene. "Heresies and Colonial Geopolitics." *Romanic Review* 103, no. 1/2 (2012): 65–80.
Simms, Norman. "Being Crypto-Jewish in Colonial Brazil (1500–1822): Brushing History Against the Grain." *Journal of Religious History* 31, no. 4 (2007): 421–450.
Siqueira, Sônia A. "O cristão novo Bento Teixeira. Cripto-judaismo no Brasil Colônia." In *Revista de História São Paulo* 90 (1972): 395–467.
———. "O Poder da Inquisição e a Inquisição como Poder." *Revista Brasileira de História das Religiões* 1, no. 1 (2008): 84–93.
Skidmore, Thomas E. *Brazil: Five Centuries of Changes*. NY: Oxford University Press, 1999.
Sluyter, Andrew. *Colonialism and Landscape: Postcolonial Theory and Applications*. NY: Rowman & Littlefield, 2001.
Smith, David Grant. "Old Christian Merchants and the Foundation of the Brazil Company, 1649." *Hispanic American Historical Review* 54, no. 2 (1974): 233–259.
Smith, Neil. "'Academic War over the Field of Geography': The Elimination of Geography at Harvard, 1947–1951." *Annals of the Association of American Geographers* 77, no. 2 (1987): 155–172.
Southey, Robert. *History of Brazil*. Vols. 1 and 2. New York: Lenox Hill Push & Dist., 1822.
Souza, Cândido Eugênio Domingues de. "'Perseguidores da espécie humana.' capitães negreiros da Cidade da Bahia na primeira metade do século XVIII." Master's thesis. Programa de Pós-Graduação em História, Universidade Federal da Bahia, Salvador, 2011.
Souza, Laura de Mello e. *O diabo e a Terra de Santa Cruz: feitiçaria e religiosidade popular no Brasil colonial*. São Paulo: Companhia das Letras, 2011.
Staden, Hans. *Hans Staden's True History: An Account of Cannibal Captivity in Brazil*, edited and translated by Neil L. Whitehead and Michael Harbsmeier. Durham and London: Duke University Press, 2008.
Stavans, Ilan. *The Seventh Heaven: Travels Through Jewish Latin America*. Pittsburgh: University of Pittsburgh Press, 2019.

Steinacher, Gerald. *Humanitarians at War: The Red Cross in the Shadow of the Holocaust.* Oxford and New York, NY: Oxford University Press, 2017.

Stern, Horace. "The First Jewish Settlers in America: Their Struggle for Religious Freedom." *The Jewish Quarterly Review* 45, no. 4 (1955): 289–296.

Stern, Steve J. *Peru's Indian Peoples and the Challenge of Spanish Conquest: Huamanga to 1640.* 2nd ed. The University of Wisconsin Press, Wisconsin, 1993.

Stuczynski, Claude B. "Preconceitos de uma hibridação: judeus e cristãos-novos em Casa-Grande & Senzala." In *Ensaios em homenagem a Alberto Dines: Jornalismo, História, Literatura*, edited by José Luiz Alqueres, 116–155. Rio de Janeiro: Casa Stefan Zweig, 2017.

Stuczynski, Claude B., and Bruno Feitler, eds. *Portuguese Jews, New Christians, and "New Jews": A Tribute to Roberto Bachmann.* Leiden: Brill, 2018.

Studemund-Halévy, Michael. "Sea is History, Sea is Witness: The Creation of a Prosopographical Database for the Sephardic Atlantic." In *Religious Changes and Cultural Transformations in the Early Modern Western Sephardic Communities*, edited by Yosef Kaplan, 487–511. Leiden, Netherlands, 2019.

Studnicki-Gizbert, Daviken. "*La Nación* among the Nations: Portuguese and Other Maritime Trading Diasporas in the Atlantic, Sixteenth to Eighteenth Centuries." In *Atlantic Diaspora: Jews, Conversos, and Crypto-Jews in the Age of Mercantilism, 1500–1800*, edited by Richard L. Kagan and Philip D. Morgan, 75–98. Baltimore: The Johns Hopkins University Press, 2009.

———. *A Nation Upon the Ocean Sea: Portugal's Atlantic Diaspora and the Crisis of the Spanish Empire, 1492–1640.* UK: Oxford University Press, 2007.

Temkin, Samuel. *Luis de Carvajal: The Origins of Nuevo Reino de León.* Santa Fe, New Mexico: Sunstone Press, 2011.

Tortorici, Zeb, ed. *Sexuality and the Unnatural in Colonial Latin America.* University of California Press, 2016.

Trivellato, Francesca. "Beyond Production vs. Consumption and Structure vs. Identity: The Case for a Renewed Jewish Economic History." *American Jewish History* 103, no. 4 (October 2019): 523–526.

———. *The Familiarity of Strangers: The Sephardic Diaspora, Livorno, and Cross-Cultural Trade in the Early Modern Period.* New Haven: Yale University Press, 2009.

Tuan, Yi-Fu. "Humanistic Geography." *Annals of the Association of American Geographers* 66, no. 2 (1976): 266–276.

———. *Topophilia: A Study of Environmental Perception, Attitudes, and Values.* New Jersey, NJ: Prentice-Hall, 1974.

Vainfas, Ronaldo. "Homoerotismo feminino e o Santo Ofício." In *História das mulheres no Brasil*, edited by Mary del Priore, 115–40. São Paulo: Editôra Contexto, 2004.

———. *Jerusalém Colonial: Judeus portugueses no Brasil holandês.* Rio de Janeiro: Civilização Brasileira, 2010.

———, ed. *Santo Ofício da Inquisição de Lisboa: Confissoes da Bahia.* São Paulo: Companhia das Letras, 1997.

———, "Santo Ofício em terra Fluminense—Cristão-novos e Inquisição no Rio de

Janeiro colonial." *Revista Instituto Histórico e Geográfico Brasileiro* 177, no. 471 (2016): 11–44.

———. *Trópico dos pecados: moral, sexualidade e inquisição no Brasil. Segunda edição*. Rio de Janeiro: Civilização Brasileira, 2014.

Vainfas, Ronaldo, and Angelo A. F. Assis. "A esnoga na Bahia: cristãos-novos e cryptojudaismo no Brasil quinhentista." In *Os Judeus no Brasil: Inquisição, imigração e identidade*, edited by Keila Grinberg, 43–64. Rio de Janeiro: Civilização Brasileira, 2005.

Vainfas, Ronaldo, and Jacqueline Hermann. "Judeus e conversos na Ibéria no século XV: sefardismo, heresia, messianismo." In *Os Judeus no Brasil: Inquisição, imigração e identidade*, edited by Keila Grinberg, 15–42. Rio de Janeiro: Civilização Brasileira, 2005.

Vainfas, Ronaldo, and Zeb Tortorici. "Female Homoeroticism, Heresy, and the Holy Office in Colonial Brazil," 77–94. Translated by Luiza Vainfas and Zeb Tortocici. In *Sexuality and the Unnatural in Colonial Latin America*. University of California Press, 2016.

Valentim, Carlos Manuel. "Uma Família de Cristãos-Novos do Entre Douro e Minho: Os Paz. Reprodução Familiar, Formas de Mobildade Social, Mecancia e Poder." Master's dissertation, Faculdade de Letras, University of Lisbon, 2007.

Varnhagen, Francisco Adolfo de. "Brasileiros no auto-de-fé de 1711 to 1767." *Revista do Instituto Histórico e Geográfico Brasileiro* 7 (1845): 52–85.

———. "Carta de Mestre Joao Physico d'el-rei, para o mesmo senhor, De Vera Cruz ao 1 de Maio de 1500." *Revista do Instituto Histórico e Geográfico Brasileiro* 5, no. 19 (1843): 342–344.

Vieira, Alberto. "Sugar Islands: The Sugar Economy of Madeira and the Canaries, 1450–1650." In *Tropical Babylons: Sugar and the Making of the Atlantic World, 1450–1680*, edited by Stuart B. Schwartz, 42–84. Chapel Hill: University of North Carolina, 2004.

Vieira, Fernando Gil Portela. "Os Calaças: Quatro Gerações de uma Família de Cristãos-Novos na Inquisição (Séculos XVII-XVIII)." Master's Thesis. Universidade de São Paulo, Faculdade de Filosofia, Letras e Ciências Humanas, Departamento de História. Programa de Pós-Graduação em História Social, 2015.

Vink, Wieke. *Creole Jews: Negotiating Community in Colonial Suriname*. Leiden: Brill, 2010.

Vogt, John L. "Fernão de Loronha and the Rental of Brazil in 1502: A New Chronology." *The Americas* 24, no. 2 (1967): 153–159.

Wadsworth, James E. *Agents of Orthodoxy: Honor, Status, and the Inquisition in Colonial Pernambuco, Brazil*. Rowman & Littlefield, [2007] 2017.

———. "Children of the Inquisition: Minors as Familiares of the Inquisition in Pernambuco, Brazil, 1613–1821." *Luso-Brazilian Review* 42, no. 1 (2005): 21–43.

———. *In Defense of the Faith: Joaquim Marques de Araújo, A Comissário in the Age of the Inquisitional Decline*. Montreal and Kingston: McGill-Queen's University Press, 2013.

———. "In the Name of the Inquisition: The Portuguese Inquisition and Delegated Authority in Colonial Pernambuco, Brazil." *The Americas* 61, no. 1 (2004): 19–54.

Walker, Timothy D. "Supplying Simples for the Royal Hospital: An Indo-Portuguese Medicinal Garden in Goa (1520–1830)." In *Portuguese and Luso-Asian Legacies in Southeast Asia, 1511–2011: The Making of the Luso-Asian World*. Vol. 1, *Intricacies of Engagement*, edited by Laura Jarnagin, 23–47. Singapore: Institute of Southeast Asian Studies, 2011.

Watkins, Case. *Palm Oil Diaspora: Afro-Brazilian Landscapes and Economies on Bahia's Dendê Coast*. NY: Cambridge University Press, 2021.

Webb, Kempton Evans. *The Changing Face of Northeast Brazil*. NY: Columbia University Press, 1974.

———. *Geography of Latin America: A Regional Analysis*. Foundations of World Regional Series. New Jersey: Prentice-Hall, 1972.

Wexler, Paul. "Ascertaining the position of Judezmo within Ibero-Romance." *Vox Romanica* 36 (1977): 162–95.

Whitehead, Neil L., and Michael Harbsmeier, eds. *Hans Staden's True History: An Account of Cannibal Captivity in Brazil*. Edited and translated by Neil L. Whitehead and Michael Harbsmeier. Durham and London: Duke University Press, 2008.

Wiznitzer, Arnold. "The Exodus from Brazil, and Arrival in New Amsterdam of the Jewish Pilgrim Fathers, 1654." *Publications of the American Jewish Historical Society* 44, no. 2 (1954b): 80–97.

———. "Isaac de Castro, Brazilian Jewish Martyr." *Publications of the American Jewish Historical Society* 47, no. 2 (1957): 63–75.

———. "Jewish Soldiers in Dutch Brazil (1630–1654)." *Publications of the American Jewish Historical Society* 46, no. 1 (1956a): 40–50.

———. *Jews in Colonial Brazil*. Columbia University Press, 1960.

———. "The Jews in the Sugar Industry of Colonial Brazil." *Jewish Social Studies* 18, no. 3 (1956b): 189–198.

———. "The Members of the Brazilian Jewish Community (1648–1653)." *Publications of the American Jewish Historical Society* 42, no. 4 (1953b): 387–395.

———. "The Minute Book of Congregations Zur Israel of Recife and Magen Abraham of Mauricia, Brazil." *Publications of the American Jewish Historical Society* 42, no. 3 (1953c): 217–302.

———. "The Number of Jews in Dutch Brazil (1630–1654)." *Jewish Social Studies* 16, no. 2 (1954a): 107–114.

———. "The Synagogue and Cemetery of the Jewish Community in Recife, Brazil (1630–1654)." *Publications of the American Jewish Historical Society* 43, no. 2 (1953a): 127–130.

Wolf, Lucien. "Crypto-Jews Under the Commonwealth." *Transactions (Jewish Historical Society of England)* 1 (1883–1894): 55–88.

———. "The First English Jew." *Transactions (Jewish Historical Society of England)* 2 (1894–1895): 14–46.

———. "Jews in Elizabethan England." *Transactions (Jewish Historical Society of England)* 11 (1924–1927): 1–91.
———. "Note on the Early History of the Dublin Hebrew Congregation." *Transactions and Miscellanies of the Jewish Historical Society of England* xi (1924–1927): 163–167.
Wolff, Egon. "Judeus, Judaizantes e seus escravos." *Revista do Instituto Histórico e Geográfico Brasileiro* 337 (October–December, 1982): 115–126.
Wolff, Egon, and Frieda Wolff. "Mistaken Identities of Signatories of the Congregation Zur Israel, Recife." *Studia Rosenthalia* 12, no. 1–2 (1978): 91–107.
———. "The Problem of the First Jewish Settlers in New Amsterdam, 1654." *Studia Rosenthalia* 15, no. 2 (1981): 169–177.
Wolff, Philippe. "The 1391 Pogrom in Spain. Social Crisis or Not?" *Past & Present* 50 (1971): 4–18.
Yerushalmi, Yosef Hayim. "Between Amsterdam and New Amsterdam: The Place of Curaçao and the Caribbean in Early Modern Jewish History." *American Jewish History* 72, no. 2 (1982): 172–192.
Young, Theodore. R. "Teaching Brazil in U.S. Universities." In *Envisioning Brazil: A Guide to Brazilian Studies in the United States*, edited by M. C. Eakin and P. R. de Almeida, 52–69. Madison: University of Wisconsin Press, 2005.
Yovel, Yirmiyahu. *The Other Within: The Marranos: Spilt Identity and Emerging Modernity*. Princeton University Press, 2009.
Zeman, Frederic D. "The Amazing Career of Doctor Rodrigo Lopez (?–1594)." *Bulletin of the History of Medicine* 39, no. 4 (1965): 295–308.
Zwerling, Uri. *Os Judeus na Historia do Brasil*. Rio de Janeiro: Outras Letras, 2013.

Index

Abenaca, Joseph, 97
Abof, Isack, 194
ABRADJIN. *See* Brazilian Association of Descendants of Jews from the Inquisition
Abranches, Giraldo de, 76
adelborst ("naval cadet"), 176
aftermath, Portuguese Inquisition, 97–102
Agents of Orthodoxy (Wadsworth), 94
agriculture, colonial Brazil, 137–39
Aguilar, Mosseh Rafael de, 179
Aidoo, Lamonte, 19, 91
Aires, Ines, 4–5
Ajuda, Engenho Nossa Senhora da, 136
Albuquerque, Jerônimo de, 136
Alcoforada, D. Ana, 152
Alencastro, Luís de, 161
All Can Be Saved (Schwartz), 94
Almeida Prado, João Fernando de, 120
Ambrasias, Moses, 194
América Española, 56
Americas, first Jewish settlements in: aftermath of Dutch rule, 191–93; first synagogues, 179–82; immigrants from Amsterdam, 183–85; importance of Jewry in northeast region, 182–83; important figures during Dutch rule in Brazil, 185–89; Jews and Dutch in tropics, 190–91; Jews from Brazil migrating North America to, 193–97; migration after Dutch leaving Brazil, 197–200; northeast Brazil under rule of Dutch, 174–79; overview, 169–73
Amstelredam galut, 123
Amsterdam: immigrants from, 183–85; migration to, 14–15; Portuguese-Jewish community in, 122–27
Anchieta, José de, 46, 121
Andrade, Manuel Correia de, 136, 159, 163
Antunes, Heitor, 22, 149–51
Antunes, Isabel, 152
Antwerp, migration to, 14–15
Archive of the Municipality of Bet Jacob in Amsterdam, 125–26
Arends, Jacques, 54
As Variedades de Proteu, 43
Assis, Angelo Adriano Faria de, 1–2, 149–51, 154
Atias, David, 190
Atlantic Slave Trade: A Census, The (Curtin), 161
Atlantic world, Potuguese Jews throughout, 128–31
Atlas Catalão, 109–10
Atlas Novus (Blaeu), 175
Atlas of the Transatlantic Slave Trade (Eltis), 161
Attig, Remy, 52
Auto da Barca do Purgatorio (Vicente), 143
auto-da-fé, Portuguese Inquisition and, 87–92
Avis, Mestre de, 109
Axis Rule in Occupied Europe (Lemkin), 96

364 Index

Azevedo, Abraham de, 190
Azevedo, José Lúcio de, 184
Azores (archipelago), 11, 76, 105, 130, 135, 144, 208, 236

Baerle, Caspar van, 170–71, 173, 174–75, 185
Bahia, 5–6, 22, 34–36, 138, 169, 189; arrests for non-Judaic crimes, 228–30; being New Christian in, 71–73; clusters of European-born populations living in, 206–12; contemporary singer-songwriter from, 100; establishing capital city of, 143; and first person arrested for crime of Judaism, 4, 90; foreign British attacks in, 121–22; indigenous and Black Populations, 217–27; Jesuit college of, 46–47; and Judaizing community of Pernambuco, 152–56; and Maccabees of Matoim, 148–52; merchants and planters, 50–51; and migration processes, 126; New Christians in, 148–52; *pau brasil* in, 119; and population density, 14; Portuguese-Jewish immigrants from Amsterdam, 183–85; regional population dynamics, 156–58; *senhor de engenhos* of, 158–61; slavery, 162; and sugar industry, 166; sugarcane boom, 144–48; sugarcane mills in, 137
bailiffs (*meirinhos*), 76, 171
bandeirantes: and Portuguese colonial enterprise, 43–48; anti-*bandeirante* sentiments, 45–46; demonizing, 43–44; famous individuals, 44–45; as slave labor, 46–48; as "subversives," 44
Banes, Daniel, 105
Barros, Manuel Álvares de, 41
Barros, Pedro Vaz de, 44–45

Battle of Guararapes, 50, 192
Beck, Mathias, 200
Beckman, Manuel and Thomas, 49–50
Beckman's Revolt (Revolta de Beckman), 49–50
Belmonte, Diogo Nunes, 160
Beracha ve Shalom, synagogue, 129
Berkiensztat, Ricardo, 100
Bethell, Leslie, 56
Bethencourt, Francisco, 24, 46, 90, 93, 95, 110
Bevis Marks Congregation, 53, 128
Bevis Marks Synagogue, 198
Bight of Benin, 162
"biography of place," using historical geography to understand, 9–11
Black Death, 81–82
Black Legend, addressing myth of, 92–97
Blackbourn, David, 130, 142
Blaeu, Willem, 175
Blake, Stanley E., 20
blood purity (*pureza de sangue*), 16, 23, 31, 92; laws (*limpeza de sangue*), 32, 40; statute establishment, 49, 59, 79, 86
Bloom, Herbert I., 191
Board of Conscience of Lisbon, 157
Bodian, Miriam, 58
Bogaciovas, Marcelo, 108
Böhm, Günter, 149
Bonfil, Ismael, 108
border fluidity, 60
Boulez, Jehovanan des, 207
Boulez, Senhor de, 121
Boxer, Charles R., 172
Boyajian, James C., 163
Brandão, Ambrósio Fernandes, 41–43, 161
Brandão, David, 190
Brazil: astronomy and, 117–18; backdrop of dossiers in, 24–26; backdrop of Portuguese Inquisition and,

Index 365

75–81; Book of National Heroes in, 51; conquering Indigenous populations in, 65–66; *degredados* and, 142–44; descendants of New Christians in, 69–73; differences between Spanish and Portuguese in, 62–69; discovery of diamonds, 48–49; Dutch invasion of, 165–67; and end of Inquisition, 200–204; *engenhos* in, 158–61; exploiting brazilwood in, 119–20; first colonial economic boom of, 7–8; first descriptions of, 114–22; first New Christians in colonial Brazil, 135–67; first sighting of, 114–15; first sugarcane plantation mills in, 152–56; first encounter with Indigenous tribes in, 118–21; foreign British attacks in, 121–22; great interest in physical/natural features of, 175–76; important figures during Dutch rule in, 185–89; industries of, 42; location of arrests for all heresies in, 224; major figures in biography of, 39–73; mechanisms of control implemented in, 76; migrating to North America from, 193–97; migration after Dutch leaving, 197–200; modern interpretation of "race" in, 20–21; most important document of landing in, 116–17; naming land of, 115–16; neighbors today, 70; northeast region of, 99–100; northeast under Dutch rule, 174–79; physical appearances in, 21; plight of Crypto-Jews in, 41–43; and Portuguese Crown, 67; racial democracy in, 19–20, 22; recording species from, 115; regional population dynamics in, 156–58; relations with Indigenous tribes in, 66–67; religious orders established in, 46; sugar industry in, 139–42; sugarcane boom in, 144–48; total arrests only for crime of Judaism by century, 226; total population increase, 14; toward geography of, 3–7; traditional conceptualization of national hybrid cultural and racial formation, 17–18; and Treaty of Tordesilhas, 115; tribunals established in, 206–7; unrecognized contributions to, 48–51. *See also* Portugal; Portuguese Inquisition
Brazilian Association of Descendants of Jews from the Inquisition (ABR-ADJIN), 98
Brazilian captaincies, 133
Brazilian Historical and Artistic Institute of Patrimony (IPHAN), 152, 181
brazilwood (*pau brasil*), 7, 15, 34, 42, 67–68, 115, 119, 121, 157, 234
brotherhoods, 47–48
Burgos, Arão, 199

Cabral, Pedro Álvares, 109, 110, 114–15
Calaça, Carlos Eduardo, 15–16, 72, 79, 95
Calle de los Lusitanos ("Street of the Lusitanians/Portuguese"), 40
Camaragibe community. *See* Pernambuco, Judaizing community of
Camarão, Antônio Felipe, 50
Camarão, Felipe, 50
Caminha, Pêro Vaz de, 115–16, 116
campanhias de emboscadas, 192
Cape Verde, 43, 67, 76, 105, 115, 143, 208, 236
Capela de Nossa Senhora das Candeias, 190
captaincies (*capitanias*), 34, 36, 68, 135, 161, 317n70; creating system of, 137–38; donating, 140–41; regional population dynamics, 156; and sugarcane boom, 144

Carpentier, S., 171
Carvalho, Manoel Lopes da, 89, 126
Casal, Aires de, 116
Casas, Bartholomé de Las, 92
Cascudo, Luís Câmara, 191
Castaño, Javier, 60–61, 82
Castro, Isaac de, 183–84
Catholic Church, 1, 11, 32, 45, 88, 91, 93, 231, 234, 291n12
Cavendish, Thomas, 121–22
cenusure officials (*qualificadores*), 76
Ceullen, M. Van, 171
Chacão, Manoel Gomes, 178
Clement X, pope, 189
clerical officials (*commisários*), 76
co-regents of districts (*coregidores da comarca*), 68
Coates, Timothy J., 138, 143–44
Coelho, Duarte, 42, 68, 135–36, 213
Coelho, Gonçalo, 140
Coelho, Jorge de Albuquerque, 42
Coelho, Nicolau, 114, 115, 118
Cohen, Jacob, 197
Colloquies on the Simples and Drugs and Medicinal Things of India (Walker), 107–8
colonial Brazil, New Christians in: backdrop of geography, agriculture, and economy, 137–39; *degredados*, 142–44; Dutch and sugar industry, 165–67; *engenhos* and African slavery, 161–63; *engenhos* in northeast, 158–61; Judaizing community of Pernambuco, 152–56; New Christians in Bahia, 148–52; overview, 135–37; regional population dynamics in, 156–58; sugar industry, 139–42; sugarcane boom in northeast, 144–48; transatlantic slave trade, 163–65
Columbus, Christopher, 114
Congregação do Oratório de São Felipe de Neri, 180–81

Congregation Kahal Kadosh Shearith Israel, 193–94
conquest, idea of, 64–65
continuity, retaining a sense of, 39–41
contributions, migrants and descendants, 41–43
Convivência, 84
Corografia Brasilica, 116
Correio Braziliense: Ou Armazém Literário, 203
Cortés, Hernán, 114
Cortesão, Jaime, 44
Costa-Gomes, Rita, 81
Costa, Jaime Lopes da, 125
Costa, Joseph da, 194
Costa, Miguel Teles da, 200
Costa, Teodoro Pereira da, 215
Costa, Violante da, 184
Costigan, Lúcia Helena, 55
Côte, Petite, 53
Count of Nassau, 171
Cresques, Abraão, 108–10, 113
Cresswell, Tim, 12
crime of Judaism, 205; accusations, 41, 49, 72, 142–43, 200, 202; first people arrested for, 4–5, 222; Indigenous and Black Populations, 217; literal translation, 4; mixed-race populations and, 17; and non-European parentage, 213, 251; place of birth for those arrested for, 246–54; total of individuals arrested for, 205; youngest individuals arrested for, 209, 211–12
cross-community migration, concept, 124
Cruz, Helena da, 4, 211
Crypto-Jews, 15, 24–25, 34–35, 100; and aftermath of Portuguese Inquisition, 101–2; in British Isles, 128; and Camaragibe community, 152–56; discussing problem of, 86; and *engenhos*, 152, 160; epitomizing experience of, 41–43; epitomizing

experience of, 41–42; examining Portuguese Inquisition dossiers, 205, 215, 225; first communities of, 37; malleability of, 72–73; mercantile professions, 130; in northeast of Brazil, 144–48; openly practicing Judaism, 171; preoccupation with, 78, 93–94; reforming, 95; research for, 99; and sugarcane boom, 144–48; surveillance of, 63–64; term, 23

cultural landscapes, considering layers of, 11–13

culture of times, term, 13

culturecide. *See* genocide, modern meaning of

Curaçao, 6, 8, 15, 73, 129, 131, 156, 181, 194, 198–200, 235

Curiel, Jacob, 128

Curtin, Philip D., 161

D. João III, king, 85–86
D. João VI, king, 202
D. Manuel, king, 117
D'Aguillar, Isaac, 197
D'Andrada, Salvador, 194
d'Orta, Catarina, 108
d'Orta, Garcia, 107–8
Dandrada, Salvador, 197
Davies, Archie, 30
Davis, N. Darnell, 198
degredados, 142–44
degredo. *See* penal exile
denunciation, Portuguese Inquisition and, 87–92
Dia Nacional da Memória das Vítimas da Inquisição, 96–97
Diálogos das Grandezas do Brasil (Brandão), 42
diamonds, Brazilian, 48–49
Dias, Bartolomeu, 110, 114
Dias, Branca, 22, 152–53
Dias, Diogo, 114

Dias, Henrique, 50
Dias, Violante, 153
diasporas, Portuguese world and: access to scientific bodies of knowledge, 111–14; Amsterdam connection, 122–27; first descriptions of Brazil, 114–22; omissions in literature of geography, 106–11; overview, 103–6; Port Jews, 131–34; Portuguese Jews in Europe, 127–28; Portuguese Jews throughout Atlantic world, 128–31

Dictionary of the History of Science, 109

Dines, Alberto, 32, 69, 180
Dodge, Cameron J. G., 68
Dormido, Aron Abravanel, 198
Dormido, Daniel, 165
Dormido, Solomon, 198
dossiers, backdrop of, 24–26
Drago, Isaac Franco, 165
Drago, Simão, 178
Dussen, Adriaen vander, 171
Dutch: aftermath of rule of, 191–93; important figures during rule of, 185–89; leaving Brazil, 197–200; northeast Brazil under rule of, 174–79; sugar industry and, 165; in tropics, 190–91. *See also* Dutch West India Company (WIC)

Dutch East India Company, 169, 175
Dutch Guiana, 54
Dutch West India Company (WIC), 169, 196; and aftermath of Dutch rule, 193; appointing governor in northeast Brazil, 174–75; diving Dutch citizens in Brazil, 174; great interest in physical/natural features of Brazil, 175–76; seeking asylum in New Amsterdam, 194–96. *See also* Brazil; Portuguese Inquisition

Eakin, Marshall C., 19, 62

Eannes, Gil, 105
Eannes, William, 127
Ebeling-Koning, Blanche T., 170
Ebert, Christopher, 130, 146
Eckhout, Albert, 174
economy, colonial Brazil, 137–39
Egipcíaca, Rosa Maria, 229–30
Eltis, David, 161
Emmanuel, Isaac S., 184
engenhos, 34, 134–37, 155, 166, 185; and African slavery, 161–63; and Brazilian sugar industry, 139; and Dutch-Portuguese conflict, 192–93; Engenho Matoim, 149; and impact of being New Chistian, 72; increase of, 156; in New World, 68; in northeast of Brazil, 158–61; and Portuguese Inquisition, 209; slave labor, 46–47; sugarcane plantation owner (*senhor de engenho*), 18, 42, 125, 155, 159, 176–77, 215–16
Enriques, Jacob Joshua Bueno, 198–99
esnoga, term, 53, 125
Espírito Santo, 41, 47, 70, 133, 137, 155–56 206, 222–25
Eurafricans, 123
Europe, Portuguese Jews in, 127–28

Falbel, Nachman, 33, 69
Fardi Bible, 110
Faria, Jacob de, 165
Faye, Aron de la, 165
Feitler, Bruno, 97, 101, 155, 172, 182
feitorias. See trading outposts
Felipe II, dom, 86
Fênix ou O Eterno Retorno: 460 anos da presença Judaica em Pernambuco, A, 69
Ferera, Abraham, 197
Fernandes, Beatriz, 152–53
Fernandes, Diogo, 152–53
Fernandes, João, 105
Fernandes, Nuno, 151

Fernandes, Tomás, 126
Fiera, David, 194
Fisher, Benjamin E., 126–27
Fishman, Talya, 58
Flory, Rae, 157
Fonseca, Baltazar da, 176
Fonseca, Isaac Aboab da, 185–89
forts, building, 177–78
France Antarctique, 121
Franco, Mestre Isaque, 127
Frazão, José, 126
Freyre, Gilberto, 16–21, 184, 199, 274n69
frontiersmen. *See bandeirantes*
Fundão, Jacob, 190
Furtado, D. Heitor, 150

Gama, Gaspar da, 117
Gama, Vasco da, 109, 110, 113, 118
Gelfand, Noah L., 198
Generale Beschrjvinge van de Capitania Paraíba (Herckmans), 174
genocide, modern meaning of, 96
gente da nação. See people of the nation
Geographical Tradition, The (Livingstone), 106–7
geography: colonial Brazil, 137–39; considering layers of cultural landscapes and palimpsest, 11–13; contribution to anglophone scholarship, 3–7; importance to anglophone scholarship, 7–9; omissions in literature of, 106–11; using to understand "biography of place," 9–11
Gerais, Minas, 73, 80
Gibson, Charles, 92
Golden Age of Exploration, 110
Golden Age of Islamic Science, 112
Goliath, Cornelis Bastaanz, 176, 179
Gomes, Gaspar, 92
Gould, Stephen J., 13
Graizbord, David L., 12–13, 23, 40, 59, 78 86, 92

Greenlee, William B., 117–18
Groesen, Michiel van, 170
Guedes, Max Justo, 66

Hamburg, migration to, 14–15
Hassig, Ross, 65
Hebrews of the Portuguese Nation. *See* Jews (Potuguese)
Hemming, John, 66–67
Henrique, dom, 86, 109
Henrique, Friar, 116
Henrique, Jacob C., 194
Henriques, Antônio Vaz, 176
Henriques, João Luís, 125
Henry the Navigator, 110–11
Herckmans, Elias, 174
Herculano, Alexandre, 82
heretical crime, 4, 90–91, 150, 205, 225
Herman, Jacqueline, 84–85
Hispanic World: predicament of term, 54–57; term, 55
Hispanic, term, 54–57
historical geography "biography of place" and, 9–11
History of Brazil Under the Governorship of Count Johan Maurits of Nassau, 1636–1644 (Baerle), 170
Hobson, John, 105
homens da nação. *See* men of the nation
Horta, José da Silva, 16–17, 53, 160, 164
hybrid population, 17–19

Iberia, term, 54–57
Iberian Jews, term, 57
Iberian Peninsula: backdrop, 82–87; discrimination of New Christians, 86; discussing "Jewish problem," 96–97; embracing Catholicism in, 85–86; Jews and Muslims ordered to lave, 82–83; Jews arriving in, 84–85; under Muslim rule, 111–12; Portuguese anti-Jewish policies, 83–84; and Portuguese Inquisition implementation, 85–86; and royal licenses, 85
IBGE. *See* Instituto Brasileiro de Geografia e Estatistica
Idea of Latin America, The (Mignolo), 55
Ilhéus, 4, 46, 133, 137, 145, 156, 206–7
In Defense of the Faith (Wadsworth), 94
independence, end of Inquisition and, 200–204
Indigenous populations: conquering, 65–66; estimates of, 68–69; first encounter of, 118–21
Inquisition, 1; backdrop of dossiers, 24–26; differences between Portugal an Spain, 64; purpose of, 24; scholarship available on, 26–28; studying dossiers from, 5–6; term, 1, 78, 93–94. *See also* Portuguese Inquisition
Instituto Brasileiro de Geografia e Estatistica (IBGE), 71
Insurreição Pernambucana, 50, 191
intermarriage, Portuguese Inquisition and, 215–16
internal secrecy, 31–32
IPHAN. *See* Brazilian Historical and Artistic Institute of Patrimony
Ireland, 127, 207
Islamic Umayyad Caliphate, 64
Israel, David, 194
Israel, Jonathan, 126
Israel, Menasseh ben, 128, 189
Israeli Syndicate of Communities of Victims of the Inquisitional Tribunals, 98
Israelite Confederation of Brazil, 99
Israelite Federation of Sao Paulo, 100
Itamaracá, 36, 136, 144, 147, 155–56, 163, 173, 177–78, 182, 185, 200

Jacob Rabbi, vilified Jew, 190–91
Jacques, Christovão, 141
Jaime, Mestre, 113

Jamaica, 6, 8, 15, 34, 56, 73, 129, 165, 167, 198–99, 235
Jarnagin, Laura, 130–31
Jesuit Order, 46
Jew, term, 45; predicament of, 54–57; problem with term, 57–59; translating as "Ashkenazi Jew," 61–62
Jewish Cultural Center of Pernambuco, 181
Jewry: Crypto-Jewry, 32, 73, 78; European, 126; Latin American, 278n136, 287n129; Lusitanian, 83–84; Luso-Brazilian, 2, 51, 97, 180; in northeast region, 182–83; Portuguese, 60, 75, 97–98, 126, 268n8
Jews (Portuguese), 233–38; and "submerged" legacy/memory, 30–33; "Eurafrican" Jewish population, 17; access to scientific bodies of knowledge, 111–14; aftermath of Dutch rule, 191–93; aftermath of Portuguese Inquisition, 97–102; "all masked Jews" (*judios encubiertos*), 45; in Amsterdam connection, 122–27; and cultural landscapes, 12; denunciation, prison, and *autos-da-fé*, 87–92; diaspora of, 2–3; discussing race regarding, 16–22; establishing first communities in Atlantic world, 129; in Europe, 127–28; first official Jewish community in North America, 129; immigrants from Amsterdam, 183–85; involvement in transatlantic slave trade, 163–65; Mexico City establishments, 129–30; migrating from Brazil to North America, 193–97; migration after Dutch leaving Brazil, 197–200; migration and mobility, 13–16; migration to Brazil, 1–3; nationhood among, 53; periodization, 33–36; Port Jews, 131–34; Portuguese Inquisition and impact on, 75–102; Portuguese-Jewish Diasporas, 103–34; quintessential "geographical" narrative of, 7–9; stereotypes, 130; terms for, 54–59; throughout Atlantic world, 128–31; toward new geography, 3–7; in tropics, 190–91; understanding "biography of place," 9–11. *See also* Brazil; Portuguese Inquisition

João I, dom, 109
João, Mestre, 109, 116–18
John II, king, 108
John II, pope, 191
John Paul II, pope, 93
John, Prester, 113
Johnson, H. B., 156
Jorge, Andressa, 154
José I, king, 201–2
Judaizers, 9, 32, 236–37; concern over one being, 21; diasporas and, 107; examination of dossiers, 207, 209, 215, 219, 221–23, 231; and first Jewish settlements in Americas, 182, 184; and first New Christians in colonial Brazil, 142, 149–53, 161; Inquisition impact on, 75, 78, 80, 85, 87, 89, 95; New Christians being, 22–24; and Portuguese Inquisition dossiers, 24–25; and Portuguese New Christian "uniqueness," 39–40, 42–44, 46, 60, 64, 71; term, 78–79
Judeo-Spanish, term, 52
Juiz Conservador das Matas ("Forest Conservation Judge"), 68
Júnior, Ademir Schetini, 202
justiça relaxada, 88

Kagan, Richard L., 131
Kahal Kadosh Magen, synagogue, 179
Kahal Kadosh Nidhe Israel, community, 198

Kahal Kadosh Zur Israel, synagogue, 179, 185
Kant, Immanuel, 107
Klooster, Wim, 122, 170
Knivet, Anthony, 121
Knowledge in Translation (Manning), 111
Koen, E. M., 58
Kogman-Appel, Katrin, 110

Lancaster, 121
Landa, Diego de, 65
LaSimon, Abram De, 194
Latin America: and aftermath of Portuguese Inquisition, 97–102; neighbors today, 70; term, 54–57
lavrador, term, 155
Law of Moses, 45
lay officials (*familiares*), 76, 333n3
LCTL. *See* Less Commonly Taught Languages
Leitão, Martim, 42
Leite, Naomi, 97
Lemkin, Raphael, 96
Léry, Jean de, 121
Less Commonly Taught Languages (LCTL), 30
Levy, Isaac, 194
Lima, Peru, 40
limpeza de sangue. *See* blood purity
Lisbon, youngest individuals imprisoned by Portuguese Inquisition in, 211. *See also* Portugal; Portuguese Inquisition
Lister, Christopher, 121
Livingstone, David N., 106–7
Lopes, Diogo Lopes, 155, 207
Lottenberg, Fernando, 99
Lucena, Abraham de, 197
Lucena, Abram de, 194
Lusitanus, Zacutus, 109
Luso-Brazilian Jewry, 2, 51, 97, 180

Machabeu, Yehudah, 190

Madariaga, Salvador, 110
Magalhães, Fernão de, 110
Magalhães, Pero de, 120
Maia, Angela Maria Vieira, 164
Maia, Salvador da, 4
Maio, Marcos Chor, 15–16, 72, 79, 95
Manning, Patrick, 111, 124
Manuel I, 83, 86
Marcgraf, Georg, 175
Marcocci, Guiseppi, 112
maritime expansions, 105–6
Mark, Peter, 16, 53, 160, 164
Markens, Isaac, 194
Marrano, term, 23
Martins, Fernão, 190
Marvel, Alan, 11–12
massapé soils, 145–46
Matoim Maccabean. *See* Antunes, Heitor
Matoim, New Christians in, 148–52
Mattos, Hebe, 50
Mauricio Nassau Bridge, 176
Maurits, Johan, 171, 174–75
Mauro, Frédéric, 50, 104
Mello, Evaldo Cabral de, 135
Mello, José Antônio Gonsalves de, 180
Melo, Sebastião José de Carvalho e, 201–2
Melville, Elinor G. K., 67
men of the nation (*homens da nação*), 57
Mendes, David, 198
Mendonça, Heitor Furtado de, 76, 152
Menezes, Francisco Barreto de, 192, 197
Mercado, Abraham de, 198
Merchant, Carolyn, 106
merchants, 11, 25, 35, 268n6; New Christian, 80, 126; Portuguese-Jewish, 49, 124, 160; top occupation for those arrested for Judaism in Brazil, 255, 260
Mesa, Isaac, 194
mestiçagem (miscegenation), 11, 19, 66, 212
Mestre Joane of Évora, 127

Mestre João, 7, 109, 116–18, 233–34
Mestre Rodrigo of Leiria, 127
Metcalf, Alida, 20, 65–66, 67–69
micro-society, 84–85
Mignolo, Walter D., 55
migration: after Dutch leaving Brazil, 197–200; and Amsterdam connection, 122–27; from Brazil to Nort America, 193–97; central theme of, 13–16; push-pull factors of, 81–82; state-sponsored movement, 144
Minas Gerais, 1, 5–6, 14, 18, 34–36; discovery of gold and diamonds in, 72, 80; and end of Inquisition, 200; first Inquisition history museum in, 98; and Portuguese Inquisition dossiers, 221–27; receiving New Christians, 73; regional population dynamics, 157–58; unrecognized contributions to colonial Brazil, 48–49
misconceptions, Portuguese-Jewish families, 51–54
Mission of Guairá, 45
mobility, central theme of, 13–16
Modena, Judah Aryeh, 124
Montoya, Antônio Ruiz de, 45
Moor, term, 21
Morais, José Ricardo de, 4, 207
Moreno-Carvalho, Francisco, 69
Morgan, Philip D., 131
Morrill, Richard, 13
Motthe, Jaques De La, 194
Mouro, term, 21
mulato, term, 21
mulatto slaves, 229
multilingualism, 52–53
municipal councils (*câmaras municipais*), 68
Muniz, Henrique, 152
Muslims, 10, 82, 111–13
myths, Portuguese-Jewish families, 51–54

Nascimento, Abdias do, 19

Nassy, David, 199
National Archives, 24–26, 116
Navarro, Jacob, 198
Navarro, Moses, 190
Nazi Germany, equating Inquisition with, 94–95
Netto, Moses, 190
Neveh Shalom, 124
New Amsterdam, seeking asylum in, 194–96
New Christians, 233–38; aftermath of Portuguese Inquisition, 97–102; in Amsterdam connection, 122–27; in Bahia, 148–52; being Judaizers, 22–24; in colonial Brazil, 135–67; common notion about, 172; communities throughout Atlantic world, 128–31; *degredados* and, 142–44; diaspora of, 2–3; dichotomy of being officially, 78; discussing race regarding, 16–22; distinction from Old Christians, 83–84; eliminating category of, 201–2; *engenhos* in northeast Brazil, 158–61; fearing Inquisition, 91–92; financial factors involved in persecution of, 91; harshest sentences reserved for, 88; impact of being, 69–73; involvement in transatlantic slave trade, 163–65; malleability of, 72–73; migration and mobility, 13–16; migration to Brazil, 1–3; most common last names, 227–28; nationhood among, 53; New World "uniqueness" of, 39–73; periodization, 33–36; Port Jews, 131–34; Portuguese Inquisition and impact on, 75–102; and Portuguese-Jewish Diasporas, 103–34; quintessential "geographical" narrative of, 7–9; regional population dynamics, 156–58; representing two-thirds of arrests in Brazil,

216; retaining a sense of Jewish continuity, 39–41; royal licenses of, 85; and sense of place, 12–13; and "submerged" legacy/memory, 30–33; and sugarcane boom, 144–48; surveillance of, 80–81; term, 23; terms for, 54–59; toward new geography, 3–7; understanding "biography of place," 9–11

New World, 1, 62, 65, 167; addressing Black Legend myth in, 92–97; differences between Spanish and Portuguese in, 62–69; encounters, 7, 29, 31, 36–37, 59, 62, 114, 276n129; interest in conquest of, 65; and Knights of Christ, 65; Portuguese and Spanish colonial encounters in, 66–67; Portuguese New Christian "uniqueness" in, 39–73; Portuguese New Christian communities throughout, 40, 129

Newitt, Malyn, 11, 111
Newport, Rhode Island, Jews in, 194
Nóbrega, Manuel da, 121
non-Judaic crimes, arrests for, 228–31
Noronha, Fernando de, 99
Noronha, Fernão de, 140–42
North America: first official Jewish community in, 129; migrating to, 193–97. *See also* Americas, first Jewish settlements in
Novinsky, Anita W., 5, 45, 100, 163, 225
Novinskym Anita W., 94
Nunes, Gonçalo, 126
Nunes, Jacob, 182

O Cruzeiro, 203
occupation: individuals arrested for Judaism, 255–59; Portuguese Inquisition and, 216–17; top occupations, 260
Old Christians, 71, 119, 148, 154; and aftermath of Dutch rule, 191; aftermath of Dutch rule, 191–93; blood purity and, 79; business practices, 130; denouncing, 87–88; distinction, 83, 86; examining Inquisition dossiers, 205–7, 211; families, 1, 31–32, 151; and first Jewish settlements in Americas, 171; indigenous and Black populations, 217–27; last names of, 52, 151–52; as merchants, 157; and miscegenation, 72–73; monolithic community, 58; network contacts in Africa, 161–62; and slave trade, 163–65; social status and "race," 212–16

Old World, 2, 32, 38, 149, 235, 237, 244
Olinda, official Jewish community in, 170–71
Oppenheim, Samuel, 89, 194
Order of Christ, 48
Orfali, Moisés, 190
Os Cristãos-Novos em Portugal No Século XX (Schwarz), 102
Ovale, David, 126
Owen, Abigail, 111

Pais, Garcia Rodrigues, 48–49
Paiva, Manoel de, 120
palimpsest, 11–13
Palmares, Zumbi dos, 51
Pardo, David, 124
Paredes, Agostinho de, 184
Paredes, Ana de, 213–14
Paredes, David, 182
pau brasil. *See* brazilwood
paulistas. *See bandeirantes*
Paz, Jorge Dias da, 153
Pedro da Costa Caminha, 182
Peixoto, Moisés, 182
penal exile (*degredo*), 71
people of the nation (*gente da nação*), 6, 8–9, 39–41, 54, 61, 123, 169, 194–95
Pereira, Matias, 107

Pereira, Pedro Nunes, 107, 108
Pereyra, Tomas Rodrigues, 126
periodization, 33–36
Pernambuco, 5–6; arrests of Judaism by century and state in Brazil, 223; Bispate of, 159, 209; Captaincy of, 36, 68, 76, 166; Dotar community in, 179–80; Dutch conquest of, 176; Judaizing community of, 152–56; occupation of, 171–72
Pina, Francisco Gomes, 125
Pinah, Benjamin de, 190
Pinto, Paulo, 126
Piso, Willem, 175
place of birth, arrests, 246–54
place, concept, 11–13
Poel, Jacob, 108
Poettering, Jorun, 53, 79–80
Pombalinas ("Pombaline reforms"), 201
Ponte, Mark, 174
popular myths. *See* myths, Portuguese-Jewish families
pork, avoiding, 51–52
Port Jews, 131–34
Porto Seguro, Bahia, 115–16, 133, 156, 206, 248
Portugal: administrative structures in Brazil, 63; encounters in New World, 62–69; heterogenous population of, 10; independence from, 200–204; investment in surveillance and preoccupation of Crypto-Jews, 63–64; push-pull factors of migration to, 80–81; during Reconquista, 64; relations with Indigenous tribes in Brazil, 66–67; and sense of place, 12–13; territories in late fifteenth century, 70. *See also* Portuguese Inquisition
Portugees-Israëlietische Gemeente, community, 53
Portuguese Age of Exploration, 108
Portuguese Crown, 66–67, 84, 86, 95, 119, 143, 172, 227, 234
Portuguese Inquisition, 233–38; affecting Indigenous and Black populations, 217–27; aftermath of, 97–102; arrests for non-Judaic crimes during, 228–30; arrests of Judaism by century and state in Brazil, 223; *auto-da-fé* during, 87–92; backdrop of, 75–81; breadth of accusations and crimes other than Judaizing, 219; circumscribing legal system, 78; denunciation during, 87–92; end of, 200–204; and *engenhos* ("sugarcane plantations"), 209; establishment of "blood purity" statutes, 79; final considerations regarding, 230–31; first arrests, 207; first arrests for crime of Judaism, 222; and Iberian Peninsula, 82–87; individuals burned in effigy as "Judaizers," 221–22; intermarriage and, 215–16; largest single cohort of heretical crimes, 205–6; mechanisms of control by, 76; miscellaneous arrests by, 245–46; motivations of, 79–80; myth of, 92–97; New Christian names, 227–28; New Christians arrested for Judaism, 219–21; New Christians in Bahia, 148–52; not following Judaic law, 215; occupation of those arrested during, 216–17; places of origin (place of birth) of those accused by, 207–9; prison during, 87–92; public and private surveillance, 80–81; push-pull factors, 81–82; race and, 212–16; results from examination of, 205–31; social status and, 212–17; total arrests only for the crime of Judaism by century, 226; total number of

individuals arrested during, 205, 210; totals for all arrests in Brazil by century, 226; tribunals, 75–77; tribunals of, 206–7; visitations to Brazil, 76; youngest individuals arrested during, 209–12
Portuguese Republic Assembly n.º 20/2020, 96
Portuguese-Hebrew Register of Regulations and Decisions, Recife, Pernambuco, 53
Portuguese-Israelite Congregation of Amsterdam, 124–25, 125–26
Portuguese-Jewish Congregation of Amsterdam, 188, 190
Portuguese, ascription, 10–11
Portuguese, regarding being, 59–62
Post, Frans, 174
Prado, Paulo, 44
presence, migrants and descendants, 41–43
Principles of Political Economy and Taxation, The (Ricardo), 127
prison, Portuguese Inquisition and, 87–92
prominence, migrants and descendants, 41–43
prosecutors (*promotores*), 76
provincial Catholic mentality, 92
pureza de sangue. See blood purity
push-pull factors, 13–15; migration, 81–82

Querido, Diogo Dias, 126, 160

race, discussing: connotations, 16–17; hybrid populations, 17–20; modern interpretation of "race," 20–21; and Portuguese Inquisition, 212–16; problems, 20; racial democracy, 19; research, 17; traditional conceptualization of national hybrid cultural and racial formation, 17; uniting Portuguese nation, 18

racial democracy, 19, 22
Raízes do Brasil, 100
Ramalho, João, 99, 119–20
Ramires, Francisco, 155
Ramos, Artur, 19
Raya, La, 60
Recife, 47; Jewish community in, 179, 190, 197, 236; main synagogue in, 179–81, 194; official Jewish community in, 170–71; synagogues in, 3, 179–82, 197
Reclus, Élisée, 141
Recôncavo Baiano, region, 145, 147–48, 202, 317n85
Reconquista, 64
Redondo, Abraham, 197
Regimento da Relação do Brasil, 68
regional population dynamics, colonial Brazil, 156–58
Register of Regulations and Decisions of the Portuguese-Jewish, 179–80
Resende, Maria Leônia Chaves de, 90, 158
reversal conversions, 178–79
Ribeiro, Afonso, 115
Ricardo, v, 127
Richardson, David, 161
Rio da Prata, 1
Rio de Janeiro. *See* Brazil
Rodrigo, Master, 108
Rodrigues, Abraham Jacob, 165, 197
Rodrigues, Ana, 4, 149–51
Rodrigues, David, 197
Rodrigues, Leonor, 41, 152
Rodrigues, Manuel, 178
Rodrigues, Martim, 44
Roitman, Jessica Vance, 124
Romeiras, Malta, 92
Rondinelli, Pietro, 141
Roth, Cecil, 90, 105, 126
Royal orders (*ordenações do reino*), 68
Rules for the Astrolabe (Zacuto), 109
"Rules for the Astrolabe" (*Regimento do astrolábio*), 117

ruling (*regimento*), 68
Russell-Wood, A. J. R., 69, 103–4, 112, 157
Ruyters, Dierick, 122–23

Sá, Mem de, 46, 149
Sá, Salvador Correia de, 122
Salvador, José Gonçalves, 1, 44, 163
Salvador, Manoel Calado do, 172
Samuel, Edgar, 51
sangue infecto. *See* taint of Jewish blood
Santa Companha de Dotar Orfãs e Donzelas (Dotar), 125
São Paulo, Brazil, 14, 27–28, 70; *bandeirantes* in, 43–47; founders of, 46; migrating to, 73; modern state of, 43, 121
São Vicente, Brazil, 34, 43, 108, 120–22, 130, 133, 135, 137
Saraiva, Antônio José, 23, 89, 91
Sarenbrenick, Salamão, 33–36
Saruco, Solomon, 53–54
Sauer, Carl O., 11
Schetz, Erasmus, 130, 142
scholarship: availability of, 26–28; omissions in, 28–30
Schorsch, Jonathan, 160
Schwartz, Stuart B., 2, 35, 47, 87, 94, 98, 114–15, 158–59, 193
Schwarz, Samuel, 102
scientific bodies of knowledge, access to, 111–14
Seed, Patricia, 105–6, 109, 112, 117, 123
senhor de engenho. *See* sugarcane plantation owner
sense of place, idea of, 12–13
Sephardic diaspora, term, 57
Sephardic Jews, 52
Sephardic, term, 57–58
Sephardim, term, 57–59
Sequeira, Abraham Machado de, 127–28
Serrana, Jacob, 197
Serrano, Isaac, 182
Sertão, Pernambuco, 147

Silva, Antônio José da, 41, 43
Silva, Custódio da, 229
Silva, Leonardo Dantes, 125
Simms, David, 11–12
Simms, Norman, 143, 172
Sítio dos Coelhos, cemetary, 179
Skidmore, Thomas, 19
slave trade: *engenhos* and, 161–63; New Christians and, 163–65; transatlantic, 16, 37, 63, 106, 134, 161–66
Slave Voyages, 161
Slavery Unseen (Aidoo), 19
Smith, David Grant, 157
social status, Portuguese Inquisition and, 212–18
Soeiro, Ephraim, 189
Sosua, Rafael José de, 90–91
Sousa, Beatriz de, 154
Sousa, Fernão, 154
Sousa, Gabriel Soares de, 120–21
Sousa, Martim Afonso de, 108
Sousa, Rafael José de, 158
Sousa, Tomé de, 143
Souza, Dona Luiza Correia de, 202
Souza, Laura de Mello e, 229
Souza, Martim Afonso de, 120, 121
Spain: administrative structures in Brazil, 63; and Dutch, 166; dynamic differences between Portugal and, 40, 57, 60, 62, 66–67; encounters in New World, 62–69; "Portuguese" as term in, 64; relations with Indigenous tribes in Brazil, 66–67; targeting, Judaizers; territories in late fifteenth century, 70; and transatlantic slave trade, 162–64. *See also* Portugal; Portuguese Inquisition
Spanish America, 45, 55–56, 63, 65, 68–69, 71, 278n142
Spanish Inquisition, 29, 40, 64, 85, 90, 92–95
Spinoza, Baruch, 188
Staden, Hans, 121

Stuczynski, Claude B., 45–46
Studemund-Halévy, Michael, 129–30
Studnicki-Gizbert, Daviken, 8, 41, 58, 61, 126
Stuyvesant, Peter, 194–97
"submerged" legacy/memory: concrete figures, 33; framework of "Hispanic world," 31; "infamous" presence of New Christians, 33; internal secrecy, 31–32; joint venture, 32–33; keeping Inquisition dossiers secret, 32; language and academic/disciplinary barriers, 30–31
subversives. *See bandeirantes*
sugar: and aftermath of Dutch rule, 192–93; backdrop of geography, agriculture, and economy, 137–39; *degredados* and, 142–44; Dutch involvement in industry of, 165–67; economic boom of, 7–8;; first sugarcane mill plantations, 148; first sugarcane mills, 135–37; industry in Brazil, 139–42; sugarcane plantation mills in Pernambuco, 152–56; sugarcane boom, 144–48; three separate products, 146; and transatlantic slave trade, 163–65. *See also* Brazil; Dutch West India Company (WIC)
sugarcane plantation owners (*senhor de engenho*), 18, 42, 125, 155, 159, 176–77, 215–16
sugarcane plantations. *See engenhos*
surgarcane, boom in, 144–48
Suriname, South America, 3, 6, 9, 15, 37; *engenhos* in, 160–61; "Eurafrican" Jewish population, 17, 123; first non-Indigenous settlers in, 128–29; leaving, 193, 197; multilingualism and, 53–54; periodization, 34; Portuguese Jews arriving in, 199; Spanish colonial legacy in, 56; and sugar industry, 165–67; UNESCO World Heritage, 181
surnames, 260–64; myths about, 52; Portuguese Inquisition and, 227–28
Synagogue Kahal Zur Israel, 73
synagogues, American emergence of, 179–82

taint of Jewish blood (*sangue infecto*), 23
Talmud Torah, 124–25
Tavares, Antônio Rapôso, 44
Tavares, Rapôso, 44–45, 99
Távora, Manuel Álvares, 109
Teixeira, Bento, 41
Teixeira, Marcos, 76
Teles, Henrique Muniz, 152
terms: predicament of, 54–57; problem with, 57–59
Thevet, André, 121
Tiaraju, Sepé, 51
Times of Israel, 99
Tiradentes, 280n10
Tirado, Jacob, 125
Tolerance of Judaism (Maurits), 171
Toortse der Zeevaert (Ruyters), 123
Tortorici, Zeb, 88, 90
Touro Synagogue, 194
Tracy, Matthew, 93
trading outposts (*feitorias*), 14
transatlantic slave trade, involvement in, 163–65. *See also* slave trade
transformation, examining, 15
transnationalism, projecting definition of, 9
Treaty of Taborda, 192
Treaty of the Hague, 192
Treaty of Tordesilhas, 43, 115
Tribunal do Santo Ofício da Inquisição de Lisboa, 75
Tristão da Cunha, 105
Trivellato, Francesca, 124
tropics, Jews and Dutch in, 190–91
Trujillo, Francisco Vesques, 45

Tupimnambás, women's work in, 139

uniqueness, New Christians: *bandeirantes*, 43–48; on being "Portuguese," 59–62; contributions of migrants and descendants, 41–43; differences between Spanish and Portuguese in New World, 62–69; impact of being New Chrisian, 69–73; misconceptions, 51–54; popular myths, 51–54; predicaments of terms, 54–57; problem with terms, 57–59; retaining a sense of Jewish continuity, 39–41; unrecognized contributions to colonial Brazil, 48–51

United Nations General Assembly Resolution 96, 96

United States, 20, 22, 29m 56–57, 100, 162, 194, 236

Vainfas, Ronaldo, 84–85, 88, 90, 124, 150
Valle de Mezquital, shifts in, 67–68
Valoroso Lucidero e o Trinfo da Liberdade (Salvador), 172–73
Valverde, Jacob, 190
Varnhagen, Francisco Adolfo de, 116
Verga, Yehuda Ibn, 108
Vespucci, Amerigo, 140, 141
Vicente, Gil, 143
Vieira, Ambrósio, 155–56, 182
Vieira, Fernando G. P., 78
Vieira, João Fernandes, 180–81
Vieira, Padre Antônio de, 189
Vila de São Paulo de Piratininga, 119

Villegagnon, Nicolas Durand de, 121
Vink, Wieke, 129
Vitória, Diogo Nunes, 126
Vizinho, José, 108
Vizinho, Moisés, 108
Vrijburg, island, 176
vrijeluijden ("free civilian"), 176

Wadsworth, James E., 24, 87, 93–94, 202–3
Walker, Timothy D., 107–8
wardens (*alcaides dos cárceres*), 76
Webb, Kempton E., 9–11, 36, 68, 103–4, 146
Wel-vaert van de West- Indische Compagnie, pamphlet, 176
White Legend, 93
whiteness, concept, 71
WIC. *See* Dutch West India Company
Willaerts, Abraham, 174
Withrington, Robert, 121
Wiznitzer, Arnold, 6, 84, 174, 184
World Heritage Site, 140

Xavier, Joaquim José da Silva. *See* Tiradentes

Yom Kippur, 129, 152
Yovel, Yirmiyahu, 59

Zacuto, Abraham, 108–9, 117–18
Zacutto, Moses, 190
Zona da Mata, sub-region, 144–46

www.ingramcontent.com/pod-product-compliance
Lightning Source LLC
Chambersburg PA
CBHW030517230426
43665CB00010B/648